The Team That Couldn't Hit:

The 1972 Texas Rangers

Edited by Steve West and Bill Nowlin
Associate Editors: Len Levin and Carl Riechers

Society for American Baseball Research, Inc.
Phoenix, AZ

The Team That Couldn't Hit: The 1972 Texas Rangers
Edited by Steve West and Bill Nowlin
Associate Editors: Len Levin and Carl Riechers

Front cover photograph courtesy Special Collections, University of Texas at
Arlington Libraries. The date of the photograph is April 22, 1972.
Back cover images courtesy of Ray Cherry.
Photographs on pages 100, 119, 157, 206, 270, and 271 are courtesy of the National Baseball Hall of Fame.
All other photographs in the interior of the book are courtesy of the Texas Rangers.
Special thanks to John Blake and Kelly Gavin of the Rangers.

Copyright © 2019 Society for American Baseball Research, Inc.
All rights reserved. Reproduction in whole or in part without permission is prohibited.

ISBN 978-1-943816-93-4
(Ebook ISBN 978-1-943816-92-7)

Book design: Wrenn Simms
Society for American Baseball Research
Cronkite School at ASU
555 N. Central Ave. #416
Phoenix, AZ 85004
Phone: (602) 496-1460
Web: www.sabr.org
Facebook: Society for American Baseball Research
Twitter: @SABR

CONTENTS

INTRODUCTION
By Steve West

1. PROLOGUE:
   THE WASHINGTON SENATORS:
   1961-71 1
   By Joseph Wancho

2. MAJOR LEAGUE BASEBALL
   COMES TO ARLINGTON 5
   By Greg Chandler

PLAYERS

3. LARRY BIITTNER 9
   By David E. Skelton

4. RICH BILLINGS 16
   By Chris Jones

5. DICK BOSMAN 24
   By Dale Voiss

6. PETE BROBERG 28
   By Gregory H. Wolf

7. JEFF BURROUGHS 35
   By David E. Skelton

8. CASEY COX 42
   By Alan Cohen

9. JIMMY DRISCOLL 48
   By Charlie Grassl

10. JAN DUKES 54
    By Clayton Trutor

11. BILL FAHEY 57
    By Kris Rutherford

12. TED FORD 63
    By Chris Holaday

13. BILL GOGOLEWSKI 67
    By Gregory H. Wolf

14. TOM GRIEVE 73
    By Steve West

15. RICH HAND 80
    By Raymond Rossi

16. TOBY HARRAH 85
    By Frederick C. Bush

17. VIC HARRIS 95
    By Paul Hofmann

18. RICH HINTON 100
    By Mark S. Sternman

19. FRANK HOWARD 106
    By Mark Armour

20. GERRY JANESKI 114
    By David E. Skelton

21. DALTON JONES 119
    By Maurice Bouchard

22. HAL KING 126
    By Chris Holaday

23. TED KUBIAK 130
    By Rory Costello

24. STEVE LAWSON 137
    By Chris Holaday

25. PAUL LINDBLAD 140
    By Paul Hofmann

26. JOE LOVITTO 146
    By Charlie Grassl

27. ELLIOTT MADDOX 150
    By Gordon Janis

28. ORLANDO "MARTY" MARTÍNEZ 157
    By Joseph Gerard

29. JIM MASON 161
    By Steve West

30. DON MINCHER 166
    By Marc Z. Aaron

31. DAVE NELSON 170
    By Rick Schabowski

32. **JIM PANTHER** 175
    By Chad Moody

33. **MIKE PAUL** 182
    By Wayne Strumpfer

34. **HORACIO PIÑA** 186
    By Rory Costello and Francisco Rodríguez Lozano

35. **TOM RAGLAND** 195
    By Bob LeMoine

36. **LENNY RANDLE** 202
    By Charlie Grassl

37. **JIM ROLAND** 206
    By Gregory H. Wolf

38. **JIM SHELLENBACK** 211
    By Paul Geisler

39. **DON STANHOUSE** 216
    By Maxwell Kates

40. **KEN SUAREZ** 224
    By Bo Carter

MANAGER

41. **TED WILLIAMS** 228
    By Bill Nowlin

42. **JOE CAMACHO** 235
    By Charlie Grassl

43. **NELLIE FOX** 239
    By Robert W. Bigelow and Don Zminda

44. **SID HUDSON** 246
    By John Bennett

45. **GEORGE SUSCE** 250
    By David E. Skelton

46. **WAYNE TERWILLIGER** 256
    By C. Paul Rogers III

OWNER

47. **BOB SHORT** 264
    By Bob Whelan and Steve West

BALLPARK

48. **ARLINGTON STADIUM** 270
    By Will Osgood

49. **PLAYERS WHO HOMERED AT ARLINGTON STADIUM AS BOTH MINOR AND MAJOR LEAGUE PLAYERS** 275
    By Alan Cohen

MEDIA

50. **DALLAS-FORT WORTH BASEBALL MEDIA IN 1972** 278
    By Steve West

BROADCASTERS

51. **BILL MERCER** 281
    By Bo Carter

52. **DON DRYSDALE** 285
    By Joseph Wancho

BEAT WRITER

53. **RANDY GALLOWAY** 291
    By Norm King

OTHERS

54. **TOM VANDERGRIFF** 294
    By Greg Chandler

55. **JOE BURKE** 297
    By Steve West

56. **HAL KELLER** 305
    By Nelson "Chip" Greene

57. BILL ZEIGLER 313
By Charlie Grassl

GREAT GAMES

58. RANGERS THROW AWAY
    THEIR FIRST-EVER GAME:
    APRIL 15, 1972:
    CALIFORNIA ANGELS 1,
    TEXAS RANGERS 0
    AT ANAHEIM STADIUM 316
    By Steve West

59. BROBERG'S EIGHT STRONG INNINGS
    GIVE RANGERS FIRST WIN
    IN CLUB HISTORY:
    APRIL 16, 1972:
    TEXAS RANGERS 5,
    CALIFORNIA ANGELS 1,
    AT ANAHEIM STADIUM 318
    By Gregory H. Wolf

60. FANS CELEBRATE THE ARRIVAL
    OF MAJOR-LEAGUE BASEBALL
    IN NORTH TEXAS:
    APRIL 21, 1972:
    TEXAS RANGERS 7,
    CALIFORNIA ANGELS 6
    AT ARLINGTON STADIUM 321
    By Duane Victor Keilstrup

61. BROBERG, RANGERS
    SUFFER HARD-LUCK LOSS TO ORIOLES:
    MAY 10, 1972:
    BALTIMORE ORIOLES 1,
    TEXAS RANGERS 0
    AT MEMORIAL STADIUM 324
    By Frederick C. Bush

62. RANGERS WIN 18-INNING MARATHON:
    MAY 17, 1972:
    TEXAS RANGERS 4,
    KANSAS CITY ROYALS 3
    AT MUNICIPAL STADIUM 327
    By Frederick C. Bush

63. NELSON, RANDLE HELP RANGERS
    SUBDUE TRIBE IN 12 INNINGS:
    JULY 16, 1972:
    TEXAS RANGERS 3,
    CLEVELAND INDIANS 2
    AT ARLINGTON STADIUM 330
    By Frederick C. Bush

64. RYAN OVERCOMES 107-DEGREE
    HEAT AND FATIGUE
    TO SHUT OUT RANGERS AND FAN 14:
    JULY 27, 1972:
    CALIFORNIA ANGELS 5,
    TEXAS RANGERS 0
    AT ANAHEIM STADIUM 333
    By Gregory H. Wolf

65. RANGERS MANAGER TED WILLIAMS
    TEES OFF IN BATTING PRACTICE
    AT FENWAY:
    AUGUST 25, 1972:
    BOSTON RED SOX 4,
    TEXAS RANGERS 0
    AT FENWAY PARK 336
    By Bill Nowlin

66. GOGO TOSSES ONE-HITTER
    AND OUTDUELS THE RYAN EXPRESS:
    SEPTEMBER 12, 1972:
    TEXAS RANGERS 3,
    CALIFORNIA ANGELS 0
    AT ANAHEIM STADIUM 338
    By Gregory H. Wolf

67. DICK BOSMAN BEATS THE WHITE SOX,
    ENDING RANGERS'
    15-GAME LOSING STREAK:
    OCTOBER 1, 1972:
    TEXAS RANGERS 1,
    CHICAGO WHITE SOX 0
    AT ARLINGTON STADIUM 341
    By Michael Huber

SIDEBARS

68. MINOR-LEAGUE BASEBALL IN THE DALLAS-FORT WORTH AREA 343
By Bruce Bumbalough

69. EMBRACING THE FUTURE: THE TRANSACTIONS OF THE 1972 TEXAS RANGERS 351
By William Schneider

70. TEXAS RANGERS 1972 SEASON SUMMARY 359
By Steve West

71. BY THE NUMBERS 371
By Dan Fields

72. THE FIRST TWO DOZEN YEARS: BAD MANAGEMENT, WORSE BASEBALL 378
By Joe Stroop

73. CONTRIBUTORS 387

INTRODUCTION

BY STEVE WEST

Just how bad were the early Texas Rangers teams? Put it this way: When reporter Mike Shropshire wrote a book about covering the Rangers from 1973 to '75, he called it Seasons In Hell, and when that book was published, two decades later, the Rangers still hadn't made the playoffs. Counting the '60s, the decade that they began as the Washington Senators, the Rangers did not go to the playoffs for the first 35 years of their existence. They threatened, finishing second six times (but never within five games of the division winners). The one time they were in first, the season ended with a strike, and they still had only a 52-62 record.

So why write a book about the 1972 Texas Rangers, perhaps the worst team in club history? Well, it's because they're the start of that history. It seems that you can't swing a bat in the team store at Rangers Ballpark in Arlington without hitting something with 1972 written on it. For a team that has been around a relatively short time, the Rangers certainly like to promote the history of the club, and it all began with this team. Many Rangers fans wear T-shirts with 1972 on them, or have key rings, or pennants, or some other memorabilia. These guys are, for good or bad, legendary. And this book is the story of why.

Perhaps one of the biggest influences on this book is one of the men who have been in the broadcast booth for so many years, Tom Grieve. Grieve was a Washington Senator who came over to Texas, was the longest-serving player from that original team, then became the general manager, before moving into the broadcast booth. Since then he regularly tells stories about the 1972 team, or about the early years, making it yet another point of interest for that first team.

THE 1972 TEXAS RANGERS

It took the vision of one man to get a major-league baseball team in North Texas. Tom Vandergriff, mayor of Arlington, a small town midway between the big cities of Dallas and Fort Worth, had that vision. Hoping to build economic opportunities in his city, he persuaded people to support his plan. It took a lot of Texas guts to pull this off, but by pitting the two big rival cities against each other, he managed to get a team into the little town in the middle.

It took a long time, though, a lot longer than he expected. He spent the 1950s and '60s trying to lure a team to move, or get an expansion team. He built Turnpike Stadium, a ballpark for the minor-league team that could quickly be converted to major-league status. He almost got Charlie Finley to bring his Kansas City A's to Texas, but Charlie eventually decided on the West Coast.

Then Vandergriff found his man. Or, maybe, Bob Short found his mark. Short was a veteran of moving sports teams, having taken the NBA's Lakers from Minneapolis to Los Angeles. Now he'd bought the Washington Senators – the expansion team, not the original, which itself had moved to Minnesota a decade before. Was it Short's plan all along? Buy a team, run it down, move it, profit? Who knows? He certainly never admitted to something like that. But he did it – twice.

Short complained about everything in Washington. The fans didn't show up. It was because of the horrible ballpark, or the neighborhood around it. He had a terrible ballpark deal, and couldn't make any money because of it. His radio and television deals tied his hands. About the only thing he had going for him was the manager, Hall of Famer Ted Williams. Until Vandergriff showed up.

Secret negotiations ensued in the middle of 1971. The Texas people were willing to give Short anything he wanted if he moved the team. They had a ballpark ready. They had broadcast deals ready. And the fans, who came out to see a minor-league team would surely flock to see a major-league one too. All Short had to do was agree to move the team.

And he did. It took some finagling, a few lawsuits, and a lot of complaining from real senators. There was an air of financial shenanigans, too. Baseball wouldn't let the Senators leave Washington without proving Short was losing money, which was easy, since he created the books. They wanted him to find local owners to buy the team instead of moving it. He found some, but they couldn't provide enough guarantees for his liking. Notably, he wanted them to cover all his losses for the last several years – which were largely paper losses anyway.

So baseball voted, and Short was allowed to go. The pot of gold at the end of the rainbow was sitting there waiting for him. All he had to do was suffer some verbal slings and arrows, along with the indignity of seeing the final game in Washington abandoned when fans invaded the field, and he could cash in. He did, by the way: the city of Arlington paid him upfront for 10 years of broadcasting fees. Not only did that $7.5 million pay off his debts, but it ensured a handsome profit, given that later investigations showed he'd put down almost no money to buy the team in the first place. And he certainly wasn't going to be around for 10 years to see how much selling the radio and TV rights would hurt the team.

The Senators moved to Arlington for the 1972 season. Rebranding called them the Texas Rangers, after the legendary state law-enforcement group. They embraced the area, using Texas symbols in all their marketing, doing everything but wearing cowboy boots and hats on the field. They did what they could to bring immediate success, but they couldn't fix one thing: the players. The team was a roster of has-beens and never-weres, with the occasional rough diamond that was either not yet polished or was quickly traded away at any sign of life.

Bad luck hit the team even before it played its first game. The first-ever players strike in the spring of 1972 delayed Opening Day, and all the plans the team had to bring in the crowds for their first game. After a week of the season was lost, instead of the first game being at home, the Rangers opened in California, and didn't get home until a few days later. But when they did, the pageantry was there, albeit to a much smaller crowd than hoped.

That first-ever Texas Rangers game? You wouldn't believe it if you read it in a novel. They lost, but they did it impressively. With the Rangers and Angels tied, 0-0, in the bottom of the ninth, Rangers reliever Paul Lindblad threw a bases-loaded walk-off wild pitch – perhaps symbolic of all the bad luck that would follow the team for decades.

When the Rangers came home for their first North Texas series, they swept the Angels in four games. Imagine the excitement in DFW for the first-place Texas Rangers. But they lost the following day and fell to fourth, and reality set in. By early June they hit last place and kept falling. Pretty much everyone quit on the team during the dog days of August, just showing up for the paychecks.

In late August the Rangers started a string in which they lost five, won one, lost four, won one, then lost five again. 2-14, if you're trying to add it up. Next they won two out of three, so they were up to 4-15. The last of those three was a one-hitter by Bill Gogolewski, who apparently used up all the luck from the baseball gods, because the very next day they started the infamous 15-game losing streak. By the end of the streak they'd completed a 4-30 run, bad enough to make any fan cry. The game to end the losing streak took another Herculean pitching effort: Dick Bosman threw a three-hit shutout to beat the White Sox, 1-0.

Toward the end of the streak the media began to report the rumor that Williams was quitting at the end of the season. The Greatest Hitter That Ever Lived had been driven crazy by this team. With a combined .217 average, they were The Team That Couldn't Hit, and there was nothing he could do about it. He would rather go fishing than manage them for another year.

Good things did happen during the season. Several game stories in this book tell of some of the better days the team had. In the June amateur draft the Rangers got Jim Sundberg and Mike Hargrove, who would each go on to long careers in the major leagues. Sunny is still around the team, having worked in the front office and in the media for the Rangers. Bobby Jones was around, too, although he was still in the minors. He'd been to Vietnam, where he'd earned a Bronze Star, and came back to play and coach for the Rangers, and spend more than two decades managing in the farm system. He retired in 2016, having spent 45 of his 50 years in baseball in the Rangers organization.

If you want to find a win for Bob Short, take a look at the attendance figures. He brashly predicted a million fans would come out, but he was wildly wrong. In the early part of the season, writers in Washington were quick to point out that compared with the prior season, Rangers fans weren't showing up as much as Senators fans had. But by the end, Short had the last laugh. Barely. Although they had four fewer home games, the Rangers had 662,974 fans through the turnstiles, 7,818 more than the Senators did the previous year. And Short proved right in the long term. There were just 25,000 more fans in 1973, but in 1974 the Rangers hit almost 1.2 million. The most the expansion Senators ever had was 918,000, while the original Senators passed a million just once. Since 1974 the Rangers have hit at least a million every season, except for the strike year of 1981, when they had 850,000 in just 56 home games. By the 1990s they were regularly hitting 2 million and passed 3 million a couple of times in the 2010s.

The on-field effort helped with attendance, of course. Short sold the team to Brad Corbett in 1974, just a few months after the fifth anniversary of his buying it. (This was not a coincidence: It was the most favorable tax window to sell, and may have been his plan all along.) Corbett owned the team until 1980. Neither of them had money to put into the team (and neither of them wanted to). They spent the decade trading good players for bad, almost always with some cash coming back to them, which was used just to fund operations. They even lied about that – when shortstop Jim Mason was sold to the Yankees at the end of 1973, Short told local media that he got $250,000. The Yankees said they paid $100,000, and the media in New York thought even that was too much.

And that's largely why the Rangers of the 1970s (and the Senators of the 1960s) were so bad. Owners operating on shoestring budgets, trying to stay afloat. The 1972 Rangers were the start of it in Texas, but they were a symptom of the malaise that was in the organization. The team had several good young players, but they were either traded away or rushed to the big leagues – David Clyde, anyone? – for financial purposes, and not developed properly. Mason and Grieve are good examples of that, too. In both cases Short wanted to put them on the major-league team, but Williams said they needed much more development in the minors.

It wasn't until Eddie Chiles bought the team from Corbett – effectively a forced sale, because Chiles had loaned Corbett money to keep the team afloat, and he couldn't afford to repay it – that the Rangers began showing some professionalism. Perhaps it was the escape from the wild times of the '70s, too. By the time George W. Bush bought the team in 1989, they were on a solid financial foundation. And then they could push on to develop teams that would be competitive in the next decade. Again partly thanks to Grieve, who spent 1984-94 as the general manager.

So, if you remember the Rangers of the 1970s, you know how bad things can be. Hopefully you stuck around to see them turn into a winning team. Of course, they still don't have a ring, 45 years later. Two World Series appearances, and twice they were one strike away from winning it all. But the curse of the Rangers continues.

DID YOU KNOW?

Some fun facts about the 1972 Texas Rangers:

They spent time in first place, and it wasn't just on Opening Day. A week into the season they won and jumped to first. The following day they lost and fell to fourth. They never got above third place again all season.

Imagine finishing 20½ games back. No, not behind the league leaders. The 1972 Rangers finished that far behind the next-to-last team, the Angels, who, at 18 games behind division champs Oakland, were closer to first than to last.

Surprisingly, the Rangers were pivotal in a division race. The Detroit Tigers were 10-2 against the

Rangers, while the Boston Red Sox were 8-4. The Tigers won the American League East by half a game over the Red Sox. Just one more loss by the Tigers, or one more win by the Red Sox, against the Rangers, and baseball history could have been completely different.

They had a 15-game losing streak, still the worst in franchise history (through 2017). That streak was part of a 4-30 run in August and September, which got them to 99 losses with three games to go. They managed to win the first two but got their 100th loss on the last day.

The team batting average was .217, the fourth lowest since the start of the twentieth century. How galling was that to manager Ted Williams, the greatest hitter of all time? The only teams that were worse? The Yankees at .214, in the Year of the Pitcher, 1968, and two Deadball Era teams, the 1908 Brooklyn Dodgers at .213, and the 1910 Chicago White Sox at .211.

Only one pitcher reached 10 wins, Rich Hand. He also led the team with 14 losses. Naturally he was traded the following May. The best pitcher may have been Mike Paul, who was 8-9 with a 2.17 ERA in 20 starts and 29 relief appearances. They traded him too, the following August.

The "best" hitters were Toby Harrah and Larry Biittner at .259 (Harrah was ahead by a few decimal points). Or, if you want to use the OPS+ stat (On-base Plus Slugging, adjusted to ballpark, with 100 being league average), it was Don Mincher, at 133. Only two others, Frank Howard and Ted Ford, were above league average in that stat.

Wins Above Replacement (WAR) is the currently fashionable stat to show how good a player is. Replacement level is zero, which means you could pick someone up from the minor leagues who should do that job just as well. The Rangers had 11 hitters and 8 pitchers at or below zero. In other words, 19 of the 38 players the Rangers used in 1972, exactly half of them, were below replacement level. The Rangers also had three hitters and three pitchers over 2 WAR. For context, a WAR over 5 puts you at All-Star level, while a WAR over 2 could be a starting player in the major leagues. Mike Paul led the team with 3.4 WAR, while Elliott Maddox was the best hitter at 2.5 WAR.

Despite all those terrible players, it was the only major-league season for just one of them. Pity poor Steve Lawson, who pitched well with a 2.81 ERA in 16 innings in his debut season. Arm trouble quickly led to the end of his career, but he at least could say that he played in the big leagues.

The ballpark was a converted minor-league park, with thousands of seats quickly added when the Rangers arrived. It was so hot in the summer that fans called it a frying pan for the two decades it somehow remained in use. When they replaced it, in 1994, they still weren't smart enough to put a roof on the new park.

WHAT'S IN THE BOOK?

All this history and more is covered in this book. The 1972 Texas Rangers were a culmination of a couple of decades of trying to get a major-league team. Dallas-Fort Worth has a long history with baseball, going back to the 1800s. Minor-league teams played in both cities for many years, indeed right up until the Rangers arrived. Articles in this book tell you that history, about the effort to bring a team to North Texas, and the story of Tom Vandergriff, the man now known as "the father of the Rangers."

The franchise began as the expansion Washington Senators, and we cover their story, which is often forgotten since it was so brief. We'll tell you about Bob Short, the wheeler-dealer who ran the team on a shoestring, and looked at Texas as a way to make a quick profit. You already know everything there is to know about manager Ted Williams, right? We'll tell you the story of Ted and his coaches, and the guys in the front office who ran the team, often despite Short's interference.

And there are the players. Biographies of everyone who played on the 1972 Rangers, whether it was their only major-league experience or if they had long careers. None longer than Tom Grieve, of course, who went on to spend five decades with the franchise, as player, general manager, and broadcaster, and earned the nickname "Mr. Ranger."

We also have several game stories from 1972. The first-ever game, which wasn't supposed to be. The first home game, cowboy boots and all. The time that Nolan Ryan struck out 14 Rangers, decades before he became a Rangers legend. And more.

Then there are all the fascinating extras we include. Stories of the guys who broadcast the games (including a Hall of Fame pitcher) in the days when the radio broadcasters took turns in the TV booth too. A newspaper beat reporter who went on to become one of the best-known writers in the Dallas media market. The story of how the team was put together, how the season unfolded, and the long suffering of Rangers fans before the team finally put a winning product on the field.

There's a lot of history here. Not all of it was good, but they were the first. Next time you're in the ballpark, look around for a 1972 logo, and think back to the people who started it, all those years ago.

ACKNOWLEDGMENTS

Many people worked together to produce this book. Every article was written by a member of the Society for American Baseball Research (SABR), all of whom volunteered their time. My original idea for the book was enthusiastically supported by C. Paul Rogers, chair of the Banks-Bragan Dallas-Ft. Worth chapter of SABR (who also gave me the book's title), and other chapter members. SABR members everywhere pitched in, providing help and advice or, more directly, writing articles for the book. The story of the 1972 Texas Rangers presented here is due to their interest in recording and preserving baseball history. You can read biographies of all the contributors at the back of the book. I thank each and every one for their time and patience as this book moved through the process from conception to publication.

Of course, there were also contacts with the players in the book. Many of them gave their time freely either to me or to writers throughout the book, and I acknowledge the importance of getting the book written with their first-person knowledge and experience.

Thanks to my wife, Marian, and son, Joshua, for their enthusiastic support during the long gestation of the book. Many times I read odd stories about the team and players, and they listened to all of them with at least polite understanding. I'm glad to have them with me, and happy they enjoy watching the Rangers both on television and at the ballpark as much as I do.

I thank Carl Riechers, the book's fact-checker, and Len Levin, the copy editor. They went through every article with a fine-toothed comb and found many things that I had missed. I would read each article two or three times before they even saw it, and they'd still catch things. Carl's ability to fact-check is amazing, making sure that someone hit .215, not .216, somewhere in the distant past. I'd get my own articles back from him and wonder how I managed to write some of the things I wrote, and glad he was there to fix it. As copy editor Len's job is to make sure everything follows SABR's Style Guide, which he must have memorized by heart, and also to ensure that everything reads properly. Often Len would subtly change a sentence I'd written and make it much clearer. Thank you both so much, Carl and Len. You definitely made this book better.

Finally, my deepest thanks go to my co-editor, Bill Nowlin, SABR director and coordinator of BioProject books. Bill invested a lot of time and effort in guiding me to produce this book, and I am grateful for his help. It took longer than we both expected from start to finish, but Bill was there all the way, and pushed it over the finish line. Maybe a baseball metaphor is better: I got the book to third base (with a lot of help), but it was Bill who drove in the winning run. Bill, thank you so much for all your work and support.

Steve West
Carrollton, Texas
March 2018

PROLOGUE:
THE WASHINGTON SENATORS: 1961-71

BY JOSEPH WANCHO

"I'd love to be the man going into Washington.
I've always felt that city is one of the top two or three franchises in the nation."
– *Frank Lane, general manager, Cleveland Indians*[1]

October 26, 1960, started a new era of Washington Senators baseball. It began auspiciously enough. Senators' president Calvin Griffith was relocating his team to Minnesota. The Senators had been an original franchise in the American League since its inception in 1901. But for years the son of Clark Griffith, a former Senators pitcher and the team's owner since 1920, had been wanting to move his club. Washington won its last pennant in 1933. Except for second-place finishes in 1943 and 1945, the Senators were a second-division club in the junior circuit. Often they were battling it out with Philadelphia or St. Louis for last place. From 1955 to 1959, they finished in the cellar. When Charles Dryden penned the phrase "Washington – first in war, first in peace, last in the American League" in 1909, it was meant to be a humorous observation. But unfortunately for Washington fans, it became a reality most seasons. "I regret leaving Washington," said Griffith, "but I just couldn't turn down the Minneapolis deal. I think we'll draw 1.3 million our first year there and we'll average more per head than we did in Washington."[2]

As part of the deal to assuage the Nats fans, an expansion team was granted to the nation's capital beginning with the 1961 season. Both the American and National Leagues were expanding to 10 teams. The American League opened for business in Los Angeles and Washington. The senior circuit put down stakes in New York and Houston. Many fans had grown weary of Griffith, and were not terribly sorry to see him leave. They were getting a new franchise, a fresh start, and that was exciting. Not to mention that a new stadium would be christened in time for the 1962 season.

However, the short turnaround time for the expansion franchises would be a burden. Most knowledgeable baseball fans expected a couple of years of futility before progress was made. Elwood R. "Pete" Quesada was named the owner of the new franchise on November 17. Quesada was an administrator with the Federal Aviation Agency (as of 1967 the Federal Aviation Administration). Before that, he had a decorated career in military aviation. Quesada immediately made overtures to Cleveland general manager Frank Lane to come to Washington. Although Lane was intrigued by the idea, he knew a bad proposition when he saw one, and stayed put. Eventually Ed Doherty was named the GM and Mickey Vernon was hired to be the manager. Vernon was an icon in Washington, one of the few stars the franchise had in the 1940s and '50s. However, over his 20 years as a major-league player, Vernon ranked third all-time in games played (2,409) without a playoff appearance. It was no fault of his own, as he owned a .286 lifetime batting average.

The expansion draft was held in Boston in AL President Joe Cronin's office. A flip of the coin for the four categories (pitching, catching, infield, and outfield) determined whether the Senators or Angels would select first. The Angels won three of the four flips; the Senators were able to get only their first pick of outfielders. Each of the existing eight AL clubs was required to make a total of 15 players available, making 120 players eligible to be drafted. As in many expansion drafts in professional sports, the names were a jumble of have-nots, also-rans, and never-were ballplayers.

The highlight of the 1961 season may have been Opening Day. Although the Nats dropped a 4-3 decision to the White Sox, President John F. Kennedy was on hand to throw out the ceremonial first pitch. The paid attendance for the last home opener at Griffith Stadium was 26,275. That total was surpassed only twice during the season, and both times the Yankees were the visitor. Led by Mickey Mantle and Roger Maris, the M&M boys' pursuit of Babe Ruth's single-season home-run record was a boon to teams needing a boost in ticket sales.

Dick Donovan led the league with a 2.40 ERA. Gene Woodling was the only player to bat over .300 (.313), and catcher Gene Green also enjoyed a good season, batting .280, hitting 18 home runs, and driving in 62 runs. The club enjoyed a winning month in May (17-12), but not much else. The Senators finished tied with Kansas City for last place in the AL. The Senators had a 61-100 record, 47½ games behind New York.

The Senators looked to improve their offense, acquiring outfielder Jimmy Piersall from Cleveland for Donovan and Green. After batting .322 for the Tribe in 1961, Piersall slumped to .244 in 1962. Donovan was named The Sporting News American League Pitcher of the Year.

The 1962 season was a carbon copy of the previous year. Not one pitcher posted a winning record and the Nats finished in last place with a 60-101 record, 35½ games out of first place. After the season, Quesada sold the team to James H. Lemon, an investment banker in Washington. Lemon hired George Selkirk to replace Doherty as the general manager. Selkirk was probably best known for taking the place of Babe Ruth in 1934, but he carved out a good career in his own right. In his nine years with the Bombers, the Yanks won six pennants.

Forty games into the 1963 season, Vernon was let go as the Senators' skipper. Piersall was traded to the New York Mets for Gil Hodges, with the understanding that Hodges would take over the reins of the club. His playing days were in the rear-view mirror. It was a curious move in that Hodges had never managed a baseball team, at any level. "He likes to work with young players, and he has the ability to teach them the things that made him a great hitter and a great defensive player," said Mets manager Casey Stengel.[3]

The Senators finished in last again in 1963, but in 1964 they crawled out of the basement into ninth place. However, they still lost 100 games for the fourth straight season. One of the highlights in the 1964 season came when right fielder Jim King hit for the cycle on May 26. He was the only player of the "new" Senators to accomplish the feat.

After the 1964 season Selkirk made a deal that gave a face to the Senators franchise. In a six-player swap with the Los Angeles Dodgers, Frank Howard was bringing his big bat east. Howard had been the 1960 Rookie of the Year. Although like many power hitters he had a penchant for striking out, Howard could also hit for average.

The Senators posted their best post-Griffith record, 70-92, in 1965 and inched up in the standings to eighth place. But for the Washington fans, the real kick in the teeth came when the Minnesota Twins won the pennant. To make it worse, their core players (Earl Battey, Zoilo Versalles, Harmon Killebrew, Don Mincher, Bob Allison, Jim Kaat, and Camilo Pascual) were all on the Washington roster in 1960. A hard pill to swallow for Nats fans, to be sure

The Senators went 71-88 in 1966, again finishing in eighth place. Sonny Siebert fired a no-hitter against Washington on August 10 at Cleveland.

The next four seasons could be termed the Frank Howard years. He was nicknamed the Washington Monument for his 6-foot-7 frame. Howard averaged 43 home runs and 108 RBIs from 1967 through 1970. His best season was 1970, when he smacked 46 round-trippers, drove in 126 runs, and drew 132 walks. All three categories led the American League.

Despite Howard's offensive fireworks, changes were being made in the Capital City. Hodges did about as much as he could with talent he was given. He was traded back to the Mets for pitcher Bill Denehy and $100,000 on November 27, 1967. Jim Lemon (no relation to the Washington owner) took over the reins of the club. A former player for the

Senators, Lemon had a solid career. He had one year of managerial experience, with York (Pennsylvania) of the Eastern League in 1964. Lemon was on the Twins coaching staff before joining the Senators. The Nats sank to the bottom of the American League standings in 1968.

Owner Lemon sold his interest in the club to Bob Short in the fall of 1968. Short, a trucking magnate from Minneapolis, had owned the Minneapolis Lakers of the NBA. He moved them to Los Angeles in 1957. He then sold the franchise to Jack Kent Cooke in 1965, making a profit of $5.2 million. Short outbid comedian Bob Hope for the majority rights to the Senators, and kept Lemon on as chairman of the board.

Would the Senators face the same fate as the Lakers? Short said all the right things when the announcement of his ownership was made. But two days later he remarked, "I am not committed to keep the team in Washington if D.C. Stadium is not made safe for the fans."[4] Selkirk was removed from his general-manager position, and Doherty was brought back into the fold, although his new responsibilities were not clearly defined. Short was his own general manager.

Jim Lemon the manager was also shown the door. Short tried to woo Kansas City manager Bob Kennedy to succeed Lemon. Kennedy wasn't interested. Short then persuaded Ted Williams to take the post. Williams signed on for a sweetheart deal to pilot the Senators. Teddy Ballgame was given a five-year pact calling for $65,000 annually. Included was a $15,000-a-year apartment in Washington and an unlimited expense account. It was surely enough for the Splendid Splinter to abandon his tackle box and reel.

In 1969 both leagues expanded by two more teams and each went to a two-division format. This created a round of playoffs before the World Series. No longer was the team with the best regular-season record guaranteed a spot in the fall classic. Not that the Senators needed to be concerned with postseason play. However, under Williams, they finished in fourth place in the American League East Division in 1969 with a record of 86-76. Howard (48 HR, 111 RBIs) and first baseman Mike Epstein (30 HR, 85 RBIs) carried the offense, while pitcher Dick Bosman led the league with a 2.19 ERA and was 14-5. Williams was named American League Manager of the Year in 1969.

Meanwhile Hodges won a world championship with the Mets, who upended the heavily favored Baltimore Orioles in the World Series.

One of the more entertaining nights for Senators fans was the All-Star Game, which was held on July 23, 1969, at Robert F. Kennedy Memorial Stadium. (Renamed from D.C. Stadium, it was commonly called RFK Stadium.) Although the National League won the contest, 9-3, Howard hit a second-inning home run to give the home crowd something to cheer about. The Senators topped the 900,000 mark in attendance for the season. There was no better advertising than a competitive team on the field.

Short saw no reason to have a general manager. He had no experience and it showed. He passed on offers to obtain Graig Nettles, instead bringing in Denny McLain and Curt Flood. Short really had no clue what he was doing. Ironically, if Bob Hope had been allowed to purchase the team they might have been less of a joke.

The Senators slumped to their old ways in 1970 and 1971. Commissioner Bowie Kuhn, who as a youth worked at Griffith Stadium, felt that it was important to keep a team in the nation's capital. American League President Joe Cronin, himself a former Senator and a great one at that, felt likewise. Kuhn made last-ditch efforts to find a buyer for the flailing franchise.

Short was asking for $12 million for the franchise, or he would not renew the lease at RFK Stadium and move the team. Short set his sights on the Southwest. He received an offer to move his franchise to Arlington, Texas, a city between Dallas and Fort Worth. Part of the deal was a 10-year broadcasting contract that paid $7.5 million in advance. American League owners also realized that it was prudent to have a team presence in that burgeoning area of the country. The owners voted 10-2 in favor of Short relocating the team to Texas. On September 21, 1971, the news became final.

The Senators played their last game on September 30, 1971. A banner that read, "Goodbye Boob Short" hung in the ballpark. Another reading "Bob Short Fan Club" was draped over a completely empty section. Fans raced onto the field in the seventh and ninth innings, causing a forfeit to the New York Yankees. Howard stepped to the plate in the sixth inning with the bases empty and hit a home run off lefty Mike Kekich. The fans went berserk, clamoring for Howard to take a curtain call. "Next time up I told (Yankee catcher Thurman) Munson to thank Mike for the gift," said Howard. "All I know is, he gave me a pitch I could hit."[5]

Notes

1. Burton Hawkins, "New Era for Baseball," *Washington Evening Star*, October 27, 1960: A-15.
2. Burton Hawkins, "Baseball Gets New Start Here as Griffs Move," *Washington Evening Star*, October, 27, 1960: A-15.
3. "Gil Has Ability to Become Successful Manager – Casey," *The Sporting News*, June 1, 1963: 9.
4. "Short Changes Tune on Move," *Washington Evening Star*, December 5, 1968: B-8.
5. Dick Heller, "Kekich's Pitch to Howard: One for the Road Maybe?", *Washington Evening Star*, October 1, 1971: E-2.

MAJOR LEAGUE BASEBALL COMES TO ARLINGTON

BY GREG CHANDLER

The On-the-field History of the Texas Rangers began on April 15, 1972, but efforts to bring major-league baseball to the Dallas-Fort Worth metroplex started more than a decade earlier. In 1953, after 50 years without expansion or relocations in either the American League or the National League, the Braves' move from Boston to Milwaukee was the first of many changes for both leagues in the next few years. Existing teams, especially those struggling in their current market, would look to new markets to improve their financial situation. Perhaps the most surprising moves were made in 1958, with the Dodgers leaving Brooklyn for Los Angeles, and the New York Giants changing their home to San Francisco, the two clubs becoming the first on the West Coast.

At the same time, both the American and National Leagues were considering adding teams. By the fall of 1960, both leagues had formed expansion committees to explore potential locations for new teams, as many as four in each league, along with the issues in adding so many new teams. The cities of Dallas and Fort Worth came together to make a proposal to both leagues. The Bi-County Park Commission, which consisted of some of the most influential people in north Texas, had assembled a comprehensive plan for a new stadium to be built in Arlington, a small town halfway between the two cities near the turnpike that connected them. They already had approval to sell bonds to raise $9.5 million for the first domed stadium for baseball. The stadium would guarantee indoor playing conditions at 75 degrees, relieving concerns over the oppressive heat of a Texas summer. The dome would also mean no threat of rainouts that would force schedule changes. Since most teams in the league would have to travel a long distance to get to Texas, and with no other teams in the area, eliminating the possibility of having to travel back for makeup games was considered a necessity by the committee. Despite a well-organized committee with financial backing and community support from one of the largest cities without a major-league team, both leagues opted for other cities. The American League added the Los Angeles Angels and replaced the Washington Senators team that was moving to Minneapolis in 1961, and the National League added teams in New York and Houston in 1962.

Tom Vandergriff, the mayor of Arlington and the chairman of the Bi-County Park Commission, continued his efforts to bring major-league baseball to north Texas. He proposed the area to club owners who were struggling and wanting to move their teams. Charley Finley was eager to move the A's out of Kansas City, but at a meeting of the American League on September 18, 1962, it was evident that a move was not going to be approved.

Determined to demonstrate support of baseball in Arlington, Mayor Vandergriff initiated construction of Turnpike Stadium in September 1964. The ballpark became the home field for the Texas League's Dallas-Fort Worth Spurs in 1965. Originally, it seated 10,000 fans, large by minor-league standards, but was designed to be easily expanded to 50,000 seats in hopes of becoming home to a major-league team. Attendance at the Spurs games was very good, but Arlington was still unable to land a major-league team.

The next serious opportunity came in 1968. Both leagues were considering adding two teams, and the Kansas City A's were now adamant about moving. Dallas-Fort Worth made a bid for a National League team but lost out to Montreal and San Diego. Roy Hofheinz, the owner of the Houston Astros, resisted a north Texas team because of the television contracts the Astros had throughout Texas, Oklahoma, and Louisiana. Vandergriff argued that an in-state rivalry would benefit Hofheinz, but it was not to be. The American League had finally approved the A's moving to Oakland, but legal threats forced them to grant Kansas City a new expansion team to replace the A's. The league chose Seattle over Dallas-Fort Worth for its second expansion team, although the Pilots would play in Seattle for only one year before moving to Milwaukee.

With further expansion not expected for several years, the only hope Vandergriff had of bringing a major-league team to Arlington was to get approval for an existing club to relocate. To that end, he continued to build relationships with owners. He garnered support from California Angels owner Gene Autry, and the owner of the Washington Senators, Bob Short. Short and the Senators were having financial difficulties, which some say were of his own doing so that he could move the team to Texas. During the 1971 season, Short petitioned the American League to be able to move the team to Arlington. He had tried to negotiate a lower lease on RFK Stadium, but even with the threat of moving the team to Arlington if a new deal could not be reached, the D.C. Armory Board would not alter the lease. Short also offered to sell the team to anyone willing to pay $12 million to keep the team in Washington. On September 21, 1971, the league convened a meeting in Boston to discuss the relocation request. Vandergriff led a contingent from Dallas-Fort Worth. While he was presenting, a messenger knocked on the door and gave them a note signed by President Nixon which read, "I implore you. Repeat: I implore you: Do not move the nation's national pastime from the nation's capital."[1] Following Vandergriff's presentation, the league excused the Texas delegation so the owners could vote. After a lengthy debate, the move was approved despite dissenting votes from the owners of the Baltimore Orioles and Chicago White Sox.[2]

News of the move was met with a flood of emotions in Washington. The nation's capital couldn't fathom how they could be losing their team to "a dinky, nowhere town between Dallas and Fort Worth with all the big-league stature of an anthill."[3] Players who enjoyed playing and living in Washington were disappointed to be moving, too. Many of the fans were very angry with Short and it was in full display in the final game of the season when the Senators hosted the Yankees. Fans hung banners all over the ballpark expressing their feelings about Short. The game ended when several hundred fans stormed the field with two outs in the top of the ninth inning. They literally stole the bases, pulled up grass, put dirt in their pockets, and grabbed anything else they could. The Senators were leading the game, but were forced to forfeit, ending a dismal season and closing the book on baseball in Washington, D.C., for 33 years.

That fall, Turnpike Stadium was expanded to a capacity over 35,000 and renamed Arlington Stadium. The team was named the Texas Rangers. It had taken 13 years of persistence, especially by Mayor Vandergriff, but Dallas-Fort Worth finally had the baseball team they coveted.

Sources
In addition to the sources in the notes, the author also consulted:
Daniel, Dan. "Finley Backs Off – Fails to Seek A.L. Approval for Shift," *The Sporting News*, September 29, 1962.
Daniel, Dan. "Let's Speed Up Expansion Plan," *The Sporting News*, September 21, 1960.
Gillespie, Ray. "Dallas-Fort Worth Join Hands in Major Bid," *The Sporting News*, September 21, 1960.

thisgreatgame.com.
baseball-reference.com/bullpen/Expansion_of_1961.
texas.rangers.mlb.com/tex/history/timeline.jsp.

Notes

1. Aaron Mathews, shutdowninning.com/boy-mayor-first-hero/.
2. "American League Owners Approve Washington Shift," *Ludington* (Michigan) *Daily News*, September 21, 1971.
3. Timothy Dwyer, "The Season Washington Was Out," *Washington Post*, August 31, 2004.

LARRY BIITTNER

BY DAVID E. SKELTON

"I'm nobody's caddy I should be playing somewhere," Larry Biittner insisted. "I don't want to be stereotyped. ... Once you get the label you can't play every day, it sticks. I've seen too many careers ruined that way, and I don't want it to happen to mine."[1] These frustrations were expressed in 1979 as the 33-year-old was concluding his 10th major-league season with fewer than 350 at-bats. In 1970-1971 Ted Williams tried to mold the left-handed hitter into something resembling his own Hall of Fame career; six years later Biittner was described as "one of the best fill-in first basemen since Lou Gehrig stepped in for Wally Pipp."[2] The lofty expectations beg the question: How was Biittner pigeonholed into just over 1,200 appearances throughout his 14-year major-league career?

Lawrence David Biittner was born on July 27, 1946, one of a dozen children of Edward Oscar and Henrietta Amollia (Stoulil) Biittner in the tiny Iowa city of Pocahontas, 200 miles southwest of Minneapolis, Minnesota. His paternal grandparents appear to have arrived separately in the United States from Bavaria as teenagers in 1879. They married 10 years later and settled in Iowa to raise their large family (the surname was changed from Büttner (pronounced "Beautner"). They farmed the "rich, dark loam ... [of] undisturbed drift soil"[3] in Pocahontas County, a pursuit that Larry's father followed.

Larry attended Pocahontas Catholic High, where he demonstrated tremendous prowess in basketball and baseball. In the former he shattered various Iowa prep-school scoring records to earn All-State honors his junior and senior years. This hardwood success won him induction into the Iowa High School Athletic Association Basketball Hall of Fame. (Through 2015 right-handed slugger Casey Blake is the only other inductee to advance to the major leagues.) After graduating from high school in 1964, Biittner received a basketball scholarship from Drake University in Des Moines, Iowa.

With a near-exclusive focus on basketball alone, Biittner tired of Drake. He transferred to Buena Vista College in Storm Lake, Iowa (30 miles west of Pocahontas), on a double scholarship to include baseball.[4] Biittner's induction into the Iowa High School Baseball Coaches Association Hall of Fame (primarily as a pitcher) demonstrated finesse nurtured further by four-time Iowa Intercollegiate Athletic Conference Coach of the Year Jay Beekman. The pair led the Buena Vista Beavers to a state championship in 1965. Three years later, Biittner's 8-0 record earned NAIA All-Star placement.[5] He had attracted professional scouts in high school. In 1968, as he neared completion of a degree in physical education, this attention intensified.

Central Scouting Bureau's Joe McDermott, a former minor-league player, manager, and owner, was one such scout. His notes on Biittner (including a remarkably frank closing assessment):

"I have followed this boy in high school and college. Saw him pitch, play [first base] and outfield. Pitched real well at Wichita Tournament. Led his college conference in all departments. I like him at [first base or outfield]. Poor family. Will sign."[6]

If McDermott believed he would easily sign Biittner, that privilege went instead to former minor-league pitcher and manager Lee Anthony. The Washington Senators scout persuaded the club to select Biittner in the 10th round of the June 1968 amateur draft. The Senators planned to send him to Geneva, New York, (short-season A) as a pitcher, but changed course after determining Biittner to be a better hitter than pitcher. He was advanced instead to Double-A Savannah, Georgia, where he played outfield and first base. Biittner's .286 average in 199 at-bats placed among the team leaders; afterward he played in the Florida Instructional League.

Biittner spent most of 1969 in the US Army. When he was discharged, the season was almost over. He made just 14 appearances with Savannah before a second assignment to the Instructional League. A standout Florida campaign earned placement on Washington's 40-man roster. In the spring of 1970 Biittner was reassigned to Double-A Pittsfield, Massachusetts, in the Eastern League. On May 20 he set the tone for the season by going 5-for-6 in a doubleheader against the Reading Phillies. On July 14 he returned from another (much shorter) military stint to again beat up on the Phillies: 4-for-6 to lead Pittsfield to an 11-7 win. After the Senators (worst in the American League in batting) lost two players to injury, they recalled Biittner.

On July 17, 1970, Biittner made his major-league debut, as a pinch-hitter against the California Angels – a weak groundout to lefty hurler Clyde Wright. Four days later, Biittner had a second pinch-hit appearance – a fly out – before returning to Pittsfield. Despite the abbreviated stay, he captured considerable attention: "[Manager Ted] Williams was enthused after watching Biittner in batting practice. Ted wants the young left-handed hitting outfielder to get about 500 more times at bat in the minors and thinks he will then be ready. ... '[Williams] talked quite a lot about the logics of hitting,' Biittner said. '[H]e advised me to bring my hips into the ball a little faster.'"[7]

Biittner returned to Pittsfield in time to capture the league's Player of the Month honor for July. On August 1 he collected two hits in the All-Star game. Ten days later he led his team to a 6-2 win over Elmira with two doubles and three RBIs. On September 22 Biittner was a triple shy of the cycle as his four hits paced Pittsfield to another win over Reading. He finished the season with a .325 average, .0001 behind Reading slugger Greg Luzinski for the batting title. Biittner's hot bat continued through a third Instructional League assignment, placing among the league leaders with a .350 average.

Biittner reported to spring training in 1971 among outfield hopefuls Jeff Burroughs and Tom Grieve. A crowded field greeted the three youngsters following the Senators' offseason acquisition of outfielder Elliott Maddox and first baseman Tommy McCraw. On March 6 Biittner made an impressive start in Grapefruit League competition with three hits and two runs scored in a 3-1 win over the Montreal Expos. But in late March all three young hopefuls were assigned to the Senators' minor-league camp.

Biittner's assignment to the Triple-A Denver Bears proved very short. He lashed out against American Association pitching at a .356 pace, including a five-RBI game against the Tulsa Oilers on April 14. At the same time Senators reserve outfielder Richie Scheinblum struggled below .155. Scheinblum was released and Biittner recalled. On May 18 Biittner collected his first major-league hit: a ninth-inning pinch-hit single off Cleveland Indians reliever Vince Colbert. Biittner came around to score. He earned his first starting assignment the next day. An 11-at-bat drought gave way to a 12-for-19 surge, including two three-hit performances contributing to two Senators victories (the team managed a mere 63 wins for the season). Another three-hit outing on June 30 included Biittner's ninth-inning walk-off single in a 2-1 come-from-behind win over the New York Yankees.

Biittner was used primarily in right field and as a pinch-hitter. On August 26 he delivered a game-winning pinch-hit double in his first at-bat following a three-week military stint. Biittner finished his rookie campaign with 44 hits in 171 at-bats (.257, with an eye-popping .368 as a pinch-hitter). Only five of the hits were of the extra-base variety. The Splendid Splinter claimed Biittner's bat evoked memories "of Johnny Mize without Mize's power."[8] Williams was determined that more heft was forthcoming from the left-handed hitter's 6-foot-2, 205-pound frame. The following February he personally directed hitting drills with Biittner (among a select few) to develop the untapped power.

In 1972 Biittner arrived at spring training possessing his "best chance of sticking"[9] with the Senators. The offseason had witnessed the exodus of a number of veteran players. By midseason a full-fledged youth movement abounded as the team – relocated to Arlington, Texas – suffered through a 100-loss campaign. The departures provided Biittner a starting role (primarily right field) but he began the season with a cold bat: .147 through May 12. A superb gloveman, Biittner was relegated to roles as a reserve fielder and pinch-hitter. In June injuries began decimating the Rangers' outfield. Biittner was pressed back into service, including a brief but uncomfortable stint in center field. "I don't mind left or right, but center field was murder," he admitted. "I really don't have enough speed for center."[10]

At this same time, life was breathed back into Biittner's bat. From June 4 through August 1 he was the Rangers' hottest hitter (.363 in 124 at-bats). On June 30 Biittner connected for his first major-league homer. The blast, off Angels pitcher Lloyd Allen, came on the heels of outfielder Ted Ford's home run, marking the first back-to-back dingers in Texas Rangers history. Williams lamented the fact that Biittner managed just two additional homers afterward and eventually gave up trying to convert the 26-year-old: "He doesn't have the swing to be a home run hitter. … Contact is his strength. He hits the ball where it's pitched. To try to change him would be stupid."[11] Though Biittner's bat cooled again in September, he finished the season tied with shortstop Toby Harrah with a team-leading .259 average. Biittner was the regular at first base after the July 20 trade of veteran Don Mincher. Dubbed the "team's first baseman of the future,"[12] Biittner prepared for the 1973 season alongside Harrah and other fellow Rangers in the Venezuelan League.[13]

Biittner's future appeared in doubt after the Rangers during the offseason acquired slugging first baseman Mike Epstein. When Epstein struggled against the wind-thwarted power alleys in Arlington Stadium, he was traded to the Angels in a deal that brought the Rangers first baseman Jim Spencer. Biittner was relegated to a utility role. On May 16, 1973, he delivered a ninth-inning, two-out, game-winning single on a check swing to beat the Kansas City Royals 2-1. But this proved one of Biittner's few highlights. With infrequent use, he struggled below .200 into June, though a late-season surge lifted his average to a respectable .252 by season's end. In November Biittner was assigned to the Rangers' Spokane affiliate. A month later, he was traded to the Montreal Expos for hurler Pat Jarvis and then transferred to Triple-A Memphis.

The driving force behind the trade was Expos general manager Jim Fanning. He correctly assessed that Jarvis's best days were behind him (Jarvis did not pitch professionally again) and hoped to secure something in return. A fellow Buena Vista alumnus, Fanning had scouted Biittner for the Atlanta Braves in 1968. "[Biittner] is a good Triple-A ballplayer with a better-than-average chance of being a major leaguer," Fanning announced after the trade. "He's an established player."[14] The Expos invited Biittner to spring training as a nonroster invitee and – apparently ignorant of Williams's earlier attempts – tried to convert him into a power hitter.

With Memphis Biittner again demonstrated his minor-league hitting credentials with a .327 average, placing among the International League leaders. Promoted to the Expos in August, Biittner found profit in the all-too-familiar pinch-hitting role: .267 in 15 at-bats. This limited success, combined with the team's loss of a number of left-handed hitters via off-season trades, made Biittner a valuable commodity in 1975. In May, when injuries and general ineffectiveness limited manager Gene Mauch's outfield options, Biittner stepped into the lineup. A .382 surge in June made it difficult to dislodge him. Biittner had his most plate appearances in three years and finished the season with a team-leading .315 (including a game-winning 11th-inning triple against the Chicago Cubs on the next-to-last day of the campaign).

In April 1976 Biittner was one of the Expos' last contract holdouts. The lingering negotiations earned him a $10,000 raise. But a concerted youth movement under new manager Karl Kuehl provided greater opportunities for rookie and sophomore prospects (Ellis Valentine, Jerry White, Larry Parrish, and Gary Carter), fewer for the 30-year-old Biittner (though he successfully foiled St. Louis righty John Denny's no-hit bid with an infield single on April 18). On May 17 the Expos acquired disgruntled 26-year-old slugger Andre Thornton from the Cubs in exchange for Biittner and veteran hurler Steve Renko. Platooned at first base and left field, Biittner found his role reduced to pinch-hitting after injuring his hand on July 26. He finished the year with an unremarkable .237-0-18 line in 224 at-bats.

Even less playing time appeared in the offing in 1977 after the Cubs traded for Los Angeles first baseman Bill Buckner. But a spring-training injury to Buckner limited the former Dodger to just 45 at-bats through June 5, to Biittner's benefit. He responded with a torrid .379 in the team's first seven games. In May he placed among the league leaders in hitting – a surge credited to a patient approach at the plate, the result of work with hitting coach Lew Fonseca during the spring. On May 17 Biittner took advantage of a 23-mph wind blowing out of Chicago's Wrigley Field to have his only career multi-homer game. (It was a 23-6 romp over the Padres in which the Cubs tied a franchise record with seven home runs.) When Buckner returned, the Cubs, a surprising contender, kept Biittner's hot bat in the lineup by putting him in left field in place of oft-injured Jose Cardenal.

On May 12 the Cubs, during a seven-game road trip from Houston to Montreal, played an exhibition against their Triple-A affiliate in Wichita, Kansas. Called upon to pitch, Biittner responded with three scoreless innings. The fine showing served as a prelude to a far less successful outing in the first game of a July 4 doubleheader in Chicago. With the Cubs trailing the Expos, 11-2, in the eighth, manager Herman Franks tapped Biittner to secure the final four outs. Pinch-hitter Larry Parrish greeted Biittner with a three-run homer, and there were two more dingers in the ninth. Though he struck out three, Biittner's 40.50 ERA, combined with a $50 fine for throwing over the head of outfielder Del Unser,[15] ensured the end of the lefty's pitching career.

But Biittner continued to contribute with the bat. His game-winning eighth-inning two-run homer against the Houston Astros on July 25 allowed the

Cubs to maintain a first-place hold over the hard-charging Philadelphia Phillies in the National League's Eastern Division. But the team's slow erosion starting in July turned into a complete collapse as the Cubs lost 28 of their final 39 contests, finishing the season with a disappointing .500 record. Excepting a dip in August, Biittner remained one of the Cubs' few consistent players. He was among the team leaders in runs scored (74), hits (147), doubles (28), homers (12), RBIs (62), and average (.298). He finished at a .341 clip in his final 91 at-bats, including a four-hit outing against the Phillies on September 26 in which he came within a triple of the cycle.

Free agent-eligible, Biittner made clear his desire to continue playing just 400 miles east of his native Pocahontas, Iowa: "I'm looking forward to finishing my career with the Cubs. … I like it here, and I'll probably move to Chicago by next year if we get together on any kind of a multiyear contract."[16] Though Biittner re-signed, the Cubs remained active in the offseason. The November 30 free-agent signing of slugging left fielder Dave Kingman put Biittner in a bind aptly captured by The Sporting News columnist Richard Dozer: "[Biittner] will try hard to maintain his 'just-glad-to-be-here' attitude in the face of the Kingman deal and the recovery of a gimpy Bill Buckner. These events guaranteed him less time at first base and in left field."[17]

Biittner's reduced role was quickly evident as the "forgotten portswinger"[18] got only 47 at-bats in the Cubs' first 42 games of 1978.[19] When the chronically injured Buckner was sidetracked in June, Biittner put together a 15-game hitting streak (the franchise's longest in two years). After a move to left field when Kingman was sidelined, Biittner was returned to a reserve role the rest of the season, achieving a .257-4-50 batting line in 343 at-bats. In December the Atlanta Braves, in the market for a left-handed-hitting first baseman, approached the Cubs about Biittner but nothing came of this.

Biittner remained in Chicago the next two years, never capturing 300 plate appearances in either season. He teamed with a pair of seldom-used teammates to anoint themselves "The Riders of the Lonesome Pines." But little use did not translate to a lack of clutch hitting. On August 15, 1979, Biittner, in a rare starting assignment, was a homer shy of the cycle in leading the Cubs to a 6-5 win over the San Francisco Giants. Two days later, his two-run pinch-hit single spurred a come-from-behind win over the San Diego Padres. With reference to Biittner's 1979 batting average, Richard Dozer offered, "How many clubs have a [guy] who hits .290 but can't find his way into the lineup half the time?"[20]

But Biittner earned distinction of a long-remembered sort on September 26, 1979. A solid defensive player, "Buckeye" (as his teammates called him) was playing right field in Wrigley when the New York Mets' Bruce Boisclair hit a sinker to right. "I caught it, but my glove opened up when it hit the ground, the ball rolled out and my cap covered it up," Biittner related in a Chicago Sun-Times interview 23 years later. He was unable to find the ball so "Jerry Martin came running over from center field [to help]. He's laughing into his glove and yelling, 'It's under your bleeping cap.' The Bleacher Bums are shouting, 'Hat! Hat! Hat!'"[21] Biittner recovered in time to throw Boisclair out at third base.

In 1979 the Cubs experienced another late-season collapse. Post-mortem speculation focused on possibly trading Buckner for a needed asset elsewhere and moving Biittner to first base. When the 1980 season began, Biittner's departure was rumored to make room for prized prospect Karl Pagel. Neither scenario developed as Biittner carved a role as a deluxe pinch-hitter for the last-place Cubs. On October 5, 1980 – the last day of the club's miserable season – Biittner stroked an eighth-inning pinch-hit single off Pittsburgh Pirates righty Don Robinson. It was his 46th pinch-hit as a Cub, tying a franchise record.[22]

For the third time in four years, Biittner entered the offseason as a free agent.[23] He had moved to Chicago three years earlier and was extremely popular among both fans and the press. He hoped to stay. But when the Cubs were slow in offering Biittner an extension – "I felt it was a slap in the face," he said[24] – he was selected in the free-agent draft by three teams. On January 12, 1981, Biittner became the first player signed by the Cincinnati Reds since the advent of free agency five years earlier. Reds general manager Dick Wagner commented, "I've always said that if I had to fight my way out of a brawl, I'd pick Larry. He has that kind of intensity."[25]

Biittner saw very limited play in the strike-shortened 1981 campaign. The next season the reserve player was the only .300 hitter for a Cincinnati team that was a shadow of its former Big Red Machine success. Biittner was released by the Reds on December 6, 1982, and signed with his first franchise three weeks later. Hopeful of receiving more play as the Rangers' designated hitter, he was primarily assigned to the all-too-familiar role as deluxe pinch-hitter. On August 8, 1983, Biittner lined a run scoring pinch-hit double to left field in Boston's Fenway Park to help lead the Rangers to a 12-7 win over the Red Sox. The hit – his 96th (and last) pinch-hit – placed Biittner 12th all-time for career pinch-hits. On September 29, 1983, Biittner made his last major-league appearance – appropriately as a pinch-hitter – in Minnesota. He was released a month later and retired. Biittner's departure left just two active players who had once worn a Washington Senators uniform: Jeff Burroughs and Toby Harrah (retired in 1985 and 1986 respectively).

Biittner returned to Chicago, where he worked as a commodity trader on the floor of the Mercantile Exchange and dabbled in real estate. In 1990 he moved to Pocahontas, where he farmed with an ex-brother-in-law. Twenty-two years earlier, Biittner had married Rowfe, Iowa, native Ann Janette Cleal shortly before his selection in the 1968 amateur draft. They met in the summer after his college sophomore year when she was a senior in high school. The union lasted 21 years and produced two sons – Thomas and Robert – before their 1989 divorce.

Biittner demonstrated both a keen sense of humor and a generous approach to fans throughout his career. In 1979, while teamed with veteran righty Ken Holtzman during the hurler's second stint with the Cubs, Biittner joked, "Holtzman has thrilled three generations of Cub fans. He helped plant the [outfield] ivy."[26] In September of that year Biittner accompanied a handful of teammates to a children's baseball clinic. In retirement he was often tapped by former teammates to participate in golf tournaments benefiting the Baseball Alumni Association and other charitable organizations. For many winters he participated as a coach at the Arizona-based Randy Hundley Fantasy Baseball Camps. Biittner was also an avid hunter and (more so) fisherman.

In 1970, when Biittner launched his major-league career, he admitted, "Being a big-league player has been my dream ever since I was a little bit of a kid."[27] This childhood dream was fulfilled with a .273-29-354 line in 3,151 at-bats over 14 seasons. During this time he played for some of the most famous managers of the period: Ted Williams, Whitey Herzog, Billy Martin, and Gene Mauch. Taskmasters all, they came to appreciate Biittner as the consummate team player, a label evidenced by the Iowa native's quotes early in his career: "I more or less try for average, rather than go for the long ball. … The home runs will come if you make contact. I like RBIs. They're the most important thing for the good of the team."[28]

Sources

The author thanks Larry Biittner for personal input provided in phone interviews on August 18 and September 4, 2015. Thanks also to Rod Nelson, chair of the SABR Scouts Committee, and Karl Green, chair of the Collegiate Research Committee, for their valuable input.

Websites

Baseball-reference.com.
Ancestry.com.
chronicletimes.com/story/1457659.html.

sites.google.com/site/iahsaasports/iowa-high-schools/defunct-high-schools/pocahontas-catholic/pocahontas-catholic-boys-basketball.
iahsaa.org/basketball/Archives/bb_hall_of_fame.pdf.
dbq.edu/media/athletics/pdfs/BS2013.pdf.
bleedcubbieblue.com/2008/1/28/92951/1830.
cubsfantasycamp.com/cubs-coaches/.

Notes

1. " 'Nobody's Caddy!' Says Cubs' Biittner," *The Sporting News*, September 8, 1979: 35.
2. "Reuschel, Biittner Deliver Big for Slipping Cubs," *The Sporting News*, August 13, 1977: 10.
3. Robert Elliott Flickinger, *The Pioneer History of Pocahontas County, Iowa* (Fonda. Iowa: G. Sanborn, 1904), 143.
4. Biittner was inducted into the Buena Vista Athletic Hall of Fame.
5. During this period Biittner appears to have played with the semipro Halstead (Kansas) Cowboys as well.
6. https://collection.baseballhall.org/PASTIME/larry-biittner-scouting-report-1968-april-09-0.
7. "Biittner Keeps Both His Eyes on Ball," *The Sporting News*, August 29, 1970: 40.
8. "Biittner – Hard to Spell, Tough at Plate," *The Sporting News*, June 19, 1971: 20.
9. "Infield Still Rangers' Danger Spot," *The Sporting News*, March 25, 1972: 40.
10. "Husky Biittner Wisely Shuns Mania for HRs," *The Sporting News*, July 29, 1972: 24.
11. Ibid.
12. "Critics Fault Ranger 'Suicide' Youth Drive," *The Sporting News*, August 5, 1972: 21.
13. Biittner took the mound as a reliever in two hopeless games for the Zulia Eagles. He went unscored upon in three innings. This was not his first professional appearance on the hill; he made made at least one similarly hopeless appearance in the Instructional League.
14. "Did Expos' G.M. Jim Fan on Jarvis?" *The Sporting News*, January 12, 1974: 39.
15. The ensuing rhubarb resulted in the ejection of Franks and player-coach Randy Hundley.
16. "Cubs Expect to Sign Six-Year Vets," *The Sporting News*, October 15, 1977: 10.
17. "Helping Cubs on New Year Resolutions," *The Sporting News*, January 14, 1978: 54.
18. "Cubs Enjoy Lefty Luxury With Gross in Groove," *The Sporting News*, June 10, 1978: 17.
19. One such at-bat included a walk-off home run in the Cubs' home opener on April 14.
20. "If Cubs Fail to Deal, It'll Be Long Season," *The Sporting News*, March 8, 1980: 24.
21. Josh Wilker, "Larry Biittner in … The Nagging Question," Cardboard Gods. (qqqqqq//cardboardgods.net/2007/05/11/larry-biittner-in-the-nagging-question/).
22. The record was broken by Dwight Smith in 1993.
23. In at least one stage of his career, Biittner was represented by partners Jim Bronner and Bob Gilhooley; from 1966 to 1970 Gilhooley played in the minor leagues.
24. "Big Cub Broom Set to Sweep," *The Sporting News*, December 6, 1980: 59.
25. "National League Flashes," *The Sporting News*, June 20, 1981: 20.
26. "Mick, a Mighty Oak Is He, Riding Cub Lonesome Pines," *The Sporting News*, May 19, 1979: 19.
27. "Biittner Keeps Both His Eyes on Ball."
28. Ibid.

RICH BILLINGS

BY CHRIS JONES

Richard Arlin Billings was born on December 4, 1942, in Detroit to Arlie and Dimple Billings, and played parts of eight seasons with the Washington Senators, Texas Rangers, and St. Louis Cardinals.[1]

The oldest of six children, Billings was recruited to play at Michigan State while playing "federation ball" in the Detroit area, teaming with fellow future major leaguers Willie Horton, Alex Johnson, and Bill Freehan.[2] His father, a factory worker in downtown Detroit, had moved the family to the Troy, Michigan, area several years before to get away from the big city, and Billings would often hitchhike along the approximately 25-mile trek to Detroit for games. When he received a ride home from Willie Horton and a coach after one game, Horton was astounded at the rural nature of the Troy area and deemed Billings' new nickname to be "cow man," a nickname Billings would carry throughout his time in that league and which Horton continued to use to refer to him even after both players had retired from the major leagues.[3]

Playing third base and outfield, Billings went on to earn accolades at Michigan State as Second Team All-Big Ten in 1964 and Third Team All-Big Ten in 1965.[4] On June 8, 1965, the Washington Senators selected Billings in the 25th round of the free-agent draft.[5] Two weeks later, Billings signed with the Senators and was assigned to Geneva in the Class-A New York-Penn League.[6] There he began his steady march toward the big leagues.

After a solid if unspectacular season in Geneva, in 1966 Billings put together an outstanding campaign for the Class-A Burlington Senators in which he batted .312, slugged 14 home runs, and was named to the all-Carolina League team.[7] Although unknown at the time, Billings developed one of his first ties to the Dallas-Fort Worth Metroplex during those first two minor-league seasons. In both Geneva and Burlington, Billings was managed by Wayne Terwilliger, who 40 years later would make history while managing the independent league Fort Worth Cats as being one of only two 80-year old managers in professional baseball history, joining Connie Mack.[8] Terwilliger would also coach Billings as a member of Ted Williams's coaching staffs with the Senators and Rangers from 1969 to 1972.[9]

Invited to big-league spring training the following season, Billings opened eyes with his bat, with *The Sporting News* reporting, "There are six outfielders and the guessing is that rookie Dick Billings will be sent down for further seasoning. Billings has impressed with his hitting this spring, but he still needs seasoning."[10] Seasoning he received after being reassigned on March 29, playing primarily as an outfielder for the York White Roses during the regular season and being assigned to the Florida Instructional League that fall.[11]

Billings received another invitation to big-league spring training as an outfielder in 1968.[12] Once again, however, Billings was reassigned to the minor leagues late in camp.[13] Playing for Buffalo in the International League, Billings spent the better part of the season providing consistent offensive production, hitting .276 with 11 home runs, and proving why his bat belonged in Washington.[14] On September 1 the Senators finally agreed and called Billings up to the big club.[15] Over the last month of the season Billings got into 12 games at third base and in the outfield, and connected on his first major-league home run on September 22 against the Tigers.[16] While his .182 batting line over a small sample size wasn't much to look at, Billings' presence generated optimism for his future in Washington, and The Sporting News commented that he and Brant Alyea "were exciting in the Senators' last home stand."[17]

After his first taste of the big leagues, Billings was originally ticketed for his second straight winter in the Florida Instructional League – this time to work out as a catcher.[18] However, when an injury opened up a roster spot on the Arecibo club in the Puerto Rican Winter League, Billings went there instead and proceeded to homer and knock in two runs in his very first game on the island.[19]

Change was afoot in the Senators dugout heading into the 1969 season, as the club signed legendary hitter Ted Williams to a five-year contract as the Senators' vice president and manager.[20] The team responded meekly in the Splendid Splinter's managerial debut in spring training, managing only a single hit – a two-out ninth-inning single by Billings.[21] Williams, for his part, was not upset at the lack of offensive firepower, stating that he was "thankful for the one hit."[22]

Billings would recall a time later in his career, though, for a period lasting approximately three days, when he was not held with such high regard by his new manager.

> Coming into the league I had a tough time with sliders … and I started just trying to focus to hit the ball up the middle and to right field. And we were in Baltimore the first month of the season, I was batting fourth behind Frank Howard and I was hitting well over .300, and the night before I got three hits off of Jim Palmer … and I come out of the dugout and go up to the batting rack where the lineup is and Ted's over in the corner next to the batting rack holding court with the reporters. And I don't even know what they're talking about but I get my helmet and I walk by and he has a bat in his hand, and he kinda pokes me and he says: "Here's a great example. He should hit 20 home runs a year and what's he do? He tries to look for the slider and hit it to right field. What kinda hitting is that?" Then he says, "Dick, I bet you didn't even read my book, did you?"
>
> And I don't know why I said this or why it even came to my mind, but I was just trying to make a point. I wasn't trying to embarrass him or anything else. … I said, "Well as a matter of fact, Ted, I did read your book, but if I read a medical book that wouldn't make me a surgeon." And everybody started laughing. And I could just see the veins in his neck start popping, it really, really ticked him off. I thought "uh-oh" and just got my helmet and went to the batting cage. And you know I didn't think that much about it. But my point was, "Yeah, Ted, I'm not like you. I can't do things that you did, most of us can't." I wasn't trying to make fun of him or anything else.
>
> So when the batting practice is over … I was in the training room getting my arm rubbed down with the hot stuff on it and Tom Grieve, my roommate, came up and said, "Before you put the hot stuff on your arm you better go check the lineup card." So I threw my jersey on and walked out to the dugout and he had scratched my name out of the lineup and put in Ken Suarez. And as I turned around to go back in the clubhouse he stopped me and pointed his finger in my chest and said, "You blankety-blank-blank-blank, you go to the bullpen and don't come back. You're not even allowed on this bench,

you go sit in the bullpen until you change your attitude."

And he benched me for three straight games. And I had to sit in the bullpen and I was not allowed to be in the dugout I guess because of that comment. And I was batting fourth and hitting over .300. There was absolutely no reason; it wasn't a platoon or anything else.

Billings did end up making the club out of spring training for the first time in 1969, but got in only 27 games for the Senators.[23] During the season, with the Senators sensing that the club was weak at the catching position, Billings received a surprise request to change positions:

> Either Wayne Terwilliger or Nellie Fox came up to me after one game and said, "What do you think about going to the minors to learn how to catch?" And I said I've never caught a game in my entire life and never had shin guards on other than catching batting practice here, and if you're going to send me out just tell me, don't make something up.

Billings was assured that it was not a gimmick and that the club saw a real future for him as a catcher.[24] And he agreed that he "couldn't field well enough to play third and didn't hit with enough power to play the outfield." So at the age of 26 and fighting for a consistent big-league role, Billings, responded, "Well, if you're going to send me to the minors anyway, then, yeah, I'll go give it a whirl."

On June 23, 1969, the Senators thus shipped Billings to Savannah.[25] The transition to catcher was not without its hiccups, however. "The night that I got in, they started me in a Double-A game and I had never caught a game in my life." Upon returning to the dugout one inning Billings noticed that that many in the dugout were laughing at him. Thinking it was just because he was getting beat up trying to catch pitcher Jack Jenkins, who "I swear threw 98 or better but just could not hit the side of a barn door," he was advised that he had actually been catching with his shin guards on backward. "That's how much I knew about catching, I didn't even know how to put the shin guards on," he would later say.

As the Southern League season wound down, Billings was involved in one game that would foreshadow a much more momentous occasion four years later. On July 26 he strode to the plate with two outs in the final inning as the only batter standing in the way of Montgomery ace John Gregory's no-hitter.[26] Billings put a scare into the entire ballpark as the ball left his bat and traveled to the farthest reaches of center field, but ultimately the ball (and the no-hitter) was hauled in with a leaping catch near the fence.[27] The next no-hitter Billings would be involved in would be much more enjoyable. He diligent efforts to learn the catcher position were rewarded as he received a September callup to Washington.[28]

Assigned to Denver to open the 1970 season, Billings and the rest of the Bears endured a dismal seven-game losing streak to begin the year.[29] Billings chipped in with a double in the seventh and a game-winning triple in the ninth to help defeat Oklahoma City in Denver's home opener, however.[30] Billings' toughness and desire to stay in the lineup was perhaps never more evident than in a late July game against Oklahoma City when, despite battling an ulcer and a virus/infection, he attempted to catch the second game of a doubleheader.[31] When his body finally gave in, Billings collapsed behind the plate and was forced to stay out of the lineup for a short time to recuperate.[32] Brushing off the brief health scare, he continued his season-long quest to frighten the pitchers of the American Association, pushing his average to .312 to go along with 10 home runs by late July.[33] On September 8 he was again recalled to Washington, though he played in only 11 games before the season came to a close.[34]

After bouncing between the minor leagues and short stints in Washington for several years, Billings was primed to take on a larger role in 1971 and made the Senators out of spring training as a catcher, wearing number 8.[35] He received consistent playing time for the first time in his career, and slugged his first home run on July 2, a three-run shot that pushed the Senators to a 6-3 win in Cleveland.[36] He followed that up on July 5 with another home run, this time a grand slam, in a 15-6 trouncing of the Indians that gave the Senators a six-game winning streak.[37] Despite the recent streak, however, the team still sat well back in the standings and was 15 games below .500 at 32-47.[38] Around the same time, and after battling through roughly the first half of the season with Paul Casanova for the starting catching position, Billings was awarded the starting job by manager Ted Williams.[39] For the season, Billings ended up putting together a .246 average in 116 games played, totaling 6 home runs and 48 runs batted in.[40]

While Billings' big-league career was just beginning, the 1971 season in Washington will forever be known for what was ending. On September 21, approximately a week and a half before the end of the regular season, the American League owners officially approved owner Bob Short's plan to move the Senators to the Dallas-Fort Worth market after the season.[41] So it was a bittersweet day for many of the 14,460 fans in attendance on September 30 when the Yankees came to town for the Senators' final home game.[42]

Billings was penciled in at catcher and batting cleanup for the finale, and proceeded to have an outstanding game, going 3-for-4 with singles in the fourth, sixth, and seventh innings and throwing out a would-be basestealer in the third.[43] Although the Senators led the game 7-5 heading to the ninth inning, the "We want Short!" chants arose in the crowd and fans began streaming onto the field in the middle of play.[44]

> They came out on the field and we just kinda, we were just mesmerized; I'd never seen anything like that before. Fans were picking up dirt in their hands and putting it in popcorn boxes and in their hat. I think one or two of them tried to steal the bases, I can't remember if they ever pulled the bases out or not. But they could just never get the crowd under control at all, they just kinda stood out on the field and milled around. We all went in the clubhouse just to wait and see what happened, and I don't know if I ever even came back out.

Unable to control the crowd, the umpiring crew "had no alternative but to award the game to New York on a forfeit. An apparent 7-5 Senators win became a 9-0 loss.[45]

After the season, Billings went to Venezuela to play winter ball and gain additional catching experience.[46] Midway through the season, he was approached to gauge his interest in managing the team if it was to part ways with manager Larry Doby.[47] Billings indicated he would be willing to take on the role, in which he was officially installed when Doby was let go.[48] The club supported Billings' ideas to improve the club, including releasing certain players who weren't all that thrilled to be playing winter ball in Venezuela, and bringing in new players who were.[49] The Zulia team responded and stormed to its first playoff appearance in team history, with Billings finishing as one of the top 10 leading hitters in the league.[50] When the team arrived at the airport in Maracaibo after clinching the playoff berth, thousands of people lined the runway to great the team and a number of fans actually carried the players from the plane.[51] Billings would return to Venezuela as a player-manager during subsequent winter-league seasons as well: "We were successful and they just had me back, basically whenever I wanted to."

As the calendar turned to 1972, the Senators' move to Texas was quite a transition for the team's players, both in geography and in accommodations. After playing in the spacious RFK stadium, Billings and others wondered how the club could possibly play at what "was basically a Class A or Double-A ballpark."[52] In addition, the players had to procure new living accommodations; although a brief trip to Texas with Denny McLain prior to the season proved to be more than sufficient for Billings in that regard:

> McLain is quite a magician and quite a marketing guy, I mean by the time we left there he had a radio/TV show lined up, he had a car dealer that had given us the use of cars, he had an apartment that was giving us free rent over in Dallas.... From that standpoint I was really excited just because of the way people welcomed us there.

The club faced two additional other hurdles before season's start. First, star Frank Howard held out before agreeing to a new contract for 1972 – it was a good thing the holdout ended, according to Billings: "They need Hondo. They don't have anyone but him and Ted as drawing cards. Who's gonna pack the park to see me and a bunch of guys named Joe until we prove ourselves."[53] Second, a league-wide player strike delayed the start of the season.[54] Billings, along with several other players, stayed in town and tried to stay in shape for the season during the strike.[55]

After the strike was resolved and after beginning the season on the road, the Rangers held the franchise's home opener with Billings behind the plate and Dick Bosman on the mound – the same battery that was in place for the final Senators game in Washington the year before.[56] The most memorable aspect of the game for Billings occurred before the first pitch was thrown, when the players were lined up on the first-base line and given cowboy hats and boots.[57]

After a rough start to the season playing on only a platoon basis, Billings was finally given the full-time starting catcher position, his bat took off, and he posted an eight-game hitting streak in early June.[58] In fact, The Sporting News noted that "during the month of June, the Rangers could trace much of their modest but increasing successes to scrappy Rich Billings."[59] And it wasn't just his bat getting attention, with manager Ted Williams commenting, "He's been the most dependable man we have – and not only with the bat. He blocks the plate with the best and his arm is far more accurate."[60] Billings finished the season as the team's leading RBI man with 58. "I led the team in RBIs, so that tells you how bad we were," he would later say.[61] The 1972 Texas Rangers finished with a record of 54-100; good for worst in the major leagues.[62]

Leading into the 1973 season, new manager Whitey Herzog was quoted as saying, "If Rich Billings is the starting catcher again, we're in deep trouble."[63] The oft-quoted response from Billings was that "Whitey, obviously, has seen me play."[64] But Billings also took issue with criticism of his defense at catcher and pre-emptive judgment of his role on the team as a backup: "All I want is an opportunity to prove myself. … I think that the catching job should be mine until I prove that I can't handle it," he said.[65] While the quotes above appear to describe an ominous beginning to their relationship, Billings later recounted that there was no ill will between the two then or now: "Whitey Herzog and I became really, really close friends, and I think that we have the highest and did then have the highest respect of each other."

Herzog's preseason comments aside, Billings was in the starting lineup at catcher on Opening Night.[66] He was sidelined shortly thereafter, however, with a broken thumb suffered on April 27 in a 4-2 win over Milwaukee.[67] Billings did return in time to play a hand in perhaps the high-water mark of the season for the Rangers, catching Jim Bibby's July 30 no-hitter against the A's, a moment he would later describe as "the twilight of a mediocre career."[68] "He was just plain explosive," Billings said, adding, "I didn't think a human being could throw a ball that fast."[69] Bibby was throwing so hard, in fact, that Billings called almost exclusively fastballs in the later innings: "I didn't see any reasons to have him throw anything else [u]nless he got in trouble [a]nd he never got in trouble."[70]

Billings also earned praise from none other than Whitey Herzog for his play during the season: "There are only two guys on this team who I feel have gone out every day and given a complete effort, the kind it takes to win. … Those two are Alex Johnson and Rich Billings," Herzog said.[71] Hampered by injuries, though, Billings finished the year with a disappointing .179 average and the Rangers ended up losing 105 games.[72]

With another new manager, Billy Martin, Billings and the Rangers looked to rebound in 1974. But for Billings the injuries kept piling on, as he suffered an ankle injury on April 27 and was placed on the disabled list.[73] He ultimately was sidelined for most of the year with a variety of injuries. "I was hurt all of that season, it was just one thing after the other," he said.[74] In August, Billings was purchased by the

Cardinals and was healthy enough to play briefly for Tulsa in the American Association and receive a late season callup to St. Louis.[75]

Considering retirement after the 1974 season, Billings received an offer from the California Angels to manage their Class-A team in 1975.[76] Still feeling the itch to give it "one more shot," and needing only 20 more days of big-league service time to reach a full five years on the major-league pension plan, Billings spurned the Angels and accepted an offer to return to the Cardinals to be a player-coach in Tulsa with the promise of being called up to the big club for at least the last 30 days of the season.[77]

Billings did play well enough in Tulsa to be called up sporadically during the season, despite suffering a separated shoulder on a play at the plate early in the season.[78] He also had the opportunity to be briefly reunited with former roommate and "magician" Denny McLain, who broadcast Iowa's minor-league games against Billings' Tulsa squad.[79] The Cardinals also honored their agreement by calling Billings up for the final 30 days of the season: "I had the upmost respect for the Cardinals and their organization," he later said. He admitted that the injuries had taken their toll on his body, however, and retired after the season. "I just wasn't the same anymore," he said.

After retiring, Billings obtained his real-estate license and began working as a broker in Texas.[80] He later obtained his real-estate license in Michigan, where as of 2018 he lived with his wife, also a licensed real-estate broker, and continued to work in the real estate industry.[81] He also remained an active member of the Texas Rangers Alumni and appeared at several events for the team each year.

Sources

In addition to the sources noted in the Notes, the author also accessed Billings' player file on Retrosheet.org and Baseball-Reference.com.

Notes

1 Interview with Rich Billings, March 4, 2018. Unless otherwise attributed, all quotations from Billings come from this interview.
2 Ibid.
3 Ibid.
4 msuspartans.com/sports/m-basebl/archive/msu-m-basebl-allbig10.html.
5 James R. Hartley, Washington's Expansion Senators (1961-1971) (Germantown, Maryland: Corduroy Press 1997, 1998), 280.
6 Ibid.
7 "Class A Averages," The Sporting News, September 24, 1966: 34.
8 "A Look at 80-year-old Fort Worth Cats Manager Wayne Terwilliger," My Plainview, July 3, 2005, myplainview.com/news/article/A-look-at-80-year-old-Fort-Worth-Cats-manager-8693434.php
9 "Twig at 80: Wayne Terwilliger Doing What Only Connie Mack Did Before Him," Billings (Montana) Gazette, July 4, 2005, billingsgazette.com/sports/twig-at-wayne-terwilliger-doing-what-only-connie-mack-did/article_74daeee0-5b2a-509f-b3ec-bec64f63622d.html
10 Bob Addie, "Billings Can Hit, but Needs Experience, The Sporting News, April 8, 1967: 20.
11 Hartley, 276; Bob Addie, "Nats, Astros Will Share Instructional Loop Team," The Sporting News, October 7, 1967: 40.
12 Bob Addie, "Senators Run on Victory Ticket," The Sporting News, March 9, 1968: 24.
13 Hartley, 277.
14 "International League Batting, Pitching Records," The Sporting News, September 28, 1968: 33.
15 Hartley, 278.
16 Hartley, 203, 176, 90; Merrell Whittlesey, "Five Nat Hurlers Started 74 Games, Finished but Two," The Sporting News, October 12, 1968, 17.
17 Whittlesey, "Five Nat Hurlers."
18 Ibid.
19 Miguel Frau, "Pickets Loaf in Timmerman Shutout," The Sporting News, November 9, 1968: 55.
20 Hartley, 93, 279.
21 Merrell Whittlesey, "Ted Tutors Promising Pupil Epstein," The Sporting News, March 22, 1969: 23.

22   Ibid.

23   Hartley, 207; "American League Rosters, Uniform Numbers," *The Sporting News*, April 26, 1969: 36.

24   Interview with Rich Billings, March 4, 2018.

25   Hartley, 280.

26   Max Mosely, "Gregory, Former Ace Reliever, Hurls No-Hit Gem for Rebels, *The Sporting News*, August 9, 1969: 39.

27   Ibid.

28   Hartley, 281.

29   Bob Hurt, "12-Inning One Hitter," *The Sporting News*, May 9, 1970: 35.

30   Ibid.

31   "No. 3 Is No. 1," *The Sporting News*, August 8, 1970: 40.

32   Ibid.

33   William J. Weiss, "American Association, Batting and Pitching Records," *The Sporting News*, August 1, 1970: 35.

34   Hartley, 283, 207.

35   "American League Rosters, Uniform Numbers, *The Sporting News*, April 17, 1971: 37.

36   Hartley, 131, 184.

37   Hartley, 131-132.

38   Hartley, 184.

39   "Senators Topple Indians, 7 to 3," *Wilmington Morning Star*, August 7, 1971: 17.

40   Hartley, 206-207.

41   Hartley, 285.

42   Hartley, 139.

43   Hartley, 139-145, 195.

44   Hartley, 143.

45   Hartley, 144.

46   Interview with Rich Billings, March 4, 2018.

47   Ibid.

48   Eduardo Moncada, "Billings Latest Venezuelan Playing Pilot," *The Sporting News*, December 25, 1971: 47.

49   Interview with Rich Billings, March 4, 2018.

50   Ibid; Eduardo Moncada, "Dick Billings: One Year Makes a Difference in Venezuela," *The SportingNews*, November 25, 1972: 55.

51   Interview with Rich Billings, March 4, 2018.

52   Ibid.

53   Merle Heryford, "Hondo Cures Short's Headache, But Gives Williams Another, "*The Sporting News*, April 15, 1972: 24.

54   Merle Heryford, "Only Fans and Players Missing at Texas' 'Bow,'" *The Sporting News*, April 22, 1972: 20.

55   Ibid.

56   Interview with Rich Billings, March 4, 2018.

57   Ibid.

58   Merle Heryford, "Mincher Can Smile with .174 Bat Mark," *The Sporting News*, July 1, 1972: 19.

59   Merle Heryford, "Late Billings Pays Rich Ranger Dividends," *The Sporting News*, July 15, 1972: 17.

60   Ibid.

61   Interview with Rich Billings, March 4, 2018.

62   Merle Heryford, "Herzog Must Plug Ranger Infield Holes," *The Sporting News*, March 3, 1973: 30.

63   Mike Shropshire, *Seasons in Hell* (Lincoln: University of Nebraska Press, 1996), 20.

64   Ibid.

65   Randy Galloway, "Billings Can't See Himself as Part-Timer With Rangers," *The Sporting News*, March 17, 1973: 48.

66   "A Season in Hell," D. Magazine, April 1991, dmagazine.com/publications/d-magazine/1991/april/sports-a-season-in-hell/

67   "Billings Lost to Rangers," *The Sporting News*, May 12, 1973: 25.

68 Shropshire, 104-107.

69 "NL Castoff No-Hits World Champions," Beaver County Times, July 31, 1973: 10, news.google.com/newspapers?id=rOtVAAAAIBAJ&sjid=2EANAAAAIBAJ&pg=790,4102988&dq=rich+billings&hl=en.

70 Ibid.

71 Randy Galloway, "Ranger Attack Consists of Alex' Bat," *The Sporting News*, May 12, 1973: 18.

72 Merle Heryford, "Seven Catchers to Vie for Rangers Job," *The Sporting News*, January 12, 1974: 39.

73 Randy Galloway, "The Rangers Are for Real, Brash Billy Warns," *The Sporting News*, May 18, 1974: 3.

74 Interview with Rich Billings, March 4, 2018.

75 Neal Russo, "It's Redbird Moving Time, With Brock Showing Way, *The Sporting News*, September 21, 1974: 13.

76 Interview with Rich Billings, March 4, 2018.

77 Ibid.

78 Ibid.; John Ferguson, "Iowa Walks Past Speedy Tulsa in A.A. Start," *The Sporting News*, May 3, 1975: 30.

79 Pete Swanson, "Pierce Finds New Lease as Triplet Power Hitter," *The Sporting News*, May 10, 1975: 32.

80 Interview with Rich Billings, March 4, 2018.

81 Ibid.

DICK BOSMAN

BY DALE VOISS

Dick Bosman finished his 11-year major-league career three games under .500. He threw a no-hitter at the age of 30, but by the age of 33 his career was over.

He was born Richard Allen Bosman on February 17, 1944, in Kenosha, Wisconsin, the only son and oldest of four children born to George and Nella (Kloet) Bosman. Kenosha is a Lake Michigan town of about 90,000 people that lies between Milwaukee and Chicago. His father was a farmer; his mother stayed home and raised the children. George Bosman later gave up farming and went to work for a trucking firm in Kenosha.

Dick grew up in Kenosha, where his father was a very good fast-pitch softball pitcher. George's prowess was so well known that a baseball field in Kenosha was named after him and his uncle Clarence, also a pitcher. George – the greatest early baseball influence that Dick had – had a dream that his son would one day be a major-league pitcher and did what he could to help him get there. Several sources list Dick as a cousin of major leaguer Duane Kuiper, a Racine, Wisconsin, native. Bosman said that while a relationship exists, it is no closer than third cousin.

Another early influence on Bosman was his high-school coach, Andy Smith, who also coached Little League. Dick pitched for the Bradford High School Red Devils and started in the 1962 state championship game, losing 2-0 on two unearned runs. One of Bosman's high-school teammates, Lance Tobert, a pitcher, signed with the Orioles but never pitched in the major leagues.[1]

Bosman received no scholarship offers from major colleges like the University of Wisconsin, and felt he would have if his high-school grades had been better. He did receive several offers from major-league clubs and opted to sign with Pittsburgh Pirates scout Paul Tretiak. Bosman decided to delay his professional baseball career by a year, however, and attend UW-Parkside, an extension of the University of Wisconsin located in Kenosha. Meanwhile he played for a semipro team in Kenosha in the summer of 1962.

After a year at Parkside, Bosman decided it was time to begin his pro career. He spent the 1963 season pitching Rookie League ball for the Kingsport (Tennessee) Pirates of the Appalachian League. That December, Bosman was chosen by the Giants in the first-year player draft. He reported to spring training with the major-league club in 1964. While he was impressive, he was one of nine pitchers cut in late March, near the end of camp. Bosman was sent to the Class-A Lexington (North Carolina) Giants of the Western Carolinas League.

The 20-year-old Bosman pitched in 35 games for Lexington, including nine starts. His 3.21 ERA apparently caught someone's attention, as the Washington Senators chose him in the December 1964 minor-league draft. Bosman spent the 1965 season pitching for York, Pennsylvania, the Senators' affiliate in the Double-A Eastern League, and after the season he pitched in the Florida Instructional

League. During his stint there he combined with Dick Loun to no-hit the Reds' entry in the league. Based on his time in the Instructional League, Bosman received an invitation to the Senators' big-league camp in 1966 as a nonroster invitee.

Senators manager Gil Hodges was quite impressed with Bosman in spring training, telling him he had a chance to be a good big-league pitcher. When club GM George Selkirk cut Bosman from the big-league roster in early April, Hodges told him to go back to York, have a good month, and they would bring him back up.

Bosman went to York, pitched well for about six weeks, and then got the call from the Senators. He made his major-league debut as a starter at Fenway Park against the Boston Red Sox on June 1, 1966. His opponent was Jim Lonborg. Bosman went 7⅓ innings, allowing three earned runs on nine hits to pick up a 6-3 win.

Over the next seven weeks Bosman made 12 appearances, including six starts. He compiled a 2-6 record with a 7.78 ERA. Included in those six losses were three saves blown by the bullpen. In late July the Senators sent Bosman back to York and replaced him with York's Barry Moore. Bosman returned to the Senators in September where he made one appearance out of the bullpen.

Bosman began the 1967 season with the Senators' Triple-A farm club at Hawaii. He went 12-11 in 26 starts with a 2.76 ERA for the Islanders, who finished the year at 60-87. Manager Wayne Terwilliger in his biography said, "Dick's fastball topped out at about 85 mph, so he worked hard at fine-tuning his two best pitches, a sinker and a 'slurve.' Whoever named that pitch got it just right – it was a combination of a slider that broke too much and a curve that didn't break enough. Bosman was managing to win despite everything, and it wasn't long before Washington called."[2] He was promoted in August. In seven starts for the Senators, Bosman went 3-1 with a 1.75 ERA. This included a five-hit blanking of the White Sox and Tommy John.

For the 1968 season the Senators replaced Gil Hodges with Jim Lemon. That year also marked the first time Bosman spent an entire season at the major-league level. He made 46 appearances, including 10 starts, going 2-9 but posting a respectable 3.69 ERA. Bosman was one of only two major-league starters that year to make double-digit starts and not throw a complete game.

Before the 1969 season the Senators replaced Lemon as manager with Ted Williams. Under Williams, Bosman flourished. This was a move that probably did as much to turn around his career as any other. Bosman credited Williams with teaching him to pitch from "above the neck."[3]

Bosman began the 1969 season by pitching 2⅓ innings of scoreless relief on Opening Day. He then alternated between the bullpen and rotation until June 18; six starts and five relief appearances. In early May, Williams said, "Dick is starting to see the light."[4] Included in that run was a 5-0 shutout of Cleveland on May 2. On June 22 Williams moved Bosman into a permanent spot in the team's starting rotation. In 20 starts after that, Bosman went 10-3 with a 2.10 ERA. He won 14 games and lost 5 with a league-leading 2.19 ERA. His wins led the staff as the Senators had their first winning season in franchise history.

In 1970 Bosman, now 26, became the ace of the Senators pitching staff. He upped his win total from 14 to 16 even though the Senators fell from 86 wins in 1969 to 70 wins in 1970. Bosman was the only member of the pitching staff to reach double digits in wins. One highlight was a one-hitter against Minnesota on August 13. César Tovar, a noted spoiler who broke up five no-hitters in the majors, led off the game with a bunt single. Bosman allowed only one walk after that, making the single run he received in the first inning stand up.

In the offseason the Senators picked up Denny McLain from the Detroit Tigers in an eight-player deal that cost them their second starter, Joe Coleman. McLain, a 31-game winner in 1968, went just 10-22 for Washington in 1971, leading the league in losses as he had led with 24 wins in 1969. Bosman went 12-16 with a 3.73 earned-run average. He led the Senators, who went 63-96, in wins, starts, and innings pitched.

While pitching for the Senators in 1967, Bosman met his future wife, Pam, a Washington native, whom he married in 1969. The couple had two daughters, Michelle and Nadine. They later adopted two others, Elizabeth and Amanda.

Before the 1972 season the Senators left Washington and moved to Arlington, Texas, where they became the Texas Rangers. Bosman made both the last start in Senators history and the first start in Rangers history.

In their inaugural 1972 season, the Rangers finished 54-100, the fifth 100-season loss since the advent of the expansion Senators in 1961. Ted Williams quit as manager after the season. Bosman turned in a respectable 3.63 ERA in his 29 starts, including a 1-0 three-hit shutout of the White Sox in his last start of the season. In four years under Williams, Bosman went 50-43 with a 3.15 ERA and a 2-to-1 strikeout-to-walk ratio.

The Rangers began the 1973 season with Whitey Herzog replacing Williams as manager. Bosman made his fourth consecutive Opening Day start. He began the season by going 2-5. On May 10 the Rangers traded Bosman and outfielder Ted Ford to the Cleveland Indians for pitcher Steve Dunning. Bosman was upset because he had spent his entire major-league career in the same organization. Friendships he developed with teammates in Cleveland eventually changed his feelings about that and he came to enjoy his time in Cleveland. He remained with the Tribe into the 1975 season. There he was joined in the starting rotation by future Hall of Famer Gaylord Perry. Bosman developed a great deal of respect for Perry, saying that Gaylord had some of the best stuff he ever saw a pitcher display.[5]

On July 19, 1974, Bosman pitched a no-hitter against the Oakland A's, winners of the 1973 World Series. It took just 79 pitches to complete the gem, and he faced just 28 batters. The only Oakland batter to reach base was Sal Bando; Bosman fielded his swinging bunt down the third-base line but his throw pulled the first baseman off the bag and Bosman was charged with an error.

In 1975 A's owner Charles Finley sent pitcher Blue Moon Odom to Cleveland for Bosman and fellow pitcher Jim Perry. Over the next two seasons Bosman went 15-6 in 49 games with a 3.80 ERA for the A's. He made a brief appearance in the 1975 playoffs for the A's.

Bosman was released by the Athletics at the end of spring training in 1977. Since his release came on March 29, it was too close to the start of the season for him to catch on with another major-league team. This left Bosman with the option of signing a minor-league contract or retiring. Despite being just 33 years old, he opted to retire.

Bosman moved to Northern Virginia, where he took a job with Johnny Koons, who owned several car dealerships. Koons had a son in Little League, so he asked Bosman to help out with coaching. This began Bosman's nine-year association with the Little League of Northern Virginia. He also took a job for three or four years as a coach for Georgetown University. During this period Bosman developed an interest in coaching at the professional level.

In 1986 Bosman was named the pitching coach for the White Sox' Triple-A affiliate in Buffalo. In June 1986, White Sox GM Hawk Harrelson fired manager Tony La Russa and pitching coach Dave Duncan. He replaced them with Jim Fregosi as manager and Bosman as pitching coach. Bosman served in this role through the 1987 season.

Before the 1988 season Bosman was approached by Orioles farm director Doug Melvin about working as a minor-league pitching instructor. He accepted and served the Orioles in that capacity from 1988 to 1991. In 1992 Johnny Oates, the Orioles' new manager, brought Bosman aboard as the team's pitching coach. Bosman served in this role for three seasons, and in 1995, when Oates left Baltimore to become the Rangers manager, Bosman went along. He served as the Rangers' pitching coach through the 2000 season. During his tenure there, the Rangers won three division championships (1996, 1998, and 1999).

Before the 2001 season Bosman accepted a position with the Tampa Bay Rays as minor-league pitching coordinator, and held the position through the end of the 2011 season. Bosman said he was very proud that the Rays' major-league pitching staff was entirely homegrown, as he had directed the minor-league pitching for the past decade.

Sources

In addition to the sources cited in the Notes, the author also consulted Baseball-Reference.com, Retrosheet.org, and various other issues of *The Sporting News*, and the *Wisconsin State Journal* (Madison, Wisconsin), June 3, 1962.

Thanks to Dick Bosman for granting the 2011 interview.

Notes

1. James Enright, "Ironman Orioles Prospect Hurls Twin-Bill Triumph for AF Team," *The Sporting News*, October 12, 1968: 16.
2. Wayne Terwilliger with Nancy Peterson and Peter Boehm, *Terwilliger Bunts One* (Helena, Montana: Globe Pequot Press, 2006), 157.
3. Author interview with Dick Bosman on August 25, 2011.
4. Merrell Whittlesey, "Higgins Gets Big Hand as Tight-Fisted Nat Fireman," *The Sporting News*, May 17, 1969: 12
5. Author interview with Dick Bosman.

PETE BROBERG

BY GREGORY H. WOLF

"It was all so new," reminisced Pete Broberg about suiting up for the Texas Rangers in their inaugural season in 1972. "A new city, new stadium, a new look. We weren't wearing the flannels anymore; we had the new stretchy ones."[1] It was the dawn of a new era in football-crazed Texas as the Washington Senators relocated to Arlington, a suburb of Dallas-Fort Worth. Broberg, a hard-throwing right-hander who joined the Senators straight from the campus of Dartmouth College the previous season, holds the distinction of winning the first game (April 16) and tossing the first shutout (April 22) in Rangers' history. "I liked pitching there – anywhere where there was humidity," said Broberg. While NL players enjoyed the comfort of the climate-controlled Houston Astrodome, players in the AL were introduced to the Texas summer heat.

Peter Sven Broberg was born on March 2, 1950, in West Palm Beach, Florida, to Gustave T. Broberg Jr. and Mary Stewart (Colwell) Broberg. The elder Broberg, whose parents emigrated from Sweden, was an attorney and municipal judge in the seaside town. An All-American basketball player at Dartmouth College and three-time Ivy League scoring champion (1939-1941), Gus Broberg was also accomplished outfielder. He turned down an offer from the New York Yankees to join their farm system in order to enlist in the Marines during World War II. As a pilot he lost his right arm in a crash in Okinawa, but he never lost his love for baseball. "My father, overtly or subliminally pushed me into baseball, and I stayed with it," Broberg the younger told the author. "We'd throw the ball to each other. He'd catch it with his left hand, sling off his glove and throw the ball back to me. He could bat one-handed, and hit popups to me."

By the time Broberg was about 14 years old, he began to recognize his baseball talents. "Tom Howser – Dick's brother – was my coach in Babe Ruth ball. He was a big influence and showed me how to pitch," said Broberg. Over the course of the next four years, Broberg established his reputation as a flamethrowing sensation pitching for West Palm Beach High School and American Legion Post 12. He regularly racked up double-digit strikeout totals, and once whiffed 23 while hurling nine perfect innings, but getting a no-decision.[2] Big-league scouts were commonplace in the fertile grounds of South Florida, but Broberg did not remember talking to any as a prep phenom, though he knew they were on his trail. Just weeks after graduating from high school, Broberg was selected by the Oakland A's with the second overall pick in the amateur draft, on June 7, 1968. "I was playing in the American Legion state tournament," he recalled. "There was a pretty good crowd and I threw a perfect game with all of the scouts there. That was probably one of the reasons they drafted me out of high school."

After several weeks of negotiations with A's owner Charles O. Finley, Broberg made national headlines when he turned down a reported signing bonus of $175,000 and enrolled at Dartmouth. "I don't remember being pushed one way or the other to sign or go to college," Broberg explained. "It was my own decision."

Broberg fell under the tutelage of Tony Lupien, longtime head baseball coach at Dartmouth. "He played with the Red Sox [in the early 1940s]," said Broberg. "I felt that he knew the ropes to the big leagues, and that's why I always asked him questions. He was a tough old timer." As a sophomore Broberg led the school to its first-ever College World Series. He struck out 11 against Florida State, but the Big Green committed six errors and lost, 6-0, in the second round.[3] Broberg gained additional experience as a member of the Fairbanks Goldpanners and played against many of the top prospects in the country in the Alaska Summer League in 1969 and 1970. "[The league] was touted as being better than the Cape Cod League," said the pitcher. "I agreed [to play] if I could bring a friend. I brought Charlie Janes, another pitcher for Dartmouth. We were the first players east of the Mississippi to play there." United Press International reported that Broberg had the "attention of every major-league scout in the business" by the end of his junior year.[4] "[He's] the fastest pitcher I've seen since Bob Feller," said Lupien of his prized right-hander, who fanned 127 in 82 innings (including 20 in a game against Boston College) and finished with a 1.42 ERA in 1971.[5]

The Washington Senators selected Broberg with the first overall pick of the secondary phase of the 1971 amateur draft (for players who had already been drafted and refused to sign). "I was honored to be chosen," said Broberg, who clarified his behind-the-scenes pre-draft negotiations with both Washington and the Boston Red Sox. "[Boston] wanted me to turn down [Washington owner] Bob Short and fall to them. That was very tempting and in hindsight perhaps I should have done that. But Washington was going to send me to the big leagues and the Red Sox were going to send me to [Triple-A] Pawtucket. The choice was easy."

"The countdown has started," wrote the Associated Press, speculating on when and if the Senators could sign Broberg, who once again was in the national spotlight.[6] But there was never any doubt in Broberg's mind where he would be. Twelve days after the lowly Senators drafted him, the flamethrowing right-hander made his major-league debut on June 20 in front of just under 20,000 spectators at Robert F. Kennedy Stadium in Washington. Broberg put on a "formidable exhibition," mused the AP, holding Boston to just two runs (both earned) in 6⅓ strong innings but got a no-decision in Washington's eventual 4-3 defeat.[7] "I wasn't nervous," reminisced Broberg, who threw 97 pitches.[8] "I was leading the game when they took me out. I called my dad and told him I had seven strikeouts, but man, I gave up three hits."

After losses in his next two starts, Broberg went on a roll, winning five of his next eight starts. During that impressive stretch of 59⅔ innings, he sported a nifty 1.81 ERA, held opponents to a .208 batting average, and completed four games, including a five-hit shutout against Cleveland. Broberg drew rave reviews: "That kid has a tremendous fastball and has tremendous poise for his lack of experience," said Jim Lonborg, former Cy Young Award winner with Boston.[9] Jim Spencer of the California Angels claimed, "He throws harder than Vida Blue."[10] Even manager Ted Williams, notoriously hard on his own pitchers, chimed in: "I've never seen a more impressive youngster come into the league."[11] But Broberg had little room for error on a team that averaged just 3.38 runs per game. He lost his final six decisions (Washington tallied just 12 runs) to finish with a 5-9 record and 3.47 ERA in 124⅔ innings while the Senators limped to a 63-96 record, good for fifth in the six-team AL East.

Like most pitchers who played for Ted Williams, Broberg's relationship with his manager was curt and to the point. "We didn't talk much," admitted Broberg. "Williams said a few nice things about me to the papers after my first few starts, but not to me." He added that Williams showed little concern and sometimes outright contempt for pitchers. Broberg recounted the time he first met Williams in the Senators' clubhouse. "I was told that Williams would ask me if I know what makes a curveball curve." Not one to play the deferential rookie pitcher to the living legend, Broberg promptly told William the answer. "Williams walked off in a harrumph after that," chuckled Broberg. "I don't think he liked it."

Broberg responded resolutely when asked if he felt pressure about jumping from college to the big leagues in 1971: "That's where I felt I should be in my natural progress. It was a comfortable state and I felt at home. I really don't think that starting in the minor leagues would have helped my career. I think some more understanding and benevolent coaches could have done a better job for me." Looking back on his big-league career, Broberg praised Sid Hudson, his pitching coach with Washington/Texas in 1971-72, as the exception to the rule.

Described by sportswriter Red Smith as "large, long haired, good looking, blond, personable, and rich," the 6-foot-3, 205-pound Broberg commanded the mound.[12] Often sporting fashionable sideburns, he relied on a three-quarters to overhand fastball to overpower hitters; he occasionally dropped to a sidearm delivery to right-handed hitters. He also threw a 12-to-6 overhand curve and a hard slider. "The pitch I wish I had learned was the circle change," Broberg confessed, referring to pitcher John Smoltz, who mentioned in his Hall of Fame induction speech in 2015 that the pitch was the difference maker in his career. "I think that is one of the greatest pitches ever invented," said Broberg, and added, "I never learned a good changeup." Broberg also looked back in awe of Bruce Sutter's split-finger fastball. When the two were teammates in 1977 with the Chicago Cubs, Broberg tried in vain to learn the pitch from coach Fred Martin, who taught it to Sutter.

The cash-strapped Washington Senators' 11-year tenure in the nation's capital came to a conclusion on September 21, 1971, when American League owners voted 10-2 to allow Bob Short to relocate the team to Arlington, Texas. "I don't think I even knew about the move until the last few games of the season when it was announced," said Broberg. "It wasn't a distraction for me."

Rechristened the Texas Rangers, in honor of the state's famous law enforcers and to establish an identity as Texas's baseball team, the club played its games in Arlington Stadium. "The stadium was like an Erector Set," joked Broberg about the former Turnpike Stadium where the Double-A Dallas-Fort Worth Spurs had played beginning in 1965. "It was just a minor-league stadium with more seats in the outfield and a big scoreboard. But I liked pitching there."

Broberg got off to a hot start in 1972. After the Rangers' tough-luck, 1-0 loss to the California Angels in the season opener, Broberg collected the first win in the history of the relocated franchise by limiting the Angels to just five hits over eight innings in a 5-1 victory at Anaheim Stadium. In his next start, he tossed the first shutout in Rangers' and Arlington Stadium's history. Praised by the AP for his "crackling fastball and a whipping curve," Broberg blanked the Angels on four hits. "He's getting confidence and he's going more to the slider and curve," said Ted Williams. "You can see him getting better and better."[13] While the Rangers proved that their early-season success by sliding to the AL West basement, Broberg improved his record to 5-4 and lowered his ERA to 2.66 on June 13 with arguably the best game of his career, a three-hit shutout of Milwaukee in Arlington. The victory was even more impressive considering that Broberg had just returned to the team after graduating from Dartmouth two days earlier. And then the roof caved in.

Broberg's degree in economics could not help the Rangers' hitting, which was dismal even by the depressed offensive output of the era. The club batted just .217, the second lowest average in the AL in the Live Ball era, and scored an average of 2.99 runs per game. After Broberg's three-hitter, the Rangers lost 70 of their next 102 games. Broberg lost his next eight decisions, and finally his spot in the rotation. Pitching out of the bullpen and primarily in mop-up situations in the last two months of the season, he concluded a once promising campaign with a 5-12 record and a 4.29 ERA in a team-high 176⅓ innings; he started 25 of a career-high 39 games. Though he ranked eighth in strikeouts per nine innings (6.8) and whiffed a career-high 11 over 7⅓ innings in a no-decision against Chicago on June

24, he also battled control problems in 1972, ranking third in walks issued per nine innings.

In the offseason, Broberg played for Aguilas del Zuila in the Venezuelan Winter League. "Rich Billings, the Rangers catcher, was the manager for Aguilas and asked me to come down and play. That's how it started," said Broberg who posted a 6-3 record and 1.73 ERA in 96⅓ innings. "I played for Leonas del Caracas (1974-1975) and Tigres de Aragua (1976-1977). They were good experiences, though Caracas was a little nerve-racking at times."

"People have a tendency to black out memories they don't want to remember," Broberg responded when asked about his second season with the Rangers. The 1973 club finished last in scoring and last in team ERA, a toxic mix that produced a franchise worst 57-105 record. New manager Whitey Herzog, a brash 41-year-old, vowed to mold the team with old-school discipline, but his approach alienated players, including Broberg. "Herzog and I did not get along," said the pitcher bluntly. Broberg got off to a rough start, losing his first four decisions, before tossing a complete game to defeat Cleveland, 3-2, on May 30 his first victory in almost a year. Broberg seemed to get on track in June, winning three straight starts; however, he felt he never gained Herzog's confidence. After a nightmarish relief outing on July 4, Broberg was unceremoniously optioned to Spokane in the Pacific Coast League. By the time he was recalled in September, Herzog had been fired and another firebrand, Billy Martin, had been hired. Known for giving his pitchers a long leash, Martin reinserted Broberg into the rotation. Broberg concluded the campaign by tossing a nifty seven-hit shutout against Kansas City for a 5-9 record and 5.61 ERA in 118⅔ innings.

In his first full season with Texas, Billy Martin transformed the club from the laughingstock of the AL to a division contender, finishing in second place with a then-team record 84 victories. The club was led by Jim Sundberg, Mike Hargrove, Toby Harrah, and MVP Jeff Burroughs, each 25 years old or younger. Broberg, after dealing with trade rumors most of the offseason, spent the campaign shuttling between Texas and Triple-A Spokane, and never found his rhythm on either team. Despite an 0-4 record and 8.07 ERA in just 29 innings over 12 appearances (two starts) with the Rangers, he maintained he never lost his confidence, even when he was demoted. "I never had one of those 'What's happening? What am I going to do tomorrow?' moments," said a reflective Broberg. "I was playing baseball and getting paid. We rolled with the punches." Broberg's tenure with the Rangers ended on December 5, 1974, when he was shipped to the Milwaukee Brewers in exchange for pitcher Clyde Wright.

The 25-year-old hurler looked forward to a fresh start in Milwaukee and the chance to escape Texas, where he thought he had not had a chance to pitch regularly the previous two years. "He can pitch," said skipper Del Crandall of Broberg, "but he has to convince me that he can be a consistent pitcher."[14] And Broberg quickly did. Earning a spot in the rotation, he held Boston to four hits (three runs) in 6⅓ innings to win his first start, on April 9. He concluded his first month in Beer City by tossing a stellar three-hit shutout against the New York Yankees at Shea Stadium (where the club played in 1974-1975 while Yankee Stadium was being renovated). In that game Hank Aaron knocked in his 2,209th run to tie Babe Ruth's record. (Ruth's RBI total has since then been adjusted.) Described by beat writer Lou Chapman as "Milwaukee's nearest version of a stopper," Broberg was arguably the biggest surprise on the 94-loss club.[15] After a rough patch in late July, Broberg unveiled a new no-windup delivery in a complete-game three-hit loss to Oakland on August 17. In his final 10 starts of the season, Broberg posted a sturdy 2.85 ERA in 79 innings, yet won just four times for the low-scoring Brewers. During that stretch he tossed a career-high 10⅓ innings against the Yankees, yielding two earned runs to pick up the loss; and blanked Detroit on six hits to record the sixth and final shutout of his career.

"I played for my favorite manager, Del Crandall," Broberg responded when asked about his seemingly unexpected turnaround. "Instead of pitching and looking over my shoulder and wondering if the pitching coach or manager was going to come get me the first time I walked somebody, Del said I'd pitch every four days." In what proved to be the first and only time Broberg pitched in the starting rotation for a full season, the big right-hander set career highs in practically every category, including starts (32), innings (220⅓), and wins (14); he also led the AL in hit batters (16), and issued 106 walks. A tough-luck loser, Broberg was saddled with 16 defeats; however, in 14 of them Milwaukee scored just 17 total runs.

Although Broberg had paced the Brewers in most pitching categories in 1975, new manager Alex Grammas was unimpressed in 1976. Citing Broberg's control problems in spring training, Grammas relegated the right-hander to swingman to start the season. Insulted, Broberg felt that he had earned a chance start regularly. "Alex and I didn't get along," said Broberg bluntly. "They wanted to tinker with my motion and windup. I lost a couple close ones in the beginning, and all of a sudden I wasn't getting a lot of work." Broberg lost three straight starts despite yielding just four earned runs in 19⅔ innings to fall to 1-4 on May 27. After dropping his fifth straight decision, on June 5 (three earned runs in six innings against Kansas City), Broberg was shunted to the far end of the bullpen and made only 12 more appearances (three starts) the rest of the season. He finished with a 1-7 record and 4.97 ERA in 92⅓ innings.

Left unprotected in the major-league expansion draft in November 1976, Broberg was selected by the Seattle Mariners with the 35th overall pick. Broberg can be seen in an airbrushed Mariners cap on his 1977 Topps baseball card, but he never actually pitched a regular-season game for the club. Near the end of spring training, Broberg was designated for assignment;[16] however, the Mariners had only a short-season Class A minor-league team. "Seattle loaned me to Wichita, the Cubs Triple-A team," explained Broberg, whose anticipated journey back to the big leagues was shorter than expected. "I pitched against the Cubs in an exhibition game and had a lot of strikeouts, and then the Cubs traded for me." On April 20 Chicago acquired Broberg. (Jim Todd was shipped to Oakland on October 25 to complete the deal.) Assigned officially to Wichita, Broberg was recalled in early July. He made 22 relief appearances, often in mopup situations, and logged 36 innings.

Broberg looked forward to camp with the Cubs in 1978 and an opportunity to prove that he was still a capable starting pitcher. "I was having too good of a spring and [the Cubs] didn't know what to do with me," said Broberg of his unexpected trade to the Oakland A's on March 29 for utilityman Rodney Scott and cash. "The Cubs had used me a reliever, and they didn't know what person they'd bump out of the rotation." Defying expectations, Broberg resurrected his career yet again by scattering four hits over 7⅓ scoreless innings against Seattle to win the first of four consecutive decisions. With a record of 9-6 (3.53 ERA) on July 3, Broberg seemed headed for his best year as the surprising A's challenged for the AL West crown, just 1½ games off the pace (41-39). But as Oakland slumped the rest of the season to finish in last place, so too did Broberg. He went winless in his next 10 starts (11 appearances), posting a 6.85 ERA and logging just 44⅔ innings, and was relegated to the bullpen. In a spot start in the second game of a doubleheader against Texas at Arlington Stadium on September 10, Broberg tossed a four-hit complete game to win, 4-1, in what proved to be his last big-league victory. He finished with a 10-12 record and 4.62 ERA in 165⅔ innings.

Just 28 years old, Broberg signed with the Los Angeles Dodgers as a free agent in 1979. "When the general manager [Al Campanis] told me they wanted to send me down, I asked about my other options," explained Broberg. "He tells me I can have my outright release. So I said just give it to me. I was released on Opening Day." The Dodgers were forced to pay Broberg his entire $65,000 salary instead of just a portion of it. But it turned out to be a blessing in disguise. Three years earlier, Broberg had been accepted to law school and received notice that he could no longer defer matriculation. That fall he began his law studies at Nova Southeastern University in Fort Lauderdale, Florida.

Spending April at home in Palm Beach for the first time since his high-school days, Broberg turned down offers from the New York Mets and Seattle

Mariners, who offered him the league minimum to pitch. "When they told me that they wouldn't pay for my apartment or help with those kinds of expenses, I told them that it would cost me more money to play ball than stay at home and start law school in the autumn. And that's what I did."

In parts of eight seasons in the big leagues, Broberg fashioned a 41-71 record, started 134 of 206 games, and posted a 4.56 ERA in 963 innings. He never suffered a baseball-related injury, but admitted with a chuckle, "I got my ego bruised." He toiled for primarily terrible teams which finished in last or next to last in six of his eight seasons. "It's a real distraction," said Broberg candidly about playing for poor ball clubs. "Guys come to the ballpark expecting to lose and that's not a good mindset. Teams I played for were 198 games under .500. A bad statistic – but the actual one."

Asked about his most vivid memory in his major-league career, Broberg gave a surprising response. "Ted [Williams] was a surly guy," he began, and then reminisced about a hitting contest and fundraiser in support of the Jimmy Fund cancer charity prior to a game between the Texas and Boston at Fenway Park on August 25, 1972. "Finally it's time for Ted to hit – he's hitting last," said Broberg. "He takes off his jacket and has his big belly hanging down. He goes up to the bat rack, going around looking for a bat. And then turns around to us in the dugout and says 'No wonder you fucking guys can't hit.'" Just shy of his 54th birthday, Williams popped up a few before the scene changed dramatically. "You could hear him yell at the batting practice pitcher [Boston's pitching coach Lee Stange], 'throw the fucking ball harder.'" recalled Broberg. "Williams started hitting line drives all over Fenway and into the seats. It was unbelievable to watch him hit."

As of 2015, Broberg has lived his entire life in Palm Beach. In July 1975 he married local resident Beverly Deitz, and together they raised two children, Erik and Elizabeth. Following his father's footsteps, Broberg became a successful attorney, focusing primarily on estate planning and real estate, and a partner in the law firm of Coe & Broberg. He has been active in the community, and has served as director of the Palm Beach Chamber of Commerce, chairman of the local recreation committee, and member of the planning and zoning board for the town.

Inducted with his father into the Palm Beach County Sports Hall of Fame in 1984, Broberg never lost his passion for baseball. He briefly revived his career when he played for the West Palm Beach Tropics in the short-lived Senior Professional Baseball Association in 1989. He often pitched batting practice to his son's high-school baseball team, and participated in reunions and old-timer's games with his former teams. In 2000 he was one of the guest speakers at SABR's national convention in West Palm Beach.

As of 2015, Broberg lived with his wife in Palm Beach.

The author expresses his gratitude to Peter Broberg whom the author interviewed on July 29, 2015. Broberg subsequently read this biography to ensure its accuracy.

Notes

1. All quotations from Pete Broberg are from the author's interview with the player on July 29, 2015.
2. "Indians Outlast PB Broberg, 1-0," *Fort Pierce* (Florida) *News Tribune*, March 25, 1968.
3. Charles Chamberlain, "Two Undefeated Teams in NCAA Baseball," *Indiana* (Pennsylvania) *Gazette*, June 15, 1970: 19.
4. UPI, "Pete Broberg Is Draft Bait," *Zanesville* (Ohio) *Times Recorder*, May 13, 1971: 8-B.
5. Ibid.; Season statistics from Dartmouth Big Green Baseball, dartmouthsports.com/ViewArticle.dbml?ATCLID=205122513. Twenty strikeouts from Will Parrish, "Broberg Ready to Give Pro Ball a Whirl," *Palm Beach* (Florida) *Post*, May 28, 1971, D4.
6. AP, "Senators Made Pitcher No. 1 Pick in Draft," *Salisbury* (Maryland) *Times Daily*, June 10, 1971: 17.
7. AP, "Broberg Makes Sox Believers; Bonus Baby Lives Up to Name," *Lowell* (Massachusetts) *Sun*, June 21, 1971: 40.
8. Pitch count from "Williams Happy; Broberg Dissatisfied by Debut," *Palm Beach* (Florida) *Post*, June 21, 1971: C1.
9. Larry Eldridge, AP, "Pete Broberg Impresses Ted," *Cumberland* (Maryland) *Evening Times*, June 30, 1971: 38.

10 AP, "One Pitch Beats Broberg," *The Capitol* (Annapolis, Maryland), August 25, 1971: 19.
11 Ibid.
12 Red Smith, "Sports of the Times. Walter Johnson II," *Warren* (Pennsylvania) *Times-Mirror and Observer*," March 21, 1971: 8
13 AP, "Peter Broberg. Ted Williams Expects Assist From Pitcher," *Lubbock* (Texas) *Avalanche-Journal*, April 25, 1872: 12.
14 Joe Saggis, UPI, "Team Sizeup: Milwaukee Brewers," *Raleigh Register* (Beckley, West Virginia), March 17, 1975: 1.
15 Lou Chapman, "Broberg Must Prove Self to Join Starting Rotation," *Milwaukee Sentinel*," April 7, 1976: 1.
16 AP, "Pete Broberg Sent to Cubs," *Progress Bulletin* (Pomona, California), April 20, 1977: 41.

JEFF BURROUGHS

BY DAVID E. SKELTON

No less an authority than Ted Williams referred to him as "the greatest young hitter I've ever seen."[1] His immense power drew comparisons to Hall of Famers Harmon Killebrew and Eddie Mathews, while his value was glimpsed in an unexecuted one-for-one swap with the California Angels' future Cooperstown inductee Nolan Ryan. (The talks collapsed only when the Texas Rangers learned of Ryan's offseason surgery in 1975.) He was the first recipient of the Most Valuable Player Award from an expansion club while earning "much of the credit for the Rangers' [1974] rise to respectability."[2] He was the next-to-last active player to wear a Washington Senators uniform. When his son was chosen as the ninth overall pick in the 1998 amateur draft, the father-son duo became one of the few pairings to garner first-round selections.

But the 16-year major-league career of Jeffrey Alan Burroughs was not all rosy. His relationship with his first big-league manager – the Splendid Splinter – turned personal and bitter (due largely to the meddling of Bob Short, the Rangers' owner). Further difficulties erupted with future Hall of Fame skipper Bobby Cox over playing time in Atlanta (this relationship was mended in Toronto in 1985). Meanwhile Burroughs' vacillating production (1974 MVP; .226 in 1975) fueled his critics and frustrated his champions. By 28 he was largely relegated to a platoon role, destroying the once overheated projections that Burroughs might one day overtake the home-run marks established by Hank Aaron and Roger Maris.

Burroughs was born to Charles Douglas and Iona Mae (Maxvold) Burroughs in Long Beach, California. The Burroughs family traced its roots to Charles's namesake in Virginia in the late eighteenth century. A series of westerly moves ensued until Charles's birth in southeast Nebraska in 1918. During World War II he moved to California, where he met Iona. On August 14, 1945, they married.[3] Six years later – on March 7, 1951 – Jeffrey was welcomed to the fold.

Burroughs' upbringing included standard teenage hijinks: in one instance gluing geese to his neighbors' mailboxes. More productive pursuits were found on the gridiron and diamonds of Long Beach's Woodrow Wilson High School. Knee surgery curtailed Burroughs' football track but did not slow his baseball chase. His prowess – as a pitcher and hitter – advanced Wilson High's baseball-rich talent that included Hall of Famer Bob Lemon, bonus baby Bob Bailey, and Burroughs' infield teammate Bobby Grich. Burroughs led his team to a city championship and in 1969, his senior year, was a California 4-A select player. Destined for Arizona State University's successful baseball program, Burroughs was soon preyed upon by the professional scouts.

Eight years removed from expansion, the Washington Senators – courtesy of a major-league-leading 96 losses in 1968 – owned the first pick in the 1969 amateur draft. This fact did not preclude the aggressive pursuit of Burroughs and other highly sought-after talent by other clubs, necessitating Commissioner Bowie Kuhn's warning concerning tampering. In mid-May the Senators, during a road swing through Anaheim, invited Burroughs to a pregame workout. Despite the youngster's "sub-par ratings in every department other than hitting,"[4] Washington's draft leanings were validated after Burroughs knocked five balls out of the cavernous park. A month later the 18-year-old became the fifth athlete to be selected first overall in the major leagues' amateur draft.

Awarded an $88,000 signing bonus, Burroughs reported to the Wytheville (Virginia) Senators in the Appalachian League.[5] Assigned to first base, the right-handed hitter wasted no time getting acclimated to the Rookie League: a near-.400 average in his first 78 professional at-bats. When the short season ended, Burroughs placed among the league leaders in nearly every offensive category while earning selection to the league's All-Rookie squad.

Ted Williams was resolute in his belief that hitters required a lengthy apprenticeship (1,200-2,000 at-bats) before advancing to the majors. This conviction did not prevent the Senators manager from wanting another firsthand look at Burroughs in spring camp in 1970. A nonroster invitee, he encountered major-league pitching for the first time on March 5 – two days before his 19th birthday – in an exhibition game against the New York Yankees. Burroughs grounded into a double play in his first at-bat and, shortly thereafter, committed an error at first base. ("I don't have a very good glove," he sheepishly admitted.[6]) All was forgiven when Burroughs connected for a towering home run. He continued to excite his veteran teammates with another blast 16 days later – a game-tying ninth-inning drive in Pompano Beach against Atlanta righty Pat Jarvis. Before spring camp, management had wrestled with Burroughs' minor-league placement. After his strong Grapefruit League performance, the slugger was advanced to Triple A with the Denver Bears.

There, Burroughs was tried at third base in a short-lived experiment. The challenges at the new position affected his offense: just one hit in his first 21 at-bats. The production picked up considerably (.354 in his next 147 at-bats) after he was moved to first base and eventually the outfield, though he also exhibited a strong propensity for striking out. On May 4 Burroughs hit his first homer of the season – a grand slam against the Evansville Triplets in a losing effort. Two days later he hoisted two more home runs to lead the Bears to a 13-6 win over the Triplets. Pacing the Bears in homers and RBIs, Burroughs earned selection to the American Association All-Star squad.

After constant pestering from owner Bob Short, Ted Williams promoted the much-heralded youngster.[7] On July 20, 1970, Burroughs made his major-league debut in right field against the Milwaukee Brewers in Robert F. Kennedy Stadium. He went hitless in three at-bats against veteran southpaw Al Downing. Four days later Burroughs collected his first big-league hit, a pinch-hit RBI single against Angels' reliever Steve Kealey. (Burroughs was thrown out trying to stretch it into a double.) An infield single in his next appearance – his second start – resulted in Burroughs' first run scored. He went hitless in his next seven at-bats and was reassigned to Denver. The big-league exposure appears to have been somewhat traumatic for the 19-year-old. Burroughs slumped to a .227-3-17 line in his final 141 at-bats, yet finished the season among the league leaders in home runs and RBIs.

Assigned to the Senators' 40-man roster in 1971, Burroughs (the youngest player) reported to spring training under a self-imposed health-food regime (seeking to shed weight from a 215-pound girth). A pawn in the tug-of-war between Short and Williams, Burroughs strengthened the former's cause after the team was compelled to install wire netting in the outfield to save the cost of balls Burroughs hit over the fence. The manager won out when Burroughs was reassigned to Denver before camp broke, but by July the young slugger was donning Senators garb after a strong American Association campaign. Starting against left-handers with the occasional pinch-hit appearance, Burroughs hit his first major-league home run on August 2, a pinch-hit three-run dinger into the upper right-field deck of Tiger Stadium to knot the score against Detroit veteran reliever Ron Perranoski. Burroughs received more playing time as Williams's confidence in the youngster grew. On August 14 Angels lefty Clyde Wright was spinning a one-hit shutout against the Senators when Burroughs drove a seventh-inning pitch for a two-run homer and a 2-0 win. Six days later he collected five hits and five RBIs in a doubleheader sweep of the Kansas City Royals. One of the Senators' hottest hitters in August (.286-4-19), he was slowed by a bruised shoulder in September. Finishing with a .232-5-25 record, he prepared for a Venezuelan winter campaign alongside teammate Toby Harrah and others.

The winter season bore dividends in 1972 Grapefruit League competition. In three games beginning March 10 Burroughs collected five hits, including two two-run homers, and seven RBIs. Burroughs was leading his club in home runs (5), and had won the starting left-field job, when he strained his lower back. The Opening Day left fielder for the newly-christened Texas Rangers became veteran slugger Frank Howard instead. Placed on the disabled list on April 26, Burroughs did not see steady play until May 16. A game-winning two-run homer off future Hall of Famer Bert Blyleven on May 21 proved Burroughs' only highlight as he continued to struggle with his back. He tinkered with a variety of batting stances and adjustments in a failed attempt to find relief. A .185-1-3 line resulted in Burroughs' assignment to Denver, where his struggles continued: .163 into July. As if throwing a switch, he experienced an extraordinary rebound with nine homers in 14 games. Burroughs finished among the league leaders with a .303 average and 24 home runs. "[W]e have one helluva player on our hands in that kid," exclaimed the Rangers' new manager, Whitey Herzog.[8]

Burroughs was not unhappy about Williams's departure. The seeds of animosity planted between manager and owner had evolved into a severe dislike between manager and player. When Burroughs reported to spring camp in 1973 he anxiously looked forward to playing for the future Hall of Fame skipper. A strong exhibition campaign included a two-homer, six-RBI outing on March 25 in a 15-7 rout of the Royals in Fort Myers, Florida. But Burroughs labored when the season began. On May 1 he led the Rangers to a 7-6 win over the Boston Red Sox with three hits and four RBIs. Eight days later his fifth-inning home run spared the Rangers from a no-hitter by Milwaukee righty Jim Colborn. But Burroughs' .217-6-19 through June 6 sparked little fear in opposing pitchers. A .400 clip in 60 June at-bats – including a 13-game hit streak – righted his average. Home runs quickly followed, including a 475-foot wallop below the left-field scoreboard in Arlington Stadium.

On July 26 Burroughs blasted the first grand slam in Rangers history.[9] His two additional slams over the next nine days tied a major-league record of three within a 10-day span. A 1-for-18 skid at the end of August did not deter the first full year player from challenging future Hall of Famer Reggie Jackson for the American League home-run crown. Remarkably, the consensus of coaches and managers (Herzog was replaced late in the season) was that the swirling right-field winds in Arlington robbed Burroughs of an additional 14 to 16 homers. Though he soon grew out of it, in 1973 Burroughs became known as much for helmet-throwing tantrums as immense power. "Those long power alleys and the wind make it almost impossible at home," Burroughs complained.[10] "I'd better not get my hands on any dynamite because I'll blow this park into the next state."[11] During the offseason the Rangers tried to remedy the situation by moving the fences 10 feet closer. They fended off numerous trade queries for the bespectacled slugger, including an aggressive and lengthy pursuit by Boston. Local news media and radio-television personnel dubbed

Burroughs the club's outstanding player, while new manager Billy Martin identified him as untouchable.

In 1974 Burroughs was one of the last to report to spring training. Newly fitted with contact lenses, he flew to Bob Short's Minneapolis home and negotiated a hefty raise. When Burroughs arrived in Florida he continued his offensive onslaught with a Grapefruit League campaign of .339-6-23.[12] Four games into the regular season, he added another grand slam to his growing résumé. In May Burroughs scorched opposing pitchers at a .352 pace, with particular relish against Chicago (.467-5-24 versus White Sox hurlers for the season). Beginning May 12, he drove in at least one run in 10 consecutive games.

Unwanted attention arrived on June 4 in Cleveland during a 10-cent-beer promotion. In the ninth inning of a knotted contest two inebriated young men ran onto the field intent on capturing Burroughs' cap. A scuffle occurred, prompting the ever-excitable Billy Martin to lead his charges out of the dugout in defense of the right fielder. The move only exacerbated the situation as more fans spilled onto the field. The ensuing riot resulted in a forfeit by the Indians, with Burroughs sustaining a jammed thumb in the brawl. Though he never used it as an excuse, the injury likely contributed to a .157 average in his next 51 at-bats. (He'd entered the game among the league leaders at .332.) A late All-Star balloting surge earned Burroughs a left-field starting berth in the midsummer classic. Before the July 23 tilt Burroughs, mired in a mild slump, requested time off. The rest proved beneficial when the re-energized slugger collected 65 hits in his final 196 at-bats (.332). Surprisingly, the home runs tailed off, with Burroughs hitting his last four-bagger on August 21 (the recurring back problems a contributing factor). He paced the franchise to only its second winning season, leading the league in RBIs (118) while placing among the leaders in homers (25) and average (.301). With reference to the postseason awards, Reggie Jackson, the league's reigning MVP, admitted, "I don't mind saying that Jeff Burroughs would get my vote if I had one."[13] Apparently the Baseball Writers' Association of America took notice as Burroughs, the only player named on all 24 ballots, outpaced three members of the World Series champion Oakland Athletics to earn the award for Most Valuable Player (becoming the first Texas player from either league to be named MVP).

An early-spring slump doomed the high-flying club's pennant aspirations in 1974. The Rangers looked to overcome such barriers in 1975. Burroughs' .310-4-13 line through April contributed to this goal. The Rangers captured sole possession of first place on May 22 only to suffer a slide of 1-7 through the rest of the month. The next two months continued to prove disastrous as the club fell out of contention. Mired in a 5-for-59 slump beginning June 10, Burroughs received an inordinate amount of blame for the collapse from aggrieved fans and feuding teammates. Having previously demonstrated a proclivity for striking out, Burroughs led the league with 155 K's in 1975 (eighth in Rangers history through 2017). "I wanted to pull the ball more ... [to] hit more homers," Burroughs explained. "You get into some bad habits and, before you know it, you've gone so far you can't correct them. I was dipping my right shoulder, getting too much of an uppercut on my swing."[14] Though he finished with strong power numbers (29 homers, 94 RBIs), the athlete who prided himself as an all-around player finished the season with a .226 average.

The next year proved remarkably similar for both player and team. The Rangers' fast start to the 1976 season cooled to midseason malaise as the club tumbled out of contention. Meanwhile Burroughs struggled to get above .229 from June through August. He ignored the many rumors of a pending trade, confident that the three-year contract extension he signed in March contained a no-trade clause. Having purchased a home in Arlington, the 26-year-old was both surprised and upset when the Rangers traded him to the Atlanta Braves on December 9 for five players and $250,000.

The Rangers reportedly received a vast number of offers for Burroughs, including trades for some of the most heralded pitchers in baseball: Yankees relief ace Sparky Lyle and future Hall of Famer Rich Gossage. The deal appears to have turned on the close relationship between Braves general manager Bill Lucas and his former boss, Rangers newly hired vice president Eddie Robinson (who vehemently denied the presence of a no-trade clause in the right-handed slugger's contract). When Burroughs recovered from the initial shock, he quickly realized the benefits derived from home games played in a stadium dubbed "The Launching Pad." In January he negotiated a three-year extension with the Braves that ensured a no-trade provision.

Over the next two years the Braves/Burroughs union proved a perfect match. In 1977 the slugger blasted nearly one-third of the Braves' home-run yield with a career-high 41 homers. Burroughs earned his second All-Star berth while becoming only the seventh major leaguer to hit 30 or more four-baggers in both leagues, and only the fourth to hit 40 or more in his first year after switching leagues. Tired of surrendering the long ball, pitchers quit throwing to Burroughs in 1978. That season he led the majors with 117 walks and a .432 on-base percentage. In both years Burroughs gained MVP consideration playing for the last-place club. He signed another three-year extension before the start of the 1979 campaign.

Sans the power, 1979 was largely a repeat performance of Burroughs' 1975 season when a promising start yielded to a 17-for-99 run through June 1. Manager Bobby Cox personally directed extra batting practice for Burroughs following a similar dip in July (.192 in 78 at-bats). The situation worsened in August when Burroughs' back problems resurfaced. Despite the no-trade clause the Braves hoped to secure Burroughs' approval for a pending swap. Anticipating an offseason departure, Burroughs received just one pinch-hit appearance in September as the team turned increasingly to Barry Bonnell in left field.

But the Braves miscalculated when Burroughs vetoed a trade that would have returned him to the Rangers. (The December 6 deal went through without him.) Burroughs' decision was a risky one: One day earlier the Braves had secured Chris Chambliss and were preparing to move first baseman Dale Murphy to the outfield. Anticipating the full-time role of prospect Eddie Miller in center, Cox and new general manager John Mullen publicly announced that Burroughs would be relegated to a reserve role.

"It's like blackmail," Burroughs complained. "They're saying, 'If you don't okay this trade, we won't play you.' It's preposterous."[15]

Miller's dismal start to the 1980 campaign prompted Cox to move Murphy to center and re-insert Burroughs in left. A 9-for-15 surge beginning April 24 briefly hoisted his average above .400 and hinted at a return to past glory (though he did not connect for a homer until June 19). On June 6 he foiled another no-hit bid with a seventh-inning double off Los Angeles Dodgers lefty Jerry Reuss. In July, as the upstart Braves moved to within 7½ games of first place following a 9-2 run, Burroughs played a pivotal role.

But when he began slipping in August, Cox – citing a desire to add more speed to the lineup – was quick to bench Burroughs. He made just 20 pinch-hit appearances (including two game-winning homers) over the season's final 52 games. Forced to acknowledge that he was not part of Cox's plans for the future, Burroughs submitted a list of eight teams he would accept a move to. Though the Mariners were not listed, the embittered slugger eagerly consented to a move to Seattle simply to get out of Atlanta. Unable to resist some parting shots, Burroughs said, "It was as if [Cox] was trying to run me out of baseball. He's been demeaning me and embarrassing me for three years. ... [T]he front office treat[s players] like we're wanted criminals."[16] The deal was held up for weeks pending resolution of a $400,000 loan Burroughs received from Braves owner Ted Turner.

In the strike-shortened 1981 season the right fielder once again received steady playing time and placed among the Mariners' leaders in most offensive categories. On August 14, 1981, Burroughs became the first player in the Mariners' short history to hit three homers in one game. He filed for free agency after the season but was one of many not selected in the re-entry draft (an early hint of owner collusion). Burroughs rejected offers from the Rangers and Mariners (the latter he deemed very insulting) and was eventually invited to Oakland's spring camp by Athletics manager Billy Martin.

Martin beamed after his former protégé signed with the club: "[Burroughs] comes to the park early, he runs, takes extra hitting. He works harder than anybody."[17] Burroughs spent the next three years in Oakland. In 1982 he set an Athletics single-season record with 11 pinch-hits, and was on the verge of shattering the American League record for pinch-hit homers when he was moved into the starting lineup. A year later the entire team escaped a near-death experience when their charter plane nearly collided with a smaller plane in-flight. But the most memorable (and humorous) occurrence came on April 8, 1984, when Martin's replacement, Steve Boros, tapped the less-than-speedy Burroughs as a pinch-runner: "I loved the look on his face when I told him he was pinch-running," Boros laughed. "Shock."[18]

On December 22, 1984, Burroughs was sold to Toronto, where he was roundly welcomed by Blue Jays manager Bobby Cox. In his first spring training at-bat in a Toronto uniform Burroughs hit a two-run homer against future Hall of Famer Tom Seaver. Among a roster of veteran players Burroughs earned the bulk of the DH responsibilities in leading the 1985 Blue Jays to their first playoff venture. When veteran slugger Cliff Johnson was acquired in August and speculation arose that Burroughs might be released, Cox rose to his defense: "He's never had the chance to be in the playoffs or World Series, he's been with us all year, and I refuse to do that to him. If winning means doing such things to people like Jeff Burroughs, winning isn't worth it."[19] In the ninth inning of Game Seven of the ALCS, Burroughs made his only postseason appearance: a pinch-hit groundout to the pitcher. It proved to be his last major-league appearance. When he retired, only infielder Toby Harrah survived as the last active player who had worn a Washington Senators uniform.

Burroughs once remarked, "I'm a pretty good ballplayer. Not a great player, but a good one. I swing a good bat, and I can drive in runs. I'm an average fielder with an average arm."[20] In spite of this modest self-assessment, Burroughs concluded a robust 16-year major-league career with a .261-240-882 line in 5,536 at-bats. Along the way he earned two All-Star berths and was the runaway selection for the 1974 AL MVP award.

Burroughs married Rhode Island native Deborah Gorman in 1977. He returned to his Long Beach roots, where they raised a family. Burroughs was an avid reader and saltwater fisherman but had a particular passion for golf. Though he never took lessons, Burroughs was an extraordinary player. In winters throughout his career he played in some of the largest tournaments (example: the Bing Crosby National Pro-Am) alongside some of sports' biggest names: Willie Mays, Joe DiMaggio, Joe Namath, and Johnny Unitas.

But baseball never strayed far from the former slugger. In 1992 he led sons Scott Alan and Sean Patrick to the Little League World Series in Williamsport, Pennsylvania. Though they lost to the Philippines entry, it was later determined that the Far East team had violated age and residency rules. The Long Beach team was awarded the title World Champions. The next year the Burroughs trio helped Long Beach to a 3-2 win over a Panama entry to become the only repeat champions in Little League World Series history. In the mid-1990s Burroughs attained additional success as a manager in the independent Western Baseball League. The family stood proudly when second son Sean, drafted by the San Diego Padres in the first round of the 1998 amateur draft, was tabbed as "the franchise's best hitting prospect since [future Hall of Famer] Tony Gwynn."[21]

Despite this success Burroughs always remained grounded. A glimpse into his outlook on life was seen in quotes shortly after he won the American League Most Valuable Player Award: "The people who know me best, like my friends in Long Beach, aren't influenced by awards or anything like that. And those are the people I'm around the most away from baseball. Success does have a tendency to change some people, and usually for the worst. But it's not going to happen to me."[22]

Sources

In addition to the sources cited in the Notes, the author also consulted Baseball-reference.com and Ancestry.com.

Notes

1. Frank Haraway, "A Teen-Age Swat Terror: Denver's Jeff Burroughs," *The Sporting News*, June 20, 1970: 37.
2. C.C. Johnson Spink, "Marshall, Hunter, Brock, Burroughs Saluted," *The Sporting News*, November 2, 1974: 3.
3. One source indicates a wedding before the move west, a possible scenario since the bride, of Norwegian ancestry, was a native of neighboring South Dakota.
4. Jack Lang, "'Quit Tampering' – Kuhn's Warning During Draft," *The Sporting News*, June 21, 1969: 5.
5. Varying reports reflect a low of $80,000, a high of $100,000.
6. Merrell Whittlesey, "Ted Warned Houk of Burroughs' Power Bat," *The Sporting News*, March 14, 1970: 26.
7. Short hoped to boost Washington's lagging attendance.
8. Randy Galloway, "Herzog Seeking 'Ballplayers, Not Boy Scouts,'" *The Sporting News*, December 23, 1972: 46.
9. The blast was the franchise's first grand slam in three years.
10. Merle Heryford, "Home Runs Just Come Naturally for Burroughs," *The Sporting News*, August 18, 1973: 20.
11. Randy Galloway, "Wind Shrivels Rangers' Homer Crop," *The Sporting News*, September 8, 1973: 4.
12. The six home runs are believed to be a Rangers spring-training record (tied by Pete Incaviglia in 1986). They included two grand slams against the New York Yankees.
13. "A.L. Flashes," *The Sporting News*, September 28, 1974: 31.
14. Randy Galloway, "Burroughs to Stop Thinking of Homers," *The Sporting News*, April 10, 1976: 30.
15. Ken Picking, "Burroughs Swings Brickbat at Braves," *The Sporting News*, February 23, 1980: 30.
16. Ken Picking, "'Treated Like Criminal,' Says Ex-Brave Burroughs," *The Sporting News*, January 3, 1981, 44.
17. Kit Stier, "Burroughs Repays A's by Staying Fit," *The Sporting News*, August 23, 1982: 29.
18. Stan Isle, "Boros' Move Raises Eyebrows," *The Sporting News*, April 23, 1984: 22; a year later Burroughs amused both teammates and fans by sliding into third base a couple of feet from the bag.
19. Peter Gammons, "Jays Have Injury Factor for 2nd Season," *The Sporting News*, October 7, 1985: 25.
20. Wayne Minshew, "Braves Placate Burroughs With No-Trade Pact," *The Sporting News*, January 29, 1977: 36.
21. Tom Krasovic, "San Diego: Prospects Analysis," *The Sporting News*, February 7, 2000: 42.
22. Randy Galloway, "Complacency No. 1 Enemy to Jeff the Ranger," *The Sporting News*, April 19, 1975: 11.

CASEY COX

BY ALAN COHEN

"Career Performance" is a term that is quite often used, and for pitcher Casey Cox, his career performance came on July 7, 1969. Casey was pitching for Washington against the Cleveland Indians. The perennial second-division Senators were having a pretty good year and their victory that night put them within 3½ games of second place in the American League's Eastern Division. Cox came into the game for Washington with one out in the top of the third inning. The bases were loaded, and Washington was trailing 2-1. Cox retired 20 all batters he faced as the Senators came from behind to win. (Lou Klimchock reached first in the eighth inning when center fielder Del Unser dropped his fly ball, but Unser gunned down Klimchock trying to advance to second base.)

Cox was not known for his hitting but in the fourth inning he laid down a perfect bunt to score catcher Jim French from third. The next day, Cox's teammates presented him with a bright red batting glove.[1]

But it was Cox's pitching that drew the real plaudits from his batterymate. "Casey has never been better," French said. "That was the best sinker he has ever had. After pitching four innings in Boston Saturday night, he was just tired enough to have his sinker working to perfection."[2]

The win was Cox's sixth of the season and dropped his ERA to a stunning 1.88.

The 1969 Senators went on to win 86 games and finish in fourth place in the AL East. The wins were their most since they began as an expansion team in 1961, and the most of any Washington team since 1945. Toward the end of the season, manager Ted Williams called Cox one of his team's two best pitchers (along with 14-game-winner Dick Bosman).[3] Cox, in his fourth season with the Senators, had arrived, posting a 12-7 record with a 2.78 ERA. The Alexandria Club of Grandstand Managers concurred with Williams, presenting Cox with a silver service set at the end of the season.[4]

In 1972 Cox traveled with the Senators as they became the Texas Rangers. It was his 10th stop in a professional career that had begun in 1962.

Joseph Casey Cox entered the world on July 3, 1941, in Long Beach, California. His parents were Joseph Casey Cox and Esther Cox. (Casey was named for his grandfathers, and was called Casey from an early age to avoid being confused with his father.) Casey's younger sister, Ann Louise, became a noted cell behavioral research scientist.

Cox's father, an accountant, wasted no time in introducing his son to baseball and by the time young Casey was 8, they were determined that young Casey would become a major-league ballplayer, just like Casey's hero, Bob Lemon. Casey starred in baseball and basketball at Woodrow Wilson High School

(Class of 1959), went to Long Beach City College for two years, then to Los Angeles State College in 1961. He pitched one season at LA State, and impressed scouts when he struck out 17 Arizona Wildcats in one outing.[5]

Cox was signed in June 1962 by scout Al Zarilla of the Cincinnati Reds for a bonus of $9,000, with an additional $8,000 to come if Cox made it to the majors. Given a choice of three minor-league destinations, he chose Rocky Mount of the Class B Carolina League. In his first appearance, on June 17, he took a no-hitter into the sixth inning against Burlington, and allowed only one run and three hits in eight innings. But Rocky Mount lost, 3-0.[6] In his second start, on June 24, he earned his first professional win, needing only 90 pitches for a 7-1 complete-game victory over Winston-Salem.[7] But despite those two gems, first-year losses outnumbered wins: 4-8 with a 4.37 ERA. Cox went to the Florida Instructional League after the season. On November 26 he was claimed by the Cleveland Indians in the annual draft of first-year minor-league players.

Cox began the 1963 season with Charleston, West Virginia, in the Double-A Eastern League, going 0-2 before being sent to Burlington of the Carolina League on May 9. Three weeks later he was sold to the Senators to make room for Early Wynn, who signed with the Indians to try to hit the 300-win mark. The Senators assigned Cox to their Peninsula farm club, making it three Carolina League teams in less than 12 months. With Peninsula, he went 9-10 with an ERA of 3.37 in 31 games.

In 1964 Washington changed its Carolina League affiliation to Rocky Mount, and Cox was back where he started. He got off to a great start, and as late as June 21, his ERA was 1.59. In his first 64 appearances, he had an ERA of 2.48, third best in the league. He tailed off in his last five appearances, but was the workhorse of the bullpen. Pitching in a league-high 69 games (only three starts), his 185 innings were third best in the league and tops among relievers. He went 9-10 with a 3.16 ERA for a team that finished at 61-77.

Cox began the 1965 season in Hawaii in the Triple-A Pacific Coast League, but after nine appearances during which his ERA stood at 5.40, he was reassigned to York, Pennsylvania in the Double-A Eastern League. Appearing in 61 games, all but one in relief, he was able to put together a 9-2 record with a 2.03 ERA. Working with roving pitching instructor Sid Hudson,[8] he was among the league leaders in ERA all season and posted a 9-2 record. Cox had hoped to be called up to the Senators at the end of the season, but went home disappointed.

"There was nothing else I ever wanted to do but get to the big leagues. Boy, this big-league life is it. It's the only way to live."[9] And in 1966 he would get to the big leagues for the first time, at age 24 with a competitive zeal that was commented on during spring training by pitching coach Rube Walker: "He has a lot of determination for a rookie. He has a lot of spirit and we're taking a long look at him."[10] Cox also impressed manager Gil Hodges with his coolness under fire. Hodges said, "Cox has shown real poise. … A couple of years ago, he was a dart-thrower. Now, he's a pitcher."[11]

Cox made his major-league debut on April 15, 1966. Recalling his debut close to 50 years later, he remembered that he was so nervous that "you couldn't shove a pin up my ass with a jackhammer." His first pitch went only 45 feet. He collected himself and went on to hurl two hitless innings in a Washington loss at Detroit. When he struck out the last batter he faced, Al Kaline, he had his first career strikeout. "I threw him a fastball and a slider for strikes. Then I tried to cut it too fine but missed and a low changeup made it 3-and-2. I got him with a low and away fastball."[12] Eight days later he picked up his first save, getting the last five outs, including a strikeout of Willie Horton for the final out, in a 5-3 Senators win over the Tigers. The Senators kept Cox busy. He pitched in 21 of his team's first 41 games, and the team was enjoying the dizzying heights of the first division. By June 2 Cox had five saves and his ERA was 2.87. The team had risen to fifth place and was within seven games of the league lead. As the season wore on, the Senators faded. Cox wound up appearing in a team-leading 66 games, compiling a 4-5 record with seven saves and a 3.50 ERA.

Sometimes a ballplayer learns a lesson from adversity and on July 19, 1966, a circumstance arose that almost 50 years later, Cox was still able to remember. He had earlier told the story to Merrell Whittlesey in 1971. "We were playing the Twins and Harmon Killebrew beat me with a hit with two out in the ninth inning (it was actually the eighth inning). The next day Hodges casually asked me how much money I thought Killebrew made, and at the time it was about $75,000, or that was my guess. I forget who the next batter was – it wasn't Tony Oliva – and he asked me how much I thought that fellow (Earl Battey) made, and I guessed $25,000. Gil told me that there must be some reason that Killebrew made $75,000 and the next hitter made $25,000, and to keep that in mind the next time I faced a big star with just an average hitter next up. I've never forgotten it, and you'd be surprised how much that has helped."[13]

Cox spent part of the winter pitching for the Licey Tigers in the Dominican League. His stay was cut short after an altercation on November 15 between Cox and some disapproving fans. He reacted to their taunts by making an "offensive gesture"[14] toward the stands. Cox was jailed, fined $50, and suspended for a week.[15] The gesture had resulted in several fans advancing toward the field. One of the fans made it as far as the dugout, and the police spent the balance of the game protecting Cox. The next day he headed home.[16] His season in the Caribbean was over.[17]

As the 1967 season approached, an optimistic Cox exclaimed, "There's something in the air in this (spring-training) camp. It's like a lot of young guys getting together and having pride."[18] But once the season started, Cox appeared in only six of his team's first 23 games, pitching only eight innings with no decisions. He was sent to Honolulu at roster cutdown time in May. After pitching in 14 games in less than a month, Cox was summoned back to Washington on June 7 and was used regularly the rest of the season. In 54 games he had a 7-4 record and a 2.96 ERA. The Senators finished the season in a sixth-place tie, 15½ games out of first place.

In 1968 Jim Lemon replaced Gil Hodges as manager and inherited a strong bullpen. The six top relievers had chalked up 310 relief appearances in 1967, but Cox would not be a factor with the Senators in 1968. Toward the end of spring training, he was assigned to Buffalo of the International League, where he went 7-5. It was not a happy time for Cox, who was unable to escape the futility of being stuck in the minors hoping for a call-up that never came. After the minor-league season ended, Cox was recalled to Washington and got into four games with the Senators.

During the offseason, the Senators acquired a new owner, Bob Short. Cox was philosophical about the change: "I hope they have a place for me. I can see this man (Short) means business, and I'd like to be part of it."[19]

Cox made the 1969 team out of spring training and had an early-season highlight on April 26 against Cleveland. He entered the game with one out in the first inning, relieving Barry Moore, who had walked four consecutive batters with one out. Cox induced Cleveland's Max Alvis to hit a comebacker that Cox turned into a 1-2-3 double play. Cox remained in the game and scattered six hits over the remaining eight innings as the Senators won, 8-1. "They told me not to be a hero, just go as far as I could. After seven or eight innings, I still felt good," he said.[20] Manager Ted Williams kept telling Cox not to be a "hero," and to tell him if he was tiring. Cox said, "I felt better in the last three innings, though, than in the middle three."[21] At bat he reached first base for the first time in his career, walking in the fourth inning. In the seventh inning he had his first career RBI when Jack Hamilton walked him with the bases loaded.

But Cox had yet to get his first major-league hit and took a fair amount of kidding. When he asked to borrow a bat from Hank Allen, the outfielder was a bit apprehensive. One of the players on the bench said, "Give it to him. He could use it for 100 years and never hurt it."[22]

Manager Williams, a fair student of hitting, was more interested in Cox being a success on the mound. One particularly memorable experience was a game against the Twins on June 8. The Twins used seven pitchers and Cox was the last of the five pitchers used by the Senators. The game went into extra innings tied 5-5. Cox entered the game in the bottom of the 11th inning. Two hits and an intentional walk loaded the bases, bringing up Cox's old nemesis Harmon Killebrew, who already had doubled and homered. The count went to 3-and-2. Walking Killebrew was not an option. Cox threw a low fastball that eluded the swinging bat of Killebrew. Del Unser's two-run homer in the 12th inning gave the Senators a lead and Cox retired the Twins in bottom of the inning to secure his fourth win of the season.

"Fortunately, playing for Ted Williams has helped me to gain the confidence and concentration that a pitcher needs in a situation like that," Cox said. "In other years, I might have beaten myself in a comparable situation. But I was thinking positive, to get the ball over. It was a big pitch. I'll never forget it." He noted the three keys to his success – Confidence, Concentration, and Control.[23]

There was a shortage of starting pitchers on the 1969 Senators and Williams on June 23 began using Cox as a spot starter. In his first start, Cox pitched 5⅓ innings of scoreless ball at Baltimore, and was in line for the win. However, the bullpen let him down and the Orioles came back to win, 5-3. On July 1 Cox threw his first career complete game, as Washington defeated Cleveland, 4-1. In 13 starts, Cox went 5-4. His record in relief was 7-3.

Between his long relief stints and occasional starting roles, Cox was getting to swing the bat more often, but his average remained at .000 (0-for-32) on July 17. On that day Cox started against the Tigers and singled off Earl Wilson in the third and fifth innings. The line drive to right in the third inning resulted in a standing ovation.[24] But the Senators' bats were cold, and Cox, who went into the game with a five-game winning streak, did not have his best stuff, surrendering a three-run homer to Willie Horton in the first inning. Cox was removed for a pinch-hitter in the seventh inning with the Senators trailing 3-1. Washington lost, 4-3, and Cox was charged with his second loss of the season, but he finally had his first major-league hits. He ended the season with five hits and a .106 batting average. He got only 10 more hits in the major leagues, and his career batting average was a dismal .099 (15-for-151).

Hitting aside, 1969 was a breakout season for Cox. He was 12-7 with a 2.78 ERA as the Senators went 86-76 under the stewardship of first-year manager Williams. The 1970 season couldn't come soon enough, and Williams promised Cox a new set of golf clubs if he got 12 hits during 1970.[25]

Cox got even more chances at the plate in 1970, starting 30 games. In his first three starts he yielded 12 runs in 21 innings for a gaudy 4.29 ERA. However, he had some offensive help and came away with three wins. He recognized his good fortune, saying, "There are some pitchers who get runs scored for them, and none of those pitchers ever gives them back."[26]

Cox stayed in the rotation for most of the season and went 8-12 with a 4.45 ERA, pitching a career high 192⅓ innings. His failure to replicate the success of 1969 was caused in part by his failure to keep the ball in the park. He gave up more homers (27) than anyone else on the Washington staff. From July 9 through August 31, Cox gave up at least one homer in each of 11 consecutive starts. His only complete game of the season, a 9-3 win over Cleveland on July 9, broke a string of 30 games in which Senators pitchers failed to complete what they started.[27] Williams did not have to spring for the golf clubs; Cox had only seven hits during the season. The team lost its last 14 games of the season to finish in last place at 70-92.

After the season Cox ventured to La Guaira, Venezuela, to play winter ball and worked on his curveball, winning three of six decisions. After the disappointing 1970 season in Washington, he expected that 1971 would be different. "I believe that (in spring training) Ted (Williams) will be more critical, and I think that will help us."[28]

By May 24 it was clear that a move to the bullpen was in order for Cox. In his first 11 appearances, 10 as a starter, he had gone 0-2 with a 4.50 ERA. After a poor performance on May 24, "I went to Ted and told him I could help the team more as a relief pitcher. He said that was fine and he would try me there. And the very next night, I got a win in relief."[29] He excelled in relief, and in 26 games from May 25 to August 3, he pitched 49 innings, and had an ERA of 1.47.

Williams said, "That's where he should have been all along, but we needed a starter and he did a good job. … Now I'll say flatly that he is the best right-handed relief pitcher in the league."[30]

Cox's poor performance as a starter in 1971 meant his overall numbers for the sixth-place Senators were not as good. He went 5-7 in 54 games with seven saves and an ERA of 3.98. He was back at home in the bullpen. In August he said, "I like what I'm doing. There is great satisfaction to saving a game as well as winning one. I have found a baseball home and I want to stay there, and hopefully with the Senators for at least five more years."[31]

But as the season ended and September became October, it was clear that neither Cox nor any of his teammates would be with the Washington Senators beyond 1971, as owner Bob Short moved the club to the Dallas-Fort Worth area in October. The Washington Senators became the Texas Rangers. Cox relocated to the Dallas area shortly after the move was announced.

By the time the move to Texas was made, Cox was one of the longest-tenured players on the team, along with Dick Bosman and Frank Howard. He went 3-5 with the Rangers, sporting an ERA of 4.41 when, at the end of August, he was traded to the New York Yankees for pitcher Jim Roland. The Yankees, who had not won anything of note since the 1964 American League pennant, were a .500 ballclub in 1972. They finished at 79-76, good for fourth place in the AL East. The 30-year-old Cox pitched in five games down the stretch, going 0-1 with a 4.63 ERA and no saves.

Cox returned to the Yankees in 1973, but after an unsuccessful outing on Opening Day, he was released on April 17. He went back to the minors, pitching that season for the Wichita Aeros, the Cubs' affiliate in the Triple-A American Association. He went 6-5 for the Aeros with a 5.05 ERA, and retired at the end of the season.

Cox has been inducted into several school Halls of Fame in the Long Beach area, and was inducted in the City of Long Beach Hall of Fame in 2007.

Cox has had multiple marriages and had one child, Carol Ann, during his first marriage. Carol Ann died at age 44 in 2008. After his playing days, he entered the world of insurance, starting out by selling life insurance. He joined a firm in Florida that paid life, medical, and dental claims for several large group clients. He eventually acquired ownership of the firm. In retirement, he has worked in various capacities for the local Republican Party near his home in Florida.

Sources
In addition to the sources cited in the Notes, the author also relied on:
Addie, Bob. "Cutdown Beefs Rock Capital," *The Sporting News*, May 27, 1967:18.
Heryford, Merle. "New Resident: Cox Relief Gun," *Dallas Morning News*, October 17, 1971: B4.

Whittlesey, Merrell. "Casey at the Bat? A Sad Sight; But He's A-OK on the Mound," *The Sporting News*, February 14, 1970: 36.

Baseball-Reference.com.

Cox's file at the National Baseball Hall of Fame and Museum library.

Johnson, Lloyd, and Miles Wolff, eds., *Encyclopedia of Minor League Baseball* (Durham, North Carolina: Baseball America, 2007),

Author interview with Casey Cox, November 1, 2015.

Notes

1. William Gildea, "This Year Cox Has Batters Buffaloed," *Washington Post*, July 9, 1969: C3.
2. Merrell Whittlesey, "French's Double Emulates Hondo Homers: Cox Joins Catcher in Star Role," *Washington Evening Star*, July 8, 1969: 33.
3. Merrell Whittlesey, "Impossible Dream: Ted's Nats Boast a Carload of '69 Pluses," *The Sporting News*, October 4, 1969: 13.
4. Merrell Whittlesey, "Ted Finally 'Convinced' Writers Nats Were for Real," *The Sporting News*, October 18, 1969: 27.
5. Bob Addie, "Cocky Young Casey Eyes Nat Relief Job," *The Sporting News*, April 9, 1966: 20.
6. "Burlington Stops Rocky Mount on Four Hits: Casey Cox Suffers Heart Breaking Loss," *Rocky Mount* (North Carolina) *Telegram*, June 18, 1962: 2B.
7. Greensboro (North Carolina) Daily News, June 25, 1962: 11.
8. Bob Addie, "Rookie Joseph Casey Cox, 24, Near Life Goal, Exudes Confidence," Washington Post, March 3, 1966: F1.
9. Author Interview with Casey Cox. All otherwise unattributed quotations come from this interview.
10. Addie, "Cocky Young Casey."
11. Bob Addie, "Cox Earns Trip North with Nats," Washington Post, March 30, 1966: C2.
12. Bob Addie, "Cox Provides Some Relief for Nats' Pitchers, Fans," *Washington Post*, April 17, 1966: C4.
13. Merrell Whittlesey, "Cox Convinces Three Doubters," *Washington Evening Star*, July 25, 1971: C-3.
14. *The Sporting News*, December 3, 1966: 59.
15. Ibid.
16. Merrell Whittlesey, "Cox' Temper a Big Problem in Latin League," *The Sporting News*, June 28, 1969: 16.
17. George Minot Jr., "Casey Cox, Nen Signed by Senators," *Washington Post*, January 26, 1967: F1.
18. *The Sporting News*, March 11, 1967: 19.
19. Merrell Whittlesey, "Short Wins Rousing A-OK in Capital Inaugural," *The Sporting News*, December 28, 1968: 27.
20. William Gildea, "This Year Cox Has Batters Buffaloed," *Washington Post*, July 9,1969: C3
21. George Minot Jr., "Long Relief Effort Gives Cox Victory," *Washington Post*, April 27, 1969: 41.
22. *The Sporting News*, June 21, 1969: 23.
23. Merrell Whittlesey, "Casey Cox Making Capital of Three C's," *The Sporting News*, June 28, 1969: 9.
24. Minot, *Washington Post*, July 18, 1969: D1.
25. Whittlesey, *The Sporting News*, March 14, 1970: 20.
26. Merrell Whittlesey, "Nat Rivals Hit Tune Sounds Like a Waltz to Casey," *The Sporting News*, May 2, 1970: 19.
27. *The Sporting News*, July 25, 1970: 30.
28. Merrell Whittlesey, "Cox Perfects His Curve in Winter Ball," *The Sporting News*, January 9, 1971: 51.
29. Randy Galloway, "'Old Man' Cox Leads Ranger Early Birds," *Dallas Morning News*, February 18, 1972: B1.
30. Merrell Whittlesey, "Nats' Cox Relief Whiz, And He Likes the Job," *The Sporting News*, August 14, 1971: 15.
31. Merrell Whittlesey, "Cox Adjusts Well to Relief Job," *The Sporting News*, August 14, 1971: 20.

JIMMY DRISCOLL

BY CHARLIE GRASSL

James Bernard Driscoll was born in the midst of World War II on May 14, 1944, in the town of Medford, Massachusetts, about three miles northwest of downtown Boston. He was the second-born of Joseph and Kathleen (O'Keefe) Driscoll, longtime residents of the Boston area. Joseph and Kathleen would ultimately produce a family of nine children – six boys and three girls. Joe Sr. was a railroad man for more than 30 years, working as a conductor on New York Central Railroad trains out of Boston. His mother, Kathleen, became a registered nurse and worked for the physician who pioneered hip-replacement surgery, Dr. Otto Aufranc of New England Baptist Hospital in Boston.

Jimmy grew up deeply immersed in the world of Boston sports. His father supplemented his income while satisfying his love of baseball as an usher at Fenway Park. His longtime access to Fenway Park enabled Jimmy to experience major-league sports and its players close-up. Joseph once asked Ted Williams to pose with Joe Jr. and Jimmy for a photo prior to a Red Sox game in 1948. The boys, 5 and 4 years old at the time, were posed on either side of the majestically tall man who had hit .406 in 1941. Jimmy retained many such rich memories of his dad and Fenway Park. He often told of how his father, when the Fenway Park gates opened before a game, Joe Sr. would stand by the Red Sox dugout and cry out to the other ushers, "They're open!" Tom Grieve, a teammate of Jimmy's on the 1972 Rangers, remembered fondly how delighted his teammates were when Jimmy would emulate his father by crying out, during batting practice, "They're open!" as the fans began to enter the ballpark.[1]

Joe Sr. often used his friendship with ushers at other venues, particularly Boston Garden, to get his family (and sometimes their friends) into events without tickets. He would have them gather an inconspicuous distance from a gate while he engaged in conversation with the gate usher. Upon "getting the high sign" from his father, the youngsters were to enter through the gate and "not look back." This procedure served the Driscoll family well over the years, exposing them to many baseball, hockey, basketball, and football games. As the boys grew older, it would be their turn to be the attraction at local venues.

Jimmy's older brother, Joe Jr., was the first to draw attention to the Driscoll family. In the spring of 1961, he broke a 68-68 tie with time expiring in the state high-school championship basketball game by sinking the game-winning basket from beyond the half-court line. The game was played before a packed house of 13,909 in the Boston Garden. In the fall of that year, Jimmy quarterbacked his Arlington High School football team to the state championship. In the spring of 1962, Jimmy's senior year, he tied baseball's Tony Conigliaro for the state high-school leadership in home runs. Other brothers, in the years to follow, would quarterback their team in a Sun Bowl football game; play in the College World Series; and umpire, calling balls and strikes, in the College World Series championship game that Roger Clemens pitched for the winning University of Texas Longhorns.

Jimmy performed well at football and basketball, but baseball was to be what shaped his future. An infielder, he was followed, starting in his sophomore year, by an ever-growing number of major-league scouts attending his high-school games. This attention culminated on graduation night in early June of 1962. His graduation ceremony began at 7:00 P.M. and by 10:30 he had signed his first professional baseball contract. (This was prior to today's amateur draft so teams had to compete for prospective talent by offering bonus money with the contract.) His father had the scouts line up outside his home, giving each of them 20 minutes to present their offer. Jeff Jones of the Milwaukee Braves made the winning presentation and obtained young Driscoll's signature on a minor-league contract in exchange for a $10,000 bonus.[2]

In high school, Driscoll played the infield, primarily shortstop. The left-handed hitter, at 18 years old, slightly built at 5-feet-11 and 175 pounds, physically resembled the Brooklyn Dodgers' Pee Wee Reese. As a result, he was often called "Pee Wee" by his teammates.

The Braves assigned Driscoll to Dublin, Georgia, of the Class-D Georgia-Florida League, managed by the snarky, seasoned Bill Steinecke, who managed in the lower minors for the Braves organization from 1937 through 1964. A player-turned-author named Pat Jordan, in his book A False Spring, described Steinecke as profane and crude in language and behavior but effective as a baseball manager.[3]

The 18-year-old Driscoll felt he was in another world as he set about to play organized ball in this small, rural Georgia town amid the civil rights strife of the early 1960s. He recalled the strangeness and puzzlement of seeing "White Only" signs, and blacks having to sit in a segregated section in right field. Adding to the strangeness of his new surroundings was a peculiar and puzzling encounter with Steinecke, awaiting Jimmy after a 10:00 A.M. workout at the Dublin ballpark.

In the lower minors, morning workouts were common to instruct the young players about the subtleties of play such as footwork around second base during a double play or infielder-outfielder communication for popups. Driscoll, having arrived in Dublin after the third inning of the team's game, did not suit up with the team, so the next morning's workout was his first uniformed activity with his new club. After the workout, the players headed to the showers. Jimmy described an event that he believed to be either an initiation or an act of unprecedented insensitivity. At the time of a 2016 interview[4], he still hadn't decided which. As he described it:

The showers next to the locker room was a small area with only five shower heads. In their haste to dress and leave for lunch at least 10 players, maybe more, gathered under those five shower heads, myself included. This scrum of naked men, elbowing and shoving each other, while vying for the most effective position under the directed water flow, got even more congested when the manager, Bill Steineke, joined his wet and soap-covered team in the disorderly fray beneath each of the limited number of shower heads. You must understand that Steineke was a consummate tobacco chewer. Not attracted by the neatly packaged and processed name brands like Red Man or Beech-Nut, he preferred chewing portions of cigars. Inserting a cigar in his mouth, he would bite off a significant portion, beginning to chew as portions of tobacco leaf fell from his lower lip because his mouth could simply not contain all the tobacco he had ungracefully shoved into the ever-growing bulge in his right cheek. Such was the condition of Steiny's mouth as he stood within a foot of my presence. Water, flowing over his face, slightly discolored the tobacco juice dripping onto the floor of the shower and upon his hairy chest. Stepping away from the direct flow of the shower head, he turned his face to mine and began to speak. Simultaneously, with the words leaving his mouth, was the fine spray of tobacco particles and juice which settled upon my face. At the same time, I became conscious of a continuous stream of warm water falling, thigh high, upon my left leg. The stream of water was hitting my leg at an angle which made me think it was not from the shower head. Turning my head downward to avoid the tobacco spray, I heard the words, 'Welcome to pro ball kid! You're going to love it here!" While appreciating the welcome message, I was disheartened to see he was urinating upon my leg. Welcome indeed!

Despite the disturbing nature of his first day in pro ball and the other cultural adjustments required of the schoolboy from Boston, he adapted to baseball among the cotton fields and played in 48 games while hitting a respectable .275. However, this was to be his only year as property of the Milwaukee Braves; in November he was selected by the Kansas City Athletics in the first-year player draft.

The first-year player draft was instituted by the major-league clubs at the 1958 winter meetings as a way to save themselves from the price war for young baseball talent that was developing after World War II.[5] Bonuses were becoming exorbitant and were even exceeding the salaries of some major-league players. At the 1964 winter meetings the rule was abandoned in favor of the amateur draft. In 1962 Driscoll was one of the 45 players drafted.

Driscoll labored long in the Kansas City/Oakland A's minor-league system, spending two years at Class A, two years at Double A, and four years at Triple A. It was a long journey but after eight years, at age 26 he got the call. It came on the night of June 16, 1970. Playing for the Triple-A Iowa Oaks (Des Moines), Driscoll doubled off the right-field wall to drive in the game-winning run. This was a special occasion for him because four of his brothers were there to see him play. They had traveled to Omaha, Nebraska, to see their brother Mark play in the College World Series for the University of Arizona. After Arizona was eliminated from the tourney, they traveled to Des Moines to see Jimmy play. After the game they bunked in Jimmy's apartment. Around 7:30 in the morning, Jimmy got a call from Charlie Finley, owner of the Oakland A's, who asked, "How would you like to be wearing a pair of white shoes in Detroit tonight?"[6] The brothers flew to Detroit and took a cab to Tiger Stadium. Arriving about 5 P.M., Jimmy found a locker with a uniform bearing the number 21 with DRISCOLL on the back of the jersey, as well as a pair of white shoes as Charlie Finley had promised. Less than 24 hours from his walk-off double, Driscoll was in uniform for the Athletics game in Tiger Stadium before a crowd of 12,541 that included his five brothers. He would never forget the night of June 17, 1970.

The 1970 Oakland A's were building the foundations of the team that would gain a playoff spot in 1971, then win the next three World Series (1972-74). Driscoll had been called up from Iowa after hitting a solid .303 in 76 games. This performance came on the heels of a .286 season in 1969.

From the bench, Driscoll watched his team take a 1-0 lead off Tigers lefty Les Cain in the top of the first. Catfish Hunter, however, could not hold the lead, failing to get anyone out in the bottom of the second. The Tigers scored five runs in the inning off Hunter and reliever Diego Segui. The A's regained the lead in the fourth only to see the Tigers retake the lead in the fifth. With the Tigers leading 8-7 in the top of the seventh inning, the A's manager, John McNamara, sent Driscoll up to pinch-hit for second baseman Tony La Russa.[7] Driscoll waited in the on-deck circle while Rick Monday batted. Monday singled to right field. As Driscoll strode to the plate, Bill Freehan, the Tigers catcher, gave him a puzzled glance, then trotted to the mound followed soon by the Tigers pitching coach. Driscoll thought they were probably discussing how to pitch to this nameless guy no one knew. After the umpire broke up the meeting at the mound, Driscoll positioned himself in the batter's box. Before seeing a pitch, he watched as Tom Timmermann, the Detroit pitcher, threw wildly to first base and Monday went to second base, in scoring position as the tying run. Nervous but focused, Driscoll dug in at the plate and awaited the first pitch. It was an inside fastball that he turned on quickly, hitting it solidly. Its path was a long, high arc down the right-field line toward the covered bleachers of Tiger Stadium, but drifted foul.

Returning to the batter's box, Driscoll thought to himself, "It might not be official but I know I hit the first pitch I saw in the major leagues for a home run!" In a few moments the inning ended with Driscoll lifting a fly ball to Mickey Stanley in center field for the third out.

He played in another 20 games for the A's that year, mostly in pinch-hitting roles, but the season was to include even more special moments and highlights for Driscoll to remember. On Sunday, July 19, the A's were in Boston to start a two-game series with the Red Sox. There was some local media notice of Jimmy Driscoll, a local boy, coming into town with the A's. He had permission from manager McNamara to stay with his folks rather than with the team at the hotel. Driscoll said he had 91 tickets held at the Fenway Park box office for family and friends. (Each player is granted 10 tickets to pass out for any game. Driscoll "borrowed" tickets from teammates to accumulate 91.

While Driscoll visited with his family, his father asked if he was starting the first game. Jimmy said he wouldn't know until right before game time. Upon arrival at Fenway Park on Sunday morning, he learned that McNamara had put him in the starting lineup at second base. With his very proud mom and dad sitting in front-row box seats by the A's on-deck circle, he went 2-for-4 against Ray Culp in a losing effort in the first game of the series and 0-for-3 in a 3-2 win for the A's in the second game. Driscoll recalled that he made a great play in the bottom of the first inning of the second game, going hard to his left between first and second base to rob Carl Yastrzemski of a hit. Yastrzemski, with a batting average of .3286 (rounded off to .329) lost the batting title to Alex Johnson of the California Angels (.3289, also rounded off to .329). Had Driscoll not made that play, Yastrzemski would have won the batting title.

At the end of that 1970 season, Driscoll experienced another special moment. In the last three games of the season, he got a taste of being a regular in the big leagues. Closing out the year against the Milwaukee Brewers, he started all three games at shortstop, replacing an injured Bert Campaneris.

In the first game of that series, on September 29, Driscoll, batting eighth in the A's lineup, went 1-for-3 with a walk. His hit was a solo home run off the Brewers' Al Downing, who four years later would be famous for his association with Hank Aaron's 715th home run,[8] to lead off the bottom of the fourth inning and put the A's ahead, 3-2. The A's, with Catfish Hunter pitching a complete game, won 4-3. Driscoll laughingly claimed, "Hank Aaron has nothing on me. Downing is on my list too!" This was his only major-league home run.

Whether it was the change in management (Dick Williams replacing McNamara as manager) or other reasons, such as too many left-handed batters, the exact reason will never be known, but the net of it all was Driscoll being returned to the Iowa Oaks for the 1971 season. Then, on June 15, 1971, the Washington Senators purchased his contract from the A's and assigned him to another American Association club, the Denver Bears. He remained in the American Association for the rest of that year, batting a combined .262 with 15 home runs.

The 1971 season was a highlight in Driscoll's minor-league career. He was named to the American Association All-Star team, and the Bears won the American Association championship, and played the Rochester Red Wings (champions of the International League) in what was then called the Junior World Series. Driscoll recalled the experience in an article in 1974 in the *Denver Post*: "We had to play all seven games in Rochester because of construction in Bears Stadium, Driscoll said. We came close to winning. We were down 3-1 and came back before Rochester won in the seventh game. We had some rain postponements, and it seemed as if we were there forever."[9]

Driscoll batted .423 with one home run, four doubles, and five RBIs in the Junior World Series.[10] That success earned him a trip to the 1972 spring-training camp of the Texas Rangers, the former Washington Senators.

Irv Moss described Driscoll's first meeting with his new manager: "On his first day with the Rangers,

Driscoll showed Ted Williams a picture taken at Fenway Park of the former Boston Red Sox slugger and a 4-year old boy. It was Driscoll some 24 years before the reunion."[11] Driscoll said that Williams was pleased he had shown him the photograph. Ted then autographed the photo with these words, "To Jim: The effort paid off. My regards, Ted Williams."

Hitless in 20 plate appearances for the Rangers, Driscoll was sent down to Denver in late May, never again to see action in the majors.

He played in his last major-league game on May 26, 1972. Third baseman Dave Nelson was hit by a Bert Blyleven pitch and had to leave in the third inning of the game. Driscoll entered the game as his replacement. Blyleven, on his way to a complete-game five-hit shutout, retired Driscoll in each of his three plate appearances that day, a strikeout in the fourth, a fly ball to right in the seventh, and a popup to shortstop in the ninth. On his last plate appearance in the major leagues, Driscoll made the 27th out to seal a 7-0 home victory over the Rangers by the Minnesota Twins before 7,383 witnesses. In his brief stay with the Rangers, Driscoll played in 15 games and reached base just twice, both on walks, never scored, and finished 0-for-18 at the plate.

In December 1972 Driscoll and catcher Hal King were traded by the Rangers to the Cincinnati Reds for pitcher Jimmy Merritt. Invited to 1973 spring training, though under a minor-league contract, Driscoll got a lot of playing time at second base in most of the Reds' exhibition games. Hitting over .400 with a couple of home runs, he was beginning to feel good about his prospects of sticking with the Reds, who were just then forming the core of Sparky Anderson's "Big Red Machine" that dominated the mid- to late '70s. But it was in a game near the end of spring training that Driscoll began to see the direction of his major-league career:

"I don't remember who hit it but a towering fly ball between first and second was coming down in short right field. A 23-year-old rookie named Ken Griffey (Sr.) was playing in right field. I was going out and Griffey was coming in. Not hearing him say anything and my eyes focused upon the descending ball, just as the ball hit my glove, Griffey hit me. Falling to the ground, feeling conscious but breathless, I held the ball for the third out. As we both lay sprawled upon the ground, I could see a concerned Sparky Anderson, Alex Grammas, and the trainer racing from the dugout toward us. Without so much as a glance or word for me, they all hurdled over my prone body to get to Griffey, also laying on his back. I struggled, unnoticed by all, to get up and walk back to the dugout unassisted. It was obvious to me where I fit into this organization. True to my feelings, the next day I got notified that Sparky Anderson wanted to see me. He told me I had played well enough to make the club but he had too many left-handed batters on the club. I was being sent down to Indianapolis."

After two disappointing seasons with Triple-A Indianapolis, (.226 and .206), Driscoll caught on with the Houston Astros' Triple-A team for the 1975 season. Ironically, he found himself in Des Moines playing for the Iowa Oaks. Hitting .205 for the year, he retired from professional baseball after the 1975 season. He was 31 years old.

After baseball Driscoll found success as an area scout for the Baltimore Orioles, while living in the Phoenix area for over 30 years. At his first game as a scout, another scout who was sitting next to him introduced himself, "Hi! I'm Joe Maddon. I'm a scout with the California Angels." They became good friends, with Jimmy being asked by Joe to be the best man at his wedding.

Upon retirement from scouting, Driscoll returned to New England in 2010, and currently lives in New Hampshire with his wife, Caroline. They have one daughter, Heather, who teaches botany at the University of New Hampshire. Driscoll is active in his church and enjoys fishing and golf.

Sources

In addition to the sources cited in the Notes, the author relied on Baseball-Reference.com.

Notes

1. Author interview with Tom Grieve, November 12, 2015.
2. Irv Moss, "'71 Season Memorable for Jimmy Driscoll," *Denver Post*, May 1, 2014.
3. Pat Jordan, *A False Spring* (New York: Dodd, Mead & Company, 1975), 114-117.
4. Unless otherwise noted, all direct quotations are from an author interview with Jim Driscoll on April 24, 2016.
5. Cliff Blau, "The Real First Year Draft," *Baseball Research Journal* 39, No. 1 (2010).
6. Oakland in 1970 was experimenting with unconventional, colorful uniforms that included white shoes in place of the more conventional black shoes.
7. Hall of Famer Tony La Russa, whose playing career in the majors and minors spanned 16 years (1962-1977), was a weak-hitting infielder whose career major-league batting average was .199 in 203 plate appearances in 132 games. After being released by the St. Louis Cardinals in 1977, he took the job of field manager for the Chicago White Sox at the end of the 1979 season. This began one of the most successful managerial careers in major-league history, spanning 33 years, over 5,000 games, six pennants and three World Series championships with three different teams (White Sox, A's, Cardinals). La Russa was inducted into the Hall of Fame in Cooperstown in 2014.
8. Al Downing, on April 8, 1974, while pitching for the Los Angeles Dodgers in a game against the Atlanta Braves, in the fourth inning of that game gave up the 715th home run of Hank Aaron's career. This broke Babe Ruth's long-standing record for career home runs.
9. Moss.
10. Ibid.
11. Ibid.

JAN DUKES

BY CLAYTON TRUTOR

Jan Dukes was a left-handed pitcher who pitched in 16 games for the Washington Senators (1969-70) and the Rangers (1972) between 1969 and 1972. Exclusively a reliever in the major leaguers, Dukes had been a highly touted pitcher at Santa Clara College, where he remains a fixture in the schools' baseball record book. The Washington Senators thought enough of his professional prospects to draft him in the first round of the January 1967 supplementary draft. Arm trouble dating back to Dukes' college days severely shortened his professional career.

Noble Jan Dukes was born on August 16, 1945, in Cheyenne, Wyoming. During his childhood his family relocated to Millbrae, California, just south of San Francisco. Dukes attended Mills High School in Millbrae, where he became one of Northern California's most highly regarded prep baseball stars of the 1960s. The slightly built 5-foot-11 lefty relied on exquisite control and excellent offspeed and breaking pitches to baffle hitters. Longtime observers of Bay Area high school baseball consider the 1963 battle between Dukes and future Baltimore Orioles and Kansas City Royals pitcher Wally Bunker to be one of the greatest pitching matchups in the state's scholastic baseball history. Mills High School defeated Bunker's Capuchino High School 1-0 in 15 innings. Bunker, the game's incredibly hard-luck loser, struck out 23 batters in 15 innings. Dukes struck out 19 in 12 innings.[1]

Dukes accepted a scholarship to play baseball at nearby Santa Clara College. The Broncos had emerged in the early 1960s as a major college-baseball program. In 1962 they advanced to the championship game of the College World Series, losing to Michigan 5-4 in 15 innings. Dukes, one of 48 Santa Clara baseball players to reach the major leagues as of 2016, played for coach Sal Taormina, who transformed Santa Clara over 15 years (1965-1979) from an upstart college baseball program at a small Catholic college into a national power that made regular appearances in the NCAA baseball tournament. During Dukes' three years at Santa Clara (1965-1967), the Broncos posted strong records (29-11 in 1965, 27-17 in 1966, and 24-14 in 1967), but were never able to win the Western Collegiate Athletic Conference title or earn an at-large bid to the NCAA tournament. Despite chronic arm injuries, Dukes put together one of the finest pitching careers in Santa Clara history. Dukes' career 2.14 ERA is the Broncos third best as of 2016. In May 1967 Dukes threw a no-hitter against UC-Santa Barbara in his final collegiate game.[2]

In June 1966 the Baltimore Orioles selected Dukes in the fifth round of the amateur draft, but the southpaw chose to return for his senior year at Santa Clara. That summer, Dukes played for the semipro Boulder Collegians, a team made up of college stars, including future major leaguer Pat Jacquez, Dukes' Santa Clara teammate who pitched for the Chicago White Sox in 1971, and future San Diego Padres manager

Greg Riddoch. In Dukes' season with the Collegians, they won the amateur National Baseball Congress championship.[3]

In January 1967 the Washington Senators selected Dukes eighth overall in the first round of the supplemental draft. He signed with the Senators in May after completing his college career.[4] Dukes advanced quickly through the Senators' farm system in 1967. He pitched primarily for the York White Roses of the Double-A Eastern League but also made two appearances for the Hawaii Islanders of the Triple-A Pacific Coast League. Dukes compiled a 5-8 record with a 1.81 ERA in 17 appearances, all starts. After the season, newly appointed Senators manager Jim Lemon observed that Dukes "doesn't seem to have too much but he gets 'em out. And that's the important thing. He has great control and phenomenal poise."[5]

In 1968 Dukes impressed Lemon enough during spring training to remain with the major-league club late into March. He was in the mix for a spot in the bullpen but the 22-year-old instead spent the season with the Buffalo Bisons of the Triple-A International League.[6] He struggled to an 11-13 record as a starter with a 4.75 ERA against the stronger competition. The following season Dukes improved considerably, going 11-10 for Buffalo with a 3.32 ERA. The 24-year-old Dukes' success in Buffalo in 1969 earned him a September call-up with the Senators, managed by Ted Williams.

Dukes made his major-league debut on September 6, 1969, against the Boston Red Sox. He allowed one earned run in three innings of relief in a 9-5 loss at Fenway Park. Dukes admitted feeling "a little shaky at first," telling the *Washington Post* that "I couldn't believe it in the bullpen that they were calling me." He ended up turning in a sufficiently solid performance to earn muted praise from his slow-to-offer-compliments manager, Ted Williams. "I think he was pretty good," Williams said of Dukes' three innings of work.[7] In eight appearances for the 1969 Senators, Dukes finished with a 0-2 record with a 2.45 ERA in 11 innings pitched in relief. In both of his losses he put the winning run on base, but the winning hits were off other pitchers.

Dukes made the Senators' Opening Day 1970 roster as a relief pitcher. He appeared in the 1970 home opener, on April 6, pitching two innings of relief in a 5-0 loss to the Detroit Tigers. Dukes surrendered two runs, threw a wild pitch, and plunked the Tigers' power-hitting shortstop Dick McAuliffe.[8] Dukes spent most of April with the Senators with no wins or losses in five appearances before being optioned to Triple-A Denver (American Association) on April 22.[9] He did not return to the major leagues that season. Hampered by the arm troubles that would cut his career short, Dukes struggled with Denver, going 5-7 with a 4.10 ERA in 28 appearances, 14 of which were starts.

Dukes toiled away in Denver in 1971 and 1972, working almost exclusively as a reliever. In 1971 he appeared in 50 games with an ERA of 3.98. In 1972, his ERA ballooned to 5.19 in 34 appearances. Dukes made a one-week return to the major leagues, from July 15 through July 22, 1972, for the first-year Texas Rangers. During his final stint in the major leagues, Dukes wore number 37 for the Rangers, a change from his old number 22 with the Senators. He pitched in three games (2⅓ innings) and did not figure in any decisions.

Dukes made his final major-league appearance on July 22, 1972, against the Tigers, pitching a scoreless ninth inning in a 6-2 defeat. After the season, the Rangers released the 27-year-old Dukes. In 1973 he pitched in 12 games for the Peninsula Whips (Hampton, Virginia), the Montreal Expos' farm team in the International League, then had brief stints with the Saltillo Saraperos and Veracruz Aguila of the Mexican League, after which he retired at the age of 28.

Dukes appeared on one widely released baseball card during his brief major-league career. Topps placed Dukes alongside fellow Senators pitcher Jim Miles on a "Rookie Stars: Senators" card numbered 154 in their 1970 set.[10]

After leaving baseball, Dukes returned to the Bay Area and had a successful career as a businessman. He settled in Sunnyvale in Santa Clara County with his wife, Arlene, and his two sons. One of his sons, Kyle, was a standout pitcher in the mid-2000s for

Homestead High School in Cupertino, California.[11] In 2005 the *San Mateo County Times* inducted Dukes into its San Mateo County Sports Hall of Fame.[12]

Sources

In addition to the sources cited in the Notes, the author also consulted baseballalmanac.com, baseball-reference.com, SantaClaraBroncos.com, and various newspapers.

Notes

1. John Murphy, "Bunker-Dukes Classic was 50 Years Ago," *PrepCat*, April 12, 2013. Accessed on November 10, 2015: prep2prep.com/prepcat/?tag=jan-dukes.
2. "Santa Clara Broncos: Baseball Record Book," *Santa Clara Broncos Baseball*, 2015. Accessed on November 10, 2015: santaclarabroncos.com/sports/m-basebl/record_book.
3. Rory Costello, "Pat Jacquez," *SABR Baseball Biography Project*, 2011. Accessed on November 10, 2015; Zak Brown, "Collegians Provided Boulder With Plenty of Series Connections," Boulder Daily Camera, October 24, 2007. Accessed on November 10, 2015: dailycamera.com/ci_13090329.
4. "Pitcher Signs," *Spokane Daily Chronicle*, May 23, 1967: 43.
5. Bob Addie, "Lemon's Hopes High," *Washington Post*, November 4, 1967: D1.
6. George Minot Jr., "Cutting Winner Tough for Lemon," *Washington Post*, March 31, 1968: C4; Edward Prell, "Senators Skipper Has Visions of First Division," *Chicago Tribune*, February 20, 1968: C2.
7. "McMullen Continues His 'Swinging Right,'" *Washington Post*, September 7, 1969: 44.
8. "Nixon Sees Senators Drop Opener, 5-0," *New York Times*, April 7, 1970, 74; George Minot Jr., "Senators Tar Ball But Lack Pitch," *Washington Post*, April 5, 1970: 5.
9. "Ramos Cut, Hannan In, Dukes Out," *Washington Post*, April 28, 1970: D1.
10. "1970 Topps Senator Rookie Stars: Jim Miles, Jan Dukes," *Rating the Rookies*, June 17, 2015. Accessed on November 10, 2015: ratingtherookies.blogspot.com/2015/07/1970-topps-senators-rookie-stars-jim.html.
11. Rick Chandler, "Jan Dukes Is a Legend in County Baseball Lore," *Oakland Tribune*, May 31, 2005. Accessed on November 10, 2015: B14.
12. John Horgan, "Ten Sports Figures to Be Honored for Their Feats," *San Mateo County Times*, June 22, 2005. Accessed on November 10, 2015: insidebayarea.com/sanmateocountytimes/localnews/ci_2816747.

BILL FAHEY

BY KRIS RUTHERFORD

When the Washington Senators arrived in Pompano Beach, Florida, for spring training in 1971, manager Ted Williams couldn't help but gush over his first overall pick in the January draft a year earlier. "That kid has major leaguer written all over him," the Hall of Famer said of 20-year-old Detroit native William Roger "Bill" Fahey. "He can catch in the big leagues right now. But he'll need more hitting experience in the minors." Then Williams doubled down on his prediction for the future of the Senators catcher. "He'll be the American League All-Star catcher in 1975."[1]

Bill Fahey was born on June 14, 1950, and grew up a fan of his hometown Detroit Tigers, idolizing the likes of Al Kaline and Bill Freehan.[2] Like most kids in the '50s, Fahey played Little League baseball before moving through the ranks to the Connie Mack level, for players of high-school age, the highest youth baseball classification in Michigan. Playing Connie Mack ball, Fahey showed the flashes of talent that led to his status as a five-sport high-school athlete at Union High in Redford, Michigan, a few miles northwest of downtown Detroit. At Union High, Fahey played both offense and defense in football (quarterback and linebacker), was co-captain of the basketball team, wrestled in the heavyweight division, was a member of the golf team, and played baseball.[3] Regardless of the sport, Fahey's 6-foot, 200-pound frame was an imposing sight, and when opponents realized he had speed other kids his size lacked, he became the type of player game plans are built to avoid.

While Fahey was successful at all sports, he concentrated on baseball, playing at the All-American Amateur Association level after the Connie Mack league and very nearly leading his team to a regional championship in 1969.[4] By that point, Fahey was already a hot commodity in professional scouting circles, catching batting practice for Detroit and having been Baltimore's 13th-round selection in the 1968 amateur draft.

"I might catch one ball during batting practice because they hit everything (in batting practice)," Fahey later said of his time behind the plate at Tiger Stadium. "The coach is just throwing it in there. But, heck, I was just a kid. My heart was pumping out of my chest."[5]

Like many players drafted in the lower rounds straight out of high school, Fahey rolled the dice, passed on the Orioles' offer, and enrolled in the University of Detroit, where he played the 1969 collegiate season. In the fall of 1969, he transferred to St. Clair Junior College.[6] St. Clair, unlike the University of Detroit, was a two-year institution, and under the rules of the baseball draft, the transfer made Fahey eligible for the secondary draft in January 1970.[7] The Washington Senators chose him with the first overall selection in the draft. After eight dreadful seasons in the nation's capital, Ted Williams's Senators were coming off their first winning season but felt slowed by the catching staff of Paul Casanova and Jim French. Fahey's signing bonus has been reported in different publications over the years as ranging from "an undisclosed substantial bonus"[8] to $40,000.[9] Based on Williams's rave reviews several weeks later, Fahey looked to be on the fast track to the big leagues.

The Sporting News commented on Fahey's selection: "Senators farm department feels they plucked a plum in the special phase of the free agent draft in the selection of Bill Fahey, 19-year-old catcher from suburban Detroit." The publication said Fahey would have been the top pick of any number of teams in the draft and opined that the Senators "apparently drafted a phenom."[10] In spite of the rave reviews of the media and Ted Williams, Fahey and most of the Senators' other "can't miss" rookies were assigned to Class-A ball. Fahey spent 1970 with the Burlington (North Carolina) Senators of the Carolina League.

While Fahey didn't tear up the Carolina League in his first professional season, he did catch 118 games for the third-place Senators, batting .244 with 3 home runs and 36 RBIs. But as Ted Williams's comments the following February indicated, Fahey wasn't drafted for his bat but for his defense. He posted a .988 fielding percentage, placing him second among everyday catchers in the eight-team circuit, and he led the league in putouts and chances accepted.[11] With one professional season under his belt, the prognosticators began to weigh in on Fahey's future, with one writer offering the comments, "…as much raw talent as any catcher in Senators' system,"[12] "…best of the crop,"[13] and "…likely to be Senators' everyday catcher in a couple of years."[14]

Fahey made the jump to the Double-A Eastern League in 1971, catching 99 games for the Pittsfield (Massachusetts) Senators and posting a .990 fielding percentage. His offensive output increased dramatically: His batting average improved to .286, and he showed flashes of the speed that had made him such a high-school standout, stealing 13 bases without being thrown out. No other Eastern League catcher even attempted to steal more than seven bases.

After being named to the Eastern League All-Star team[15] late in the season, Fahey was briefly promoted to Triple-A Denver, where he got four hits in four games and fielded to perfection. Before the season ended, Ted Williams called his catcher of the future to Washington for his first major-league appearance. His two appearances, against the Red Sox and Yankees in late September, yielded no hits in eight plate appearances and even a rare error in the field. That short would be his only one in a Senators uniform. During the offseason the franchise relocated to Arlington, Texas, and prepared to begin play in 1972 as the Texas Rangers.

Team owner Bob Short, notorious in Washington for promoting young players to draw fan interest,[16] continued the pattern in Texas, often rushing players to the majors before they were ready. Fahey was among the rush jobs in 1972.[17] He spent the first half of the season with Denver, continuing his stellar defensive play. The Rangers called Fahey up in late July, and he stayed with them the remainder of the season,[18] playing in 39 games. Fahey's defensive prowess shined brightly with a fielding percentage of .992, and he threw out 44 percent of would-be basestealers, five points above the league average. Offensively, Fahey was dreadful, batting just .168 with three extra-base hits and 10 RBIs in 119 at-bats. His first major-league hit and RBI came off California Angels pitcher Clyde Wright as a pinch-hitter in the eighth inning of a 3-2 Texas loss on July 28. On September 4, Fahey slammed his first home run, a two-run shot off Kansas City's Ted Abernathy in front of 3,710 fans at Arlington Stadium. Despite Fahey's lack of offensive punch, statistically he outplayed Hal King and Ken Suarez, who also auditioned for the new label "Texas's catcher of the future."

In 1973 new Rangers manager Whitey Herzog elected to go with experience at catcher, keeping Dick Billings and Suarez on the roster. Fahey was assigned to Spokane of the Pacific Coast League and remained in Triple A all season. He was the starting catcher for the PCL West All-Star team, and had two RBIs in his squad's 9-6 win. Fahey lived up to Herzog's praise for his ability to block the plate, a skill he'd shown off at Pittsfield in 1971 when the burly catcher held onto the ball in a violent home-plate collision.[19] On August 9, 1973, Fahey again blocked the plate, only this time the result became a turning point in his career.

With the Hawaii Islanders visiting Spokane, Hawaii outfielder Chris Coletta sped toward home on a single to the outfield. As Fahey reached for the approaching throw, Coletta's knee struck him in the side of his torso. This time Fahey didn't hold onto the ball for the out, and he didn't stand up. Instead, he was carried from the field to the hospital, where he remained for 10 days. With five broken ribs and a punctured lung, the collision led to a string of injuries that plagued Fahey for three seasons. Just two weeks later, after Spokane swept Tucson for the PCL championship, Indians fans named the injured Fahey the team's most valuable player.[20]

Despite the Rangers trainers and team doctors questioning whether Fahey would be ready for spring training, in early January the team declared him fully healed. No doubt Fahey was eager to get back on the field. Whitey Herzog hadn't lasted the season as the Texas manager before being replaced by Billy Martin. With a new skipper, Fahey expected a better shot at making the Rangers roster. He headed for camp as one of seven catchers, a group that included Jim Sundberg, a second-year professional who had burst onto the scene with an outstanding 1973 season at Double-A Pittsfield. It didn't take long for Fahey to lose traction in his bid for a roster spot. On the first day of spring training, a thrown ball hit him directly in the face, breaking his nose, and because of complications, landing him in the hospital for another extended stay.[21] While the remaining six catchers auditioned for Billy Martin, Fahey lost valuable playing time, and no doubt Martin began to wonder if the player previously called the catcher of the future wasn't injury-prone. When Sundberg grabbed the starting catcher's slot and Duke Sims beat out the contenders for the backup position, once again Fahey opened the season in Spokane. He remained with the Indians for all but six games.

Fahey had another excellent season at the Triple-A level, but talk of him as the future catcher of the Texas Rangers faded. Jim Sundberg developed more quickly than Fahey, matched his ability defensively, and added more to the lineup as a hitter. In November 1974, The Sporting News noted that Fahey, "once rated as the Rangers' future catcher, must be considered in trade talks."[22] Two weeks later, TSN called him "expendable" due to Sundberg's development, although it said he might hang on as the Rangers' backup catcher.[23] That is exactly what Bill Fahey did.

With most teams, Fahey's status as backup catcher would have earned him a decent amount of playing time. Unfortunately for him, the 1975 Rangers had a catching machine in Sundberg. The budding star started 148 games, with the remainder split between Fahey and Ron Pruitt. Fahey played in 21 games with only 39 plate appearances, although he did bat .297, the best batting average of his professional career. He might have gained more playing time if not for another injury, a broken hand suffered from a foul tip that landed him on the 21-day disabled list.[24] For the third time in three seasons, Fahey lost significant playing time because of an injury. He also endured another managerial change as Robert Short fired Billy Martin midway through the season in spite of the Rangers' finishing just five games behind Oakland in the American League West and drawing over a million fans in 1974.

In 1976, Billy Martin's replacement, Frank Lucchesi, chose Fahey as the Rangers' regular backup catcher. He played in 38 games, his most in a major-league season to date, and batted .250 in 94 plate appearances. Again, he was stellar in the field with a .993 fielding percentage while throwing out a respectable 32 percent of runners attempting to steal a base. Fahey maintained his position and posted similar numbers in 1977, but when 1978 arrived, he once again found himself playing Triple-A ball, this time with Tucson in the PCL. John Ellis, a former Yankee and a three-year starting catcher for the Cleveland Indians, beat Fahey out as Sundberg's backup. For Fahey, the writing was on the wall. In December 1978, he was traded along with Mike Hargrove and Kurt Bevacqua to San Diego in exchange for Oscar Gamble and

Dave Roberts. Many considered Fahey the player "thrown in" by the Rangers to make the trade for Gamble and Roberts equal.[25] At the time, an argument could definitely be made that Texas needed to rid itself of Fahey to clear the way to develop new catching prospects.

For San Diego, Gene Tenace held down the catcher's position, and veteran Fred Kendall, in his second stint with the team, was a serviceable backup. But when speaking of Fahey, San Diego manager Roger Craig commented, "I like his attitude. He has great desire. ... Maybe all he's needed was to be healthy and have a chance to play every day."[26] Of course, Craig also pointed out how much he liked the way his new catcher blocked the plate, a primary source of Fahey's injuries. When Gene Tenace moved to first base in August of 1979, Craig offered Fahey his first chance to be an everyday catcher. Fahey responded to the challenge, batting .287 in 73 games, with a career-high 3 home runs and 19 RBIs. He maintained a .994 fielding percentage and threw out 36 percent of would-be basestealers.

In 1980, although his batting average and fielding percentage fell, Fahey had finally become a somewhat regular player, appearing in 93 games for the Padres. Late in the season, teams like the Red Sox showed interest in obtaining Fahey for a pennant run, but it wasn't until March 1981 that the Padres turned their backup catcher loose. For Fahey, his dream came true with the change in scenery.[27]

In December 1980, San Diego sent Gene Tenace, Rollie Fingers, Bob Shirley, and a player to be named to St. Louis in return for seven players including backstops Terry Kennedy and veteran Steve Swisher. Two weeks before Opening Day, the Padres sold Fahey to Detroit for $90,000 cash. After a decade bouncing between the minors, Texas, and San Diego, Fahey headed home to where he'd caught batting practice his senior year in high school. Now he would be a backup to Lance Parrish, the Tigers' regular catcher.

From 1981 through most of 1983, Fahey played sparingly, as utilityman John Wockenfuss caught a good share of the games Parrish sat out. By 1982, Roger Craig had arrived in Detroit as the Tigers' pitching coach and began working with Fahey. On August 24, Craig and Fahey were involved in what may have been the most notorious moment of Fahey's career.

Craig called Fahey that morning and told him he'd be playing in Oakland in place of Parrish, who had flown home for the birth of his child. The Athletics, managed by Fahey's old Texas manager Billy Martin, were simply playing out the string in the midst of a horrible season. The A's Rickey Henderson was pursuing Lou Brock's single-season record of 118 stolen bases. Henderson entered the August 24 game needing just three to tie Brock's record, and after getting on base early and stealing second and third off Fahey's normally powerful arm, only one stolen base remained for the tie. Henderson had a chance to break the record in front of the home crowd.

Henderson was on deck for the bottom of the eighth inning, when Fred Stanley drew a walk. Stanley, who in 17 professional seasons stole only 48 bases and only 11 of those at the major-league level, was what baseball coaches often call a "base clogger." When Rickey Henderson hit what he called a "seed" to left field, Stanley hadn't touched second before the ball was back in the infield.[28] So, Henderson stood on first, blocked from even attempting to tie Lou Brock's record by one of the Tigers' slowest baserunners. When Stanley received the steal sign from third-base coach Clete Boyer, he knew his odds were slim. Indeed they were, as Stanley was caught in a rundown that Detroit third baseman Enos Cabell considered merely an attempt to open a base for Henderson and he didn't even run to tag Stanley out.

Fahey said Craig came to the mound and told pitcher Jerry Ujdur to toss over to first base three times, then throw Fahey a pitchout. All went as planned, and on the pitchout Henderson took off like lightning for second base. It took everything Fahey had in his arm to make it a close play even on a pitchout, but when Henderson arrived at second base in a head-first slide, umpire Durwood Merrill, a native of Hooks, Texas, emphatically called him out. Bedlam ensued. Before it was over, Billy Martin, Oakland coach Charlie Metro, third baseman Wayne Gross, and Dwayne Murphy were all tossed from the game. Henderson claimed Merrill told him that if he was to break Lou Brock's record, he'd have to earn it. Merrill denied making the comment. In any case, as C.W. Nevius wrote, "Henderson tied and broke the record in two games in Milwaukee, and hardly anyone remembers … the catcher. …"[29] There's no telling how many remember Bill Fahey's role in preventing Henderson from granting the home fans a little pleasure in an otherwise forgettable Oakland season.

Fahey began the 1983 season in Detroit, but with 1980 11th-round draft choice Dwight Lowry set for his major-league debut soon after the All-Star break, the Tigers released Fahey on August 5. After 11 major-league seasons and just 383 games played, the one-time catcher of the future for the Washington Senators and Texas Rangers retired as a player just a season before his hometown Tigers rolled through the American League on the way to a World Series title.

Fahey did not completely cut ties with Detroit. In 1984 he managed the Tigers' Lakeland team in the Class-A Florida State League. Lakeland's .319 winning percentage fell quite a bit short of the parent club's success. It was the last team Fahey managed.

In 1985, Fahey remained with the Detroit organization, serving as an aide to pitching coach Roger Craig. A year later, when Craig was named manager of the San Francisco Giants, he took Fahey along, eventually making him third-base coach. The move bred success for everyone involved, and in 1989, after nearly 20 years in baseball, Fahey got his first taste of the postseason and the World Series when San Francisco faced off against Oakland in what has become known as the Loma Prieta Earthquake Series. Oakland swept the Giants in a four-game Series that took 14 days to complete.

In 1991, while still coaching with Roger Craig, Fahey decided it was time he returned to the Dallas-Fort Worth area, where he and his wife, the former Carla Matthews, raised their sons, Scott and Brandon. Fahey believed that with the Rangers having parted ways with manager Bobby Valentine, coaching slots would be open on the club. He asked Craig for permission to speak with the Rangers, a request to which Craig responded by firing Fahey with three days left in the season.[30]

Fahey did return home, but no position with the Rangers was in the offing. Eventually, Texas offered a minor-league position that Fahey turned down. Other offers came from Cleveland, the White Sox, and the Mets, the most tempting an offer to manage the Mets' Triple-A team. Fahey turned down all the offers, having found coaching Little League and Duncanville High School totally satisfying as he watched his sons grow up.[31] He also served many years in leadership positions with the Duncanville Baseball Booster Club. In 2015, the Duncanville Independent School District inducted Fahey into its Hall of Honor.[32]

Scott, Bill and Carla's oldest son, graduated from Duncanville High in 1997 and played four years of college baseball before returning to his high-school alma mater as a teacher and head baseball coach.[33] Brandon, two years younger than Scott, also graduated from Duncanville and was drafted in the 17th round by San Diego. Like his father, Brandon passed on signing a contract, instead attending Grayson Community College in North Texas. A season later Baltimore, the team that had chosen his father over 30 years earlier, drafted him in the 32nd round. Again, Brandon Fahey passed up the opportunity to turn professional and transferred to the University of Texas, where he played for the 2002 College World Series champion Longhorns. Baltimore again chose him in the 12th round. This time Brandon signed and made his debut with the Orioles in 2006. After three seasons bouncing between Triple A and the Orioles, Brandon retired from baseball.

Looking back on his career and what might have been, Bill Fahey took it all in stride. He even gloated a little. After all, he said, he proved that Ted Williams, among the greatest baseball players ever to take the field, didn't know as much about baseball as he thought he did.

"I proved him wrong," Fahey said. "Williams said I'd be an All-Star catcher. I proved him wrong."[34]

Sources

All statistical information, transactions, seasons various teammates played, and comparisons of statistical data are based on information from Baseball-Reference.com. The author thanks Paul Geisler for supplying a number of sources used in this article.

Notes

1. "Almost Skipper Fahey Picked for Stardom," *Port Huron Times Herald*, February 19, 1971.
2. Paul Post, "Fahey's Ultimate Dream Was Playing for Hometown Team," *Sports Collectors Digest*, October 13, 1990.
3. Merrell Whittlesey, "Nats' Coleman Second Half Bearcat," *The Sporting News*, February 7, 1970.
4. "Redford Whipped in Final, 12-9," *Detroit Free Press*, August 19, 1969.
5. Paul Post.
6. Bill Fahey player file at the National Baseball Hall of Fame.
7. Jeff Brazier, "The Truth About Junior College Baseball," www.baseballcoaches.org, accessed, February 7, 2018.
8. "Fahey Is Signed by Senators," Port Huron Times Herald, February 17, 1970.
9. "Almost Skipper," February 19, 1971.
10. Merrell Whittlesey, "Nats' Coleman."
11. Bill Fahey player file.
12. Merrell Whittlesey, "Southworth Sleeper on Nat Hill List," The Sporting News, January 30, 1971.
13. Ibid.
14. Merrell Whittlesey, "Will Nats Prima Donnas Ruffle Ted?" The Sporting News, February 27, 1971.
15. Bill Fahey player file.
16. Merrell Whittlesey, "Will Nats." February 27, 1971.
17. Merrell Whittlesey, "Lefty Starter Tops Nat Shopping List," The Sporting News, November 6, 1971.
18. "Tigers Drop 3-1 Game to Lowly Texas Rangers," Sault Saint Marie Evening News, July 24, 1972.
19. "Eastern League," The Sporting News, August 7, 1971.
20. "Fahey Recuperates From Injuries to Ribs, Lung," The Sporting News, September 8, 1973. See also "Coast Toasties," The Sporting News, September 8, 1973.
21. "Ranger Ramblings," The Sporting News, March 16, 1974.
22. Merle Heryford, "Rangers Put Two Infielders on Trade Saddles," The Sporting News, November 2, 1974.
23. Jim Hawkins, "Tigers Willing to Gamble in Their Quest for a Catcher," The Sporting News, November 16, 1974.
24. Randy Galloway, "Gaylord Reduced to Sad Serf Role as Ranger," The Sporting News, July 12, 1975.
25. Phil Collier, "Throw-In Fahey Now Padre Prize," San Diego Union, September 15, 1979.
26. Ibid.
27. Paul Post.
28. C.W. Nevius, "Return of the Okey Dokey," San Francisco Chronicle, September 22, 1990.
29. Ibid.
30. Paul Post.
31. Ibid.
32. Duncanville Independent School District, "Duncanville Athletics Hall of Honor." duncanvilleisd.org/Page/254, accessed, February 13, 2018.
33. Ibid.
34. Paul Post.

TED FORD

BY CHRIS HOLADAY

Ted Ford decided on his career path when he was 8 years old; he told his father he was going to be a baseball player.

"Of course my dad didn't believe me," said Ford in 2015. "I thought it would be easy but he knew how hard it would be to make that happen."

Born in Vineland, New Jersey, to Theodore and Doreen Ford on February 7, 1947, Theodore Henry Ford Jr. grew up in a baseball-loving family with two brothers and one sister. With natural talent and hard work, it wasn't long before it became apparent there might actually be something to his youthful career ambitions.

Though baseball was his first love, Ford also excelled at football, basketball, and track. "I played quarterback for one game," he recalled with a laugh, "but the coach said I didn't like to give up the ball so he made me a halfback."[1] When he was a senior at Richland High School, scouts were frequently in the stands to watch the 5-foot-10, 180-pound outfielder with the big arm. Ford was drafted by the Indians in the first round (11th overall) of the January 1966 amateur draft. (The Indians selected the most notable player in the draft that year, pitcher Joe Niekro, with their seventh selection.)

After spring training, the Indians assigned Ford to their Midwest League club in Dubuque, Iowa. In 71 games with the Packers in 1966, he hit .263 with 6 home runs and 25 RBIs in 262 at-bats. After the season the Indians loaned him to the Oakland Athletics' club in the Arizona Fall League. Since the club had a strong outfield (top prospects Reggie Jackson, Rick Monday, and Cito Gaston), Ford spent most of his time at third base that fall.

Ford spent that winter playing in the Dominican Republic and after spring training with the Indians, earned a promotion for the 1967 season to Pawtucket of the Double-A Eastern League. There he hit .210 with 42 RBIs in 132 games in 1967.

Ford's baseball career was interrupted after the '67 season by a letter from Uncle Sam. Drafted into the US Army, Ford received orders to deploy overseas after basic training. Ready to ship out – probably to Vietnam – Ford learned that his orders had changed and he was sent to Fort Polk, Louisiana. Assigned to be a cook, he spent much of the next year and half working on his culinary skills instead of baseball skills.

TED FORD

Discharged in late 1969, Ford rejoined the Indians organization. The club sent him to the Florida Winter Instructional League to get back in baseball shape. From there he went back to the Dominican Republic to get more plate appearances. The hard work over the winter paid off, and a strong spring training in 1970 won Ford a spot on the big-league roster. On April 7 he made his major-league debut. Facing star pitcher Dave McNally of the Baltimore Orioles, Ford went 0-for-2 with a walk in his first game.

With the Indians, Ford was used mostly as pinch-hitter and late-game replacement. In 1970 he made 50 plate appearances in 26 games and hit .174. Most of the season, however, was spent at Triple-A Wichita. There, he had a standout season for the Aeros and batted .326 with 12 home runs and 57 RBIs in 106 games.

The 1971 season again saw Ford shuttle back and forth between Cleveland and Wichita. With the Indians for 74 games, he hit .194 in 196 at-bats. With the Aeros for 49 games he hit .330 in 176 at-bats.

"I really liked Cleveland but I spent a lot of time sitting on the bench," said Ford in 2015. "But they had good players like Vada Pinson ahead of me."

Over the winter of 1971-72, Ford went to Venezuela to keep his skills sharp. There he joined the Tigres de Aragua, where he was a teammate of Rod Carew, Dave Concepcion, and Graig Nettles.[2]

Despite the lack of playing time with the Indians, Ford did get a hit that changed his baseball fortunes. "In a game against the Senators in '71, I hit one off the wall," recalled Ford. "I think that caught the eye of their manager, Ted Williams. When they moved to Texas and were looking to make some moves the next spring, Williams recommended me."

Ford reported to the Indians spring-training facility in Arizona in 1972 but on April 3 he was traded to the Texas Rangers. Williams and general manager Joe Burke apparently saw great promise in Ford because they gave up Roy Foster and veteran Tommy McCraw to get him. McCraw had played in Washington the year before after spending the previous eight seasons with the White Sox. Foster had actually been Ford's teammate in Cleveland but was traded to the Rangers in December, then ended up back with his previous club.[3]

As many players do when traded, Ford had mixed emotions. "I liked the Indians organization," he said, "but I was happy I was going somewhere I might get a chance to play regularly."

The Rangers assigned Ford to the Denver Bears, their Triple-A affiliate. He was there for only nine games, however, before getting the call to Arlington. "We had gone to Wichita for a game and we got snowed in and couldn't leave," he recalled. "It was there I got the call from Ted Williams to come to Arlington."

On April 28, 1972, Ford made his Rangers debut against the Boston Red Sox in Arlington.

He pinch-hit for Larry Biittner in the sixth inning and drew a walk off Bill Lee. Replacing Biittner in right field, he came up again in the bottom of the seventh with the game tied, 6-6, two men on and two outs. Facing veteran Bobby Bolin this time, Ford connected on a long home run to right-center field. Driving in Tom Grieve and Frank Howard, the homer put the Rangers up 9-6, which stood as the final score.

Ford remained in the Rangers' lineup for the rest of the season and played in 129 games, starting 97 times in right field and 17 in left. At the plate he hit .235 and led the team with 14 home runs and 19 doubles while driving in 50 runs. Always known for his strong arm, Ford led the American League with 10 assists from right field.

Ford credited two of the game's all-time greats, Williams and Don Drysdale, for his success that season. Drysdale, who was the KRLD/KDFW announcer for the Rangers in 1972, had a close relationship with manager Williams. "They were buddies and always together," said Ford. "They would both give me advice and encouragement."

After the season Ford went back to Venezuela. With Tigres de Aragua again, he built on his solid season with Rangers and hit .303 with 7 home runs and 36 RBIs in 56 games.[4]

Spring training in 1973 saw the emergence of Jeff Burroughs, who took over the starting role in right field. So despite his solid performance the previous season, Ford began the 1973 season with Spokane, the Rangers' new Triple-A affiliate. He started strong and was hitting .361 after 20 games but on May 10 was traded (with Dick Bosman) back to the Indians for pitcher Steve Dunning. The Indians assigned Ford to Oklahoma City. There he hit .324 with 59 RBIs in 101 games, a performance that earned a September call-up to Cleveland. Ford appeared in 11 big-league games late that season, hitting .225 in 40 at-bats.

What proved to be his last major-league game was against the same team he faced in his debut, the Baltimore Orioles. Batting leadoff in the second game of a doubleheader on September 29, 1973, Ford went 1-for-5 with a single off star left-hander Mike Cuellar. It was final game of season for the last-place Indians.

Ford began the 1974 season at Oklahoma City but on April 24 was traded back to the Rangers for pitcher Charlie Hudson. Told he was going to be remaining in the minor leagues, Ford decided to leave the game and go home. After being granted his release by the Rangers, Ford was talked into signing with the Hawaii Islanders of the Pacific Coast League. Technically a San Diego affiliate, the Islanders received only a few players from the Padres and were free to sign whomever they liked to fill out their roster. The deal worked out well for Ford, who had one of his best seasons at the plate (.309, 17 home runs, 70 RBIs).

After the season, Ford entertained offers to play in Japan and Mexico. The money was better in Mexico and it was closer, so in 1975 he headed south and signed with Jalisco. In eight seasons in Mexico, Ford also played for Durango, Reynosa, Saltillo, the Mexico City Reds, and the Mexico City Tigers.

"The people were nice and they treated me well in Mexico. But eventually the other teams just started walking me all the time. That took all the fun out of the game. So after the 1982 season I went home to New Jersey."

After baseball Ford worked as a blueberry farm contractor in Hammonton, New Jersey, for several years. Eventually he returned to Texas and settled in McAllen, where he operated a baseball camp for youngster 10 to 15 for six years.

When his youngest son, Tim, signed to play baseball for Huston-Tillotson University in 2012, Ford followed him to Austin. There he continued to coach children while also serving as an assistant to Coach Alvin Moore with the Huston-Tillotson Rams. The 2016 season was Ford's third with the NAIA school.

Ted Ford's younger brother, Lambert, also pursued professional baseball as a career. He was drafted out of Vineland High School by the Cleveland Indians in the first round (fifth overall) of the January 1968 draft but didn't sign. The Houston Astros then selected him in the fifth round of the June 1968 draft. Lambert made it as high as Double A and spent the 1972 and '73 seasons in the White Sox organization with Knoxville in the Southern League. Like Ted, he spent several seasons playing in Mexico before retiring in 1983.

Ted Ford's grandson, Darren, continued the family tradition and was drafted out of Vineland High School by the Brewers in 2004. Known for his speed, Darren Ford made his major-league debut in 2010 with the San Francisco Giants as a pinch-runner. He won a World Series ring that season and played part of the next with the Giants. After a couple of years in other organizations, Darren returned to the Giants and spent the 2015 season at Triple-A Sacramento.

Ted Ford still has fond memories of his playing days. "I think Cleveland was my favorite city to play in," he said in 2015. "But they were great to me in Texas. I had my own fan group out in right field and that was fun." Ford never lost his passion for the game and kept contributing to it by his work with young players. And no one can ever say his childhood dream of being a baseball player didn't come true.

Sources
Besides the sources cited in the Notes, the author consulted Baseball-Reference.com.

Notes

1. The author interviewed Ted Ford by telephone on November 16, November 18, and December 30, 2015. All quotations attributed to Ford are from these interviews unless otherwise indicated.
2. Estadisticas Beisbol Profesional Venezolano (purapelota.com).
3. Associated Press, "Indians, Rangers swap outfielders," *St. Petersburg Times*, April 4, 1972.
4. Estadisticas Beisbol Profesional Venezolano.

BILL GOGOLEWSKI

BY GREGORY H. WOLF

On September 12, 1972, Bill Gogolewski, a 24-year-old right-hander who had struggled thus far in his second full season in the big leagues, was pitching the game of his life against fireballer Nolan Ryan and the California Angels. While the Ryan Express was racking up 15 strikeouts, Gogolewski held the Halos hitless through 7⅔ innings. "I made one bad pitch, one bad decision, and it cost me a hit," recalled the pitcher in an interview with the author.[1] He settled for a one-hit shutout, and the best pitched ballgame in the Texas Rangers' first season in Arlington.

Part of the baby-boomer generation, William Joseph Gogolewski (pronounced Gogo-les-ski) was born on October 26, 1947, in Oshkosh, a city of 40,000 residents nestled on the western banks of picturesque Lake Winnebago, about 90 miles north-northwest of Milwaukee. He was the third and final child (following Karen and Gerald) of Alois and Theresa (Kempinger) Gogolewski, both native Wisconsinites who married in 1939. Alois, whose grandparents emigrated from Poland at the turn of the 20th century, worked as an assemblyman for Rockwell International. Of German stock, Theresa had been a seamstress in a local dress factory and was a full-time homemaker.

As a youngster Bill played baseball, football, and basketball as the seasons progressed. By the time he was about 10, he started playing organized baseball in a local recreation league. His coaches soon recognized that the tall, lanky youth had a strong right arm, and made him a pitcher. "When I was in high school," explained Gogolewski, "I got my first real coaching from Harlan Quandt. He was quite a good pitcher at the University of Wisconsin." With Quandt's mentorship at Oshkosh High School and under coach Norm Kumbier for his local American Legion team, Gogolewski made a name for himself as a hard thrower who regularly racked up double-digit strikeout totals. As a junior, he tossed a no-hitter and struck out 17, but that was just a prelude to his senior season.[2] He hurled three one-hitters, two two-hitters, and one four-hitter to go 5-1, and then fired another one-hitter and whiffed 17 to help his club capture the district championship.[3]

On the day he graduated from high school in 1965, Gogolewski was selected by the Washington Senators in the 18th round of Major League Baseball's first amateur draft. He wasn't surprised that he was selected – scouts had been following him for two years – but he was surprised by which team chose him. "We never knew [Senators' scout] Burt Thiel was around," said Gogolewski, who signed his first professional contract as a 17-year-old. "[Thiel] came to our home. We didn't know what to expect. He made an offer with a bonus, I think it was $3,500. Back then we didn't have agents; and being drafted in the lower rounds, we didn't expect a lot. I was just happy I was drafted and going to play professional baseball." Gogolewski's parents supported his decision to pursue his dream. "No matter where we played," recalled Gogolewski, "they were there."

Gogolewski began his long journey to the big leagues with the Wytheville (Virginia) Senators in Rookie-class Appalachian League. "That was the first time I was ever away from home," admitted the pitcher. "It was a little scary. Lee Anthony, my coach, was very laid back and understood that players needed to go through a transition. I stayed at a house – four of five of us – and that helped out a lot." Standing 6-feet-4, but rail-thin at just 165 pounds, Gogolewski was the youngest player on the team, and got by with a fastball. He went 5-1, led the team with 92 strikeouts, and carved out a 4.50 ERA in 82 innings.

Promoted to the Burlington (North Carolina) Senators of the Class A Carolina League in 1966, Gogolewski responded with a team-high 24 starts, producing an 11-9 record and 3.18 ERA in 164 innings for skipper Wayne Terwilliger. Washington added the 18-year-old hurler to its 40-man roster after the season.

Gogolewski's career began just as America's involvement in the Vietnam War began to intensify. As they had during World Wars I and II, as well as the Korean War, professional ballplayers had to reckon with the prospect of military service. Wanting to balance his duty to his country and continue playing baseball, Gogolewski decided to enlist in the National Guard after discussing matters with his former coach Harlan Quandt. "If I wouldn't have signed up, I would have been drafted," he said. "They had just started the lottery, and my number was 3." Gogolewski served beginning in November 1966, and went on active duty in January 1967. He was with the 1157th Transportation Company, stationed in Oshkosh.

Discharged in late April, Gogolewski missed spring training with the Senators and joined the York (Pennsylvania) White Roses in the Double-A Eastern League. Needing time to transition back to baseball, he made just nine starts (12 appearances) and went 4-3 with a sturdy 2.55 ERA in 60 innings. The Senators were still impressed with their 19-year-old hurler and assigned him to the Florida Instructional League for extra seasoning in the fall.

The most important pitch Gogolewski threw in 1967 was to Susan Paulick of Oshkosh. They married that year, and raised two boys. For the remainder of Bill's professional baseball career, his wife and children accompanied him to spring training and then on to where ever he was assigned to play, providing both support and levity to an often-hectic lifestyle. In the offseasons, the family returned to Oshkosh, except for 1972-1974 when they lived in the Dallas metropolitan area year-round.

In 1968 Gogolewski participated in his first big-league spring training, with the Senators at Pompano Beach. "I don't know if I was intimidated," he replied when asked about his first impressions. "I was a little in awe of the players and the facilities. What we had in the minors – that wasn't real good like it is today." Gogolewski had little chance of landing a spot in the starting rotation, which already included three young starters from the previous year (Joe Coleman, Frank Bertaina, and Barry Moore). "The coaches watched us pitch on the side and BP," said Gogolewski, "but they didn't pay too much attention to us." He was assigned to Savannah in the Double-A Southern League, where he was still the youngest player on the club. Gogolewski's numbers (7-7, 112 innings, 4.42 ERA) lost some of their luster.

The mood at the Senators' spring training in 1969 was transformed by team owner Bob Short's improbable hiring of living legend Ted Williams as manager. Gogolewski, given another look-see in camp, did not impress the Splendid Splinter, who dismissed the young hurler as erratic and lacking control, and transferred him to the minor-league affiliate camp at Plant City.[4] "I was young, and had some time to make it," said Gogolewski of his demotion. "It was disappointing, but I thought I'd overcome it." But just as his season with the Buffalo Bisons of the Triple-A International League got under way, Gogolewski came down with elbow problems that plagued him the entire year. Just a step away from his dream, the good-natured hurler's ERA soared to 5.25 (a team high among starters) and he was limited to just 84 innings in 18 appearances (13 starts). Given Gogolewski's ethnic heritage, it was fitting that he tossed a complete-game victory over

Louisville at Niagara Falls on Polish-American Night on August 19.[5]

Gogolewski arrived at the Senators' spring training in 1970 with his career at a crossroads. He had been left unprotected in the Rule 5 draft the previous December, but was not selected. In camp, Gogolewski's elbow still ached, making pitching difficult. "I was getting hit all over the place," he told the author. "I was concerned that I wasn't going to make it to the big leagues." He needed a break, and was about to get one from an unexpected source. "My catcher, Rich Stelmasczek, came to me and asked if I can throw a slider," recalled Gogolewski, who had been playing around with one for a few years but had not thrown one in games. "So I say, 'I can now.' I started gripping the ball differently and it became my out pitch."

The slider eventually proved to be Gogolewski's ticket to the big leagues. "Ted Williams was a true believer that every pitcher should throw a slider," explained the Wisconsin native. "That was the most difficult pitch for him to hit. When I came up [in 1965] I threw more of a slow, big breaking ball, a slurve." Gogolewski's pitching arsenal also included both a two- and four-seam fastball, thrown predominantly from an upper three-quarter delivery. "I threw a knuckle curve, too," recalled Gogolewski. "That got changed by [Texas Rangers pitching coach] Sid Hudson in the spring of 1971. I started throwing a conventional curve, snap the wrist and pull the shutter down."

Armed with an explosive fastball and an emerging, dangerous slider, Gogolewski had the best year in his career in 1970 with the Pittsfield (Massachusetts) Senators in the Eastern League. He was frustrated about being dropped down a class to Double-A, but he took it in stride. Finally pain-free, Gogolewski fanned 14, 13, and 15 batters in his first three starts, and quickly proved that he was the best pitcher in the circuit, winning his first eight decisions.[6] Despite missing almost three weeks in July fulfilling his obligations to the National Guard, Gogolewski led or co-led the league in wins (14), complete games (15), and strikeouts (146), while posting a career-low 2.47 ERA in 171 innings. He was the only player chosen unanimously to the Eastern League all-star team.[7]

"We were on the road," reminisced Gogolewski about promotion to the majors in 1970. "Joe Klein was my manager and he called me in and told me, 'You've been called to the big leagues.'" Somewhat perplexed, Gogolewski responded, "'What do I do? I've got a wife and child sitting at home back (in Pittsfield). Does someone give me a car to go back home and get them?' Well, I stayed with the team until we returned home. When I packed to leave, the water pump broke in my car, and we were delayed another day. By the time I got to Washington, they say 'Where have you been? We called you up a week ago.'"

On September 3 Gogolewski, who had now bulked up to about 205 pounds, made his major-league debut for the last-place Senators in front of a sparse crowd of just 5,550 spectators at Robert F. Kennedy Stadium in the nation's capital. He scattered three hits in 3⅔ innings of relief and gave up a run in an eventual loss to Cleveland. "I remember getting in the bullpen car," recalled Gogolewski about his debut. "We had a Corvette. We drove to the first-base dugout and I handed the batboy my jacket, and took the mound." Eight days later, he picked up his maiden victory in his first start, despite surrendering seven hits and walking four in 5⅔ innings (two runs) against Detroit in Tiger Stadium. Lauded by Washington beat writer Merrell Whittlesey as a "September sensation," Gogolewski held Baltimore to two hits over seven innings to win his next start for another victory.[8] He finished with a 2-2 record and 4.81 ERA in 33⅔ innings.

Gogolewski seemed destined for a spot in the starting rotation in 1971, but suffered a gruesome injury at the beginning of the season. "When we were doing our outfield drills, [recently signed pitcher] Denny McLain spiked me and almost ruptured my Achilles tendon." He missed almost three weeks. Assigned to the bullpen upon his return and then missing almost three weeks in June with the National Guard, "Gogo," as he had been called since his high-school days, moved into the starting rotation on July 6. He made 16 consecutive starts and produced a stellar 2.67 ERA in 101 innings in the best stretch of pitching in his big-league career. He tossed his first shutout, a four-hitter against the New York Yankees on September 1. "I felt really good about my pitching," said the hurler, whose final numbers (6-5, 2.75 ERA in 124⅓ innings) suggested an even better season in 1972.

Though many pitchers have complained about Ted Williams as a manager, Gogolewski had a surprisingly different take. "I had a good relationship with him," said Gogolewski. "He didn't think real highly of pitchers, but he was smart about pitching." The lanky Wisconsinite recalled an episode with Williams in spring training to prove his point. "He called me over to sit next to him in the dugout. He started to call the pitches that the opposing pitcher was going to throw. He was correct about 90 percent of the time."

"I was disappointed that we were leaving D.C.," admitted Gogolewski about Bob Short's decision to relocate the struggling club to Arlington, a suburb in the Dallas-Fort Worth metropolitan area, after the 1971 season. "We heard about the rumors, but that wasn't a distraction for me." Gogolewski liked pitching in RFK Stadium. "We had good infield grass and dirt. It wasn't a hitter's park. It was basically enclosed, and there was no wind taking balls over the fences."

Gogolewski wasn't sure what to expect in Arlington and North Texas, where baseball played second fiddle to the state's unrivaled pastime, football, but he was pleasantly surprised. "The fans embraced the team, and also Tom Vandergriff, the mayor of Arlington and the big backer who worked with Bob Short to get the (team's relocation) done." Arlington Stadium, where the rechristened Texas Rangers played their games, had been built in 1965 and, as Turnpike Stadium, served as the home of the Double-A Dallas-Fort Worth Spurs. The seating capacity had been increased from 10,000 to over 35,000 by 1971, but retrofitting was not yet completed by the time the season kicked off. "They had to redo both of the locker rooms to meet major-league standards," recalled Gogolewski. "We dressed out in the center-field locker room until the new ones under the stands were finished." But the biggest transition, according to the pitcher, was getting used to the weather. "They had some day games scheduled and they had to (reschedule) them because even for the players being out there in 104-degree heat trying to play a ballgame was hard."

Gogolewski's first season in Texas, however, was anything but smooth. After the season started 13 days late because of the first players' strike in baseball history, Gogolewski was pummeled in his first start (eight hits and eight runs in 3⅔ innings) in a loss to Chicago, and lasted only a third of an inning in his next one. It appeared as if he turned it around, yielding only four runs in 28⅓ innings in his next four starts, winning three of them. But the big right-hander pointed to a relief outing during that stretch as the beginning of his troubles. "[Sid Hudson] called down in the third in a game against Cleveland [May 14], and I started to warm up and then again in later innings. I finally got in in the ninth inning," said Gogolewski who pitched a 1-2-3 frame. "After that, I told him I was done. But I went back out in the next inning and gave up a home run to Chris Chambliss to lose the game. That was the start of my slide and all my losses. I don't blame that game, it was just a coincidence." Shunted to the bullpen for much of July and August, Gogolewski returned to the starting rotation on August 26 to hurl three straight strong starts (six runs in 22 innings), yet came away winless with two losses to drop his record to 3-9. In his next start, against California at Anaheim Stadium, "Gogo" pitched the game of his professional career. He held the Angels hitless for 7⅔ innings before light-hitting Billy Parker doubled. "We had a joke between pitchers," said Gogolewski with a chuckle. "If you throw a shutout, you'd have a chance for a no-decision." Settling for a one-hitter and a 3-0 victory, he outdueled the game's hardest thrower, Nolan Ryan. The masterpiece proved to be Gogolewski's last of two shutouts and six complete games in his career. For the cellar-dwelling, 100-loss Rangers, Gogolewski posted a 4-11 record and a 4.24 ERA in 150⅔ innings, and started in 21 of 36 games.

The Rangers' second season in Arlington got under way with a new skipper, Whitey Herzog, who replaced the unhappy and increasingly apathetic Williams. "Great manager," responded Gogolewksi when asked about his reaction to the 41-year-old first-time skipper. "He was a player's manager. Whitey surrounded himself with good baseball people (such as coaches Chuck Estrada, Del Wilber, Frank Lucchesi, and Jackie Moore). And he proved himself." With the offseason acquisition of starters Jim Bibby and Jim Merritt, and Sonny Siebert in early May, Gogolewski was moved to the bullpen. "I didn't mind relieving as long as I was in the major leagues pitching," said the hurler, who didn't view the assignment as a demotion. "If that's where they need me, that's where I'll go." Capable of warming up quickly, Gogolewski was well suited for long relief, a necessity for the league's worst ranked pitching corps (4.64 team ERA). After he saw action in 14 games through May, Gogolewski's workload increased when two unfortunate incidents happened. "[Rookie] Steve Foucault dislocated his shoulder [on June 30]; he was our short right-hander. And Charlie Hudson, the left-hander, shot himself in the hand [on June 9]."[9]

That summer Gogolewski pitched in one of the most storied games in Rangers history. Bob Short, in financial straits since he had purchased the Senators in 1968, drafted Texas high-school phenom David Clyde with the first pick in the 1973 amateur draft. In an effort to drum up interest for his club, Short signed the 18-year-old, who made his big-league debut on July 27 in front of the first-ever sellout crowd in Arlington Stadium. "I was in the bullpen," said Gogolewski. "They called down and told me exactly what they were going to do. If Clyde gets through the fifth, they'd send him out in the sixth, but take him out so he could get an ovation. And then I'd come in." Teenager Clyde got the headlines (one hit in five innings, plus seven walks), while Gogolewski scattered three hits over four innings, yielding just an unearned run to preserve the victory and earn his sixth save.

Gogolewski admitted that he didn't think Clyde was ready for the big leagues. "That was one of the biggest mistakes that the organization made – bringing guys [up] too early," he said. "Let 'em get seasoned a little. Bob Short needed the money and didn't care about winning." Gogolewski also pointed to the crippling effect the acquisition of Denny McLain had on the club as the most egregious example of Short's lack of baseball acumen. In order to obtain McLain (whom Commissioner Bowie Kuhn had recently reinstated and pronounced "not mentally ill"[10]) and three toss-ins (Elliott Maddox, Norm McRae, and Don Wert), the Senators surrendered workhorse right-hander Joe Coleman and future Gold Glove infielders Ed Brinkman and Aurelio Rodriguez, as well as right-hander Jim Hannan, in a trade many consider among the worst in baseball history.

In last place, 33½ games behind Oakland in the AL West, the Rangers replaced Herzog with Billy Martin, who had been suspended by Commissioner Kuhn and subsequently fired by the Detroit Tigers after ordering his pitcher, Joe Coleman, to throw spitballs in a game against Cleveland on August 30. The busiest reliever in Herzog's bullpen, Gogolewski appeared in only four games for Martin. "I must have ruffled his feathers because I didn't pitch much for him." For one of the worst big-league clubs of the decade (57-105), Gogolewski led the team with 49 appearances (tied for 10th most in the AL), ranked third on the club in innings (123⅔), while posting a 3-6 record and 4.22 ERA.

On March 23, 1974, Gogolewski was shipped to Cleveland to complete a trade for Steve Hargan from the previous December. "I found out about being traded from my neighbor, [teammate] Steve Dunning," said a bemused Gogolewski. "It was in the paper. No one [in management] told me. We had purchased a home in Texas in '72. That was supposedly a no-no if you wanted to stick around with the club. As soon as you buy a house, you get traded." Gogolewski joined the Indians for their final week of spring training before they reassigned him to Oklahoma City, their Triple-A affiliate in the American Association. He posted a 10-11 record and 3.63 ERA in 181 innings with the 89ers and was a September call-up with the Tribe, logging 13⅔ innings in five relief outings.

Gogolewski, just 27 years old, was released in the offseason, but was not yet ready to give up what he had worked his entire life to attain. "I got hold of [Chicago GM] Rollie Hemond and told him my situation," said Gogolewski. "He signed me to a contract." Playing just a few hours' drive from his home town, Gogolewski was on the White Sox roster the entire season, but was used little, appearing in 19 games and logging 55 innings (5.24 ERA) without a decision.

In the offseason Gogolewski decided to hang up his spikes. "My body couldn't take the physical stress anymore," he admitted. "I had developed elbow problems, and then I had back problems. I couldn't throw that much without my elbow swelling up. Back then you didn't have the surgeries like you do now." In parts of six big-league seasons, Gogolewski went 15-24 and posted a 4.02 ERA in 501 innings. He won 54 games and logged 854 innings in seven seasons in the minors. "I don't regret the decision," Gogolewski said. "I felt it was time. The transition wasn't that bad. I had two young boys getting ready to start school, and didn't want to drag them around."

A Wisconsinite by heart, Gogolewski returned to Oshkosh with his wife and two boys and transitioned to his post-baseball career. After working at a big and tall clothing store for a few years, Gogolewski began a 28-year tenure as inventory specialist at Oshkosh Trucking Corporation. Beginning in 2000, he also served on the advisory board of the city parks in Oshkosh. He still held that position and resided in Oshkosh as of 2016.

Since retiring from baseball, Gogolewski has participated in various events sponsored by the Major League Baseball Alumni Association, including golf tournaments and baseball clinics. He also returned to Arlington for the 40th anniversary of the Rangers' first season.

When asked about one of his most vivid memories in his professional baseball career, the modest Gogolewski took a few seconds to think and provided an insightful answer that gave testimony to his love and passion for baseball. "The overall experience of playing major-league baseball, and having managers like Ted Williams, Whitey Herzog, Billy Martin, and Chuck Tanner. Just being in contact with those kinds of people."

The author expresses his gratitude to Bill Gogolewski, whom he interviewed on August 17, 2015. Gogolewski subsequently read this biography to ensure its accuracy.

Sources

In addition to the sources cited in the Notes, the author also accessed Retrosheet.org, Baseball-Reference.com, and SABR.org.

Notes

1. All quotations from Bill Gogolewski are from the author's interview with the player on August 17, 2015.
2. *Oshkosh Daily Northern*, April 27, 1964: 10.
3. *Oshkosh Daily Northern*, May 22, 1965: 16; May 29, 1965: 5.
4. *The Sporting News*, October 3, 1970: 12.
5. *The Sporting News*, September 6, 1969: 36.
6. *The Sporting News*, May 30, 1970: 39.
7. *The Sporting News*, August 8, 1970, 44.
8. *The Sporting News*, October 3, 1970: 12.
9. Hudson blew off the middle finger of his left hand cleaning his .38 pistol at his apartment in Texas. Surgeons saved part of the finger by grafting bone from his elbow. He had posted a 6.00 ERA over 12 appearances and 24 innings. Amazingly, he returned on July 29, and was more effective after the injury (3.99 ERA in 38⅓ innings in 13 appearances). See UPI, "Southpaw Shoots Right Digit," *Chicago Tribune*, June 10, 1973: Section 3, 1.
10. Ira Miller (UPI), "Denny McLain Sent to Senators in Eight-Player Transaction," *Cumberland* (Maryland) *News*, October 10, 1970: 15.

TOM GRIEVE

BY STEVE WEST

Tom Grieve has passed 50 years in baseball, 49 of them spent with the Texas Rangers franchise. He played, was general manager, and worked as a broadcaster for the Rangers, rightfully earning him the sobriquet "Mr. Ranger."

Thomas Alan Grieve was born on March 4, 1948, in Pittsfield, Massachusetts, to Alan and Polly (Hopkins) Grieve. After military service, Alan worked in clothing manufacture, then as an automobile salesman and as a fleet manager. Tom grew up with two sisters, Laurie and Cande. He was known for much of his life by the nickname Tag, for his initials. Tom remained close to his family all his life. As a commentator with the Rangers, for many years he had a tradition of calling his mother every Mother's Day, talking to her while on the air broadcasting the Rangers game.[1]

Pittsfield is known to baseball historians, because a 1791 town ordinance barred the playing of baseball near the town's meeting hall. This ordinance is the earliest known written reference to baseball.[2] During his broadcasting career, Grieve mentioned this fact on several occasions. He said that he and his friends regularly played on the field by the meeting hall but had no idea of the historical significance of the location.[3]

In high school Grieve played football, basketball, and baseball, in which he pitched, caught, and played in the outfield. In baseball and football, in which he was a quarterback, he was named to All-Western Massachusetts teams. He played on Pittsfield High's 1966 state champions, hitting over .400 and driving in the only run in the championship game, and won an award as the top scholar-athlete in Western Massachusetts. "He's always been a quiet competitor with a burning desire to do well," Buddy Pellerin, his high-school coach, said many years later.[4] Grieve went on to play for the Chatham Anglers in the Cape Cod League that summer, hitting .416 in 89 at-bats.

Drafted in the first round (sixth overall) by the Washington Senators, Grieve had already committed to go to the University of Michigan. He refused to sign with the Senators until they agreed that he could finish his college degree. Senators farm director Hal Keller agreed to let him complete the school year before reporting to the minor leagues each summer. He also gave Grieve a $60,000 bonus.[5]

Assigned to Burlington in the Class-A Carolina League in 1967, Grieve struggled. He hit .138 in 13 games before being sent down to Geneva of the Class-A New York-Pennsylvania League, where he hit .236 with six home runs.

After missing the early part of the 1968 season while at college, Grieve reported to Salisbury in the Class-A Western Carolinas League. He started hot, hitting .429 with three home runs in his first 14 games. He was selected to the All-Star team, but broke a finger in practice on the morning of the game.[6] He still earned a trip back to Burlington, hitting .296 with three home runs in nine games at the end of the season.

In 1969 Grieve jumped to Buffalo in the Triple-A International League, where he hit just .245 with 11 home runs. He spent the fall in the Florida Instructional League, where he also hit .245. But that was enough to earn Grieve an invitation to the Senators spring training for 1970, where he performed very well, hitting .365. On March 18 he reached base seven times on four hits, two of them doubles, and three walks. Despite being the standout rookie in camp, his manager brought him back to earth. "Where would we play him? Certainly not over Howard, Unser, or Lee Maye. The kid should play every day," manager Ted Williams said.[7]

Grieve understood, knowing he was still a young player. He was happy just with the training he had already received from Williams. "That man … he's just great. The biggest thing he has done for me is to get me mentally ready to hit."[8]

As expected, Grieve was sent to Triple-A Denver, where he hit .280 with 13 home runs in half a season, interrupted by military service. He caught a break when Senators outfielder Wayne Comer sprained his wrist and went on the disabled list. Grieve was recalled to replace him.

On July 4 Grieve played a night game in Denver, then had a sleepless night, having to catch a plane to New York. He arrived barely an hour before the 1 P.M. start of the first game of a doubleheader, and was put in the starting lineup for his major-league debut. He grounded to short, third, and second before being lifted for a pinch-hitter in the ninth. Grieve was later observed dozing on the bench during the second game.[9]

The following day Grieve got his first two major-league hits, both off Sam McDowell of the Cleveland Indians. On July 9 he hit his first major-league home run, off the Indians' Rick Austin. His three-hit day raised his average to .316, but it was all downhill from there. Playing in 47 of the Senators' last 84 games, Grieve hit just .198 with three home runs. This hot-or-cold pattern would continue throughout his career.

In 1971 Grieve was sent back to Denver for more seasoning. Despite breaking a finger in May, and missing time due to military commitments, he hit .272 with 19 home runs and brought himself back into the team's focus. The Bears won the American Association title, but while Grieve went 9-for-27 with seven RBIs, they lost the Little World Series to Rochester.

At the end of the 1970 season the Senators had been contacted by a Venezuelan team that hoped to sign Grieve for their winter season, but Williams said no. "Grieve is tired and should not even be playing in this league," Williams said.[10] But after 1971 Grieve did head to Venezuela, and returned there several more times throughout his career. During the 1973-74 winter he hit .340 with nine home runs and 60 RBIs in Venezuela, prompting teammate Toby Harrah to say, "I thought Tom should have gotten the MVP award down there. … He was doing it all, both defensively and offensively."[11]

In 1972 Grieve was out of options, and stayed with the major-league club, which had relocated from Washington to become the Texas Rangers. "Our scouts have long considered him to have the potential to be a good hitter. … If you let him get away, and he happens to find himself, you could regret that move for a number of years," general manager Joe Burke said. In fact, Grieve wasted 1972 on the bench, getting just 158 plate appearances in 64 games, although he was with the team the whole season. "I certainly didn't accomplish anything worthwhile," he said. "I just hoped that somewhere along the line I would get a chance to play every day."[12]

Back in Venezuela for the winter, Grieve hit .309 with 10 home runs for Zulia, and attracted attention from the Rangers, with scouts reporting his improved performance. He got even less playing time in 1973, though, just 136 plate appearances. It took until July 27, when he hit a three-run shot against the Angels, for him to get not only his first home run but also his first RBIs of the season.

Up to then he had just 30 at-bats all year, but things changed in the last couple of months of the season. "When he got his chance after Rico (Carty) got hurt, he suddenly went up there swinging with authority. You can see the difference in him now," manager Whitey Herzog said.[13] From July 27 to the end of the season, Grieve hit .333 with seven home runs. With that performance, Herzog suggested that Grieve had a chance to win the right-field position the following season.

Come the spring of 1974, Grieve had expectations. "I'm not coming to camp hoping for a chance to play this season. I'm expecting that chance this time," he said. He also noted that both new manager Billy Martin and owner Bob Short had told him he would have the chance to play, and that Short said that if he didn't, the club would look to trade him. "I really hope it doesn't come to that. I hope I can make it here, because I want to play here," Grieve said.[14]

Unfortunately for Grieve, he hurt his ankle in the first exhibition game and missed some time in the spring. He shook it off, though, and began the season with eight hits in his first three games. Hitting .323 through April, Grieve seemed to have cemented his spot in right, but he cooled off, falling all the way to .255 by season's end. He hit two home runs in the infamous 10-cent-beer night in Cleveland in June, but that was a rare highlight. In the second half he was back on the bench, getting just 65 plate appearances.

Finally, in August of 1975 new manager Frank Lucchesi gave Grieve a shot, and he had 100 plate appearances in a month for the first time in his career. "I want to throw him in there every day and see what he can do," Lucchesi said.[15] Grieve responded by hitting .283 with seven home runs, and the thinking was that finally he would be a regular in 1976. But still questions surfaced. Though he thought he had a full-time job, trade rumors arose. Reportedly the Tigers asked for Grieve in return for Joe Coleman, and there was speculation about interest from the Indians.[16]

Grieve started 1976 on a tear, continuing his history of being a streaky hitter. He would have weeks or months in which he could hit anything, and follow up when "a Little Leaguer could get him out tossing a basketball."[17] It had been assumed that the streaks were due to being off the bench so much, but it continued when he got regular time. "I don't like it, but it's always been that way and probably always will be,"

Grieve said. "If I understood what happens, maybe I could do something about it, but I have absolutely no idea."[18] His manager agreed. "You just have to leave him in there when things aren't going well. ... He can hit any pitcher alive, from either side, when he's hot," said Lucchesi.[19]

Grieve's ups and downs continued all year, and he finished at .255 with 20 home runs (leading the team) and 81 RBIs. Showing his level head, he said, "Those aren't the greatest statistics in the game, but for me and my ability, they're good enough."[20] Despite his being named the club's player of the year, the rumors continued, with his trade value as high as it had ever been. But he stayed, although a pulled muscle in his rib cage limited him early in the season, a broken hand cost him six weeks in June and July, and a slump to .225 reduced his playing time even further.

The trade rumors intensified, and they finally came true at the winter meetings. Grieve was sent to the New York Mets as part of a four-team, 11-player deal.[21] Even then the Rangers were reluctant to trade Grieve. On his arrival at the winter meetings, Rangers owner Brad Corbett had said there was no way that Grieve would be traded.[22]

The problem for Grieve was that the Mets had a glut of outfielders. Manager Joe Torre said he would like to keep six of them on the roster. Unfortunately for Grieve he ended up being the sixth man, so although he was with the team the whole season, he got just 110 plate appearances, the lowest total of his career so far. Of his 54 games, 27 were as a pinch-hitter (when he hit just .080). Opportunity lost, again.

At the end of 1978 the Mets traded Grieve and pitcher Kim Seaman to the St. Louis Cardinals for pitcher Pete Falcone. Still a spare part, Grieve spent a month on the Cardinals' bench before being unconditionally released, having gone 3-for-15 in limited duty with the team. Although other players didn't want to see him leave, Grieve said, "It was a pretty logical decision on their part."[23]

He returned to Texas, signing a minor-league deal with the Rangers' Triple-A Tucson team. Grieve hit .266 with 14 home runs there, including three in one game, but the writing was on the wall. He considered playing in Japan, but instead ended his playing career and joined the Rangers' front office.

Grieve spent 1980 as director of group sales for the Rangers, then was promoted to assistant farm director. At the end of 1982 Joe Klein was promoted to general manager, and Grieve moved up to farm director. In 1983 he became the first former first-round pick to make a first-round selection in the draft, when he chose Jeff Kunkel. (Kunkel's father, Bill, was a former major-league umpire who had once called Grieve out on strikes.[24])

On September 1, 1984, Klein resigned as general manager, and team President Mike Stone promoted Grieve. Klein had been unhappy that Stone had changed the structure of the club so that manager Doug Rader reported directly to him, instead of to Klein. Grieve didn't have a problem with it. "Obviously, I am comfortable with that arrangement, or I wouldn't have accepted the job," he said.[25]

Grieve at 36 became the youngest general manager in the major leagues, but that didn't faze him. "I'm very excited and thrilled by the opportunity," he said. "Quite frankly, this is better than facing Nolan Ryan." Stone gave him his full support. "Tom Grieve is the embodiment of our statement of purpose," he said.[26] Grieve later said, "I don't care about being the youngest GM. I want to stick around to be the oldest."[27]

Grieve expressed his philosophy early on. He said he would not trade "one good player for a lot of mediocre ones. I'd rather trade one good one for another good one, given needs."[28] On the other hand, he immediately went into the free-agent market and brought in several mediocre players. Describing the need to quickly build depth, Grieve said, "We had some things we had to do, and we didn't see any other way."[29]

The Rangers stumbled starting 1985, and with a 9-23 record in early May, Rader was fired. Bobby Valentine, a former Mets teammate of Grieve, succeeded him. The hiring included a switch back in the chain of command, with Valentine reporting directly to Grieve, instead of to Stone.

At the end of the year Grieve signaled a change in attitude, stating that the team needed to develop its own players instead of signing free agents. He said, "I can't say we won't be active at all, but we're not pursuing anybody at this time. ... It's more practical to develop our young players."[30] He began to focus on young pitching, gathering arms through trade and the draft. Grieve had recognized how far from being competitive the Rangers were.

Although the Rangers had quick success in 1986, finishing second in the American League West Division, they fell back to sixth the following two seasons, and the building continued. After 1987 Grieve said, "We'd like to improve our pitching, but I don't have any great ideas on how to do that."[31]

Grieve had some gambles, such as signing Steve Howe, a pitcher with a history of drug problems. Howe pitched decently for the Rangers at the end of 1987, but relapsed and the team terminated his contract. Grieve and the Rangers had defied Commissioner Peter Ueberroth in bringing up Howe, and the team got a $250,000 fine for doing so.[32]

By 1988 Grieve was starting to make more moves, and admitted that the pressure to win was beginning to build. "As the years go by, you have to place more emphasis on winning," he said. "You still want to develop talent, but it is a fact of life that you can't be in a rebuilding program forever."[33] At the end of the season he gave shortstop Scott Fletcher the largest contract in franchise history, then a few days later went all in at the winter meetings.

In a string of trades and signings, Grieve remade the team, bringing in first baseman Rafael Palmeiro, second baseman Julio Franco, pitcher Jamie Moyer, and, surprising everyone, Nolan Ryan. "We had stayed pat for three years and we didn't show the improvement we wanted," Grieve said. "I'm confident we improved."[34] "This is the one most important transaction the Texas Rangers have ever made," said Valentine of the Ryan signing.[35]

During the 1989 season, as the team struggled to keep up with the leaders, Grieve made another trade. Acquiring DH Harold Baines and infielder Fred Manrique from the Chicago White Sox, he gave up Fletcher along with two prospects, pitcher Wilson Alvarez and outfielder Sammy Sosa. As both prospects went on to stardom, this deal defined Grieve's time as GM for many years to come. Worse, it didn't help the team, which finished fourth that season and third the next two.

New owner George W. Bush believed in Grieve, though. "You can assume we're very pleased with their performance," Bush said, referring to contract extensions for both Grieve and Stone.[36] Especially pleasing for Bush was the attendance figures, which passed two million for the first time in 1989. "What the fans are saying is that they agree with the path we're taking," Grieve said. "They're starting to see some results, and they're excited about the future."[37]

But Bush shook things up after the 1990 season, firing Stone and bringing in Tom Schieffer as president. Bush said neither Grieve or Valentine should fear for his job, but the writing was on the wall. The team was above .500 for three seasons in a row, 1989-91 (just the second time that had happened in franchise history), but their best record in that time was just 85-77. In July 1992, with the team in third place, 6½ games out, Valentine was fired, and Grieve gave Harrah the job for the rest of the season. They slumped after that, even though Grieve tried to spark things with another big trade, acquiring Jose Canseco from Oakland for Ruben Sierra, Jeff Russell, and Bobby Witt. The Rangers ended up going 32-44 under Harrah to finish 19 games out of first.

At that point Bush was still high on Grieve. "I've always felt good about Tom Grieve," he said. "He's a good man and a good, solid general manager."[38] Grieve brought in Kevin Kennedy to manage in 1993. They contended, finishing second, and were in first place in their division – with a 52-62 record – when a strike ended the 1994 season. And that was it for Grieve: The day the strike began, the Rangers decided to make changes and fired him as general manager.

Grieve quickly got a change in career. In 1995 Schieffer suggested that he try broadcasting. He had done a couple of games in 1980 and decided to go ahead and do more.[39] That season Grieve did 57 games as color analyst on the Rangers' Prime Sports cable-television broadcasts, beginning a long career in the booth. Over the years his role expanded; he spent more than two decades in the position, alongside numerous play-by-play partners. He became the public face of Rangers broadcasts, and earned the nickname "Mr. Ranger."

In 2008 Grieve announced that he had prostate cancer, but after surgery he returned to work just a couple of weeks later. In 2014 he let others take some of the road trips. Over the next few years he reduced his workload, down to about 65 games in 2017, while also appearing on some pre-and postgame shows, and making numerous appearances in the community for the team.

Grieve married Kathy Conry of Pittsfield in 1969. Their three children all went on to successful sporting careers. Daughter Katie played volleyball, in which she was all-state in high school then played at Auburn University, and later worked in the Rangers front office. Son Tim pitched at Texas Christian University and was selected in the 23rd round of the 1994 draft by the Kansas City Royals. He played several seasons in the minor leagues for the Royals and Arizona Diamondbacks, reaching as high as Double A. He then moved on to a scouting career, recently working for the Detroit Tigers.

Younger son Ben was drafted second overall in the 1994 draft by the Oakland A's, making him and Tom the only father-son combination to be first-round draft picks. Ben made his major-league debut in 1997. In 1998 he was the American League Rookie of the Year, and made the All-Star team. He went on to a nine-year career with Oakland, Tampa Bay, Milwaukee, and the Chicago Cubs.

Tom Grieve received numerous honors over the years. In 1985 he became one of the first three members of Pittsfield's newly formed Baseball Hall of Fame.[40] In 1987 he was inducted into the Texas Baseball Hall of Fame. In 2010 he was inducted into the Texas Rangers Hall of Fame. In 2017 he was elected to the Western Massachusetts Baseball Hall of Fame.

On Opening Day in 2016 Grieve and Rangers coach Bobby Jones threw out the first pitch, each being honored for his 50th season in professional baseball. They had become friends while playing together at Geneva in 1967, and each spent most of their careers within the Rangers organization. During that Opening Day ceremony Grieve reflected on his life in the game. "When you're little you dream of being a player and when you're a player you just assume that you'll go back to school or get a job. … You don't have the slightest idea of what you're going to do," he said. "The longer you play, the more it's what you know and do. To be able to stay in it after all this time, there's no way you could see that coming."[41]

Notes

1. Author's recollection of numerous broadcasts.
2. John Thorn, Baseball in *The Garden of Eden* (New York: Simon & Schuster, 2011), 54-55.
3. The author recalls hearing this anecdote a number of times over the years.
4. Brian Sullivan, "Pittsfield's Own Ranger," *Berkshire Eagle* (Pittsfield, Massachusetts), October 27, 2010.
5. Bob Addie, "Senators Ink Kid Slugger," *The Sporting News*, September 3, 1966: 20.
6. "Class A Leagues," *The Sporting News*, July 27, 1968: 42.
7. Merrell Whittlesey, "Swift Unser Sharpens Bunting Skill," *The Sporting News*, April 4, 1970: 11.
8. Garry Brown, "The Morning Line," *Springfield* (Massachusetts) *Union*, April 3, 1970: 36.
9. Merrell Whittlesey, "Nats Add Sunday Punch on Rick's Pinch-Homers," *The Sporting News*, July 25, 1970: 21.
10. Merrell Whittlesey, "Nats to test Maddox at Third and in Left Field," *The Sporting News*, November 28, 1970: 44.
11. Randy Galloway, "Now or Never for Grieve in Drive for Ranger berth," *The Sporting News*, March 2, 1974: 30.
12. Randy Galloway, "Grieve Wins Ranger Applause with Hot Bat in Winter League," *The Sporting News*, February 24, 1973: 50.
13. Randy Galloway, "Grieve Locking Up Ranger Picket Post," *The Sporting News*, September 1, 1973: 13.
14. Randy Galloway, "Now or never."
15. Merle Heryford, "Grieve Shows Rangers He's Ready for Steady Job," *The Sporting News*, November 1, 1975: 21.
16. Randy Galloway, "Rangers Swamped with Offers for Toby Harrah," *The Sporting News*, November 8, 1975: 51.
17. Merle Heryford, "Tom Grieve's Batting Tale – Either Red Hot or Ice Cold," *The Sporting News*, June 12, 1976: 15.
18. Ibid.
19. Ibid.
20. Randy Galloway, "Rangers Shed No Tears for Grieve," *The Sporting News*, October 9, 1976: 12.
21. The full trade. The Texas Rangers sent Grieve and a player to be named later to the New York Mets. The Atlanta Braves sent Willie Montanez to the Mets. The Rangers sent Tommy Boggs, Adrian Devine, and Eddie Miller to the Braves. The Rangers sent Bert Blyleven to the Pittsburgh Pirates. The Pirates sent Nelson Norman and Al Oliver to the Rangers. The Mets sent Jon Matlack to the Rangers. The Mets sent John Milner to the Pirates. In March the Rangers sent Ken Henderson to the Mets as the player to be named later.
22. Randy Galloway, "Kid's Name Kills Ranger Trade Talks," *The Sporting News*, February 18, 1978: 62
23. Rick Hummel, "Brock of Ages Like Reborn Redbird at Plate," *The Sporting News*, May 26, 1979: 15
24. Peter Gammons, "Owners' Feud Costs Red Sox," *The Sporting News*, June 20, 1983: 15.
25. "Klein Resigns as Rangers G.M.," *The Sporting News*, September 10, 1984: 56.
26. "A.L. West," *The Sporting News*, September 17, 1984: 16.
27. "Insiders Say," *The Sporting News*, March 21, 1988: 9.
28. Peter Gammons, "Wanted: 'Managers in Industrial Sense,'" *The Sporting News*, October 22, 1984: 20.
29. Peter Gammons, "Is Texas Just Buying More Mediocrity?," *The Sporting News*, January 14, 1985: 51.
30. Jim Reeves, "Rangers Won't Pursue Free Agents," *The Sporting News*, November 25, 1985: 53.
31. "Rangers," *The Sporting News*, December 14, 1987: 57.
32. "Rangers to Appeal Fine," *New York Times*, September 17, 1987.
33. Phil Rogers, "Texas Saga: 8 Men Out," *The Sporting News*, July 4, 1988: 16.
34. Moss Klein, "Grieve Deals Rangers the Look of a Contender," *The Sporting News*, December 19, 1988: 47.
35. Phil Rogers, "Texas-Size Deals by Rangers," *The Sporting News*, December 19, 1988: 51.

36 "Rangers," *The Sporting News*, October 9, 1989: 22.

37 Phil Rogers, "No Flag, but Texas Fans Buy the Plan," *The Sporting News*, March 12, 1990: 14.

38 T.R. Sullivan, "Texas Rangers," *The Sporting News*, September 14, 1992: 28.

39 Barry Horn, "'Mr. Ranger' Tom Grieve Still a Fixture in Rangers' TV Booth – Not Bad for a Guy 'Who Had No Idea What to Do,'" *Dallas Morning News*, sportsday.dallasnews.com/texas-rangers/rangers/2016/03/11/hot-air-mr-ranger-tom-grieve-still-fixture-rangers-tv-booth-bad-guy-idea.

40 Peter Gammons, "It's Time to Appreciate Jays' Versatility," *The Sporting News*, August 12, 1985: 21.

41 John Henry, "Rangers Journal: Tom Grieve, Bobby Jones Celebrate 50 Years in Baseball," *Fort Worth Star-Telegram*, April 4, 2016.

RICH HAND

BY RAYMOND ROSSI

Rich Hand showed a lot of promise early in his career, but he damaged his own prospects with bitterness every time he felt slighted, and that, along with arm injuries, caused his pitching career to be over by the time he was 26.

Richard Allen Hand was born on July 10, 1948, in Bellevue, Washington. He was the third of four sons of Betty (née Morse) and Leo Hand, a plumber. Always athletic, Hand dreamed of a career as a professional basketball player, although he also played baseball at Lincoln High School in Seattle. He was good enough at baseball to be selected by the Pittsburgh Pirates in the 38th round of the 1966 amateur draft, but didn't sign. "I wasn't physically prepared to play professional baseball," he later said.[1]

He chose instead to go to the University of Puget Sound, which offered him a scholarship for both baseball and basketball. While there he realized that baseball was the sport that would give him better opportunities. In the summers of 1967 and 1968 Hand went to Alaska to pitch for the semipro Alaska Goldpanners, winning state championships both seasons. In 1967 they finished tied for fourth at the National Baseball Congress tournament in Wichita, Kansas. Back in college, the New York Mets drafted him in the fifth round of the secondary draft in 1968, but again he didn't sign. "They insulted my intelligence with their offer," he said.[2]

Things got even better in 1969. Hand threw a no-hitter against Western Washington and a one-hitter against Washington State, and was named an All-American. In his three seasons in college, he was 21-6 with 216 strikeouts in 215 innings. In June he was drafted first overall in the secondary draft by the Cleveland Indians.

Drafted on June 6, 1969, Hand was quickly signed by Indians scout Loyd Christopher for a bonus of $17,000. "Christopher didn't offer me the world – but he offered me a chance and that's what I wanted most."[3] After signing the contract on June 14, Hand was assigned to the Triple-A Portland Beavers, and made his professional debut on June 15, giving up two runs in 1⅔ innings in relief. It took until July 15 before he got his first win, giving up one run in eight innings to beat Spokane. He then got going, winning four more in a row. He finished the season 7-4 with a 3.60 ERA.

In November of that year Hand married Stephanie French, but it didn't work out and they divorced in early 1972. Also that winter he continued his studies by correspondence, continuing through the spring and summer of 1970 when he gained enough credits to complete his political-science degree.

Hand's performance at Triple A in 1969 got him a spring training invitation for 1970, but he was a longshot, listed as one of eight pitchers for three open spots in the Indians' rotation. He believed in himself though: "I believe I have as good a chance as anyone to make this team. I've made every team I've tried out for."[4]

Talking about Hand and fellow pitcher Ed Farmer, manager Alvin Dark said "Each will have to make it as a starter or go back to the minors. Both have got to pitch regularly in order to develop as they should."[5] Hand was almost immediately slowed by a sore back, hurt while swinging a bat, but he soon showed his athleticism by running three miles in 21 minutes, just the second pitcher in camp to do that during the spring.

Just before camp broke, Dark announced the biggest surprise of spring training, naming Hand the third starter. "I've seen all I need to see. The kid has done everything we could possibly ask him to do and I'm convinced he can help us as a starter or a long reliever. Any experience he needs, he can get up here with us."[6]

Hand made his major-league debut on April 9, 1970, against Baltimore, taking the loss as he gave up six runs in 3⅓ innings. Switched back and forth between the rotation and bullpen, he made 25 starts and 10 relief appearances during the season. He got his first save on May 3, but had to wait until June 7 for his first win. On July 16 he got his first shutout, throwing a four-hitter to beat the Kansas City Royals, 6-0, while allowing just one runner to reach second base. On August 28 he one-hit the California Angels, with the only hit a home run to the second batter of the game, Roger Repoz.

Hand completed the 1970 season with a 6-13 record but a 3.83 ERA, leading him to be considered a good prospect for the future. Indians ace Sam McDowell, talking about the team's prospects for the coming season, said, "Rich Hand will be our third starter and I know he's going to be a lot better. Remember, he was just a rookie last summer."[7]

The following spring, Hand set lofty goals for himself, saying that in 1971 his goal was "either 20 victories, 20 saves, or a combination of victories and saves equaling 20, depending upon how I'm used."[8]

Hand failed at reaching that goal, not just in 1971, but for the rest of his career.

He was slowed in spring training by a muscle strain in his forearm, which put him on the disabled list to start the season. Once he came off he struggled, and with a 1-4 record and 4.65 ERA he was sent to Triple A in early July to get more consistent work in.

That worked out well for Hand as on August 19 he threw a no-hitter against the Tulsa Oilers. He had three walks (all to the same batter) and one error behind him, but noted that he had several instances where fielders made good plays. "This is a big thrill for me, but I had a lot of help. Naturally, I'd have preferred this in the American League," Hand said. He also said he was aware all the way of the no-hitter: "The guys on the bench were extra quiet and I tried to get them to talk it up a bit."[9]

Tulsa manager Warren Spahn said, "[H]e pitched a good game, and it looks to me as if he's a little too good for this classification," while Wichita manager Ken Aspromonte said, "This is the happiest moment in my four years of managing." His pitching coach, Clay Bryant, said, "He's an intelligent boy. He knows what he has to do and has done it by himself. He deserves the credit."[10]

Hand got a dig in at his major-league manager, saying he had been disappointed when Dark sent him to the minors. "I came here determined to prove Dark wrong, but he's gone now," referring to Dark's firing at the end of July.[11] Hand still had to wait until the end of the Wichita season – where he had gone 8-2 with a 1.88 ERA – before being recalled to Cleveland. "They just left me there to rot," he later said. By the time he was recalled, "I had thrown so much that I was really physically depleted. I didn't do too well, and that made me mad."[12]

Hand pitched in five games (four starts) in September, but an ERA of 8.10 brought his season record to 2-6, 5.79. He was disappointed and so were the Indians, who traded him to the Texas Rangers in December. Going to Texas with Hand were Roy Foster, Mike Paul, and Ken Suarez, while in return the Indians got Gary Jones, Terry Lee, Denny Riddleberger, and Del Unser. The trade was characterized as primarily Foster for Unser, although the

81

Rangers said they had held out until Hand was included in the deal.[13]

"I was real surprised about being traded and, at first, had some mixed emotions about it," Hand said. "But now I feel it's the greatest thing that ever happened in my baseball career." He looked forward to playing for Rangers manager Ted Williams, feeling that Williams must have confidence in him to trade for him. "I feel I've had the confidence in myself and my ability, but other people haven't had that confidence, or at least enough to give me every start and leave me alone when I get in there."[14]

Early in his career Hand was a fastball pitcher, but with his arm problems in 1971 he had to change. "After I had my arm trouble, I knew I couldn't overpower people. I had to work on my control, on just getting the ball over, in order to get people out. So I came up with better control than I had ever had and even after my arm came back, I still had it."[15] He later claimed that the changeup was his most effective pitch, and it helped his fastball too. "With the changeup, the hitter has something else to worry about," he said.[16]

After an average spring in 1972, Hand was disappointed once more to be sent to the Rangers' Triple-A team, the Denver Bears. "Nothing in baseball ever has surprised me more," he said. "Bitter? yes, I think that's a fair appraisal. I didn't have a great spring, I know that, but then who did on our staff?"[17]

He got two starts in Denver (1-1, 3.46) before being recalled at the beginning of May when Don Stanhouse went on the disabled list. Apart from two relief appearances in late May, Hand spent the whole season in the rotation. He pitched well, ending with a 3.32 ERA, although his 10-14 record showed more about the terrible team he was on, which he led in wins. In fact, the Rangers did not score a single run in support of him during the first 23⅓ innings Hand was on the mound. Talking about that run support toward the end of the season, Williams said, "Look at Hand. He could be a 15-game winner right now with no effort at all."[18]

Although respectful of Williams, Hand was not intimidated by him. When Williams once told him, "I hate pitchers," Hand replied, "'Ted, I've heard that all year, and I've never met a manager I liked.' He thought that was hilarious."[19]

Hand admitted that he had trouble when he first came back up to the major leagues. "When I returned, I went out there pitching scared. I was worried about doing good and staying up here." But he changed his attitude, and that's when success returned. "I just said to hell with it. … I just started pitching … reaching back, letting it fly and putting things out of my mind, like going back to Denver."[20]

During 1972, things changed for Hand personally, too. His first marriage ended at the start of the year, and in September he married Terrie Molnar, a schoolteacher he had met while in Cleveland. Several of his teammates and their wives attended, including Mike Paul, with whom he'd been traded from Cleveland, as best man. Over the next few years the couple had a son and a daughter together.

The 1973 season started slowly for Hand; he was 2-3 with a 5.40 ERA on May 20. On that day he was traded to the California Angels, along with first baseman Mike Epstein and catcher Rick Stelmaszek, for first baseman Jim Spencer and pitcher Lloyd Allen. Once again Hand was upset with being traded. "I couldn't have been happier where I was. It's not the greatest team right now, but it's headed in the right direction. I wanted to grow with this team and I hate to leave Arlington. That's a fine place to live."[21]

Used by the Angels mostly as a long reliever, Hand pitched decently, although he spent more time on the disabled list with arm problems. He returned, though, and in four starts at the end of the season he was 2-1 with a 2.77 ERA. On September 26 Hand started and had a 4-3 lead after seven innings. Going out for the eighth, he pitched to one batter, Jeff Burroughs, who homered to tie the game. That ended up being Hand's final batter faced in the major leagues.

His performance in September led to the thought that he might make the rotation in 1974, but once again, at the end of spring training Hand was sent to Triple-A Salt Lake City. He considered not reporting, but did, and struggled through the season with Salt Lake, also spending the last couple of months on option to Pawtucket in the Boston Red Sox farm system.

After a forgettable season, in October Hand was sent to the St. Louis Cardinals organization as the player to be named later, completing a September deal which had brought Orlando Pena to the Angels.

As 1975 arrived, Hand decided he had had enough of baseball. His arm hurt and he was tired of the minor leagues. He decided not to report to the Cardinals, and although there were teams interested in him – Oakland reportedly offered him a contract – he chose instead to retire from baseball. "I probably exited the game too soon, but I had a lot of pain. … I still had some years left."[22]

Home, now, was Arlington, Texas, which Hand had called a fine place to live when he was traded from the Rangers to the Angels in 1973. As of 2018 Hand had made the Dallas-Fort Worth area his home since he retired from playing.

Hand had begun working in business while still playing baseball, and now his efforts expanded. He became involved in real estate, owning construction companies, and partnering in real-estate ventures around North Texas, and as a managing director in an asset-management company.

His marriage to Terrie had ended, and in 1987 he married Susan Hardin. Over the next decade the couple had four daughters, all of whom were athletically successful. With Hand involved as a parent and coach, the children performed on select basketball teams, won various championships across the country, and all went to college on basketball scholarships. His daughter Whitney was a star player at Oklahoma and was drafted by the WNBA, but decided not to go pro because of several knee injuries. She married Oklahoma quarterback Landry Jones, who went on to play in the NFL with the Pittsburgh Steelers.

As of 2018 Hand remained involved with baseball. He has been a board member of the Major League Baseball Players Alumni Association for many years, and appeared several times a year at Rangers functions on behalf of the team.

Sources

In addition to the sources cited in the Notes, the author consulted Baseball-Reference.com.

The author gratefully acknowledges the assistance of Steve West in completing this article.

Notes

1. Russell Schneider, "Dark Counts on Right Hand for No. 3 Hill Job," *The Sporting News*, April 18, 1970: 23.
2. Ibid. Players who had previously been drafted but not signed were not eligible for the regular phase of future drafts. Instead they were included in a secondary phase, which took place after the regular draft. This system lasted through 1986, when all players were consolidated into a single draft.
3. Ibid.
4. Ibid.
5. Russell Schneider, "Indians Turn 'Camp Cheerful' Into 'Iwo Jima' for Pitchers," *The Sporting News*, March 7, 1970: 20.
6. Russell Schneider, "Dark Counts."
7. Russell Schneider, "Mound Award Excites and Delights Sudden Sam," *The Sporting News*, November 14, 1970: 58.
8. Russell Schneider, "Brown Trying Sims' System on Dark," *The Sporting News*, February 20, 1971: 37.
9. John Ferguson, "AA's Second No-Hitter: Hand Chokes Off Tulsa," *The Sporting News*, September 4, 1971: 35.
10. Ibid.
11. Ibid.
12. Randy Galloway, "Young Hurler Hand Rated Rangers' Prize Catch," *The Sporting News*, December 25, 1971: 38.
13. Merle Heryford, "Rangers Size Up Foster as Home-Run Threat," *The Sporting News*, December 18, 1971: 47.
14. Randy Galloway, "Young Hurler Hand."
15. Ibid.
16. Randy Galloway, "Ranger Rich Gets His Men with Tight-Hand Policy," *The Sporting News*, July 8, 1972: 18.

17 Ibid.
18 Merle Heryford, "Rangers Lasso Wins with Castoff Hurlers," *The Sporting News*, September 9, 1972: 21.
19 Dan Raley, "Where Are They Now: Rich Hand, Former Lincoln High, UPS Standout," *Seattle Post-Intelligencer*, seattlepi.com/sports/baseball/article/Where-Are-They-Now-Rich-Hand-fomer-Lincoln-1247298.php#photo-677682, retrieved January 31, 2018.
20 Randy Galloway, "Ranger Rich."
21 Randy Galloway, "Epstein Knapsack Full of Kind Feelings," *The Sporting News*, June 9, 1973: 20.
22 Dan Raley, "Where Are They Now."

TOBY HARRAH

BY FREDERICK C. BUSH

Who was the last player to bat for the Washington Senators in the franchise's final game and also the last active player from that team? Who played both complete games of a doubleheader at shortstop without handling a single chance? Who became one-half of the first set of American League teammates – and only the second duo in major-league history – to hit back-to-back inside-the-park home runs? Who was one of the three players who combined to hit a major-league-record three grand slams in one game? The answer to all of these questions is Toby Harrah, a former infielder for the Senators/Texas Rangers, Cleveland Indians, and New York Yankees.

In addition to being in the right place at odd times, Harrah also developed a reputation as a practical joker over the course of his career. He once sneaked up behind Rangers teammate and future Hall of Famer Gaylord Perry and sprinkled itching powder on his neck and shoulders between innings. Outfielder Tom Grieve recalled, "So when Gaylord goes back out to the mound, he's going through all these fake spitball maneuvers that he does and he's itching the back of his head uncontrollably while he's out on the mound. And everybody was just dying laughing at it."[1] On another occasion, Harrah used a razor blade to cut several of the stitches in the seat of first baseman Mike Hargrove's pants, so that they split as he was boarding the team bus. On this occasion, the hilarity ended abruptly as Harrah had to confess his misdeed when Hargrove was prepared to punch out an innocent teammate whom he suspected of pulling the prank.[2]

It would be wrong, however, to consider Harrah – whose surname is arguably the best-known palindrome in baseball history – to be little more than a walking trivia answer and merry prankster. He is also, according to sabermetrician Jay Jaffe's WAR Score system (JAWS), the 25th best third baseman in major-league history as of 2016.[3] Although Harrah has not received as much recognition as might be expected from a top-25 ranking, he is appreciated in Arlington, Texas, and Cleveland, the locales where he spent the majority of his career.

Toby Harrah, one of nine children born to Burton and Glenna Harrah, entered the world on October 26, 1948, in Sissonville, West Virginia. Harrah's given name is Colbert Dale, but he explained, "My grandmother didn't like it and nicknamed me Toby, and I've been Toby ever since."[4] Burton Harrah had begun working in West Virginia's coal mines at the age of 12, but he moved his family to La Rue, Ohio, about 140 miles southwest of Cleveland, where he found work in the nearby industrial town of Marion. According to Toby, La Rue "was so small the phone book only had one Yellow Page."[5]

Harrah lettered in four sports – baseball, basketball, football, and track – at Marion's Elgin High School, and he soon gained the attention of major-league scouts for his play at second base. In spite of the interest in Harrah, he was not signed upon graduation because he had been offered a football scholarship to Ohio Northern University and the scouts all assumed that he would play college ball.[6] Scout extraordinaire Tony Lucadello checked in on Harrah in the late fall and, when he found out that Harrah was not attending college, signed him to the Philadelphia Phillies on December 27, 1966.[7] Harrah was uncertain about his desire to play baseball, saying, "My high-school coach told me, 'Go down there [spring training] and give it all you've got for one month and, if after that you want to come home, come home.'"[8] Harrah went, and his first spring training led to a 17-year career in the major leagues.

Harrah spent the 1967 season with the Class-A (short-season) Huron Phillies of the Northern League, where he played primarily at second base but also saw some time at shortstop. He batted only .256 but had a .394 on-base percentage thanks to a high rate of bases on balls. The good eye that Harrah demonstrated at the plate as an 18-year-old would remain one of his greatest assets, resulting in 1,153 walks over the course of his major-league career and only 868 strikeouts. The Washington Senators saw enough potential in Harrah that they snatched him away from the Phillies in the minor-league draft on November 28, 1967.

The Senators intended Harrah to be their shortstop of the future, and that is where he started 132 of the 135 games in which he played for Class-A Burlington in the Carolina League in 1968. In 1969, he batted .306 in 46 games for Burlington, advanced to Double-A Savannah, and had an eight-game cup of coffee with the Senators.

After one more year in the minors with the Double-A Pittsfield Senators in 1970, Harrah became Washington's starting shortstop in 1971 at the youthful age of 22. Ted Williams was the Senators' manager. He had a reputation for not wanting to have rookie players on his team, and Harrah knew he faced a challenge, saying, "I know I must show a lot of improvement, but I think I can do it."[9]

On April 5, 1971, the Senators opened their season at home with an 8-0 victory over the Oakland Athletics. Harrah, who according to Williams was "in there as tight as a drum," batted in the leadoff spot and finished 2-for-4 with a walk and two runs scored.[10] It was a great season opener for both the Senators and for Harrah, whose father, Burton, and fiancée Pamela Mohr were both in attendance. After the game, Williams asserted, "We will go as far as our young shortstop takes us."[11]

On April 7, a mere two days after Harrah's Opening Day exploits, Harrah and Pam were married. They had two children together, son Toby in 1974 and daughter Haley in 1978, but their marriage ended in divorce in September 1979.

Williams placed a great burden on Harrah since the 1971 Senators team was as woeful as the previous 10 squads of this second Washington franchise had been. They finished 63-96 and avoided last place in the American League East only because of the Cleveland Indians' 60-102 mark. Years after his career ended, Harrah credited Williams for aiding his development as a player, asserting, "Well, he was the best hitter I ever saw in my life, and he made me a better hitter."[12] The results of Williams' teaching were not immediately evident, however, as Harrah batted .230 in 1971. He had yet to flash the combination of power and speed for which he would become known as the decade progressed.

Harrah spent only one season in Washington. Senators owner Bob Short packed up his franchise and moved it to Arlington, Texas, a city between Dallas and Fort Worth, in time for the 1972 season with the team renamed the Rangers. Perhaps the most noteworthy moment of Harrah's short tenure in the nation's capital occurred on September 30, 1971, at Washington's Robert F. Kennedy Stadium, in the season's final game. The Senators had already scored two runs in the bottom of the eighth inning to take a 7-5 lead against the New York Yankees before Harrah came to bat with two outs and teammate Tommy McCraw on first base. McCraw was thrown out at second on a steal attempt, which resulted in the first of several oddities in Harrah's career: Though he was the Senators' last batter, Harrah did not receive credit for an at-bat or even a plate appearance.

Washington fans were unhappy that the franchise was leaving and, with two outs in the top of the ninth, they decided to give Short and his team what they considered to be a fitting sendoff. They stormed the field in such numbers and began to vandalize it with such force that, in order to ensure the players' safety, the umpires declared the game a forfeit to the visiting Yankees so that both teams could exit the field quickly. After the fans had helped the Senators snatch one final defeat from the jaws of victory, it was off to Texas for Harrah and the rest of the team.

A new city and a new name did not lead to an improvement in the standings for the same old cast of characters. The 1972 Texas Rangers stumbled to a 54-100 record and a last-place finish in the AL West under Williams, in the first major-league season ever to be shortened by labor unrest between the players and owners. Though the team floundered, Harrah's play improved, and he was chosen as an AL All-Star Game reserve at shortstop. He missed out on his chance to play in the July 25 midsummer classic because of a shoulder injury he suffered in a game against the Indians shortly before the game. The injury limited Harrah to 116 games in what might otherwise have become his breakout season, but he still finished with a .259 batting average, 29 points higher than he had hit the previous year.

Williams, unhappy with the Texas heat and the Rangers' losing brand of baseball, retired after the 1972 season, and Whitey Herzog became the new manager. Herzog did not inherit a talented roster – Harrah and outfielder Jeff Burroughs were the only players he thought had All-Star futures – and the Rangers actually fared worse in 1973, finishing in last place again with a 57-105 record.[13]

Harrah made great strides after playing winter ball in Venezuela for the second consecutive year to hone his defensive skills, which had been his shortcoming. He credited his Zulia (Venezuela) Eagles teammate Cookie Rojas (the Kansas City Royals' second baseman) for helping to bring about vast improvement in his glove work. Rangers catcher Rich Billings, who had managed the Zulia squad, enthused, "He was just sensational down there. Toby might be developing into the best shortstop in the American League. I've never seen anyone improve as much as he has."[14]

While Harrah was being lauded for the strides he had made on defense, he started slowly with the bat in 1973. Then, on June 23 against the Royals in Kansas City, he caught fire against lefty Paul Splittorff. Harrah was 3-for-3, including a double and a home run, and walked twice. His homer tied the game at 4-4 in the top of the ninth inning and chased Splittorff from the game. The Rangers took a 7-4 lead, but the Royals stormed back in the bottom of the ninth to win the game, 8-7.

One great game normally does not make or break a player's season; however, in this case it did, though it was not the kind of break Harrah would have liked. The next time he faced Splittorff – in Arlington on July 1 – the pitcher intended to send a message to Harrah that he would not be embarrassed again. Splittorff aimed a fastball at Harrah's chin, which resulted in a break in the left hand that he raised to protect himself. It was Harrah's second consecutive season to be interrupted by an injury, but he handled it in stride and quipped, "Better a broken hand than a broken face."[15] Harrah finished 1973 with a .260 batting average, 10 home runs, and 50 RBIs.

Herzog did not finish the season as the Rangers' manager. He was fired after a 14-0 loss to the Chicago White Sox on September 4 left the Rangers with a 47-91 record. The Rangers fell under the managerial leadership of Billy Martin, who was already building a résumé that was composed of equal parts fame and infamy. Harrah, who lauded Williams as the best hitter he had ever seen, was equally effusive in his praise for Martin, avowing, "He was the best manager I ever played for, because he made baseball fun."[16] In Texas, as was the case in most of Martin's other managerial stops, that was true for all of one season.

In 1974, the Rangers had a new owner in Brad Corbett, a full season of new manager Billy Martin, and a suddenly competitive team that was aptly dubbed "The Turnaround Gang" in the team's preseason media publication.[17] Martin worked his momentary magic, and the Rangers pushed the two-time defending champion Oakland Athletics for the majority of the season and posted an 84-76 record, but they had to settle for finishing in second place, five games behind the A's.

Stars were born, or reborn, across the Rangers' roster. Future Hall of Famer Fergie Jenkins, who had been acquired in a trade with the Chicago Cubs in October 1973, won 25 games and the AL Comeback Player of the Year Award. Jeff Burroughs batted .301 with 25 home runs and 118 RBIs to earn the AL Most Valuable Player Award. Mike Hargrove finished the season with a .323 batting average and 66 RBIs to win the AL Rookie of the Year Award.

As for Harrah, he played in every game in 1974 and again batted .260 while more than doubling his home-run total to 21 and driving in 74 runs. Harrah's increased offensive output was a welcome improvement that did not go unnoticed. Prior to the 1975 season, one Dallas reporter wrote:

> The old Toby Harrah used to choke way up on his bat and slash singles all over the outfield; when former owner Bob Short used to pronounce his last name "hurrah," Toby, the singles hitter, just cringed and went along. The new Toby Harrah hits home runs and the park announcer rolls out the last name just the way Toby likes it.[18]

Harrah attributed his newfound power to a change in his approach at the plate in which he opened up his stance to become more of a pull hitter. He explained, "I got to thinking [that] if I'm only going to hit .260 or so, I might as well hit with more power. So now I have confidence in myself as an extra-base hitter."[19] He also credited encouragement from Martin, explaining, "Billy felt I could be a home-run hitter for him and he urged me to be aggressive at the plate and take my best cut every time."[20]

The Rangers looked primed to field a competitive team filled with All-Stars for years to come. However, as was ever the case with Martin, his petulance and controversial persona affected his team and ended in his dismissal. Harrah defended Martin, claiming:

> He loved the turmoil, he liked the chaos. That was just the way it was with Billy. He kept things stirred up all the time, which kept the attention off of us. That made it a lot easier to play, because there was enough pressure on us young players as it was.[21]

Owner Brad Corbett, on the other hand, did not appreciate the bedlam that surrounded his team in 1975, and he fired Martin after 95 games; at the time, the Rangers were 44-51 and were mired in fourth place in the AL West, 15½ games behind the A's. Third-base coach Frank Lucchesi became the new manager and guided the Rangers to a 35-32 record the rest of the way.

The only Rangers player to improve his performance in 1975 was Harrah, who finally had his breakout season. He batted .293 with 20 homers and 93 RBIs, scored 81 runs, stole 23 bases, and drew 98 walks. He was selected as an All-Star Game reserve for the second time, though he was not inserted into the game by AL manager Alvin Dark of the Oakland A's, and he finished 15th in the AL MVP vote after the season.

Prior to 1976, Harrah signed a three-year escalated contract that would pay him $100,000 for the first year, making him and the Phillies' Larry Bowa the only two shortstops to be paid six-figure salaries.[22] In addition to the new contract, Harrah was inserted into a new place in the batting order. Lucchesi often used Harrah in the cleanup spot, which made him an anomaly in the 1970s when weak-hitting shortstops like the Baltimore Orioles' Mark Belanger and the Detroit Tigers' Tom Veryzer were the norm in the AL.[23]

On June 25, Harrah constituted a one-man wrecking crew in a doubleheader against the White Sox in Arlington. In the first game, an 8-4 Rangers' victory, he went 3-for-5 with a home run and five RBIs. He followed that with a 3-for-3 performance that included another homer, three RBIs, and two walks in a 14-9 loss in the nightcap. Harrah may have been fresh and aggressive at the plate due to the fact that he was completely inactive in the field. Incredibly, although he played all nine innings of both games at shortstop, he did not get a single fielding chance. Though Harrah had not had the opportunity to demonstrate any fielding prowess in the doubleheader, his stellar play was noticed around the league. He was voted the AL's starting shortstop in the 1976 All-Star Game; as a starter, he finally got to play in the actual game, though he went 0-for-2 at the plate.

In spite of the All-Star honor, Harrah's offensive numbers were down slightly in 1976 as he finished with a .260 batting average, 15 homers, and 67 RBIs. As a team, the Rangers struggled to a 76-86 record and a fourth-place finish. In November, Texas signed free-agent shortstop Bert Campaneris away from the Oakland A's and informed Harrah that he was being moved to third base for the 1977 season. Harrah had resisted previous attempts to turn him into a third baseman, but this time he agreed to the switch, saying, "My move to third strengthened us in two infield positions – there and at shortstop – so obviously it has to be the right move."[24]

Whether or not Harrah truly believed the clichéd "it's what's best for the team" line applied to his move to third base, it actually held true this time. In spite of the fact that the 1977 Rangers went through a major-league record four managers during the season, they finished 94-68, which was the best record in franchise history to that point.[25] Their fine season went for naught, however, as they had the misfortune of being in the same division as the Kansas City Royals, who won the AL West with a 102-60 record. In the pre-wild-card era, there was no playoff opportunity for the Rangers.

Harrah, while manning the hot corner, put up the best all-around offensive numbers of his career. His batting average was still in the .260s – .263, to be exact – but he hit 25 doubles and 27 home runs, drew an AL-leading 109 bases on balls, stole 27 bases in 32 attempts, and scored 90 runs. Harrah's numbers were All-Star-worthy, but he was bypassed for the AL team as he was now playing the same position as stalwarts like the Royals' George Brett and the Yankees' Graig Nettles.[26] Though Harrah did not get to participate in the All-Star Game, he did take part in yet another odd moment that made baseball history. On August 27, in an 8-2 victory at New York, Harrah and second baseman Bump Wills hit back-to-back inside-the-park home runs against Yankees reliever Ken Clay in the seventh inning. It was the first time the feat had been accomplished in the AL and only the second time it had happened in major-league history.[27]

Though Harrah had reason to dislike Kansas City, what with the Royals winning the division and Brett being voted the AL's All-Star third baseman, it was there that he met the woman who became his second wife, Janet Beane. In 1978, while visiting Kansas City, Jan met a man who claimed to be Toby Harrah of the Texas Rangers, but she was unimpressed. One night after the encounter, Jan and her friends saw some Rangers players at a local watering hole. She told one of the players, "I met your third baseman last night," only to be informed that the Rangers had not yet arrived in Kansas City on the previous evening.[28] Jan was then introduced to the genuine Toby Harrah; they struck up a romance and were married a year and a half later.

In addition to meeting Jan, Harrah soon experienced another life-changing event, a trade. The Rangers had finished 87-75 in 1978, which had left them in a second-place tie with the California Angels, five games behind the division champion Royals. Not only was the season's outcome disappointing, but Harrah's batting average had dipped to .229 with 12 homers and 59 RBIs. Under Corbett's ownership, the Rangers teams of the late 1970s and early 1980s seemed to have a revolving-door policy, and they often made baffling trades in which they simply swapped one star for another without any clear plan for improvement. The four-team trade that had sent pitcher Bert Blyleven to Pittsburgh in exchange for outfielder Al Oliver on December 8, 1977, had been a prime example of one such transaction. One year later to the day, Texas sent Harrah – the last holdover from the inaugural Rangers team – to the Cleveland Indians in exchange for third baseman Buddy Bell. The two players were similar in many ways, though Bell was considered to be the better defensive third baseman.

The trade to Cleveland was a homecoming for Harrah. He recalled listening to Indians games on the radio as a child and believed the trade to be a dream that had come true. Harrah was happy that his family and old friends could now make regular trips to Cleveland to see him play. He also supposed, "And Buddy Bell was a pretty good player, so I must have been not that bad myself to get traded for Buddy Bell."[29]

Harrah's dream did not quite turn into a nightmare, but the specter of Bell loomed over him during his time with the Indians as the Cleveland fans and media misdirected their animosity over the popular Bell's departure toward him. Harrah has said, "I always felt that during my career in Cleveland, I was a much more complete player than I was in Texas."[30] A comparison of Harrah's numbers in Texas versus Cleveland confirms his belief, but it took four full seasons for him to be accepted as the player who replaced Bell.

The change of scenery did not result in a change in the standings for Harrah. In fact, the Indians were reminiscent of the early-1970s Rangers teams on which he had played and dwelt in the cellar of the AL East. In the five years Harrah spent in Cleveland, the Indians finished in sixth place four times and seventh place once.

In 1979, Harrah started slowly but recovered to finish the season with a .279 batting average, 20 homers, and 77 RBIs. He also stole 20 bases, making him and teammate Bobby Bonds (25 homers/34 steals) the first 20-homer/20-steal players in the Indians' history. Cleveland finished 81-80 that season; however, in the tough AL East that was only good enough for sixth place, 22 games behind the first-place Orioles.

Toward the end of Harrah's first season in Cleveland, his divorce from Pam became final. He married Jan Beane on October 27, 1979, and she became a beacon of emotional stability for him amid the turmoil of his time in Cleveland. Though Toby and Jan were happy together, the transition in Harrah's personal life created greater turmoil than any criticism he received at the hands of unhappy Clevelanders. Harrah gave evidence of Pam's ongoing enmity toward him when, while discussing Jan in May 1982, he told a reporter, "That's J-a-n. Don't confuse her with Pam, my first wife, or Pam might sue me. She's already sued me for everything else I have."[31]

In 1980, the Indians again finished in sixth place with a 79-81 record. Harrah hit .267, with 11 home runs and 72 RBIs, and scored 100 runs. He also played alongside his second AL Rookie of the Year teammate, "Super Joe" Charboneau, who became a sensation in Cleveland that year. Harrah has asserted that Charboneau is the most memorable of his Indians' teammates:

> He made baseball fun. ... He brought some interest to the Cleveland Indians, which they didn't really have at that time. There were a lot of good ballplayers, but nobody really had that personality – somebody who was different, and was good, like Joe Charboneau.[32]

Even Charboneau could not turn the Indians' fortunes around, though; his star burned out after only one season due to back injuries he could not overcome.

The Indians again hovered around .500 in the strike-shortened 1981 season, once more finishing in sixth place with a 52-51 record. Harrah's batting average climbed to .291, but he hit only five home runs in 361 at-bats. The power outage was a result of injuries he had suffered when he fell off a ladder while painting his Fort Worth-area house on – this would be too odd to be believable with anyone else

– Friday, February 13, 1981. Harrah injured his wrists, kneecaps, and elbows and, though the players' strike gave him some time to recuperate, he had not fully regained his strength when the season resumed.[33]

The injuries Harrah suffered in 1981 set the stage for a fantastic 1982 season. Harrah said of the turnaround, "After the season ended I tried to build myself up by swinging the lead bat – Ted Williams has always been real big on swinging the lead bat – and I started working out on the Nautilus a little. And I got stronger than I'd ever been."[34] The 1982 season got off to a tense start, however, as Harrah finally had enough of the Cleveland media's lingering love for the departed Bell. As fate and the major-league baseball schedule had it, the Indians opened the season with a two-game series against the Rangers. Harrah homered in the opener, but Bell homered twice in the Rangers' 8-3 victory, and the Cleveland media focused on their former third baseman's exploits. After Harrah went 3-for-4 with four RBIs in the Indians' 13-1 clobbering of Texas the next day, Harrah groused to the press, "Buddy would have had six RBIs."[35]

Cleveland finished in sixth place for the fifth consecutive year, posting a 78-84 record in 1982. The team's poor performance was by no means a reflection of Harrah's efforts, though. Strengthened by his new offseason exercise regimen, Harrah played in all 162 games and batted a career-high .304 with 25 homers, 78 RBIs, and 100 runs scored. He earned the final All-Star berth of his career as he and Bell were picked to back up George Brett at third base for the AL. Though it seemed that Harrah could never escape Bell's presence, his fantastic 1982 season finally won over the Cleveland faithful.

After the 1982 season, on October 4, Harrah had surgery to correct a heart murmur as a preventive measure to avoid infections that his condition could have caused.[36] He emphasized the fact that the surgery was a minor procedure – it was not open-heart surgery – but he could not know that he had two greater trials in store for him. On February 19, 1983, a fire did more than $100,000 damage to his home and forced his family to live in a hotel for four months. The next day, Harrah had to sign autographs at a baseball card show in Dallas. When he returned to his hotel room, he received word that his father had been killed in a car accident earlier in the day. Jan Harrah described the shock of the dual tragedies: "Because of the fire, Toby did not have enough clothes or a suitcase to take to Marion. We had to go out and buy those things. After it happened, we were so busy that I don't think there was time for it to sink in."[37]

In addition to the off-the-field hardships, Harrah missed a month of the season when he suffered the second broken hand of his career – courtesy of an errant pitch from the Orioles' Dennis Martinez – in an early-April game. All of these factors contributed to a decline in Harrah's performance – his batting line fell to .266-9-53 – and the team's fortunes fell even further as the Tribe finished 1983 in seventh place with a 70-92 ledger.

Harrah's time in Cleveland came to an end when he agreed to waive his no-trade clause and was dealt to the Yankees on February 5, 1984. The Yankees had posted a 91-71 record in 1983, so Harrah and his new team both had playoff aspirations. He soon found out that he would not be a full-time starter for the Yankees, though, as he and Roy Smalley formed a platoon at third base. Harrah has said, "… [E]verybody should play for the Yankees for one year, because they have a great tradition," but he seemed unhappy during his time in New York and his play reflected his frame of mind.[38] He batted only .217-1-26 in 88 games in 1984 while the Bronx Bombers' record dropped to 87-75, which resulted in a third-place finish in the AL East. After one lost season in the Big Apple, the Yankees traded Harrah back to the Rangers on February 27, 1985.

Texas fans were happy to see Harrah return, though they most likely thought that he would fulfill a backup role or be part of a platoon as he had been with the Yankees. In a surprise move, Harrah became the Rangers' starting second baseman in 1985 and showed that, even at age 36, he still had one good season left in his tank. In 126 games, he batted .270-9-44 and drew a career-high 113 bases on balls; if sabermetrics had been around in 1985, Harrah's .432

on-base percentage would have made him a highly prized commodity. Once again, however, his best efforts were to no avail as the Rangers finished in the basement of the AL West with a 62-99 record.

Harrah returned in 1986, but Father Time finally caught up to him. He batted only .218-7-41 for a much-improved Rangers team that finished 87-75 and moved up five spots to second place, five games behind the Angels. In his final season, Harrah became part of yet one more historic moment. On August 6, in a 13-11 victory over the Orioles in Baltimore, Harrah went 5-for-5 with a double, a grand slam, and four RBIs. Harrah's homer came in the second inning, and Baltimore teammates Larry Sheets and Jim Dwyer both hit slams in the fourth inning to set a record for most grand slams hit in a major-league game.[39] It was the last hurrah for Harrah as a player.

During his 17-year career, Harrah never once got to participate in the playoffs. Nonetheless, he looked back on his career and said, "There are no regrets at all, man. ... That's [playoffs] just kind of icing on the cake. Just to get a bite of the cake. ... I was pretty happy just with that."[40]

Although Harrah's playing days were over, baseball continued to be his profession. In 1987, he was named the manager of the Oklahoma City 89ers, the Rangers' Triple-A affiliate. Two years later, he became the Rangers' first-base coach under Bobby Valentine, who had been his last manager as a player. The 1992 season brought new changes to Harrah's job status: he moved from first-base coach to bench coach and then became the Rangers' manager after Valentine was fired with 76 games left in the season. The Rangers went 32-44 under Harrah and finished in fourth place with a 77-85 record. Kevin Kennedy replaced him as the Rangers' manager in 1993.

After a two-year hiatus, Harrah rejoined the managerial ranks with the Triple-A Norfolk Tides, a New York Mets affiliate. He guided the Tides to an 86-56 record and a first-place finish in the International League's West Division, for which he was named the league's Manager of the Year for 1995. In 1996, Harrah became Cleveland's third-base coach under his old Rangers and Indians teammate Mike Hargrove, where he replaced Buddy Bell, who had been named the Detroit Tigers manager. This time around, Harrah suffered no backlash from Clevelanders for stepping into a position that Bell had manned.

Harrah spent the next 17 years plying his trade in various coaching capacities for numerous organizations, including the Detroit Tigers, Cincinnati Reds, Colorado Rockies (where he served as the bench coach from 2000-02 for manager Buddy Bell), and the independent Fort Worth Cats. His last position was as an assistant hitting coach with the Detroit Tigers from June 2012 through the end of the 2013 season. When Tigers manager Jim Leyland retired after 2013, Harrah learned that his contract would not be renewed because new manager Brad Ausmus was hand-picking his coaching staff.

Harrah is often underrated as a player, but he has received numerous honors, especially in Texas. He was inducted into the Texas Baseball Hall of Fame in 1988 and into the Texas Rangers' Hall of Fame in 2009; he was also named the 13th-best player in Rangers history in 2011 and the 41st-best player in Indians history in 2013. Additionally, a 2006 book published by Baseball Prospectus determined that Harrah was the second-best clutch hitter in the major leagues – behind only Mark Grace – from the period spanning 1972 to 2005.[41]

Harrah expressed his love for the game of baseball in a 2009 interview, saying, "Baseball is a great game, man. I mean, we all have that little-bitty kid in us and it never leaves. I'm 60 years old and that little-bitty kid is still there. If I could start all over and do it again, I would."[42] As of 2015, Toby and Jan lived in Azle, Texas, northwest of Fort Worth; they have two grown children, daughter Katie and son Thomas. Jan owned the Heirloom and Antique Shop in Azle, which she and Toby ran together. According to Harrah, small-town life suits him, and he enjoyed working in the antique shop, saying, "You never know what treasure is going to come through the door. Like baseball, it makes life fun and exciting."[43]

Sources

In addition to the sources provided in the Notes, the author also consulted the following:

Crowe, Ryan. "21 Best Rangers Ever: Toby Harrah," dfw.cbslocal.com/2011/07/01/21-best-rangers-ever-toby-harrah/, accessed June 14, 2016.

Lukeheart, Jason. "Top 100 Indians: #41 Toby Harrah," letsgotribe.com/2013/8/1/4548584/top-100-indians-41-toby-harrah, accessed June 14, 2016.

Markusen, Bruce. "Let Go by the Tigers, Toby Harrah Deserved Better," detroitathletic.com/blog/2013/12/03/let-go-by-the-tigers-toby-harrah-deserved-better/, accessed June 14, 2016.

State of Texas Vital Records.

Notes

1. SportsDayDFW.com, "Rangers Announcer Tom Grieve Recalls Toby Harrah's Itching-Powder Prank on Gaylord Perry: 'Everybody on the Bench Is Just Dying Laughing,'" sportsday.dallasnews.com/texas-rangers/rangersheadlines/2013/06/01/rangers-announcer-tom-grieve-recalls-toby-harrah-s-itching-powder-prank-on-gaylord-perry-everybody-on-the-bench-is-just-dying-laughing, accessed June 14, 2016.

2. John Woestendiek, "Last Men Out: Thirty-Four Years Later, Baseball and the Final Senators Game Still Resonate in the Lives of the Men In Washington's Last Lineup," articles.baltimoresun.com/2005-04-03/entertainment/0504020017_1_elliott-maddox-life-after-baseball-washington-senators/2, accessed June 14, 2016.

3. Jay Jaffe's WAR Score system (JAWS) is used to compare a player against other players at his position who are Hall of Famers. As of August 2016, Harrah was ranked 25th among all third basemen in major-league history; however, he could move higher or lower in the future, depending upon where currently-active third basemen are ranked after their playing careers have ended. For an explanation of how JAWS is measured, see baseball-reference.com/about/jaws.shtml. To view the current JAWS ranking for third basemen, see baseball-reference.com/leaders/jaws_3B.shtml.

4. Bruce Anderson, "Not Enough Hurrahs For Harrah: Toby Harrah Has Got Good Wood and Bad on the Ball, but Few Cheers in Cleveland," .si.com/vault/1982/05/17/624073/not-enough-hurrahs-for-harrah, accessed July 28, 2016.

5. Joe Stroop, "The Other Third Baseman – Toby Harrah,", shutdowninning.com/the-other-third-baseman-toby-harrah/, accessed June 14, 2016. La Rue, Ohio has not grown since Harrah's youth. The 2010 US Census determined the population of La Rue village to be approximately 747; see factfinder.census.gov/faces/tableservices/jsf/pages/productview.xhtml?src=bkmk.

6. David L. Porter, ed., Biographical Dictionary of American Sports: Baseball, G-P, revised and expanded edition (Westport, Connecticut: Greenwood Press, 2000), 630.

7. Tony Lucadello (1912-1989) signed 50 players who eventually graduated to the major leagues, including Hall of Famers Fergie Jenkins and Mike Schmidt, 1974 NL Cy Young Award winner Mike Marshall, and 1970 AL batting champion Alex Johnson. On May 8, 1989, Lucadello committed suicide. There was speculation that he was distraught at the prospect of losing his job, but both Lucadello's widow, Virginia, and the Phillies' organization denied that he was in any such danger (See Articles.Philly.Com/1989-05-15/Sports/26111032_1_Scout-Police-Car-Tony-Lucadello).

8. Anderson, "Not Enough Hurrahs for Harrah."

9. Merrell Whittlesey, "Long-Shot Harrah Pays Off in Nats' Shortstop Gamble," The Sporting News, April 3, 1971: 35.

10. Merrell Whittlesey, "Nats' Harrah Hears Cheers in Capital Debut," The Sporting News, April 17, 1971: 5.

11. Ibid.

12. David Laurila, "Prospectus Q&A: Toby Harrah, Part 2," baseballprospectus.com/article.php?articleid=8912, accessed July 28, 2016.

13. Mike Shropshire, Seasons in Hell with Billy Martin, Whitey Herzog and "The Worst Baseball Team in History" – The 1973-1975 Texas Rangers (New York: Donald I. Fine Books, 1996), 21.

14. Randy Galloway, "Tip-Top Toby Receives Titanic Texas Hurrah," The Sporting News, March 10, 1973: 41.

15. Shropshire, 73.

16. David Laurila, "Prospectus Q&A: Toby Harrah, Part One," baseballprospectus.com/article.php?articleid=8905, accessed June 14, 2016.

17. Shropshire, 181.

18. Tom Stephenson, "Ten Reasons Why the Texas Rangers Will Win the Pennant," dmagazine.com/publications/d-magazine/1975/may/ten-reasons-why-the-texas-rangers-will-win-the-pennant/, accessed July 28, 2016.

19. Ibid.

20. Randy Galloway, "Rangers Cheer Homer Surge by Surprise Swatter Harrah," The Sporting News, September 14, 1974: 10.

21. Laurila, "Prospectus Q&A: Toby Harrah, Part One."

22   Randy Galloway, "Rangers Elevate Toby Harrah to Big Cash Class – $100,000," *The Sporting News*, April 17, 1976: 9.

23   Bruce Markusen, "Card Corner: A Long Road to NY for Toby Harrah," baseballhall.org/discover/card-corner/a-long-road-to-new-york-for-toby-harrah, accessed June 14, 2016.

24   Randy Galloway, "Campy's Arrival Convinces Harrah to Switch to Third," The Sporting News, March 26, 1977: 20.

25   Frank Lucchesi, the Rangers' Opening Day manager, was fired after the team stumbled out of the gates to a 31-31 record. Texas lured Eddie Stanky out of retirement, but Stanky said he was homesick and quit after only one game; the Rangers won that game, leaving Stanky with a 1-0 record for Texas. Connie Ryan, a Rangers coach, then took over on an interim basis and amassed a 2-4 record before Billy Hunter took the reins on a permanent basis and led the team to a 60-33 record the rest of the way. For a complete breakdown of the 1977 Rangers season, see baseball-reference.com/teams/TEX/1977-schedule-scores.shtml.

26   Though Brett and Nettles had great seasons in 1977 and were worthy of being All-Stars, the choice of Oakland A's rookie Wayne Gross over Harrah as the second reserve third baseman for the AL was questionable. Gross finished the 1977 season with a .233-22-63 batting line with 66 runs scored while Harrah's line was .263-27-87 with 90 runs scored.

27   On June 23, 1946, Chicago Cubs left fielder Marv Rickert and first baseman Eddie Waitkus were the first to accomplish this feat, against New York Giants pitcher Nate Andrews. They hit their homers in the fourth inning of the first game of a doubleheader at New York's Polo Grounds; in spite of the historic event, the Cubs lost a slugfest to the Giants, 15-10. For the box score and play-by-play, see retrosheet.org/boxesetc/1946/B0623NY11946.htm. The true-life story of Waitkus, who was shot by a crazed female fan in 1949, provided part of the plotline for the character Roy Hobbs in Bernard Malamud's 1952 novel The Natural and Robert Redford's 1984 movie adaptation with the same title.

28   Woestendiek, "Last Men Out."

29   Laurila, "Prospectus Q&A: Toby Harrah, Part One."

30   Ibid.

31   Anderson, "Not Enough Hurrahs for Harrah."

32   Laurila, "Prospectus Q&A: Toby Harrah, Part One."

33   Anderson, "Not Enough Hurrahs for Harrah."

34   Ibid.

35   Ibid.

36   Terry Pluto, "Harrah to Undergo Heart Surgery," *The Sporting News*, October 11, 1982: 35.

37   Terry Pluto, "A Trying Winter for Tribe's Harrah," *The Sporting News*, March 7, 1983: 35.

38   Laurila, "Prospectus Q&A: Toby Harrah, Part One."

39   Associated Press, "BASEBALL; 3 Slams Set Record for Game," New York Times, August 7, 1986.

40   Ibid.

41   Nate Silver, "From Chapter 1-2: Is David Ortiz a Clutch Hitter?", espn.com/espn/page2/story?page=betweenthenumbers/ortiz/060405, accessed July 28, 2016.

42   Laurila, "Prospectus Q&A: Toby Harrah, Part 2."

43   Joshua Adams, "Talkin' with Toby Harrah," issuu.com/azlenews/docs/heritage_mag_5_2015, accessed July 28, 2016.

VIC HARRIS

BY PAUL HOFMANN

A utility player is one capable of playing several different positions. Often utility players are not great hitters, yet they are valuable in their ability to fill in for injured regulars, give others in the lineup a much-needed rest, serve as late-inning defensive replacements, and occasionally pinch-hit. In short, they provide teams with a greater level of flexibility. Vic Harris evolved into a prototypical utility player. During a major-league career that spanned eight years, he played in at least 28 games at six different positions.

Victor Lanier Harris was born on March 27, 1950, in Los Angeles, the only child of Fred Martin and Sue Winifred (Adams) Harris. Fred was a compressor operator for the City of Los Angeles and Sue worked as a beautician. The most important life lesson he learned from his parents was to respect and value people. "I was taught to love people," Harris said.[1]

Vic grew up as a Los Angeles Dodgers fan and began playing baseball around the age of 7. He began switch hitting at the age of 12. Harris described himself as quiet and attributed his success in baseball to two key ingredients. "I was a natural athlete and I was a team player."[2]

A graduate of Los Angeles High School, Harris starred in baseball at Los Angeles Valley College. He was a two-time All-Metropolitan Conference selection and an All-Southern California and Junior All-American.[3] The fleet-footed Harris was first drafted by the New York Mets in the 25th round of the 1969 amateur draft. However, he did not sign and elected to return to the school for his sophomore year.

In January 1970 the Oakland Athletics selected Harris in the first round of the 1970 secondary draft. After he signed with the A's on May 9, scout Phil Pote asked him to return to school and earn his associate's degree. Harris heeded Pote's advice and was grateful to him.[4] Crediting Pote, Harris said, "He understood I would have a life after baseball."[5] He said he considered accepting a scholarship to play baseball at University of Southern California. Looking back on it, he said, "I wish I had finished my education and gone to SC."[6]

Harris was assigned to the Coos Bay-North Bend (Oregon) A's of the short season Class-A Northwest League for the remainder of the 1970 season. He played in 75 games (67 at second base) and led the team in batting (.326) and stolen bases (30). He struggled defensively and made 19 errors at second base for a .947 fielding percentage.

In 1971 Harris was promoted to the Burlington (Iowa) Bees of the Class-A Midwest League. Joining an infield that included third baseman Phil Garner and shortstop Tommy Sandt, the Bees finished in first place in the circuit's South Division. Harris led the Bees in games played (120), plate appearances (535), at-bats (444), runs (84), hits (129), doubles (27), walks (77), and stolen bases (39). He finished the year with a .291 batting average, .392 on-base percentage, and .811 OPS.

Harris started the 1972 season with Birmingham of the Double-A Southern League. He played 32 games at second base and was batting .294 with 12 RBIs and 6 stolen bases before being promoted to Iowa of the Triple-A American Association. In 64 games, Harris batted .293 with 6 home runs, 25 RBIs, and 12 stolen bases. Harris said, "I was having a great year. That is, until I reached the major leagues. Then it all came at me."[7]

On July 20, 1972, Oakland traded Harris with Marty Martinez and a player to be named later to the Texas Rangers for Ted Kubiak and Don Mincher.[8] The trade was first announced on the afternoon of the 19th, yet Martinez played for the A's that night and got three hits in a 9-6 win over the Milwaukee Brewers. The Brewers filed a protest with the American League, but it was disallowed.[9] In the meantime, Harris was en route to Arlington, Texas, where he became the Rangers' everyday second baseman.

Harris made his major-league debut on July 21 when he came on as a defensive replacement in the top of the seventh inning. Lenny Randle, who started the game at second, replaced Martinez at shortstop, while Harris played second base and occupied Martinez's spot in the batting order. In the bottom of the eighth, Harris had his first taste of major-league pitching when he was struck out by southpaw Mickey Lolich.

The young second baseman had a dubious start to his major-league career as he endured a 0-for-36 drought before collecting his first major-league hit. As of 2018 this remained a modern record for debut futility.[10] He finally collected his first big-league hit when he delivered an RBI single off White Sox right-hander Stan Bahnsen. The hit came in Harris's 13th major-league game.

Things didn't get much better for Harris, or the Rangers, during the remainder of the season. In 61 games he hit an anemic .140 and with only 10 RBIs. He made 10 errors and finished with a .960 fielding percentage, significantly below the .977 fielding percentage for all AL second basemen. The Rangers, who had relocated from Washington before the 1972 season, were 16-45 (.262) with Harris in the lineup. At 54-100, they finished in last place in the AL West, 38½ games behind the eventual World Series champion Oakland A's.

Despite his monumental struggles at the plate in 1972, during spring training in 1973 Harris earned a roster spot as an outfielder and utility infielder. The season proved to be his best in the major leagues. In 152 games he hit .249 with career highs in runs (71), doubles (14), triples (7), home runs (8), RBIs (44), and stolen bases (12). Harris credited the offensive turnaround to manager Whitey Herzog: "Whitey put me out there every day and gave me a chance."[11] However, his defensive woes continued. He made 10 errors in 25 games at third base and another 4 in 18 games at second. Harris attributed many of his errors to throwing difficulties.[12]

The 1973 season brought with it both memorable and forgettable events in Harris's major-league career. On May 11, he hit his first major-league home run, off A's left-hander Vida Blue, a seventh-inning solo shot that cleared the left-field wall at Arlington Stadium. (Harris occasionally reminded Blue of the fact when the two were later teammates with the San Francisco Giants.[13])

It was also during the 1973 season that Harris fell victim to the hidden-ball trick. The play occurred in a game between the New York Yankees and Rangers at Arlington Stadium on June 6. The Rangers had just trimmed the Yankees' lead to 3-1 on a Toby Harrah sacrifice fly when the play occurred. According to The Sporting News, "With Texas runners at first and second base, two out and Rico Carty prepared to bat in the fifth inning, New York right-hander Steve Kline circled the mound pretending to rub the baseball. When Vic Harris led off second base, shortstop Gene Michael moved in for the tag and the inning was over. 'Michael had the ball, but I had to make it look good,' Kline said."[14] Harris was Michael's fifth victim of the hidden-ball trick.[15] Harris chuckled when remembering the event. "It was the most embarrassing thing I ever did," Harris recalled with a chuckle. "Although it wasn't that funny at the time."[16]

Later that season, Harris had the less dubious distinction of scoring the winning run in a no-hit, no-run ball game. On July 30, right-hander Jim Bibby no-hit the World Champion Oakland A's at the Oakland-Alameda County Stadium. Harris was the starting center fielder and batted second. In the first inning, he drew a one-out walk off Blue and came around to score the game's first run when Jeff Burroughs hit a grand slam. Eight innings later, Bibby retired Gene Tenace on a popfly to second to complete the masterpiece.

During his year-and-a-half tenure with the Rangers, Harris played under three high-profile managers. Ted Williams managed the Rangers in 1972, Herzog managed the Rangers for most of the 1973 season, and Billy Martin for the final 23 games of the season. When asked who his favorite manager was, Harris gave the nod to Herzog while acknowledging that the notoriously difficult Williams and Martin were "good people."[17]

During the 1973-74 offseason Harris and Bill Madlock were traded to the Chicago Cubs for future Hall of Fame pitcher Ferguson Jenkins. In acquiring the pair from Texas, the Cubs were hoping they had added an everyday third baseman and second baseman to the lineup. Richard Dozier's preseason analysis of the Cubs' revamped infield highlighted the speed the two brought to the club: "Madlock and Harris are the main speed merchants, both with the potential of upwards of 30 stolen bases if given the green light with some regularity."[18]

Harris started 30 of the Cubs' first 33 games at second base, but a season-long slump resulted in diminished playing time as the campaign went on. He was hitting .195 with 11 RBIs and 9 stolen bases when he was injured in a collision at second with the Braves' Darrell Evans on July 7.[19] Season-ending knee surgery followed.

During the 1975 season Harris split time between the Cubs and Wichita of the Triple-A American Association. In 32 games with the Aeros he was primarily used in the outfield and batted .242 with one home run and 11 RBIs. He played in 51 games with the Cubs and was used almost exclusively as a pinch-hitter. In 56 at-bats he hit only .179 with 5 RBIs. On December 22, 1975, the Cubs dealt Harris to the St. Louis Cardinals for light-hitting utility infielder Mick Kelleher.

Harris got off to a great start with the Cardinals in 1976. He was named NL Player of the Week for the week ending May 9 after going 13-for-28 (.464) with 7 RBIs. Entering play on May 15, the second baseman was hitting .315. However, as often was the case throughout his career, he went into another deep slump (.115 over his next 44 games) and increasingly found himself playing a utility or pinch-hitter role. He finished the season with a .228 average with one home run and 19 RBIs. Notably, Harris stole only one base as the knee injury that ended his season prematurely two years earlier had slowed him on the basepaths.

Once again Harris was on the move during the offseason. On October 20, 1976, the Cardinals traded him along with Willie Crawford and left-handed pitcher John Curtis to the San Francisco Giants for right-handed pitchers Mike Caldwell and Jonn D'Acquisto and catcher Dave Rader. The Giants were coming off a 74-88 season and needed to fill a number of holes. Spec Richardson, the Giants' director of baseball operations, declared that the Giants got the better of the trade. "We got us a spot lefthanded pitcher and two men who can come off the bench and do something, Crawford and Harris. These are people who know what to do all the time," said Richardson.[20]

Harris started the 1977 season with Phoenix of the Triple-A Pacific Coast League in a utility role. He played in 24 games in the outfield, 7 at second base and 5 at shortstop. He was hitting .266 with one home run and 18 RBIs when he was called up to San Francisco in late May. Used primarily as a pinch-hitter and utility infielder, Harris finished the season with a .261 average, 2 home runs, and 14 RBIs.

Capable of playing second, short, third, and all three outfield positions, Harris won a position as a pinch-hitter and utilityman coming out of spring training in 1978. However, he started the season in a 0-for-19 funk and never really got going. On July 18, hitting .152 with one home and 11 RBIs, Harris was optioned to Phoenix, where he stayed until major-league rosters expanded in September. After the season he was granted free agency.

On March 6, 1979, Harris signed a minor-league contract with the Milwaukee Brewers. He failed to make the Brewers roster out of spring training and spent the entire season with the Triple-A Vancouver Canadians. Harris was a veteran presence with the team. He played in 142 games and batted .275 with 82 runs scored, 25 doubles, 9 home runs, and 66 RBIs, helping the Canadians capture the Pacific Coast League's North Division title.

Harris went to spring training with the Brewers again in 1980 with the hope of earning a spot as an extra outfielder. His efforts were stalled when he crashed into a wall and opened a gash behind his right ear that required three stitches and resulted in a concussion and overnight stay in the hospital.[21] Harris started the 1980 season at Vancouver and played in 69 games with the Canadians in which he was used defensively in the outfield. He was hitting .273 with 3 home runs, 37 RBIs, and 13 stolen bases when he was called up by the Brewers. After his return to the majors, Harris hit .213 with a homer and 7 RBIs.

Harris's last game in a major-league uniform was one of his most memorable. On October 5, the last day of the regular season, in a sparsely attended affair against the Oakland A's, the team that originally drafted him, he closed out his major-league career with a 2-for-6 effort that included the only walk-off hit of his career. The A's and Brewers were locked in a 4-4 tie in the top of the 15th inning. Against A's rookie right-hander Dave Beard, Ben Oglivie singled to right with one out and stole second. After Gorman Thomas flied out to left field, the A's walked John Poff to take their chances with Harris. The Brewers' right fielder responded with a walk-off single to right, plating Oglivie with the winning run. "It was the only walk-off hit of my career," Harris said.[22]

Harris became a free agent after the 1980 season and with no offers from major-league teams, he signed with the Kintetsu Buffalos of the Japanese Pacific League. Joining fellow American Ike Hampton on the Kintetsu roster, the switch-hitting Harris was the Buffalos everyday second baseman. He enjoyed a solid year, batting .268 with a team-leading 22 home runs and 74 RBIs. He also became only the fourth player in Japanese baseball history to hit home runs from both sides of the plate in a game. He accomplished the feat on July 5, 1981, in a game against the Seibu Lions.[23]

Harris moved from second base to the Buffalos' outfield for the 1982 season. While he batted .272, his power declined, and Harris totaled only 9 home runs and 35 RBIs. His offensive production declined once again in 1983 (.198-4-23). Despite his struggles at the plate, he became only the second player in the history of Japanese baseball to hit home runs from both sides of the plate in a game twice when he accomplished the feat for the second time on September 1 in a contest against the Nankai Braves.[24]

Harris looked fondly on his years in Japan, saying, "I really felt comfortable there. I knew I was going to be playing every day." He also credited the Japanese training regimen for some of his success. "I was in the best shape I was ever in. Over there they get you in condition."[25]

With his career in Japan now over, Harris returned to the United States and attempted to reach the majors once more. Now 34 years old, the aging journeyman spent the 1984 season with the Louisville Redbirds of the Triple-A American Association. Harris finished his final season of professional baseball with a .231 average, 5 home runs, and 29 RBIs in 75 games with the Redbirds.

Harris was married twice and has one son. After retiring from baseball, he returned to Los Angeles and worked in the aerospace industry with Rockwell and later Boeing as an emergency fire dispatcher. From 2006 to 2013 he was an instructor for the Major League Baseball Urban Youth Academy in Compton, California.

Sources

In addition to the sources cited in the Notes, the author also relied on Baseball-reference.com and Retrosheet.org.

Notes

1. Vic Harris, personal correspondence, January 29, 2018.
2. Ibid.
3. "Hall of Fame: Inductees," lavc.edu/athletics/Hall-of-Fame/Inductees.aspx.
4. Untitled document, mlblogsmlburbanyouthacademy.files.wordpress.com/2013/02/victor-harris.pdf.
5. Vic Harris, personal correspondence, January 29, 2018.
6. Vic Harris, personal correspondence, February 1, 2018.
7. Ibid.
8. On July 26, 1972, the Athletics sent Steve Lawson to the Rangers to complete the trade.
9. "Marty Martinez," sabr.org/bioproj/person/e7951fc7.
10. "The Lineup Card: 10 Milestones to Look Forward to in 2013," baseballprospectus.com/news/article/20040/the-lineup-card-10-milestones-to-look-forward-to-in-2013/.
11. Vic Harris, personal correspondence, January 29, 2018.
12. Vic Harris, personal correspondence, February 1, 2018.
13. Ibid.
14. "Yankees Use Trickery," *The Sporting News*, June 23, 1973: 34.
15. Bill Deane, "Gene Michael, Master of the Hidden-Ball Trick," September 14, 2017, dizzydeane.wordpress.com/2017/09/14/gene-michael-master-of-the-hidden-ball-trick/.
16. Vic Harris, personal correspondence, January 29, 2018.
17. Ibid.
18. Richard Dozier, "Kessinger Cubs' Infield 'Stranger,'" *The Sporting News*, January 26, 1974: 31.
19. "N.L. Flashes: Harris Sheds Cast," *The Sporting News*, August 10, 1974: 30.
20. Art Spander, "Spec Sees Giants Profiting on Swap," The Sporting News, November 6, 1976: 22. Crawford and Rob Sperring were traded to the Houston Astros prior to the start of the 1977 season for second baseman Rob Andrews.
21. Tom Flaherty, "Buck Rodgers: Earth Mission," The Sporting News, March 29, 1980: 33.
22. Vic Harris, personal correspondence, January 29, 2018.
23. "kaku shu hon rui da ki roku shu (Part I)," 2u.biglobe.ne.jp/~akichan/hr1.htm.
24. "kaku shu hon rui da ki roku shu (Part I)."
25. Vic Harris, personal correspondence, January 29, 2018.

RICH HINTON

BY MARK S. STERNMAN

Like cats, many left-handed pitchers seem to have multiple lives. Drafted by four clubs five times over five years in the 1960s, lefty Rich Hinton pitched for five clubs in six years in an erratic career that largely spanned the 1970s. A star at the University of Arizona who also played in Mexico, Hinton pitched just well enough to stay on the fringes of the majors for nearly a decade.

In addition to being in the right place at odd times, Harrah also developed a reputation as a practical joker over the course of his career. He once sneaked up behind Rangers teammate and future Hall of Famer Gaylord Perry and sprinkled itching powder on his neck and shoulders between innings. Richard Michael Hinton was born on May 22, 1947, in Tucson, Arizona, to Duncan and Bernice (Honea) Hinton. The second of five children, he grew up on the family farm, while his father also worked in the maintenance department of Marana Public Schools in Tucson, and his mother owned a barber shop. Hinton began playing baseball when he was little, and once struck out 17 batters in six innings in American Legion ball. A 1965 graduate of Marana High School, he played baseball, basketball, and football.

Hinton attended the University of Arizona, where he went 32-8 over three seasons. He refused to sign the first four times teams drafted him (the Dodgers in the 23rd round in 1965, the Indians in the fifth round in 1967, the Padres in the fourth round in 1968, and the Indians in the fourth round in 1969). Hinton succumbed after the White Sox, the team to which he would frequently return, picked him in the third round of the 1969 June secondary draft. White Sox scout Gordon Maltzberger inked Hinton to his first contract.[1]

After going 4-3 with two minor-league teams in 1969, Hinton earned a nonroster invitation to spring training in 1970 and first received notice for "his second consecutive impressive outing"[2] after hurling three scoreless innings over a pair of games, giving up just two hits and striking out three.

Hinton returned to Tucson for the 1970 season and went 10-12. After the season, he played in the Florida Instructional League, where he "had the best winning percentage (7-1 for .875)"[3] and struck out 56 in 55 innings with a 1.96 ERA. Hinton again received a nonroster invitation to spring training in 1971, but again returned to Tucson.

But thanks to the 20.25 ERA of rookie Stan Perzanowski, the cousin of Ron Perranoski, the White Sox recalled Hinton in mid-July. Pitching coach Johnny Sain deemed Hinton a "terrific prospect," largely due to his demeanor: "He looks at you real straight."[4]

The focused Hinton made his major-league debut on July 17 against the New York Yankees and pitched a perfect inning of relief against the heart of the New York order (Bobby Murcer, Roy White, and Ron Blomberg). Two days later, in the opener of a doubleheader, Hinton won his first game by pitching the eighth and ninth innings of a game Chicago won

8-3 in 10 innings over Mel Stottlemyre. The White Sox turned double plays in both innings to bail out Hinton, who got his first strikeout by fanning Gene Michael.

Hinton dropped his first game later that same week, losing the second game of a doubleheader against the Senators. Entering the ninth inning of a tie game on July 24, he gave up a bunt single, a sacrifice, and a walk before exiting the game. Frank Howard's double drove in the winning runs in a 5-3 Washington victory.

Hinton died by the bunt and lived by the bunt. Trailing 6-5 against the Yankees in the bottom of the 12th on July 27, he successfully executed the first of his two major-league sacrifices to put the tying run in scoring position. Pat Kelly's double tied the game, which Chicago and Hinton won 9-6 later that frame on a homer by Bill Melton.

Hinton even pinch-hit to sacrifice in the bottom of the 10th inning on August 11. Although he did so successfully, Hinton, who stayed in to pitch, gave up a home run to Ray Fosse as Cleveland triumphed 3-2 in 12 innings.

On August 27, Hinton made his first start in the majors in a brief but eventful outing against the Detroit Tigers. He scored the only run of his career after reaching on a failed bunt/fielder's choice and stealing the only base of his career to give the White Sox a 1-0 lead in the top of the third. But in the bottom of the inning, disaster struck. Consecutive RBI hits put Detroit up 2-1. With two outs and nobody on, Hinton hit Willie Horton "in the left eye.... Horton was sent rolling over and over in the dirt in pain. He was taken to Ford Hospital where the injury was determined not to be serious. X-rays of the eye revealed no fracture."[5]

Hinton finished 1971 with a 3-4 record, with a 4.44 earned-run average. Although Chicago had planned for Hinton to pitch in Puerto Rico over the winter,[6] the White Sox instead traded him on October 13 to the Yankees for outfielder Jim Lyttle. New York general manager Lee MacPhail explained, "We have to rebuild our second-line pitching and feel we have started with this move. Hinton is only 24, has a fine arm and we like his potential. We were especially interested in lefthanders and Rich will get a full chance to make our club."[7]

Looking good in pinstripes, Hinton threw five shutout innings to start spring training in 1972.[8] Seeking to strengthen his left-handed pitching, MacPhail made a bigger move to acquire a portsider with AL experience by trading Danny Cater for Sparky Lyle, which pushed Hinton out of the bullpen and into the starting rotation. Manager Ralph Houk pointed to the acquisitions of Lyle and Hinton as two of the three most promising developments for New York just prior to the last week of spring training.[9]

And then Hinton got sick. He "had been suffering from a 'low-grade infection' for more than a week and was finally sent back to New York ... for further examination."[10] The diagnosis: mononucleosis. That proved incorrect, but he did have "a virus that whittled six pounds off his six-foot-two, 185-pound frame."[11]

Not until May 24 did Hinton start a game for the Yankees. He "originally was supposed to make his first start against Milwaukee April 20, but the game was rained out. Then he was scheduled to start one of the games of Sunday's [May 21] double-header against Boston, but he lost out ... because Saturday's game was rained out and Fritz Peterson ... was nudged back to Sunday."[12]

Hinton threw seven innings of five-hit ball to beat Cleveland in what would turn out to be his best game in pinstripes and his only win of 1972. "I didn't feel tired out there," said Hinton. "The ball felt sticky at first, but I washed my hands between innings to get the rosin off. From then on, things went just right."[13]

Making two more starts on three days of rest each time, Hinton pitched poorly, giving up eight runs (seven earned) in just 5⅓ innings combined as New York lost both games. Hinton then went to the bullpen. While he gave up just one run over three innings in two games, he walked five. The Yankees sent Hinton to Syracuse of the International League, where he spent a memorable few months. In the opening game of a June 30 doubleheader, he appeared as a pinch-runner but got picked off second base. In the nightcap, he threw a no-hitter. "I'm always aware of how many hits I give up," he said with a grin. "I felt I had a strong fast ball and I went with it most of the way, mainly because of the lead the guys gave me. It wasn't really moving that well. But I kept it down consistently."[14]

In spite of this gem, Hinton went only 3-9 with a 4.78 ERA for the Syracuse Chiefs, so New York sold him on September 7 to Texas. Hinton pitched five times in relief for the Rangers, all in losing efforts. Three times he faced his former Chicago teammates, picking up the loss in the middle effort despite "a fine relief stint"[15] that blew up when Pete Broberg allowed two of Hinton's inherited runners to score.

Manager Whitey Herzog said, "Hinton is the type of guy who could blossom overnight for you. I've talked to a lot of people who like his potential."[16] But Hinton spent just six months and one day as Texas property. On March 8, 1973, the Rangers traded Hinton and Vince Colbert to the Cleveland Indians for Alex Johnson. "Hinton's only victory in 1972 was over the Indians … and probably was the big reason for their continued interest in him."[17]

Due to the worst of his 10 minor-league seasons in terms of his 5.10 ERA, Hinton never pitched for Cleveland, which released him on April 1, 1974. A fortnight later, the White Sox again signed him, but he spent 1974 and the first half of 1975 entirely in the minors until Chicago reliever Terry Forster suffered an arm injury that led to Hinton's returning to the majors for the first time since 1972.[18]

Manager Chuck Tanner used Hinton exclusively in relief although he tried to move him from the mound to right field in the middle of an appearance and then bring him back to pitch to gain a platoon advantage. The umpires would not allow the move. "Wouldn't have bothered me to play the outfield," said Hinton. "When I was in Denver, I hit a homer and double one night, then came in from the outfield and pitched the last two innings."[19] Hinton's return to the South Side ended on December 12, 1975, when Chicago traded him and Jeff Sovern to the Cincinnati Reds for Clay Carroll. "The Reds were loaded with fine relievers, and shedding the veteran's salary was the economical choice."[20]

Praising the "spectacular" winter-league performance of his new acquisition, Cincinnati pitching coach Larry Shepard cautioned, "But, Hinton still had to prove he can get major leaguers out."[21]

In spring training, Hinton "had pitched well" but nevertheless "was sent to Indianapolis" because "both Santo Alcala and Pat Zachry were out of options, making [Hinton's] departure almost a cinch."[22]

The Reds recalled Hinton, who pitched for the team from June 18 to July 28. He started one game, against Houston on June 25, but gave up three homers in less than three innings, ballooning his ERA to 10.80. Hinton finished the 1976 season with a 7.64 ERA and spent 1977 in Mexico City, where he went 14-8. He returned to the American League after that season when the White Sox signed him as a free agent on November 28, 1977.

Trying to make the team in spring training, Hinton argued with umpire Nestor Chylak. Hinton "threw his fist in the air in a mock 'strike' call on a serve that Chylak had declared a 'ball.' 'Don't you show me up,' screamed Chylak. 'Don't put your fist in the air on me.' Nestor gained quick revenge. Hinton's 3-and-1 pitch … seemingly split the heart of the plate. 'Ball four,' said Chylak."[23]

Hinton "finished the exhibition exercises with a 0.93 ERA and won a three-way race with Rich Wortham and Eddie Bane for a lefty relief job."[24] Pitching coach Stan Williams raved about Hinton: "He has improved every time out this spring. He has a sneaky fast ball … it kind of jumps on you out of a deceptive pitching motion. He has a good curve and uses a screwball for a changeup. He can either start or relieve, but I think he's more effective as a reliever, because his fastball isn't that tough when you see it the second time around."[25]

In his season's debut on April 16, Hinton faced New York's Reggie Jackson at Yankee Stadium with runners in scoring position and one out. Chicago manager Bob Lemon praised Hinton's approach: "He gets him 2-and-2 and then drops down and cuts loose with that big underhanded curve ball. Reggie starts to stride, and finds himself frozen. The pitch was just outside for ball three but Reggie looks over to our dugout and yells: 'Where in hell did he come up with that one!' Then on the 3-and-2 pitch, Hinton smokes him inside for the strikeout and we get out of the inning."26

With excellent efforts against the eventual division champions, Hinton got off to a strong start in 1978, with an ERA of 1.69 at the end of April and 0.87 at the end of May. On May 15 against the Yankees again, Hinton set down all 14 batters he faced.27

Hinton's ERA dipped to a season-low 0.75 after June 3, when he saved a game (his first in the majors) against the Royals and extended a three-game streak during which he had faced 20 batters and retired them all. After the game, Hinton confessed, "I was wilder than a March hare. ... I was lucky to retire five in a row because I knew they'd be taking the first pitch and I went to 2-and-0 on at least three of the hitters."28

In spite of this superb start, Hinton sat for 10 days before picking up the victory on June 13 after the White Sox transformed a 9-0 deficit against the Indians into a 10-9 win. After stretching his perfect streak to 22 straight batters retired, Hinton gave up the ninth Cleveland run before pitching "6⅓ superb innings for his first victory of the season and only the seventh of his roller-coaster major league career. ... 'It's kind of tough keeping your concentration when you're pitching with an 8-0 deficit,' said Hinton. ... 'At that point, naturally, I never considered that we'd win it.'"29

Oddly, Hinton's next appearance also spanned 6⅓ innings of one-run relief, but Chicago dropped that game, a fate that it would suffer in most of his appearances for the 1978 White Sox. Of Hinton's 29 games that season, Chicago won just six.

On July 14 in the Bronx, Hinton relieved Ken Kravec in the bottom of the sixth with the White Sox leading 5-4 against Ron Guidry, who would win the Cy Young Award that season with a 25-3 record. Hinton protected the lead until the bottom of the eighth when Chris Chambliss's sacrifice fly tied the game. Chicago rallied to retake the lead in the top of the ninth when Don Kessinger singled off Guidry. Hinton retired the first batter in the bottom of the frame before pinch-hitter Cliff Johnson "fouled off a 2-2 pitch, and I thought I'd throw him one more high fastball," Hinton told a reporter after the game. "He swings at those but can't hit them. If I missed, I was going to curve him."30 Johnson did not miss but homered to make the score 6-6 and force extra innings. In the bottom of the 11th, Reggie Jackson doubled and scored on Graig Nettles' single as the White Sox and Hinton took a tough 7-6 loss.

One week later in Chicago, Hinton fared no better against the Yankees, lasting less than one inning in relief and taking another loss. Trying to protect a 4-3 lead, "he was a strike away from retiring [Mickey] Rivers when he hit him on the shoulder to force in the tying run"31 and then gave up a two-run single to Roy White that proved decisive in a 7-4 New York win.

Hinton went to the minors in August and started four games for the Iowa Oaks. He won all of them, completing three, and came back to the majors when the rosters expanded on September 1. After two relief appearances, Hinton started three times in a row to close out the season and completed the first two, the only two complete games of his major-league career. In beating Minnesota 6-1 on September 12, "Hinton threw 147 pitches while working much of the evening under a drizzle."32 In a strange effort, Hinton gave up seven hits, walked seven batters, and struck out only two. The Twins left 13 men on base.

In 1979, Hinton did not make the White Sox out of spring training and went back to Iowa, where he pitched mostly as a starter.33 Recalled in May, he lost as a starter on May 12 against Kansas City, when he failed to last five innings in a 5-4 defeat. Ten days later, Hinton won the ninth and last game of his major-league career by shutting out Oakland over the last four innings. He gave up just two hits, walked none, fanned five, and seemed destined for a larger role: "The Sox now consider him to be the left-handed stopper they have long sought."34

Hinton did pick up the last two saves of his career in his last month in Chicago. He pitched the final four innings of a 13-3 rout against Milwaukee on June 10, pitching into and out of trouble by giving up eight hits and one walk. He threw much more effectively in his second save, stopping Seattle on one hit over 3⅓ innings on June 21. "Joe Sparks, his Iowa manager last year, has tried to get him to hide the ball longer and turn more in his delivery. It's a lot to remember, Hinton noted."[35]

Hinton's last two appearances for Chicago went disastrously. In retiring only four batters against the Twins, he yielded seven hits, one walk, and six runs (five earned) in a 16-4 loss on June 30. The next day Hinton came on with two out and one on against Minnesota. He struck out Hosken Powell looking before giving up a walk-off single to Glenn Adams as Chicago lost 2-1. On July 6, the White Sox traded Hinton to Seattle for Juan Bernhardt. After pitching in 16 games for Chicago, Hinton appeared in 14 more for the Mariners, reaching 30 games for the only time in his career, which gained him a $5,000 bonus.[36]

After this rewarding effort, Hinton never again appeared in a professional game. Having married first Karen and then Rita, he has six children, three boys and three girls. Unlike their father, all three of Rich's sons threw right-handed. Milwaukee selected Rich's oldest son, Robert, in the 40th round of the 2003 draft, but Robert never got beyond Triple A.[37]

According to his LinkedIn profile, Hinton has worked in Arizona and Florida since his retirement from baseball. Since 1995, he has been president of RM Hinton Inc., which builds environmentally friendly residences. Hinton writes, "I personally run each job and still enjoy putting on my tool belt when needed."[38]

Notes

1. The information in this paragraph comes from the National Baseball Hall of Fame and Museum's file on Hinton. Thanks to Reference Librarian Cassidy Lent of the Hall for scanning the Hinton file.
2. George Langford, "Sox Whip Twins, 9-4," Chicago Tribune, March 17, 1970: C2.
3. "Pirate Prospect Stennett Grabs FIL Bat Crown," The Sporting News, January 16, 1971: 61.
4. Pat Jordan, "In a World of Windmills," Sports Illustrated, May 8, 1972.
5. George Langford, "Tigers Beat Sox, Horton Hit in Eye," Chicago Tribune, August 28, 1971: B5. Horton missed a month due to the injury. Dan Holmes, "Willie Horton," sabr.org/bioproj/person/e320ca42 (accessed August 27, 2015).
6. George Langford, "Sox' Big 3 Pan for Gold in Sea of Young Talent," Chicago Tribune, September 3, 1971: C1.
7. Jim Ogle, "Three Yankees Line Up for Pay Boosts," The Sporting News, October 30, 1971: 22.
8. Murray Chass, "A Passing Grade for Stottlemyre," New York Times, March 10, 1972.
9. "For Houk, Little Things Make Contender," New York Times, March 26, 1972.
10. "Yankees Awaiting Report on Hinton," New York Times, April 1, 1972.
11. Joe Donnelly, "Rich Hinton: Odd Man Washed Out," Newsday, April 21, 1972: 119. An article in the New York Times on the same day claimed that Hinton did indeed have mono. See Murray Chass, "Rain Falls on Hinton's Debut as Yanks' Fifth Starter," New York Times, April 21, 1972. A third report referred to the illness as a "mysterious infection." See Jim Ogle, "Yanks' Beene Eyes Strike, Decides to Join Syracuse," The Sporting News, April 22, 1972: 22.
12. Murray Chass, "Yanks' Hinton Sure to Get a Start, Weather or Not," New York Times, May 23, 1972.
13. Associated Press, "Weather OK, So Is NY Rookie," Boston Record American, May 26, 1972: 66.
14. Bill Fox, "Chiefs' Hinton 'Makes Up' With No-Hitter," The Sporting News, July 15, 1972: 38.
15. Richard Dozer, "Allen Slams 37th, Sox Triumph 7-4," Chicago Tribune, September 25, 1972: C3.
16. Randy Galloway, "Rangers to Switch Gogo to Relief Duty," The Sporting News, February 10, 1973: 44.
17. Russell Schneider, "Tribe Gets One Johnson, Sells Another," The Sporting News, March 31, 1973: 53.
18. "Forster Out for 21 Days," Chicago Tribune, July 27, 1975: B3.
19. Bob Verdi, "Sox Stock Plummets," Chicago Tribune, August 3, 1975: B1. Hinton did play six minor-league games in the outfield, including three in 1975.
20. Derek Norin and Mark Armour, "Clay Carroll," sabr.org/bioproj/person/7fa1137e (accessed December 28, 2015).
21. Earl Lawson, "Darcy, Carroll Grow Edgy Checking Reds' Timetable," The Sporting News, March 20, 1976: 30.
22. Bob Hertzel, "New No. 36," Cincinnati Enquirer, June 19, 1976.

23 Dave Nightingale, "Sox, Yanks Play As If It Counted," Chicago Tribune, March 17, 1978: E2.

24 Dave Nightingale, "White Sox Prove That Numbers Don't Always Count," Chicago Tribune, April 6, 1978: C1.

25 Dave Nightingale, "Williams Delivers Pitch for Sox Staff," Chicago Tribune, April 16, 1978: B4.

26 Dave Nightingale, "Hinton Benefits From Schueler's One Extra Pitch," Chicago Tribune, April 20, 1978: C3. This article also describes Hinton as a "Clint Eastwood look-alike" and calls him "the first 'submariner' to grace the Chicago relief pitching scene since Ted Abernathy," who had pitched for the Cubs in 1965-1966 and 1969-1970.

27 Thomas Rogers, "Yankees Defeat White Sox, 4-1; Rivers Is Benched by Martin," New York Times, May 16, 1978.

28 Dave Nightingale, "Sox Pound Lumps on Royals," Chicago Tribune, June 4, 1978: B14.

29 Dave Nightingale, "Sox Battle All the Way Back," Chicago Tribune, June 14, 1978: E1.

30 Richard Dozer, "Yanks Guess Right, Nip Sox in 11," Chicago Tribune, July 15, 1978: 11.

31 Richard Dozer, "Yanks Don't Need Reggie Against Sox," Chicago Tribune, July 22, 1978: F3.

32 Richard Dozer, "Hinton Pleases Himself," Chicago Tribune, September 13, 1978: E3.

33 Richard Dozer, "White Sox Look to the 20s to Build Their Pitching Staff," Chicago Tribune, April 15, 1979: C3. Richard Dozer, "Soderholm's Punch, Proly's Save at Bell Stop Texas," Chicago Tribune, May 6, 1979: C3.

34 Richard Dozer, "Sox Win on Orta Homer," Chicago Tribune, May 23, 1979: E1.

35 Richard Dozer, "Sox Beat Seattle – Finally," Chicago Tribune, June 22, 1979: D1.

36 An unattributed article dated October 20, 1979, from the National Baseball Hall of Fame and Museum's file on Hinton.

37 Tom Haudricourt, "Getting to Know: RHP Robert Hinton," jsonline.com/blogs/sports/116536593.html (accessed October 12, 2015).

38 www.linkedin.com/pub/rich-hinton/5b/181/350 (accessed October 19, 2015)

FRANK HOWARD

BY MARK ARMOUR

He was not the first man to be recognized as a threat to break Babe Ruth's record of 60 home runs in a season, but Frank Howard was surely one of the first to draw such attention while still in the minor leagues, or even in college. This gentle, humble man would be no match for Ruth in personality nor, it would turn out, in ability. Howard got a relatively late start on his professional career, and took several additional years struggling to reach the heights baseball observers had predicted for him. But in the end, he became an All-Star, a home run champion, a World Series hero, and one of the game's most feared, and most admired, sluggers.

Frank Oliver Howard was born on August 8, 1936, in Columbus, Ohio, to John and Erma Howard. John was a large man (6-foot-4, over 200 pounds) and a machinist for the Chesapeake and Ohio Railway in Columbus, while Erma was a homemaker. Frank was the third of six children who lived with their parents in a modest frame house. "There was always lots of food on the table," Howard remembered, "but if we kids wanted money, we had to earn it." Frank shined shoes, caddied, and did the hard manual labor befitting his size. "When I was 14," he recalled, "I worked a hundred-pound jackhammer in the streets for the city of Columbus, got paid maybe a dollar and a half an hour and was glad to get it."[1] By the middle of his tenure at Columbus South High School, he had grown to 6-foot-5, 195 pounds.

John Howard had played semipro baseball around Columbus, and encouraged his son's interest in the game. Despite his size, Frank had no interest in football, but he played both basketball (at which he excelled) and baseball (which he preferred). Howard was good enough to be widely recruited to play college basketball, but he decided to stay at home and play at Ohio State. "Frank was anxious to get an education," recalled Floyd Stahl, his basketball coach at OSU, "but he had almost no money. We didn't have the grants-in-aid and the sports scholarships that we have today. I told Frank I thought we could find jobs for him." Howard did get some assistance from the school, but also worked around campus for four years. When Stahl got him a job working on a cement crew, the foreman told him, "Frank does twice as much work as any laborer I've had."[2] Stahl was soon concerned that Howard would work too hard and overtrain. Howard became a basketball star for the Buckeyes, earning All-American honors as a junior, and setting a Madison Square Garden record in a holiday tournament with 32 rebounds in a game, and 75 for the three games.[3] The next year Howard was drafted by the Philadelphia Warriors of the NBA.

He also played baseball for Ohio State, eclipsing the .300 mark in two seasons and displaying occasional glimpses of the power for which he would become known. The Brooklyn Dodgers first scouted him in 1956, and the next year, when Howard was a junior, Cliff Alexander filed a telling report: "Good arm. Fielding below average. Hitting below average (good potential). Running speed slightly below average. Major league power. Definite follow." What Alexander saw was an unfinished product, with a lot of potential. Howard played that summer of 1957 for Rapid City in the Basin League, a circuit that drew a lot of attention from big-league scouts. He almost signed that summer, but had promised Stahl he would return to Columbus for his final year of basketball.[4]

After his basketball season ended, he let major-league scouts know that he was ready to sign. He had a lot of offers, but the Dodgers (now in Los Angeles) had been talking to him for a couple of years and he never seriously considered anyone else. Alexander remembers Howard calling him up to tell him that Paul Richards, who was running the Baltimore Orioles at the time, had offered a $120,000 bonus. Howard asked Alexander for $108,000—$100,000 for himself, and $8,000 to be put toward a new house for his parents. Alexander agreed, and Howard was on his way.[5] He left Ohio State one semester short of a degree in physical education.

The Dodgers sent their big recruit to their Green Bay team in the Class-B Three-I League, where he played for former Brooklyn star outfielder Pete Reiser. This first stop proved no difficulty at all, as Howard hit .333 and led the league with 37 home runs and 119 RBIs. At the end of the year he was named the league's Most Valuable Player. One evening at a local pizza parlor he met Carol Johanski, a secretary for the *Green Bay Gazette*. Six months later they married, and Howard soon bought a house in Green Bay and settled there.

In September the 22-year-old was brought up to Los Angeles to finish the season. He made his debut on September 10, 1958, at Philadelphia's Connie Mack Stadium. Batting against Robin Roberts, he finished 2-for-4, including a mammoth two-run home run in his second big-league at-bat. The drive hit a billboard atop the left-field roof, causing left-fielder Harry Anderson to say he was afraid the billboard was going to fall over onto his head.[6] On the 16th, he came to bat in Cincinnati with teammate Duke Snider on third base. Up in the radio booth, Dodgers announcer Vin Scully commented wryly that Snider was standing way off the foul line in deference to Howard's propensity for pulling line drives down the line. Just as Scully said this, Howard hit a vicious foul liner that hit Snider in the head, knocking him briefly unconscious and ending the Duke's season.[7] Howard finished his brief trial hitting .241 in 29 at-bats.

In 1959 the Dodgers sent Howard to Victoria of the Texas League, which also proved to be no challenge. Through 63 games he looked to be on his way to a Triple Crown, with 27 home runs, 79 RBIs, and a .371 average. Dodgers GM Buzzie Bavasi paid the club a visit, watched Howard hit a 520-foot homer to win a game, and brought him back to Los Angeles. Howard only stayed a week, going just 2-for-19 before getting sent to Spokane (Triple-A Pacific Coast League). He hit .317 with 16 more home runs with Spokane in the second half, then returned to the Dodgers in mid-September. The club was in the middle of a pennant race so Howard only got two at-bats, including a pinch-hit home run off the Cardinals' Lindy McDaniel on the 23rd. The Dodgers ultimately won the pennant and the World Series. After the season *The Sporting News* named Howard their Minor League Player of the Year.

By the spring of 1960, with 50 big league at-bats to his credit, Howard's size, strength, and power had already led to a fair bit of commentary. Tales of 500-foot minor-league home runs, and his line drives that threatened base runners and infielders, were told repeatedly. In a day when many major leaguers were not even six feet tall, and when the biggest stars in the National League—Willie Mays, Hank Aaron, Ernie Banks, Frank Robinson—were no more than 180 pounds, Howard had reached 6-foot-8, and was a full 250 pounds. In later years he would occasionally be heavier. Jim Gilliam, Howard's 5-foot-10 teammate, spoke for many when he said, "a man that big should hit fifty homers every year—and I mean every year."[8] He was still a work in progress in the outfield and first base (a fine arm but slow to get moving), and he swung at way too many bad pitches. As one scribe noted, "Huge Frank has little comprehension of his own mammoth strike zone and but slight control over his all-or-nothing uppercut swing. Until he develops a modicum of finesse, Los Angeles will string along with its present quota of mere mortals."[9]

As ballyhooed as Howard was, he still faced the task of landing a spot on a world championship team. He did fairly well in spring training in 1960 (.278 with two home runs), but had a minor run-in with manager Walter Alston about his lack of playing time and ended up back in Spokane to start the year. In 26 games there he hit .371, and returned to the Dodgers in May, this time to stay. He soon became the regular right fielder and, despite a late-season slump, ended up hitting .268 with 23 home runs. After the season he was named the National League Rookie of the Year.

His 1961 season began slowly because of a chipped bone in his thumb. Alston had intended to move him to first base, but the injury and recovery kept Howard out of the lineup early, and he ended up mainly platooning in right field, starting just 72 times. He actually hit better than his rookie year — .296 with 15 home runs in just 267 at-bats, but grew increasingly frustrated when he could not stay in the lineup.

After the 1961 season the Dodgers lost both of their first basemen, Gil Hodges and Norm Larker, in the expansion draft, causing them to move Ron Fairly to first and open up more playing time for Howard. Although he still only started 123 games, he hit .296 with 31 home runs (seventh in the league) and 119 RBIs (fifth). He was still an undisciplined hitter, with 108 strikeouts and just 39 walks. The Dodgers were a great offensive team, finishing second in the league in runs while playing in the pitcher-friendly Dodger Stadium (in its first year), and won 102 games before falling to the Giants in a best-of-three playoff series to decide the pennant.

A big change for Howard came about in early 1963. "For years," wrote Sports Illustrated, "he has tried to hit 90-mph pitches with 20/40 vision in his good eye and 20/60 in his left. He was second in the league in strikeouts last year, and his relations with fly balls were no better, particularly those appearing out of the L.A. smog. Last week Howard put on glasses and immediately whacked three home runs in four games."[10] Howard stayed hot for a while (.384 in April), but a bad slump (.167 in May, .194 in June) cost him his full-time job, as he alternated the rest of the season with Wally Moon in right field. He still managed 28 home runs (by far the most on the team) and a .273 batting average in 417 at-bats. Glasses or no, he set an all-time Dodgers record with 116 strikeouts at the plate. He wore glasses for the rest of his career.

Thanks mainly to their great pitching staff, the 1963 Dodgers returned to the World Series and swept the New York Yankees, who had won the Series the previous two seasons, in four straight game. Howard finished 3-for-10 in his three games, including two memorable shots. In the first game, facing Whitey Ford, he crushed a fastball 460 feet to deep left-center field for the "longest double in the 41-year history of Yankee Stadium," reaching the fabled monuments that were on the playing field in that era. In the fourth game, in Dodger Stadium facing Ford again, he hit a slow curve 450 feet into the upper deck in deep left field.[11]

After the 1963 season Howard was 27 years old and people no longer believed he would turn into Babe Ruth. In his four years he had been on the field about two-thirds of the time for the Dodgers, and had hit .282 and averaged 24 home runs per year. While others had called him the new Ruth, and then came down on him when he was less than that, Howard had a more measured view. "I think I am a realistic guy," he said. "I have the God-given talents of strength and leverage. I realize that I can never be a great ballplayer because a great ballplayer must be able to do five things well: run, field, throw, hit and hit with power. I am mediocre in four of those — but I can hit with power. I have a chance to be a good ballplayer. I work on my fielding all the time, but in the last two years I feel that I have gotten worse as a fielder. My greatest fear was being on the bases, and I still worry about it. I'm afraid to get picked off. I'm afraid to make a mistake on the bases, and I have made them again and again, but here I feel myself getting better."[12] His throwing arm, once a strength, had been hurt when he shoved himself into a locker in a fit of anger.

Nonetheless, he wanted to know where he stood, and he went to see general manager Bavasi. "I didn't go in and give it that old nonsense about play me or trade me, because the Dodgers have some mighty fine players," said Howard. "I told Mr. Bavasi that these were my peak years as an athlete and that an athlete doesn't get two or three sets of peak years. I wanted to play regularly, and Mr. Bavasi said I would get that chance this year. Manager Alston said it, too. Now it's up to me."[13]

Howard started the first 49 games of the 1964 season, but hit just .215 despite 14 home runs (second in the league to Willie Mays). At that point Alston began sitting Howard occasionally against right-handed pitchers, and he ended up with 433 at-bats, 24 home runs, and a .226 average. Alston and Bavasi had both come to believe that they could not win in Dodger Stadium with power; they needed pitching, defense, and speed. When Howard asked to be traded after the season, the Dodgers obliged. On December 4, they dealt Howard, third baseman Ken McMullen, and pitchers Phil Ortega and Pete Richert, to the Washington Senators for pitcher Claude Osteen, infielder John Kennedy, and $100,000. Without Howard, and ably abetted by Osteen in the starting rotation, the Dodgers went on to win the 1965 World Series without a single player who hit more than 12 home runs. "Disappointed in the trade? Oh, no," recalled Howard. "I knew it was time. I was at the stage of my life where I had to find out if I could play every day."[14]

The Washington Senators were an expansion team with four years under their belt — they had lost at least 100 games every year, and had reached no higher than ninth place. No matter. Howard was excited about going where he was wanted, and excited to play for Gil Hodges, his teammate from a few years earlier. Howard remained his own toughest critic, especially where his defense was concerned. "I'm not a complete player," Howard admitted. "I can't throw like a complete player should. And I don't always hit the ball like I should. I do try, though." Replied Gil Hodges: "Frank's being paid to hit."[15] In 1965, Howard battled injuries all year, but played 149 games and hit .289 with 21 home runs and 84 RBIs, all team-leading figures. For the first time, he played mainly left field rather than right.

The next season his statistics were fairly similar (.278, 18, 71 in 146 games). In judging his record today, it is important to remember just how depressed run scoring was in the 1960s, especially in the American League. Although Howard was not a star, his OPS of .790 compared favorably to the AL's .670. And he continued to make news, and add to his legend, with his long home runs — such as one he hit against the White Sox at D.C. Stadium in April. "Tommy John threw him something," recalled teammate Fred Valentine, "and he hit a line drive back at him. John fell off the mound trying to get out of the way of the ball. [Center-fielder Tommie] Agee started in like he was going to catch a line drive. It was like a 2-iron, and it ended up in the upper deck in centerfield. They painted another seat."[16] (The Senators had begun painting seats in the upper deck to represent some of Howard's long home runs.)

Before the 1967 season, Hodges worked with Howard to retool his swing. He felt that Frank's level swing was producing hard ground balls, and asked Frank to try a slight uppercut and to stand closer to the plate so he could pull the ball more.[17] The results were obvious, as Howard had 24 home runs by midseason in 1967, and ended with 36 (third in the league) and a .256 average. He led the league with 155 strikeouts, and walked only 60 times, but his OPS of .849 was still eighth in the AL. It was his best season to date.

In 1968 Hodges moved to New York to manage the Mets, and was replaced by Jim Lemon, a former outfielder for the old Washington Senators who had been an all-or-nothing slugger like Howard, hitting as many as 30 home runs and leading the AL in strikeouts three times. This year, 1968, is historically recognized as the Year of the Pitcher, as the AL hit .230 and had shutouts in 20 percent of its games.

Bucking this trend, Howard took a step forward and became the hitter people had predicted he would become a decade earlier.

He hit .338 in April, but his best stretch came in early May when he collected 10 home runs and 17 RBIs in a span of six games. In so doing, he set records for home runs in four games (7), five games (8), and six games (10). Detroit pitcher Joe Sparma, who gave up the eighth home run in this streak, said, "He always was good for 30 home runs anyway, but this year he's clobbering my best pitches. I think he'll hit 70." "No," contradicted teammate Jim Northrup, "he'll hit 75."[18] As late as June 9, Howard held league leads in home runs (22), runs batted in (47), and batting average (.342). As the AL had had Triple Crown winners in each of the last two seasons (Frank Robinson and Carl Yastrzemski), Howard's statistics were getting quite a bit of attention. As usual, the slugger himself was less impressed than the media. "All I'm trying to do is get three good cuts each time up. I haven't changed my swing, and I don't kid myself — I'm a streak hitter and I'm hot."[19]

For the season, Howard settled down to hit .274, which was still 10th in the AL. He led the league with 44 home runs, 330 total bases, and a .552 slugging percentage, huge numbers for 1968, and finished second with 106 RBIs. He started his first All-Star Game, playing right field and batting fourth, going 0-for-2 in the AL's 1-0 loss in the Astrodome. In August he turned 32, and people were writing like he had finally figured out how to hit. For the first time in his career, he also played quite a bit of first base, starting 51 times there. "Jim Lemon did a marvelous job with me," Howard recalled. "He just took it a little further than Gil took it in '67. He moved me a little closer to the plate, spread me out a little bit more, cut down on the overstride, and as a result, I was starting to get a little more selective at the plate, and probably had my first really good year in the big leagues."[20]

Howard had picked up the nickname "Hondo" early in his career, and it endured. Once he joined the Senators, and especially once he became a star, he picked up two more nicknames: the "Washington Monument" and "Capital Punisher." The names played on his new environs along with his strength and formidable presence in the batter's box, but both sobriquets belied his gentle nature. He was nice to everyone but pitchers.

After the Senators' 10th-place finish, new owner Bob Short took over in January 1969 and decided to replace Lemon after his single season. To replace Lemon, Short lured Ted Williams out of his eight-year retirement, surprising everyone around the game. For Howard, this would be another turning point, perhaps the most important one. Williams believed he knew how to make Howard a better hitter. "He called me into his office one day in the spring of '69," Howard recalled. "He said, 'Bush! Come on in here.' I'd only been in camp a couple of days, and I'm thinking, 'Gee, I'm not in his doghouse already, am I?'"

"Can you tell me how a guy who hit 44 home runs only got 48 walks?" asked Williams. After Howard offered some explanation, his manager got to the point. "Well, let me ask you. Can you take a strike? I'm talking about if it's a tough fastball in a tough zone, first pitch. Or if it's a breaking ball, you're sitting on a fastball … Can you take a strike? You know, try to get yourself a little better count to hit in?" Howard said he could. "Well try it for me."[21]

In the event, Howard increased his walk total from 54 to 102, while his strikeouts fell from 141 to 96. He took advantage of more hitter's counts, and ended up hitting .296 with 48 home runs and 111 RBIs. He led the league with 330 total bases, and finished among the leaders in on-base-percentage (.402) and slugging percentage (.574). He hit a home run off Steve Carlton in the All-Star Game, held at his home park of RFK Stadium.

"I did it without even trying to walk," said Howard. "I was ready to hit, if it was my pitch, but if it was something other than I was looking for, I took it. I was laying off some bad pitches, getting more counts in my favor, and all because of Ted Williams. He's one in a million! A marvelous, marvelous, man!"[22] One wonders what kind of career Howard might had if he had learned to do this 10 years earlier. People had been trying to get him to lay off bad pitches his entire career. Williams, with a very simple piece of advice, succeeded. Williams was impressed. "He still hit more home runs, some of them out of sight. I mean he crushed the ball. I think without question the biggest, strongest guy who ever played this game."[23] Williams had quite an influence on the rest of the team as well, as they finished in third place in the new six-team AL East with an 86-76 record. Williams was named the league's Manager of the Year.

The next year the team fell back to 70 wins and last place (losing their final 14 of the year), though Howard kept hitting. Playing 161 games in left field and first base, he led the AL in home runs (44), RBIs (126), and walks (132). Twenty-nine of his walks were intentional, as pitchers had begun to realize that they could no longer get him to chase bad pitches with runners on base. Indians manager Al Dark walked him intentionally 12 times in 18 games. His star pitcher, Sam McDowell, was particularly afraid of Howard, who hit .368 with five home runs in 68 at-bats off McDowell in his career. It might have been worse; McDowell walked Howard 25 times, including nine times intentionally. Twice in 1970 Dark moved McDowell to another position with Howard due up, then moved him back to the mound when the coast was clear.

Although Howard had just had his three best seasons, he had turned 34 years old. He dropped back at bit in 1971, hitting .279 with 26 home runs, though his 83 walks helped him remain one of the league's most valuable offensive forces. His dropoff might have been aided by showing up in camp weighing 297 pounds. He worked hard in the spring to remove the weight, though it might have weakened him to start the season. The big story in Washington that season was the protracted public effort to find a local buyer for the team, a story that resolved itself late in the season when Short received permission from the American League to move the Senators to Arlington, Texas. In the team's last game, on September 30, 1971, Howard hit the final home run by a Washington Senator, though the game was ultimately forfeited to the Yankees when the angry fans stormed the field in the ninth inning. After Howard hit the home run, he received a standing ovation, and waved to the crowd from the dugout steps with tears in his eyes.[24]

Major-league baseball did not return to Washington for 34 years.

Howard had become one of the higher-paid players in the game, reaching $125,000 by 1970 and staying there for a few years. In early 1972, prior to reporting to the brand new Texas Rangers, he held out for a small raise but likely settled for maintaining his $120,000 salary. He still lived in Green Bay, where he owned several shopping centers, but at least one scribe thought he ought to head to camp: "Considering the prevailing temperatures in Green Bay this time of year, it's a wonder Howard doesn't settle just to get warm."[25] After he did so, and after a brief player strike that spring, on April 21, 1972, Howard appropriately hit a home run in his first home at-bat for the Rangers, the first hit in Arlington Stadium, a long drive to dead center. "A guy just does the best he can," said Howard. "We're aware you can't peddle a poor product to the public. It's nice to think that these people's first memory of major league baseball might be my home run, but I really hope that their memory is the win."[26]

It was not a harbinger, as Howard's days of stardom were behind him. He hit just .244 with nine home runs in 95 games before being sold to the Detroit Tigers on August 31. The Tigers were in a fight for the AL East title, and acquired Howard to platoon at first base with Norm Cash. Howard hit .242 for the month, but had one big day — a 3-for-4 performance against the Orioles on September 21 that included a home run off Dave McNally. As the Tigers won the division by a half-game, Howard's contributions were important. Because he did not report to the Tigers until September 1, he was ineligible to play in the AL Championship Series against Oakland, which defeated Detroit in an agonizingly close five-game series.

The next season marked the advent of the designated hitter rule in the AL, a change tailor-made for the 36-year-old Howard — or the 26-year-old Howard, for that matter. He played 85 games for the Tigers, only three times in the field, and hit 12 home runs and batted .256. In October he drew his release, ending his major-league career. He signed for 1974 to play with the Taiheyo Lions of Japan's Pacific League, but he hurt his back in his very first at-bat, and never played again. Howard's playing career was over at age 37.

With his popularity, it is not surprising that Howard enjoyed an extensive post-playing career in the game. He managed the Spokane Indians in 1976, but returned to the major leagues as a coach with the Milwaukee Brewers the next and remained in the majors for most of the next 20 years. He had two brief trials as manager. He led the San Diego Padres in the strike-marred 1981 season, but was let go after the team finished last in both halves of the split season. Two years later he took over the New York Mets when George Bamberger was fired 46 games into the 1983 season, but Howard was not offered the job after the Mets finished last. Howard was well respected as a coach, but his employers seemed to feel that he was too nice a guy to be a successful manager. Besides the Brewers and the Mets, he also served as coach with the Seattle Mariners, the New York Yankees and the Tampa Bay Devil Rays.

After spending offseasons in Green Bay for many years, by the early 1990s Howard had resettled in Northern Virginia where his years of stardom in Washington made him a popular and revered figure. He and Carol raised six children, but their marriage later ended and in 1991 he remarried, and he and second wife Donna were still happily together in 2012. When the major leagues returned to Washington in 2005, with the relocation of the former Montreal Expos, Howard became the most visible link to the previous major-league teams that had played there. Especially in the Nationals years at RFK Stadium, Howard's old park, fans got a visible reminder of the old star anytime they looked at the painted seats, still visible in the upper deck. In 2008 the Nationals began play in the brand-new Nationals Park, and the next year unveiled three statues in their center field plaza, depicting Walter Johnson (who pitched for the first 20th- century version of the Washington Senators), Josh Gibson (who starred in the Negro Leagues for the Homestead Grays, who played in Griffith Stadium), and Howard (representing the expansion Senators). When the Nationals reached the postseason in 2012, Howard threw out the ceremonial pitch of the Division Series before Game Four.

Long after he had retired, Howard was often called upon to look at back on his career, especially the years prior to his stardom, and he always did so objectively. "To be totally honest, had I made some adjustments -- hitting-wise -- earlier in my career, instead of just going up there [swinging at everything], I would have had better years. When people look back on their careers, they say they wouldn't change a thing. I would have. I would have made the adjustments. I would have given myself the chance to put up big numbers."[27]

But let us not dwell on what Frank Howard did not accomplish, and instead marvel at what he did: 382 home runs, two home run titles, an RBI title, a World Series home run and championship, three All-Star Games, and the admiration of most of greater Washington, D.C. The man has a statue outside of a big-league ballpark, an honor not bestowed on many players. For a few years there, a big-league pitcher would rather face just about anyone in the world instead of Frank Oliver Howard, the Capital Punisher.

Notes

1. John Devaney, "Frank Howard: Goliath Grows Up," *Sport*, September 1968: 65.
2. William Leggett, "The Dodgers' Troubled Giant," *Sports Illustrated*, May 25, 1964.
3. Al Hirshberg, *Frank Howard—The Gentle Giant* (New York: Putnam, 1973), 22.
4. Ed Linn, "Frank Howard—The Man Behind the Babe Ruth Myth," *Sport*, April 1961: 61. The Cliff Alexander report is included in this article.
5. Mike Bryan, "Reflections on the Game," *Sports Illustrated*, May 25, 1989.
6. Ed Linn, "Frank Howard," 67.

7   John Schulian, "The Boys Of Summer Were The Boys Of Slumber The First Year In Los Angeles," *Sports Illustrated*, April 14, 1975.
8   Allan Roth, "Frank Howard's Baseball Diary," *Sport*, July 1960: 21.
9   "Los Angeles DODGERS," *Sports Illustrated*, April 11, 1960.
10 "Baseball's Week," *Sports Illustrated*, May 6, 1963.
11 William Leggett, "Koo-foo the Killer," *Sports Illustrated*, October 14, 1963.
12 William Leggett, "The Dodgers' Troubled Giant," *Sports Illustrated*, May 25, 1964.
13 Ibid.
14 James R. Hartley, *Washington Senators* (Washington, D.C.: Corduroy Press, 1998), 45.
15 Mark Mulvoy, "Baseball's Week," *Sports Illustrated*, June 14, 1965.
16 James R. Hartley, *Washington Senators*, 54.
17 "Rising Dynasty for the Birds," *Sports Illustrated*, April 17, 1967.
18 Peter Carry, "Highlight," *Sports Illustrated*, May 27, 1968.
19 Ibid.
20 James R. Hartley, *Washington Senators*, 91.
21 James R. Hartley, *Washington Senators*, 94.
22 James R. Hartley, *Washington Senators*, 105.
23 John Underwood, "Ted Williams—My Year," *Sports Illustrated*, January 26, 1970.
24 Don Oldenburg, "No Place Like Home," *Washington Post*, March 22, 2005: C1.
25 "People," Sports Illustrated, March 6, 1972.
26 Harold Peterson, "New Home on the Range," *Sports Illustrated*, May 1, 1972.
27 Bill Ladson, "Q&A with Frank Howard—Former Senators Slugger discusses career in Washington," Washington Nationals Website (http://washington.nationals.mlb.com), January 22, 2009.

GERRY JANESKI

BY DAVID E. SKELTON

In his April 27, 2014, major-league debut, righty Scott Carroll tied the Chicago White Sox record for the longest initial outing by one of its pitchers: 7⅓ innings, last established by Gerry Janeski in 1970. After a dubious start to his major-league career – four hits and a hit-by-pitch to his first six batters – Janeski settled down to surrender just one run in his next 20⅓ innings. Buried in the Boston Red Sox organization for five years, Janeski's 2-0, 1.65 mark in his first two big-league appearances, including a three-hit shutout over the Oakland Athletics, drew instant attention. Not an overpowering pitcher, Janeski prided himself on his control. "I pitch low, the sinker," Janeski explained. "[I] try to make them hit the ball into the ground."[1]

But control problems contributed to Janeski's early exit from the majors when, inexplicably, his walks-per-inning ratio nearly doubled during his sophomore season. Though he found some later success as a reliever (particularly after returning to the minors) Janeski never rebounded to the majors after four brief appearances in 1972.

Gerald Joseph Janeski was born on April 18, 1946, the younger of two children of Joseph Francis and Stanistawa C. "Sophia" (Grygier) Janeski, in Pasadena, California. He was the grandson of Polish and German immigrants, the paternal surname shortened from Janiszewski by his father.[2] Gerald and his sister attended La Salle High School in Pasadena, a private institution founded in 1956 in the Roman Catholic Archdiocese of Los Angeles. The La Salle Lancers established their first varsity baseball team in 1959. During his junior and senior years (1963-64) Gerry Janeski, under the guidance and no-nonsense approach of baseball coach Phillip "Duffy" Lewis, was named as a pitcher to the Santa Fe All-League first team. Janeski moved on to nearby California State University Los Angeles, where the English major[3] honed his talent under the watchful eye of famed Golden Eagles baseball coach Jim Reeder. It was from these collegiate fields that scout and former major-league catcher Joe Stephenson signed Janeski to a Boston Red Sox contract in 1965.

Janeski was assigned to the Waterloo (Iowa) Hawks in the Midwest League (Class A). In the pitching-dominant circuit, the 19-year-old made a strong professional debut: eight wins and a 2.56 ERA in 16 appearances (league average: 3.21). When the season ended Janeski was named the Hawks' most valuable pitcher. Excepting a brief stint in the Double-A Eastern League in 1966, Janeski bounced among the organization's varied Class-A affiliates the next two years. Personal highlights included a 13-strikeout venture on June 30, 1966, against the Dubuque Packers – believed to be a single-game career high – and a heartbreaking 1-0 loss to the Greensboro Yankees in 1967 in which Janeski retired 21 consecutive batters before surrendering a ninth-inning homer. While pitching for Winston-Salem in the Carolina League in 1967, Janeski placed among the league leaders in

ERA for portions of the season until a second-half dip took him out of the running. He still finished well below the league average with a 2.95 mark.

Greater success came in 1968 in Janeski's second stint in Pittsfield, Massachusetts (Double A): 7-3, 1.32 in 15 appearances. In June the Louisville Colonels' Ken Brett, the Red Sox' prized lefty prospect, was shelved with what was feared to be a career-threatening elbow injury. The organization promoted Janeski to Louisville as Brett's replacement on the Triple-A roster. Used exclusively in relief, Janeski was challenged when he did not have time to loosen properly. "Usually it takes me an inning or two to get loose," Janeski confessed (though he did co-author a June 21 shutout over the Syracuse Chiefs).[4] When Brett recovered sufficiently to rejoin the Colonels, Janeski was sent back down. He won five straight games to lead Pittsfield's effort to overtake the slumping Reading Phillies and capture the league flag. In September the two teams competed in the championship playoffs. Janeski got his team's only series win, a 2-1 contest in which the righty scored the winning run in the 10th inning.

Reassigned to Louisville in 1969, Janeski set an early tone for his finest professional campaign with a shutout of the Toledo Mud Hens on April 28. One month later he impressed teammate Bob Montgomery with a two-hit shutout over the hard-hitting Tidewater Tides: "I could have caught [Janeski] in a rocking chair today," the batterymate joked. "He was so relaxed that I thought we might have to go out and wake him up a couple of times."[5] On July 14 Janeski became the first 12-game winner in Triple A. He was selected as the International League's starter in the August 7 All-Star tilt against the Washington Senators. In Tidewater manager Clyde McCullough's plan to use one pitcher per inning in the circuit's midsummer classic, Janeski needed just eight pitches in the first frame to dispose of the Washington batters. As Louisville manager Eddie Kasko explained, "[Janeski] looks good to hit. The hitter likes what he sees but, when the ball gets to the plate, the bottom drops out of it."[6] The durable hurler finished the season with an International League-leading 14 complete games while placing among the leaders in wins (15), innings pitched (186), shutouts (3), and walks per nine innings (1.7).[7] Though the parent club struggled from the mound in the 1969 campaign, there is no evidence that the Red Sox considered promoting Janeski during the season (though he was placed on the 40-man roster during the offseason).

In 1970 Janeski reported to the club's Winter Haven, Florida, spring camp. He shared a passion for kite flying with slugging prospect Billy Conigliaro, oblivious to the ongoing negotiations of a December 13, 1969, four-player swap between Boston and the Chicago White Sox. Minor-league pitcher Billy Farmer had refused to report to the White Sox and the teams sought a suitable replacement. On March 9 the clubs agreed upon Janeski. The previous year the White Sox were spared the league's worst pitching solely by the existence of the expansion Seattle Pilots. Little improvement was expected in 1970 when, with reference to veteran starters Tommy John and Joe Horlen, the phrase heard often around Chicago's Sarasota, Florida, camp was "Tommy and Joe and pray for snow."[8] Three innings of shutout ball by Janeski against the Detroit Tigers on March 14, followed eight days later by four innings of the same against Kansas City, attracted much attention. "I think we've got a pitcher there," said manager Don Gutteridge. "The more I see of him, the more I like him. ... he has good poise."[9] The Chicago scribes fawned on him as well, describing Janeski as "quite a refreshing sort ... intelligent and articulate."[10] On April 1 Janeski's fate was sealed with a "standout perform[ance]"[11] against the Pittsburgh Pirates. He was provided an opportunity to continue flying kites in the Windy City when he accompanied the club to Chicago as the White Sox' number-three starter.

An Opening Day 12-0 thumping by the Minnesota Twins accented the plight of the White Sox' 1970 campaign. A season-long mediocre offense, coupled with the majors' worst ERA, contributed to a 106-loss season (a franchise worst through 2017). Janeski's debut performance was the club's first win of the season, and a successful 5-2 run beginning May 12 provided the rookie with a team-leading seven victories. This included a strong June 9 outing against the organization that had buried him for so many years (a two-run homer by future Hall of Famer Carl Yastrzemski was the only barrier between the hurler and his second career shutout). Eight days later Janeski, at best a fair hitter, helped his own cause by driving in three runs on a single and a squeeze bunt to corral the New York Yankees, 6-3. He lacked run support in what might have been two additional wins.

Another attribute that made Janeski popular with the sportswriters was his keen sense of humor. In his first 60⅔ innings, Janeski surrendered just two home runs, both three-run shots by Baltimore slugger Boog Powell, who was on his way to his only MVP season. After the second blow, Powell "said Janeski was a very impressive pitcher 'and throwing harder' than the first time. [The righty r]etorted … 'If I throw any harder, he'll hit it to the moon.'"[12] Dubbed a "sensational rookie"[13] by reporters, Janeski drew favorable comparisons to fellow first-year players Thurman Munson and Bert Blyleven.

But hitters started to zero in on the rookie hurler. Beginning on June 27, Janeski won just one of 11 decisions as his ERA approached five. Pitching coach Les Moss began working with Janeski on a slip pitch. "He has a good fastball and slider," Moss explained. "[B]ut he's been around the league twice now and everyone knows that's all he can throw. It's time for him to develop a pitch to fool some people."[14] The additional instruction took. Excluding an August 30 outing against Boston – a game in which no pitcher was spared as the teams combined to score a near-record 32 runs – Janeski finished the season 2-2, 3.22 over his last six appearances. He concluded the year among the team leaders in appearances (35), innings pitched (205⅔), wins (10), and losses (17) to earn White Sox' Rookie of the Year honors.

Under the watchful eye of Johnny Sain, the White Sox' new pitching coach, Janeski ventured south where he played for the Zulia Eagles in the Venezuelan Winter League. The experience proved challenging for Janeski as he performed poorly under Eagles manager Luis Aparicio. The White Sox began shopping the hurler. On February 9, 1971, Janeski was traded to the Washington Senators for outfielder Rick Reichardt.[15] Janeski's arrival, combined with the earlier acquisition of former 30-game winner Denny McLain, caused manager Ted Williams to gush, "We just might have the best pitching in the American League."[16]

The only thing the Splendid Splinter knew about pitching was how to hit it. Grand expectations fell far short as the 1971 Senators plunged to their annual second-division finish; the staff in general, and Janeski in particular, realizing their own challenges. Janeski's trials began in spring training when a brilliant outing was often balanced against a less distinguished one. Williams vacillated between plugging Janeski into the rotation and using him in relief. The manager's mind was made up on April 2 when the Atlanta Braves pummeled the righty for 13 hits and seven runs in five innings.

In his first nine relief appearances, Janeski pitched brilliantly: nine hits and one run surrendered over 10⅔ innings (there were two less successful starts). On April 21 he earned what became his last major-league win with 2⅔ innings of two-hit relief against the Yankees in New York. Williams's confidence in Janeski grew and he inserted the righty into the rotation. Despite a high walk yield and two losses, Janeski made an adequate showing (3.64 ERA) in five starting assignments through June 9. Far less success ensued. He did not survive the second inning in a start against the Baltimore Orioles on June 22. Five days later, Williams used a quick hook in New York after Janeski walked the first two batters. The righty was optioned to the Triple-A Denver Bears after a June 29 relief appearance against the Red Sox.

Janeski earned four wins, including an August 15 shutout over the Tulsa Oilers, to lead the Bears to a first-place finish in the West Division of the American Association. But his bigger contributions came in the playoff series that followed. On September 9 manager Del Wilber turned to Janeski in the decisive Game Seven for the league championship against the Indianapolis Indians. The righty hurled a five-hit complete-game victory (surrendering no earned runs) to advance the Bears to the Junior World Series. A week later he was just as effective against the Rochester Red Wings: a 3-2 complete-game win in which Janeski induced 19 outs via infield grounders. But the string of playoff success ran out when Wilber again turned to Janeski for a Game Seven win to no avail.

Janeski enjoyed continued success in Denver in 1972 after a dreadful spring training. On April 18 he fired a five-hitter against Tulsa in a 3-2 win, then two weeks later pitched a three-hit victory over Indianapolis. Placing among the league leaders at 4-1, 2.72, he earned promotion to the parent club (relocated to Texas) when rookie reliever Don Stanhouse was injured. Janeski made four appearances, including a strong start in a losing effort against the White Sox on May 23. But the healthy return of Stanhouse, combined with the acquisition of infielder Dalton Jones from Detroit, caused a roster logjam. Janeski made what turned out to be his last major-league appearance on May 28, 1972 (a successful two innings of relief against the Twins), before being optioned back to Denver. Encumbered by a second-half swoon, he finished the Triple-A season with a record of 11-10, 4.79.

With the exception of one starting assignment in 1973, Janeski concluded his professional career from the bullpen. Pitching for the Spokane Indians in the Pacific Coast League (the Rangers' newly located Triple-A affiliate) Janeski began a brilliant 1973 campaign (4-1, 1.89, and a league-leading 14 saves) before suffering another second-half swoon. Postseason success was again realized on September 6 when Janeski captured the win in relief in the last of a three-game sweep over the Tucson Toros to capture the league championship. In May 1974, Janeski moved to the San Diego Padres' Hawaii affiliate, where once again a strong start yielded to a second-half swoon (1-3, 5.63 in his last 26 appearances). The disappointing finish convinced Janeski to seek other endeavors.

During the major leagues' 1970 All-Star break, Janeski married Suzanne Virginia "Suzie" Prater. A native of Alhambra, California (Los Angeles County), Suzie's spent her childhood in close proximity to the Pasadena haunts of Janeski's youth. The couple returned to California, where Janeski (joined later by his wife and son) launched a successful career in real estate. In the 1980s he formed an investors group with Hall of Famer Hank Greenberg. Throughout this time Janeski was active alongside fellow major-league alumni in a campaign to ensure financial assistance to players who found far less success after baseball. The campaign realized success in 2011 when Commissioner Bud Selig announced that the new Collective Bargaining Agreement would include annual annuities up to $10,000 to baseball's "lost boys."

In 62 major-league appearances (280 innings) Janeski earned 11 wins against 23 losses and a 4.73 ERA. Bypassed and seemingly ignored for five years in the Boston Red Sox organization, he defied the odds by emerging on the big-league scene with a splash. His inability to master more than a terrific slider and pedestrian fastball, combined with the inexplicable control problems encountered after his rookie season, stymied what might have been a much longer career.

Sources

In addition to the sources cited in the Notes, the author also consulted Baseball-Reference.com, Ancestry.com, and the following websites:

baseballlibrary.com/ballplayers/player.php?name=Gerry_Janeski_1946.

knightfever.wordpress.com/2015/08/18/knights-knotes-august-17-2015/.

lasallehs.org/s/639/start.aspx.

lancerbb.org/La_Salle_Lancers_Baseball/History.html.

ocweekly.com/2012-03-29/news/major-league-baseball-players-medical-pension-richard-lee-dick-baney/.

realtor.com/realestateagents/Jerry-Janeski_Laguna-Niguel_CA_49384_965894497.

The author wishes to thank Rod Nelson, chair of the SABR Scouts Committee.

Notes

1. "Janeski in Control," The Sporting News, June 28, 1969: 42.
2. Though they lived just 40 miles apart in Pennsylvania in the 1930s, the author was unable to make any familial ties between Gerald's father and minor-league player Robert J. Janeski (baseball-reference.com/register/player.cgi?id=janesko01rob).
3. An avid reader, Janeski was particularly fond of author John Steinbeck.
4. "American Assn.," The Sporting News, September 4, 1971: 36.
5. "International League," The Sporting News, June 7, 1969: 34.
6. "International League," The Sporting News, August 16, 1969: 38.
7. On the downside, Janeski also led the league with 218 hits surrendered.
8. This echoed a popular tagline from the Boston Braves' 1948 pennant run: "Spahn and Sain and pray for rain" (sometimes rendered as "Spahn and Sain and two days' rain.")
9. "Chisox '70 Chant: 'Tommy and Joe – Pray for Snow,'" The Sporting News, April 4, 1970: 8.
10. Ibid.; A health enthusiast, Janeski earned the nickname The Wheat Germ Kid when reporters noticed that his locker resembled a health-food store.
11. "Exhibition Games," The Sporting News, April 18, 1970: 35.
12. Nothing Chilly About Mac's Chisox Bat," The Sporting News, May 23, 1970: 21.
13. Ibid.
14. "Major Flashes," The Sporting News, August 15, 1970: 30.
15. Reichardt, acquired by the Senators just the year before, appears to have rankled feathers in a salary dispute that precipitated his early exit from Washington.
16. "Denny Wins Gold Star as First-Week Nat," The Sporting News, March 6, 1971: 39.

DALTON JONES

BY MAURICE BOUCHARD

In groups of twos and threes at first and then, little by little, in larger groups, the fans rose and cheered for their hometown team. It spread throughout Fenway Park until virtually every one of the 35,000 fans had joined in the spontaneous standing ovation. The top of the ninth inning on October 12, 1967, was about to start. The score was 7-2; the St. Louis Cardinals were leading the Boston Red Sox in the seventh game of the World Series. The way Bob Gibson was pitching, there was little doubt about the final outcome, but the fans wanted to say "Thank You" to their Red Sox, who had brought so much joy and excitement in the wild ride that was the summer of 1967. Dalton Jones, who was getting ready to play third base, remembered it well nearly 40 years later. "Talk about bringing a tear to your eye," Jones reminisced.[1] One could still hear the emotion in his voice four decades removed. Mississippi native Dalton Jones, still two months shy of his 24th birthday, had played on baseball's biggest stage, yes, played and thrived.

Twenty-four summers before, Mrs. Louise Jones was concerned. Although they were living in Baton Rouge and had access to good medical care, Clinton and Louise Jones did not trust the big city doctors.[2] The former Louise Purl had, in fact, lost a baby during her first pregnancy while in the care of Baton Rouge doctors. Not about to let that happen again, the Joneses moved back to their hometown in southern Mississippi to be in the care of a familiar, trusted doctor. James Dalton Jones was born on December 10, 1943, in McComb, Mississippi. Dalton, as he was to be known, was named for his father's brother, James Dalton, an Army Air Corps flier who had been killed in action in North Africa a year earlier.[3] Dalton was the first child in the Jones family. A brother, Melvin, arrived three years later.

While growing up in Baton Rouge, baseball was an integral part of young Dalton's life. Dalton's father loved baseball. Clinton H. Jones was then an assistant chemist for the Esso (now Exxon) Oil Company.[4] In addition to his official duties at work, he resurrected the company baseball team and help lead the team to a semipro championship. Previously, Clinton had been a star in the Class-D Evangeline League. Clint, as he was known, played first base and was the batting champion in 1934 for the Opelousas (Louisiana) Indians.[5] Clint Jones led that league in runs scored and hits in 1934 as well. He moved up to the Class-A Des Moines Demons in 1935 and would likely have gone on to higher-level minor league teams, perhaps beyond, had not an arm injury ended his baseball career.[6] In addition to Clinton's experience in the minors, Dalton's great-uncle, Leroy "Cowboy" Jones, played in the Texas League. Family vacations often centered on baseball. The Jones family would travel to St. Louis to see the Cardinals play; they traveled to Kansas City and even to Cleveland to see the Red Sox play on the road. Consequently, as a youngster, Dalton became a Stan Musial fan and a Ted Williams fan.

The Jones family was present in Cleveland when Ted Williams tied and then passed Mel Ott for third place on the major-league career home run list.

In addition, Clinton Jones coached Dalton from Little League up through American Legion ball. Dalton also benefited from countless one-on-one sessions with his father, who always had time to hit fungoes or throw batting practice. When scouts started flocking around the 14-year-old Jones, it was his father who kept everything in the "right perspective".[7] From an early age, Dalton wanted only to be a major-league baseball player.

Dalton was a star shortstop for his high school team in Baton Rouge, the Istrouma Indians. In 1961, Jones led Istrouma to the Louisiana state championship game (future major-league star Rusty Staub led the opposing team, Jesuit High School of New Orleans). After graduation, Red Sox scout George Digby signed the 6-foot-1, 180-pound, left-hand hitting shortstop for a $60,000 bonus, a considerable amount in 1961 but about half what some top prospects received. Still, Jones felt a responsibility to perform up to the high expectations of the Red Sox.

Jones immediately reported to the Alpine (Texas) Cowboys of the Class-D Sophomore League, managed by former Red Sox pitching great Mel Parnell. In his first professional game, Jones hit two triples off the 425-foot fence at Tingley Field in Albuquerque. The second triple came with two out in the ninth inning. The hit started a three-run rally as the Cowboys beat the Dukes, 4-3.[8] After this promising debut, Jones went into a prolonged slump, the first time Jones had experienced mediocrity (or worse) in baseball. He was feeling the pressure, most of it self-inflicted. He seriously considered quitting baseball, thinking he could not make it at the professional level. However, after some soul searching, prayer, and not a few calls home, Jones decided to persevere. He went on to hit .322 in 77 games, including 18 doubles, 8 triples, 6 home runs, 48 RBIs, and 58 runs scored.

The next year, 1962, Jones was promoted to York (Pennsylvania) of the Double-A Eastern League. The teenager had a good year for the White Roses, hitting .309 in 127 games. The young shortstop led the league in triples with 13. He scored 77 runs and knocked in 52.

In 1963, after a very good spring training in which he nearly made the Red Sox opening day roster, Jones was promoted to the Seattle Rainiers of the Triple-A Pacific Coast League. Jones, switched to second base with the emergence of Rico Petrocelli (who would be Jones' roommate in the major leagues), had a decent year. His average dropped to .255 but he scored 78 runs while clubbing 7 home runs and 11 triples.

Spring training in 1964 was a very good one for the 20-year-old Jones, but he expected to be in the minors that year. As spring training marched on, however, Jones was still with the big club. One day, late in the spring season, pitching coach Bob Turley found Jones working out in center field. As he walked by, the former Yankee pitching star joked to Jones, "I heard you're going to be rooming with me this season."[9] That was how Dalton Jones learned he was heading north with the Boston Red Sox.

Jones made his major-league debut on April 17, 1964, the home opener at Fenway Park. He contributed his first major-league hit, an RBI triple. It came in the third inning off White Sox hurler Joe Horlen. The Red Sox went on to beat the White Sox, 4-1, in a game that also featured another Red Sox rookie, Massachusetts native Tony Conigliaro, who hit the first pitch he saw at Fenway Park for a home run. The next day, also at Fenway, Jones hit his first major-league home run, a solo shot in the ninth inning off White Sox left-hander Don Mossi. After the game, Boston manager Johnny Pesky called Clinton Jones to celebrate Dalton's home run. Red Sox announcer Curt Gowdy gave Jones and Tony Conigliaro videotapes of the games in which each hit his first home run.[10] In those days before VCRs and before universal TV coverage, that was a rare gift.

1964 proved to be an acceptable debut year for Dalton Jones. He was hitting over .300 late in May but then saw his average drop to as low as .218 in early August before settling at .230 for the year. Jones scored 37 runs and batted in 39 in 118 games for the eighth-place Red Sox. The highlight of his season came on May 19 at Fenway Park against the

Los Angeles Angels. The Sox were losing 3-0 in the bottom of the ninth. Jones, who had not played in the game to this point, kept walking in front of manager Johnny Pesky to get noticed. Pesky relented and told Jones he would bat for Red Sox pitcher Bob Heffner.[11]

Heffner was due up seventh in the inning. After two quick outs, it looked as though Jones would not hit. Dick Stuart walked, however, and then went to third on Tony Conigliaro's double. A hit batsman and another walk produced a run and left the bases loaded for pinch-hitter Dalton Jones. As Jones told the *Boston Globe*'s Ray Fitzgerald three years later, "Pesky sends me up to pinch-hit and I'm scared out of my mind."[12] Jones whistled a double past Angels pitcher Don Lee on a 3-2 count. The hit cleared the bases giving the Red Sox the walk-off victory, 4-3. It was Jones' most meaningful hit yet as a Red Sox pinch-hitter and it helped propel him into a role for which he would achieve some fame, at least among Red Sox fans.

While Jones had some success at the plate, he had some trouble in the field, committing an error in each of his first three games, and was beginning to be labeled, perhaps unfairly, as a defensive liability, a label that was to stick with him throughout his career. He played 85 games at second in 1964, sharing time with Chuck Schilling and Felix Mantilla. Second base was still a new position for Jones, and in 1964 he committed 16 errors for a .959 fielding percentage.

The next two years, 1965 and 1966, were lackluster seasons for the Red Sox. Tom Yawkey's so-called "country club" may have been pleasant for the players, but it didn't do much for the winning percentage or the gate receipts. The Red Sox finished ninth in a 10-team league both years. Jones had a slightly better year in 1965 than in 1964. In '65, Jones was still batting over .300 in late August before finishing at .270. He also had his career high-water marks in hits (99) and total bases (137).

Highlights for the season include a five-hit day against the Senators in Washington on July 9 and an RBI triple off Luis Tiant, providing the only run Dave Morehead would need when he pitched his no-hitter against the Cleveland Indians on September 16 at nearly empty Fenway Park. Nine days later, in another historic moment, Jones batted (he reached on an error) against the 59-year-old Satchel Paige in Kansas City.

Jones improved offensively despite tearing a hamstring muscle and despite moving to his third infield position in four years. He suffered his injury rounding first at Fenway while legging a double against Luis Tiant in early May. Jones would play with his leg wrapped the rest of his career.[13] When Frank Malzone hurt his foot early in the season, manager Billy Herman put Jones at third base. Jones played so well at the position that he earned the starting spot against right-handed pitching after Malzone returned.[14] Jones played 81 games at third base and made 17 errors in 243 chances.

In 1966, Jones lost his starting job to rookie Joe Foy, and his offensive production dropped off. He batted only .234 in 252 at-bats, more than 100 fewer than in either of his previous two major league seasons. It was a struggle all year. Jones' average never reached .240; he was batting .200 on the Fourth of July. Jones played in 70 games at second base and just three at third base. He committed 10 errors in 260 chances, improving his second-base fielding percentage from two seasons previous. Jones' batting highlight for the year came on July 6 in the first game of a doubleheader at Yankee Stadium. With the score tied, 3-3, Jones batted for the pitcher in the ninth inning and hit a one-out, two-run home run to make the score 5-3, which held up when the Yankees were retired in the bottom of the frame.

The Red Sox in the spring, summer, and fall of 1967 have been much chronicled. While most of the accolades deservedly go to Yaz, Lonborg, Tony C., Boomer, Rico, and a few others, fans remember Dalton Jones' clutch hitting, especially pinch-hitting late in the 1967 campaign. In terms of raw offensive output, it was his least productive major-league season so far. He played in only 89 games and had 159 at-bats. While he hit .289, he had only 65 total bases. Jones was a man without a position in 1967 and was relegated almost entirely to pinch-hitting. Rookie

Mike Andrews was the starter at second, while Foy held down the hot corner. Freshman manager Dick Williams gave Jones a start when he could. For example, when Foy was in Williams' doghouse for being overweight late in April, Jones had five consecutive starts (April 21-25). Jones responded. He hit .368 during that stretch, scoring at least one run in each game as the Sox won four of the five games.

On May 24, in a rare start, Jones hit a solo home run off Denny McLain at Tiger Stadium. It was enough for Jim Lonborg, who blanked the Tigers, 1-0. Between June 8 and September 4, however, Jones started only one game. In addition to being forced out of the starting lineup for baseball reasons, there was also Uncle Sam to contend with. In 1967, the war in Vietnam was raging. The Red Sox and other teams were keen to keep their players out of the military draft. They made sure all of their eligible players were assigned to Reserve units. Lonborg, Jones, and other players did two-week stints during the season. Even though his playing time was limited, Jones made the most of his spot starts and pinch-hitting opportunities. He was especially productive late in the season as one of the closest pennant races in American League history unfolded.

Jones' average had dipped to .220 by August 17. Starting with a pinch hit on August 19, Jones went 24 for 59 (a .407 clip) the rest of the season, with one home run, 14 RBIs, and six runs scored. On August 20, he came off the bench and had two key hits to help the Sox erase an 8-0 deficit against California as the Sox went on to win 9-8. On August 22, he broke a scoreless tie with a pinch-hit, two-run triple in the seventh inning off Phil Ortega of the Washington Senators. The Sox won, 2-1, which put them in second place, just a percentage point behind the White Sox. On September 18, the Red Sox played the Tigers in Detroit. Going into the game, the Sox were trailing the first-place Tigers by one game. Jones got the start at third because he hit well in Tiger Stadium and had hit a home run off McLain, the Tiger starter, earlier in the year. The move to start Jones paid off. He had four hits in five at-bats with two RBIs, including a 10th-inning home run off Mike Marshall.

Jones speared Bill Freehan's line drive for the final out in the bottom of the 10th, giving the Red Sox a 6-5 victory and a share of first place. "This had to be the best game of baseball I've ever played in the big leagues," Jones told the *Boston Globe*'s Clif Keane.[15] On September 24, Jones got the start at third again. This time he went 4-for-6 with a double and triple and five RBIs as the Sox beat the Baltimore Orioles, 11-7.

When the Red Sox had to beat the Twins on the final two games of the 1967 season to ensure at least a playoff game for the American League pennant, Jones had a key role to play. In the penultimate game, with the Twins leading 1-0, Jones had a pinch-hit single in the bottom of the fifth inning, moving Reggie Smith to third. Jerry Adair knocked in Smith; Carl Yastrzemski drove in Jones for the go-ahead run. The Sox never trailed after that and won, 6-4, giving them a share of first place with the Twins. On October 1, the last game of the regular season, Jones got the start at third and batted in the second spot in the order. He had two hits in four at-bats, including a single to keep the rally going in the five-run sixth inning. Jones scored one of the five Red Sox runs as they beat the Twins 5-3. The win and the Tigers' loss later that afternoon gave the Red Sox their first pennant in 21 years.

Given that Jones had so few starts in the regular season, it seems somewhat surprising he started four of the seven World Series games. Dick Williams wanted the left-handed hitting Jones in the lineup against St. Louis right-handers Bob Gibson, Dick Hughes, and Nelson Briles. With that vote of confidence, Jones responded. He hit .389 for the Series, second only to Yastrzemski among Red Sox hitters. Jones had a key pinch hit in Game Six, with the Red Sox facing elimination, down three games to two. Jones did not start even though the right-handed Hughes was the starting pitcher for the Red Birds. (Jones unsuccessfully lobbied Dick Williams for the chance to start. At the time, he was the leading Red Sox hitter at .353. "I told him that I thought I deserved to play, I thought I had done the job".)[16] With one out in the bottom of the seventh inning, with the score tied, 4-4, Jones was sent up to hit for John Wyatt. Facing former teammate Jack Lamabe, he singled to right field. The next batter, Joe Foy, plated Jones with a double to left for the go-ahead run. The Red Sox went on to score four in the inning, won the game, and forced a Game Seven the next day. Jones pinch-hit in the eighth inning of the deciding game, with the Red Sox down, 7-1, and drew a walk. He stayed in the game to play third in the top of the ninth. It was the last time Jones appeared in a postseason game.

Dalton Jones thought, after the way he played third base in the World Series, he would compete with Joe Foy for the starting job in 1968.[17] Jones did start the first six games of the season at third base. He was batting only .071, however, when Joe Foy got the starting nod against White Sox lefty Gary Peters on April 18. Foy played well and became the regular third baseman the rest of the season. Williams gave Jones a chance to be an everyday player, but it meant learning a new infield position. By midseason, first baseman George Scott was struggling at the plate (as were many players in the "Year of the Pitcher.") Jones started at first against Oakland on July 1 and played first base in 55 of the final 88 Red Sox games in 1968. He acquitted himself very well, handling 478 chances with only two errors.

While his fielding was improving, Jones' batting average was going in the other direction. He had decided he was going to hit more home runs and tried to pull everything.[18] Pitchers started pitching him outside. In the past, Jones would have taken the pitch the other way, to left field. Now he was hitting ground balls to second. Jones had 354 at-bats in 1968, nearly 200 more than in 1967, but his average plummeted to .234. One bright spot was his specialty, pinch-hitting; he had 11 pinch hits and a .407 average. Jones struck out 53 times though, a career high.

As the offensive struggles continued, Jones put more and more pressure on himself.[19] The only person who could pull Jones out of his batting funk, Clinton Jones, was dying of leukemia 1,500 miles away. Clinton Jones succumbed to the disease the next year. Jones had more time at first in 1969, playing very well

there, but his batting average dropped to .220. While he cut back on the strikeouts, he was not providing the offensive power major-league teams expect from a corner infielder. The two-year experiment at first base was over and it was time for a change. On December 13, 1969, the Red Sox traded Jones to the Detroit Tigers for utility infielder Tom Matchick. Overall, Jones hit .243 with the Red Sox with 26 home runs and 186 RBIs. He hit well in pressure situations, compiling a .271 average as a pinch-hitter. He remains the Red Sox all-time pinch-hit leader with 55.

At first, Jones was happy about the trade.[20] He was ready for a change. Jones had always hit well in Tiger Stadium. When the 1970 season started, however, it was clear the Tigers' plans did not include Jones. The Tigers already had a left-handed pinch-hitting specialist, Gates Brown. Jones was used sparingly as a utility infielder, appearing in only 62 games in the field, 89 overall. One "highlight" of the season came on July 9 against his former team. Jones came in as a pinch-hitter in the bottom of the seventh inning. With the score tied, 3-3, and the bases loaded, Jones hit what should have been the first grand slam of his career. Inexplicably, Don Wert decided to tag up at first and Jones passed him while rounding first. Jones was called out and given credit for a single. He did get three RBIs, however, and the Tigers went on to beat the Red Sox, 7-3. Jones hit .220 for the second straight year but he led all Tigers with 11 pinch-hits and a .379 average as a pinch-hitter.

In 1971, Jones' playing time was reduced even further. He played only 32 games in the field, including, for the first time, the outfield. Jones was batting .375 when Al Kaline was slowed by a pulled hamstring. Jones hit .500 with a home run in three starts in right field. After maintaining a .300 average into mid-June, Jones finished the year at .254. Due to limited playing time however, he had career lows in most offensive categories, including runs, hits, RBIs, doubles, and total bases. He was the team pinch-hit leader again, though, with 13 pinch hits and a .289 average.

After going hitless in his first seven games of 1972 (seven at-bats), Jones was traded by the Tigers to the Texas Rangers for pitcher Norm McRae. It was a reunion of sorts for Jones, getting to play for manager Ted Williams. It was a difficult year for Jones. He was used sparingly again, getting only 151 at-bats for the last place Rangers. He hit a career low .159 for "one of the worst teams in baseball history."[21] Although only 28 years old, Jones was running out of chances. In fact, his last chance had come and gone. On January 25, 1973, Dalton Jones was released by the Rangers.

Jones, who had married a Cambridge, Massachusetts, native and former Miss John Hancock, Joanne Korezniowski, moved his wife and two boys, Brian and Darrin, back to Baton Rouge.[22] Jones could not find a job outside baseball. He contacted Mel Didier, director of scouting and player development for the Montreal Expos, and begged his way back into baseball.[23] Jones was given a minor-league contract for the 1973 season. He reported to the Expos' Triple-A affiliate in Hampton, Virginia, the Peninsula Whips. Jones, by his own admission, was not very good. He appeared in 59 games and batted just .208 with seven doubles and two home runs. His stint in the Expos organization was over. Jones finished his nine-year, major-league career with a .235 batting average, 41 home runs, and 237 RBIs. He batted .262 in his career as a pinch-hitter. When he retired, his 81 pinch hits placed him second all-time among American League pinch-hitters.

After baseball, Dalton Jones has had several careers, including banking, mutual fund and investment sales, and finish carpentry. He worked for several years for his father's former employer, Exxon, as an electronic instrument technician. In the late 1980s, Jones and his new wife, Barbara, moved to Plymouth, Massachusetts, where Jones started a financial services company.

In 1989, he was an infielder and coach for the Winter Haven team in the Senior League, managed by former Red Sox pitcher Bill Lee. His teammates included Ferguson Jenkins, Gary Allenson, and Bernie Carbo. Jones also played in several softball games organized by the enterprising Lee.

Barbara Jones, who has a Ph.D. in education, took a job in the Charlotte, North Carolina school system. After living in Charlotte for a few years, Dalton and Barbara moved to Liberty, Mississippi, not far from McComb, where Dalton was born.

Sources
In addition to the sources cited in the notes, the author also consulted:
Coleman, Ken and Dan Valenti. *The Impossible Dream Remembered* (Lexington, Massachusetts: The Stephen Greene Press, 1987), and the websites: www.baseball-reference.com, www.baseballlibrary.com, www.baseball-almanac.com, www.nicholls.edu/baseball, www.retrosheet.org, and www.sabr.org.

Notes
1. Interview with Dalton Jones, February 28, 2006.
2. Interview, February 2006.
3. Interview with Dalton Jones, March 29, 2006.
4. Fitzgerald, Ray. "Pressure Pinches Year-Round," *Boston Globe*, August 21, 1967: 23.
5. www.nicholls.edu/baseball
6. Sec Taylor, "Demons Need Infield Material," *The Sporting News*, February 28, 1935: 8.
7. Fitzgerald, *Boston Globe*, August 21, 1967: 23.
8. Salazar, "Red Sox Scout Signs Prize, Then Manages Kid in Debut," *The Sporting News*, June 21, 1961: 30.
9. Interview, February 2006.
10. Interview, February 2006.
11. Ibid.
12. Ray Fitzgerald, "Pressure Pinches Year-Round," *Boston Globe*, August 21, 1967: 23.

13 Interview, March 2006. The hamstring tear likely occurred May 7, 1965.
14 Clif Keane, "Jones Hitting Wins Third Base Position," *Boston Globe*, May 23, 1965.
15 Clif Keane, "'Best Game I Ever Played,' Proclaims Happy Jones," *Boston Globe*, September 19, 1967: 27.
16 Dave Anderson, "Second Guessers Are Left Up Tree," *New York Times*, October 12, 1967: 60.
17 "Jones Feels Sure He Can Oust Foy," *Washington Post*, March 6, 1968: E2.
18 Interview, February 2006.
19 Ibid.
20 Ibid.
21 Ibid.
22 Diane White, "No more miniskirts for her," *Boston Globe*, August 21, 1967: 27.
23 Interview, February 2006.

HAL KING

BY CHRIS HOLADAY

In the late 1960s and early '70s, Hal King defined the moniker of journeyman catcher. A left-handed hitter with some pop in his bat, King played for the Houston Astros, Atlanta Braves, Texas Rangers, and Cincinnati Reds for parts of seven seasons. Never quite consistent enough with either bat or glove to keep a starting job, King worked hard and could always be counted on to contribute with a solid effort. At times, however, he delivered in spectacular fashion. King never played in more than 89 games in a major-league season and only 322 games for his career. He is notable for being the first major-league player to appear for both Texas teams, but perhaps most famous for a 1973 pinch-hit home run that sparked a Reds winning streak which resulted in a divisional title.

Born February 1, 1944 in Oviedo, Florida, Harold "Hal" King was one of 14 children, nine of whom were boys. "Four of my brothers also played baseball seriously," said King in 2015. "There wasn't much else to do back then in a small town like Oviedo except play baseball."[1]

After high school in 1962, Hal followed his brother John and tried out for the barnstorming Indianapolis Clowns, the same organization with which Hank Aaron had his start. Both brothers signed with the club and traveled the country, playing games against local teams wherever they could be scheduled. John King eventually left but Hal remained and in 1964 caught the eye of scouts for the Los Angeles Angels. Seeing great potential in the young catcher, the Angels purchased King's contract from Ed Hamman and Syd Pollock, owners of the Clowns, for $8,000.[2]

For the 1965 season, the Angels assigned King to Quad Cities in the Midwest League. There, in his first season of Organized Baseball, he played 90 games and hit .241 with 6 home runs. He was even called on to pitch an inning in three games. Promoted to El Paso in the Texas League in 1966, King saw less playing time. With catching prospects Tom Egan and Elrod Hendricks also on the roster, there was little room for him to make an impact and he hit only .156 in 96 at-bats. With other players ahead of him, King was left unprotected in the Rule 5 draft after the season and was selected by the Houston Astros.

The Astros assigned King to the Asheville Tourists of the Class-A Carolina League for the 1967 season. There he found his swing and hit .288 with 87 RBIs while leading the league with 30 home runs. That display of power earned King a September promotion to Houston. He made his major-league debut at age 23 on September 6 with an eighth-inning pinch-hit groundout against future Hall of Famer Gaylord Perry. His first hit came four days later with a single off the Dodgers' Bill Singer. Later in the game he notched both his first triple and first run batted in, also against Singer, driving in Rusty Staub. In all, King appeared in 15 games for the Astros and showed promise with a .250 average, 11 hits, and 6 RBIs.

After the season he went to San Pedro de Macoris in the Dominican Republic to play winter ball. "That was my first time out of the country and it was a real awakening," said King in 2015. "It was like the lights were turned on for me that winter, it was so different. There were some great players, though, and the people were nice."3

King reported to Astros spring training in 1968 ready to battle for a big-league roster spot. Not only did he make the roster, but he was named the starting catcher on Opening Day. On the second day of the season, batting third between Joe Morgan and Rusty Staub, King went 3-for-4 with an RBI and two runs scored.

On April 15, King was involved in a record-setting game between the Astros and New York Mets at the Astrodome. Starting behind the plate, he ended up catching the complete 24-inning marathon that lasted 6 hours and 6 minutes. At 1:37 A.M. the Astros finally scored to win, 1-0. No game had ever gone longer than 20 innings without a score. At the plate in that game, King went 1-for-9 with a double off Mets starter Tom Seaver.

"I think I set a record in that game for going 24 straight innings with no passed balls and no errors. I couldn't do that now," said King with a laugh in 2015. "But when you're 24 years old you don't feel it in your knees so much."4

The Astros eventually decided to stick with their established catching combination of John Bateman as starter and Ron Brand as his backup that season. King played in 27 games for Houston with 10 starts behind the plate but he spent most of the season in the minors. He played in 56 games for Dallas-Fort Worth in the Double-A Texas League and 43 games for Triple-A Oklahoma City.

In 1969 King made the short trip from his home in Oveido to the Astros' spring-training facility in Cocoa, Florida. It was a short stay, however. On March 11 he was traded to the Boston Red Sox for minor-league pitching prospect Mark Schaeffer. King reported to Winter Haven and was in contention for a big-league roster spot but the Red Sox went with Russ Gibson and Jerry Moses behind the plate. Sent to Triple-A Louisville, King hit .322 with 9 home runs in 342 at-bats but he never got the call to Boston. Instead, the Red Sox promoted a promising young catcher from Double A at the end of the season. His name: Carlton Fisk.

Opportunity smiled on King that December when he was selected by the Atlanta Braves in the Rule 5 draft. "Boston didn't protect me and the Braves took me. I was happy to go, though," recalled King. "I had a really good season in Louisville and they still didn't protect me."5

King made the Braves roster out of spring training in 1970 as the backup to veteran Bob Tillman. It would prove to be his best year in the major leagues. Appearing in 89 games (51 of them as the starting catcher), King posted a .260 batting average with 11 home runs and 30 runs batted in. After the season he played winter ball in Venezuela. There, playing for Navegantes del Magallanes, he hit .300 with 7 home runs and 32 RBIs in 57 games.6

With the trade of Bob Tillman to Milwaukee, King looked to be in the running for the starting catcher job in Atlanta in 1971. A rookie backstop named Earl Williams had other plans, however. In spring training, King, Bob Didier, and Williams, who had made his big-league debut the previous September, battled for the job. King won the job and got the start on Opening Day, a game in which he went 2-for-4 with a double and a run. He started the first 11 games of the season but eventually became the second choice to Earl Williams, who would win the National League Rookie of the Year Award that season. In total, King played in 86 games, starting 48 behind the plate, and hit .207 with 5 home runs and 19 RBIs.

Over the winter of 1971-72, King returned to Navegantes del Magallanes in Venezuela. Again he played well, hitting .297 with 8 home runs and 33 RBIs, in 59 games.7 Back in the States, King had yet another major-league organization's spring training to report to: the Texas Rangers, the franchise just relocated from Washington.

King reportedly caught Ted Williams's eye during spring training in 1971 and during the winter meetings the Rangers acquired him for catcher Paul Casanova. Though Casanova had more major-league experience, he was never a power hitter and had batted only .203 in 1971. King was a similar type player but his left-handed bat made him a better fit for the Rangers.

When asked about the trade by an Associated Press reporter during 1972 spring training, Williams replied, "I don't think anybody has allowed King to catch as much as he should have in the past. All the reports on him were the same, good hit, no glove. But heck, no one ever gave him a chance to get some experience behind the plate. So far he hasn't been the butcher behind the plate he was cracked up to be. He's not the most graceful catcher you'll ever see, but he hustles and gives you a workmanlike job each day and he's improving. His bat will be a big help to us, especially since he hits from the left side, where we needed some punch. Right now I plan to use him as a starter against all right-handed pitchers and use Dick Billings against lefties."[8]

Said King in the same article, "This camp is just as tough as all the others I've been to, I've run just as much as anywhere else, but I've run harder because I'm happy to be here playing for Williams."[9]

On April 15, 1972, the club played its first official game as the Texas Rangers and Hal King was the starting catcher. He walked twice and had one of only two hits off Angels starter Andy Messersmith in the 1-0 loss. By late July, Dick Billings was getting much of the playing time behind the plate and the Rangers decided to give a look to another young left-handed-hitting catcher, Bill Fahey. King and fellow catcher Ken Suarez were sent to the Triple-A Denver Bears. King had appeared in 50 games with Texas and hit .180 with 4 home runs and 12 RBIs. With Denver he hit .283 in 23 games.

On December 1, 1972, King was traded by the Rangers along with utility infielder Jim Driscoll to the Cincinnati Reds for pitcher Jim Merritt. It was a move that did not bode well for King's playing time. With All-Star (and future Hall of Fame) catcher Johnny Bench firmly entrenched behind the plate in Cincinnati, and Bill Plummer his established backup, it left little room for another catcher.

King began the 1973 season at Triple-A Indianapolis but after 38 games got the call to report to Cincinnati. He made his debut on June 20 against the Giants. Starting at catcher (Bench played outfield in that game), he drew a walk in the second but in the fourth connected on a solo homer off starter Elias Sosa.

On July 1 King hit one of the most famous home runs in Reds history. Entering the first game of a doubleheader at Riverfront Stadium, the Reds trailed their National League West rivals the Los Angeles Dodgers by 11 games. King came to the plate as a pinch-hitter for fellow catcher Bill Plummer with the Dodgers and pitcher Don Sutton one out away from a win. With Tony Perez and Darrel Chaney on base, King slugged a three-run homer for a 4-3 Reds win. "It was a changeup," said King in 2015. "I still remember the pitch Don Sutton threw."[10]

Ignited by King's homer, the Reds rapidly made up ground on the Dodgers. They followed that win with a 3-2, 10-inning victory in the second game of the doubleheader. The next night the Reds won yet another thriller over the Dodgers, 4-2, on Tony Perez's walk-off homer. King contributed two more pinch-hit home runs down the stretch, including a grand slam on July 9 against the Montreal Expos and a 10th-inning game-winner against the New York Mets on August 17. King played in 35 games (only nine as catcher) but his contributions were huge in the Reds' drive to take the NL West championship.

In the NLCS, King played in three games against the Mets. He singled in the Reds' Game Three loss and in Game Five, pinch-hitting for Ross Grimsley, drew a ninth-inning walk. He was on second base when Dan Driessen grounded out to end the Reds' dream of a pennant. "I thought for sure I'd get a ring that year. We had a great team and I thought surely we'd beat the Mets," said King in 2015.[11]

Over the winter of 1973-74, King decided to go back to Venezuela. He joined Aguilas del Zulia and in 47 games hit .255 with 7 home runs and 22 RBIs.[12] He reported to spring training with the Reds' catching situation the same as it had been in 1973; with Bench and Plummer ahead of him there was little chance of big-league playing time. As in the previous season, King was assigned to the Indianapolis Indians. Splitting his time between catching and serving as designated hitter, he turned in a .256 average with 10 home runs and 35 RBIs in 69 games.

Recalled to Cincinnati in midseason, King again primarily served as a pinch-hitter and caught in only five games. With just 17 at-bats, he hit .176 with 3 RBIs. On October 1, King played what would prove to be his final big-league game; pinch-hitting in the seventh inning for relief pitcher Pat Darcy, he struck out against Buzz Capra.

Another chapter in Hal King's baseball career began after the 1974 season. "The Reds sold my contract, that's how I ended up in Mexico," he recalled in 2015. "It wasn't that bad but I think I could have had three or four more years in the big leagues as a DH for someone. The fans were good in Mexico but the worst thing was the long bus rides."[13] King had several successful years in the Mexican League. The 1975 season was split between the Cordoba Cafeteros and Puebla Pericos while the next two were with the Coahuila Mineros. In 1978 he signed with the Saltillo Saraperos. With that team in 1979 he hit .320, slugged 19 homers and led the league with 124 walks.[14]

At the end of the 1979 season, King hung up his spikes and returned home to Oviedo. He eventually went into business for himself and started a power-washing and home-maintenance business. He remained active in the local sports community, and served as president of the athletic boosters club of Oviedo High School when his son was on the football team. With his bat traded for a set of clubs, King turned his focus to the game of golf.[15]

As for Hal King's baseball-playing family, younger brother Nate King signed with the Minnesota Twins in 1964. He spent six seasons in the minors and made it as high as Charlotte in the Southern League but was out of professional baseball after the 1969 season. Brother Johnny, who had barnstormed on the Indianapolis Clowns, also signed with a major-league organization and spent part of the 1966 season in the Chicago Cubs system. A nephew, Brion King, was drafted by Baltimore in 1995 and spent a couple of seasons in the farm systems of the Orioles and the Toronto Blue Jays. Said King in 2015, "My son preferred football but Brion has a couple of young sons who look like they could be fantastic baseball players."[16]

"The secret to success in the major leagues is you've got to get relaxed," King said in reflecting on his career in 2015. "You've got to settle down. I'd say I only got relaxed somewhat. If I could have completely, I think my career would have been very different."[17]

Notes

1. Telephone interviews with Hal King in December 2015.
2. Alan J. Pollock, *Barnstorming to Heaven: Syd Pollock and His Great Black Teams* (Tuscaloosa: The University of Alabama Press, 2006), 336-338.
3. Telephone interviews with Hal King in December 2015.
4. Ibid.
5. Ibid.
6. Estadisticas Beisbol Profesional Venezolano (purapelota.com).
7. Ibid.
8. Associated Press, "King Trying to Shake Tag He Can't Catch," *Gadsden* (Alabama) *Times*, March 27, 1972.
9. Ibid.
10. Telephone interviews with Hal King in December 2015.
11. Ibid.
12. Estadisticas Beisbol Profesional Venezolano (purapelota.com).
13. Telephone interviews with Hal King in December 2015.
14. Bill Weiss and Marshall Wright, "Top 100 Teams – #75: 1979 Saltillo Saraperos," The Official Site of Minor League Baseball (milb.com/milb/history/top100.jsp).
15. Telephone interviews with Hal King in December 2015.
16. Ibid.
17. Ibid.

TED KUBIAK

BY RORY COSTELLO

"Being a utility player wasn't a pleasant way to spend your time in the major leagues," said Ted Kubiak in 1987. "But it was a living."[1] Twenty years later, he said, "There's no doubt in my mind that my ten-year major-league career was because of my defensive ability."[2] In 2011 he expanded further. "It took quite a while for me to be comfortable with the role and I don't think I ever really did. I hit enough to keep a job but it was my glove that made my career."

The infielder hit a mild .231 with just 13 homers from 1967 to 1976. Even so, he made a useful contribution to the Oakland A's dynasty that won three straight World Series from 1972 through 1974. The highest praise came from a former teammate in Oakland. In 1980 Tony La Russa said, "I always thought Kubiak was the most valuable player on that team because he could fill in for Dick Green at second or Campy Campaneris at short or Sal Bando at third and the team would go on winning."[3]

Starting in 1989, Kubiak began molding young players as a minor-league manager and instructor. "When I quit [in 1977], I wasn't interested in staying in the game," he said in 2011. "I'd had enough of the contractual battle in San Diego and having my salary cut the full 20 percent after being told I'd done a great job for them was the last straw. When they refused to even talk to me about it, that was all I needed to end it. I was 34 years old, wasn't happy with how I was playing and was struggling with being able to keep my abilities sharp, something that used to be so easy for me. But after being away from the game for 12 years I decided it was still something I loved. I made a couple of phone calls and was hired by my old Oakland club. It was a good decision because I enjoy managing and working with and developing the young players."

Theodore Rodger Kubiak was born on May 12, 1942, in New Brunswick, New Jersey. His family lived in nearby Highland Park, a small borough that provided a great place in which to grow up.[4] "I don't know how old I was when I would play catch with my dad when he got home from work, but at the age of 7 I was invited to play on an unofficial Little League team in Highland Park." Growing up an hour from New York, he was a fan of the Yankees. In 2011 he said, "Even with the Dodgers and Giants in New York, the Yankees got all the media coverage, plus they won the World Series every year, so I naturally gravitated to them and Mantle in particular. He was an amazing player and though I got to know a little of his personal life, reading the latest biography of him revealed just how hard it was for him to play the game every day because of his leg problems. That made everything he accomplished so much more amazing. It was eventually incredible to play against him in the major leagues."

"I was on our high-school basketball team but didn't play much. As a shortstop at Highland Park High, I didn't think I was anything special, just one of the guys, trying to do the best I could. Somehow I hurt my back as a junior and had a terrible year, but my senior year saw me chosen as the MVP of the team. When my name was called for that honor in our school assembly, I was shocked and the cheers from the audience a complete surprise."

Kubiak was invited to a tryout camp by the Kansas City Athletics while playing in a tournament game his final year. While on the bench between innings, he was tapped on the shoulder and turned around to face Ray Sanders, a Kansas City scout, who issued the invitation. He was shocked and couldn't believe what he'd just heard. Sanders worked with scout Tom "T-Bone" Giordano, who played 11 games in the majors for the Athletics in 1953, when they were still in Philadelphia. "Tom was active with the Indians organization at the same time I was and I still keep in touch with him." After his pro career ended, Tom was a high-school teacher in Copiague (Long Island), New York, but baseball proved to be his enduring livelihood. Fifty years after he signed Kubiak, Giordano was still active, in the Texas Rangers organization.

"I would have signed for nothing, but when I hesitated Tom offered a modest bonus of $500. I was going to Pratt Institute to become an architect but with Instructional League and winter ball, I never did get back, which I regret." Even without a college degree, though, this man's flair for language was apparent. He embarked on a book about his life in baseball, its changes over his 40-plus years in the game, and its effect on him as a person and a man. The format of the book centers on the 300-page infield manual he developed for the Cleveland organization when he was their defensive coordinator for five years.

Kubiak's apprenticeship in the minors lasted six seasons. While with the Sarastoa Sun Sox, he made the Florida State League All-Star team during his first year, leading the league in putouts, assists, chances accepted, and double plays. His batting was solid enough too at .253, and though he did not hit any home runs, he had 53 RBIs. He went to spring training with the Athletics in 1962, which was quite a thrill, and jumped to Binghamton in the Double-A Eastern League.

Against the higher competition, the young pro's batting slipped to .203. "Kansas City jumped me three levels in 1962 and I was way over my head. At the end of the season I began switch-hitting, hoping to lessen the effect of the breaking ball, and it was a good decision. In 1963 they sent me to Lewiston, where I hit .295. Switch-hitting complemented my glove work enough to help me stay in the major leagues for ten years."

Kubiak was a Northwest League All-Star in 1963, but he was still developing. During each of his first three years, he made more than 40 errors at short. In a 2007 interview with David Laurila of *Baseball Prospectus*, Kubiak said, "I received one suggestion – the smallest amount of instruction – in my first spring training, and after that, everything I learned, I taught myself. In order to make myself into a good defensive player, I had to dissect what I was doing and make changes on my own. I had to determine how to maximize my talents while judging what my talents were."[5] He did so successfully, cutting his errors down to the high 20s from 1964 through 1966.

He also showed just enough with the bat to keep advancing. The 1964 season was another step back (.214 in 105 games in the Texas League and .171 in 16 games in the Pacific Coast League). But he stepped forward in 1965 (.281/7/38 with Birmingham in the Southern League) and held his own when he returned to Triple-A in 1966 (.260/2/38 with Vancouver). He was one of four PCL players to appear in every one of his team's games that year. Vancouver manager Mickey Vernon said, "He is an excellent competitor. He has great hustle and is a major league shortstop all the way. I think he can hit quite well in the majors."[6]

In the spring of 1967 Kubiak made the Kansas City roster, and he never appeared in another minor-league game. He played sparingly (hitting just .157 in 117 plate appearances in 53 games) behind Bert Campaneris at shortstop and John Donaldson at second base. Occasionally he filled in at third, where Sal Bando was trying to unseat Danny Cater. "When I got to the majors I had to learn how to play second and third base," Kubiak said in 1987. "A more important thing I had to learn was how to sit on the bench and keep myself mentally prepared to come into a game if I was needed. That was something to which I really had to adjust."[7]

The following winter Ted went back to the Dominican Republic. It was his third taste of winter ball; he had played 14 games in Venezuela for Tigres de Aragua in 1965-66 and was with the Dominican club Estrellas Orientales in 1966-67. "In Venezuela, I dislocated my thumb tagging a runner in a rundown," Kubiak recalled in 2011. "So I was only there about a month. The Venezuelan and Dominican Leagues are very good – the competition is on a major-league level. I was a rookie just trying to get along and did well enough to get invited back, which tells you something."

The return to San Pedro de Macorís, cradle of shortstops, was very satisfying. Estrellas won the league championship in 1967-68. The team's biggest local star was Rico Carty. The pitching staff was led by Cuban Mike Cuéllar – who faced just 28 men as he threw a one-hitter in Game Six of the finals versus Escogido – and Larry Dierker.[8]

"The Dominican was great," said Kubiak. "The people down there are great. I've gone back in recent years for work. The league has blown up so much, although there is still the poverty. But the people are still as nice and friendly as can be. One of my good friends now is Minnie Mendoza, who also works for Cleveland and was the third baseman on our Estrellas team. We gloat over the team never having won again for the past 40 years."

Kubiak continued in his reserve role for the A's, who had moved to Oakland, during 1968. Campaneris remained a fixture at short – he held the position for 12 straight years with the A's – but for three games in April, manager Bob Kennedy experimented with the Cuban in left field because he wanted to get Kubiak in the lineup. Campy hated the change, though, and was soon back at his familiar spot. Kubiak was often the subject of trade talks. That year the Baltimore Orioles were interested in acquiring him because they were worried that Mark Belanger's unit might be called into service in Vietnam. Ted himself was serving in the National Guard, which he had joined in 1967.[9]

A natural shortstop, Kubiak didn't play second base until he got to the big leagues. "Everything was backwards at second base, and it took time to separate the two positions, but second base was so much easier." One rival pitcher said, "Ted Kubiak is the best shortstop OR second baseman in either league."[10] In 1969, however, smooth-fielding Dick Green reclaimed his natural second-base position. Kubiak's starting opportunities typically came when either Campaneris or Green was injured. His hitting had picked up to .250 in 1968 and remained at .249 in '69. On June 22, 1969, he hit his first big-league homer, off Minnesota's Jim Kaat.

On December 7, 1969, Oakland traded Kubiak and pitcher George Lauzerique to the Seattle Pilots for Ray Oyler and Diego Segui. "I knew when I was traded from Oakland the first time the team was eventually going to do well," Ted said in 1987.[11] Segui had been the Pilots' best pitcher, but "the weeping need was for a shortstop who can play every day. Kubiak can; Oyler could not. Ted is 27, Oyler is 31. Ted batted .249, Oyler hit .165."[12]

The 1970 season marked Kubiak's career highs in just about every category and it was that year that convinced him he was a major-league player; nothing more than an average player but one nonetheless. After the Pilots moved to Milwaukee, he played in 158 games for the Brewers – but he started 88 times at second base and just 68 times at short. In June manager Dave Bristol decided that he needed a new second baseman. Kubiak got the call, and in 2011 he said, "I hated the change at first. I'd lost much of the edge I had in 1967, my first year in the majors, because I had to sit on the bench and did so for three years before the trade to Seattle. I was never as good as I was after my Triple-A season. The year in Milwaukee was giving me a chance to maybe regain some of my ability, but then I was moved to second. It was a battle." In August 1970 he had said, "I suppose I should be grateful for the change because at least I'm a regular in the big leagues."[13]

Given regular duty, Kubiak hit 4 homers, drove in 41 runs, and hit .252. He also enjoyed his finest day at the plate in the majors on July 18, 1970, at

Fenway Park. He was 4-for-5, driving in seven of the Brewers' runs (and tying the club's single-game record) in a 10-5 win over the Red Sox. The highlight was a ninth-inning grand slam off Ed Phillips, a righty whose big-league career consisted of 18 games with Boston that year. Kubiak had also reached him for a homer at County Stadium on May 6. In 2011 Ted quipped, "Phillips was unfortunately sent down; I guess they figured if I could hit home runs off him, he didn't have quite enough."

Ted played much the same role for the Brewers during the first four months of the 1971 season – except in reverse. Dave Bristol switched him back to short in June. On July 29 Milwaukee traded Kubiak and minor leaguer Charlie Loseth to the St. Louis Cardinals for José Cardenal, Bob Reynolds, and Dick Schofield. "I was glad to be going to a good club," said Kubiak after the trade. "Here they don't let you play – there's too much pressure on you. I knew I was going to be traded, but I didn't expect it now at this stage in the season."[14] Ted didn't stay long in St. Louis, though, as the Cardinals sent him to the Texas Rangers on November 3 for pitcher Joe Grzenda. Ted Williams, then the Rangers manager, liked Kubiak as a second baseman and inquired with St. Louis. Cardinals general manager Bing Devine said, "You know, we had tried for a couple of years to get Kubiak. He did his job with us, but it was just one of those things – we needed an experienced left-handed reliever so badly." But before they could spare Kubiak, they obtained another utilityman, Marty Martinez, from the Astros.[15]

Ted was in Texas for only a few months as well. On July 20, 1972, the Rangers dealt Don Mincher and him to Oakland for Vic Harris, Marty Martinez, and a player to be named later (Steve Lawson). "I could see a big change when I returned," Kubiak said in 1987. "I was pleasantly surprised to see some of the guys I had come through the minors with had matured so much and at the right time."[16]

Dick Green missed nearly all the season with a herniated disc before coming back in mid-August. He was replaced by Larry Brown, who hurt his back. Tim Cullen played more second base than anyone for Oakland that year, but when he pulled a hamstring, the A's needed depth. Kubiak stepped in and started 15 straight games at second. At the end of August Dal Maxvill came in through the revolving door. Seven different men started at the position for the team that year.

Kubiak offered interesting insights into the A's contentious clubhouse atmosphere and owner Charles O. Finley. Author Bruce Markusen, who has chronicled the A's dynasty in a book and many articles, quoted Ted. "A lot had to do with the intensity of the ballclub and the fact that the players were there to win games. I think Charlie Finley had something to do with that because he was so outspoken. I don't know whether it was his design or whether it was just his method or just his personality, but he allowed the players to speak out also. There were guys who'd get pissed off at him, get angry and say things in the papers."[17]

The manager of the A's, Dick Williams, was another forceful personality. "I really liked playing for Dick," said Kubiak in 2011. "I can't say I had much contact with him, but I thought he managed extremely well. I always liked playing for someone like Dick was. He was hardnosed and commanded respect. I had questions about some of my other managers – although Ted Williams was a great guy – but on the A's, everybody knew their job and did what it took to get the job done."

Kubiak made it to the postseason for the first time in 1972. In the AL Championship Series against Detroit, he appeared in four games and went 2-for-4. He added a single in three at-bats against Cincinnati during the World Series.

Mainly backing up Dick Green, Kubiak got into 106 games during the 1973 season, though he came to the plate just 198 times (.220-3-17).[18] During the postseason, Kubiak got into three games in the ALCS against Baltimore, going 0-for-2. In the World Series, he appeared in four games versus the New York Mets, going hitless in three at-bats. However, he scored the winning run in Game Three at Shea Stadium. He drew a one-out walk off Harry Parker in the top of the 11th inning, advanced on a dropped third strike by Jerry Grote, and scored on a single by Campaneris.

The most notorious moment in the Series was Finley's scapegoating of another second baseman, Mike Andrews, whose errors helped lose Game Two after he had replaced Kubiak in the eighth inning. In 2011 Kubiak still remembered well how Finley tried to remove Andrews from the roster and replace him with Manny Trillo. "I was in shock. We were on the plane getting ready to fly to New York and we realized Mike wasn't with us. We eventually heard what was happening but eventually Mike made the plane. The next day during our workout in New York, we wore black armbands with Mike's number as a show of support." The Mets fans gave Andrews a standing ovation in Game Four when the reinstated player entered as a pinch-hitter.

In between the 1973 and 1974 seasons, Kubiak was part of a pioneering group: the first 29 major-leaguers who went to salary arbitration with the owners. The amounts were peanuts by today's standards. The biggest demand came from Reggie Jackson, who asked for (and got) $135,000 instead of Charlie Finley's offer of $100,000. Ted, who had made $30,000 in 1973, asked for $42,500. He had to settle for $37,000.[19]

Kubiak remained a frequent fill-in for Dick Green in 1974, also spelling Campaneris on occasion. He said, "Sure it bothers me, but over the years, I've become accustomed to being a utilityman and I contribute as best I can." He added, "As soon as Greenie is ready, even on one leg, he's in there. There are times when I get ticked off, but if I go out there and try to play like that, I can't do as good a job. Maybe it's maturity, but I can separate my play now from my feelings."[20] In part because of some long idle stretches, his hitting languished (.209/0/18 in 220 at-bats).

Ted "sat out the [1974] playoff with a swollen left ankle and hurt feelings. Although he was in uniform in both Oakland and Baltimore, he said back then that the A's wouldn't allow him to be introduced with his teammates before the game."[21] "I have no recollection of that," said Kubiak in 2011. "But I was hurt. I was upended trying to turn a double play in Chicago about three weeks before the playoffs [on September 22]. My leg was all swollen; it took a long time for the blood to get out of it and I was on crutches for a while. I was (on the active roster) in the World Series, I just didn't get in the games because of the way they went." Dick Green, though he went hitless in the Series, was outstanding in the field. Dal Maxvill, who had returned to Oakland, subbed briefly for Green in the first two games.

On May 16, 1975, Oakland traded Kubiak to the San Diego Padres for pitcher Sonny Siebert. He joined the Padres when their infield was a shambles as a result of illness and injuries. "Ted will do a good job for us at third or second and he can fill in at short if we need him," said San Diego manager John McNamara, who had managed Kubiak at Binghamton, Dallas, and Oakland.[22] "Why they figured I was going to be a regular third baseman with no home-run power, I couldn't figure," Ted said in 2011. "Once again, I was asked to play a position on a daily basis that I really never played before and it was not easy." He played mainly third for the remainder of the year, since 22-year-old Mike Ivie really wasn't suited for the hot corner.

In 1976 Kubiak filled in behind the Padres' new third baseman, Doug Rader, and behind Tito Fuentes at second. Both years in San Diego, his hitting numbers were right around his career average: .224 and .236. *The Sporting News* commented, "Kubiak has been a first-rate fill-in for the Padres, but they don't feel he could play every day for any length of time."[23] Heading into the 1977 season, he and the Padres could not come to terms by the March 10 deadline, so the Padres renewed his $38,000 contract at the maximum pay cut. He "walked out of the Yuma spring training camp on March 30 ... was never heard from again and was placed on the disqualified list."[24]

That was it: Ted Kubiak never played another game in the majors. In 2011 he commented, "I didn't like the experience. They treated me exactly the way they treated most of us in those years. They wouldn't say anything – take it or leave it. But I was 34 then, it was probably time to go."

In the 1978 season, Kubiak returned to the A's, doing some color work on TV broadcasts along with Hank Greenwald. "That was just spot appearances, fill-in color jobs. Finley called me up." He was then involved in various other businesses before returning to real estate, renovating houses and apartment buildings. Back in 1971, he had taught real estate in Milwaukee; he went into that business in Oakland in 1973. But he hoped to get back into baseball, perhaps as a scout.[25]

In 1989 he returned to the field, again with the Oakland organization. It's tempting to think that Tony La Russa (then managing the A's) might have had a hand in this, as he had previously with Joe Rudi's return to the team as a coach. But Kubiak said, "No. I sent out two résumés and made two calls: one to the Giants and one to the A's, because I was living in the Bay Area. The A's sounded like they were going somewhere with Sandy Alderson. I also still had some friends in the organization, like Wes Stock. He called up Karl Kuehl, the farm director, they interviewed me and offered me a position."

Kubiak started with Southern Oregon in the Northwest League (rookie ball) and then took over in midseason for Lenn Sakata at Modesto, an A's affiliate in the California League. After four more seasons with Modesto, he moved to the Cleveland Indians organization in 1994, managing at the Double-A and A levels through 2003.

When asked if he had ambitions of becoming a big-league manager, Kubiak responded, "Because I'd left the game for 12 years, the game was not being run any more by my contemporaries. So often in the game you need a friend to take you along with him, so I was a very new face to the new people. I had a lot to learn when I first began managing and don't think I even presented myself as managerial material. As the years have gone by, I've learned a lot more and it would be interesting to do so – but the game has changed so much, I wouldn't fit in with the new technology and computerized look everyone seems to think is so important now. The game is very different."

From 2004 through 2008, Ted served as the minor-league defensive coordinator for the Indians. Each of his infielders and staff members received the 300-page personalized infield manual that he wrote.[26] In the interview with David Laurila, he offered many intriguing observations – notably on how well-conditioned legs are the foundation of a good infielder, influencing all other parts of body positioning. He called Omar Vizquel "the consummate infielder of these times."[27]

In 2011 he added, "There are some very acrobatic players in the major leagues these days. I see things that would be helpful to many of them, but there's no doubt today's player is a better athlete than we were. Not smarter but better athletes, and that doesn't mean their fundamental play is better. Look at the mistakes made in the game today. I played in an era when there were many of the best players of all time. It's hard for me to comment on anyone specific because I just don't see them enough. I did get to watch Vizquel when he was with us in Cleveland, and he and Roberto Alomar were as good as they were said to be."

Kubiak returned to managing in 2009 with Cleveland's rookie-ball club in Arizona. In 2010 and 2011 he managed the Lake County Captains in the Midwest League; they won the league championship his first year. "There's not as much pressure as when I was a player. It wasn't easy at first because there is so much you have to be aware of, but everything has fallen into place and I love it," he said in 2011. "I love the puzzle of the game, battling the other teams. Winning is a huge part of development, and playing for our Oakland club and the St Louis Cardinals taught me a lot about winning." In 2012 the Indians made him the manager of the Mahoning Valley (Niles, Ohio) Scrappers of the short-season New York-Penn League, and he was still at the helm in 2014.

At 70-plus, Ted Kubiak was still filled with energy and desire. "It's not really a job. Baseball is still the game I enjoyed when I was a kid. It's a great game. In many other ways it's changed a lot, but it's still the same game on the field. I work out every day, I keep in shape, and hearing from the people who've been under my tutelage and gone on – that's an energy boost. They're going to have to take the uniform off me."

Grateful acknowledgment to Ted Kubiak for his memories (telephone interview, September 12, 2011, plus extra input via e-mail, October 11, 2011). Thanks also to Tom Barthel for the introduction.

Sources

baseball-reference.com

retrosheet.org

Notes

1. Randy Schultz, "Where Are They Now?" *Baseball Digest*, March 1987: 83.
2. David Laurila, "Prospectus Q&A: Ted Kubiak." Baseball Prospectus website, April 22, 2007 (baseballprospectus.com/article.php?articleid=6131).
3. Bob Markus, "Pryor Waxing Hot Over His Utility Billing," *The Sporting News*, August 16, 1980: 27.
4. Ted was the only child of Theodore Kubiak (no middle name), a traffic manager for Gerber Plumbing, and Margaret "Marge" Pochinski.
5. Laurila.
6. Joe McGuff, "A's Offer Swap Bait In Spare DP Duo-Kubiak, Donaldson," *The Sporting News*, December 24, 1966: 32.
7. Schultz.
8. Juan Carlos Musa, "Recuerdan la conquista de la corona de las EO en 1968," *Hoy* (Santo Domingo, Dominican Republic), February 2, 2011.
9. Ron Bergman, "Kubiak Leads Rising A's," *The Sporting News*, June 15, 1968: 17.
10. Ibid.
11. Schultz.
12. Hy Zimmerman, "Milkes Gambles to fix Pilots' Defense," *The Sporting News*, December 27, 1969: 36.
13. Larry Whiteside, "Heise a Blue-Chip Shortstop, Brewers Will Drink to That," *The Sporting News*, August 21, 1971: 10.
14. "Kubiak Sent to St. Louis by Brewers," Associated Press, July 30, 1971.
15. Neal Russo, "Bird Bullpen Lists Sharply to Portside," *The Sporting News*, November 20, 1971: 47.
16. Schultz.
17. Bruce Markusen, *Baseball's Last Dynasty: Charlie Finley's A's* (Indianapolis: Masters Press, 1998), 139.
18. That year, he also married the daughter of former big leaguer Irv Noren, who was one of the Oakland coaches. Bruce Markusen, "Here's What Happened to '73 World Champion Oakland A's," Baseball Digest, October 1998: 69. Kubiak's two children, Justin and Kristi, are from a prior marriage.
19. Jerome Holtzman, "Arbitration a Success, Players and Owners Agree," The Sporting News, March 16, 1974: 53.
20. Ron Bergman, "Kubiak, Gilt-Edged Utilityman, Pays Handsome Dividend to A's," The Sporting News, August 10, 1974: 22.
21. Ron Bergman, "Player Barbs and Pressure Fail to Jar A's Pilot Dark," The Sporting News, October 26, 1974: 11.
22. Phil Collier, "Kubiak Plugs Big Hole at Padres' Hot Corner," The Sporting News, June 14, 1975: 13.
23. Phil Collier, "Padres Back Off on Talk About Metzger Deal," The Sporting News, January 1, 1977: 36.
24. Phil Collier, "Padres Give Blessing to 'Reborn' Hendrick," The Sporting News, April 16, 1977: 11; Collier, "Novice Gives Padres the Look of a Champion," The Sporting News, April 23, 1977: 9.
25. Schultz.
26. David Hall, "The Sleeper," Kinston (North Carolina) Free Press, April 6, 2008. Subject: Carlos Rivero, then an Indians prospect.
27. Laurila.

STEVE LAWSON

BY CHRIS HOLADAY

At the end of the 1972 season, rookie pitcher Steve Lawson's stat line looked very promising. The Texas Rangers' left-hander pitched 16 innings in 13 games, struck out 13, and had an ERA of 2.81. Not bad for a 21-year-old on a last-place team. Unfortunately, fate didn't smile on Lawson and those numbers would remain his final ones in the major leagues.

Steven George Lawson was born on December 28, 1950 in Oakland, California, to Joseph and Barbara Lawson, and grew up in nearby San Lorenzo with his older brother, Jeff. Joseph, who owned a gas station in San Lorenzo, had pitched a season in Class-C ball in the Cincinnati Reds organization in 1939, then stayed in independent baseball until World War II began. Steve Lawson said he "played baseball from the time I was able to stand."[1] At San Lorenzo High School he was a standout basketball player but it was his performances on the pitching mound that began to draw the attention of professional scouts. San Lorenzo baseball coach Howie Thompson said, "Steve is the best pitcher I'll ever have the pleasure of coaching."[2]

On June 5, 1969, shortly after graduation, Lawson got a call from the Oakland Athletics; he had been selected in the third round of the amateur draft. Lawson turned down a full baseball scholarship from Arizona State University when he was signed by Oakland scout Eli Grba for a "substantial bonus."[3] In an organization with a deep pool of pitching talent that included the likes of Catfish Hunter, Blue Moon Odom, Rollie Fingers, and Vida Blue, competition would be tough. "When called by Oakland," recalled Lawson in 2015, "I still remember their statement that I needed to be good or I would be traded."

After signing, Lawson was sent to Pasco, Washington, to join the Tri-City A's of the short-season Northwest League. There, his first professional coaching came from manager Billy Herman, the former National League infielder who was inducted into the Baseball Hall of Fame in 1975.) Lawson pitched in 13 games with 11 starts that rookie season. His won-lost record was only 1-6 but with 63 strikeouts in 63 innings, the Athletics' management must have been reasonably satisfied with their draft choice.

In 1970, the A's affiliate in the Northwest League was located in Coos Bay-North Bend, Oregon, and Lawson was assigned there. Led by manager Harry Bright, the team had a strong pitching rotation that also included future major leaguers Glenn Abbott and Mike Barlow. Lawson contributed with a 3-4 record, a 3.68 ERA, and 71 strikeouts in 66 innings. He even found success at the plate, hitting .333 and contributing 8 RBIs.[4]

In 1971, Lawson followed manager Harry Bright to the Midwest League and the Burlington Bees. It proved to be his breakout season; Lawson started 14 games and went 7-2 with a 3.07 ERA and seven complete games. The performance earned him a big promotion and in 1972, he began the season with the

Iowa Oaks of the Triple-A American Association. In 20 starts, Lawson was 7-9 with 106 strikeouts in 122 innings.

On July 26 of that season, Lawson became the "player to be named later" in a deal made between the Athletics and the Texas Rangers six days earlier. Oakland had sent rookie second baseman Vic Harris and veteran utility infielder Marty Martinez to the Texas Rangers for infielder Ted Kubiak and veteran first baseman Don Mincher. The A's owed the Rangers one more player in the deal and the Rangers selected Lawson.

Instead of being sent to Denver, the Rangers' Triple-A club, as expected, Lawson was told to report directly to Arlington. Given uniform number 24, he took a spot on the bench in the bullpen. "It was fantastic," said Lawson in 2015. "Ted Williams was the coach and I was thrilled to be realizing my dreams."

On August 3, in the fifth inning of a game against the Minnesota Twins, the call came in to the bullpen: Lawson was to take over for starter Dick Bosman. With the bases loaded and one out, it was not an enviable situation for a major-league debut. Lawson proceeded to give up singles to Rich Reese and Bobby Darwin, which cleared the bases and put the Twins up 6-0. He got out of the inning by getting both Charlie Manuel and Danny Thompson to ground into force outs at second base.

The sixth inning went much smoother; catcher Glen Borgmann flied out to left, then pitcher Jim Perry and outfielder Cesar Tovar both grounded out to short. Bill Gogolewski took over in the seventh but the Twins were on a roll and went on to win 9-1.

Two days later, in Chicago, Lawson appeared in his second game. In a much lower pressure situation than his debut, he took over for Rich Hand in the eighth with one on and one out but the Rangers up 11-4. Lawson struck out pinch-hitter Tom Egan and got Luis Alvarado to ground to third, resulting in a force out of Mike Andrews at second.

In the ninth, Lawson made what would be the only plate appearance of his major-league career. Facing fellow rookie Jim Geddes, he hit an infield single to third. He advanced to second on a walk to Toby Harrah but a popup to short by Ted Ford ended Lawson's sole adventure on the basepaths.

Back on the mound in the bottom of the ninth, Lawson gave up back-to-back singles to Buddy Bradford and Pat Kelly, followed by a walk to Jay Johnstone. Despite the bases being loaded with no outs, Ted Williams stuck with Lawson, perhaps wanting to see how the rookie would handle the situation. The next batter, Rick Reichardt, hit a grounder that resulted in a force out at second but Bradford scored. Up next was All-Star outfielder Carlos May. Lawson ended the rally and the game – and was credited with the save – when he got May to ground into a double play.

On Friday, September 15, Steve Lawson had the opportunity to pitch against his former organization in front of a hometown crowd. In the eighth inning he got the call to take the mound against the Athletics at Oakland-Alameda County Coliseum. With a 10-0 lead, the eventual World Series champs had the game well in hand but it was still a memorable event for the Bay Area native. "I definitely remembered that game," recalled Larson. "I was glad to be in my hometown and celebrating my wife Sandi's birthday."

The outing started well; Larry Haney grounded back to the mound and Lawson threw him out at first. Sal Bando was up next and drew a walk, which was followed by a single from Ted Kubiak. Pitcher Ken Holtzman (who tossed a complete game) grounded out but the runners advanced. Shortstop Tim Cullen then cracked a single to center that scored both runners. Lawson then got Angel Mangual to ground to short for a force out of Cullen at second.

Lawson's last major-league appearance came on October 4. With the Rangers facing the Royals in Kansas City on the last day of the season, Lawson got the call to the mound in the seventh with the home team up 4-0. Steve Hovley led off with a single but Lawson struck out Jim Wohlford, then retired Amos Otis and John Mayberry with fly outs. In the eighth, Lawson remained on the mound. After a walk to Lou Piniella and a single to Ed Kirkpatrick, however, he was pulled in favor of Jim

Panther. The Rangers failed to mount a comeback and the Royals won, 4-0.

At the end of spring training in 1973, Lawson was assigned to the Rangers' Triple-A affiliate in Spokane. A shoulder injury soon began to take a toll. He started only 10 games that season and pitched 54 innings; a 1-8 record and 7.50 ERA were certainly not reflective of the promise Lawson had shown the previous season.

Despite his struggles of the previous season, the Rangers stuck with Lawson and sent him back to Spokane in 1974. He continued to struggle with shoulder problems and never regained his touch. In 17 games, Lawson was 3-8 with a 5.40 ERA.

"Sports medicine was an infant compared to today's options," said Lawson in 2015. "I felt uncertain about my injury and elected to retire from professional baseball. It was a good decision."

Lawson had married his wife, Sandi, in 1971 and the couple eventually settled in Oregon.

"I started my business called Contract Sweepers," recalled Lawson of the company he sold in 2005. With its sweeping equipment the company cleaned shopping-center parking lots. "It was something I knew nothing about until my cousin decided he did not want to keep the business. I bought it and it worked out for everyone, thus the reason we now live in Oregon. We thought we'd try living in Oregon and have never looked back."

In 2015 Lawson said he spent much of his spare time golfing and fishing but still enjoyed watching baseball.

Though his playing career didn't pan out as he would have hoped, Lawson is still remembered for his prowess on the mound. When San Lorenzo High School established an athletic Hall of Fame in 2006, Lawson was among the inaugural inductees. He was the only baseball player so honored.[5]

Said Sandi Lawson, "Steve was fortunate to play professional baseball because of his skill level. He loved playing but was humble and didn't say much. He was just having fun."

Sources

The author relied heavily on email correspondence with Steve and Sandi Lawson in December 2015 and data provided by Baseball-Reference.com.

Notes

1. Author email correspondence with Steve and Sandi Lawson, December 2015. All direct quotations are from this correspondence, unless otherwise noted.
2. Lowell Hickey, "Joe Lawson Relives Dreams," Hayward (California) Daily Review, January 22, 1969: 23.
3. Steve Ames, "SLz Ace Lawson Signs A's Pact," Hayward (California) Daily Review, June 20, 1969: 21.
4. George Artsitas, "The A's Era," The World, Coos Bay, Oregon, July 16, 2015.
5. "San Lorenzo High School Establishes Athletic Hall of Fame" San Lorenzo (California) Express, May 4, 2006.

PAUL LINDBLAD

BY PAUL HOFMANN

Paul Lindblad wasn't one of the Oakland A's most celebrated stars or eccentric personalities, but he was a valuable part of a formidable bullpen that contributed to the team's string of five consecutive division championships and three consecutive World Series titles. Though somewhat overlooked in the annals of Athletics history, Lindblad was without question an integral part of the Swingin' A's dynasty of the early 1970s.

Paul Aaron Linblad was born on August 9, 1941, to George and Helen (Walters) Lindblad in Chanute, Kansas.[1] He was the oldest of five boys. Chanute, a mill town in the southeast corner of the state, had 11,000 residents at the time. The Lindblads settled in Chanute after George was discharged from the Navy and went to work for the Santa Fe Railroad. The job required George to spend a great deal of time away from the family, commuting to and from Kansas City. George Lindblad was a strict and highly critical father.[2] Although he always wanted Paul to play professional baseball, he rarely encouraged him or was satisfied with his son's performance on the field. Over time, this contributed to a strained relationship between the two. Paul's mother was a homemaker.

Paul Lindblad's journey to the major leagues is a story of love, persistence, and faith. His baseball career began on the baseball diamond in Katy Park. He began playing Little League baseball, progressed to American Legion baseball, and was introduced to the world of semipro baseball on the Kansas prairies. It was there that he fell in love with the game of baseball and also the woman he would marry.

Paul, known as Junior, was a standout athlete.[3] He attended Chanute High School, where by all accounts he was a good student. He did well in math and drafting, subjects that would serve him well when he entered the construction business after baseball. Paul was a three-year letterman on the basketball team and the 1959 state high school champion in the javelin.[4] The school did not have a baseball team.

American Legion baseball dominated the landscape of rural Midwest America and Lindblad led the Chanute Legion team to a regional title and a berth in the state tournament, where the team lost by one run in the first round.

After high school, Lindblad attended Chanute Junior College, which was conveniently located in the same building as the high school. He played semipro baseball, threw the javelin (he finished second at the National Junior College Championships in 1961), and continued his relationship with his high-school sweetheart, Kathy, who was still attending high school.

After earning an associate's degree in business from Chanute Junior College, Lindblad was awarded an athletic scholarship to play baseball at the University of Kansas. He arrived in Lawrence, Kansas, in the fall of 1961 and found it difficult to be away from Kathy. He frequently made the 100-mile trip back home to

Chanute to see her on weekends, and they decided to marry. The Lindblads were married on November 4, 1961. Soon after, Lindblad withdrew from school, moved to Kansas City, and took a job with the Sante Fe Railroad. He worked for the railroad for almost a year before signing a contract with the Kansas City Athletics prior to the 1963 season. His $2,000 signing bonus helped the young couple who by this time were the proud parents of a daughter they named Cindy.

The Athletics sent Lindblad to the Burlington Bees of the Class A Midwestern League, where the 21-year-old established himself as a bona-fide major-league prospect, winning 10 games with a 1.58 earned-run average before a sore elbow forced the Bees to shut him down. The elbow pain was severe enough for the A's to send Lindblad to the Mayo Clinic to have it checked. The pain was so severe, his wife said, that he questioned his future in baseball.[5] But there was no structural damage to his arm and a winter of rest was all that was required.

In 1964 Lindblad was assigned to the Birmingham Barons of the Double-A Southern League. The Barons were the first integrated professional sports team in Alabama, and Lindblad observed firsthand the segregation that continued to dominate the South. His teammates included future Athletics Bert Campaneris, Tommie Reynolds, and John "Blue Moon" Odom. (The team's story and the 1964 Southern League pennant race are chronicled in Larry Colton's *Southern League: A True Story of Baseball, Civil Rights, and the Deep South's Most Compelling Pennant Race.*)

Lindblad had an up-and-down season for Birmingham, winning his first five starts, then falling into a slump in June and dropping four straight. It was the first time the lefthander had to deal with the ebbs and flows of pitching professionally. Despite struggling in June, Lindblad earned a $1,000 promotion bonus after sticking with Birmingham for more than 90 days. The bonus again came in handy as the Lindblads were expecting their second daughter, whom they named Paula. He finished 1964 with a respectable 11-8 season, 3.32 ERA, and 139 strikeouts, the highest strikeout total of his career. Lindblad was never an overpowering pitcher. His fastball topped out at around 90 mph and his best pitch was his slider. His greatest asset on the mound was his pinpoint control, the ability to put any pitch wherever he wanted it. Lynn Ranabargar, a longtime Chanute resident, said, "If he wanted a curveball low and outside, that is exactly where it was. If he wanted a fastball high and tight, all he had to know was how far off the chin they want it and that's where it went."[6]

Understanding that he was not an overpowering pitcher and that his future in baseball depended on his ability to stay healthy and be a fundamentally sound player, Lindblad jogged daily basis and ran extra wind sprints to keep himself in the best shape possible. He also took great pride in making sure he made the routine plays.

The 1965 season brought with it a promotion to Kansas City's Triple-A affiliate, the Vancouver Mounties of the Pacific Coast League. In 28 starts Lindblad posted a 12-11 record and a 3.67 ERA, which earned him a late-season call-up to the A's, a team on its way to and finishing last in the American League. On September 15, 1965, he made his major-league debut against the soon-to-be crowned American League champion Minnesota Twins. He tossed a perfect seventh inning, striking out Bob Allison and Jimmie Hall. He pitched in three more games for the Athletics that fall. On September 22 he suffered his first major-league loss after yielding a fifth inning, two-run homer to Washington Senators shortstop Eddie Brinkman. Despite an unimpressive 11.05 ERA in 7⅓ innings, he was in the major leagues to stay.

During his early years in professional baseball, Lindblad played winter ball in Venezuela and the Caribbean. During this time he became interested in collecting coins. When he wasn't playing ball, Lindblad explored his surroundings and often purchased old coins from the local people. Later he took his numismatic interests to the extreme of buying a metal detector, which he carried with him on road trips. Bruce Markusen wrote regarding Lindblad's penchant for searching for hidden treasures in *Baseball's Last Dynasty: Charlie Finley's Oakland A's*:

Don Mincher, who played with Lindblad in Washington, Oakland, and Texas remembered the left-handed reliever as a man of boundless energy, who always needed to keep busy. Mincher recalled Lindblad's trademark habit of searching for money with a metal detector. "He'd go to the ballparks and look for pennies and nickels all day long." By Lindblad's own estimation he collected an average of $11 per city on road trips and gave the money to his children, who like Lindblad himself enjoyed collecting coins. When the metal detector beeped, Lindblad used a small screwdriver to dig into the turf and warning track. Yet, Lindblad had to be careful not to dig too deep, for fear of striking a water hose or electrical line. Trips to Cleveland's Municipal Stadium posed a special problem, since groundskeepers Harold and Marshall Bossard took special pride in maintaining the grass field. "If I dig too deep into the Indians' field," Lindblad said, "those two guys would tan my hide."[7]

The A's broke camp in Bradenton, Florida, in 1966 with the 23-year-old Lindblad on the pitching staff. As a minor leaguer he had been used almost exclusively as a starter. However, his role with the A's was less defined and the next two seasons would go a long way toward shaping his role as a long and middle reliever. In 1966 and 1967 he started 24 games and worked in 60 as a reliever. On August 12, 1966, against the Minnesota Twins, Lindblad threw wild on a pick-off attempt at second base, allowing the Twins' Cesar Tovar to advance to third. Tovar then stole home off a rattled Lindblad. The throwing error was noteworthy because Lindblad would not commit another error until May 6, 1974, a record 385 errorless games streak that covered nearly eight years. He finished 1967 with a 5-8 record, with six saves and a 3.58 ERA.

On July 16, 1967, Lindblad tossed a three-hit shutout against the Chicago White Sox at Comiskey Park. It was the only complete game of his career. He made only 12 more starts the rest of his career. The Athletics struggled on the field and at the gate in 1967, winning only 10 of their final 40 games and drawing just 726,639 fans all season. Fearing a collapse of the franchise, baseball owners allowed owner Charles Finley to relocate the team to Oakland. The Lindblads were excited and nervous about moving their young family so far away from Kansas.[8]

Lindblad's first season in Oakland saw him settle into a role that would define the remainder of his major-league career. He appeared in 48 games, 47 in relief, and compiled a 4-3 record with two saves and a 2.40 ERA. He followed with two more solid seasons in 1969 and 1970. In 1969 he pitched in 60 games, winning nine and losing six with a 4.14 ERA. Soon after the end of the 1969 season, Paul and Kathy welcomed their third child, a son they named Troy. In 1970 Lindblad made 62 appearances on his way to recording an 8-2 mark with three saves and a 2.70 ERA. Just as the 28-year-old Lindblad was establishing himself as a major leaguer, so too were the A's establishing themselves as contenders. The perpetual doormats of the American League finished 1970 in second place, nine games behind the Twins in the American League's West Division.

Early in the 1971 season Lindblad's career took an unexpected turn. On May 8 he was dealt with Frank Fernandez and Mincher to the Washington Senators for first baseman Mike Epstein and left-handed reliever Darold Knowles. Both players were key acquisitions that allowed the A's to get over the hump. After being an integral part of the Athletics rebuilding process, Lindblad now found himself playing for a Senators club that was battling the Cleveland Indians for last place in the American League East. A year later the team relocated to Arlington, Texas, and became the Texas Rangers. Lindblad spent two productive seasons with the Senators/Rangers franchise. In 1971 he appeared in 43 games for the Senators, finishing with a 6-4 record with eight saves and a 2.58 ERA. With Texas in 1972, he led all American League hurlers with 66 appearances and finished the season with a 5-8 mark, nine saves, and a 2.62 ERA. During these two years Lindblad solidified himself as one of the most reliable left-handed relievers in the American League. Meanwhile, his former teammates in Oakland were celebrating their 1972 World Series title.

In November 1972 Finley reacquired Lindblad in exchange for A's farmhand Bill McNulty and outfielder Brant Alyea. Finley's revolving-door style of managing player personnel often resulted in his re-acquiring players he had previously traded, and when Finley dealt Lindblad to the Senators, he told Paul that he would try to reacquire him. Despite the many well-documented disputes Finley had with many of the players he employed, Kathy Lindblad said Paul's relationship with Finley was always friendly and respectful. The relationship extended beyond his playing days. Finley occasionally called Paul just to "catch up on things."[9] Lindblad's first season back with the A's was not one of his better ones. He pitched in only 36 games, making three spot starts. He finished the year 1-5 as his ERA rose more than a run per game, to 3.69. Heading into the postseason, Darold Knowles was the first left-handed option out of the bullpen and Lindblad did not appear in the A's five-game ALCS victory over the Baltimore Orioles.

Lindblad did pitch in three games during the 1973 World Series against the New York Mets. In Game Two he relieved in the 12th inning after the Mets had taken a 7-6 lead off Rollie Fingers. Lindblad induced back-to-back groundballs to second baseman Mike Andrews, both of which Andrews fumbled, leading to three more runs that put the game away.

In Game Three, also an extra-inning affair, Lindblad came on in the ninth inning, worked two innings, and earned the victory, one of the greatest moments of his life, according to his wife.[10] In addition to earning the victory, Lindblad became a footnote in baseball trivia when he became the last pitcher to face Willie Mays. In the bottom half of the tenth the Mets' aging slugger pinch-hit, and Lindblad got him to ground into a fielder's choice. The A's scored the winning run in the top of the 11th. The victory was Lindblad's only postseason win. He pitched once more in the Series, throwing a scoreless inning in Game Four.

Among the three World Series rings won by Lindblad, the 1973 ring was the one he was most proud of and routinely wore, despite the fact that it originally contained no diamonds.[11] He felt he had contributed more to this team's success than the other two teams that won World Series titles. The ring was lost when Lindblad placed it in a briefcase that was later stolen. Kathy Lindblad still has her husband's rings from the 1974 and 1978 World Series.[12]

The Athletics and Lindblad followed up their 1973 World Series title with another championship season in 1974. Lindblad pitched more than 100 innings for the first time since 1967 and had a 4-4 record with a career-low 2.06 ERA as he filled the void created by the struggles of fellow lefty Knowles. However, his contributions ended at the conclusion of the regular season. The A's received such solid starting pitching performances throughout the American League Championship Series and the World Series that Lindblad didn't make a single postseason appearance.

The 1975 season was perhaps Lindblad's finest. With Knowles having been traded to Chicago, his workload increased significantly. He came out of the bullpen 68 times and pitched 122⅓ innings, both career highs, on his way to posting a 9-1 record with seven saves and a 2.72 ERA. The effort earned the attention of sportswriters across the country as Lindblad garnered a handful of votes and finished 18th in the American League MVP voting, during a season when the A's won their fifth consecutive American League West championship.

On September 28, 1975, the final day of the 1975 season, Lindblad combined with Vida Blue, Glen Abbott, and Fingers to toss a no-hitter against the California Angels. Lindblad pitched a 1-2-3 seventh inning, retiring Leroy Stanton on a groundout to third, striking out John Balaz, and getting Bruce Bochte to ground out to second. It was the first time in the major leagues that four pitchers combined for a no-hitter.

The A's were swept by the Boston Red Sox in the 1975 ALCS. Lindblad, who pitched in two of the three games, was one of the few A's pitchers who were remotely effective. In 4⅓ innings he allowed one run to a heavy hitting Red Sox lineup that included Carl Yastrzemski, Fred Lynn, and a host of other big bats.

The 1976 season was Lindblad's last in Oakland. The 34-year-old again proved to be a reliable member of the bullpen as he went 6-5 with a 3.06 ERA. The A's championship run ended as the team finished with an 87-74 record, 2½ games behind the Kansas City Royals. With many of the key pieces of the A's dynasty already departed, the franchise's glory days were clearly in the rear-view mirror. In an effort to cut costs, Finley sold off as many of the A's assets as possible. Lindblad still had value and before the start of the 1977 season he was sold to the Texas Rangers for $400,000.

Lindblad spent a little more than a season and a half with the Rangers before being purchased by the New York Yankees on August 1, 1978. The Yankees needed to bolster their bullpen in an effort to chase down the front-running Red Sox. The Yankees caught the Red Sox and went on to win a one-game playoff to advance to the American League Championship Series and eventually the World Series. Lindblad made his final appearance in the majors in Game One of the 1978 World Series. Coming on in relief in the fifth inning he pitched 2⅓ innings and gave up three earned runs as the Dodgers battered four Yankees pitchers for 11 runs in the opening game blowout.

The Yankees' acquisition of Lindblad reunited him with his good friend and longtime A's roommate, Jim "Catfish" Hunter. In addition to collecting coins, Lindblad loved the outdoors, particularly hunting and fishing, activities he and Hunter relished together.

After the season the Yankees sold Lindblad to the Seattle Mariners, who released the 37-year-old left-hander at the end of spring training. After 14 seasons in the majors, Lindblad's career had ended, and he retired to his home in Arlington, Texas. Lindblad finished his career with a 68-63 record and 64 saves in 385 games, with a 3.29 ERA and the admiration of many who remembered him as the perfect teammate.

Lindblad became a custom homebuilder in Arlington. He returned to baseball as a minor-league pitching coach in the Milwaukee Brewers organization in 1987 and worked in that capacity until 1993, when he was diagnosed with early-onset familial Alzheimer's disease (FAD), the same disease that afflicted his mother and later three of his brothers. Early-onset Alzheimer's is a rare form of the disease that is known to be entirely inherited.[13]

The disease progressed rapidly and had a dramatic impact on Lindblad's behavior and his physical appearance. He began to get progressively more upset at little things and was unable to control his anger, often lashing out at Kathy.[14] According to Kathy, he didn't recognize her or his children and wasn't the same gentle, caring man she had married.[15]

In 1997 Lindblad was moved to a facility that specialized in assisted-living care for those suffering from Alzheimer's. Lindblad spent the final nine years of his life in Peach Tree Place in Arlington.[16] He died from complications of the disease on January 1, 2006. He was 64 years old.

After Lindblad's death, the field at Katy Stadium in Katy Park in Chanute was renamed Paul Lindblad Field. On October 5, 2008, Lindblad was inducted into the Kansas Sports Hall of Fame.

Sources

Colton, Larry, *Southern League: A True Story of Baseball, Civil Rights, and the Deep South's Most Compelling Pennant Race* (New York: Grand Central Publishing, 2013).

Markusen, Bruce. *Baseball's Last Dynasty: Charlie Finley's Oakland A's* (Indianapolis: Masters Press, 1998).

McDowell, Brian, "Legion tournament honors Lindblad's legacy," *Chanute Tribune*, July 5, 2013. Retrieved from chanute.com/sports/article_593e439e-e5c1-11e2-9e26-001a4bcf6878.html

Wolters, Levi. "Hall of Fame Induction Ceremony Sunday," *Wichita Business Journal*, October 2, 2008.

Chanute Area Chamber of Commerce and Office of Tourism (2012). Retrieved from chanutechamber.com

Chanute Historical Society. Retrieved from chanutehistory.org/

Chanute, Kansas. Retrieved from en.wikipedia.org/wiki/Chanute,_Kansas

Kansas City Athletics: Historical Moments. Retrieved from sportsencyclopedia.com/al/kcityas/kca_s.html

Markusen, Bruce, "Thinking of Paul Lindblad." Retrieved from bruce.mlblogs.com/2006/01/17/thinking-of-paul-lindblad/

Paul Aaron Lindblad 1941-2006. Retrieved from thedeadballera.com/Obits/Obits_L/Lindblad.Paul.Obit.html

Paul Lindblad. Retrieved from baseballlibrary.com/ballplayers/player.php?name=Paul_Lindblad_1941&page=chronology

Types of Alzheimer's: Early-Onset, Late-Onset and Familial (2013). Retrieved from webmd.com/alzheimers/guide/alzheimers-types

Wade Funeral Home, Arlington, Texas, Paul Aaron Lindblad August 9, 1941-January 1, 2006. [Funeral Program, 2006].

W.E. Alford, personal communications, December 10 and December 12, 2013

Lindblad, Kathy, personal communications, December 11, 16, and 17, 2013

Notes

1. Wade Funeral Home, "Paul Aaron Lindblad 1941-2006."
2. Personal correspondence with Kathy Lindblad, December 17, 2013.
3. Personal correspondence with W.E. Alford, December 10, 2013.
4. Larry Colton, *Southern League: A True Story of Baseball, Civil Rights, and the Deep South's Most Compelling Pennant Race* (New York: Grand Central Publishing, 2013).
5. Personal correspondence with Kathy Lindblad, December 16, 2013.
6. Brian McDowell, "Legion tournament honors Lindblad's legacy," *Chanute Tribune*, July 5, 2013.
7. Bruce Markusen, *Baseball's Last Dynasty: Charlie Finley's Oakland A's* (Indianapolis: Masters Press, 1998), 177-178.
8. Personal correspondence with Kathy Lindblad, December 16, 2013.
9. Personal correspondence with Kathy Lindblad, December 11, 2013.
10. Personal correspondence with Kathy Lindblad, December 17, 2013.
11. Personal correspondence with Kathy Lindblad, December 11, 2013.
12. Ibid.
13. Types of Alzheimer's: Early-Onset, Late-Onset and Familial (2013).
14. Colton.
15. Personal Correspondence with Kathy Lindblad, December 17, 2013.
16. Colton.

JOE LOVITTO

BY CHARLIE GRASSL

Joseph Lovitto Jr. was born on January 6, 1951, in the Los Angeles County harbor town of San Pedro. Joe was the oldest of two sons with a brother, Robert, born in 1959. His parents, Joseph and Anthonette Lovitto, enrolled their son into San Pedro's Catholic, all-boys Fermin Lasuen High School and saw Joe become a star athlete, excelling in football and baseball, in the years 1966-68. A switch-hitting catcher in high school, Joe discovered he would be selected in the first round of the January 1969 major-league amateur draft by the Washington Senators provided he could find a way to be eligible by graduating from high school. Since graduation at Fermin Lasuen was only in June, Lovitto was forced to consider another way.

Lovitto found he needed only one semester to graduate from public high school, so he transferred to San Pedro High School in the fall of 1968. This enabled him to graduate in January of 1969 and become eligible for baseball's January Amateur Draft.[1] True to their word, the Senators selected Lovitto as the second player picked in the first round of the 1969 draft. Picked first before Lovitto by the Houston Astros was another switch-hitting Californian high schooler, Derrel Thomas. Thomas went on to enjoy 15 seasons in the big leagues as a versatile player who played every position but pitcher during his career. Of the first 50 players picked in that draft, eight made it to the majors while only three played professional baseball longer than 10 years.

At the time of his signing by the Senators in 1969, Lovitto was believed to possess all the physical tools to reach stardom in the major leagues. In high school all of this came easy. He was the fastest. He could hit anyone's pitcher. He could throw anyone out on the bases. As he stepped up into another level of the baseball talent pool, expectations were very high that Lovitto would soon be the next Mickey Mantle.[2] His physical gifts were genuine but his understanding of them was lacking. Not realizing all professional baseball players were high-school or college stars, Lovitto, it soon became apparent, had an attitude and approach to the game that in high school was endearingly called "confidence," but was soon to be sarcastically labeled "brash," "cocky," and even "arrogant."

Mike Shropshire in his biting book about the 1973-75 Texas Rangers teams made this observation: "Lovitto could run, throw, hit and hit with power. The problem was that while he could do all these things, Lovitto seldom did."[3] Some would say he was a victim of injuries that limited his physical abilities and playing time. Certainly that is a part of his story but his development as a major-league hitter never was realized as he was accelerated through the Rangers farm system, playing only 168 games in Class-A ball, 44 games in Double-A, and 34 games in Triple A. The Rangers' desperate need for more fans in the seats and for exciting talent that could be hyped, their financial investment in him as a first-round pick in the draft, his rock-star-like external demeanor, his good looks and "confidence," as well as the high expectations of the ballclub's talent evaluators, all served to cause the Rangers to insert an inexperienced and unproven 21-year-old Joe Lovitto into the starting lineup of the 1972 Rangers, where he would struggle mightily to fulfill "expectations." Lovitto's career foreshadowed the arrival in 1973 of another high schooler, 18-year-old David Clyde. Same motives. Same results.

Lovitto's first taste of competition was in Shelby, North Carolina, in the Class-A Western Carolinas League. At 18, he was the youngest player on the team. Losing some playing time to injuries, he appeared in about half of the team's 124 games, starting 14 games as a catcher and 49 games in the outfield. This was his last experience as a serious candidate for the catching position as the Senators wanted to utilize his excellent speed in the outfield and not squander it crouching behind the plate. Hitting .229 in 271 plate appearances with six home runs, Lovitto showed flashes of his speed on the basepaths by stealing 22 bases in 29 attempts.

Concerned about Lovitto's light hitting and needing to find a fielding position best suited to his outstanding speed and throwing arm, the Rangers sent Lovitto to the Florida Instructional League after the season. Playing in a place where young prospects could develop or learn new positions, and older veterans could rehabilitate from injuries under game conditions, Lovitto again was the youngest player on the roster, and in 24 games, hit only .179 with a meager two RBIs in 91 plate appearances.

The Senators moved their Class-A team to Burlington, North Carolina, in 1970. Under Joe Klein, who had also managed Shelby in 1969, Lovitto had a more promising season at the plate, hitting .266 with 5 home runs and 45 RBIs in 101 games. In the field, he split time between the outfield and a new position, second base. Relatively injury-free, he played in 101 of the team's 137 games.

The 1971 season saw Lovitto reunited with his manager for a third consecutive year, when he and Klein were moved up to Double-A Pittsfield. Playing exclusively at second base, in 44 games Lovitto showed evidence of meeting those high "expectations" by hitting a solid .301 with 27 RBIs. Anxious to see if this was evidence of progress, the Rangers moved him up to the Triple-A Denver Bears. Though limited by injury to only 34 games and 111 plate appearances, Lovitto responded with an average of .326 and an on-base percentage of .414 while playing mostly in the outfield. It seemed the real Joe Lovitto had finally appeared.

At spring training of 1972, in the new uniform of the Texas Rangers, Lovitto was a member of a major-league team, playing for manager Ted Williams who, along with most of baseball, agreed that he was certainly destined for stardom. He had been groomed to play both infield and outfield, and the only question was where he would play in the field.

On April 15, 1972, Lovitto made his major-league debut. Batting seventh and starting in center field, he went 0-for-2 at the plate, with a walk and a stolen base as the Rangers lost, 1-0, to the California Angels. In the next game, April 16, he singled to center for his first big-league hit, off the Angels' Tom Murphy. His only home run in 1972 came on June 10 against the Orioles' Dave McNally – a two-run homer to right-center in Arlington Stadium. The season, however, became a continuous struggle at the plate. It was July 10 before Lovitto's average rose above .200, and to do that it took a 4-for-5 night at the plate to climb from .194 to .212. He ended the season batting .224 in 375 plate appearances. When he did get on base he was able to steal only 13 bases in 24 attempts.

Lovitto's flippant attitude continued to exhibit a careless approach to development as a player. It was viewed by some as just his "sense of humor," which only served to affirm his career-destroying pattern of behavior. Ted Williams and his coaching staff likely did not see it as just a quirky sense of humor. An example was Lovitto reportedly telling Williams, when asked if he had read Williams' book on baseball, "Hell, Ted, I didn't even know you wrote a book."[4] Another is the photo of Lovitto, in uniform, sitting in the dugout, with his mouth completely filled with a baseball.[5] To complete the picture, there is another story of Ted Williams telling Lovitto he was wasting his talent, which resulted in Lovitto storming from the room and slamming the door in his manager's face!⁶

In November 1972, Williams resigned and Whitey Herzog was hired to replace him. Brutally honest, Herzog sized up his 1973 Rangers as follows, "Defensively these guys are really substandard, but with our pitching staff, it really doesn't matter."⁷

The 1973 season was perhaps the worst start imaginable for Lovitto. His performance reached new lows and, over the space of 2½ months, forged a one-way plane ride from Arlington to Spokane, Washington. How bad was Lovitto in April of 1973? With a batting average of .152, he made 28 outs during the month. The opponents' outfield had four of the putouts, four of the outs were strikeouts, and 20 were made within the infield. In 33 official April at-bats, Lovitto had five hits (one of them an infield hit) without a run batted in and with just one stolen base. Only eight times did Lovitto get the ball out of the infield. In May, he was 0-for-8 in nine games. In June, he was 1-for-3. His last game was June 10, after which he was soon on his way to his new position as an outfielder for the Triple-A Spokane Indians. Herzog had seen enough.

At 23, Lovitto arrived at a new place in his professional career. No longer being coddled because of his potential, he now was expected to produce, both at bat and on the field. At Spokane, Lovitto remained relatively healthy, batting a respectable .279 with 4 home runs and 38 RBIs. This was enough for Lovitto to be invited to the 1974 spring-training camp with another opportunity to make the major-league club.

With third base now covered by Lenny Randle and Jim Fregosi, Lovitto was competing for a spot in the outfield. The slower speeds of Jeff Burroughs, Alex Johnson, and Tom Grieve limited them to the corner outfield spots, so with a 33-year-old Cesar Tovar his only competition for the center-field spot, Lovitto made the team for the 1974 season. However, the wording under the photo of Lovitto in the 1974 Texas Rangers game program clearly revealed that the Rangers were close to ending their relationship with Lovitto. In a document that typically goes to great length to be positive in its descriptions of player exploits and potential, it was chilling in its wording about the future of Joe Lovitto as a Texas Ranger: "A big project in spring training will be this cocky youngster, who was the Rangers' No.1 pick in the …1969 draft. Switch-hitting Joe has played second base, the outfield, third base and caught, but has been slowed by a variety of ailments – elbow, shoulder, tonsils, flu, etc. He has more talent than has surfaced, can run and throw, needs only to hit a bit more to stick around." In contrast, the publication said of catcher Dick Billings, who hit .179 in 1973: "Rich broke his right thumb on April 27, missed 15 days, and that set the tone for his entire 1973 season. He didn't have a good year, but he's a gutsy guy who plays with pain and never complains."

Playing in 113 games in 1974, Lovitto batted .223 with 2 home runs and 26 RBIs, and 6 stolen bases in 14 attempts, numbers very similar to his 1972 season. Lovitto remained with the team through the 1975 season but saw action in only 50 games while batting .208 in 123 plate appearances. In his final season he was on the disabled list from June 15 through August 31, missing 76 games. His last at-bats in the majors occurred in a game against the Chicago White Sox on September 14, 1975, when he pinch-hit in the ninth inning for the DH, Tom Robson. He walked and scored a run. He batted twice more, grounding out to short and flying out to center field, before the game ended in the bottom of the 13th on a walk-off single by Roy Howell. His last appearance in a game came two days later, on September 16, when he ran for Mike Hargrove in the bottom of the ninth in a 6-4 loss to Oakland.

On December 12, 1975, Lovitto was traded to the New York Mets for Gene Clines. On March 26, 1976, at the end of spring training, he was released by the Mets. The career that once held such promise and interest ended without fanfare or notice. Lovitto retired, at the age of 25, and did not play again. His baseball career was marred by his health, his immaturity, and the Rangers' need to rapidly build a new fan base. Their need and his lack of maturity were a formula that proved lethal to the vulnerable career of a talented athlete.

On July 8, 1974, in the middle of his third season with the Rangers, the 23-year-old Lovitto took a step toward stability in his life when he married Melissa Jan Farmer, a 21-year-old former high-school beauty queen and American Airline flight attendant from Grand Prairie, Texas. The marriage ended three months short of six years on April 9, 1980.

Maturity has a way of encroaching upon life as one grows in age. It began to come for Lovitto one year after his divorce and some five years after his retirement from baseball. At the age of 31, he married Katherine Lynn Madden at her parents' home in Mansfield, Texas, on April 4, 1981. The couple had two daughters, Lauren and Leslie.

Ten years later, in 1991, Lovitto's health introduced a new challenge into his life: He was diagnosed with testicular cancer.[8] The battle against cancer consumed the next 10 years of his life as the cancer began to spread into other parts of his body. In this battle, Lovitto's strength of will, which had made him less coachable in baseball, served to preserve his life far beyond what the doctors at Houston's M.D. Anderson would predict. Utilizing every experimental drug available combined with Lovitto's strong will to live, his doctor said, prolonged his life for at least four years past any reasonable medical predictions based upon his physical condition. Lovitto died on May 19, 2001. He is buried in the Moore Memorial Gardens Cemetery, Arlington, Texas.

Lovitto is remembered by his family, his teammates, Rangers fans, and the city of San Pedro. San Pedro placed a plaque bearing his name on the "Sportswalk to the Waterfront" to honor his sport exploits. Others honored on this Hollywood Boulevard-style sidewalk are athletes from the San Pedro and Los Angeles area including Joey Amalfitano, Alan Ashby, and Garry Maddox. The biography associated with Lovitto's plaque reads, in part, "Joe Lovitto was a star football and baseball star at San Pedro's Fermin Lasuen High. … Although Lovitto had blazing speed, his career was hampered by injuries. … Billy Martin said, 'Lovitto would have been a great player, but he was plagued by injuries.'"[9]

Bill Zeigler, the Rangers' trainer during Lovitto's tenure with the team, provided a perspective on him that most of his teammates shared: "Joe was a guy who played hard and aggressively. As I recall he hurt his shoulder on several occasions diving for balls in the outfield. He dressed flamboyantly, with gold chains and such, but his teammates loved him. A very popular guy with all of us."[10]

Sources

In addition to the sources cited in the Notes, the author also consulted Baseball-Reference.com, 1974 Texas Ranger Souvenir Program and Scorecard from author's personal files, and *The Baseball Encyclopedia* (ninth edition) from Macmillan.

Notes

1. The January amateur draft was begun in 1965 and discontinued in 1986. Baseball's amateur draft is now conducted only once per year, in June.
2. A statement (unsupported) attributed to Ted Williams and quoted in an online obituary posted on July 5, 2002, by Debbie Cromwell. findagrave.com/cgi-bin/fg-cgi?page=sh&GRid=5463135, accessed December 20, 2015.
3. Mike Shropshire, *Seasons in Hell with Billy Martin, Whitey Herzog and "The Worst Baseball Team in History"… The 1973-1975 Texas Rangers* (Lincoln: University of Nebraska Press, 1996), 21.
4. Caption under a photo of Lovitto and Williams that was posted online at findgrave.com by Lovitto's sister-in-law, Debbie Cromwell.
5. Eric Nadel, Texas Rangers: The Authorized History (Dallas: Taylor Publishing Company, 1997), 68.
6. Shropshire, 21.
7. Ibid.
8. *Los Angeles Times*, May 23, 2001.
9. sportswalkwaterfront.com, accessed December 20, 2015.
10. Author interview with Bill Zeigler, January 24, 2016.

ELLIOTT MADDOX

BY GORDON JANIS

From the moment he was born in the back seat of a car in the parking lot of the East Orange (New Jersey) General Hospital, during a snowstorm on December 21, 1948,[1] Elliott Maddox showed a knack for doing things on his terms. He was a premier defensive outfielder who had just begun to show his offensive talent when a cruel date with destiny paid him a visit one rainy night at Shea Stadium. Maddox's story is not merely one of promise cut short by injury. In an 11-year major-league career, he would have the unusual distinction of being traded from three different teams by manager Billy Martin and playing for four other managers who are in the Baseball Hall of Fame. He was a college-educated man who did not let baseball define or control him. He was also an outspoken figure who had the courage to stand up for what he believed in.

Jackie Robinson had just broken baseball's color barrier the year before Maddox was born, and even though his parents rooted for the Brooklyn Dodgers and took him to games at Ebbets Field, young Elliott developed a lifelong connection to another team, the New York Yankees, whom he remembered cheering for during the 1958 World Series. Years later he would not only don Yankee pinstripes, but play in the World Series for his favorite team. Still, the only autograph he received or even requested when he was young was that of Jackie Robinson.[2]

His parents, Willie and Martha,[3] both grew up in Georgia and settled in New Jersey after World War II when his father returned from overseas service with the US Coast Guard. His father was an auto mechanic.[4] Elliott's family, which included an older brother, Willie Jr.,[5] and a younger sister, lived in Vauxhall, a predominantly African-American section of Union. He played Little League, Teener League, and American Legion ball in Union, New Jersey, and semipro ball for the East Orange Soverels of the Essex League.

During high school, Elliott lettered in baseball, basketball, soccer, and track. By 10th grade he was the starting third baseman for Union High School. In his senior year, as the starting shortstop, he batted cleanup and led his team to the state championship in 1966. That year, he was picked by the Houston Astros in the fourth round of the amateur draft. Following the advice of baseball great and fellow New Jerseyan Larry Doby, he did not sign, instead preparing for college and his future, believing he would be drafted again.[6] In contrast, a high-school teammate, pitcher Al Santorini, who signed a contract that same year as a first-round pick of the Atlanta Braves, would be out of baseball at age 24 after amassing only 17 big-league wins.

After receiving scholarship offers from more than 100 colleges, Maddox chose the University of Michigan, based on its reputation both athletically and academically as well as its proximity to relatives in Detroit. Initially a premed major with aspirations of being an orthopedic surgeon, Elliott switched to prelaw when it was evident that he could not play baseball and maintain such a demanding academic schedule.[7] While Maddox was the first black student at Michigan on a baseball scholarship, he was actually the third black major leaguer to have played baseball for the university.[8] The first two, trailblazing brothers Moses Fleetwood Walker and Welday Walker, played for Toledo of the American Association in 1884 until it became apparent that the league would not tolerate players of color or teams that employed them.

In his sophomore year (1968), his only season playing for Michigan, Maddox led the Big Ten in batting with an average of .467 while playing the outfield. The Detroit Tigers made him their number-one pick in the Secondary Phase of the June 1968 amateur draft, and Maddox was signed by Tigers scout Rabbit Jacobson for $40,000. The Tigers allowed him to report late to spring training to accommodate his academic schedule.

After reporting, Maddox batted .314 in 40 games with Lakeland in the Florida State League before moving to Rocky Mount in the Carolina League, where he hit .297. The memorable highway billboard outside Rocky Mount read: "You Are Entering Klan Country."[9] Unable to rent a motel room there, he found lodging with a local black family.[10] Nevertheless, in 1969 his .301 average was eighth best in the Carolina League. In late 1969, while playing in the Florida Instructional League, Maddox and his four black and Puerto Rican teammates had to sleep in their cars for three days because no motel would give them rooms. The 20-year-old Maddox called Tigers general manager Joe Campbell and, introducing himself as the number-one draft pick, declared, "We're tired of sleeping in cars; we're not going to sleep in cars any more."[11] Within two hours they had rooms on the beach like the other ballplayers. Maddox's outspokenness raised concerns with the Tigers when they learned he had participated in civil-rights sit-ins at the University of Michigan, and the GM "warned me about any future demonstrations."[12]

Maddox made the Tigers' big-league club in 1970 spring training. His major-league debut came as a pinch-hitter on April 7, when he grounded out against the Senators' Joe Grzenda. Batting against the Indians' Dean Chance in the fourth inning on April 21, Maddox singled home the tying run with his first major-league hit. He then got an infield hit in the ninth and scored the decisive run. He hit his first big-league homer nine days later off the Royals' Mike Hedlund in the ninth inning to seal a Tigers win. By June, manager Mayo Smith had Maddox batting second between Dick McAuliffe and Al Kaline.[13] He showed his versatility by playing six positions that season. In September, Maddox returned to Michigan for his senior year while simultaneously playing for the Tigers 40 miles away. As he later described it, "I was literally playing and going to college at the same time. I did homework on the road trips and always had my books around the locker room. Some of the guys, like Gates Brown, used to kid me about using big words in the dugout, but everything went pretty smoothly."[14] For the season he had an on-base percentage of .332 despite batting only .248, and was voted the Tigers' rookie of the year by the Detroit Sports Broadcasters Association.

After the 1970 season, manager Smith was fired and was replaced by Billy Martin, who in his only season of managerial experience, had guided the Minnesota Twins to the American League West title in 1969, during the first year of divisional play. Under Martin, the Tigers immediately traded Maddox along with pitchers Denny McLain and Norm McRae and third baseman Don Wert to the Washington Senators for pitchers Joe Coleman and Jim Hannan and infielders Ed Brinkman and Aurelio Rodriguez. Of the players the Senators received in the deal, only Maddox would still be playing by 1973. Denny McLain, who had been suspended for associating with gamblers, was one year removed from back-to-back Cy Young Awards, including the first 30-win season in 34 years.

This deal paid dividends for the Tigers, who won the American League East title in 1972. The Senators had just been purchased two years earlier by Bob Short, who over-leveraged himself in a deal that saw him outbid comedian Bob Hope for bragging rights to a major-league team in the nation's capital.[15] In order to help attract fans to the lowly Senators, whose ticket prices were the highest in the league,[16] Short hired Ted Williams, who had been retired from baseball for nine years and had never managed before.

Maddox was hardly intimidated by the legendary Williams, and was not afraid to challenge his orthodoxy about baseball or politics. "He was lecturing us on hitting one day and I said that's not the way Clemente and Aaron do it, and that made him mad," Maddox said. "He couldn't understand that not everyone is 6-3 and 200 pounds and has his reflexes. And I'd agitate him about Nixon. He thought Nixon was the greatest, and when I said something about him, he'd sputter all over the place."[17]

Maddox recalled reporting to the Senators in 1971 during the Vietnam War, thinking he would be drafted. He described showing up in Pompano Beach for spring training with a big Afro and "looking like Jimi Hendrix with the tassels hanging down. And which just irked Ted to no end my coming in dressed like that."[18] When Maddox displayed a "Free Angela Davis" bumper sticker on his locker, referring to the radical activist who was jailed and later acquitted in a high-profile murder case, he was told to remove it, and believed he was from then on labeled a troublemaker, and was threatened with being sent down to the minors.[19]

One player in spring training who liked the bumper sticker and presumably the courage in displaying it was Curt Flood, himself no stranger to bucking authority.[20] That spring, Maddox briefly roomed with Flood, whose own courage to fight baseball's reserve clause made him a pariah in the baseball establishment and forced him to miss the 1970 season. Flood was signed by Bob Short as a big-name attendance draw after refusing to play for Philadelphia when the Cardinals traded him to the Phillies. Maddox greatly admired the way Flood took a principled stand against the baseball establishment,[21] and almost certainly regarded Flood as an inspiration years later when he too would take baseball to court. Maddox said his later experience as a player representative could be attributed to Flood's example, among other factors.[22]

Maddox soon proved himself a valuable fixture in center field, as he led all American League outfielders in 1971 with 3.05 Range Factor per Nine Innings. In early 1971, Williams said of Maddox: "He's going to be some player in two years."[23] At the plate, Maddox hit an anemic .217 for the season. But the disappointment that would be seared into the collective memory of DC baseball fans in 1971, and for decades to come, was when owner Bob Short moved the team to Arlington, Texas, where they became the Texas Rangers. A blog account of the riotous last Senators game at RFK Stadium recalled that after two teenagers' homemade banner cried, "How Dare You Sell Us SHORT," several players showed their support. "Outfielder Elliot Maddox gave the Black Power Fist Salute with his batting glove on – to the youngsters – to great admiration from the fans."[24] Maddox hit an eighth-inning sacrifice fly that put the Senators ahead, 7-5, and proved to be the last Senators at-bat, when a runner was caught stealing. In fact, as the Yankees batted in the top of the ninth inning, angry fans, feeling betrayed by the owner's move to greener pastures, rioted to the extent that the game could not be finished and the Senators lost by forfeit.

With the Rangers, Williams called Maddox "perhaps the best defensive center fielder in the American League."[25] The Rangers experimented with Maddox as a switch-hitter during spring training, though that was soon abandoned when his low average cost him the Opening Day center-field job to rookie Joe Lovitto. Maddox became the regular center fielder in late April. He was batting just .224 on June 12 when a pulled muscle kept him out of the lineup for 17 games. After many games as a pinch-runner or defensive replacement, Maddox started games in left and right before regaining the center-field job on August 4. During a 13-game span in August, Maddox batted .327 and raised his average to a modest .252. His season ended abruptly on August 29 when he broke his hand while diving back to first base at Yankee Stadium.[26] Still, in just 98 games, he stole 20 bases, tied for 12th in the American League. The Rangers finished sixth in their division with a record of 54-100.

In 1973 Maddox was optimistic that his injuries and underperformance from the year before were behind him and that he would establish himself not only as the regular center fielder, but as a decent hitter. Ted Williams departed and was replaced by rookie manager Whitey Herzog. In spring training Maddox predicted he would hit .280. Herzog downplayed such expectations, saying, "We'll take .250 or .260 with all his other assets."[27] Indeed, Maddox started off well and was among the league leaders at the end of April with an average of .326. Then his productivity declined sharply. In May and June of 1973, he missed 20 games with a sore shoulder and pulled hamstring.[28] He was batting .228 in September when Herzog was replaced by Billy Martin for the final 23 games of the season. Maddox played in just 11 of those games, starting two, and going 4-for-10, ending the season at .238. For the season he stole only five bases, and none after July 1.

The Rangers sold Maddox to the Yankees for $40,000 in March 1974. It was a welcome opportunity for the New Jersey native to show the team he cheered for as a boy that he was better than his major-league career to that point, and worthy of the first-round draft pick he had been six years earlier.

He also was starting with a clean slate under manager Bill Virdon, who commented, "After we got him, I heard he was a militant. But I don't pay attention to that stuff."[29] In late May, the Yankees skipper caused a stir by moving veteran Bobby Murcer from center field to right and naming Maddox as the regular center fielder. As Virdon, himself a former outfielder, recalled years later, "Maddox was one of the best while he was physically able."[30] Many believed that Murcer belonged in center, the rightful heir to former teammate, Yankee legend, and fellow Oklahoman Mickey Mantle. Maddox was already hitting .283 at the time of the switch, but afterward both he and Murcer showed increased production and the Yankees won 13 of their next 19 games. The decision to move Murcer from center field to right field in favor of Maddox was even mentioned on Maddox's 1975 Topps baseball card: "One of Mgr. Virdon's most controversial moves of 1974 was inserting Elliott in centerfield and moving Bobby Murcer to right. Elliott responded with superb hitting and flawless fielding."[31]

In July 1974 Maddox had the satisfaction of two four-hit games two days apart, against teams he had formerly played with, on July 3 in a loss to the Tigers and on July 5 in a 14-2 triumph over Billy Martin's Rangers. The Yankees battled for the division lead all year, and held first place into the latter half of September, but ultimately finished second, two games back of the Baltimore Orioles. For Elliott Maddox, 1974 would go down as his career year as he finally stayed healthy and showed he could hit as well as field. His .303 average was fifth best in the American League, and his .395 on-base percentage ranked fourth. Despite only three homers and 45 RBIs, he ranked fourth in Wins Above Replacement (WAR) among position players with 5.4. He was second among league outfielders with 18 assists. He finished eighth in the American League MVP voting. The New Jersey Sportswriters Association named him Player of the Year.[32]

While Elliott Maddox the ballplayer was finally realizing his potential through consistency on the field, Elliott Maddox the man decided to convert to Judaism so that his religious affiliation would be consistent with his personal beliefs. The son of a Baptist father and Methodist mother, Maddox was first exposed to Judaism through several childhood friendships and visits to the home of his Little League coach, Mr. Shapiro, whose family warmly welcomed him. He believed that the upbringing of Jews and blacks alike made them "more willing to accept people for who they are."[33] His sense of spiritual kinship between Jews and blacks was solidified during a Judaic history class at the University of Michigan. "Talk about slavery, the [E]xodus ... coming out of Africa, you may want to call it Egypt."[34] His parents were supportive of his newfound spiritual identity: "They thought it was great that I finally believed in something."[35] In a 2004 article that coincided with his upcoming appearance at a Baseball Hall of Fame event honoring Jews in baseball, Maddox addressed "anti-Semitism on the field, in the clubhouse, from management. It's alive and well in a very sick way."36 In a 2010 documentary on Jews in baseball, Maddox quipped, "I always considered myself a good two-strike hitter. Being black and a Jew I got the two strikes. So, now I can handle anything."37

While playing in New York, Maddox upheld his reputation for being outspoken in addressing the racial divides even on integrated teams. He said that when a black football player was mobbed by teammates following a touchdown, "half those guys would probably stab him in the back if they had the chance. The only reason they're patting him on the back is that he's putting money in their pockets."38

During spring training, when Maddox accused Billy Martin of lying to him about his chance to play when he was with the Rangers, he became the target of a couple of errant pitches, and a brawl ensued.39 The feud continued into the regular season when the Yankees and Rangers first played in New York. When Maddox was predictably plunked by a Rangers pitcher in May, he asked Commissioner Bowie Kuhn to intervene "before somebody gets seriously hurt."40 That would be the last time he would play against Martin's Rangers, though he would still have to deal with Martin again.

During the 1974 and '75 seasons, while Yankee Stadium was closed for renovation, the Yankees played all their home games at Shea Stadium, the Mets' ballpark in Flushing, Queens. Playing on a soggy Shea Stadium outfield on Friday night, June 13, 1975, with the Yankees clinging to a narrow lead in the ninth inning, Maddox slipped while catching a fly ball and suffered a season-ending injury. He tore cartilage and two ligaments in his right knee. Still, the Yankees, who were battling for first place and desperately needed outfielders following injuries to Bobby Bonds, Lou Piniella, and Roy White, wanted Maddox to return that season and put off surgery until after the season. The day after his injury, the team fell out of first place and only briefly returned. In August, less than three months later, the Yankees fired Bill Virdon and replaced him with Billy Martin, who at least publicly said all the right things about wanting a healthy Maddox back in the lineup.41 On September 3, with the team already 12½ games out, surgery was finally performed when it was obvious how serious the injury was. That season, which had started out with such promise, ended with Maddox batting .307 in just 55 games. The Yankees finished in third place, 12 games behind the Red Sox.

Maddox, wearing a heavy metal leg brace, received a standing ovation from appreciative fans in his first home game at Yankee Stadium on June 22, 1976, over a year after his devastating injury, when he was announced as a pinch-hitter, before responding with a double. Not performing as well as hoped, he returned to the disabled list on July 1. He was returned to the active roster by September 1 in order to be eligible for the postseason. He hit just .217 in 18 regular-season games in 1976. In three ALCS games against the Kansas City Royals, he was 2-for-9 with a double and an RBI. As the starting right fielder in Game One of the World Series, Maddox hit a triple in his second at-bat. The World Series that year was the first one to employ the designated hitter, a role that Maddox filled in Game Two. (He was 0-for-3.) Although the Yankees were swept in four games by the Cincinnati Reds, nobody on the team was happier and had worked harder to be there than Elliott Maddox.

Maddox wound up suing the Yankees, the Mets, the City of New York and others for $12 million in damages for the unsafe playing conditions he had to play under at Shea Stadium that fateful night that changed everything. Though he had alerted the manager and grounds crew to the wet field conditions before the incident, that fact was used to argue that he assumed the risk because he could have refused to play.42 That legalistic argument may be unrealistic in the context of a player who does not want to hurt his team's chances during a pennant race, or jeopardize his job security, or compromise his teammates' trust by refusing to play in unsafe conditions. In 1985 the New York State Supreme Court ruled against Maddox.43

In November 1976, Maddox had a second surgery to remove seven chips in his knee, without the consent of Yankees doctors. In January, the Yankees traded him along with outfielder Rick Bladt to the Orioles for Gold Glove outfielder Paul Blair. Maddox said that upon learning of the trade, he jokingly told Orioles manager Earl Weaver to sell his house. "It stood to reason that as soon as I got there, Billy Martin would be on his way to Baltimore."[44] From his debut in July until the end of the season, Maddox batted .262 in 49 games for the Orioles.

Maddox was not away from New York long. He signed a five-year $950,000 free-agent contract in November 1977 with the National League Mets. There were a few noteworthy aspects of his signing, one of which was that he would be returning to Shea Stadium, the site of his devastating injury. Even though the Mets were a party to his lawsuit, as leaseholders of Shea Stadium, it did not stop them from signing him. Also, Maddox was among the first major-league free agents ever signed by the Mets, who had been known for their parsimonious refusal to pay Tom Seaver and other stars their fair market value. Maddox played with the Mets from 1978 through 1980, under manager Joe Torre, posting averages of .257, .268, and .246 respectively. He endured a couple more stints on the disabled list during that time. In 1980 he played in 130 games, mostly at third base, which he found harder on his knees than playing the outfield. Despite his discomfort at the hot corner, his .956 fielding percentage was fourth among league third basemen. In 1980 he was hit by pitch a league-leading six times. In February 1981, the Mets released Maddox with two years remaining on his contract. For his career, he hit .262 with 18 homers and 234 RBIs over 11 seasons.

After retiring from baseball, Maddox worked as an investment banker on Wall Street for seven years and managed an ice-cream parlor that went bankrupt.[45] He coached for the Yankees in Fort Lauderdale and as a roving instructor in 1990-1991. He then worked for eight years as a senior foster-care counselor in Broward County, Florida. As a single father, he had to stop when it interfered with his family time. Maddox had three children with two wives.

In 1989, as the Soviet Union began to unravel, Maddox traveled to Poland to help establish Little League baseball.

In 1997 he was inducted into the Union County, New Jersey, Baseball Hall of Fame. In 2004, the Jewish Sports Hall of Fame inducted him and his former Yankee teammate Ron Blomberg as honorees. In 2003, a circuit judge in Florida acquitted Maddox of grand theft and perjury charges in connection with income received while on disability leave from his counselor position with state Department of Children and Families.[46] In 2006, he taught baseball fundamentals to Israeli youths in preparation for the short-lived Israel Baseball League.

In 2010, 35 years after his conversion to Judaism, Maddox had a bar mitzvah ceremony attended by more than 300 youngsters at the Ron Blomberg Baseball Camp in Milford, Pennsylvania, where Maddox had run clinics for five years.[47] Over the years, he has had no fewer than 13 surgeries on his knee.[48] As of 2018, Maddox lived in Coral Springs, Florida.

Notes

1. Transcript of Elliott Maddox interview by Rebecca Alpert, for Jewish Major Leaguers, Inc., conducted March 7, 2005. The 26-page oral history can be found in Maddox's player file at the National Baseball Hall of Fame Library. All existing baseball databases show Maddox as being born on that date in 1947.
2. Ibid.
3. Dave Hirshey, "Elliott Maddox: 'I Always Say What's on My Mind,'" *New York Times Magazine*, April 23, 1978.
4. Peg Stomierowski, "Bias Plagues Sports Like Other Fields, Says Maddox," *Binghamton Press*, February 13, 1975.
5. njsportsheroes.com/elliottmaddoxbb.html, retrieved March 5, 2015.
6. Elliott Maddox, "Blending Athletics and Academics," *New York Times*, June 15, 1980.
7. Peter Ephross with Martin Abramowitz. *Jewish Major Leaguers in Their Own Words* (Jefferson, North Carolina: McFarland & Co, Inc., 2012), 170-71.
8. baseball-almanac.com/college/university_of_michigan_baseball_players.shtml.

9   Hirshey.

10 Sam Abady, "Appeal Play – Maddox in Mudville," baseballlibrary.com, May 28, 2007, retrieved on March 5, 2015. Note: As of early 2018, this site now seems to be in accessible.

11 Ephross, 172-73.

12 Hirshey.

13 Watson Spoelstra, "Maddox Quick to Learn – Tiger Tutors Taking Bows," *The Sporting News*, June 27, 1970: 16.

14 Maddox. "Blending Athletics."

15 nats320.blogspot.com/2006/11/night-my-washington-senators-died_26.html.

16 Ibid.

17 Larry Merchant, "The Yanks' Main Man," *New York Post*, undated September 1974 newspaper clipping in Maddux's player file at the National Baseball Hall of Fame.

18 Ephross, 172.

19 Ibid.

20 Brad Snyder, A Well-Paid Slave: Curt Flood's Fight for Free Agency in Professional Sports (New York: Viking, 2006), 214.

21 Ibid.

22 Interview by Rebecca Alpert.

23 George Minot Jr., "Williams Looks to Knowles for Longer-Lasting Relief: Maddox Tickles Manager's Fancy," Washington Post, February 25, 1971 retrieved from ProQuest Historical Newspaper Online Archive.

24 nats320.blogspot.com/2006/11/night-my-washington-senators-died_26.html.

25 Randy Galloway, "Maddox Eyes '73: Start of Something Big," The Sporting News, September 23, 1972: 36.

26 Merle Heryford, " 'Forgotten Man' Maddox Producing," The Sporting News, May 26, 1973: 10.

27 Merle Heryford, The Sporting News, May 26, 1973: 14.

28 Randy Galloway, "Ranger Ramblings," The Sporting News, June 2, 1973: 4.

29 Merchant.

30 Murray Chass, "To Break a Man's Heart, Take Center Away," New York Times, March 1, 2005.

31 75topps.blogspot.com/2010/02/113-elliott-maddox.html.

32 Hirshey.

33 Ephross, 170.

34 Ibid.

35 Ron Kaplan, "A Switch Hitter's Conversion," *New Jersey Jewish News*, August 26, 2004.

36 Ibid.

37 "Jews and Baseball: An American Love Story," *Clear Lake Historical Productions*, 2010.

38 "Education Gives Me Free Voice, Ballplayer Says," *Binghamton Press*, February 14, 1975.

39 Murray Chass, "Maddox, Martin: No Love Lost," *New York Times*, May 24, 1975.

40 Phil Pepe, "Maddox Tired of Ducking, Wants Kuhn to Stop Billy," *New York Daily News*, May 25, 1975.

41 Phil Pepe, "Martin Admits Error, Cottons Up to Maddox," *New York Daily News*, August 16, 1975.

42 Abady. See also Adam Nagourney, "Ex-Yankee Strikes Out in Lawsuit," *New York Daily News*, November 23, 1985.

43 See Abady and Nagourney.

44 Hirshey.

45 "Maddox Pays Up for a Bad Check," *New York Post*, June 27, 1989.

46 "Elliott Maddox: Who Knew?," Blogpost, July 15, 2003 contained article by Paula McMahon, South Florida Sun-Sentinel (Fort Lauderdale), July 15, 2003. Retrieved from forums.nyyfans.com/showthread.php/45792-Elliott-Maddox-who-knew, on March 5, 2015.

47 Nate Bloom, "Interfaith Celebrities" column, August 17, 2010, Retrieved from interfaithfamily.com/arts_and_entertainment/popular_culture/Interfaith_Celebrities_Is_Sedgwick_Closer_to_an_Emmy_or_Will_Margulies_Make_Good.shtml.

48 njsportsheroes.com/elliottmaddoxbb.html.

ORLANDO "MARTY" MARTÍNEZ

BY JOSEPH GERARD

Orlando "Marty" Martínez Oliva was a major-league baseball player, coach, manager, and scout who was best known for scouting Edgar Martinez and signing him to a professional contract with the Seattle Mariners in 1982. Orlando Martínez played for six teams in the major leagues, beginning with the Minnesota Twins in 1962 and ending with the Texas Rangers in 1972. After his major-league playing career was over, Martínez played, coached, and managed in the Rangers minor-league system for four years before becoming player-manager of the Double-A Tulsa Drillers in 1977. He managed the Drillers for two years and won a first-half championship in 1977. Afterward, he became a scout and coach for the Seattle Mariners, and was named interim manager of the team for one day in 1986.

Orlando Martínez was born on August 23, 1941, in the Batabano section of Havana, Cuba, in what is now Mayabeque province. At the Instituto Civico Militar in Marianao, he lettered in baseball, track, and basketball. He set a national record for striking out 23 batters in one game and was named to the All-Cuba national team. In 1957 he traveled to Mexico with a team of Cuban high-school players, compiling a batting average of .306 during the trip.

After graduating from high school in 1959, Martínez attended the University of Havana for one year and the University of Mexico in Mexico City for another, but his academic studies came to an end when he was discovered by Joe Cambria, the scout who helped open up Latin America for the major leagues. Cambria signed hundreds of players, mostly of Cuban descent, to inexpensive contracts for the Washington Senators and their successors, the Minnesota Twins, including Bobby Estalella, Tony Oliva, and Camilo Pasqual.

Martínez signed with Cambria in 1960 and was sent to play for the Erie Sailors, the Senators' affiliate in the Class-D New York-Penn League. He got off to an inauspicious start, hitting only .222 in 297 at-bats, but improved the following season with the Wilson Tobs (short for Tobacconists) of the Class-B Carolina League, where he hit .265 with 24 extra-base hits (one a grand slam) and 56 RBIs. He led the league's shortstops in putouts and assists, and was named to the league All-Star team. The Tobs, managed by Jack McKeon – who went on to win more than 1,000 games as a big-league manager – captured the league championship by 11 games. (There were no playoffs.)

The former Washington Senators, in their second year in Minnesota, were impressed enough by Martínez to jump him straight to the big leagues in 1962. He spent all season with the Twins, though he got only 18 at-bats in 37 games. The Twins returned him to their farm system in 1963. He played briefly for Dallas-Fort Worth in the Triple-A Pacific Coast League before being sent down to Double-A Charlotte of the South Atlantic League. He failed to hit .200 at either level and repeated Triple-A at Atlanta in 1964.

Martínez was assigned to Triple-A Denver in 1965, and spent two years with the Bears under manager Cal Ermer, who made a recommendation that resulted in Martínez returning to the big leagues, albeit with another team. In July of 1966, Ermer noticed the left-handed Martínez taking some swings right-handed in batting practice, and asked, "Why don't you try that in games, against left-handers?"[1] Despite an 0-for-14 start, Martínez said "Ermer stuck with me. When I started batting both ways, I was hitting around .218, as I remember, and I hit about .380 the rest of the way."[2] Martínez ended the season hitting .313. The Atlanta Braves took notice, and selected Martínez off the Twins roster in that winter's Rule 5 player draft. When Twins president Calvin Griffith trivialized the loss of Martínez, Braves manager Billy Hitchcock responded, "All I know is we weren't the only club interested in drafting Martínez. I know of at least two other clubs who wanted to make him their first draft choice."[3]

The Braves eyed Martínez as a late-inning defensive replacement at shortstop. During 1967 spring training Hitchcock said, "He has shown us here that he can make the plays, both at shortstop and second base."[4] The Braves manager also liked the enthusiasm and spirit that came to be known as Martínez's calling cards. "He's alive when he's in the dugout, too, always chattering and keeping everybody in the game," the manager said. "Little things like that are extremely important."[5] Martínez became a utility player with the Braves, a role he would fill for the rest of his major-league career. He appeared in 44 games, and hit .288 in 87 plate appearances before he hurt his left ankle while sliding into second base on August 26, an injury that ended his season.

After the season, the Braves sought a catcher to back up Joe Torre. After failing to land one at the winter meetings, they took the advice of Cal Ermer, Martínez's manager at Denver, who was now skipper of the Twins. Ermer told Braves manager Lum Harris at the winter meetings that Martínez could handle the backup catcher position. "He has the arm, he has the hustle and he is agile enough that he handles himself behind the plate well," Ermer said.[6] Bullpen coach Ken Silvestri seconded Ermer's opinion, as Martínez had filled in as both bullpen and batting practice catcher the prior year, and had done well catching Braves knuckleballer Phil Niekro. "When we get to spring training next February, Martínez will be our No. 2 catcher. That will be one of my first projects," Harris concluded.[7]

As it turned out, Martínez appeared in only 14 games behind the plate in 1968, but he was the Braves' primary infield reserve, amassing 395 plate appearances, his major-league season high. He hit .230 playing mostly at shortstop, third base, and second base.

After the season, the Braves traded Martínez to the Houston Astros in return for Bob Aspromonte, the last original member of the Colt .45s. In 1969 Martínez hit a personal high .308 in 213 plate appearances. However, his playing time diminished considerably over the next two seasons. In 1970 he had only 159 plate appearances and batted only .220, and in 1971 he was relegated to the bench for much of the season. After 67 games he had been to the plate only 52 times, and made known his desire to be traded. "I like Houston and the organization has been good to me. I have no complaints, but everyone wants to play," said Martínez.[8]

Houston manager Harry Walker meanwhile had let it be known that the team was beset by internal problems caused by what he called three to five troublemakers, and suggested that Martínez was one of them, despite the fact that no such assertion had ever been made by anyone else associated with the club. In fact, Martínez had begun a popular program that grew to include all of the Astros players, in which they made regular visits to hospitals. "We are a part of society," he said. "It is a chance to be a part of the community, to repay something for what we have."[9]

Not surprisingly, the Astros complied with Martínez's request and traded him in November to the St. Louis Cardinals in exchange for Bob Stinson. The 1972 season turned out to be Martínez's last in the major leagues. His stint with the Cardinals lasted only nine games before he was traded to the Oakland Athletics on May 18 for Brant Alyea. Martínez played only two months for the A's before he was traded to the Texas Rangers on July 20 with Vic Harris and a player to be named for Ted Kubiak and Don Mincher. (The trade was first announced on the afternoon of the 19th, yet Martínez played for the A's that night and got three hits in a 9-6 win over the Milwaukee Brewers. Brewers director of baseball operations Frank Lane filed a protest with the American League, but it was disallowed.)

While Martínez may have been denied an opportunity at a world championship with Charlie Finley's developing dynasty in Oakland, his time in Texas led to the next phase of his career. In 1973 Martínez became a player-coach for the Spokane Indians of the Pacific Coast League, a Rangers farm team. He batted .303 in 152 at-bats for the Indians, the last season in which he saw significant playing time.

In 1974 Martínez returned to Spokane as a coach, and in 1975 he was assigned to Pittsfield of the Double-A Eastern League. On July 24 he replaced Jackie Moore as manager. In 1976 he managed San Antonio, which had replaced Pittsfield as the Rangers' Double-A affiliate. The team kept him on as manager in 1977, when they relocated their Double-A team to Tulsa. The Drillers made the Eastern Division playoffs as a result of winning the first-half title, but lost the division championship series to the second-half winner, the Arkansas Travelers.

Martínez was involved in an unfortunate incident during the 1977 season that may have been representative of the racist tendencies still prevalent in the South at that time. A fan, Jerry Sterling, sued Martínez, the Drillers, and the Texas Rangers, alleging that Martínez and several players had punched him during a game on May 10 at Little Rock. In his defense, Martínez claimed that Sterling had been using racial invective against him throughout the game. The suit was settled two years later for $1,125.

Martínez left the Drillers after the 1978 season. In 1980, he began his association with the Seattle Mariners when he managed the Wausau (Wisconsin) Timbers of the Class-A Midwest League to a 57-82 record. The Timbers were a co-op club whose roster was stocked by several teams, but was predominantly made up of Seattle prospects.

Martínez subsequently went to work for the Mariners as a minor-league instructor and scout, and it did not take long for his impact to be felt. In 1982 he spotted Edgar Martinez playing in a semipro league in Puerto Rico and arranged for a tryout. "He was a third baseman at the time and had great hands," Martínez said. "I honestly thought at the time that he would be a great second baseman. That shows how much I know. He was a good hitter, not a power hitter, and handled the bat well."[10]

Edgar Martinez, who was a college student and worked at a pharmaceutical company, signed a $5,000 bonus contract with the Mariners and turned out to be one of the best hitters of his era, but not without Marty Martínez's help. "He was a big part of my development throughout the minor leagues," Edgar said. "He was almost like a father figure to many of the Latin players, and anyone who played in the infield. They were all like his sons. He took his work very personally and very serious."[11]

Marty believed strongly in Edgar, and after Edgar hit only .173 at Class-A Bellingham in 1983, Marty persuaded Mariners general manager Hal Keller to send the player to the instructional league in Arizona. Keller didn't see why he should, but later said, "I was wrong on Edgar. I never thought he'd hit in the big leagues."[12] Edgar, who hit .340 in Arizona, said, "Marty was fighting for me. He asked them to give me another opportunity. I'll always be grateful for that."[13]

Martínez also signed Omar Vizquel to a contract with the Mariners in 1984, and tutored him in the minor leagues. Vizquel had a 24-year major-league career, and his fielding percentage of .985 as of 2014 was the best ever recorded by a shortstop. Martínez was credited with assisting future Mariner major-league infielders Harold Reynolds and Spike Owen as well.

Martínez joined the Mariners coaching staff in 1984 under manager Del Crandall, and stayed on in 1985 when Crandall was replaced by Chuck Cottier. On May 8, 1986, Cottier was fired, to be replaced by Dick Williams. While Williams was in transit, Martínez was named interim manager for one game on May 9, which the Mariners lost to the Boston Red Sox, 4-2. Mariners president Chuck Armstrong remembered, "We felt like he would be a sentimental favorite among the players. Marty was so well-liked, no one could resent the fact we had asked him to do that for a game."[14]

Martínez was not included on Williams's coaching staff in 1987. In 1988 he managed the Triple-A Calgary Cannons after manager Bill Plummer was promoted to be the Mariners' third-base coach in midseason.

Martínez was named supervisor of Latin American Scouting for the Mariners in 1989, and held that role until 1992 when he became the Mariners' third-base coach under Plummer.

In addition to his scouting responsibilities, in 1993-94, Martínez managed the Mariners' Arizona League rookie team, based in Peoria, Arizona, where he helped develop a young Dominican player named David Ortiz.

After retiring, Martínez and his wife, Jessie Faye, split their time between homes in Tulsa, Oklahoma, and the Dominican Republic. He died in Santo Domingo of an apparent heart attack on March 8, 2007, at the age of 65. He was buried in Green Acres Cemetery in Skiatook, Oklahoma. At the time of his death, Martínez was reportedly attempting to find a new job in baseball

Chuck Cottier conferred Martínez with the nickname, Baseball Marty, and it soon stuck. "Just a wonderful, happy, guy," said Cottier. "He was, first and foremost, a great baseball man."[15]

Sources

In addition to the sources cited in the Notes, the author consulted Ancestry.com, Baseball-almanac.com, Baseball-reference.com, Retrosheet.org, and the National Baseball Hall of Fame Library player file for Orlando "Marty" Martínez.

Notes

1. Wayne Minshew, "Martinez Strikes Happy Tepee Note with Two-Way Bat, Glove," *Atlanta Constitution*, April 1, 1967.
2. Ibid.
3. Ibid.
4. Ibid.
5. Ibid.
6. Furman Bisher, "Lum Catches Martinez," *Atlanta Journal*, December 2, 1967.
7. Ibid.
8. John Wilson, "Just a Sub, Marty Leaves Mark on Astros," *The Sporting News*, July 10, 1971.
9. Ibid.
10. Jim Street, "Mariners Fans Salute Martinez," Seattle mariners.mlb.com, October 3, 2004.
11. Larry Stone, "Baseball Marty Left Big Impression on Mariners," *Seattle Times*, March 19, 2007.
12. Ibid.
13. Ibid.
14. Ibid.
15. Ibid.

JIM MASON

BY STEVE WEST

Confidence was a word used a lot in reference to Jim Mason. When he played well – which was rare – it was because he had his confidence. When he struggled, it was because he'd lost it. Dick Young said he was "a big guy with a small tolerance for pressure,"[1] and that may explain why, in an era known for bad players, Mason was one of the worst, a below-replacement-level player for his career.

James Percy Mason was born on August 14, 1950, in Mobile, Alabama. He was one of seven children (four girls, three boys) of Myril (pronounced Merle) and Patricia Mason. Myril worked for the Louisville & Nashville Railroad. As a child Jim was a baseball fan, and later related his admiration for Mickey Mantle. "Mickey was a favorite of mine when I was a kid," he said, "and I've always wanted to meet him. I sorta did meet him once but that was when I was 2 years old. The Yankees played an exhibition game in Mobile and I got his autograph."[2]

Mason attended Murphy High School in Mobile, playing baseball, football, and basketball. He also played in the Mobile Babe Ruth league, coached by his father. The team was the state champion in 1965 and 1966, and went to the Babe Ruth World Series in 1965. In 1966 Mason pitched the state championship game, throwing a two-hit shutout with nine strikeouts.

Shortly after graduating from high school, Mason was drafted by the Washington Senators in the second round (28th overall) of the June 1968 draft. He briefly attended the University of Southern Alabama but had already switched his focus to baseball.

Mason began his career with Geneva of the New York-Penn League in 1968. The everyday shortstop, he hit just .217, although his 33 walks led the team and he showed good work with the glove. It was perhaps the glove the Senators were thinking of in the spring of 1969 when, with the threat of a players strike looming, they brought seven minor leaguers to the major-league camp, Mason among them.

The strike did not materialize, but Mason took advantage of the exposure. He started the spring going 7-for-17, attracting a lot of attention. "When I came here I didn't think I'd do this well, because on television it looks like those pitchers throw so much harder," he said.[3] Manager Ted Williams was more enthusiastic, predicting that Mason would be a regular in the majors in three years. "Can't miss," said Ted.[4]

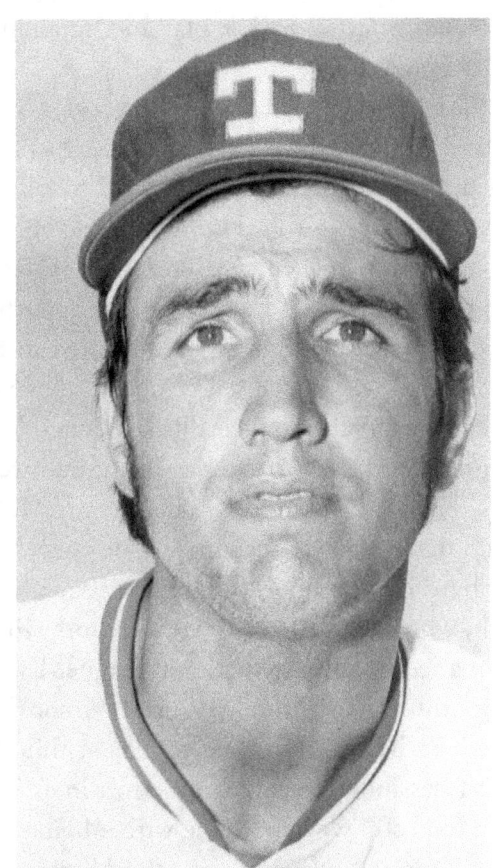

Mason was a shy but popular young man who Williams said reminded him of former Senators star Cecil Travis. For his part, Mason was awed just being around the Hall of Famer. In his deep Alabama drawl, according to one reporter, he remembered seeing Williams on television. "Ah reckon I was 9 or 10 years old. Ah thought he was the greatest ballplayer who ever lived. And as for playing for him, who would ever dream that?"[5]

With no room for him, since there was no strike, and having performed so well in the spring, the Senators ticketed Mason for Triple-A Buffalo, where at 18 he was one of the youngest players in the league. He struggled, but military commitments due to the Vietnam War meant that he played in only 35 games, missing most of the second half of the season. Even so, owner Bob Short thought Mason should start in the majors in 1970, but listened when Williams told him that Mason wasn't ready.[6] Sent back to Triple A, now in Denver, he did better, hitting .241, but his reputation with the glove suffered as he made 48 errors. His season highlight came in a game on September 1 when he both started a triple play and hit an inside-the-park home run.

At the end of the 1970 season the Senators invited Mason to the Florida Instructional League, but he declined. Instead, the Senators decided to take their Double-A shortstop, Toby Harrah, who accepted the invite. General manager Joe Burke said, "We invite the players we want and give them an opportunity to develop faster."[7] The decision appeared to harm Mason's chances, especially when, just a few weeks later, the Senators traded their third baseman, Aurelio Rodriguez, and shortstop, Ed Brinkman, to the Detroit Tigers in return for pitcher Denny McLain.

With the left side of the infield wide open, Mason might have had his shot, but he was beaten out by Harrah, who had impressed the Senators with his performance in the instructional league. Even so, Harrah still felt the more advanced Mason would get the job.[8] Mason also tried to play at third base, but unsuccessfully. He made four errors in one game at third (and still won the game with a home run in the 13th inning). "Ah'm just not a third baseman," he drawled.[9]

Mason felt that the team had made the decision before camp even opened. "I really didn't get a chance. It was apparent they had their minds made up," he said.[10] Frustrated when he was sent down, he threatened to quit and go back to college, but quickly changed his mind and reported to Denver once more.[11] He tried to put a positive spin on things. "I'm determined to show them I can play ball. I'm just going to give it all I've got and the future will take care of itself," he said. "He's got the right spirit and the future looks bright," Denver manager Del Wilber said.[12]

Mason did much better this time in Denver, hitting .268, drawing 77 walks, and making just 23 errors. "You try to get to the point where you throw that ball over there and not even think about it," he said of his improvement on defense.[13] The team did very well, too, winning the American Association championship before losing the Junior World Series to Rochester. Mason earned a reward, being called up to the Senators for the end of the season. He made his major-league debut in Fenway Park against the Boston Red Sox on September 26, going 0-for-3 with a walk. Two days later he got his first hit, at home off the New York Yankees' Stan Bahnsen, and the following day added two hits off Mel Stottlemyre to end his first big-league season 3-for-9.

Talking about having been sent back to Denver in 1971, Mason thought the demotion had helped him: "Going back there may have been the best thing that could have happened to me." He said he learned more than he thought he would.[14] For spring training in 1972, he was more circumspect. "This year I'm going to Florida with the idea that there are 10 people fighting for that job and I'm just one of them."[15] This time he did better, while Harrah spent much of the spring hurt. "Mason is looking better every day, but maybe I wouldn't feel that way if Harrah had been playing," said Williams.[16] Indeed, when the season began Harrah was in Arlington with the newly moved Texas Rangers, and Mason was on his way back to Denver.

He hit .272 there, and was called up in late July, staying in the majors for good this time. He played most of the games for the rest of the season, including 10 appearances at third base. He struggled at the plate, hitting just .197.

Mason made the team out of spring training in 1973, but as Harrah's backup. In May the team switched Harrah to third and made Mason the starting shortstop. He was hitting well early, over .300 as late as June 9, but he went into a slump, hitting just .141 the rest of the season, and lost his starting job in

July. "I wasn't playing and lost interest," he said. "If you don't play every day, you can't psych yourself up for when you do play. I wound up playing once a week usually and I guess showed that I was dissatisfied."[17]

With Harrah saying he preferred to play shortstop, the team had to choose between the two players, and they did. In December they sold Mason to the Yankees for $100,000. "It's kinda hard to price yourself, but I think $100,000 is a lot of money to anybody," he said.[18] The Yankees needed someone to compete with Gene Michael at short. They had tried to trade for the Phillies' Larry Bowa, but when they couldn't get him, Mason was the best available. "I don't think they would have paid that much money if they didn't want me to play," he said.[19]

Mason won the starting position in the spring, and stayed there all year. Given the opportunity to play every day, he put up the best numbers of his career. He started slowly but things began to pick up. "He's doing much better than he did in the beginning of the season," Michael said.[20] In 152 games he hit .250 with five home runs. He even got some payback against his old team when on July 8 he hit four doubles against the Rangers, tying a major-league record. Mason knew why he was performing so well. "I've got my confidence," he said.[21]

The 1975 season turned into a nightmare, though. Although he said, "I'm not the kind of guy who needs to be pushed to do my best. I'll push myself,"[22] whatever pushing he did was in the wrong direction. His bat disappeared; he hit just .152. The Yankees sporadically tried others at short, but it wasn't until late July that Mason lost the job for good. At that point sportswriter Young called him "a big guy with a small tolerance for pressure," and it seemed to be true.[23] Any time things went wrong, or he felt he didn't have the full confidence of the team or manager, his performance disappeared. "I completely lost my confidence last year. I got to the point where I didn't want the ball to come at me. If it did, I knew I was going to mess it up," he said.[24]

At the end of 1975, the Yankees' Triple-A manager, Bobby Cox, needed a shortstop for his Venezuelan winter-league team, and called Mason. "I went down because I wanted to find out if I can still play," Mason said, and play he did. He hit .356 and fielded well. "He did a terrific job for me," Cox said. This brought back the confidence in Mason once more, although a year later he said, "I'm not going to play winter ball this year. … All it got me was another year with the Yankees."[25]

Returning to the Yankees in 1976, Mason made his thoughts clear. "I thought I might be thrown in some trade. But I'm here and now I want to play."[26] Talking about his new-found confidence, he said, "If I make an error, I'm going to forget about it and make sure I don't make another one."[27] He spent the first few months platooning with Fred Stanley, but poor performance made manager Billy Martin give Stanley the starting job full-time in July. Mason ended the season hitting just .180, although the Yankees made the playoffs. They beat the Royals three games to two in the ALCS, with Mason making two late-inning defensive appearances, then went to the World Series against the Cincinnati Reds. They were swept in the Series, with Mason getting into three of the four games.

In Game Three Mason got the only playoff at-bat of his career, and made the most of it, homering off Reds pitcher Pat Zachry. "He missed with a slider and I was looking for the fastball," said Mason. "I thought he'd be taking," said Zachry.[28] Despite hitting the only Yankees home run of the Series, two innings later Mason was removed for a pinch-hitter. He became the 15th player to homer in his first World Series at-bat, and until 2005 was the only player to homer in the only World Series plate appearance of his career. His later reaction may have been to the outcome of the Series: "It was more exciting getting to the World Series than being there."[29]

Billy Martin twice dropped Mason from his teams. When he took over in Texas, Mason lost the shortstop job and was then sold to the Yankees; and when Martin came back to New York, Mason lost the starting job, then spent a season platooning. Mason was mystified as to why. "I never had a cross word with the man. Maybe he just doesn't like my personality. … If I deserve the job, I'm sure he'll give it to me."[30] But Martin didn't give him anything. After the 1976 season

Mason was left exposed in the expansion draft, and the Toronto Blue Jays selected him, 30th overall.

Mason looked forward to another opportunity. The Yankees "didn't tell me anything, but I knew I wouldn't be going back to New York," he said.[31] "I just did not have a good year last year. I don't think I played enough. Last season I'd get rolling and they would throw in a pinch-hitter. I think getting a chance to bat regularly will help restore my confidence."[32] He did have one regret, though. "The only thing I'll miss about leaving New York is Catfish Hunter. We became real close friends and ran around together."[33]

Visiting New York with the Blue Jays in April 1977, Mason received cheers from Yankees fans. "The fans have been very nice this week," he said, perhaps oblivious to the fact that the cheers were ironic, more due to the Yankees' poor start (they were 2-8 after the first two Toronto games) than anything Mason did. He commented on the difference between the expectations of the two cities. In New York, "the constant getting on you makes you press, even though you're really putting the pressure on yourself a little bit," whereas for Toronto, "win or lose, they're for you, and I hope it stays like that."[34]

Hope or not, the cheers didn't last long for Mason in Toronto. Hitting .165 in May, he was traded along with pitcher Steve Hargan and cash back to the Rangers, in return for third baseman Roy Howell. "I'm going down there to do the best I can and try to get in the lineup as much as possible," he said.[35] He spent the rest of 1977 and all of 1978 as a backup to Rangers starter Bert Campaneris.

The Rangers inexplicably gave Mason a four-year contract at the end of 1977, given his backup status. They then gave up on him at the end of 1978, trading him to the Montreal Expos for minor-league outfielder Mike Hart. "I'm looking forward to finding out the differences between the American and National Leagues," he said. On his recent string of moves (four teams in three seasons), he said, "It's just a change of jobs. It's pretty interesting moving around and seeing different places."[36] Perhaps overestimating his worth, when asked about his contract he said, "I feel obligated by the contract I signed, whether or not it is good or bad."[37]

Mason spent 1979 with the Expos as a backup, getting into just 40 games and hitting just .183. Looking to upgrade, in the spring of 1980 the Expos released him. Unable to find another team, he returned home to Mobile.

Mason married his hometown sweetheart, Cathy Cassidey, in 1970. Cathy worked as a teacher, and the couple had two daughters. At home he continued to play rec-league baseball, while he and his father were inducted together into the Mobile Youth Baseball Hall of Fame in 1975.

Notes

1. Dick Young, "Young Ideas," *The Sporting News*, July 19, 1975: 16.
2. Murray Chass, "Mason: New $100,000 Yankee," *New York Times*, March 4, 1974: 40.
3. Merrell Whittlesey, "Raw Rookie Mason Is Hit of Ted's Camp," *Washington Evening Star*, March 25, 1969: D1.
4. Merrell Whittlesey, "Short Unfurls Bankroll, Building for Lengthy Reign," *The Sporting News*, April 5, 1969: 17.
5. Merrell Whittlesey, "Mason Is on Cloud Nine," *Washington Evening Star*, March 11, 1969: D1.
6. Merrell Whittlesey, "Short Just Won't Stand Still, Seeks More Nat Faces," *The Sporting News*, November 21, 1970: 49.
7. Frank Haraway, "Determined Jim Mason Bears Down at Denver," *The Sporting News*, May 15, 1971: 35.
8. Merrell Whittlesey, "Two Rookies to Tussle for Nat Shortstop Job," *The Sporting News*, December 26, 1970: 40.
9. Merrell Whittlesey, "Ted Keeps 'Em Guessing on Nat Infield Scramble," *The Sporting News*, March 27, 1971: 38.
10. Haraway.
11. Merrell Whittlesey, "Harrah to Learn While on the Job," *Washington Evening Star*, March 17, 1971: C9.
12. Haraway.
13. Randy Galloway, "Rookie Jim Mason Typifies Rangers," *The Sporting News*, February 26, 1972: 41.

14 Ibid.
15 Ibid.
16 Merle Heryford, "Rangers Make Room for Randle's Bat," *The Sporting News*, April 1, 1972: 44.
17 Chass.
18 Ibid.
19 Ibid.
20 Phil Pepe, "Mason Builds on Confidence and Smashes Yankee Critics," *The Sporting News*, August 24, 1974: 7.
21 Ibid.
22 Phil Pepe, "Mason Now Indispensable Man in Yankee Lodge," *The Sporting News*, April 12, 1975: 15.
23 Young.
24 Phil Pepe, "Mason Claims Yank Shortstop Job," *The Sporting News*, April 3, 1976: 38.
25 Eddie Menton, "Mason Happy with Toronto," Mobile (Alabama) *Press Register*, November 6, 1976: C1.
26 Pepe, "Mason Claims Yank Shortstop Job."
27 Ibid.
28 Lowell Reidenbaugh, "Rookie Zachry, DH Driessen Torpedo Yanks," *The Sporting News*, November 6, 1976: 5.
29 Menton.
30 Pepe, "Mason Claims Yank Shortstop Job."
31 Menton.
32 Neil MacCarl, "New Blue Jays Delighted as Opportunity Knocks," *The Sporting News*, November 27, 1976: 61.
33 Menton.
34 Herschel Nissenson (Associated Press), "Jim Mason Isn't Bothered by Jeers: He's Blue Jay Now," *Mobile Press Register*, April 21, 1977: G1.
35 Dave Reichart, "Mason Confident with Rangers," *Mobile Press Register*, February 19, 1978: E1.
36 Eddie Menton, "Traded Jim Mason Looks Ahead to NL as Montreal Expo," *Mobile Press Register*, December 9, 1978: B1.
37 Ibid.

DON MINCHER

BY MARC Z. AARON

Donald Ray Mincher was a two-time member of the Oakland Athletics. In 1970 he was the team leader in home runs with 27. Before being traded for the second time to the Athletics on July 20, 1972, Mincher homered off Joe Coleman at Detroit on July 10. It was a personal career milestone, his 200th home run. It was also to be his last.

Minch,[1] as he was often called, "is the only man who played for both the original Twins and the original Rangers, 11 seasons apart. And, for that matter, he was the only player to see the end of both Senators' runs in Washington."[2]

Born on June 24, 1938, in Huntsville, Alabama, Mincher was of German-Irish-Indian descent. At Butler High School (Class of 1956) he played baseball, basketball, and football. In his senior year he captained both the baseball and football teams. He was a good enough football player to make both All-State and High School All-American. Mincher turned down a football scholarship at the University of Alabama to pursue his love of baseball.[3] At 6-feet-3 and 205 pounds, he was built for the sport. An American Legion baseball player, Mincher was signed by former major leaguer Zack Taylor to a Chicago White Sox contract for $4,000 after high school and was sent to Duluth-Superior of the Class C Northern League.[4] That year he married his high-school sweetheart, Patsy Ann Payne.[5] Mincher returned to Duluth-Superior in 1957 and led Northern League first basemen in putouts, assists, and double plays. In 1958, playing for Davenport in the Class B three-I League, he finished fourth in batting (.330) and was named to the league All-Star team.[6]

After spending the 1959 season at Charleston of the Class A Sally League (.272, 22 home runs), Mincher was sent on April 4, 1960, with Earl Battey and $150,000 to the Washington Senators for Roy Sievers. On the 18th, Mincher was in the Opening Day lineup at first base, going hitless in front of the home crowd against the Boston Red Sox. In his third game, at Baltimore on the 20th, Mincher got his first two major-league hits. On the 25th, at home against Baltimore, he hit his first major-league home run, off Milt Pappas, to deep right field. In mid-May, batting .230 with 2 home runs, Mincher was sent to Charleston in the American Association. Recalled in late September, he had two hits in five pinch-hitting appearances.

Before the 1961 season the Senators franchise was moved to Minneapolis-St. Paul, to play as the Minnesota Twins. Mincher hit five home runs for the Twins but spent most of the season at Triple-A Buffalo. In 1962 he was back with the Twins. On April 28, playing at Cleveland, he hit a pinch-hit home run off Ron Taylor, then, remaining in the game at first base, he homered for a second time, off Frank Funk. (Mincher was to finish his career with ten pinch-hit home runs, four of them in 1964.) Mincher had another two-home-run game on July 20, 1963, at Minnesota's Metro Stadium, taking starter Steve Ridzik of the expansion Senators deep twice as the Twins won 11-3. The next day he did it again, homering twice off Senators starter Don Rudolph as the Twins won 3-2. (Mincher, a left-handed batter, had no problem that day off the lefty Rudolph. However, throughout his career he always fared better against right-handers, and was often out of the starting lineup against left-handed starters.) Four days later, on July 24 at Cleveland Stadium, Mincher again hit two home runs, off Pedro Ramos and Jerry Walker.

Mincher made Ridzik a particular target. On August 26, 1963, he homered off the right-hander again, at D.C. Stadium, and on August 18, 1964, homered twice in consecutive at-bats off Ridzik, again in Washington.

Mincher settled in as the Twins' first baseman. He told an interviewer in 2010 that his biggest thrill in baseball came in the first game of the 1965 World Series when he hit a home run of the Los Angeles Dodgers' Don Drysdale. "To bat against Koufax and Drysdale when it really meant something," Mincher said. "I didn't realize what a big thrill it was until I got older and started thinking back on these things."[7] His wife, Patsy, knew Mincher was slightly nervous as he was extremely quiet as she drove him to the ballpark. Usually he was talkative.[8] In the bottom of the second inning, in his first Series at-bat, Mincher homered to deep right field off Drysdale. Mincher spoke of the feat often, his wife said.[9] In Game Two, Mincher tied a World Series record with four assists at first base. (Three of the assists were on groundballs by lefty Willie Davis.)

On June 9, 1966, Mincher was part of baseball history again when he was one of five Twins who hit home runs in one inning, an American League record. The Kansas City Athletics were the victims; the others besides Mincher to go deep in the seventh inning that day were Rich Rollins, Tony Oliva, Zolio Versalles, and Harmon Killebrew.[10]

After the 1966 season Mincher was traded by the Twins with pitcher Peter Cimino and outfielder Jimmie Hall to the California Angels for infielder Jackie Hernandez and pitcher Dean Chance. With the Angels Mincher had his best major league season in 1967. He hit 25 home runs and was selected to the All-Star team for the first time.

On April 11, 1968, in the second game of the season, Mincher was hit on the cheek by a fastball thrown by the Cleveland Indians' Sam McDowell. The blow was a glancing one and Mincher missed only nine games, but he was plagued by headaches and dizziness and struggled at the plate for the rest of the season.[11] On September 4, after he reeled backward while swinging at a pitch, he was removed from the game. X-rays and tests were inconclusive, but Mincher was given the rest of the season off.[12] Mincher's average for 1968 was .236, down from .273 in 1967; his home run and RBI production suffered likewise.

Though Mincher was cleared after tests at the Mayo Clinic, Angels manager Bill Rigney considered him damaged goods after his struggles during the season, and did not feel that the reports provided positive assurance as to Mincher's full recovery.[13] The Angels left Mincher unprotected in the expansion draft after the season and Mincher was selected as the Seattle Pilots number-one pick. He played in 140 games for the Pilots hit 25 home runs, and was named to the American League All-Star squad. Mincher was the Pilots player representative.[14]

On January 15, 1970, as the Pilots were becoming the Milwaukee Brewers, Mincher was traded to the Athletics with infielder Ron Clark for outfielder Mike Hershberger, pitchers Lew Krausse and Ken Sanders, and catcher Phil Roof. With Oakland he hit 27 home runs, his career high. His walk-off home run on August 2 off Horacio Pina of Washington with two outs in the ninth inning of a scoreless game in Oakland was one of 27 he hit that season – a career high.

The following season, on May 8, 1971, Mincher was traded by the Athletics along with catcher-outfielder Frank Fernandez, pitcher Paul Lindblad, and cash to the Washington Senators for first baseman Mike Epstein and pitcher Darold Knowles. On July 17 at RFK Stadium in Washington, Mincher, not in the lineup that day against the Twins, was in the outfield bullpen when in the fourth inning home-plate umpire Hank Soar motioned him to move away from the bullpen fence in center field, where he could pick up Minnesota's signs. Mincher's gesture in response 410 feet away was not to Soar's liking. In what could be a distance record for an ejection in baseball, Soar ejected Mincher without hesitation.[15] Patsy Mincher said that her husband was only motioning back to mean, "What do you want?," but it was taken differently by Soar.[16]

After the 1971 season the Senators moved to Texas to become the Rangers. On July 20, 1972, Mincher was traded back to Oakland with infielder Ted Kubiak for utilityman Vic Harris, infielder Marty Martinez, and pitcher Steve Lawson. Mincher was not too happy. "I'm not ready to sit on the bench," he said, noting that Athletics first baseman Mike Epstein was hitting well.[17] "I've been around a long time and I've learned to expect almost anything, but this trade knocked me off my feet," Mincher said.[18] But Epstein went out with an eye infection, and Mincher was placed at first base and in the cleanup spot. He got off to a poor start, going 2-for-22 with no home runs or RBIs. When Epstein returned, Mincher was relegated to pinch-hitting for the balance of the season.[19] He did contribute in the World Series; his pinch-single in Game Four drove in the tying run in the ninth inning against Cincinnati. The next batter, pinch-hitter Angel Mangual, singled home the game-winning run.

With little hope for his role to change in 1973, Mincher decided to retire. "I just have no desire to play the role I did last year," he said. "I don't care to be that kind of player. I enjoyed being on a world championships club, but I didn't want to sit on the bench watching my more mature years slip by."[20] (Patsy Mincher said in 2013 that Don's shoulder at this time hurt so much that he could hardly comb his hair without being in pain.[21]

During Mincher's two stints with the Athletics he played in 210 games, hit 29 home runs (27 of them in 1970 that led the club), knocked in 87 runs and batted .236. Described by one sportswriter as "intense and introverted,"[22] Mincher may have been his own worst enemy. He admitted in 1968 to putting too much pressure on himself both when he was doing well (worrying about keeping it going) and when he was not (staying in the slump). He applauded his supportive wife, Patsy, for spending long nights listening to him spilling his guts out.[23]

After 13 seasons Mincher's retirement allowed him to spend more time with his wife and three children at home in Huntsville. It also provided Mincher with time to pursue his hobbies, which included fishing and hunting.

Mincher ran a sporting-goods store, specializing in trophies and awards for about ten years before returning to baseball in 1985 as the general manager of the Huntsville Stars of the Southern League.[24] The Stars were an Athletics affiliate from 1985 to 1998. When there was a chance in 1994 that the franchise might be moved out of the city, Mincher put together a group of investors to buy the team from owner Larry Schmittou. After the 1998 season the Stars and Athletics parted ways and the Milwaukee Brewers became the Stars affiliate. During Mincher's time with the Stars they won two Southern League championships. During all these years Patsy worked with him at the ballpark. In October 2000 Mincher was elected interim president of the Southern League when Arnold Fielkow left for the NFL. His interim position was made permanent before the start of the 2001 season. Later Mincher and his group sold the Stars to a New York attorney. During his time with the Stars, Mincher was twice elected Executive of the Year and in 2008 was inducted into the Alabama Sports Hall of Fame.

Mincher had a deep interest in the development side of baseball. He made it the mission of the Southern League to promote minor-league baseball as wholesome family fun and entertainment at a reasonable cost.[25]

In October 2011 Mincher stepped down as president of the Southern League. In January 2012 he felt pain in both arms that proved to be symptoms of serious heart problems. He underwent surgery to take care of blockages. Then pneumonia kicked in. He died on March 4, 2012.[26] He is buried in Maple Hill Cemetery, Huntsville, Alabama.

Mincher was preceded in death by his parents, George and Lillian. He was survived by his wife, Patsy; and three children, Mark (head baseball coach for almost 30 years at Huntsville High before becoming principal), Lori Lumpkin, and Mincherna Hopper; and many grandchildren and great-grandchildren. At the 2012 Winter Meetings Patsy was honored as "The First Lady of Southern League Baseball." Not only had she worked at the ballpark during Mincher's tenure with the Huntsville Stars but she also handled the logistics and much of the child-rearing during Mincher's major-league career.[27]

Notes

1. 1974 player file fact sheet contained in Mincher's Hall of Fame Library Player file. (Hereafter cited as HOF file).
2. John Branch, "A Twin, a Ranger and, Most of All, a Senator," *New York Times*, October 6, 2010.
3. Telephone interview with Pat Mincher on December 10, 2013. (Hereafter cited as Pat Mincher interview.)
4. Maury Allen, "Mincher Enjoys HR and Series Chance," *New York Post*, October 7, 1965.
5. Pat Mincher interview.
6. 1974 player file fact sheet.
7. John Branch, "A Twin, a Ranger and, Most of All, a Senator."
8. Pat Mincher interview.
9. Pat Mincher interview; Oakland Athletics Press Release; HOF file.
10. Max Nichols, "Mele's Maulers Tie Mark, Clout Five HRs in Innin,g" *The Sporting News*, June 25, 1966.
11. John Branch, "A Twin, a Ranger and, Most of All, a Senator"; Hy Zimmerman, "Pilots Looking Toward Mincher to Get Em over The Sporting News, Choppy Seas," *The Sporting News*, February 1, 1969; Hy Zimmerman, "Mincher Fired Up to Clip Angel Wings," April 19, 1969.
12. "Mincher Goes to Hospital, Suffers from Dizzy Spells," *The Sporting News*, September 21, 1968; John Wiebusch, "Mincher Dismayed, Excited on Leaving Angels for Pilots," *The Sporting News*, November 2, 1968.
13. John Wiebusch, "Mincher Dismayed."
14. Hy Zimmerman, "Krausse Wants to be Starter … Pilots Will Give him a Chance," *The Sporting News*, January 31, 1970.
15. "Soar's Vision Sharp," *The Sporting News*, August 7, 1971.
16. Pat Mincher interview.
17. Randy Galloway, "Critics Fault Ranger 'Suicide' Youth Drive," *The Sporting News*, August 5, 1972.
18. Ibid
19. Ron Bergman, "Mincher Weary of Bench Duty, Retires as 200-Homer Belter," *The Sporting News*, January 13, 1973.
20. Ron Bergman, "Mincher Weary of Bench Duty."
21. Pat Mincher interview.
22. Ross Newhan, "Mincher Sings Happy Tune With Long Bow to Rigney," *The Sporting News*, March 30, 1968.
23. Ibid.
24. John Branch, "A Twin, a Ranger and, Most of All, a Senator"; Pat Mincher interview.
25. Southern League website.
26. Mark McCarter, April 13, 2011: al.com/sports/index.sst/2011/04/opening_night_remains_special.html.
27. Mark McCarter, December 5, 2012: al.com/sports/index.ssf/2012/as/pat_mincher_proclaimed_first_l.html

DAVE NELSON

BY RICK SCHABOWSKI

David Earl Nelson was born on June 20, 1944, in Fort Sill, Oklahoma. He loved sports and played in the Little League, the Babe Ruth League and Connie Mack ball. Basketball was also a favorite sport. Nelson's idols growing up were Oscar Robertson and Jackie Robinson. Nelson graduated from Junipero Serra High in Gardena, California, in 1963. He had an outstanding athletic career, playing baseball, basketball, and football, and running track. Nelson was on the baseball and track teams at the same time. One day he had a baseball game followed by a track meet in which he competed in the 100-yard dash. He wasn't too fatigued after the baseball game, winning his event with a time of 9.6 seconds.

Commenting about his football skills, Nelson remarked, "A lot of people don't know about my football career. I have kept it a secret. I played a lot of football in high school and had a lot of success with it. I had more success with it than I did baseball. I had all kinds of football scholarship offers. I had scholarships from Notre Dame, Brown University, Oregon State, and a number of other schools, but I wanted to stay close to home."[1]

Nelson attended Compton (California) Junior College for one year. His parents were going through a divorce, and he wanted to stay close to his mother. He played football and was selected as a back on the 1963 Junior College All-American football team. From Compton Nelson accepted a baseball scholarship to Los Angeles State College (now Cal State LA). After his two years in college, Nelson decided that he wanted to pursue a professional baseball career. At a tryout he caught the eye of Cleveland Indians scout Bob Mattick and signed a contract. Assigned to the Dubuque Packers of the Class A Midwest League in 1964, Nelson batted .253, was second in stolen bases with 53, and was the league's All-Star second baseman. In 1965 Nelson played for the Salinas Indians and led the Class A California League in stolen bases with 41. He was promoted to the Pawtucket Indians of the Double-A Eastern League, again led his league in stolen bases (57) and earned a spot on the league all-star team. Promoted to the Triple-A Portland Beavers in 1965, Nelson led his league in stolen bases (29) for the third time in a row, and in a poll of managers was voted the league's fastest baserunner.

The Indians' new manager Alvin Dark liked Nelson because of his speed, and a great spring training, in which he was voted the most outstanding player by writers and broadcasters covering the team, resulted in Nelson making the move to the major leagues for the 1968 season. On April 11, 1968, he made his major-league debut when he ran for catcher Duke Sims in the eighth inning. In his first major-league start, on April 20 at Fenway Park in Boston, playing second base and leading off, Nelson made his presence known. He walked to open the game and promptly stole second base. In the third inning he had his first hit, a single off Jerry Stephenson. An injury to starting second baseman Vern Fuller gave Nelson more playing time. He finished the season batting .233 in 189 at-bats and stealing 23 bases, and was chosen to the Topps Major League Rookie All-Star Team at second base.

A confident Nelson arrived for spring training in 1969. "I'm just trying to win a job," he said. "Last season, even though I was in the big leagues, I didn't know myself if I belonged here or not. Now I feel like I fit into the picture. Now I feel so confident I could play any place except catcher or pitcher – and it's a great feeling."[2] A torn hamstring muscle, suffered in the next to last spring training game, bothered Nelson all season, and he batted .203 in 123 at-bats, stealing four bases. After the season, the Indians traded Nelson, Horacio Pina, and Ron Law to the Washington Senators for Dennis Higgins and Barry Moore.

Senators manager Ted Williams remembered Nelson from an at-bat against his team the previous summer. Nelson pulled a Casey Cox slider for a hit, prompting Williams to say, "Anybody who can handle a pitch like that can play for me."[3] There was a lot of competition for the starter's job at second base, but Nelson hit around .400 in spring training and won the job. Williams said of Nelson, "He has done everything expected of him and more. He is a most pleasant development."[4] But Nelson had a tough season, batting .159 in 107 at-bats, and in May was sent to Triple-A Denver, where he batted .369 in 236 at-bats. Nelson bore no animosity toward Williams, saying, "Whenever I got a chance, I always sat near him on the bench and listened. I really learned a lot that way. He teaches you a lot about confidence, attacking the ball and picking on your pitch. I told him I'd work hard and come back a better ballplayer."[5]

Going into the 1971 season, Nelson was confident about winning back the second-base job, but after a few exhibition games he was shipped to Denver. "That was the biggest disappointment of my career," he said. "Ted kept saying he had to have a long look at Richie Scheinblum because he had the best credentials on the club with his .337 batting average. I kept hearing that and reading that. I batted .369!"[6] At Denver Nelson batted .307 and was recalled on June 15. He started at third base the next night. Three days later, on June 18, Nelson hit his first major-league home run off Boston's Sonny Siebert at Washington's RFK Stadium. He went on a tear and a month later on July 15, he was batting .327 with three home runs, after having 419 times at bat over 2½ seasons without one. He finished the season batting .280 with 5 home runs and 17 stolen bases.

The transition to third base wasn't easy for Nelson, but he worked hard. "It didn't come naturally to me as it does to some people," he said. "I had to work at it. I still have to. I don't feel that I'm overconfident or lazy, but I can't take my mind off what I'm doing. There's no such thing as a reflex play for me with the glove."[7]

In 1972 the Senators moved from Washington to the Dallas-Fort Worth, Texas, area, becoming the Texas Rangers, and Nelson made sure they got off to a running start by stealing seven bases in eight attempts in the first 13 games of the season. Rangers TV broadcaster Don Drysdale observed, "Nelson studies the pitchers, and for the first two or three steps he has tremendous explosion. That's what Maury (Wills) had in his prime. He didn't have blazing speed, but he could get into high gear quickly."[8]

Manager Ted Williams respected Nelson's ability on the basepaths, commenting, "This year I gave him his head on the bases. He has the go-ahead anytime he feels he's ready. He's not a glory hog and he won't go unless he thinks it will help us. I'm not surprised he's off to a good start hitting and stealing bases. That's the way he ended up last year."[9] Speed is an obvious factor for basestealing, but there are some intangibles also. Nelson elaborated, "You got to know your pace and the catchers and pitchers. You get the feel of it. You can figure your odds pretty well before you take off."[10]

Nelson's batting average hovered in the .280 range for the first two months of the season, then fell off, dropping to .235 by the All-Star break. He finished the season with a .226 batting average and 51 stolen bases, one behind league leader Bert Campaneris.

After the season Nelson moved from Los Angeles to Texas and helped the Rangers with promotions.

He also would be playing for a new manager, Whitey Herzog, and returning to second base in 1973. Herzog wanted to try Joe Lovitto at third base, with Nelson going back to his old position. The move wasn't easy for Nelson, who said, "When I first moved back this spring, nothing felt right. I was butchering plays I should have made easily. It was tough, but everything feels natural again. I like it."[11] Rangers third-base coach Chuck Hiller was amazed at Nelson's transition, saying, "I never saw a guy so handcuffed find himself so fast."[12]

The 1973 season proved to be the best of Nelson's career. He batted .286 with 43 stolen bases, and was selected to play in the All-Star game in Kansas City, an honor that Nelson called his greatest baseball thrill. Among the highlights of the season were homering twice off the White Sox' Eddie Fisher on April 17, becoming the first Rangers player to hit two homers in a game, and being selected in a vote by the media covering the Rangers as their Most Valuable Player. At least two clubs approached the Rangers seeking to acquire Nelson, but the Rangers weren't interested.

Billy Martin managed the Rangers in 1974. On April 14 he drove in six runs against the Athletics with a three-run homer, a single, and a sacrifice. But injuries were a big part of his season. In a game against the Chicago White Sox on May 10, Nelson and Lenny Randle collided on a short fly ball off the bat of Ron Santo. Nelson was knocked unconscious and carried off the field with a broken nose, sprained ankle, and a whiplash injury. He was in the hospital for five days. (Randle suffered a severe shoulder sprain.) Nelson didn't return to the playing field until June 12. On July 21 he injured a knee against the Red Sox when Rick Miller slid into him trying to break up a double play.

Things were back to normal on August 30 when Nelson stole second, third, and home in the same inning. Nelson was happy, "It was very satisfying. It proved that, at long last, I can move again," he said.[13] He stole 25 bases during the season but batted only .236.

Nelson pulled an unusual hidden ball trick against the Brewers' Bob Coluccio on June 14. Teammate Tom Grieve recalled it a few years later: "Dave was playing second base, he takes the throw and Coluccio is safe. So Dave tells him, 'Step off the bag for a second, I want to kick the dirt off it.' So Coluccio steps off the bag and Dave tags him out, pulls the hidden ball trick on him."[14] Remembering the play Nelson said, "At first he just laughed about it. Then he went into the dugout and his manger, Del Crandall, just chews him out. So the next inning, he comes running out of the dugout and mad and he says, 'You embarrassed me and you embarrassed my team.' I said, 'I didn't embarrass your team, you did.' He said, 'I'm going to get you back. You watch out, one day you're going to be playing second base and I'm going to get you.' I said, Why wait, let's get it on right now!"[15]

After his injury-plagued 1974 season, the Rangers wanted Nelson to prove without a doubt that he was the starter at second base. Nelson responded with one of the best spring trainings of his career in 1975, both at bat and in the field, and kept his starting position.

Nelson got off to a great start, stealing six bases in the first 11 games, but on April 19 he reinjured his ankle sliding into second base in a game against the Royals. After conferring with Martin, Nelson decided to have another surgery.

Dr. Harvey O'Phelan, the Minnesota Twins physician and a close friend of Martin's performed the surgery on April 29. Nelson remained on crutches until May 19, and was in a walking cast until early June. After therapy and a conditioning program, it was hoped Nelson would be as good as new. On August 15 he returned to the active roster, but started only 10 games the rest of the season, batting only 39 times. He finished the season with a .213 batting average. Reflecting on the 1975 season Nelson said, "Last season was a lost one for me. When I finally was ready to play, I didn't get to. I started so well in '74, but the injury messed me up."[16]

After the season Nelson was traded to the Kansas City Royals for pitcher Nelson Briles. "Dave is going to be a great addition to our club," said manager Whitey Herzog, who had been his skipper in Texas. "He goes all out all of the time. Not only will he give us more maneuverability, but he can hit and steal bases. I won't be afraid to use him leading off as the designated hitter."[17]

Nelson was elated to be reunited with Herzog, reflecting after his career, "Whitey Herzog was without a doubt the best manager I ever played for. He did all phases of the game well. As a manager he was a great communicator. He was able to let everybody know what their roles were, and they played hard for him."[18]

Before 1976 spring training, Nelson met with Royals general manager Joe Burke and, according to Burke, said he wouldn't complain if he wasn't a regular. "… I'm confident he can help us," Burke said.[19] An injured leg muscle put Nelson on the disabled list early in the season. While he was on the DL, he joined the Royals' TV crew as a color man.

Back in action, he had a big game on June 15 in a 21-7 victory over the Tigers at Tiger Stadium. He went 3-for-4 and drove in four runs. He finished the season with a .235 average and 15 stolen bases.

The Royals were playoff-bound. Nelson recalled, "It was exciting. I felt we had one of the best teams in baseball that year. We struggled at the end to win the Western Division. We ended up playing the Yankees in the playoffs, and it was one of the most exciting playoff series I have ever been involved in."[20] The Royals lost to the Yankees when Chris Chambliss hit a walk-off homer in Game Five.

Injuries again limited Nelson's playing time in 1977, limiting him to 55 plate appearances in 27 games. He suffered a pulled leg muscle early in the season, and a pulled groin muscle in midseason. On September 27 he doubled off Oakland's Matt Keough in what turned out to be his last major-league at-bat. After winning the AL West again, the Royals faced the Yankees in the 1977 ALCS. Because of injuries, Nelson was not on the playoff roster.

After the season, the Royals offered Nelson a job managing their rookie-league team in Fort Myers, Florida, but he wanted to try to play one more season with the Royals. The Royals gave Nelson his release on April 1, 1978. Nelson turned down an offer to play in Japan, and sought a nonbaseball career. Through friends in Washington he landed a job with the Department of Housing and Urban Development helping redevelop low-income homes. The job was interesting and fun, but not what he wanted to do for the rest of his life. Nelson joined the Royals TV booth for the 1979 season, then after the season he took a job as an assistant coach for Texas Christian University near his offseason home in Fort Worth. He liked coaching, but he yearned to return to the majors in that capacity.

Good fortune came Nelson's way. A baseball's winter meetings in Dallas, former teammate Tom Grieve asked Nelson if he could fill in for Dick Howser who was scheduled to do a speech on infield play. Nelson did such a great job talking about not infield play, baserunning, and stealing, that he got a number of job offers to coach. Nelson signed with the White Sox as a minor league infield and baserunning instructor. Chicago manager Tony La Russa was so impressed with Nelson's work during spring training that he used him with the White Sox from 1981 to 1984.

In 1985 Nelson left to work as minor-league coordinator for the Oakland Athletics for two years. He returned to the broadcast booth with the Chicago Cubs for two years, in 1988-1989. He missed the playing field and served as the Montreal Expos minor-league baserunning instructor for two seasons.

In 1992 Nelson returned to the majors as a coach for the Cleveland Indians, a position he held through the 1997 season. Longtime Indians announcer Herb Score retired, so the Indians moved Nelson to the broadcast booth, working with Mike Hegan and Tom Hamilton. Nelson missed the playing field. "Working with the players, being in uniform, down on the field – that's my first love," he said. "Working with Tom and Mike was tremendous fun, as was being involved in the media side of baseball. But my heart is on the field."[21]

Nelson spent the 2001 and 2002 seasons as an outfield instructor in the minors for the Milwaukee Brewers before working as the Brewers' first-base coach from 2003 to 2006. He returned to the broadcast booth in 2007, serving as an analyst for Brewers games for Fox Sports, a position he still held in 2016.

Outside of the broadcast booth, Nelson stayed busy as the director of Brewers alumni relations, and joined the board of directors of Open Arms Home for Children, which provides homes to orphaned children affected by the AIDS pandemic in South Africa.

Dave Nelson passed away on April 23, 2018 after a battle with liver cancer. He was 73 years old.

Brewers chief operating officer Rick Schlesinger summed up Nelson's life: "Davey took every opportunity to turn a casual introduction into a lifelong relationship, and his legacy will live on in the positive impact he had on the lives of so many people. Davey's love of life and commitment to helping those in need were second to none, and we are so grateful for the time that we had with him."[22]

Notes

1. Chuck Greenwood, "Licensed to Steal: Nelson Stole Three Bases in One Inning." *Sports Collectors Digest*, October 28, 1994.
2. Russell Schneider, "Nelson Puts Headlock on Second Sack," *The Sporting News*, April 5, 1969: 10.
3. Merrell Whittlesey, "Nelson Gives Nats a Solid Midway Lift," *The Sporting News*, April 11, 1970: 37.
4. Ibid.
5. Frank Haraway, "Nelson's Big Bat, Glove Brought on the Spurt of the Grizzlies," *The Sporting News*, September 5, 1970: 33.
6. Merrell Whittlesey, "Nats Rejoice Over Nelson Bat Revival," *The Sporting News*, July 7, 1971: 11.
7. Merle Heryford, "Nelson's Flying Feet, Hot Bat Win Plaudits of Ranger Fans," *The Sporting News*, June 10, 1972: 33.
8. Major Flashes: "Nelson a New Wills?" *The Sporting News*, July 8, 1972: 30.
9. "Nelson's Flying Feet."
10. Ibid.
11. Merle Heryford, "Nelson's Quick Shift Ends Ranger Keystone Problem," *The Sporting News*, April 21, 1973: 22.
12. Ibid.
13. Merle Heryford, "Triple Theft Signals Return," *The Sporting News*, September 21, 1974: 19.
14. T.R. Sullivan. "Ex-Ranger Nelson Embodies Spirit of Robinson," "Texas Rangers.com," April 13, 2012.
15. Ibid.
16. Joe McGuff, "Royals Pad Their Keystone With 'Full' Nelson," *The Sporting News*, November 29, 1975: 53
17. Ibid.
18. Greenwood.
19. Joe McGuff, "K.C. Cools Toward Cleon, But Warms to Nelson," *The Sporting News*, February 11, 1976: 39.
20. Greenwood.
21. "Tribe's pitching Coach Regan Resigns; Nelson Quits," *Cleveland Plain Dealer*, October 14, 1999: 6D.
22. Tom Haudricourt, "Brewers' TV analyst Nelson dies at 73," *Milwaukee Journal Sentinel*, April 24, 2018: 3B.

JIM PANTHER

BY CHAD MOODY

Although pitcher Jim Panther never appeared on a Topps baseball card, he nonetheless was able to stake a claim in baseball history as one of the original members of the Texas Rangers. After his relatively brief big-league career came to an unceremonious end, a new career in baseball began for Panther as a decorated high-school coach. "Yep, you can take Jim Panther out of baseball, but you can never take baseball out of Jim Panther," sportswriter Patricia Babcock McGraw wrote – a fitting way to describe a man who has dedicated his life to the game.[1]

James Edward Panther was born of German descent on March 1, 1945, in Burlington, Iowa, but grew up in the Chicago suburb of Highland Park, Illinois, where his parents had settled. His mother, Mary, worked as a buyer at a department store, and his father, Mark, worked in the education field – eventually climbing the ranks from teaching and coaching to an administrative position at Highland Park High School.[2] Panther's brother, Mark Jr., rounded out the family in the Catholic household. Athletic genes ran in the family, as Panther's father was a one-time Big Ten Conference record holder in javelin for the University of Iowa (where he also played football), and an aspiring 1936 US Olympian until his hopes were dashed by an arm injury.[3] Jim Panther was an accomplished amateur athlete in his own right at Highland Park High School, garnering an All-State Honorable Mention as a running back and quarterback in football, and being labeled a "tremendously clever ball handler" as a member of the varsity basketball squad.[4] He was also selected as All-Conference in baseball, the recognition no doubt aided by what Panther deemed as one of his "biggest baseball memories": a perfect game he pitched against Libertyville High School in 1963 – the very school for which Panther later became head baseball coach.[5]

Panther had planned to accept an offer to play both baseball and football at the University of Miami (Florida) after graduating from high school in 1963. A broken leg suffered in his senior year while sliding into a base at the end of the baseball season derailed those plans, however. Although Miami offered him a spot on the roster for the following season once he had recovered, Panther decided to stay closer to home and enroll at Southern Illinois rather than deferring college for a year. In opting to become a college student, Panther felt it provided protection from being drafted into the military during those tumultuous political times.[6] Despite passing on the opportunity at Miami, he did find his way onto the baseball squad at SIU, and made a positive impact for the squad's starting pitching staff. At one point during his junior season in 1966, the right-handed hurler boasted an impressive 19-inning scoreless streak as one of coach Joe Lutz's "top four pitchers."[7] And at season's end, Panther's outstanding 0.94 ERA in 57⅓ innings was the second best all time for the Salukis (and remains fifth best on the all-time list through their 2016 campaign).[8]

Panther's fine performance at SIU during his junior year piqued the interest of the St. Louis Cardinals, who drafted him in the 26th round of the June 1966 Amateur Draft. He did not sign, however, opting to remain in school. "First of all, I didn't like the Cardinals. And second of all, they were loaded with too many other good pitchers," Panther later explained.[9] Only a little more than seven months later, another big-league club came calling. On January 28, 1967, the Kansas City Athletics drafted him in the fifth round of the Amateur Draft (Secondary Phase) at the behest of scouting director Joe Bowman.[10] This time, Panther decided to sign. "I signed with (Kansas City) and looking back, I probably should have just signed with the Cardinals," he reflected. "The A's were even more loaded than the Cardinals. But I went anyway."[11] Although Panther therefore had to forgo his final year of college baseball eligibility, the Sigma Pi fraternity member still prioritized his education.[12] He continued to take classes at SIU during the offseasons while playing professional baseball, and ultimately attained a master's degree in 1969.[13]

Panther had a hectic first season in professional ball in 1967, spending time with three of Kansas City's minor-league affiliates: the rookie-league GCL Athletics of the Gulf Coast League, the Leesburg A's of the Class-A Florida State League, and the Peninsula Grays of the Class-A Carolina League. The 6-foot-1, 190-pound "side-arm fastballer" had consistent success at each stop, not posting an ERA higher than 2.84 for any team.[14] Between the three teams, Panther finished the year with a 3-2 record, a 2.09 ERA, and a 1.02 WHIP. He allowed only 25 hits while striking out 45 in his 43 innings of work over 16 appearances. Although he started only two games, one was a complete-game four-hit victory for Peninsula in late August – in which he featured an "excellently-controlled sinking curve" – to put the cap on his promising initial minor-league campaign.[15] Panther initially had reservations about pitching primarily out of the bullpen, but grew to like it. "I really enjoyed pitching in relief last year," he said after the season. "I was afraid I wouldn't get enough work in relief, but it's so different from college ball as you get called upon much more often."[16]

Back with Peninsula for the entire 1968 season (by then an affiliate of the Oakland Athletics, who had relocated from Kansas City), Panther pitched mostly in relief again due to a logjam of capable starters on the Grays' staff.[17] Although his 8-4 record in 38 appearances (3 starts) at season's end appeared impressive, examination of Panther's subpar ERA and WHIP – 4.61 and 1.52, respectively – indicated that he had suffered a sophomore slump of sorts. Notwithstanding this step back, Oakland promoted Panther to the Birmingham A's of the Double-A Southern League. He spent the entire 1969 campaign there, during which time teammate Pete Koegel tagged Panther with the nickname "Pink." Despite facing more formidable competition, the 24-year-old saw improvement as he settled into his now-familiar bullpen role. In 21 appearances, he finished the year with a 5-5 record, collected six saves, and dropped his ERA to 3.65 – nearly a full point lower than in his disappointing sophomore stint.

In addition to his time on the mound at Birmingham, 1969 was also a busy and important year personally for Panther. As he worked to complete his master's degree at SIU, he coached the Salukis' freshman baseball squad while he was a graduate assistant.[18] And in the fall, Panther began what became a long career as an educator at Libertyville (Illinois) High School. The school's administration was able to accommodate the scheduling conflicts that naturally arose with having an aspiring big-leaguer on its teaching staff. "I've had the best situation here at Libertyville and when I leave, I'm just going to have to tip my hat to everyone," Panther later reflected on his unique employment situation.[19]

After his bounce-back year at Birmingham, Panther found himself promoted to the Triple-A level for the 1970 season. Once his teaching obligations had been met for the school year, he reported in June to the Iowa Oaks of the American Association.[20] Panther acquitted himself nicely at the highest level of minor-league baseball. He became a mainstay in the Iowa bullpen, along the way posting an impressive late-season streak of 26 scoreless innings while the Oaks were in division pennant contention.²¹ In 35 appearances, Panther finished the year with a 1-1 record, a 2.64 ERA, and six saves.

Panther's fine season at Iowa was rewarded with his addition to Oakland's 40-man roster for the beginning of the 1971 season. Granted a leave of absence by his school so he could attend spring training with the big-league club in Mesa, Arizona, the side-armer performed reasonably well there.²² And with new Oakland manager Dick Williams dissatisfied with the performance of his relievers during the spring games, the bespectacled Panther found himself in a battle with his old teammate from Iowa, LaDon Boyd, for the final spot on the Athletics' pitching staff.²³ Ultimately, the future Hall of Fame manager decided to retain the services of Panther. "We decided that Panther would be a little better in relief because of his good sinker pitch," Williams explained.²⁴ Panther did not have to wait long to see his first big-league action. In Oakland's first game of the season, on April 5 in Washington against the Senators, he was inserted into the game in the second inning to replace struggling starter Vida Blue. Inheriting a bases-loaded situation, Panther promptly uncorked a wild pitch that allowed a run. He got the next batter to fly out to end both the inning and his major-league debut. Making his second appearance for the Athletics only two days later in relief of starter Rollie Fingers, Panther allowed a disastrous six earned runs (including four from a grand slam) in only 1⅔ innings of work in being tagged with the loss to the Chicago White Sox. After two additional unremarkable appearances, Panther was sent back to Iowa in mid-April, with his roster spot taken by pitcher Marcel Lachemann. Manager Williams reportedly wanted to give Panther "regular pitching assignments," while believing the veteran Lachemann would be more effective in spot relief for the club.²⁵ Panther's disappointing final statistics in his first stint in the big leagues included an 0-1 record and 11.12 ERA in 5⅔ innings pitched.

Resuming his 1971 campaign in Iowa, Panther initially returned to his comfortable bullpen role. But as the Oaks hit a bit of losing skid against division rival Indianapolis, Panther was given a rare start in late-May. "Panther deserves a start," team owner Ray Johnston succinctly explained.²⁶ Making the most of his first start since 1968, Panther provided "tight pitching" in picking up a complete-game victory over Evansville, and with subsequent solid starts earned his way into the starting rotation. "I've put Jim in our starting rotation because anybody with an arm as strong as his deserves a chance to use it in a lot of innings," manager Sherm Lollar said. "Besides, he might earn himself a call from the Oakland club."²⁷ Although that call never came, Panther was given the honor of a selection to the American Association All-Star team in July.²⁸ Panther finished the year with a 10-10 record and a 3.63 ERA in 30 games (21 starts) for the Oaks. He completed six of the starts, including one shutout.

Back on Oakland's 40-man roster for the 1972 season, the "subdued and almost introverted" Panther was a holdout during spring training because of "money problems with [Oakland team owner] Charlie Finley."²⁹ At the same time, the Athletics were dealing with a thin starting pitching staff due to the lingering holdout of Vida Blue and an injured Chuck Dobson.³⁰ Hoping to strengthen its starting staff, on March 4 Oakland decided to acquire controversial one-time 31-game winner Denny McLain from the new Texas Rangers franchise – formed when the Washington Senators relocated to Arlington for the 1972 season. In exchange, Texas received Panther and fellow minor-league pitcher Don Stanhouse. "We made the trade for youth," Rangers owner Bob Short said.³¹ While Stanhouse was viewed by many as the "big man" for Texas in the deal, Oakland scout George Bradley felt Panther was being unfairly overlooked. "Panther is a smart pitcher who just might make the jump," Bradley opined.³² Owner Short also expressed confidence in his new side-armer, stating that he believed Panther "could win for us this year."³³ Panther himself was pleased about the opportunity to join the Rangers. "I felt the trade was good for me because of the fact that I'd get a better chance to pitch over here. Actually, getting traded was a big break for me," he said.³⁴ Expert analysis of the deal generally indicated that Panther would likely be vying for a spot in the Rangers' bullpen – despite his success as a starter in Iowa during the previous season. Panther was open to any role presented to him, although concerned about having missed a significant portion of spring training because of his contract dispute in Oakland. "Here [Texas], anything they want me to do is all right. But I know I'm off to a late start and I'm worried about catching up with the rest," he confessed.³⁵

Panther did indeed catch up, opening the season on the big-league roster. "I had my doubts about (Panther), although coming out of spring training I thought he could help us," said Rangers pitching coach Sid Hudson.³⁶ Panther made an immediate impact, picking up his first major-league win in relief against Nolan Ryan and the California Angels in only his second appearance of the year. After the game, Panther believed teammate Horacio Piña was awarded the victory. "You mean they gave me the win, not Pina? Well I'll be darn. Gee, that makes me happy, but I would've never expected it," Panther said upon learning he was in fact the winner.³⁷ Feel-good victory aside, Panther struggled during the first month of the season, posting a 9.45 ERA through mid-May. He settled down from that point, however, not allowing an earned run in 13 of his next 14 games. Panther's improvement was attributed in part to his work with Hudson on creating a variety of release points in addition to his usual side-arm delivery. "Really, I didn't think I was throwing that bad at the first of the season, but I can see a definite improvement now," Panther said. "Confidence, of course, is a big thing, and I've got a lot more of that now, particularly since I'm getting to pitch pretty regularly. But also I'm pitching smarter now, I think."³⁸ His pitching coach echoed his sentiments. "Jim was real nervous those first couple of times, you could tell that. But he kept working at it, kept plugging away and now he looks like a different pitcher out there. He's got a lot of poise and confidence. He's challenging people," coach Hudson said.³⁹ Panther became a mainstay in the Texas bullpen for the rest of the season, and finished the season strong, not allowing an earned run in 12 of his final 13 appearances. By season's end he had compiled a 5-9 record with a 4.13 ERA over 93⅔ innings pitched in 58 games.

Finishing its inaugural season in 1972 with a dreadful 54-100 record, Texas sought to add some punch to its listless lineup in the offseason in hopes of improving on their major league-worst .217 team batting average.⁴⁰ To do so, on October 27 the Rangers dealt Panther to the Atlanta Braves for former batting champion Rico Carty. Although he did not know he would be dealt, Panther was not completely blindsided by the transaction. "It's no secret the Braves want more pitching and the Rangers need more hitting, so the trade wasn't surprising," he said.⁴¹ Braves director of player personnel Eddie Robinson confirmed Panther's view, admitting Atlanta was "doing this in hopes of bolstering our pitching staff."⁴² Robinson had a favorable opinion of the 27-year-old hurler, adding that he believed Panther possessed "a lot of potential."⁴³ New Texas skipper Whitey Herzog had a differing view of Panther's prospects had he stayed with the Rangers, however. "Panther didn't figure to make our club," the future Hall of Fame manager said.⁴⁴

Despite having a "good spring training" to prepare for the 1973 season, Panther did not make the Atlanta ballclub, either.⁴⁵ Instead, the "disappointed" pitcher was assigned to the Richmond Braves of the Triple-A International League to open the year, where he resumed his familiar role as a relief specialist.⁴⁶ Panther struggled in the early going, posting a substandard 5.63 ERA in his first nine appearances. According to Richmond manager Bobby Hofman, the cause of the sinkerball pitcher's difficulties was simple: His "ball wasn't sinking."⁴⁷ Panther began working on a new release point in an attempt to remedy the problem. "Now he's getting the ball to sink," manager Hofman proclaimed after Panther's successful work with Atlanta's minor-league pitching instructor Harry Dorish.⁴⁸ He quickly lowered his ERA by more than a full point, and attracted the attention of the struggling parent club that was still feeling the effects of having a pitching staff with the worst team ERA in baseball during the prior season. Called up in late May to replace Tom Kelley in Atlanta's bullpen, Panther started strong, not allowing an earned run in 10 of his first 11 games. "I think I can do a good job for the Braves in relief if they pitch me and it looks like they will," he said.[49] Panther did not continue to do a good job for the Braves, however. Allowing earned runs in nine of his next 12 appearances – and culminating with a disastrous outing against the Cincinnati Reds in which he allowed six hits, one walk, and six earned runs in only a third of an inning pitched – Panther's statistics for Atlanta included a 2-3 record and dreadful 7.63 ERA over 30⅔ innings. He was returned in early August to Richmond's bullpen, where he finished the season.

Panther's poor performance with Atlanta stemmed from a stabbing pain he felt in his shoulder during a game earlier in the season. "I felt something in my shoulder," Panther recalled. "It was right before the All-Star break, so I had three days off. I kept my mouth shut, but after that I couldn't throw hard. I finished that year, but the next year I couldn't play. I've had two surgeries on that shoulder for labrum tears."[50] Panther was well aware of the precarious realities of life as a marginal big-leaguer. "I was one of those bottom-of-the-line guys," he admitted. "If you had 10 pitchers, I was eight, nine, or 10. In Oakland they had 10 pitchers, and I was 11. If you got hurt, you kept your mouth shut. At least I did."[51] Panther never again played professional baseball after this serious injury. "It was tough," he said regarding being forced to hang up his spikes. "The hardest part was when February rolled around and you didn't leave for spring training."[52]

After leaving the game, Panther continued his work as a teacher at Libertyville High School – albeit without the interruptions from moonlighting as a professional baseball player. He also was able to continue to stay close to the game, initially as an assistant baseball coach at Libertyville before assuming varsity head-coaching responsibilities in 1983. At the end of his 20-year coaching tenure there, Panther was Libertyville's all-time winningest head coach, posting an outstanding 528-169-4 record.[53] As a testament to his coaching abilities, Panther was inducted into the Illinois High School Baseball Coaches Association Hall of Fame in 1999 and the Lake County High School Sports Hall of Fame in 2002. "I had more success coaching than I did playing," he reflected. "Working with young people, teaching, and coaching was the most rewarding career I could ever have had. I loved every minute of it."[54] Outside of his careers in baseball and education, Panther also enjoyed spending time with his family. He and his wife, Bonnie – whom he married in 1967 – raised three children, Tami, Amanda, and Tim. Tragically, Tim – nicknamed "Mountain Man" due to his love of nature and the outdoors – died at age 23 after mistakenly eating a toxic plant while hiking.[55] "No one should ever have to suffer the loss of a child," Panther said. "After that nothing else could ever be as difficult. It changes your life forever."[56] After retiring from teaching and coaching in 2002, he and Bonnie relocated from Illinois to the warmer climes of Fort Myers, Florida. In 2011, Panther was diagnosed with prostate cancer, which he ultimately overcame through extensive radiation treatment, keeping a positive outlook all the while. "You do what you have to do," he said regarding his battle with the disease.[57] Panther counts golfing, traveling, and exercising among his favorite post-retirement pursuits.

Although he spent only one year in Texas, Panther accumulated a lifetime of great experiences with the Rangers during their inaugural 1972 season – despite the club finishing with an awful 54-100 record and playing in a converted minor-league ballpark. "It was a good place and the fans were great," he said. "It was a lot of fun even though we weren't very good."[58] Panther continued to follow the Rangers closely after his retirement, and in 2012 participated in the club's 40th-anniversary reunion ceremony on Opening Day at the Rangers Ballpark in Arlington with 12 of his former teammates from the inaugural 1972 team. "They gave all [of us] a jersey with your name on it, and we threw out the first pitch," Panther recalled. "We threw to people who were '72 season-ticket holders. This was by far the best one [Opening Day]

I've ever seen."[59] Some of Panther's fondest memories of his playing days in Texas included the opportunity to spend time with the club's manager – and Hall of Famer – Ted Williams, whom he occasionally witnessed still putting on impressive batting-practice feats while in his mid-50s.[60] "I got along with (Williams) well and I liked him," Panther said. "It was tough for him to manage [the 1972 Rangers]. We were behind in too many games."[61] It was also tough to manage to stay cool in the extreme Texas heat. "Once we played the White Sox there and I'll never forget, at 7:30 [P.M.] it was 105 degrees," Panther said. "We would still do a lot of running no matter how hot it was."[62] Nevertheless, the heat was a small price to pay for the good times he had as one of the first Texas Rangers. "I played with a lot of good guys and I wish we would have stayed there," Panther said. "We really enjoyed ourselves down there."[63]

In addition to the sources noted in this biography, the author accessed Panther's file from the library of the National Baseball Hall of Fame and Museum in Cooperstown, NY. Ancestry.com; Baseball-Reference.com; GeneologyBank.com; NewspaperArchive.com; Newspapers.com; and Retrosheet.org.

Notes

1. Patricia Babcock McGraw, "Panther Delivers His Final Season," *Daily Herald* (Arlington Heights, Illinois), March 22, 2002: 4-1.
2. Prugh Funeral Service, "Welcome to the Memorial Page for Mary Frances Panther," prughfuneralservice.com/notices/MaryFrancis-Panther, accessed April 13, 2017; Sec Taylor, "Sittin' In With the Athletes," *Des Moines Register*, August 26, 1955: 17.
3. "Mark Panther Again Hurls the Javelin," *Council Bluffs* (Iowa) *Nonpareil*, June 19, 1944: 7; Maury White, "Maury White," *Des Moines Register*, June 28, 1987: 11D.
4. College of Lake County Athletics, "Lake County High School Sports Hall of Fame – Jim Panther," clclancers.com/HShallOfFame/126.php, accessed April 13, 2017; Ralph Leo, "7th Place Highland Park Has No. 1 League Scorer," *Chicago Tribune*, February 21, 1963: 12.
5. Ross Forman, "Jim Panther – Teaching Baseball and Enjoying It," *Sports Collectors Digest*, June 10, 1994: 150.
6. "Panther Delivers His Final Season."
7. "SIU Baseball Team Playing in Quincy Meet," *Southern Illinoisan* (Carbondale), April 22, 1966: 13; "Stingy Staff Biggest Asset for Southern," *Alton* (Illinois) *Evening Telegraph*, April 21, 1966: B-13.
8. Associated Press, "Ohio State Near Title in Regional," *Daily Pantagraph* (Bloomington-Normal, Illinois), June 4, 1966: 11; *Southern Illinois University Salukis Baseball 2017 Media Guide* (Carbondale, Illinois: Southern Illinois University, 2017), 117.
9. "Panther Delivers His Final Season."
10. Anup Sinha and Bill Lajoie, *Character Is Not a Statistic: The Legacy and Wisdom of Baseball's Godfather Scout Bill Lajoie* (Bloomington, Indiana: Xlibris, 2010), 288.
11. "Panther Delivers His Final Season."
12. Jay Langhammer, "Sigma Pi Sports," *The Emerald of Sigma Pi Fraternity*, Spring/Summer 1984: 17.
13. Jeanne Pauly, "Jim Panther, Player, Coach & Cancer Survivor," *Between the Palms*, April 2012: 3.
14. "Bulls Down Grays, Yanks Here Tonight," *Daily Press* (Newport News, Virginia), August 2, 1967: 13.
15. Bob Moskowitz, "Panther, McNulty, Holt Get Grays Past Tobs, Near 1st," *Daily Press* (Newport News, Virginia), August 31, 1967: 12.
16. Larry Odell, "Prep Star Visits SIU," *Southern Illinoisan* (Carbondale), January 21, 1968: 10.
17. Bob Moskowitz, "Grays Look 'Right' for 2 Here Tonight," *Daily Press* (Newport News, Virginia), May 13, 1968: 13.
18. Larry Odell, "Two Preps Pass Up Gridiron for Baseball," *Southern Illinoisan* (Carbondale), May 12, 1969: 10.
19. "Panther Delivers His Final Season,": 4-4.
20. Larry Odell, "Another Gable, a Wrestler, Packed House," *Southern Illinoisan* (Carbondale), March 31, 1970: 11.
21. Pete Swanson, "Big Crowd Sees Trips Lose, 4-3," *Evansville* (Indiana) *Courier*, August 30, 1970: 1-C.
22. "Jim Panther – Teaching Baseball and Enjoying It."
23. Associated Press, "Rookie Panther Winner for Athletics," *Eureka* (California) *Times-Standard*, April 2, 1971: 13; Bill Bryson, "Jim Panther Stays; Boyd Back to Oaks," *Des Moines Register*, April 2, 1971: 1-S.
24. Bryson: 3-S.
25. United Press International, "Athletics to Open Series With Angels," *San Rafael* (California) *Daily Independent Journal*, April 20, 1971: 24.

26 Ron Maly, "Owner Still Likes Skidding Oaks Over Indianapolis," *Des Moines Register*, May 19, 1971: 2-S.

27 "Oaks' Reliever Fires Shutout in New Role," *The Sporting News*, July 3, 1971: 37.

28 United Press International, "Oaks Win," *Ames* (Iowa) *Daily Tribune*, May 20, 1971: 10; Associated Press, "Add Schubert to All-Stars," *Des Moines Register*, July 15, 1971: 1-S.

29 Mike Schwebel, "Stanhouse's Long Hair No Problem to Williams," *Southern Illinoisan* (Carbondale), March 26, 1972: 15.

30 Bruce Markusen, "Oakland A's Diary – Archive," BaseballGuru.com, baseballguru.com/markusen/oak2.html, accessed April 18, 2017.

31 Associated Press, "Stanhouse May Be Starter in Texas," *Southern Illinoisan* (Carbondale), March 5, 1972: 9.

32 Larry Odell, "Stanhouse Too Inexperienced?" *Southern Illinoisan* (Carbondale), March 31, 1972: 13.

33 Sid Hartman, "Sid Hartman," *Minneapolis Tribune*, March 7, 1972: 2C.

34 Randy Galloway, "A Panther on the Prowl," *Dallas Morning News*, June 19, 1972: 3B.

35 "Stanhouse's Long Hair No Problem to Williams."

36 "A Panther on the Prowl."

37 Newspaper article from Panther's file from the library of the National Baseball Hall of Fame and Museum in Cooperstown, New York.

38 "A Panther on the Prowl."

39 Ibid.

40 Merle Heryford, "Rangers Get Carty to Beef Up Attack," *The Sporting News*, November 11, 1972: 50.

41 Newspaper article from Panther's file from the library of the National Baseball Hall of Fame and Museum in Cooperstown, New York.

42 Associated Press, "Braves Trade Rico Carty to Rangers," *San Antonio Express and News,* October 28, 1972: 3-D.

43 United Press International, "Controversial Baseball Star Traded to Texas," *Ogden* (Utah) *Standard-Examiner*, October 28, 1972: 7A.

44 Associated Press, "Rangers' Carty Tagged With 'Beeg Boy' Title," *Abilene* (Texas) *Reporter-News*, April 4, 1973: 8-B.

45 Larry Odell, "Trading Trials and Tribulations," *Southern Illinoisan* (Carbondale), June 3, 1973: 11.

46 Ibid.

47 Bob Moskowitz, "Braves' Rally in 5th Downs Peninsula, 5-1," *Newport News* (Virginia) *Daily Press,* May 15, 1973: 12.

48 Ibid.

49 "Trading Trials and Tribulations."

50 Roger Wallenstein, "Fresh, Eager and Outclassed," *Beachwood Reporter* (Chicago), beachwoodreporter.com/sports/fresh_eager_and_outclassed.php, accessed April 21, 2017.

51 Ibid.

52 Barry Temkin, "Panther Leaving Legacy of Fun, Fundamentals," *Chicago Tribune*, May 5, 2002, articles.chicagotribune.com/2002-05-05/sports/0205050405_1_fundamentals-spring-training-pitchers, accessed May 7, 2017.

53 "Libertyville Wildcats Baseball Coaching Records," Libertyville High School Baseball, wildcatsbaseball.com/team_records.htm, accessed April 21, 2017.

54 "Jim Panther, Player, Coach & Cancer Survivor."

55 "Obituary: Timothy James Panther of Libertyville," *Daily Herald* (Arlington Heights, Illinois), February 9, 1999, genealogybank.com/doc/obituaries/obit/0FFA292284F97316, accessed May 7, 2017.

56 Ibid.

57 Ibid.

58 Marty Maciaszek, "Libertyville's Panther Recalls Rangers' Start," *Daily Herald* (Arlington Heights, Illinois), October 18, 2011, dailyherald.com/article/20111018/sports/710189686/, accessed May 7, 2017.

59 "Fresh, Eager and Outclassed."

60 Lew Freedman, "Ex-Big Leaguer Jim Panther Savors His Past," Call to the Pen, calltothepen.com/2013/06/06/ex-big-leaguer-jim-panther-savors-his-past/, June 6, 2013, accessed April 23, 2017.

61 "Libertyville's Panther Recalls Rangers' Start."

62 Ibid.

63 Ibid.

MIKE PAUL

BY WAYNE STRUMPFER

Mike Paul, a veteran of a half-century in professional baseball, was born on April 18, 1945, in Detroit. Michael George Paul was the oldest of seven children born to George and Theresa Paul. George Paul was a police officer in Detroit, but thought it was becoming too dangerous there and moved the family to Compton, California, when his oldest child was in the eighth grade.

Mike attended Pope Pius X High School in Downey, California. There, as a senior starting pitcher, he was named the Catholic League's Most Valuable Player in 1962. After high school he was a starting pitcher at Cerritos Junior College in Southern California. The left-hander was 13-0 and named the Most Valuable Player of the Metropolitan Conference in 1965. That year, Paul received a two-year scholarship to attend the University of Arizona. Although plagued early with some arm troubles, Paul was 8-2 and helped lead the Wildcats into the College World Series in 1966. His highlight was pitching a complete-game "do or die" 6-1 victory over an Arizona State University team featuring Reggie Jackson late in the season. In the College World Series, Paul led Arizona over Northeastern University in its only victory in the tournament.

During these years, Paul played in the summer leagues and in 1967 his team in Tucson had the chance to face the Cleveland Indians' Double-A club. It was at that game that Indians scout Hank Peters first spotted Paul. Later that year, the Indians drafted him in the 20th round of the amateur draft. He signed a contract with a $500 bonus and reported to Reno in the California League. In Reno, Paul's arm strength and velocity improved and he was promoted to Triple-A Portland at the end of July. There Paul began a lifetime friendship with teammate Ray Fosse. In his first year of professional ball, Paul had a 2.34 ERA and, most impressively, struck out 140 batters in 104 innings pitched.

The Indians invited Paul to spring training in 1968. His spring performance, including four shutout innings against the Chicago Cubs on March 16, was so promising the Indians were ready to bring him up. But Paul was only two months away from graduating from the University of Arizona. So the Indians assigned him to Reno and Paul commuted and pitched on the weekends until he graduated from the University of Arizona with a bachelor of science in physical education in May. After graduating, Paul was quickly promoted and joined the Indians in Minnesota.

Less than a year after being drafted by Cleveland, Paul made his major-league debut, against the Twins in Minnesota. That night, May 27, 1968, Paul replaced Stan Williams on the mound in the seventh inning and was credited with a save by allowing one hit in 2⅔ innings to secure a 3-1 victory. Paul went on to pitch in 36 games for the Indians that season with a 5-8 record and three saves. Near the end of the season, Paul started and won a game in New York against the Yankees that helped secure the Tribe's third-place finish in the American League. Although he started seven games, the young left-hander couldn't break into the starting rotation that year as Cleveland's staff included Sam McDowell (1.81 ERA), Luis Tiant (1.60), Sonny Siebert (2.97), and Williams (2.50). In his rookie season, Paul roomed with young slugger Tony Horton, who had also gone to high school in Southern California.

Paul threw a fastball, a curveball, and a change-up, but his fastball was what led to his early success. Shortly after his major-league debut, his batterymate, Duke Sims, noted: "(Paul's fastball) moves only a couple of inches, but that's all you need to keep it off the fat part of the bat and mix up a hitter. It's his surprisingly good control that makes the difference. He's sneaky fast. Slow windup and the ball explodes."[1]

After the 1968 season, Mike Paul married Rosalie Ruiz and they spent their honeymoon in Venezuela, where he pitched in the Venezuelan winter league. Playing winter ball in Venezuela, Puerto Rico, and Mexico was an annual ritual for Paul and it was made easier by having a wife who spoke fluent Spanish. Playing in the winter also allowed Paul to make extra money during a time when the major-league minimum salary was $10,000. He also hoped it would give him an advantage in spring training the following season in trying to make the major-league club.

The 1969 season began poorly for the Indians, who lost 15 of their first 16 games and never recovered, losing 99 games. Paul was a spot starter and long reliever, striking out 98 batters in 117⅓ innings pitched. In 1970, Paul struggled and was sent to Triple-A Wichita after the All-Star break until September. After a season in which he was 2-8 with a 4.81 ERA in 30 games for the Indians, Paul headed again to winter baseball. There he hurt his shoulder and came to spring training in 1971 injured and in pain. As Paul put it, "There were no surgeries back then – it was cortisone shots and pain pills."[2] The Indians sent the lefty to Wichita to start the season and he remained there until he was recalled in midsummer. Paul continued to struggle with a sore arm and his strikeout rate plummeted to 33 in 62 innings pitched.

At the busy Winter Meetings in December of 1971, there were 15 trades involving 53 players in five days. In one of those trades, the Indians swapped Paul, pitcher Rich Hand, catcher Ken Suarez, and outfielder Roy Foster to the Texas Rangers for pitchers Terry Ley, Gary Jones, and Denny Riddleberger and outfielder Del Unser. The Rangers had just finished their last season as the Washington Senators and would begin playing in Arlington, Texas, in 1972. Mike Paul learned of the trade while pitching in winter ball in Puerto Rico. His manager, Eddie Lopat, pulled him aside and told him he had received a telegram announcing the trade. The left-hander remembered thinking it was probably time for a change after several years with Cleveland. Paul said he thought the Rangers traded for him because he always pitched well against the Senators.

At spring training in 1972, Paul experienced a number of changes. For the first time, spring training was in Florida and the Grapefruit League, his new team was managed by Hall of Famer Ted Williams, and the players went on strike just before the season started. The main issue was pension benefits. Paul recalled that back then, with small salaries, pension and health care benefits were very important to the players. During the strike, Paul returned home to Tucson and pitched batting practice for the University of Arizona while living off his earnings from winter ball. After a couple of weeks, the strike ended and the players returned to play a slightly shortened season with a number of additional doubleheaders scheduled.

The 1972 season was Williams's last as a manager. Paul said he thought Williams was tired and lost interest after managing for four seasons, and was not thrilled with the team's move from Washington to Texas. Teammate Tom Grieve joked that the Rangers were so bad that year that they made the world's greatest hitter quit.[3] Although the Rangers ended with a 54-100 record, it was Mike Paul's finest season. Williams used a lot of pitchers and Paul thrived in that system. The lefty pitched in 49 games, starting

20, and was sixth in the AL with a 2.17 ERA. Paul gave up only four home runs in 161⅔ innings. Paul described his success that year as "decent pitching and a lot of luck."[4]

Ted Williams believed breaking balls were the hardest pitch to hit and he was always encouraging his pitchers to throw more. After pitchers gave up extra-base hits, Williams would often ask them what pitch they threw. If it was a fastball, the pitcher would get a tongue-lashing. Once, after Paul gave up a home run, Williams asked him the dreaded question. Knowing what was coming if he admitted he threw a fastball, Paul lied and told his skipper that he had thrown a curveball. Williams told Paul to make sure to get the ball to move more next time and walked away.[5]

In 1973, the Rangers hired Whitey Herzog as a first-year manager. Mike Paul liked Herzog. "He treated everyone fairly – he treated me the same whether I had a good outing or a poor outing," the lefty recalled.[6] Paul started the year as the number-two starter but struggled, pitching in 36 games, including 10 starts, for the Rangers and had a 5-4 record with a 4.95 ERA. It was a disappointment after his strong 1972 season. On August 31, the Rangers sent Paul to the Chicago Cubs for a player to be named later to strengthen their bullpen. Coming to the Cubs was an easy transition because Paul knew many Cubs players from his years in spring training in Arizona with the Indians. It was also the first time Paul was in a pennant race; the Cubs were in contention until the last week of the season. Paul pitched in 11 games for the Cubs and had a 3.44 ERA in 18⅓ innings.

Paul started the 1974 season with the Cubs, but after two games he was released. Without a job in baseball for the first time in his adult life, Paul called Dallas Green, the Philadelphia Phillies farm director. Green placed Paul with Triple-A Toledo. There, Paul pitched for manager Jim Bunning and amassed a 7-2 record as a spot starter and long reliever. That winter, Paul continued his tradition of pitching in winter ball, this time in Mexico, with the hopes that he might make the Phillies' major-league roster the following year. But it wasn't to be; Paul never returned to pitch in the major leagues.

Instead, Paul pitched in Toledo for the season as a veteran who ate up innings. In 1976, Paul started playing summers in the Mexican League. One of his friends told him the league "isn't pretty, but they are paying," and that was enough for Paul to continue his career south of the border.[7] Paul pitched for several teams including Juarez and Mexico City and won 20 games several times through 1982. By then, Paul said, his arm was "trashed" and he "was tired of playing for pesos."[8] In 1983, Paul landed a job as the pitching coach for Reno in the San Diego Padres minor-league system. He stayed there for two years and coached up-and-coming star Mitch Williams. In 1985 and 1986, Paul was the pitching coach for Triple-A Vancouver in the Brewers' system.

Through his friend Dave Duncan, Paul was hired by manager Tony La Russa of the Oakland A's as their bullpen coach in 1987. Paul had that job for two seasons, including the 1988 World Series team. (The famous Kirk Gibson Game One-winning home run landed about 50 feet from Paul, who was in the right-field bullpen at Dodger Stadium.)

Paul was hired as the pitching coach for the Seattle Mariners in 1989 and was in that role for three years with manager Jim LeFebvre. While in Seattle, he coached a young, wild, left-handed flamethrower named Randy Johnson. Paul said Johnson was a "very intense competitor" and struggled with his mechanics early in his career.[9] In 1992, Paul returned to Oakland as a bench coach and advance scout. After three years with Oakland, Paul was the Texas Rangers' advance scout from 1995 to 2001. After scouting for several teams, Mike Paul landed a job with Colorado in 2006 and as of 2018 continued to work for the Rockies, scouting both the major- and minor-league players of four teams in the Southwest. Paul and his wife, Rosalie, have two daughters, Amanda and Allison, and as of early 2018 he and his wife still reside in Tucson.

Sources

In preparing this biography, the author relied primarily on telephone interviews conducted with Mike Paul on March 26, 2017, and April 12, 2017. Also helpful were articles in The Sporting News on March 30, 1968: 28; June 8, 1968: 24; June 15, 1968: 27; December 18, 1971: 43; and September 22, 1973: 14; as well as Baseball-Reference.com.

Notes

1. *The Sporting News*, June 15, 1968: 27.
2. Mike Paul, telephone interviews with the author.
3. Ibid.
4. Ibid.
5. Ibid.
6. Ibid.
7. Ibid.
8. Ibid.
9. Ibid.

HORACIO PIÑA

BY RORY COSTELLO AND FRANCISCO RODRÍGUEZ LOZANO

This lanky pitcher was the first Mexican player to win a World Series ring. El Ejote – The Stringbean – was a member of the Oakland A's bullpen in 1973. His motion was quirky and memorable: Whipping the ball from a low side-arm/submarine angle, Piña then swung wide and landed hard with his trailing right foot. NBC's broadcasts of the 1973 World Series focused on the impact crater that Horacio created.

Piña pitched in 314 big-league games from 1968 to 1978, starting just seven times. After 1974 he then went back to Mexico, where he was a very effective starter in both summer and winter ball. His best season was the summer of 1978, highlighted by a perfect game on July 12. His 21-4, 1.94 record earned him a final two-game stint in the majors that September. Horacio then pitched on in Mexico through 1980 until he hurt his shoulder. He entered his homeland's Baseball Hall of Fame in 1988.

Horacio Piña García was born in Matamoros de La Laguna, in the state of Coahuila. This Matamoros is not the city directly across the Rio Grande from Brownsville, Texas (400 miles east, in the state of Tamaulipas). It is half an hour east of Torreón, the center of Mexico's ninth-biggest metro area. The Laguna region surrounds Torreón and its twin city Gómez Palacio, just across the Nazas River in the state of Durango.

Horacio's father was Roberto Piña Trujillo, a cornmill operator on a communal farm called Ejido las Maravillas. On March 12, 1945, the fourth of Roberto and Nohemí García Castro's seven children entered the world.[1] Before Horacio came José, Óscar, and Silvia; after him were Cuca, Roberto, and Jaime.

Note the tilde (~) in the family name, which the American press left out in his playing days. He never had it on his uniforms in the US either; they read only PINA. Looking back in 2009, though, Piña said it never mattered to him. "I had a lot of discipline. I came in running from the dugout to the field and I left running. What's more, I didn't know what that little thing above the 'n' was even called! It was only later I found out it's called a tilde."

Matamoros is a baseball-loving city, as is much of northern Mexico. Roberto Piña was a semipro pitcher (with a conventional overhand delivery). Horacio, however, barely touched bat and ball growing up – he favored soccer. He played goalie and sweeper because of his height. He only came to baseball by chance at age 17 after picking up a foul ball from a local field called Campo Cámara. His return throw was impressive enough to prompt someone to ask if he wanted to play ball. Horacio demurred, but the additional promise of 50 pesos – good money for the time – got him to join his first team. La Paletería Galindo (a purveyor of paletas, or Mexican popsicles) was the sponsor.[2] He later pitched for another team called "Los Chicos del Once."³

There were other local clubs in Gómez Palacio. During a 1963 game there, the gangling teenager got nicknamed for life. He stood well over 6 feet tall but then weighed little more than 150 pounds.⁴ A friend named Joaquín Gómez first called him "slice of watermelon" and then Ejote. The latter tag stuck.⁵

In 1964 Piña played for the "Frankie" team of Gómez Palacio, as well as the Matamoros team in La Liga Mayor de Béisbol de La Laguna. After a regional championship game in the city of Guadalupe Victoria (also in Durango), scouts from the Puebla Pericos organization in the Mexican League approached him.⁶ One was Nazario Moreno, who played just 32 games at the nation's top level but remained on the scene in various capacities, including manager. Horacio told them, "I don't know how to play." They replied, "We'll teach you there." His mother signed the contract, since his father had passed away.⁷

For the 1965 season, Piña joined Zacatecas in the Mexican Center League (Class A), a Puebla farm club also known as the Pericos (Parrots). He pitched 116 innings in 38 games, winning four and losing six. Control was a problem, as he walked 72 men, fueling a fat 6.60 ERA.

Horacio appeared in just six games with Zacatecas in 1966. He wanted to join the big club in Puebla, then managed by former Cleveland Indians star Beto Ávila (known as "Bobby" in the US). The Pericos reassigned him to the farm team, though, and so Piña went instead to the Monclova Acereros in La Liga del Norte de Coahuila. He also played for Matamoros in La Laguna's top league again.⁸

In 1967 Piña made the Puebla team. Even after he threw a 1-0 shutout, the Pericos had their doubts about whether he could be a starter. Horacio therefore decided to return to La Liga del Norte, but Cuban manager Tony Castaño persuaded him to stay.⁹ Piña went on to win 16 games against 11 losses for the last-place club, while posting a 3.28 ERA. The Mexican Baseball Writers Association did not make its annual MVP and Rookie of the Year selections that year, owing to an internal dispute.

The Mexico City sports paper La Afición polled the league's managers, though, and they named Horacio top rookie.¹⁰

Regino "Reggie" Otero, a scout for the Cleveland Indians, was paying attention, Otero, a Cuban who had played briefly with the Chicago Cubs in 1945, had moved into scouting after serving as a coach with the Tribe in 1966. Cleveland worked out a deal with Puebla, and Horacio then joined Reno in the California League (Class A). There he went 1-0, 4.00 in 18 innings across three games.

After the summer season ended, Piña played winter ball at home for the first time in La Liga Mexicana del Pacífico (LMP). The owner of the Culiacán Tomateros, merchant Juan Ley Fong (known as "Chino" for his Chinese birth) brought him aboard. In December 1967 Horacio reeled off an impressive streak of 46⅓ scoreless innings, still (as of 2014) a league record. It started with 13⅔ innings in relief on the 12th; three straight shutouts followed before opponents finally got to him in the sixth inning of his next start. Piña also pitched a no-hitter that winter, winning 2-1.

Horacio pitched in spring training with the Indians in 1968. He opened the season on loan to the Portland Beavers, Cleveland's Triple-A affiliate, and made five sharp starts, including a one-hitter with nine strikeouts his first time out. Overall, he was 3-1, 0.69 in 39 innings before returning to Puebla in mid-May. That was the deal he made with the Indians front office – under threat of fine and/or suspension – because his salary was lower in Triple-A than the Mexican League.¹¹

El Ejote continued to do well with the Parrots. He went 9-6, although he lost his last four decisions, with a 2.22 ERA. That prompted Cleveland to purchase his contract in mid-August. They were supposed to wait until after the Mexican League season ended on August 16, but manager Alvin Dark wanted his help.¹² "There was talk on the team that he was a racist," said Piña in 2009, "but it wasn't certain, because there were various Latinos. He gave a chance to everyone, and those who got the job done, we got in."

Piña made his big-league debut at Cleveland's Municipal Stadium on August 14. In relief of Luis Tiant, he retired all six Detroit Tigers who faced him, striking out four. Three days later, again at home, he relieved his fellow Mexican Vicente Romo and picked up the last two outs against the Chicago White Sox. It was his first of 38 saves in the majors.

On August 21, Piña made his first big-league start, against the Boston Red Sox at Municipal Stadium. He allowed two runs (one unearned) in 8⅔ innings and left to a standing ovation from the crowd of 8,991. Vicente Romo returned the favor, finishing off the 8-2 victory. One point of interest was that the US papers listed his age as 21 rather than 23.

After the game, Horacio said, "I tired a little in the last inning and I believe this was the hottest night I have ever pitched. It is a little cooler in Mexico where I pitched this year. I was a little nervous at the start and also wild because I couldn't control my overhand fastball."[13] It is notable that he varied his motion in his earlier years. Also, one of his Latino teammates must have translated, because the rookie spoke little if any English then. Perhaps it was Luis Tiant; in 2009 Piña remembered how good the Cuban was to him. "In any way or whatever thing he would help us. On days off we would get together with the family – a very good person."

Author Bruce Markusen, who chronicled the Oakland dynasty of the early '70s, described Piña. "At six feet, two inches, and 160 pounds, the reed-thin right-hander .earned the nickname 'Ichabod Crane' during his early major league days. An impressive physical specimen he was not."[14] During the '70s, Horacio filled out to nearly 180 pounds. His wiry hair also grew quite bushy at times (as depicted on his Mexican Hall of Fame plaque and his bust at Campo Cámara).

Piña made the Indians staff in spring training 1969 and pitched in 31 games for them over the first four months, although he spent a brief spell with Portland in April. On the surface, his ERA was an unimpressive 5.21, but a couple of bad outings inflated that number. At the end of July, after the White Sox hit him hard, Cleveland sent Horacio down to Double-A Waterbury.[15] He did not appear in a single game there, though – rather, he went home. "I pitched more effectively than others, but I was demoted while they stayed," he said in 1990. "They (Cleveland) threatened to suspend me."[16] In fact, *The Sporting News* said he was suspended after refusing to report.[17]

On December 5 the Indians traded Piña along with pitcher Ron Law and infielder Dave Nelson to the Washington Senators. In return, they received Dennis Higgins and Barry Moore. The relatively minor deal received little attention at the time, as it was a busy day at the winter meetings and there was other news from the business side of the game: the move of the Seattle Pilots and a power struggle within the league offices.

That winter Culiacán won the first of two LMP titles during Horacio's time there (unfortunately, Mexico was not part of the Caribbean Series revival in 1970). He ranked these alongside his World Series as the best things that ever happened to him in baseball. About being a Tomatero, Piña said in 2007, "They were 12 unforgettable seasons. I don't forget that after each season in the big leagues, I arrived in my beloved Culiacán to defend the house of the Tomateros. We came to have the best pitching in the league for many years."[18]

Piña was late reporting to the Senators camp in 1970, until manager Ted Williams threatened to fine him $100 a day.[19] But when he did arrive, Williams became his benefactor. Although the general public was unaware back then, at least some of the Senators knew that Williams (who spoke some Spanish) had Mexican heritage. They did not know that it was on his mother's side, though, because Ted almost never spoke of family. Horacio has said that it was not a surrogate father-son relationship, yet the Splendid Splinter may still have seen something of his former self in El Ejote.

Piña described their rapport in ProMex, a San Antonio-based Hispanic sporting monthly of the early '90s. He told how "Williams became a close friend who helped him adjust to life in the United States. Since Pina didn't feel very secure about his English, he would get to the ballpark very early.

Naturally the manager Williams was also there." Horacio also learned how to fish from the noted angler. He spoke fondly of "their talks while casting their rods into a tin can inside the dugout. '[Williams] would complain about guys like Frank Howard who were making a lot of money and weren't half as good as he was.'"[20]

In 2009 Piña added his memories of how Williams would invite him to the movies if a game got called. ("What are you doing?" "Nothing.") It would be just the two of them, and Ted would buy popcorn and a gallon of milk. They shared a lot of laughs even if they didn't understand the film. "I really appreciated him. He was a tremendous person and he gave me a job," said Horacio in summary.

Working strictly in relief, Piña appeared often with the Senators in 1970 (a career-high 61 games) and again in '71 (56 games). His stints were short by the standards of the day, as he totaled 128⅔ innings pitched. Though he continued to walk a good few batters, he was still generally effective.

Even so, author Thomas Boswell is fond of recounting one unflattering (yet funny) memory of an outing at Griffith Stadium. "Once, we saw the Senators' flamboyant submarine pitcher, Horacio Pina, as he caught his spikes and tripped in mid-delivery. He rolled down the mound in a sideways tangle as though he'd somehow nailed his own hand to the ground. For years, when somebody tried to be too flashy and fell on his face, my mother would intone, 'Horaaaacio Piiiina.'"[21]

Piña stayed with the franchise in 1972 as owner Bob Short moved it to Texas. That season he recorded a career-high 15 saves in 60 games. Though he had earned Ted Williams' confidence, Horacio said modestly, "I am just a mediocre pitcher. I could not be a starter, but I could go in for a few innings and help the team. A relief pitcher has to throw strikes more than a starter and he has to use his brains more. … I just try to throw strikes aiming at the batter's weak points." The same article noted his "quick smile" and "friendly character" – and that he was making more money with Culiacán than he was with the Rangers.[22]

On November 30 the Rangers traded Piña to Oakland for a former Washington teammate, first baseman Mike Epstein. The A's sought room in their lineup for Gene Tenace, whose shoulder ailment was limiting his ability to catch.[23] The *Oakland Tribune* took a dim view of the deal – "Epstein [was] surrendered rather cheaply, it seemed"[24] – but it worked out well for the A's. The disgruntled slugger played only 27 games for Texas in '73 before they peddled him to the Angels, where he struggled for the rest of that season. "Superjew" was out of the majors after just 18 games with California in 1974.

On the other hand, Horacio was pleased. From Culiacán, he said, "Ted Williams was great to me and I was happy in Washington and in Texas, but pitching for the world champions will be something special."[25] He got off to a strong start in the East Bay, with some help from Oakland pitching coach Wes Stock. Bruce Markusen wrote:

"Initially, Pina had also failed to impress Stock, who noted his past inability to handle left-handed batters. Pina, an effective side-arming pitcher against right-handed hitters, seemed unwilling to use that style against lefties. 'He was coming over the top to left-handers and his ball always was up,' Stock explained to *The Sporting News*. 'His natural motion is side-arm, and his ball sinks when he throws it that way.'

"Stock quickly convinced Pina to rid himself of the overhand delivery and show courage in using his side-winding motion at all times. Pina had been given such advice in the past, but the recommendations never stuck – until now. With his long fingers and large hands, Pina already threw his best pitch, a sinking palmball, more effectively than most pitchers. Pina's palmball now became lethal to left-handed hitters, as well."[26] He had learned the pitch from bullpen mate Joe Grzenda with the Senators and mastered it in winter ball.[27]

In later years, Horacio commented, "I believe the submarine ball was a gift that God gave me ever since I started. When I went to the U.S., many people said they wanted me to change that style, but the reality is that they told me, "Forget it, you're getting outs and that's why we're keeping you with us."[28]

Piña complemented Rollie Fingers, Darold Knowles, and Paul Lindblad nicely in the Oakland bullpen. He pitched in 47 games (6-3, 2.76) and picked up eight saves. Oddly enough, this was the first season since 1969 in which lefties had a higher batting average against him than righties.

In 2009 Horacio underscored how A's manager Dick Williams liked discipline. "He was good people but there was a lot of discipline, and that's why Oakland became champions. He didn't hang out with the team, just on the field, and outside he was apart."

He mentioned how Williams gave him chances to pitch, including various save opportunities when Rollie Fingers was not available. For a while, however, he was in Dick's doghouse. In a key situation against Baltimore, the skipper approached the mound and told him that he didn't want to see any curves or changeups, just fastballs. Piña disobeyed and gave up a home run. This appears to have been in Oakland on July 16, as aging Brooks Robinson hit a three-run homer in the seventh to give the Orioles a 7-5 lead that they then held.

"Dick Williams got mad. He had me a month [actually 11 days, but no doubt it felt longer], go warm up, sit down, warm up, sit down. He was right, I didn't pay attention. He told me, 'Here, what I say goes.' They told me that for this they could send me to Triple A."

Finally Piña returned to action on July 27 when Dave Hamilton got knocked out of the box in the first inning at Minnesota, following a doubleheader on the 26th. Williams came in and said, "Only fastballs." This time Horacio obeyed. In his view, the biggest thing he learned from Williams was his sharp strategy in making changes. "He made some tremendous changes, good for the team and for winning."

Advancing to the postseason for the first time in the US, Horacio pitched in one game in the AL Championship Series against Baltimore. In Game Two, the Orioles knocked Vida Blue out in the first inning. Piña replaced him and pitched two scoreless innings, though he allowed one inherited runner to score.

The A's then faced the surprising New York Mets in the World Series. Horacio became the second Mexican to make it to the fall classic, following Bobby Ávila in 1954. In Game Two, Vida Blue was leading 3-2 in the sixth inning but put two runners on with one out. As Joseph Durso of the *New York Times* put it, "Blue was replaced, briefly and disastrously, by Horacio Pina and his right-handed, underhanded-whip delivery."[29] His first pitch hit Jerry Grote; he then gave up a 10-foot scratch single to Don Hahn. Bud Harrelson followed with a clean single and that was it for Piña. Darold Knowles then entered and got Jim Beauchamp to hit a comebacker that should have been a 1-2-3 double play. Instead, he slipped and threw it away, and two unearned runs were charged to Horacio. The Mets eventually won in 12 innings, 10-7, as Mike Andrews made two errors and became a scapegoat for owner Charles O. Finley.

Piña relieved for three innings in Game Four, which the Mets won 6-1. Mike Andrews, reinstated on the Oakland roster, pinch-hit for him in the eighth inning. Knowles and Fingers were the only relievers whom Dick Williams used after that. When the A's took Game Seven, though, Horacio pocketed a full winner's Series share: $24,617.57. He went home to the acclaim of all Mexico.

Not long after the Series ended (December 3), Oakland traded Piña to the Chicago Cubs, re-obtaining Bob Locker. It was a curious swap in a couple of ways. First, Locker was also a side-armer. In addition, "the trading of Locker fulfilled a promise the Cubs had made him when they swapped Billy North to Oakland for the veteran righthander [the previous offseason]. Locker … had said he would not report unless the Cubs promised to trade him back to a Coast club."[30]

Charlie Finley, who acted as his own general manager, also apparently liked what Locker had done his first time around with the A's. Reportedly, however, Dick Williams was "dazed" by the deal, even though Piña had "fallen out of favor" with him. "How could Charlie make that trade?" Williams said. "He says he wants me back as manager and then he goes and trades Pina ... [who] is seven years younger."³¹ Events would prove the manager mostly right. Locker missed the entire 1974 season after an elbow operation; Oakland then shipped him back to Chicago, along with Darold Knowles and Manny Trillo, for Billy Williams.

Meanwhile, in the National League for the first time, Piña appeared in 34 games for the Cubs in 1974. The team had envisaged him as their short reliever, but there were few save opportunities that year. Most of those went to Oscar Zamora after he was promoted to Chicago in June. Worse, Horacio had a sore shoulder (something that had also bothered him during 1973). On July 28 the Cubs traded him to the California Angels for lefty-hitting catcher Rick Stelmaszek, a Chicago native. Pitching under Dick Williams once again, he saw little action the rest of the way, pitching just 11⅓ innings in 11 games.

At the end of spring training 1975, the Angels released Piña (who had reported late). The A's reacquired him on waivers, but allegedly he refused to report because he didn't want to pitch in the minors.³² According to Horacio, though, he was told that his fastball wasn't what it used to be. In addition, he refused to take a cortisone shot.³³

Still not yet 30, the pitcher returned home to Matamoros. He wanted 40,000 pesos (US $3,200 at the prevailing exchange rate) and a Dodge Royal Monaco car to play in the Mexican League. His local team, Unión Laguna, wouldn't meet those conditions – but Aguascalientes did.³⁴ He paid dividends almost immediately, throwing a seven-inning no-hitter at Ciudad Juárez on May 1, 1975.

Piña would spend the next five seasons with the Rieleros, largely as a starter but also coming out of the pen, which was his primary role in 1977. From 1975 to 1977 he was only one game over .500 (32-31), but his ERAs were excellent, including a league-leading 1.70 in '77.

Horacio's second LMP championship with Culiacán came in the winter of 1977-78, and he got to play in the 1978 Caribbean Series in Mazatlán. Host nation Mexico went just 1-5, though, with Piña losing one game in relief to the Dominican Republic. His time with the Tomateros also ended after a run-in with Juan Manuel Ley, eldest son of Juan Ley Fong and the team's co-founder. "Three other players and I demanded of Chino Ley that he put us up on the beach and that he give us the $40 per diem that he gave the foreign ballplayers. But he got pissed off and ran us off the club. He sent me to Mexicali."³⁵

Piña's greatest game came that summer in Aguascalientes, at Estadio Alberto Romo Chávez before a crowd of more than 25,000. He was aware he had a no-hitter – when the manager's young sons told him, he replied, "Go over there and bring me a coffee." However, he had no idea that the 86-pitch masterpiece was a perfect game, only the second of nine innings in league history. He was perhaps most pleased that he had set a career high with his 17th victory.³⁶ Horacio followed up by pitching six more perfect innings in his next start.³⁷ He capped his career year by helping the Rieleros win the Mexican League championship, although he lost a duel in the finals to Unión Laguna's ace, Antonio Polloreno.³⁸

That September 14, the Philadelphia Phillies purchased Piña's contract. Rubén Amaro, Sr., then a Latin American scout with the Phillies, recommended him.³⁹ Horacio pitched in two games down the stretch for the NL East winners, but he was not on the postseason roster. After Philadelphia lost the NLCS to the Los Angeles Dodgers, they returned him to Aguascalientes.

In February 1979 one US article quoted Phillies manager Danny Ozark as unconcerned that Piña was not yet in camp,⁴⁰ suggesting that at some level he was still in the club's plans. He stayed with the Rieleros, though, and had a decent year (13-9, 2.80). Horacio's last full season in the pros was 1980; for the Yucatán Leones, he was 9-8, 1.51. That winter, however, he tore his rotator cuff while playing for Guaymas. Even though Dr. Eluterio Valencia operated, he knew it was a career-ender as it happened.⁴¹

Piña's final summer statistics in Mexico were 100 wins, 68 losses, and a 2.35 ERA. He started 160 of his 235 appearances, pitching 98 complete games and 24 shutouts. In 2007 the Mexican Pacific League celebrated its 50th anniversary and issued a list of the top 50 players in its history. One of those names was Horacio Piña.

After retiring, Piña served two seasons as a pitching coach for Unión Laguna.[42] He then stayed home in Matamoros. In addition to drawing his big-league pension, Horacio established a cantina alongside his house, together with one of his brothers. In his leisure time, he still spent many hours fishing.[43]

Piña and his wife, Zoila Ávila, whom he married in Matamaros in 1967, had six children: Horacio, Hilda Patricia, Rosa Isela, Roberto, Yazmín Anel, and José Iván. Sad to relate, they also lost an infant who was less than a month old. Horacio was away playing in the US at the time and he did not even know until the burial had already taken place. The same happened when his grandmother died. Piña suffered another tragedy when the son he had with a woman in Aguascalientes died at age 12 in a freak horseback riding accident. (He also had a daughter from this relationship.)[44]

In March 2009 Matamoros re-inaugurated La Unidad Deportiva Horacio Piña, the multisport facility that honors the town's best-known athlete. After several years of discussion, the center received much-needed government funding for repairs and upgrades, as time and the elements had taken a severe toll over three decades of use.[45] The young men of the city also play baseball in La Liga Municipal Horacio Piña.

By his early 60s, the once-skinny Ejote had put on a pleasing amount of weight (he liked his Corona beer). He remained lively, full of laughter, and interested in baseball. For example, he commented in 2007 that steroids don't make the ballplayer. "I'm going to put it to you very simply. To bat, first you have to hit the ball, and to get outs, first you have to throw strikes. Steroids don't give you either of those things."[46]

Looking back on his time in the majors – specifically with Oakland – Piña said in 2008, "They taught me to give it everything I've got, not to be wishy-washy, always give it your best shot, like the boxers."[47]

Francisco Rodríguez Lozano's article ("Horacio Piña: El hijo pródigo de Matamoros"), based on an interview at home with Piña, was originally published in the magazine Semanario Vanguardia (Saltillo, Coahuila, Mexico), August 4, 2008. It may be found with accompanying photos at semanariocoahuila.com/pdf_sem/semanario_131.pdf and also on Paco's blog (pacorolo.blogspot.com/2009/08/el-hijo-prodigo-de-matamoros.html). Paco also re-interviewed Piña on November 25, 2009, and December 3, 2009, providing additional input.

Thanks also to Fernando Ballesteros of the Puro Béisbol website.

Sources
paperofrecord.com (other small pieces of information from *The Sporting News*)
retrosheet.org
ligadelpacifico.mx
salondelafama.com.mx
Treto Cisneros, Pedro, editor, *Enciclopedia del Béisbol Mexicano* (Revistas Deportivas, S.A. de C.V., 1998).
Bjarkman, Peter, *Diamonds Around the Globe: The Encyclopedia of International Baseball* (Westport, Connecticut: Greenwood Press, 2005).
Araujo Bojórquez, Alfonso, *Series del Caribe: narraciones y estadísticas, 1949-2001* (Colegio de Bachilleres del Estado de Sinaloa, 2002).

Notes

1. "Pina Is Articulate Moundsman." Associated Press, August 11, 1972 (information on number of siblings and father's occupation); Rodríguez Lozano, Francisco, "Horacio Piña: El hijo pródigo de Matamoros." The photo of a plaque in Matamoros, on the blog version of Rodríguez's story, showed Piña's parents' names.
2. Rodríguez Lozano, op. cit.
3. "25 años de una hazaña perfecta." *El Siglo de Torreón*, July 12, 2003.
4. Ibid.
5. Fernando Ballesteros, "Desestima Piña los esteroides." Puro Béisbol website (purobeisbol.com.mx/content/blogcategory/10/28/), published in 2007.
6. Ibid.
7. Rodríguez Lozano, op. cit.
8. "25 años de una hazaña perfecta"
9. Ibid.
10. Roberto Hernandez, "Relief Star Suby Wins ERA honors," *The Sporting News*, September 9, 1967: 36.
11. ussell Schneider, "Gabe Nabs Another Tamale From Mexico in Horacio Pina," *The Sporting News*, September 7, 1968, 17.
12. Ibid.
13. "Tribe Scores Eight Times In Fifth inning For Win," United Press International, August 22, 1968.
14. baseballthinkfactory.org/files/cooperstown/discussion/markusen_2003-04-25_0/
15. "Cleveland's Indians Send Pina to Minors," Associated Press, August 1, 1969.
16. Raul Flores and Mario Longoria, "Mexican Hall of Famer – Horacio Pina," *ProMex*, issue unknown, 1990.
17. Russell Schneider, "Tribe Finds Relief From Bullpen Ache," *The Sporting News*, December 20, 1969: 40.
18. Ballesteros, op. cit.
19. Merrell Whittlesey, "Hot Tamales – Rodriguez and Pina Fuel Nats," *The Sporting News*, May 23, 1970: 33. During the 1970 season, before he was traded to Detroit, fellow Mexican Aurelio Rodríguez was Horacio's roommate both in a Washington hotel and on the road.
20. Flores and Longoria, op. cit.
21. "The Church of Baseball," in Geoffrey C. Ward and Ken Burns, *Baseball: An Illustrated History* (New York: Alfred A. Knopf, 1994), 191. In another telling of the story (*Los Angeles Times*, May 13, 2001: D-2), Boswell had a gust of wind blowing Piña sideways.
22. "Pina Is Articulate Moundsman."
23. Ron Bergman, "Epstein Exit Traced to Tenace Shoulder Ailment," *The Sporting News*, December 23, 1972: 37.
24. "Baseball Winds Up Big Week," *Oakland Tribune*, December 3, 1972, 51.
25. Tomás Morales, "Trade to A's Pleases Mexican Starter Pina," *The Sporting News*, January 6, 1973: 47.
26. Markusen, op. cit.
27. Ron Bergman, "Athletics Avoid Deep Water When Horacio Is on Bridge," *The Sporting News*, May 19, 1973: 13.
28. Ballesteros, op. cit.
29. Joseph Durso, "Mets Get 4 Runs in 12th to Beat A's, 10-7, and Even Series at 1-1," *New York Times*, October 15, 1973: 1.
30. "Giants, A's get relievers," United Press International, December 4, 1973.
31. Ron Bergman, "Williams Dazed by Finley Deal for Locker," *The Sporting News*, December 29, 1973: 29.
32. "A's Acorns," *The Sporting News*, April 19, 1975: 8.
33. Rodríguez Lozano, op. cit.
34. Ibid.
35. Ibid.
36. Ibid.
37. Sergio Luis Rosas, "Recibe homenaje Horacio 'Ejote' Piña," *El Siglo de Torreón*, November 4, 2007.
38. Claudio Martínez Silva, "De Jaboneros a Vaqueros," *El Siglo de Torreón*, March 21, 2008.
39. "25 años de una hazaña perfecta."
40. "Phils report for duty," Associated Press, February 28, 1979.
41. Rodríguez Lozano, op. cit.

42 "25 años de una hazaña perfecta."
43 Ballesteros, op. cit.
44 Ibid.
45 Joel Flores Maltos, "Inaugurarán obras en la UD de Matamoros," *El Siglo de Torreón*, March 3, 2009.
46 Ballesteros, op. cit.
47 Rodríguez Lozano, op. cit.

TOM RAGLAND

BY BOB LEMOINE

"Always smiling, made you feel good to be around him."
Cleveland sportscaster Joe Tait on Tom Ragland.[1]

Tom Ragland wanted his mother to get him a baseball glove when he was 5 years old. There was no money for one, and it was a few years later when he found a discarded one on a Detroit street. For a boy who would be picking cotton when not in school, nothing ever came easy for Tom Ragland. He knew what it took to persevere. His journey to the major leagues took six years of bus rides in the minors, and once he made it to the top he mostly sat on the bench waiting for his opportunities. Ragland played 10 seasons of professional baseball, but in only one of them was he solely on a major-league roster. He played in only 102 games at the major-league level, including 25 with the 1972 Texas Rangers. The boy who found, cleaned, and stitched up his first glove after finding it on the street became a man called "Rags" who used his grit and glove to make it to the major leagues.

Thomas Junior Ragland was born on June 16, 1946, in Talladega, Alabama. His parents, Thomas Garrett and Catherine Ragland, never married, and young Thomas split his childhood between Alabama with his sharecropper maternal grandparents and Catherine, who lived in Detroit. He had several half-brothers and half-sisters. He also for a time lived in Cleveland with an aunt, Claudia Borden, who "helped raise me and was a great influence in my life."[2] When he was 5 years old, Ragland, living in Alabama, asked for a baseball glove for Christmas. His grandmother "almost had a stroke," Ragland recalled. In Alabama, he lived in his grandparents' house with about 15 others. A baseball glove was a pure luxury. "I needed clothes," Ragland said, acknowledging that that was the common item on their Christmas list. "To want a baseball glove at five years old," he laughed. "I was born to do it."[3]

His surroundings in Alabama were devoid of baseball. The family would sit in the living room, some playing dominoes or checkers, but he was up close to the radio, listening to a ballgame with his grandfather. He remembered hearing Washington Senators games and Mickey Vernon playing.[4] When Rags found that glove on a Detroit street, he was living with his mother and stepfather. He attended Breitmeyer and Sherrard, two Detroit elementary schools. Because of an abusive situation involving his stepfather, Ragland lived in Detroit and then Gadsden, Alabama. "I was living with my mother and stepdad, who was a real bad person to me and my mother," Ragland recalled. Then came a moment that changed his life forever. Jim Bibbs, Ragland's elementary-school gym teacher, had already been a godsend to Ragland, paying his travel when he needed to leave home for Detroit and Gadsden. This time, Bibbs sent him $25 for Christmas, a gift that came with a choice. The $25 could be used to get himself something nice for Christmas, or it could buy a bus ticket back to Detroit. Bibbs offered to let Ragland live with him while finishing his junior and senior years of high school, and also play baseball. Ragland bought the bus ticket, and Bibbs got him a spot in a Babe Ruth League. Ragland was grateful. Bibbs "always put me in the right spot," he said. "He became my dad." In high school, Ragland was the MVP of the league in both his junior and senior years, leading Northern High School to back-to-back East Side championships in 1964-1965.[5] Bibbs went on to become a track coach at Michigan State, the first African-American coach in the university's history. He was inducted into the Michigan State Athletic Hall of Fame in 2010, and the Track & Field and Cross Country Coaches Hall of Fame in 2015.[6] "I know that God sent Mr. Bibbs to me," Ragland said. "Mr. Bibbs is a living angel."[7]

Ragland was discovered by Charles "Tommy" Thompson, a scout for the Washington Senators. After graduating from high school, he was drafted by the Senators in the 15th round of the inaugural June 1965 amateur draft. With his $4,500 signing bonus, Ragland showed his thankfulness by sending $1,000 to his mother and buying his grandparents a car. He offered money to Bibbs, who refused, "but he told me to help another kid whenever I got the chance."[8] He took his first airplane ride in July, landing in Virginia, where he began his professional career with the Wytheville Senators of the Rookie Appalachian League. Ragland batted an impressive .301 and his 17 doubles tied him for second in the league. He hit eight home runs, two in one game, and played 53 games at shortstop with a .925 fielding percentage, best among shortstops.[9] He also tied for the league lead in being hit by a pitch (6). Ragland was surprised at the amount of segregation and racism he saw that existed not only in the South, but also within baseball teams themselves. Ballplayers on the same team were segregated according to hotel accommodations. "I discovered how ugly things were," Ragland said. "I didn't realize how things were like that in baseball. I thought it would be different in the pros."[10]

In 1966, Ragland moved up to the Geneva (New York) club in the Class-A New York-Pennsylvania League. Manager Gordon MacKenzie reported in April that Ragland "is a good hitter and he shows some power. He improves every time I see him play second base. He's got a good flip motion on his throws which should help him make the tough plays."[11] Ragland batted only .216, but in 123 games at second base, his .969 fielding percentage, putouts (254), and assists (285) were tops in the league for second basemen. Ragland represented Geneva at the league's all-star game in July.[12] At the last home game of the season, he was presented with a suitcase for winning the fans' vote as the most popular player on the team.[13] Even more impressive for Ragland was that his hero, Pete Rose, had won the award in 1960. "Pete Rose was my idol. I loved Pete Rose. I still do."[14]

Ragland would need that suitcase in 1967. On January 28, he wed Ida Mae Goldman. He began the season with the Burlington (North Carolina) Senators of the Class-A Carolina League. Ragland continued to find discrimination, as white players on the Burlington team were able to stay in a nice trailer park, while he and Ida had to rent a room from a high-school principal. He called this the "tail end" of the days of Jim Crow and segregation.[15] He batted .237 in 49 games, 39 of them at shortstop with a fielding percentage of .916. Geneva tried several players at second as a replacement for Ragland but was unsuccessful, so they reacquired him from Burlington at the end of July.[16] "I like it here," Ragland said of playing in Geneva.[17] After the season, the Raglands had an addition to their family, as daughter Althea was born.[18]

In 1968 Ragland remained at the Class-A level, playing for High Point-Thomasville (North Carolina), managed by Jack McKeon, in the Carolina League. Ragland showed his durability by leading the league in games played (141) and was second in being hit by a pitch (10). He batted only .240 but led all second basemen in putouts (355) and in turning double plays (98). "We finished second in our division, then won five straight in the playoffs," Ragland remembered of the championship club.[19] That winter, Ragland spent time in Bradenton, Florida, with the Senators team in the Florida Instructional League.

Ragland made the jump to Buffalo of the Triple-A International League in 1969, despite the original plans that he would remain in Double A. That all changed when Washington manager Ted Williams paid a visit to the minor-league camp. Williams "saw me hit a double off the Tigers' Triple-A team. He told the farm director Hal Keller to play me at second base for Buffalo," Ragland remembered.[20] "Tom Ragland didn't figure very prominently in the Bisons' 1969 plans when spring training opened," wrote Joe Alli of the Buffalo Courier-Express, "but the 22-year-old second baseman is attracting a lot of attention with his excellent play in exhibition games."[21] Ragland was batting .368 near the end of March and manager Hector Lopez was impressed. "That boy Ragland is doing a good job," he said. "He handles the bat pretty good, can run, and makes the plays in the field."[22] In game one of an Opening Day doubleheader, he batted in the top of the ninth at Louisville with the bases loaded and the score 3-3. He looped a single to center, driving in the go-ahead run in what would become an 11-3 laugher for Buffalo. "I want to tell you I was nervous when I went to the plate," Ragland admitted. "When I reached first base I said, 'Thank you, Lord!'"[23] The hit calmed his nerves and he doubled and singled in his first two at-bats in the second game.

In Buffalo's home opener, Ragland smashed a three-run home run. "He's our second baseman until he plays himself out of a job," Lopez promised.[24] Ragland went 3-for-5 on his 23rd birthday to lead Buffalo to a 7-3 win.[25] His biggest contribution, however, was his steady play at second. "Ragland isn't hitting as much as some of the other second baseman," Lopez said, "but he makes the double play better than anyone in the league."[26] Ragland led the team in stolen bases (13), walks (65), games (135), and plate appearances (521), and was second in runs scored (57). He led all second basemen in the International League in assists and double plays, and tied for the league lead in putouts. He batted .252 with 3 home runs and 40 RBIs. Ragland left a game on May 8 and raced to the hospital, where Ida gave birth to their second daughter, Kimberly.[27] He returned to Florida at the end of the season and played again in the Instructional League.

In 1970 Ragland played for the Senators' Triple-A farm team, the Denver Bears of the American Association. He again led his team in games played (126) and in plate appearances (503), and was second in walks (61) and doubles (19). He had a .979 fielding percentage at second base, and also played some at shortstop and helped turn 75 double plays. His 10 hit-by-pitches led the league again. He batted .259 with 2 home runs and 40 RBIs. His pinch-hit bases-loaded double in the ninth powered Denver to a win over Wichita on May 25.[28] Denver won the Western Division title and met Omaha in the playoffs. Ragland doubled in a five-run first, then doubled home two in a Game Four 8-3 win.[29]

After six years of toiling in the minor leagues, Ragland made it to the Senators out of spring training in 1971. A veteran power hitter who stood 6-feet-7 made sure the young, light-hitting 5-foot-10 Ragland was taken care of in this new experience. "He's just the greatest person in the world," Ragland said of his towering yet compassionate teammate, Frank Howard. "When I first came north, he took me aside. He said, 'Rags, listen to Hondo. For the next two weeks, wherever Hondo goes, you go. Whatever Hondo eats, you eat. It takes two weeks for the first paycheck. I know you're not making any money.' He carried me for two weeks. I'll never forget him for that."[30]

Ragland made his major-league debut on Opening Day, April 5, 1971, as a defensive replacement at second base. It was the Senators' final Opening Day. He handled two putouts in the 8-0 win over Oakland, but did not get an at-bat. "I finally made it to the show," he recollected in 2005. "To hear that national anthem, that was just awesome."[31] He entered three more games as a late-inning replacement, going hitless in two at-bats. He was optioned to Denver on April 20 when Don Wert came off the disabled list.[32]

Denver won the American Association title in 1971. Ragland contributed by slamming an inside-the-park home run in the ninth inning in a 3-2 win over Omaha on May 27.³³ He doubled in the winning run in the bottom of the ninth in a 6-5 win on July 25.³⁴ The Bears trailed Indianapolis three games to two in the best-of-seven championship series. The final two games were a doubleheader at Denver's Mile High Stadium. Ragland went 2-for-3 in the first game, a 4-2 victory.³⁵ Denver won the second game, 5-2, to take the title and move on to the Junior World Series, which they lost to Rochester (New York). He finished the season batting .301 with 4 home runs and 32 RBIs. He also had a strong .986 fielding percentage at second base. Ragland briefly played winter ball in Venezuela for the Zulia team, but was released during their season.³⁶

Ragland was recalled to Washington for the final games of the season. These were the final games played by the expansion Senators franchise that began in Washington in 1961, and the end of the 71-year history of the combined teams known as the Washington Senators. The original Senators (1901-1960) left for Minneapolis, and this team was now headed to Arlington, Texas. Ragland's first game back was a start in Boston on September 24. Batting eighth and playing second base, he singled off Roger Moret to get his first major-league hit. On September 30, Ragland started at second base in the last game of the Senators' franchise. He went 1-for-4 and scored a run in the eighth inning that would be the last run scored in Washington for a long while. The run gave Washington a 7-5 lead, but because fans stormed the field in the top of the ninth, the game was forfeited to the New York Yankees. The statistics counted, except that there were no winning or losing pitchers. Ragland finished with a .174 batting average with four singles in 10 games.

While the Senators moved to Texas and became the Rangers, Ragland, after spending spring training with them, went back to Denver to start the season. "Ted [Williams] was big on experience," Ragland said, noting that the Texas manager felt there were too many right-handed hitters on the team.³⁷ In 88 games with Denver, he batted .245 with 6 home runs and 38 RBIs. On July 23, Ragland was recalled by the Rangers. Because he was called up after the All-Star break, he didn't receive a $5,000 bonus he had been hoping for. From July 27 to August 22, he started four games and finished five others, going 0-for-16 at the plate. "But in those four (starts) I faced Vida Blue, Wilbur Wood, Dave Lemonds, and Ken Holtzman. I got a few hits after that and they started to fall in a little better."³⁸ He had a nine-game hitting streak from August 25 to September 5 in which he batted .357 (10-for-28) with a .400 on-base percentage. He finished the final seven games of the season 0-for-14 to drop his season average to .172. He had an impressive .982 fielding percentage, however, committing only one error in 89 innings.

Ragland's time in the Washington/Texas organization came to an end after eight seasons. On November 30, 1972, he was traded to the Cleveland Indians for pitcher Vince Colbert. Assigned to Cleveland's Triple-A team at Oklahoma City, he was invited to spring training as a nonroster player. A .303 batting average won him a spot on the Cleveland roster, which impressed manager Ken Aspromonte. "Tom has done everything we've asked of him," the manager said. "I like the boy very much."³⁹ Ragland was overjoyed. "I don't see how anybody could possibly be any happier than I am," he said. "I appreciate this chance and I hope I can continue to please Kenny. I've worked hard and I'll keep on working hard. This is what I've always wanted."⁴⁰ It also meant he finally received the $5,000 bonus, which the Raglands used to purchase a home in Detroit.⁴¹

Ragland didn't get into a game until the first game of a doubleheader against Boston on April 22. He entered to play second in the eighth inning. With one on and one out, Cleveland trailed 7-4 in the bottom of the ninth. Ragland singled off John Curtis in his first at-bat of the year. After a walk loaded the bases, pitcher Ron Lolich hit a walk-off grand slam to win 8-7. In May, with Jack Brohamer injured, Ragland took advantage of more playing time, starting 19 games and batting .338 with a .373 on-base percentage. He went 3-for-4 in an 8-3 win at Chicago on May 25.

"I knew what Tommy could do because I saw him play for Denver in 1970 when I was managing Wichita," Aspromonte said. "I figured he could provide us with back-up insurance at both second base and shortstop, but I never figured him for this." The manager mentioned a time when he wanted to lift Ragland for a pinch-hitter and wanted to explain it to him. Instead, Ragland replied, "I'm just so grateful to you for bringing me up here and giving me this chance, you don't have to explain anything to me. You're tops and you do anything with me you think best." Aspromonte said, "How can you beat a guy like that? He's one in a million."[42]

Ragland was reflective of how far he had come: "This is the first time in nine years of pro baseball that any organization or any person has shown any faith in me. Why shouldn't I be very grateful? It's also the reason I feel like I've got to go out there every day and prove myself over and over again … to justify that faith."[43] More than 40 years later he still had a special place in his heart for teammate Gaylord Perry, who thought Ragland was the best defensive infielder the Indians had. "If I'm pitching tomorrow," Perry said, "I want Raggy at second base."[44]

Ragland's average plummeted through the rest of the season, however, from .347 on May 31 to .269 on June 30 as he went 3-for-32 over the month. Much of the blame could be placed on a hyperextended right knee as well as other bumps and bruises that he refused to let sideline him. "Rags is the guy who's really hurting," Aspromonte said. "He has a sore knee, back and arm, but never once did he ask to come out of the lineup. He's the one who deserves credit."[45] When Jack Brohamer returned, Ragland's playing time decreased, and so did his optimism. "When I was starting out in the minors," he said, "it wasn't sitting on the bench in Cleveland that I was dreaming of. It hurts, man, because I've proved I can do the job."[46] His final batting average was .257 with 12 RBIs, and his fielding was once again steady with a .984 fielding percentage.

Seeing little room for Ragland on the roster in 1974, Cleveland sold him to the Houston Astros for the $20,000 waiver price. Houston assigned him to Denver, now their minor-league affiliate.[47] He played his fourth season in the familiar surroundings of Mile High Stadium, batting .249 with 3 home runs and 49 RBIs. Playing 120 games at second base, he had a .970 fielding percentage. It would be his final season, as the demotion to the minor leagues meant his salary was cut from $18,000 to $11,000 for the season. Denver offered him a contract. "I declined the contract, politely," Ragland said. "I told them to give another kid a chance. My wife and I had our fourth child by then (in addition to Althea and Kimberly, the family also included a daughter, Katrina, and a son, Thomas Jr.). I was 28. I wasn't ready to quit ball, but we had a mortgage payment and I had to provide for my family."[48] Ragland went home to Detroit and began working full-time at his offseason job: making ice cream at a Kroger milk-processing plant. He worked his way up to distribution manager.[49] He also scouted in the Detroit area for the Rangers from 1977 to 1979. In 1999, after more than 20 years away from the game, Ragland decided to take a trip to spring training. "I had taken two weeks' vacation and I was going to go to Florida and mingle, get my name back in the hat. Everybody in my family was grown. It was the right time to get back in the game." While en route, however, he received word from back home that his son, Thomas Jr., was in critical condition following a car accident. Ragland returned home. His son died three weeks later. "It took me five years to get my cry out," he said.[50]

Ragland said he still had a longing for baseball, and wished his career had taken a different path. "That's my wish, that I could get back in the game again," he said in 2005. "Not a week goes by that I don't dream about baseball. It hurts sometimes."[51] Besides scouting for the Rangers, he also coached Little League and high-school baseball, including the St. Martin de Porres High School team that Thomas Jr. played for.[52] Ragland also appeared with other former major leaguers in the Youth Baseball Clinic Series, sponsored by the Major League Baseball Players Alumni Association. At one such gathering, organizer Jason Glasgow said, "We want to focus on the inner-city kids, because there's not a lot of fields and coaches in Detroit, and we feel like the kids there are missing out on playing a great game."[53] Underprivileged kids can learn a lot from a guy named "Rags" who found his first glove on the street.

After 41 years working at Kroger, Ragland retired in 2009. He was humbled when company vice presidents attended his retirement ceremony. Many of them had tears in their eyes recalling the relationships they built with him over the years. "That made me feel good," Ragland said.[54]

As of 2017 Tom and Ida Ragland had three grown daughters with four grandchildren and continued to live in Detroit. He was inducted into the Detroit High School Hall of Fame in 2017.[55] Always with a thankful heart, when asked what one item he would definitely want in this biography, Ragland replied, "I just want to give a shoutout to all the people who stuck up for me."[56] No doubt, they would give a shoutout to Rags as well.

Sources

In addition to the sources cited in the Notes, the author was also helped by Baseball-reference.com, Retrosheet.org, and Tom Ragland's file from the Giamatti Research Center at the Baseball Hall of Fame. Special thanks to Rod Nelson for research assistance.

Notes

1. Terry Pluto and Joe Tait, *Joe Tait, It's Been a Real Ball: Stories From a Hall-of-Fame Broadcasting Career.* (Cleveland: Gray & Co., 2011), 83.
2. Russell Schneider, "Happiest Indian: 'Daddy Rags,'" *Cleveland Plain Dealer*, April 6, 1973: 34.
3. Author interview with Tom Ragland, April 26, 2017.
4. Ibid.
5. Ibid.
6. Ibid.; msuspartans.com/sports/c-track/spec-rel/081115aaa.html; msuspartans.com/genrel/093010aau.html.
7. Author interview.
8. Ibid.
9. "Know the Nats: Tommy Ragland," *Burlington* (North Carolina) *Times-News*, April 27, 1967: 2B.
10. Author interview.
11. "Infield Could Be Key to Senators 1966 Hopes," *Geneva* (New York) *Times*, April 23, 1966: 14.
12. Norm Jollow, "Wild Pitch in 10th Scuttles Senators, 3-2," *Geneva Times*, July 16, 1966: 9.
13. "Popular Fellow," *Geneva Times*, August 31, 1966: 3.
14. Author interview.
15. Ibid.
16. "Tom Ragland Arrives to Plug Hole at 2nd," *Geneva Times*, July 26, 1967: 14.
17. "Mezich 'Heps Out' to Sink Senators Twice," *Geneva Times*, July 27, 1967: 27.
18. "Highlightin'," *Burlington* (North Carolina) *Times-News*, April 11, 1968: 12.
19. Joe Alli, "Ragland 'Loose' After First Hit," *Buffalo Courier-Express*, April 28, 1969: 18.
20. Author interview.
21. Joe Alli, "Ragland Leads Herd Over Tidewater, 3-1," *Buffalo Courier-Express*, March 27, 1969: 35.
22. Ibid.
23. "Ragland 'Loose.'"
24. Ibid.
25. "Bisons Snap Wings' Streak at Five, 7-3," *Buffalo Courier-Express*, June 17, 1969: 21.
26. Joe Alli, "Herd Has Hopes for Star Berths," *Buffalo Courier-Express*, July 21, 1969: 20.
27. Joe Alli, "Bisons Jeff Terpko Halts Columbus, 7-1," *Buffalo Courier-Express*, May 9, 1969: 22.
28. "Denver Bears Top Wichita, Romp to Fifth Straight Win," *Greeley* (Colorado) *Daily Tribune*, May 26, 1970: 25.
29. "Bears Down Omaha, 8-3, in Fourth Playoff Game," *Greeley Daily Tribune*, September 9, 1970: 26.

30 John Woestendiek, "Last Men Out – Thirty-Four Years Later, Baseball and the Final Senators Game Still Resonate in the Lives of the Men in Washington's Last Lineup," *Baltimore Sun*, April 3, 2005: 1F.

31 Ibid.

32 "Washington Takes Wert Off List," *Abilene Reporter-News*, April 21, 1971: 22.

33 "Ragland Homer Pushes Denver Past Omaha," *Greeley Daily Tribune*, May 28, 1971: 28.

34 "Pitcher Gets Winning Run for Denver," *Colorado Springs Gazette-Telegraph*, July 26, 1971: 14.

35 "Bears Win Title – in Junior World Series," *Colorado Springs Gazette-Telegraph*, September 10, 1971: 14.

36 Eduardo Moncada, "Missing Stroke? Brant Finds It in Venezuela," *The Sporting News*, November 20, 1971: 55. Eduardo Moncada, "Carew: Interim Pilot, Top Venezuelan Hitter," *The Sporting News*, November 27, 1971: 55.

37 Author interview.

38 Russell Schneider, "Indians Tap Their Toes to Rags Time," *The Sporting News*, June 9, 1973:19.

39 Russell Schneider, "Happiest Indian: 'Daddy Rags,'" *Cleveland Plain Dealer*, April 6, 1973: 34.

40 Ibid.

41 Author interview.

42 Russell Schneider, "Schneider Around," *Cleveland Plain Dealer*, May 27, 1973: 50.

43 Ibid.

44 Author interview.

45 Russell Schneider, "Schneider Around," *Cleveland Plain Dealer*, June 2, 1973: 34; June 6, 1973: 76.

46 Chuck Hickman, "Utilityman Suffers on Bench," *Daily Iowan* (University of Iowa), August 28, 1973: 7.

47 Russell Schneider, "Schneider Around," *Cleveland Plain Dealer*, March 30, 1974: 52.

48 Woestendiek.

49 Ibid.

50 Ibid.

51 Ibid.

52 Author interview.

53 Jason Carmel Davis, "Former Major Leaguers to School Youngsters in Baseball Clinic," *C&G Newspapers* (Warren, Michigan). Retrieved April 5, 2017. candgnews.com/sports/former-tigers-school-youngsters-baseball-clinic.

54 Author interview.

55 Author interview.

56 Ibid.

LENNY RANDLE

BY CHARLIE GRASSL

The MLB Network produced a television special calling versatile switch-hitting infielder-outfielder Lenny Randle "The Most Interesting man in Baseball."[1] The 12-year major-league veteran learned to speak five languages; wrote, published, and performed a hip-hop song;[2] worked as a stand-up comic for free steaks; was principally responsible for the popularity of baseball in Italy; and ran a baseball academy in California, Italy, and other locales in Europe.

Lenny's father, Isaac Randle, was a longshoreman and a veteran of World War II. Isaac's wife, Ethel, helped with the finances by working as a seamstress for various families in the Southern California community where they lived. During the war, Isaac met a French chef while stationed in the Anzio-Nettuno region of Italy, who introduced him to the delights of European food. He promised the chef, out of gratitude for his friendship and wonderful meals, that if he ever had a son he would give him his name, Schenoff. After the war, Isaac fulfilled that promise as Leonard Schenoff Randle came into this world in Long Beach, California, on February 12, 1949. Isaac and Ethel's family eventually grew to eight: four boys and four girls. The parents emphasized education, and all eight of the Randle children obtained college degrees.

Growing up around the stories of his father's military experiences and later playing with military veterans like Ted Williams, Billy Martin, and others provided Lenny Randle with a perspective of dedication, sacrifice, and appreciation of life itself that perhaps combat experience helped provide. Randle reflected that Williams, in the clubhouse, would talk about hitting, fishing, and war. These stories fascinated and illustrated how these players took a military approach to playing baseball: "Those guys played baseball as if it was war. Each game brought the intensity of combat. You played a game as if it was the last game on earth and you were getting taken over by another country. We were not concerned about our batting averages. It was about the team and winning the game. That's how I learned to play the game."[3]

Randle grew up in Compton, California. At Centennial High School he was a star athlete in football and baseball. In 1967, his senior year, was captain of both teams. Drafted by the St. Louis Cardinals in the 10th round of the 1967 amateur draft, he chose to attend Arizona State University to further hone his baseball skills under the venerable Sun Devils coach Bobby Winkles. Despite his slight 5-foot-10 and 169 pounds, Randle continued to be involved with football. Seeing action as a wide receiver in the 1969 season, he was credited with five receptions for 65 yards and one touchdown. His real contribution was as a kickoff and punt-return specialist where his speed was best utilized.

Randle's presence on the ASU baseball team was much more impactful; he batted .298 as the starting shortstop in 1968, .225 at second base in 1969, and .335 at second base in 1970. The highlight of Randle's college baseball career was the 1969 season. The Sun Devils went 56-11, leading the Western Athletic Conference, defeating Brigham Young and Idaho in the conference tournament, and advancing to the College World Series. After losing, 4-0, to a 33-4 Texas Longhorns team that included Burt Hooton and James Street, the Sun Devils won their next five games to claim the College World Series title. In Randle's final season, 1970, the Sun Devils fell to a 30-22 record and missed qualifying for the playoffs. That disappointment was soothed for Randle when the Washington Senators drafted him in the first round of the 1970 amateur draft, the 10th player selected.

The 21-year-old switch-hitting infielder signed immediately and was assigned to the Denver Bears of the Triple-A American Association. Playing in 34 games at second base, Randle batted .208. Back at Denver in 1971, he had played in 48 games, mostly at second base and was batting .288 when he was called up to the Senators and made his major-league debut on June 16, 1971.

A tough assignment it was, for Randle's first game was against first-place Oakland with Vida Blue, 13-2 at the time, on the mound for the A's. Playing second base and hitting seventh in the lineup, Randle flied out to left field in his first at-bat, in the top of the second inning. After being called out on strikes in the fifth inning, Randle got his first major-league hit, an infield single, when he beat Bert Campaneris's throw to first from deep in the hole at shortstop in the seventh inning. He batted again in the top of the ninth and struck out swinging to end the game. Blue pitched a complete game and the A's prevailed, 5-1.

Randle played in 1,137 more games, for the Senators, Texas Rangers, New York Mets, New York Yankees, Chicago Cubs, and Seattle Mariners. His 12-year career included standout performances in 1974 with the Rangers and 1977 with the Mets, hitting .302 (sixth in the American League) and .304 respectively.

Randle was a gifted, athletic player both in positional flexibility and durability. Seldom injured, he played in an average of 143 games per year over a five-year span from 1974 through 1978. Though principally an infielder, Randle also was a valuable insertion into the outfield, starting 60 games there in 1975, mostly as the center fielder, recording eight assists and four double plays from that position. In that same year he caught six innings. His speed on the basepaths was reflected by 199 stolen bases in the five-year span.

Drafted as a seasoned college player, Randle never played below Triple-A ball in the minor leagues. After getting his feet wet in 46 games with Denver in the American Association in 1970, he began the 1971 and 1972 seasons at Triple A but was called up to the major-league club by the middle of each season. A solid 1973 season of 140 games with Spokane in the Pacific Coast League, where he stole 39 bases and hit .283 with an on-base percentage of .373 clearly showed Randle was ready for full-time duty in the big leagues.

Though Randle eventually played for six major-league teams, he knew only one franchise from 1970 until April 26, 1977, the Washington Senators/Texas Rangers. In '77, after a highly publicized incident in which he assaulted his manager, he was traded to the New York Mets, where he enjoyed his best year, batting .304 with 33 steals in 136 games in 1977. But the 1978 season saw his batting average sink to .233 with only 14 steals in 132 games. On March 29, 1979, at the end of spring training, Randle was released by the Mets. For Randle, 1979 became a whirlwind odyssey of associations with two minor-league teams and four major-league clubs who sent him to the minors in May and returned him to the majors by August.

On May 16 of that year, Randle signed a minor-league contract with the San Francisco Giants and was assigned to the Phoenix Giants of the Pacific Coast League. On June 28 he was included in a trade that returned the Giants' Bill Madlock to the Pittsburgh Pirates. The Pirates assigned Randle to their Portland PCL affiliate, where Randle played until his contract was purchased by the New York Yankees on August 3. He was with the Yankees for the remainder of the season. Let go by the Yankees after the season, Randle finished his career with the Chicago Cubs and Seattle Mariners.

Randle's major-league career involved more than just statistics. It was sprinkled with circumstantial oddities that worked over time to support an image of someone who just "bumbles" through life. In fact, in the MLB Network Presents show about Randle he is referred to as the "Forrest Gump of baseball."[4] That was a reference to an innocent, childlike person who is exposed, shaped, and controlled by life's circumstances as opposed to a person of intelligence and maturity who shapes and manages his own life. Consider these unusual circumstances:

Since 1971, five major-league baseball games have ended in a forfeit. Randle played in two of them. The first was on the last day of the 1971 seasons when fans stormed the field with two outs in the ninth inning, angry over the team's decision to move the franchise to Texas in 1972. In 1974 he played in the infamous Ten Cent Beer Night game in Cleveland when drunken fans began to come on the field. While with the Mets, Randle was at bat on July 13, 1977, when the lights went out in New York City. Shea Stadium lights failed around 9:30 P.M. with Randle at bat and the Cubs' Ray Burris on the mound. Randle would claim years later that he had just hit the ball between third and short for a single when the darkness descended so it was never scored officially. This was the second game of a scheduled three-game series. When the game was resumed, 64 days later, on September 16, a scheduled offday, Randle did hit the ball toward the shortstop and was thrown out at first.

Randle's public image threatened to be defined by two other incidents that occurred during his playing career.

On May 27, 1981, Amos Otis of the Kansas City Royals hit a dribbler down the third-base line. As it rolled along the baseline, Randle, on his hands and knees, blew the ball into foul territory. After much consultation, the umpires ruled his action illegal. (This act was repeated on a bunt down the third-base line in 1987 by Royals third baseman Kevin Seitzer. On that occasion, he was unsuccessful in making it go foul.) Randle's antics have been portrayed as evidence of his being unconventional, weird, crazy, and strange. One might suspect such labels were solidified when viewing yet another side of Randle from an event that took place on March 27, 1977, before a spring-training game in Orlando, Florida.

This is the well-known attack by the 28-year-old Lenny Randle on his 49-year-old manager, Frank Lucchesi. After holding down the Rangers' second-base position for 113 games in 1976, Randle was told he would lose that position in 1977 to another first-round pick from Arizona State, Bump Wills, an unseasoned rookie with only two minor-league seasons on his résumé.[5] When Randle complained, Lucchesi expressed surprise that someone so well paid and fortunate enough to be a major-league ballplayer should complain about such matters and went further, calling Randle a "punk." The on-field confrontation turned violent with Lucchesi suffering a broken jaw before the "fight" could be stopped by teammates. Randle was suspended, fined, and traded to the Mets. In a pair of ironically related events, the Rangers in 1977 enjoyed their best season to date with 94 wins and a second-place finish to the Kansas City Royals in the AL West. And Randle went on to enjoy his best season, hitting .304 in 136 games for the Mets. The lights may have gone out at Shea Stadium in 1977 but Lenny Randle shined brightly in the midst of a gloomy season of 98 losses for the Mets.

Randle's major-league career came to an end in 1982, at the age of 33, while he was with the Seattle Mariners. On June 18 he pinch-hit for Paul Serna, the Mariners shortstop, in the ninth inning and lined a single to center off Kansas City reliever Dan Quisenberry for the 1,016th hit of his major-league career. On the 20th, he was a ninth-inning defensive replacement at second base and didn't come to bat. On June 28, he was given his unconditional release by the Mariners. And thus was born the second life of Lenny Randle.

At the urging of Ted Williams and some friends in the military, Randle was encouraged to try a year of Italian baseball. In the spring of 1983, he became the regular second baseman for Nettuno of the Italian Baseball League and enjoyed great success, winning that season's batting championship with a audy average of .477.⁶ He was the first major-league player to compete professionally in Italy. It was love at first sight for Lenny and he soon had his whole family brought over to live there. He was affectionately known as "Cappuccino" because of his seemingly endless energy and reliance on little sleep each night. He said, "After I die there will be plenty of time to sleep. While I'm here, two to four hours is plenty!"⁷ In a Rolling Stone posting in 2015 Randle said, "I'm blessed and staying away from stress. It's the Fountain of Youth here. This is home to me. It's like utopia!"⁸

Randle, his wife, Linda, and sons Kumasi, Ahmad, and Bradley seem to have ventured into many different areas of life. Bradley enjoyed a brief fling in the NFL and the Canadian Football League after starring in football at the University of Nevada at Las Vegas. A cousin, Marques Johnson, played in the NBA. The eight Randle siblings own a nonprofit service that helps students discover and apply for college scholarships.

In 1980, Randle was elected to the Arizona State University Sports Hall of Fame for his football and baseball contributions.⁹ The citation mentioned his major-league career, and noted that as a football return specialist, he scored six touchdowns on kickoff and punt returns.

Randle travels frequently to Italy, where he promotes and conducts baseball clinics, and searches for that next Joe DiMaggio. He remains convinced that it is only a matter of time until some 10-year-old, receiving instructions at his baseball academy, grows into the first super star major-league ballplayer from Italy.

Randle was asked in an interview how he viewed his life. His surprising answer was, "I don't really think about it. I just do it! I live every day as if it was my last day on earth."¹⁰

Sources

In addition to the sources cited in the Notes, the author also consulted Baseball-Reference.com and the following:

Kantowski, Ron. "Frenetic Father Relishes Randle's Breakthrough," *Las Vegas Review-Journal*, November 4, 2012.

Miller, Mark. blitzweekly.com/lenny-randle-still-crazy-years/.

Stephen, Eric. sbnation.com/mlb/2015/12/11/9887920/lenny-randle-documentary-mlb-network-review.

Notes

1. MLB Network, *MLB Presents: Lenny Randle*, "The Most Interesting Man in Baseball," aired December 15, 2015.
2. In an interview reported on the blog "OAG Only a Game," Randle related how he and some teammates helped a victim of cerebral palsy, Davey Finnegan, buy a voice communicator with the song, "Just a Chance, Kingdome." He said they raised $20,000. wbur.org/onlyagame/2015/05/30/lenny-randle-mlb-history-kingdome.
3. Author interview with Lenny Randle, July 29, 2016. Unless otherwise indicated, all quotations attributed to Randle come from this interview.
4. Ibid.
5. Elliott "Bump" Wills was the son of Dodgers great Maury Wills.
6. Nettuno is located on the Mediterranean coast of Italy approximately 30 miles south-southeast of Rome. Named after Neptune, god of the sea. It is considered the birthplace of Italian baseball after American soldiers near the end of World War II taught the locals the game. Since 1948, the first year of the Italian Baseball League, Nettuno has been represented by a team in that league. web.archive.org/web/20101228220659/; centerfieldmaz.com/2010/02/former-met-of-day-lenny-randle-saga.html.
7. Norm Ordaz, interview with Lenny Randle, *Clubhouse Chatter*, February 28, 2016. clubhousechatter.mlblogs.com/2016/04/23/clubhouse-chatter-lenny-randle-2/.
8. Dan Epstein, "Lenny Randle's Italian Baseball Renaissance," *Rolling Stone*, April 16, 2015. rollingstone.com/sports/features/lenny-randles-italian-baseball-renaissance-20150416
9. thesundevils.com/sports/2000/8/16/208252919.aspx.
10. Norm Ordaz.

JIM ROLAND

BY GREGORY H. WOLF

Signed by the Minnesota Twins in 1961, left-hander Jim Roland debuted as a 19-year-old in a September call-up the following season and tossed a three-hit shutout in his first big-league start, in 1963. "[He] has a blazing fast ball and is effectively wild," wrote Twins beat reporter Arno Goethel.[1] Battling injuries and control issues throughout his ten-year big-league career, most notably with the Twins and Oakland A's (1962-1972), Roland never realized the potential his inaugural start suggested and was relegated to the unglamorous role of long reliever and mop-up artist. He was also unlucky: Seven years after Roland missed the Twins' pennant in 1965 when he spent the year in Triple-A, the A's sold him to the New York Yankees in 1972, the season they won their first of three consecutive World Series.

James Ivan Roland, Jr. was born on December 14, 1942, in the small town of Franklin, nestled in the Smoky Mountains of western North Carolina. His parents were James Ivan Sr., a pipefitter by trade, and Florence Virginia (Henson) Roland. By the time Jim was in the fourth grade in the early 1950s, the family had relocated to Raleigh, more than 300 miles to the east, where Jim Sr. found employment as a guard and maintenance man at a local prison. Like many youths, Jim Jr. got his start on the diamond in a local Little League. By the time he was a junior at Broughton High School in Raleigh, the tall (6-feet-3), yet thin (160-pound, though he grew bigger) hard-throwing southpaw had the attention of scouts. On the recommendation of scout Al Evans, Minnesota Twins executive vice president Joe Haynes signed Roland upon his graduation in 1961 for a $50,000 signing bonus. It was widely reported that the hefty financial incentive was the largest the Twins/Senators ever paid to a pitcher.[2] (The Washington Senators relocated to Minnesota for the 1961 season.)

Just weeks removed from high school, the 18-year-old Roland began his professional baseball career in the Class B Carolina League with the Wilson Tobs, a team located less than 50 miles from his hometown. Roland impressed the Twins brass by winning seven of 13 decisions and posting a fine 3.15 ERA in 123 innings for the first-place Tobs. After the season, he was added to the Twins' 40-man roster and sent to the Florida Instructional League to work on his control (4.9 walks per nine innings) with manager Del Wilber, a former big-league catcher and respected developer of young pitching prospects.[3]

Roland, coming off an ankle operation in the offseason, reported to Minnesota's spring-training facility in 1962. The Twins had finished with a lackluster 70-90 record (seventh place) in the first year of expansion in the AL, and desperately needed a hard-throwing lefty to compete with the likes of the New York Yankees and Detroit Tigers. With less than a full season of Class B ball under his belt, Roland was sent along with other prospects (outfielder Tony Oliva and another hard-throwing lefty, Gary Dotter)

to the Class A Charlotte (North Carolina) Hornets of the South Atlantic League (Sally). Roland struggled against more experienced competition (1-3, 4.17 ERA in 41 innings) and was reassigned to Wilson. Roland excelled for the below-.500 club. Named to the league's all-star team, he sported only a 10-8 record, but was the hardest-to-hit hurler in circuit (5.4 hits per nine innings), ranked second in ERA (1.98), and was third in strikeouts per nine innings (10.6). Twice the southpaw struck out 14 batters in a game to go along with 12 and 13 punchouts in two other contests.

Roland's performance with the Tobs earned him a late-season look-see with the Twins. On September 20 he made his major-league debut (and his only major-league appearance of the season). In relief of Jim Kaat, Roland tossed two scoreless innings, yielding a hit and striking out one.

The young lefty was back with Del Wilber in the Florida Instructional League in the fall of 1962. For all of his potential, Roland also walked 6.1 hitters per nine innings for the Tobs. Along with teammates Oliva, Orlando Martinez (infield-utility), and Joe McCabe (pitcher), Roland was named to the league's all-star team. He was also chosen as the "Rookie Pitcher" in the Florida Instructional League. He was widely expected to be the Twins' fifth starter in 1963.[4]

Roland made a big splash in his second camp with the Twins. "[He's] blossomed as the surprise of spring training," praised *The Sporting News*.[5] The newspaper also tabbed him as the "Best Young Pitcher" and the "Most Personable Newcomer" in light of his constant smile, talkative personality, and infectious enthusiasm.[6] "Lots of good natural stuff," said manager Sam Mele of his youthful prospect.[7] Roland earned his first big-league win in a wacky game on April 16, 1963, at Metropolitan Stadium. The eighth Twins pitcher of the contest, he tossed the last two frames against the Los Angeles Angels. He gave up a go-ahead run in the 13th inning, but was bailed out by the powerful Twins offense in the bottom of the frame. Roland tossed a masterful three-hit, 144-pitch shutout in his first major-league start, on April 21 against the Chicago White Sox at Comiskey Park.

He whiffed seven, but also walked nine, and got out of bases-loaded jams in the first and fifth innings. After struggling in his next four starts, Roland hurled a complete-game five-hitter on June 1 to defeat the Detroit Tigers, and seemed even stronger in his next outing, on June 5, when he held the Kansas City A's to just two hits in seven innings. However, that game proved to be disastrous for his career. "Something snapped," said Roland about the pain he felt in elbow after a pitch in that game.[8] "My elbow was swollen so much I couldn't wear a suit coat because the sleeve wouldn't fit over the elbow."[9] Save for a brief one-third-inning outing six weeks later, Roland was inactive for the rest of the season. Team physician Dr. Bill Profitt diagnosed the injury as ripping "scar tissue in his muscle," but not a tear, and prescribed rest.[10]

Sportswriter Arno Goethel, described Roland as "one of the biggest question marks in the Twins camp" in 1964.[11] The question mark got even bigger when Roland arrived in camp more than 40 pounds overweight – at about 223 pounds – drawing the ire of Mele.[12] The Twins had two dependable left-handed starters, Jim Kaat and Dick Stigman; consequently, Roland was tabbed as a swingman. He had counted primarily on his overhand fastball, curve, and effective changeup through his first three years in the pro ball, but added a slider to his repertoire in spring training. He unveiled the pitch in a spot start against New York in Yankee Stadium on May 19. He hurled a career-high 12 innings (and faced 50 batters), holding the eventual pennant winners to seven hits and two runs, while striking out eight and walking six. He was replaced by pinch-hitter Lenny Green in the 13th inning when the Twins exploded for five runs, making Roland the winner. Roland's 12-inning effort has been surpassed only twice in Minnesota Twins history (Camilo Pascual went 12⅔ innings against Cleveland in 1963 and Jim Merritt logged 13 innings against the Yankees in 1967.) "I've never seen a pitcher pick up [the slider] any faster," said pitching coach George Maltzberger about Roland's outing.[13] Two starts later the southpaw tossed an overpowering two-hitter against the Boston Red Sox, but struggled thereafter, losing four of his next five starts and his spot in the rotation. Confined to mop-up duty for the remainder of the season, Roland posted a 2-6 record and a 4.10 ERA in 94⅓ innings, while battling control problems (6.0 walks per nine innings).

Roland's once promising career had been marred by injuries (ankle and elbow), and by 1965 he seemed washed up at age 22. Dabbled as trade bait in the offseason, Roland struggled in spring training in 1965 under new pitching coach Johnny Sain. A pulled thigh muscle set him in further back in competition with Dwight Siebler, Dave Boswell, and Jim Merritt for a spot on the staff. He was optioned to the Denver Bears of the Triple-A Pacific Coast League, where a series of immature incidents made manager Cal Ermer question his commitment to the game. Roland injured his knee jumping in protest of a call by a first-base umpire in July. And he committed the cardinal sin of walking off the mound on several occasions while Ermer was on his way to remove him.[14] In primarily a starting role, the left-hander won eight, lost six, and posted a 3.81 ERA in 156 innings. He was recalled by the Twins in September but did not pitch.

Called a "problem kid" by Twins beat reporter Max Nichols, Roland reported to the Twins' spring training hoping for a new beginning.[15] He had been "disillusioned and discouraged" by his year in Denver, but appeared stronger and healthier in 1966.[16] "Roland is throwing the way he did in 1963 – hard and low," said team owner and general manager Calvin Griffith optimistically.[17] Roland also donned spectacles for the first time, claiming that poor depth perception had contributed to his erratic pitching. Despite the praise, Roland couldn't crack the deep Twins staff, and was sent back to Denver to start the season. Splitting his time with the Bears and the Syracuse Chiefs of the International League, Roland endured a horrific campaign, winning just six times, leading all Triple-A hurlers with 19 losses, and finishing with an unsightly 4.80 ERA in 163 innings. A September call-up, Roland made his first big-league appearance in more than two years by tossing two scoreless innings of mop-up duty in his only outing with the Twins.

Out of player options, Roland stuck with the Twins in 1967 and 1968. During spring training in 1967, an Associated Press story described Roland as "one of the most disappointing investments Calvin Griffith ever made."[18] Relegated to the unceremonious role of mop-up man, he logged only 35⅔ innings spread over 25 relief appearances in 1967 and 61⅔ innings (in 28 games) in 1968. His final win in a Twins uniform was a complete-game five-hitter (one of his four starts in the 1968 season) against the Washington Senators on August 27.

During those two years, the Twins tried everything to help Roland rekindle the magic his first start suggested. He joined less experienced prospects in the Florida Instructional league in 1967 in order to work extensively with Twins pitching coach, Early Wynn. The little-used Roland had developed bad habits and poor mechanics. "He's been bending his waist," said the future Hall of Fame pitcher, who admitted that it might be too late to reform the lefty.[19]

Roland's approach to life changed radically during his season with Aragua in the Venezuelan winter league in 1967-1968. He pitched well (5-3 with a 2.24 ERA, plus three more victories in the playoffs), but lying awake at night in his one-room accommodation made him take stock in his career and purpose in life. "Suddenly I felt that if I couldn't have my family with me, I needed somebody else on my side. I became a believer," he told Arno Goethel. "Since I've become more serious about Christianity, I've eased my mind."[20] For the remainder of his life, Roland was guided by his religious convictions.

The sale of Roland to the Oakland A's on February 24, 1969, merited little press coverage. In parts of six big-league seasons he had posted a 10-9 record and logged just 244⅔ innings. Nonetheless, the A's were willing to take a chance on the hard-throwing left-hander, especially since he was just 26. After 13 consecutive losing seasons in Kansas City (1955-1967), the A's were a team on the rise. In their maiden season in Oakland (1968), they enjoyed their first winning campaign since 1952, when they were located in Philadelphia and still owned by Connie Mack. Led by a young pitching staff including Catfish Hunter, Chuck Dobson, Blue Moon Odom, Jim Nash, Lew Krausse, and Rollie Fingers, the A's seemed poised for an even better season in 1969.

In his first year with Oakland, Roland enjoyed his best season in the big leagues. While right-hander Fingers and left-hander Paul Lindblad were the first two firemen out of the bullpen, Roland was assigned to long relief and often pitched in mop-up games. The A's lost 27 times in his 36 relief appearances (the team's overall record was 88-74), but Roland sparkled with a 2.82 ERA in 60⅔ innings out of the bullpen. With the pennant out of reach, manager John McNamara gave Roland a chance to start. The southpaw responded by winning a career-best three consecutive starts, beginning with a complete-game four-hitter against the California Angels in Anaheim on September 21. "This is the best year I've got control of both my slider and fastball every time I go out there," he said.[21] Roland will forever hold the distinction of pitching the final game against the Pilots in their brief, one-year tenure in Seattle. In the 162nd game of the season, Roland limited the Pilots to seven hits and matched his career high with nine strikeouts in a 3-1 victory in front of just 5,473 spectators in the final major-league game in Seattle's Sick's Stadium. An atrocious hitter, Roland also recorded his last hit in the big leagues (he went 6-for-84 with one RBI in his career). A's beat reporter Ron Bergman described Roland's showing as a starter as "impressive," while team brass promised to take a closer look at him as a fifth starter the next season.[22] He finished the season with a 5-1 record and career- and staff-low 2.19 ERA in 86⅓ innings.

Breaking into the A's starting rotation was easier said than done. The trio of Hunter, Dobson, and Odom had started 102 games between them and logged 713⅔ innings in 1969. However, the team lacked a left-handed starter. In spring training Roland competed for a job with hard-throwing Al Downing, acquired in the offseason from the New York Yankees. But Roland had an awful camp, struggled with mechanics, and was back in long relief, save for two ineffective starts.[23] Downing won the job, but was ineffective, and ultimately was sent to the Milwaukee Brewers at the trading deadline. Ron Bergman called Roland "one of the best (long relievers) in the business" and noted that the role is "one of the least respected jobs in baseball."[24] Roland hurled 2⅓ and 3⅔ innings to earn victories in August, but the latter win was costly. In that game, on August 11, he collided with the Cleveland Indians' Ray Fosse at home plate and tore ligaments in his right knee. "It was like hitting a wall," said Roland, who tried to jump over Fosse, instead of barreling over the catcher as Pete Rose had done about a month earlier in the All-Star game.[25] Roland landed on the disabled list and pitched just twice after that, finishing with a robust 2.70 ERA in 43⅓ innings spread over 28 appearances. His injury opened the door for the highly-touted prospect lefty Vida Blue, who was summoned from Triple-A Iowa.

With the triumvirate of Fingers, Bob Locker, and rubber-armed lefty Darold Knowles firmly ensconced as the A's relievers, Roland occupied his position at the far end of the bullpen bench in 1971. Manager Dick Williams called on him 31 times, and 26 of those were in mop-up losses. Roland went 1-3 with a 3.18 ERA in 45⅓ innings.

Plagued by recurring arm pain, Roland was a baseball nomad in 1972. After just two appearances for the A's, he was sold to the New York Yankees on April 28. A little more than four months (and 16 mainly ineffective appearances) later, he was traded to the Texas Rangers for pitcher Casey Cox. A combined 5.28 ERA in 30⅔ innings earned Roland his outright release from the Rangers. At just 29 years of age, Roland's professional career was over.

Roland chalked up a 19-17 record over parts of ten seasons, and compiled a 3.22 ERA in 450⅓ innings. In four seasons in the minor leagues, he went 32-42 with a 3.48 ERA in 651 innings.

After his playing days, Roland returned to North Carolina and began a long and successful career as a business representative for a sporting-goods company. He was active in the Elizabeth Baptist Church in his hometown of Shelby, North Carolina. Diagnosed with cancer, he retired from his job in January 2010.

On March 6, 2010, Roland died in Shelby. He was survived by his wife, Vicki (Whiten) Roland, and four adult children, James III, Jan, Lori, and Megan.26 He was buried in Oakland Cemetery, in Gaffney, South Carolina, his wife's hometown, about 20 miles from Shelby.

Sources

Chicago Tribune, New York Times, The Sporting News

Ancestry.com, BaseballAlmanac.com, BaseballCube.com, BaseballLibrary.com, Baseball-Reference.com

SABR.org

Notes

1. *The Sporting News*, February 1, 1964, 22.
2. *The Sporting News*, May 4, 1963, 9.
3. *The Sporting News*, October 11, 1961, 26.
4. *The Sporting News*, April 13, 1963, 5.
5. *The Sporting News*, April 6, 1963, 2.
6. *The Sporting News*, April 20, 1963, 14.
7. *The Sporting News*, May 4, 1963, 9.
8. *The Sporting News*, February 1, 1964, 22.
9. Ibid.
10. *The Sporting News*, December 7, 1963, 22.
11. *The Sporting News*, February 1, 1964, 22.
12. *The Sporting News*, March 26, 1966, 12.
13. *The Sporting News*, June 4, 1964, 8.
14. *The Sporting News*, July 17, 1965, 50.
15. *The Sporting News*, March 26, 1966, 12.
16. Ibid.
17. Ibid.
18. Associated Press, "Jim Roland May Yet Repay Twins," *The Daily Republic* (Mitchell, South Dakota), March 28, 1967, 9.
19. *The Sporting News*, October 28, 1967, 20.
20. *The Sporting News*, September 21, 1967, 9.
21. *The Sporting News*, September 27, 1969, 16.
22. *The Sporting News*, October 18, 1969, 36.
23. *The Sporting News*, April 18, 1970, 12.
24. *The Sporting News*, September 5, 1970, 10.
25. Ibid.
26. Obituary, *Shelby* (North Carolina) *Star*. legacy.com/obituaries/shelbystar/obituary.aspx?n=jim-roland&pid=140499740.

JIM SHELLENBACK

BY PAUL GEISLER

The tall, lanky left-handed pitcher started with youth baseball, excelled in the minor leagues, played for four major-league teams, then continued as a pitching coach at various levels to complete a 50-year career in baseball.

Standing 6-feet-2 and weighing 200 pounds, James Philip "Jim" Shellenback, born November 18, 1943, in Riverside, California, grew up in a baseball family and had quite a legacy to follow. His father's younger brother, Frank, pitched briefly in the major leagues, won 316 minor-league contests, and had a long career as a major-league pitching coach and minor-league coach and manager.

James's great-grandparents emigrated from Germany to settle in Ohio, probably originally with the name Schellenbach. His grandfather, John Albert Shellenback, married Carolyn "Carrie" Nolte and settled in the Joplin, Missouri, area, where they had five children, including next-to-youngest Paul (Jim's father) and Frank (his uncle). The family moved to Riverside, California, and Paul married Beatrice LeBlanc Henry, from Plymouth, Massachusetts, and of French background. Paul worked in auto sales and later as an accountant for the US Department of the Interior. Paul and Beatrice had six children – four boys and two girls.

Young Jim, the next to youngest of the six kids, progressed through the ranks of Little League, Pony, and Colt baseball, with his Riverside team going to the 1960 Colt League World Series. Although he never met his uncle Frank, who stayed busy as a major-league pitching coach, Frank gave his nephew a new glove at the start of each season.[1]

Jim became a standout at Riverside Ramona High School as both a pitcher and right fielder. He once hit a 435-foot grand slam.[2] Although he claimed he "goofed around too much" and "should have done better," the school inducted this 1962 graduate into the Ramona Sports Hall of Fame in April 2015.[3]

One of Jim's Little League coaches, Ray Viers, scouted for the New York Yankees, as a "bird dog," hoping to find local talent for the big club. In 1961, on Viers' recommendation, a Yankee scout came to see the high schooler pitch, and soon signed him to a $4,000 contract. Jim promptly used the money to buy a new car.[4]

Shellenback began his professional career in 1962 in the Class-D Appalachian League with the Harlan Smokies. He advanced the same season to the Class-C Pioneer League, with the Idaho Falls Yankees. Drafted by the Pittsburgh Pirates from the Yankees in the 1962 first-year draft, he went to the Gastonia Pirates (Class A) of the Western Carolinas League, where he spun a string of seven consecutive wins and earned a spot on the league All-Star team. He moved to Double A the next year with Asheville of the Southern League, and again earned a spot on the All-Star squad. He split time in 1965 with Asheville and Triple-A Columbus of the International League.

After the 1965 season, Shellenback played winter ball in Nicaragua and developed into one of the best pitchers in the league, until the US military summoned him away. Abraham Gorn, owner of the Boer team in the Nicaragua League, called the US ambassador with an unsuccessful bid to arrange a 30-day deferment for the young pitcher, who saw himself inching closer to a spot on the Pittsburgh roster.[5]

After completing training with the Marine Reserve, Shellenback drove from San Diego, then to his home in Riverside, then on to training camp in Florida. The last battery man to report, Shellenback went straight to bed with flu symptoms.[6] Although he competed for a spot on the Pirates that spring, he ended up in Columbus again, where he pitched himself onto the All-Star team with the league-leading Jets.

The Pirates called him up in September, and he made his major-league debut at Dodger Stadium on September 15, pitching the eighth inning in a losing cause. A week later, he made one more appearance with two innings pitched in another Pirates loss. Shellenback excelled in the Dominican League that winter and continued to make Pittsburgh general manager Joe L. Brown's top list of prospects.

Shellenback began the 1967 season on the Pirates roster. He pitched in relief three times in April without allowing a run, then the team shipped him back to Columbus. The Marines called him away that summer for a 17-day commitment.

After he completed the Columbus season, Shellenback returned to the Pirates in September. On the 25th he made his first major-league start and gained his first big-league victory with a dazzling 11-inning complete game, beating the Los Angeles Dodgers 2-1, allowing just six hits and two walks. He suffered his first losing decision on September 30, the next-to-last day of the season.

On the evening after that loss to Houston, Shellenback had dinner with a date at a friend's house in a suburb of Pittsburgh. The evening drizzle made the roads slick. He remembered crossing a bridge in the passing lane "at a safe speed with both hands on the wheel. All of a sudden I could feel the rear wheels spin. Within a couple of seconds I was staring at oncoming headlights." His car met head-on with another one.

"I was in a daze after the impact," Shellenback said. "My chest hurt mostly, and I felt shooting pains in my right leg. I was slumped against the steering wheel, and I was scared. I really thought I'd 'had it,' and this was a helluva way to go."[7]

Shellenback went to Braddock General Hospital with a compound fracture of his right leg, a rib fracture, and internal injuries. He spent 11 days in the hospital. His passenger, Carolyn Arizberger, taken to Columbia Hospital, suffered head injuries and lacerations. The other driver had cuts and bruises.[8]

Pirates team physician Joseph Finegold reported that Shellenback "did not appear to be in danger and there should be no further complications."[9] Shellenback had established himself as a very viable member of future Pittsburgh pitching staffs, yet his pitching career faced some major questions.

In mid-January of 1968 Shellenback went to Florida, determined to return to his former pitching form. The cast remained on his right leg until February, when team doctors reported him "progressing well" and allowed him to continue his plans to prepare for spring training.[10] Unable to run, he limped into training camp 10 days ahead of the other players. He spent "endless time in the training room, in the whirlpool, and having massage treatments on his leg."[11]

Shellenback missed most of the first half of the 1968 season and made his first start back in Columbus on June 16. He marked his first victory in July, after five straight losses. By mid-August his comeback seemed complete; he had evened his record at 6-6.

"Nobody expected me to be able to pitch this season," commented Shellenback. "We didn't think he would be able to pitch an inning this season," added general manager Brown. "He's shown a lot of courage with this year's performance."[12] Shellenback finished the 1968 season with Columbus with a 9-8 record, making 18 starts in 25 appearances over 142 innings with an ERA of 2.85. "It has been a minor miracle," concluded team physician John Stephens, who worked with Shellenback on his recovery.

Shellenback started 1969 with the Pirates and pitched 16⅔ innings in eight appearances before being traded to the Washington Senators on May 17 for another left-handed pitcher, Frank Kreutzer. In Washington Shellenback got more opportunity, mostly as a reliever. He won his first American League start, 4-1, on June 12 against the Oakland Athletics, but finished the year with a mediocre record of 4-7 and a 4.04 ERA.

In his first full season in the major leagues, Shellenback found himself under rookie manager Ted Williams, whose first manager in professional baseball had been Jim's Uncle Frank at San Diego in 1936. Frank gets credited with converting Williams from a pitcher to an outfielder, who hit .406 for the Boston Red Sox five years later, on the way to a career batting average of .344 over 19 seasons. As Jim recalled the story, one day Frank went to the mound to talk with his pitcher, Williams. "Ted told him, 'I think I'd do better in the outfield,' and that's where he stayed."[13]

Williams remembered Frank fondly. "Remember, I was just a 17-year-old kid, and this man was good to me."[14] The last pitcher to throw a legal spitball in Organized Baseball, Frank had an amazing career himself, mostly in the Pacific Coast League. He played the first part of the 1919 season with the Chicago White Sox, and avoided the World Series scandal that year, pitching the rest of the season with Minneapolis of the American Association. In 1920, when he was 21 years old, the major leagues declared his spitball illegal. He spent the next 19 years, throwing his spitball successfully in the PCL. Frank remains one of the winningest pitchers in professional baseball. Bill James referred to him as perhaps "the best pitcher in the history of the minor leagues."[15]

Jim Shellenback remembered Williams as a manager who liked the curveball, but said little to the pitching staff, relying a lot on pitching coach Sid Hudson. Ted "wasn't too bad," Shellenback said. "He wasn't really hard on you or anything like that. He gave me a lot of chances." The team included several veterans and coaches like Nellie Fox, who helped compensate for Williams's lack of managing experience. Joe Camacho stood together with Williams in the dugout and helped make lineup moves.[16]

On an offday in July 1969, Jim married Jo Ann Carol Wilshe in Fairfax, Virginia. On the marriage certificate he listed the street address of his "usual residence" as RFK Stadium. They had a son, James Philip Shellenback Jr., born in 1970 in Florida. The marriage ended in divorce in 1978. He married a second time in November 1982, to Mary Theresa Meigs in Florida. The couple divorced in 2001.

Shellenback continued with the Senators through the 1970 and 1971 seasons with 6-7 and 3-11 records, respectively. His pitched his first shutout on July 25, 1970, against the California Angels. All three of his victories in 1971, one of them a shutout, came against the New York Yankees. Jim changed his approach midway through the 1971 season by focusing on a strong first pitch to each batter, instead of nibbling. He worried about a possible trade or a demotion to the minors. "No matter what they tell me, I knew I was on the way to the minors if I didn't start doing something different."[17]

During the 1971 season, some of the Senators players formed "The Underminers Club," dedicated to getting Williams replaced as manager. They held clandestine meetings and dressed in sheets, resembling Ku Klux Klan members.[18] According to Shellenback, "[Denny] McLain was the perpetrator of the whole thing. He used to go out of his way to break every rule that Ted had on the ballclub." Williams expected his players to follow close to his own lifestyle, of getting up early and getting busy. He allowed a nap in the afternoon, if necessary, before getting to the ballpark. Shellenback remembered him being pretty lenient and needing to enforce many of the rules, until McLain joined the team. "Then [Williams] pretty much started dropping fines and stuff like that. McLain was pretty much out of control."[19]

In 1972, with Williams still manager and most of the dissidents traded, the Senators relocated to Texas. A member of the initial Texas Rangers roster, Shellenback set the record for the number of letters on a Texas uniform with 11. Eight others tied that record until 30 years later, when Todd Hollandsworth joined the Rangers in 2002.[20]

Shellenback started the season with Texas as a spot starter and reliever and began to have some growing success. Leaving his 3-11 season behind him, he began to show "every sign of being the southpaw starter that Williams wants."[21] Then on July 11, tragedy struck again. Jim broke his ankle in a game in Detroit against the Tigers on a play covering first base on a ground ball. He had his leg in a cast for six weeks and did not pitch again that season.[22]

He spent most of 1973 with the Spokane Indians, the Rangers affiliate in the Pacific Coast League. Winning 13 games there, mostly as a starter for the 1973 PCL champions, Shellenback returned to the Rangers for two relief appearances in September. After 11 relief appearances with Texas to start 1974, Shellenback returned to Spokane, winning another PCL championship with the Indians.

The San Diego Padres bought Shellenback's contract from the Rangers before the 1975 season and assigned him to the Hawaii Islanders, their affiliate in the PCL. On a PCL championship team for the third season in a row, Shellenback also helped set a team record when the pitching staff notched 28 consecutive scoreless innings. In 1976, he stayed with Hawaii as both starter and reliever with a 7-5 record and a 4.29 ERA.

Released by the Padres, Shellenback signed with the Minnesota Twins in the spring of 1977 as a minor-league pitching coach, replacing Ray Berres. He pitched two innings for the Twins in the annual Hall of Fame exhibition game in Cooperstown as they beat the Philadelphia Phillies, 8-5. He had his final opportunity to pitch in the big leagues when the Twins signed him as a free agent in August. Called up in September, he made five appearances, all in relief, with no decisions and a 7.94 ERA.

In 1978, Shellenback returned to his role working with minor-league pitchers in the Twins organization with the Triple-A Portland (Oregon) Beavers. In June 1988, when Jim Mahoney abruptly resigned as manager, Shellenback took charge of the team for the rest of the season. He returned to his pitching-coach position to start 1989. In 1994 he moved to the Twins rookie-level team in Elizabethton, Tennessee, in the Appalachian League, where he stayed until he retired after the 2011 season. As of 2018, he lived in Arizona.

Shellenback played and coached baseball his whole life. His major-league career covers parts of nine seasons with four different teams. He compiled a record of 16 wins 30 losses, and two saves, with a 3.81 ERA. He pitched 454 innings in 165 games, including 48 starts, eight complete games, and two shutouts. He produced no spectacular numbers, but his baseball career remains a testimony to what strong determination and a love for baseball can accomplish.

Notes

1. "Major Flashes," *The Sporting News*, August 9, 1961: 23.
2. "Rams Crush Bucs, 18-2," *San Bernardino County Sun*, April 12, 1961: 8.
3. David Zink, "Shellback Joins Ramona's Sports Hall of Fame," *Riverside* (California) *Press-Enterprise* (scng.com), April 21, 2015.
4. Ibid.
5. Horacio Ruiz, "Loss of Shellenback and Dees Damages Boer Pennant Push," *The Sporting News*, January 15, 1966: 25.
6. Les Biederman, "Pirates Eye Sleeper in New Gonder," *The Sporting News*, March 12, 1966: 22.
7. Eddie Fisher, "Gimpy, Gutsy Jim Shellenback Is Comeback Kid at Columbus," *The Sporting News*, September 11, 1968: 27.
8. "Buc Pitcher Injured in Auto Crash," *Pittsburgh Post-Gazette*, October 2, 1967: 5.
9. "Pirates' Shellenback in Car Crash," *Pittsburgh Press*, October 2, 1967: 39.
10. *Pittsburgh Post-Gazette*, January 9, 1968: 17.
11. Fisher.
12. Bob Black, "Farmhands Make Most of City Visit," *Pittsburgh Press*, August 13, 1968: 34.

13 Bill Nowlin, interview with Jim Shellenback, June 8, 1997.
14 Merrell Whittlesey, "Ted-Shelly Combo Revives Old Tune," *The Sporting News*, August 16, 1969: 18.
15 Brian McKenna, "Frank Shellenback," Society for American Baseball Research BioProject.
16 Nowlin, Shellenback interview, June 8, 1997.
17 "Nats Shower Broberg with Stream of Kudos," *The Sporting News*, July 12, 1971: 27.
18 Wells Twombly, "A Hard Fall for the Super Pitcher," *The Sporting News*, June 3, 1972: 17.
19 Bill Nowlin, interview with Jim Shellenback, June 15, 1997.
20 "Notebook – Another Late Collapse?" *Democrat and Chronicle* (Rochester, New York), August 4, 2002: 9.
21 Randy Galloway, "Rangers Hurlers Sharp; Hitters Take a Vacation," *The Sporting News*, June 3, 1972: 29.
22 "Tiger Notes," *Lansing* (Michigan) *State Journal*, July 13, 1972: 36.

DON STANHOUSE

BY MAXWELL KATES

Although his tenure in Baltimore was limited to two good seasons and a comeback year, both of the nicknames for which Don Stanhouse became famous were earned while wearing an Orioles uniform. Manager Earl Weaver, overly apprehensive every time Stanhouse was retrieved from the bullpen, called him "Full Pack" after the number of cigarettes he was known to smoke each time he pitched.[1] Stanhouse's teammate Mike Flanagan called him "Stan the Man Unusual" as a play on words to rhyme with the surname of a St. Louis Cardinals' Hall of Famer. There was, however, far more to the pitching career of Don Stanhouse than a pair of colorful nicknames. During his decade in the major leagues, as he sported a red afro and occasional walrus moustache, he perfected his skills both as a starting pitcher and as a short reliever in a career which took him from Cowtown to Tinseltown by way of la Belle Province and the Land of Pleasant Living. Stanhouse reached the pinnacle of his performance in 1979, the year he earned both an All-Star berth and a trip to the World Series with the Orioles. Injuries may have cut short his career after winning a free-agent jackpot with the Los Angeles Dodgers but he remains a unique character in the memories of his fans and the media.

Donald Joseph Stanhouse was born on February 12, 1951 in DuQuoin, Illinois to a family of Scottish-Irish background.[2] As a high school student, Stanhouse earned All-American honors in baseball and football and was regarded as the best athlete the school had ever produced in both sports. As John Croessman reported in the *Evening Call*, "DuQuoin could find itself on the 4th down, 12 or 15 yards out, and the confident Stanhouse would drop back, roll out the side, and throw a 'Hail Mary' pass 56 yards from the Murphysboro 44."[3] In light of his heroics on the Van Meter Field gridiron, Stanhouse was recruited by Dan Devine at the University of Missouri on a football scholarship and also was selected by the Oakland A's as a third baseman with number nine pick in the first round of the June 1969 draft. He faced a decision most aspiring athletes would drool over: whether to accept a football scholarship at Missouri or sign a contract with the Oakland Athletics. It was a win-win situation with Devine and Charlie Finley working things out where Stanhouse could get a college education and pursue a major-league career.

In his first professional season in the Northwest League, he was redeveloped as a pitcher while continuing to play third base. Though reluctant to switch positions initially, he was convinced by manager Billy Herman that while it could take four to six years to reach the major leagues as a third baseman, that time would be halved as a pitcher. Stanhouse made the switch and emerged as the top pitching prospect in the Oakland organization within three years.

"I know the Oakland people were high on me and I also knew there was an opening for a 5th starter in their rotation of Vida Blue, Ken Holtzman, Catfish

Hunter, and Blue Moon Odom. So I went to spring training [in 1972] feeling like I would get a good shot at making the rotation."[4] The A's were coming off a record of 101-60 with a division title in 1971. Since Vida Blue, the reigning Most Valuable Player and the man responsible for 24 of those victories, was holding out for a better contract, Stanhouse was warmly welcomed to the group and had reasons to feel cautiously optimistic about cracking the rotation. What he never expected was a trade before Opening Day, least of all to the "new" Texas Rangers.

"I was really surprised when they told me about the trade, but when I learned who it was for, I knew the Rangers must have a lot of confidence in me."[5] Oakland sent Stanhouse and Jim Panther to Texas on March 4, 1972 for Denny McLain. After the season opener was protracted by labor action, Stanhouse lived up to scouting expectations in his major-league debut on April 19, 1972, a bleak 40-degree afternoon in Chicago. Stanhouse introduced himself to the American League by striking out the side in the first inning. Relying mainly on fastballs, his totals for the day included five hits, one run, nine strikeouts, and three walks in 6 2/3 innings. Despite a 2-1 triumph by the White Sox, Stanhouse beamed with pride that he "got [Dick] Allen twice on the fastball."[6] For the season, he posted a respectable 3.78 earned run average despite a record of 2-9. The Rangers, meanwhile, posted a ghastly record of 54-100 playing before empty bleachers in unbearable heat in their first season after transferring from Washington. Manager Ted Williams resigned after the season and was replaced by Whitey Herzog. The relationship Stanhouse endured with his new manager tested his mettle during his sophomore season.

The 1973 Rangers picked up right where they left off in 1972, in the basement of the American League West. As Herzog told Mike Shropshire of the Fort Worth Star-Telegram, he did not know if he were managing a baseball team or a Mexican bus station.[7] Stanhouse did not exude confidence in his new manager. In his first appearance of the season in Kansas City on April 11, the 22-year-old right-hander yielded a walk-off home run to Paul Schaal.[8] By Memorial Day, Stanhouse's record deteriorated to 0-5. His job appeared secure, at least temporarily, as his earned run average of 4.23 was sufficient to lead the team.[9] Stanhouse was still a bachelor and his manager grew concerned that his concentration was focused on diversions away from the baseball diamond: "The other day, when Stanley was pitching in Minnesota, I swear, he kept on staring at this [striking woman] sitting behind the Twins' dugout. Well, everybody on our bench was staring at her too. But we weren't trying to pitch to Harmon Killebrew!"[10]

Stanhouse had no problem focusing on June 13, 1973 in Cleveland when he and starter Pete Broberg outpitched Hall of Famer Gaylord Perry to achieve his first save in organized baseball. Exhibiting the confidence he displayed playing high school football, as he sat on the bench before the ninth inning, "...I had a real strong feeling and I told myself I was going to strike out the side."[11] After fanning John Lowenstein and Buddy Bell, he surrendered a single to Jack Brohamer before George Hendrick was called out on strikes. Despite the poise Stanhouse demonstrated on the mound, it was his mischievous attitude that rankled the conservative Rangers' establishment. Later that night on a flight to Baltimore, Shropshire remembers that "...Stanhouse, still flush from his resounding ninth inning in Cleveland, prowled the aisles, autographing paper napkins and stuffing them into the shirt pockets of the various passengers who had no idea who Stanhouse was or what convention he and his bizarre cronies were headed to."[12]

Entering a July 2 contest to preserve a 3-2 lead for phenom David Clyde, Stanhouse surrendered two runs and dropped his record to 1-7. By now, Herzog was resolved to demote his colourful pitcher at the first opportunity. Within two weeks, Jackie Brown had been summoned from AAA Spokane at the expense of Stanhouse's spot on the roster.[13] While pitching for Spokane, an incident on a flight retuning from Hawaii unfairly cemented Stanhouse's reputation with the Rangers as an agitator: "One player got mouthy with a [stewardess] and she went and got the agent. The agent wanted to kick the guy off the plane. It was not the player that had caused the problem but he mouthed off. I defended the player because I figured we were all together. The agent said 'OK, you're off too.'"[14] The local media had misinterpreted the story, accusing Stanhouse of anything from attempting to fly the plane to luring a stewardess into the latrine with him. The Rangers bought the media's side of the story and never recalled Stanhouse when the rosters expanded.

By 1974, Billy Martin had replaced Whitey Herzog as the manager. Having already won division titles with reclamation projects in Minnesota and Detroit, Martin had little interest in punishing players for their actions off the field; he told Stanhouse that "Those things don't matter as long as you play well for me." Stanhouse once again split the 1974 season between the Rangers and Spokane. The Montreal Expos saw enough potential in his fastball to acquire him and infielder Pete Mackanin on December 5, 1974 for Willie Davis. He began the 1975 season in Memphis for Karl Kuehl and quickly made a believer in his new manager. On May 12, Stanhouse one-hit the Richmond Braves, 8-0, on only 95 pitches. By the time he was promoted to Montreal in June, he had amassed a record of 6-5 with a sterling earned run average of only 1.92. Injuries limited Stanhouse to four Montreal appearances for Gene Mauch in 1975 and as training camp broke the following season the Expos nearly outrighted him off the major-league roster. Stanhouse was out of options, but the team's new manager insisted on keeping him. That manager's name was Karl Kuehl.

Stanhouse proved to be one of the few pleasant surprises on the 1976 Montreal Expos. Although his record of 9-12 would ordinarily appear modest, he was particularly valuable considering how injuries and inexperience limited the Expos to a record of 55-107. Beginning the season in the bullpen, Stanhouse was promoted to the starting rotation in June when ace Steve Rogers was injured with a broken hand. In his first start, he snapped a six-game losing streak by limiting the Pirates to five hits in a 7-1 victory. Stanhouse helped his cause by belting a two-run single and was treated to a standing ovation by the sparse crowd at Jarry Park. Kuehl complimented Stanhouse, affirming that "he's always pitched well for me. That's the way he pitched at Memphis last year."[15]

After losing his next start to the Giants, Stanhouse pitched an impressive 3-0 shutout over the Padres. He was now 4-2 for a team 12 games under .500, responsible for two of the four complete games for the entire rotation. Stanhouse continued to pitch well, and after defeating the Giants at home on August 9, his record stood at 8-5 while his 2.60 earned run average was second in the National League only to Fred Norman's 2.38.[16] Stanhouse had rewarded Kuehl and his coaches for staying the course and ignoring criticism. As he conveyed to Bob Dunn of the *Montreal Star* early in the season, "I'm erratic. I know that. Consistence is the name of the game. Give me a little time."[17] In 26 consecutive starts, Stanhouse was an unsung hero for the Expos. It was a battle every day, every game and he was ready to do his part.

Stanhouse had additional challenges as training camp broke for the Expos in 1977. Replacing Kuehl as manager was Dick Williams, who arrived in Montreal with a reputation as a style of hardnosed, no-nonsense leadership. Stanhouse was determined to erase Williams' opinion of the Montreal rotation as "Steve Rogers and a bunch of no-names."[18] As he discussed with Ian MacDonald of the Montreal Gazette, "I know I can win. I just have to get my act together and prove it again this spring."[19] Despite his lacklustre performance in Daytona Beach, Stanhouse was rewarded by Williams as the Number 2 starter behind Steve Rogers.

"I've always believed that Rogers was the one pitcher here who thought I could be number 2. I have to believe in myself. I have always believed [that] if there were going to be two right-handed starters here, I had to be one of them."[20]

In his first start of the 1977 season at Veterans Stadium, Stanhouse surrendered five earned runs in five hits before Bill Atkinson won the game in relief over Philadelphia. His next start on April 15 would be the first game played at the cavernous new Olympic Stadium. A two-run homer by Ellis Valentine marked the entire offensive output for the Expos as they were defeated 9-2, also by the Phillies. Although

Stanhouse later admitted he was struggling with a virus, Williams was not impressed. But, Williams knew he had a great arm and a pitcher with a no quit attitude, but, could he get hitters out.

"Maybe he belongs in the bullpen," the manager quipped.21 Stanhouse was not pleased with Williams' decision, though one would not know it from his pitching record. In 31 relief appearances, he went 6-2 with 10 saves and a 1.52 earned run average.22 Although rated by one publication among the 10 most effective relief pitchers in baseball, Stanhouse was paid less than 70% of the Expos' pitching staff. 23 After struggling with contract negotiations, the Expos traded Stanhouse, along with pitcher Joe Kerrigan and outfielder Gary Roenicke, to the Baltimore Orioles for pitchers Rudy May, Randy Miller, and Bryn Smith on December 7, 1977.

Initially, a carefree bachelor such as Stanhouse might have been disappointed to relinquish the Ste. Catherine Street nightlife – the envy of Major League Baseball – for a city where entertainment had been described by Norm Cash as going "down the street and [watching] hubcaps rust."24 However, the trade to Baltimore allowed Stanhouse the opportunity to reach an accomplishment he could never have achieved had he stayed in Montreal – to pitch in a World Series. Years after Stanhouse retired, he explained to Baltimore Sun writer Mike Klingaman the significance behind his 'Unusual' nickname:

Stanhouse's unorthodox nature extended far beyond his pitching delivery. He would arrive in spring training in a black Cadillac to match his outfit and the paint scheme of his apartment. He used to bring a stuffed gorilla to the games, perhaps the inspiration for the primal screams he would yelp as batting practice concluded and the game was about to start.25 Then there was the 'sleeper' egged on by teammates Lee May and Terry Crowley. "I'd go into the stretch and drop my head, like I'd fallen asleep. Eventually the hitter would stomp out of the box and the umpire would come out and say 'Wake up!'"26 When he did, the game was over!

Antics aside, the 1978 Orioles found themselves in a pennant race with the defending World Champion New York Yankees, an iconic Boston Red Sox team, and the surprising Milwaukee Brewers. Ironically, the strength of Orioles teams of the past – pitching – proved to be their undoing, preventing the Charm City squadron from finishing higher than fourth-place. The bullpen was particularly suspect as relievers Joe Kerrigan, Tim Stoddard, and Tippy Martinez all struggled early in the season. On the other hand, in spite of Weaver's outward anxiety whenever Stanhouse pitched, he expressed great confidence in his new right-handed bullpen specialist: "He's my short man, whether it be right-handed or left-handed hitters." When asked if Weaver had ever stayed with a closer for an entire season, he replied, "I can't remember that I ever did," adding that Stanhouse "[has] shown that he can get the job done, so I'm going to stay with him." Pitching coach Ray Miller further illustrated Weaver's remarks, "he won't give into the hitters, even if he gets behind on the count. He continues to go after them with his pitch. That may be why he walks a few, but it's also why he gets people out."27

Indeed, Stanhouse walked nine batters in his first 13 innings of the season. On the other hand, by April 30, he registered five saves – five more than any of his teammates – while limiting the opposition to a minuscule 0.67 ERA. On July 4 in Cleveland, Stanhouse notched his 12th save, thus matching the season record for any Orioles relief pitcher under Weaver. However, the way he pitched might have been enough for Weaver to single handily propel the share price of his Raleigh cigarettes. As Jim Henneman of the Baltimore Sun reported, Stanhouse was forced to convert two double plays in order to save himself from base running situations that were his own doing. He put them on so he would know where they were at!

"I know I have too many walks for a relief pitcher and I know the reason I walk so many," Stanhouse pleaded with Henneman. "It's because I won't throw for the middle of the plate. It's just the way I pitch."28 On a lighter note, he later admitted that he thought he was cheating the fans if he enticed the batter to pop out on one pitch when he could work the count on six or seven.²⁹ Stanhouse also admitted culture shock in adjusting to Weaver's style of managing his bullpen, asking his relievers to warm up three or four times before he would bring them into a game. He could have also used a little luck from the batting order. During the first half of 1978, the Orioles scored only twice after Stanhouse entered the game. His record for the season was 6-9 with a 2.89 ERA and 24 saves, one short of the franchise record set by Stu Miller. It is said that Weaver taunted him about the record to get him ready for the next year.

Following the 1978 season, the Orioles tweaked their roster by signing free agent pitcher Steve Stone and purchasing the contract of John Lowenstein from the Texas Rangers. In spite of these personnel moves, expectations for 1979 were modest as owner Jerold Hoffberger put the team up for sale. Stanhouse remembers the anticipated competition to become the top American League team: "You look at the Yankees, Boston and California and their personnel they had that year and you think, 'Wow, were they good!' But you know something? We beat 'em all."³⁰ Baltimore generated a record of 102-57, the best in baseball for 1979. After a typically slow April, the Orioles catapulted themselves into a comfortable first-place lead by the end of May, claiming 11 of their 23 June victories in the eighth inning or later. Under the banner of "Oriole Magic," it seemed a different player was the game's hero every night. Large crowds became the norm at Memorial Stadium rather than the exception, the most vocal of whom was William G. "Wild Bill" Hagy. Hagy led cheers from Section 34 at the Orioles' old stadium during the 1970s and 1980s. He spelled out O-R-I-O-L-E-S with his body while fans yelled each letter in unison. You knew you were at an Orioles home game when you heard 40,000 Baltimore accents exclaim "O!" in unison during the "Star-Spangled Banner."

For at least 21 of those victories, Don Stanhouse could count himself among the Orioles' heroes – one for every save he achieved in 1979. In July, he was invited to accompany Ken Singleton as Orioles representatives at the All-Star Game in Seattle. Singleton pinch hit and Stanhouse did not get into the game.

Both unhappy with the 6-5 loss to the senior circuit, it was time to move on to more important things for the two All Stars. And, they and the Baltimore Orioles went on to win the American League East and won more games (102) that any team in major-league baseball that year.

After posting a record of 7- 3 with a 2.85 ERA during the regular season, Stanhouse was summoned from the bullpen to relieve Jim Palmer in Game One of the ALCS against the California Angels. True to the fundamentals of "the Oriole Way," Stanhouse won the opener on pitching, defense, and a three-run homer – hit by Pat Kelly in the bottom of the 10th inning. Victory was no easier for the Orioles in Game Two, as Stanhouse entered the game with nobody out in the bottom of the eighth inning to preserve a 9-4 lead for Mike Flanagan. A run scored on a double-play ball, a sacrifice fly, and two RBI singles later, the Orioles lead had now dwindled to 9-8 before Stanhouse ended the game with the bases loaded. When asked why he had not sent his ace reliever to the showers, Weaver candidly answered, "I still had three cigarettes left!"³¹ The Orioles went on to win the ALCS series on a complete-game shutout by Scott MacGregor.

Stanhouse saw action in three games of the 1979 World Series. In Game Two, he yielded an RBI single to Manny Sanguillen to give the Pirates a 3-2 lead. He also pitched in Game Five and the deciding Game Seven in which Pittsburgh claimed the World Championship. It was a classic World Series with the Pirates coming back to win after being down three games to one. Stanhouse was not a factor during the series as he had been most of that year. It was said the Chuck Tanner, the Pirates manager, had to keep Stanhouse out of the game in the late innings.

Stanhouse would find his name in far more headlines after the conclusion of the season as an impending free agent. After losing key free agents Reggie Jackson, Bobby Grich, and Wayne Garland under Hoffberger, the Orioles were now under new management. In a classic battle of words between attorneys, however, new owner Edward Bennett Williams proved to be no match for Morden "Cookie" Lazarus.

Stanhouse's Montreal-based agent demanded a five-year, $1.5 million contract, which was comparable to what the Atlanta Braves were paying closer Gene Garber, also a Lazarus client.[32] Williams scoffed at Lazarus' demands, which average to $300,000 a season. Since Jim Palmer earned $265,000 in 1979, argued Ken Nigro of the Baltimore Sun, Palmer "would be the first at [GM Hank] Peters' doorstep should Stanhouse be offered more."[33]

Talks soon broke off between Lazarus and the Orioles. Meanwhile, after appearing in both the 1977 and 1978 World Series, the Los Angeles Dodgers were rebounding from their first losing season in over a decade. At the apex of general manager Al Campanis' shopping list were a starting pitcher and an effective closer. The 1979 free agent blitz would be the Dodgers' first after the death of Walter O'Malley. Under the senior O'Malley, the Dodgers were risk averse against signing high profile free agents. On November 17, two days after breaking the bank to lure starter Dave Goltz from Minnesota, the Dodgers inked Don Stanhouse to a five-year, $2.1 million contract. As he told Gordon Verrell of the *Long Beach Press Telegram*, "I've got the pot of gold at the end of the rainbow."[34] His new manager, Tommy Lasorda, did not smoke, but his love for Italian food was already well known throughout baseball. Would "Full Pack" become "Full Plate" each time he was called upon to pitch?

Living in an exclusive ocean-view ninth-floor condominium in Marina del Ray, Stanhouse was in awe of his newfound lifestyle, "I sit at home ... looking out at the pretty girls in shorts, the sailboats, the ocean, and here I am, a young millionaire bachelor right in the middle of it all."[35] In spite of his levity with the press, Stanhouse took pride in his uniform and made it clear why he signed with the Dodgers. As a member of a healthy Los Angeles team, he was confident he would return to a second consecutive World Series in 1980: "Everyone wants to play in the Ravine. It's beautiful. I've been [to the World Series] once and I can't wait to get back. I don't see any reason why we can't be there in 1980."[36]

The converse of Stanhouse's prediction became the reality as injuries cost the Dodgers the 1980 National League West division title by half a game. Among the more severe injuries were shoulder, back, and pitching arm ailments to Don Stanhouse. After only four appearances in Dodger Blue, Stanhouse was placed on the disabled list on April 16. Three months would pass before he became activated: "It feels good just to be back," he told Verrell in late July. "I was telling [trainer] Bill Buhler the other day while we were working out, it was a whole lot easier pitching."[37] Stanhouse pitched two solid innings in his return to the active roster, a 3-2 Dodger victory in 12 innings over the Chicago Cubs on July 27. However, it was evident to those who saw him pitch that his injuries limited his effectiveness. Stanhouse struck out only five batters in 21 relief appearances, posting a 2-2 record with 7 saves and a 5.04 ERA. By the end of the season, rookie Steve Howe had replaced him as the bullpen ace.

In April 1981, the Dodgers had a difficult decision ahead of them. With the roster decimated by injuries to starters Jerry Reuss, Burt Hooton, and Dave Goltz, they needed a healthy arm to carry the rotation. Consequently, in order to create a space for Dave Stewart's recall from Albuquerque, the Dodgers released Don Stanhouse. Rick Monday remembers the Catch-22 situation faced by Al Campanis: "We were sad to see Don leave; he had been shelved by arm troubles but he was still a part of the team and a pretty good guy to have around. There were not too many dull moments in our clubhouse with Stanhouse [around]."[38]

The Dodgers did return to the World Series in 1981, defeating the New York Yankees in six games. However, Stanhouse was left no choice but to watch the games on television as his former teammates celebrated. At the same time, 1981 did offer Stanhouse a diamond milestone of a different sort when he married the former Kyle Stevenson, a flight attendant from Dallas, Texas. Thirty years later, that might have been his best pitch.

His old manager, Earl Weaver offered his career a lifeline to return to the Orioles in 1982. Effective enough in spring training and with injuries to many of the Orioles pitching staff, Stanhouse sign a contract on April 5. Returning to Baltimore, he was unsure of the reception he would receive from the fans he had left as a free agent two years earlier. On Opening Day, he received an emphatic answer. The PA announcer hadn't even finished saying Stanhouse's name in the pregame introductions when the capacity crowd at Memorial Stadium rose for a standing ovation, welcoming home their quirky but beloved prodigal son. "That," Stanhouse says, "was the biggest thrill of my whole career."[39] But, it was not a year to remember, Stanhouse was 0-1 with a 5.40 ERA in 17 appearances.

Stanhouse gave it one more shot the following year as a player-coach for the Hawaii Islanders. A season of work had made his arm strong again and things were looking good for a call back to the big leagues, ironically with the Pittsburgh Pirates. But a car running a red light hit Stanhouse's car on the way to the ball park. Whiplash took its toll on a rebuilt arm and body. He was rained out of the last game of that season, he knew he just could not come back again. After ten years of pitching and pranks, agents and airports, he knew it was time to hang up his spikes. Earl Weaver's package of cigarettes was now empty. His lifetime statistics were 64 saves in 294 appearances, a record of 38-54 and an ERA of 3.84.

As of 2012, Don and Kyle Stanhouse live in Trophy Club, Texas with their son Duke. Daughter Kameryn is in advertising and marketing in New York City and their married daughter, Kelsey Heil, delivered their first grandchild in June of 2012.

After 12 years as an investment banker, he established Stanhouse & Associates in 1995 which in turn generated two additional businesses, Pro Players Legacy Group and Pro Players Power and Gas. He is a lifetime member of the Major League Baseball Players Alumni Association and the Texas Rangers Legacy Group, having attended the 40th anniversary celebration on Opening Night 2011. Between his 60th birthday, his 30th wedding anniversary, and the return of his Rangers to their second consecutive World Series, 2011 was a year of celebrations for Stanhouse.

The odyssey of Donald Joseph Stanhouse is paradoxical but at the same time, common among baby boom American males; a free spirit who marched to the beat of his own drum and defied authority. "When I was in the big leagues, I thought it would last forever," he remembers. "I didn't think about life after baseball. But even if I had, this is light years away from where I'd ever thought I'd be."[40] But, he awoke one day to find himself the establishment figure he would have hated when he was 21. His Harpo Marx hairstyle and moustache have been replaced by white hair and a clean shaven profile. As he conveyed to Mike Klingaman of the *Baltimore Sun*, "I put on a suit and tie and drive a white SUV and do things I never thought I would do."[41]

In a 10-year major-league career, Stanhouse held the distinction of pitching for five managers who are in the Hall of Fame: Ted Williams, Whitey Herzog, Dick Williams, Earl Weaver, and Tommy Lasorda. He pitched in a World Series and was selected to an All-Star team. He shared a baseball field with over 60 Hall of Fame players and coaches and, for a time, held his own, with a "full pack" of wild ideas and in his own "unusual" way. For Stanhouse, the pitcher's mound remains a special place, which is why he can't resist an epilogue to his statement of good fortune.

"But you know something?" he says, chuckling lightly. "Someday, I could be back in that dugout, and Earl will be looking over at me and saying 'Better get Fullpack up again.' And I'd be ready to go. The game's always changing. If you can just relax and change with it, life will be good." For Stanhouse, the infielder turned starting pitcher turned relief pitcher turned entrepreneur and father and husband, changing with an ever-changing game seems to be just business. Business as … unusual!"[42]

Notes

1. Dan Epstein, *Big Hair and Plastic Grass: A Funky Ride Through Baseball and America in the Swinging '70s*, (New York: Thomas Dunne Books, 2010), 174.
2. Ian MacDonald, "Ex-Starter Stanhouse a Kingpin in Expo Bullpen," *The Sporting News*, August 27, 1977: 19.
3. John Croessman, "Don Stanhouse 'The Closer' in DuQuoin 40 Years Later," The DuQuoin Evening Call; par 4; available from www.duquoin.com; Internet; accessed January 9, 2011.
4. Randy Galloway, "New Ranger Stanhouse Silences the Skeptics," *The Sporting News*, May 6, 1972: 3.
5. Galloway, 3.
6. Galloway, 3.
7. Mike Shropshire, *Seasons in Hell* (New York: Dutton Publishing Company, 1996), 42.
8. Shropshire, 66
9. Shropshire, 43.
10. Shropshire, 73
11. Shropshire, 47.
12. Shropshire, 48.
13. Shropshire, 103.
14. Ian MacDonald, "'Want to Put My Act Together,' Stanhouse Informs the Expos," *The Sporting News*, March 12, 1977: 34.
15. Dunn, 15.
16. MacDonald (March 12, 1977), 34.
17. Dunn, 15.
18. Jacques Doucet, *Il etait une fois les Expos – Tome 1: Les annees 1969-1984* (Montreal: Editions Hurtubise Inc., 2009), 296.
19. MacDonald (March 12, 1977), 34.
20. Dunn, 15.
21. MacDonald (August 27, 1977), 19.
22. MacDonald (August 27, 1977), 59.
23. Ian MacDonald, "Expos' Offer 'Embarrasses' Stanhouse," *The Sporting News*, December 17, 1977: 59.
24. Maxwell Kates, "Norm Cash" in Mark Pattison and David Raglin, eds., *Sock It To 'Em, Tigers* (Hanover, Massachusetts: Maple Street Press, 2008), 24.
25. Klingaman, par 8.
26. Mike Klingaman, "Catching Up With…Former Oriole Don Stanhouse," Baltimore Sun; par 10; available from http://weblogs.baltimoresun.com; Internet; accessed 9 January 2011.
27. Jim Henneman, "Stanhouse Is Mr. Big in Orioles' Bullpen," *The Sporting News*, May 20, 1978" 17.
28. Jim Henneman, "Reliever Stanhouse Props Up Shaky Orioles," *The Sporting News*, July 22, 1978: 11.
29. Gordon Verrell, "Dave and Don Rich Odd Couple," *The Sporting News*, April 5, 1980: 42.
30. Klingaman, par 18.
31. Klingaman, par 5.
32. Ken Nigro, "Lazarus Seeking to Raise Stanhouse," *The Sporting News*, October 6, 1979: 22.
33. Nigro, 42.
34. Verrell (April 5, 1980), 42.
35. Verrell (April 5, 1980), 42.
36. Gordon Verrell, "Dodgers Grab Two Prizes," *The Sporting News*, December 1, 1979: 52.
37. Gordon Verrell, "'It's Time We Got Going,' Says a Healthy Stanhouse," *The Sporting News*, August 16, 1980: 22.
38. Rick Monday, and Ken Gurnick, *Rick Monday's Tales from the Dodgers Dugout* (Champaign, Illinois: Sports Publishing LLC, 2006), 71-72.
39. Stanhouse, January 18, 2012.
40. Ibid.
41. Klingaman, par 16.
42. Stanhouse, January 18, 2012.

KEN SUAREZ

BY BO CARTER

KEN SUAREZ, ONE OF THE "CAN'T-MISS" catching prospects of the 1960s and a member of the Rangers' inaugural squad in 1972, took a roundabout trip to arrive at his Arlington destination.

Kenneth Raymond Suarez was born on April 12, 1943, in Tampa, Florida, the son of Joseph R. and Gladys M. (Wadsworth) Suarez, who married in 1941 in Tampa while Joseph was on Army leave. Kenneth had a younger brother, James, born in 1945. Mother and children lived with their family in Tampa as Joseph served his Army duty.

Ken's late wife was Irene Lopez, whose father was Emilio Lopez – the brother of Alfonso "Al" Lopez who played and managed in the majors and is in the National Baseball Hall of Fame. They were married in Tampa in 1965 after being high school sweethearts. She was a vice principal for 35 years at sports-famous Fort Worth Bishop Nolan Catholic High School and active in diocesan education for four decades.[1]

Kenneth showed big-league potential as a right-handed hitter in college at Florida State. He had starred earlier at Tampa Jesuit High School and played American Legion summer baseball with Baseball Hall of Famer Tony La Russa and Lou Piniella.

Getting his first starting role for the perennial powerhouse in Tallahassee, Florida, as a sophomore in 1963, Suarez responded by pacing the Seminoles to their third NCAA World Series appearance under legendary coach Danny Litwhiler and then enjoyed his best collegiate season in 1964.

That year he hit .404 in 44 games for the nationally fifth-ranked FSU squad under new head coach and nine-season major leaguer Fred Hatfield, belted 6 home runs, had 30 RBIs, scored 25 runs, and walked 21 times to pace the Seminoles in each of those statistical categories. He earned consensus first team All-America honors and was selected for the 1964 US Olympic baseball team (a demonstration sport in Tokyo that year) before signing as a free agent for an undisclosed sum with the Kansas City Athletics in the spring of 1965, just before the first major-league free-agent draft in June.

While Suarez paid his minor-league dues on several occasions while being called up and sent down, he got off to a sizzling start with Lewiston, Idaho, in the Class-A Northwest League. In 55 games he batted .321 with 10 homers and 35 RBIs and was promoted in midseason to the Birmingham (Alabama) Barons of the Double-A Southern League, where his numbers decreased in the face of stronger competition.

Suarez's defensive skills and projected power (his first hit at Lewiston was a grand slam) earned Suarez a spot on the A's 40-man roster and the possibility of being manager Al Dark's everyday catcher.[2]

In 1966, Suarez made the team out of spring training but did not adapt well to major-league pitching. He made his major-league debut on April 14 and collected his first base hit on the 19th. His first run batted in came in a losing effort on April 24, but his second won the game for Kansas City. It came in the first game of a doubleheader at Yankee Stadium. Whitey Ford was pitching for New York and in the top of the fifth inning Ossie Chavarria hit a two-out double to left and Suarez singled to center to drive him in with the only run of the game.

In 35 games for the A's through July 9, however, Suarez was batting only .145 with 2 RBIs. He was sent down to Mobile, Alabama, to fill in for the injured Rene Lachemann. Phil Roof seized the starting assignment for the A's. On July 28, Suarez was struck in the face by a pitch and suffered a broken cheekbone and the loss of two teeth.[3] In the nine games he'd played for the Double-A Southern League team before the injury, he had batted only .125. While waiting for the 1967 season to begin,[4] he returned to Florida State to earn his degree in finance.[5]

In the fourth game of the 1967 season, Roof suffered a split finger and Suarez put on the starting catcher's togs for eight games with a .235 average, 2 homers (his first in the majors was off 1968 World Series standout lefty Mickey Lolich of the Detroit Tigers), and 4 RBIs. When Roof returned from the disabled list, the A's returned Suarez to Birmingham.

In November, the Athletics assigned Suarez to Triple-A Vancouver. Then they chose not to protect Suarez in the Rule 5 draft and the Cleveland Indians claimed him. Al Dark again became Suarez's manager, having been fired by A's owner Charles O. Finley and become manager of the Indians. Suarez was barely used at all by Cleveland, though, appearing in 17 games in 1968 with one single and a walk in 10 at-bats, and he wasn't used at all after August 30.

Suarez also was under the tutelage in the professional ranks in 1968, 1969, and 1971 of the inimitable Alvin Dark. Dark, who also served as the Indians general manager in 1968 and '69, managed all or parts of 13 major-league seasons for five teams in the 1961-77 era.

In the offseason, Suarez worked for the sheriff's office in Tampa, in the juvenile division. "It's the most rewarding work I've ever done," he said. "My job is to counsel kids ... try to get 'em out of trouble and keep 'em out of trouble."[6]

Suarez split 1969 between the Indians and the Portland Beavers of the Pacific Coast League. With Portland he hit .239 with 2 homers and 10 RBIs in 49 games, and he saw his most extensive playing time to date with the Indians, 36 games, hitting .294 with a homer and nine RBIs. Suarez spent all of the 1970 season with Wichita in the Triple-A American Association, where he enjoyed his best campaign at bat (.301 in 84 games, named to the league all-star team), and earned a trek back to the majors in 1971. As Ray Fosse's backup, he played in 50 games and batted .203 with one homer, and nine RBIs.

The 28-year-old backstop went to the Rangers from the Indians in a December 1971 deal. The Indians received Roy Foster, Rich Hand, Mike Paul, and the 28-year-old Suarez for Del Unser, Denny Riddleberger, Terry Ley, and Gary Jones.

The offseason deal with the Rangers for the Rangers inaugural 1972 season allowed Suarez to be the third catcher for manager Ted Williams's team. It was a team so lacking in offense that Williams often stepped into the batter's box during batting practice and demonstrated the fine art of hitting and eye-to-bat control in an effort to encourage his batters to generate some runs.

When the Washington Senators moved to Texas, Suarez became somewhat of a fan favorite as the fourth catcher on the roster and started developing lifelong friendships in the Arlington area.

The first-year Ranger did squeeze in 25 games, 33 at-bats, 4 RBIs, and a .152 batting average before being optioned to Texas's farm club at Denver in the Triple-A American Association. He responded with a career-high .341 batting average in 35 games. Suarez's solid defense earned him the initial playing time in 1972 behind veteran catchers Rich Billings and Hal King, and callup Bill Fahey. Suarez was 5-for-33 (.152).

His Denver showing and better-than-average defensive skills over the course of 1972 helped Suarez leap into a key backup role for Billings in 1973, and Suarez played in 93 games, a major-league season high for him. He had 278 at-bats and registered a .248 batting average. He broke up Jim Palmer's potential perfect game for the Baltimore Orioles on June 16 by hitting a single with one out in the ninth inning after the righty retired the first 25 batters.

Suarez's $20,000 salary in 1973 for the cash-starved Rangers was not what he felt he was due in 1974, and when he became the first Ranger to file for arbitration he was subsequently traded back to the Indians on February 12, 1974, for Leon Cardenas. The disappointed Suarez never trekked to Arizona for 1974 spring training after filing a formal grievance with the Major League Baseball Players Association and essentially retired at the age of 30. The grievance never was resolved.[7]

While his ongoing negotiations and filings continued, the Indians dealt Suarez to the California Angels along with Rusty Torres on September 12, 1974, for Frank Robinson. Suarez never played a game in an Angels uniform either and left baseball.

The 5-foot-8, 175-pound catcher had a career batting average of .227 with 5 homers and 60 RBIs in 295 major-league games over all or parts of seven seasons.[8]

In later life Suarez worked as a pregame guest on WBAP radio broadcasts. He also was involved in the aviation industry with experimental aircraft, home-grown vegetable gardens, youth baseball-park projects, and scouting for the Rangers in the Tarrant County (Fort Worth) area.[9]

He also has been an active member in the Dallas–Fort Worth Ex-Pros Baseball Association in raising funds for inner-city baseball park construction and assistance for needy former major leaguers.

"Ken has been an active participant in the DFW Ex-Pros for many, many years after Eddie Robinson and Dr. Bobby Brown began the original chapter in the 1990s," said the current DFW Ex-Pros president, former major-league pitcher Jack Lazorko.[10]

"Though I got drafted by the Rangers out of Mississippi State in 1978, I knew of his legacy with the original team in 1972," Lazorko said. "He laid the groundwork for many great teams over the next 45 years and was proud of his association with Ted Williams and that first team in Arlington."[11]

Suarez was part of a scouting combine that cross-checked Will Clark and Rafael Palmeiro while they were juniors and draft-eligible at Mississippi State in 1985. His reports proved correct as that duo led their team to a 50-15 mark and third place in the NCAA World Series. The eventual starting first basemen at different times for the Rangers later combined for 853 homers and 3,040 RBIs over a composite 35 seasons in the big leagues.[12]

And charting many of their at-bats and defensive moves from a perch in the old press box behind home plate at old Dudy Noble Field in Starkville, Mississippi, was none other than Ken Suarez.[13]

"Ken Suarez was one of the most professional people I have met in scouting players," Mississippi State coach Ron Polk recalled after the 1985 season. "We knew Clark and Palmeiro were going to be special even they came to Mississippi State in 1983, and by the time they were juniors, every team in the majors was scouting them. Ken did the usual charts, spoke to the players' parents, our coaching staff and teammates and gathered as much information as anyone on the two players."[14]

The Rangers and Suarez probably took great delight that the 1985 first-rounders (Clark to the Giants, Palmeiro to the Cubs) eventually made it to Arlington. Both earned spots in the College Baseball Hall of Fame and delighted Rangers fans with their power hitting for several seasons.

"It has been a great run since I first played sandlot ball in Tampa," said Suarez, "and now I have made many new friends over the years in Texas and I'm just living the life. It was great to see many of them at the Ex-Pros holiday banquet and looking forward to more good times with these fellows and their families."[15]

Sources

In preparing this biography, the author consulted BaseballReference.com, BaseballAlmanac.com, MLB.com, PointAfter.com, and FanGraphs.com.

Notes

1. Obituary, *Fort Worth Star-Telegram*, November 13, 2012.
2. Russell Schneider, "A Wish Comes True – Suarez, Dark Reunited," *The Sporting News*, February 24, 1968: 27. The grand slam came in a game against Salem.
3. "Suarez Injured by Pitch," *The Sporting News*, August 13, 1966: 38.
4. Schneider.
5. Sid Bordman, "Rifle-Armed Suarez Fills A's Mitt Gap," *The Sporting News*, May 6, 1967: 18.
6. Schneider.
7. Email to author from Major League Baseball Players Association on March 2, 2018.
8. Most standard baseball databases list Suarez as 5-feet-9, but he himself said, "Yeah, but I'm 5-8." See Bordman.
9. Conversations with Texas Rangers media relations executive John Blake, May 21, 2015, and September 16, 2016.
10. Conversations with Jack Lazorko on December 20, 2017, and January 11, 2018.
11. Ibid.
12. Ibid.
13. Conversations with Ken Suarez on April 23, 1985, April 30, 1985, and December 10, 2017.
14. Conversation with coach Ron Polk of Mississippi State on June 20, 1985.
15. Conversations with Ken Suarez.

TED WILLIAMS

BY BILL NOWLIN

Any argument as to the greatest hitter of all time always involves Ted Williams. It's an argument that can never be definitively answered, but that it always involves Williams says a lot. One could probably count the legitimate contenders on the fingers of one hand. Most would narrow the field to just two players, Babe Ruth being the other. One could make a good case for Lou Gehrig, and a very small handful of others. Ted himself ranked Ruth, Gehrig, Jimmie Foxx, Rogers Hornsby, and Joe DiMaggio as the top five (he elected not to include himself in any such ranking).[1]

If the name of the game is getting on base, no one ranks above Williams. His lifetime on-base average was .482, and think what that means. He reached base safely 48.2% of the time he came up to bat – almost half the time. Ruth comes in second, at .474. One of the reasons Williams ranked first was his self-discipline; he refused to swing at pitches outside the strike zone. In time, he developed such a reputation that more than one catcher complaining about a pitch being called a ball was told by the umpire, "If Mr. Williams didn't swing at it, it wasn't a strike." But The Kid had the strike zone down cold from the first. Even in 1939, his rookie year, Ted walked 107 times, ranking second in the American League (he led the league that first year in total bases – by a big margin). Across his entire career, which touched four decades (1939-1960), Williams had a walks percentage of 20.75. More than one out of every five times, he took a walk.

Even with a pitch in the strike zone, he wouldn't take a cut at it unless he felt it was a pitch he could drive. "Get a good pitch to hit" – the philosophy imparted to Ted in Minneapolis by hitting instructor Rogers Hornsby, meant more than just a pitch in the strike zone. If the pitcher dropped in a good curveball low and away (which he knew was his most vulnerable spot in the zone), he would figuratively tip his cap, take the strike, and wait for a better pitch. Unless there were two strikes on him, he would take his chances that there was a better pitch coming.

Ted had strong opinions about what made for a great hitter, and it involved hitting for a combination of average and power. Had he been willing to sacrifice power for batting average, one suspects, he could have ranked right at the top instead of just fifth among "modern era" (post-1901) players. Had he been willing to sacrifice average and just swing for the fences, he would have hit more than 521 home runs. As a young man, he knew what he wanted. At age 20, he said, "All I want out of life is that when I walk down the street folks will say, 'There goes the greatest hitter that ever lived.'"[2] In conversation late in life, when someone asked whether he thought he'd accomplished that, he simply said he didn't know but that it was a great honor just to hear his name in the same sentence as a Ruth or a Gehrig.

Becoming a great hitter was a goal Ted set for himself at a very early age. Born in San Diego on August 30, 1918, he was the first-born son of professional photographer (and former U.S. cavalryman)

Samuel Williams and his wife, a Mexican-American who dedicated her life to Salvation Army work, May Venzor Williams. It wasn't the happiest of marriages and both parents were frequently out of the home, often leaving Ted and his brother, Danny (two years younger), to fend for themselves. Fortunately, neighbors welcomed Ted in, but he spent endless hours playing ball on the North Park Playground in the Southern California city where the climate allowed one to play pickup ball all year round. A dedicated playground director, Rod Luscomb, saw Ted's drive and took him under his wing. By the time Ted reached high school, he was an exceptional player who attracted the attention and support of coach Wofford "Wos" Caldwell.[3]

It was his bat that first caught coach Caldwell's eye, but Ted excelled as a pitcher for the Hoover High Cardinals. He often struck out a dozen or more batters in a game, but he hit well, too, and found a place in the lineup for every game. Even while still a high school player, Ted signed his first professional contract – with the locally-based San Diego Padres, of the Pacific Coast League. With the Padres, Ted got his feet wet in 1936, hitting a modest .271 but without even one home run in the regular season. Ted completed high school and then played for the Padres again in 1937, upping his average to .291 and showing some power with 23 homers. Boston Red Sox general manager Eddie Collins had spotted Ted while looking over a couple of Padres players and shook hands with owner Bill Lane on an option to sign the young player, which he exercised in time for Ted to go to the big-league training camp in Florida in the spring of 1938.

Williams was a brash and cocky young kid who was deemed to need a full year in the minors and he was assigned to the Minneapolis Millers, where he proceeded to win the American Association Triple Crown with a .366 average, 43 home runs, and 142 RBIs. There was no question that he would be with the Red Sox in 1939, and the buildup in Boston's newspapers was unprecedented. The Kid was all that had been promised, and then some. Playing right field, he hit 31 home runs and batted .327. Not only did he lead the league in extra-base hits and total bases, he also led the league in runs batted in in his rookie year with 145, setting a major-league rookie record that has never been beaten. His fresh and evident love of the game won the hearts of many Boston fans.

The following year, 1940, Williams switched permanently to left field and improved his average to .344, though he dipped a bit in home runs (23) and RBIs (113). He placed first in both on-base percentage and runs scored. It was the first of 12 seasons that he led the league in on-base percentage; remarkably, he led in OBP every year through 1958 in which he was eligible. From his very first trip across country to spring training in 1938, Ted became known for his relentless questioning of other players about situational baseball – what was Ted Lyons' "out pitch" to a left-handed hitter late in the game with runners on base? What would Bobo Newsom start you out on first time up? Williams seemed to live and breathe baseball and it rang true when he later acquired the nickname "Teddy Ballgame."

Maybe he seemed just too good to be true. After a brief honeymoon with the press in the highly competitive newspaper town that was Boston, the critical stories began to come out. Taking on Ted sold newspapers, and writers like Dave Egan and Austen Lake could get under Ted's skin, sometimes provoking a story where none had existed before. He was easy to mock, taking imaginary swings out in the field and letting a fly ball drop in. He was so cocksure that he turned off some of the crusty ink-stained wretches, and a little sanctimonious – declining an interview with one of the deans of the press corps, columnist Bill Cunningham, because the writer had been drinking.[4] Some of the writers had it in for Ted, and let him have it. There commenced a feud with the writers that lasted Ted's whole career, and beyond. He enjoyed barring the scribes from the Boston clubhouse, sniffing the air distastefully as one walked by, and more than once spit toward the press box in contempt. He earned some other monikers – "Terrible Ted" and the "Splendid Spitter" – the latter being a reference to his widely-known nickname as a lanky, gangly kid – The Splendid Splinter.

There were fans who enjoyed egging Ted on, too, and during this second season he turned against the fickle fans. He later admitted he had "rabbit's ears" and could hear the one loud detractor over the hundreds of cheering fans, and he let it get to him. He admitted he was "never very coy, never very diplomatic. As a result I would get myself in a wringer. ...I was impetuous, I was tempestuous. I blew up. Not acting, but reacting. I'd get so damned mad, throw bats, kick the columns in the dugout so that sparks flew, tear out the plumbing, knock out the lights, damn near kill myself. Scream. I'd scream out my own frustration."[5] He just could not abide the fair-weather fans who'd be for him one day and against him the next. One thing he determined never to do was tip his cap to the fans; even though there were days that he truly wanted to, he just couldn't bring himself to do so. He was a complicated man and yet, despite all the tumult and turmoil, he never showed up an umpire by arguing a call and never once got tossed from a game. And, though he preferred to keep to himself, he got along fine with other ballplayers, both on his own team and on opposing teams.

It was in 1941 that The Kid had a season for the ages – batting .406 despite the sacrifice fly counting against the hitter's average. Few players had achieved the .400 mark, and no one has done so since. Ted also set a single-season on-base percentage mark (.553) that was never topped in the 20th century. (Barry Bonds now holds the highest mark.) Williams led the American League in runs and home runs. Two months after the season ended, Japanese warplanes attacked Pearl Harbor.

As sole supporter of his mother (his parents had divorced), Ted was exempt but that didn't prevent some from questioning his courage when he chose to play baseball (and pay off an annuity he'd purchased for his mother) in 1942. He had already achieved national stature as a star baseball player at a time when baseball was unrivaled by any other sport. This made him a convenient target for criticism, but servicemen attending ball games cheered for Williams. Once he'd made his point, he signed up in the Navy's V-5 program to begin training as a naval aviator when the season was over. In his fourth year of major-league ball, Ted hit for the Triple Crown in the major leagues, leading both leagues, as it happened, in average (.356, down a full 50 points from the prior year), home runs (36) and RBIs (137). And then it was off to serve. For the second year in a row, Williams came in second in MVP voting.

Ted Williams spent three prime years training and becoming a Navy (and then Marine Corps) pilot – and becoming so good at flight and gunnery that he was made an instructor and served the war training other pilots. The day he received his commission, he married Doris Soule – the first of three marriages. He kept active to some extent, playing a little baseball on base teams but only as time permitted given his primary duties. Lt. T.S. Williams ended his stretch at Pearl Harbor and never saw combat.[6]

After the war, Ted returned to the Red Sox and received his first MVP award from the baseball writers, helping lead Boston into its first World Series since 1918. He led the league in OBP, total bases, and runs, but an injury to his elbow while playing in an exhibition game to keep loose for the upcoming Series hampered his ability to compete effectively in the fall classic. Boston lost to the Cardinals in seven games, and Ted's weak hitting helped cost them the championship.

In 1947, Ted had his second Triple Crown year, leading the A.L. with .343, 32, and 114. The Red Sox didn't come close to the Yankees that year, and in each of the next two years, they lost the pennant on the final day of the season. Williams led the league in both average and slugging both seasons, among other categories. In 1949, he earned his second Most Valuable Player award – and only missed an unprecedented third Triple Crown by the narrowest of margins. He led in homers and RBIs, but George Kell edged him by one ten-thousandth of a point in batting average.

The year 1950 might have been on tap to become his best ever – he had already hit 25 homers and driven in 83 runs when he shattered his elbow crashing into the wall during the All-Star Game. He missed most of the rest of the season, and said he never fully recovered as a hitter – though one would hardly know it to look at the stats he posted. In 1951, he led the league once more in OBP and slugging.

Come 1952, as the war in Korea mounted, the Marines recalled a number of pilots to active duty. Among them was the less-than-pleased T.S. Williams, now a captain in the Reserve. He was to turn 34 that August, and Doris and he had a young daughter, Barbara Joyce (Bobby-Jo.) When it was clear there was no choice but to comply, Ted determined to do his best. He requested training on jets and was ultimately assigned to Marine Corps squadron VMF-311 which flew dive bombing missions out of base K-3 in South Korea. Capt. Williams flew some 39 combat missions, though he barely escaped with his life on the third one when his Panther jet was hit and had to crash-land. The plane burned to an irretrievable crisp but Williams was up on another mission at 8:08 the next morning. It truly was an elite squadron to which Williams was assigned; on more than half a dozen missions, Williams served as wingman to squadron mate John Glenn.

A series of ear infections consigned him to sick bay for two stretches and when it was obvious the war would be over in a matter of weeks, Williams was sent back Stateside and mustered out – in time to be an honored guest at the 1953 All-Star Game. He threw himself into preparation to play and he got in 91 at-bats before the season was over – batting .407 in the process.

Ted broke his collarbone in spring training in 1954 and missed so many games at the start of the season that come season's end, he fell 14 at-bats short of having the requisite 400 to qualify for the batting crown he would have otherwise won with his .345 average. Ted appeared in only 117 games, but still drew enough walks to lead the league (136). The walks hurt him, though, since the batting title was based on "official" at-bats alone. This seemed so unfair that the criteria were changed in later years to be based on plate appearances. After the 1954 season, he "retired" (the term is placed in quotation marks because it seemed as though retirement was a strategic move in a divorce) and did not make a start in the 1955 season until May 28. He completed the year with 320 at-bats, but hadn't lost his touch as indicated by his .356 average and 83 RBIs in the two-thirds of a season he played. In 1956, he had what by Williams standards seemed like a pedestrian, even somewhat lackluster year, accumulating an even 400 at-bats with 24 homers, but still hit at a .345 clip. A.L. pitchers were no fools; he drew over 100 walks and led the league in on-base percentage.

The year 1957 is what was arguably the year in which Ted Williams proved what a great hitter he truly was. No longer the Kid who turned 23 while hitting .406 back in 1941, Ted entered his 40th year in that season. He might have been "splendid" but he was no splinter. He'd filled out his physique, gone through war and divorce, suffered broken bones and pneumonia. Despite all the accumulated adversity, Ted hit .388 (just six more hits would have given him .400 again, hits that a younger man might have legged out) and led the league by 23 points over Mickey Mantle. His .526 OBP was the second highest of his career and so was his .731 slugging average. So, too, were the 38 home runs he hit. It was truly a golden year.

His final three seasons saw a decline, though batting .328 as he did in 1958 would for almost any other player be spectacular. In fact, it was enough to win Ted the batting championship even if it was some 16 points below his ultimate .344 lifetime average. The batting title was his seventh, not counting 1954 as per the rules of the day. 1959 was his one really bad year; he developed a very troublesome stiff neck during spring training that saw him wear a neck brace and have a very difficult time trying to overcome it. He never truly got on track and batted a disappointing .254 with only 10 homers and 43 RBIs in 272 at-bats. It was sentiment alone that placed him on the All-Star squad, one of 18 times he was accorded the honor. Everyone expected him to retire; even Red Sox owner Tom Yawkey, with whom Williams had a good if distant relationship, suggested it might be time.

Ted Williams didn't want to leave with a season like 1959 wrapping up his career. He came back for a swan song season, but insisted that he be given a 30 percent pay cut because of his underperformance in 1959. He felt he hadn't earned the money he was being paid, at the time – as it had been for many years – just about the highest salary in all of baseball, understood to be around $125,000. Williams had hard work in 1960 but he produced, batting .316 with 29 home runs – the last of which was hit in what had been announced as his very last at-bat in the major leagues.

In his latter years, Williams had played for a Red Sox team that offered him little support in the lineup, had not much in the way of pitching, and didn't draw many fans. Even Ted's final home game drew just over 10,000 fans to Fenway Park. How much better he would have done had he played in a park with a friendlier right field, like Tiger Stadium or Yankee Stadium, remains unknowable. How much better he might have done had he had a Lou Gehrig hitting behind him in the lineup, or had he not missed five seasons to military service, remains unknowable.

Leaving on such a high note, Williams couldn't resist a final shot at the Boston press corps with whom he had so frequently feuded since his second year with the Red Sox. The "knights of the keyboard" wouldn't have Williams to kick around anymore. And Ted Williams left town, though in lieu of any farewell dinners he quietly, and without publicity, stopped to pay a visit to a dying child stricken with leukemia. Teddy Ballgame, as he was known, had been the leading spokesman for Boston's "Jimmy Fund" for many years. Ted had appeared on behalf of Dr. Sidney Farber's children's cancer research efforts since the late 1940s, in fact since before Dr. Farber (the "father of chemotherapy") first achieved remission in leukemia. Today, over 85 percent of children with leukemia are cured.

Save for appearances for the Jimmy Fund, Ted took time off and spent the next several years catching up on his fishing while bringing in some endorsement income through a long association with Sears Roebuck, which produced an extensive line of Ted Williams brand sporting equipment – all of which Ted insisted on testing personally, right down to the tents and sleeping bags that would bear his name. Ted married a second time, to Lee Howard of Chicago in September 1961. It was a short-lived marriage, perhaps in part because Ted had already met the woman who was perhaps his soulmate in life, Louise Kaufman. Though they never married, she loved Ted through both his second and third marriages (the third, to Dolores Wettach, occurred in 1968, when she was apparently already pregnant with the son who became John-Henry Williams.) Dolores and Ted later had a daughter, Claudia Franc Williams, born shortly after Ted and Dolores separated a few years into the marriage. Always in the background was Lou Kaufman, who – though six years older than Ted – was a fishing champion in her own right and apparently had enough salt to spar with Ted with the sort of banter he liked to dish out. There were other women, of course. In many ways, Ted Williams was a "man's man" and perhaps didn't have the patience for a relationship. Visiting one afternoon in the late 1990s at Ted's house in Florida, this author was presented with a blunt, candid, and unanswerable remark when – out of the blue – Ted declared, "Yeah, I guess I was a great hitter, but I was a lousy husband and a crummy father."

After the requisite five years following his playing career, Ted Williams was elected to the National Baseball Hall of Fame in his first year of eligibility. When he was inducted in the summer of 1966, Williams wrote out his speech by hand the evening before (the original is in the Hall of Fame) and after thanking those who helped him on his way, he devoted part of the core of his speech to an impassioned plea that the Hall of Fame recognize the many Negro League ballplayers who had not been allowed to play in the segregated major leagues prior to 1947.

He wrote in his autobiography *My Turn At Bat* (published in 1969) of his Mexican-American mother, "If I had had my mother's name, there is no doubt I would have run into problems in those days, the prejudices people had in Southern California." One can speculate that his own awareness of prejudice may have informed his remarks at the Hall of Fame. The first African American in the American League, Larry Doby, says that Williams went out of his way to make him welcome – not grandstanding but with the simplest of private gestures on the field. When the Red Sox finally integrated by adding Pumpsie

Green to the big-league roster in 1959, Ted chose Pumpsie as his throwing partner before games.

In the same year as his remarkably self-revealing autobiography was published, Williams became manager of Bob Short's Washington Senators ball club. The team showed a fairly dramatic improvement in team batting his very first year and, while on safari in Africa, Ted received word that he had been named Manager of the Year. It was good timing for Ted's second book (written as had been the first with author John Underwood) – *The Science of Hitting*. The book demonstrated the Ted Williams approach to the game and, as with *My Turn At Bat*, has remained in print ever since – no small feat in the world of books. Even in the 21st century, *The Science of Hitting* is often the book of choice for aspiring batters.

Ted had signed on as manager for five years, but he lost interest after the Senators failed to further improve (and some of the ballplayers chafed under his regime to the point of near-insubordination).[7] Ted traveled to Texas with the franchise and served as the first manager of the Texas Rangers in 1972 but he begged out of the fifth and final year of the deal.

Throughout his years as player and as manager, he was always a colorful "larger than life" figure with a booming voice and a presence that defined charisma. He was often a lightning rod of sorts, loved or hated by fans, and a reliable source of controversial copy for sportswriters and reporters. He was loud and boisterous, but as he himself admitted in his autography, he was "never very diplomatic. …I did a lot of yakking, partly to hide a rather large inferiority complex."[8]

After leaving full-time employment in baseball for good, Ted served for years and years as a "special assignment instructor" with the Boston Red Sox. Typically, this meant he would show up at spring training for a few weeks and look over the younger hitters, occasionally taking a player aside later in the year as well. When Carl Yastrzemski was struggling in his first year of trying to fill Ted's shoes as Boston's left fielder, the team flew Williams in from where he was fishing in Canada and he spent a few days working with Yaz. Yastrzemski says, "He really didn't say anything; he was just trying to build me up mentally. He says, 'You've got a great swing – just go out and use it.'" Yastrzemski realized he was trying too hard to emulate Williams as a home run hitter, but Ted helped him settle down and helped him become himself. Over time, Yaz says, "I think the big thing that I learned from him, which he talked about, was the strike zone, strike zone, strike zone."[9]

For many years, Ted lived in a small but comfortable cabin on New Brunswick's Miramichi River where he was able to fish for his beloved Atlantic salmon, a fish he so admired that he became a leader of the fight to preserve the species from overfishing and other encroachments on its habitat. An annual "Ted Williams Award" is presented to others who have joined in the cause. Ted enjoyed the companionship of Lou Kaufman in his later years.

Ted Williams was active on the Hall of Fame's Veterans Committee (and sometimes criticized for being too vocal an advocate for players he championed such as Phil Rizzuto and Dominic DiMaggio). As he grew older, many of the hard attitudes toward Ted softened and, in the words of Doris Kearns Goodwin, "It seemed like his stature…his stature was always there – I don't think anyone ever disputed how great he was – but the kind of emotions he generated in the fans got stronger as time went by rather than weaker, which is really nice. I'm glad he's lived to see all that. It seems to have mellowed and made him a happier person, too."[10]

He always engendered strong opinions and harbored many of his own. This was a man of many interests and an intellectual curiosity perhaps surprising in a ballplayer, a man whom his Marine Corps instructor could conceive of as a Shakespearean scholar and whom Tommy Henrich of the New York Yankees could envision as a brain surgeon or nuclear scientist.[11] Biographer David Halberstam once said that Ted "won 33,277 arguments in a row…the undisputed champion of contentiousness" – but then went on to write a book about the friendship between Ted, Bobby Doerr, Dominic DiMaggio, and Johnny Pesky that endured for six decades.[12]

For the last several years of his life, Ted became active in the memorabilia market, attracting very large sums to appear for occasional signings at industry shows. Some took advantage of his natural generosity and in one case Ted pursued a man who had defrauded him, the case becoming an episode on the America's Most Wanted television show. Ted's son, John-Henry Williams, took over management of the marketing of his father with mixed success. Many criticized John-Henry for being too zealous in his father's behalf and for some of his business schemes, but there was no doubt that Ted very much loved his son and was prepared to turn a blind eye to any faults. Ted suffered a stroke and a subsequent heart operation sapped his health, and he entered a period of decline that ended with his passing on July 5, 2002. In death, as in life, controversy swirled around Ted Williams as two of his three children had his body cryonically frozen for the possibility of some later revival if science someday learns a way to restore life to those who have been so preserved. Many of Ted's closest friends were aghast but efforts by his eldest daughter to reverse the decision were in vain. An outpouring of more than 20,000 people attended a memorial at Boston's Fenway Park later in July 2002 and the memory of the man they called The Kid lives on.

NOTES

1. See Williams' ranking, and his system, in Ted Williams and Jim Prime, *Ted Williams' Hit List* (Indianapolis: Masters Press, 1996), reissued by McGraw-Hill, 2003.
2. One place where he made a similar statement is in his autobiography, written with John Underwood. See *My Turn At Bat* (New York: Firestone, 1988), 7.
3. In 2005, nine members of the Society for American Baseball Research collaborated to tell the story of Ted Williams' family and life growing up in San Diego. See Bill Nowlin, ed., *The Kid: Ted Williams in San Diego* (Cambridge, Massachusetts: Rounder Books, 2005).
4. See Jim Prime and Bill Nowlin, *Ted Williams: The Pursuit of Perfection* (Champaign: Sports Publishing, 2002), 57.
5. *My Turn At Bat*, 11.
6. The story of Williams' military years, both in World War II and the Korean War, is told in Bill Nowlin, *Ted Williams at War* (Burlington, Massachusetts: Rounder Books), 2007.
7. For a look at the start of his time with the Senators, see Ted Leavengood, *Ted Williams and the 1969 Washington Senators* (Jefferson, North Carolina: McFarland, 2009).
8. *My Turn At Bat*, 13.
9. Author interview with Carl Yastrzemski, August 31, 1977.
10. uthor interview with Doris Kearns Goodwin, May 3, 1997.
11. Bill Churchman was the Marine Corps instructor in question. See his remarks in *Ted Williams: The Pursuit of Perfection*, 81, and those of Tommy Henrich in the same volume on page 103.
12. David Halberstam, *The Teammates* (New York: Hyperion, 2003). The best biographies of Ted Williams are Ed Linn, *Hitter: The Life and Turmoils of Ted Williams* (New York: Harcourt, Brace, 1993), Leigh Montville *Ted Williams: A Biography of An American Hero* (New York: Doubleday, 2004), and Ben Bradlee, Jr., *The Kid: The Immortal Life of Ted Williams* (New York: Little, Brown, 2013).

JOE CAMACHO

BY CHARLIE GRASSL

The New Bedford, Massachusetts, area is home to one of the largest Portuguese-American communities in the United States. Known as the Whaling City due to its pre-eminence as a whaling port during the nineteenth century, New Bedford attracted many immigrants from Portugal and its dependent territories to work in the whaling industry and later to the textile mills. In the early 1900s cotton weaving became a very vibrant industry in New Bedford and nearby Fall River as whaling declined. These American cotton mills grew so large as to become an economic threat on the world market to the long-established British cotton mills of Manchester and others in Lancashire county, England.

In 1916 Jose Camacho, born of Portuguese parents in British Guiana (now an independent nation, Guyana, in South America), came to settle in New Bedford to find work in its cotton mills. In New Bedford he married Augusta Piedade, whose ancestry stemmed from Madeira, a Portuguese possession off the African coast. On May 29, 1928, their son Joseph Gomes Camacho was born. As Joseph grew up in New Bedford, it was not whales or cotton that attracted his focus and energy but baseball.

As a professional baseball player, Camacho never advanced beyond Double-A, achieving far more success as an educator. Yet, from a business association with one of baseball greatest hitters, Ted Williams, he later tasted life in the Big Leagues as a bench coach. From that relationship grew a lifelong friendship between the Hall of Famer and the Camacho family.

As a 15-year-old sophomore at New Bedford High School, Joe attended a local tryout camp of the Philadelphia Athletics in 1944. Believing he made a good impression he had reason to believe a baseball career awaited. His father insisted he delay his dream until after graduating from high school, so Joe completed his high-school baseball career. In his last two games he pitched a 13-inning 4-3 victory, and then a no-hitter. After graduating from high school, Camacho worked in the local mills and played baseball in 1946 and 1947 in the Twilight League, a semipro circuit of teams sponsored by area mills. Major-league scouts often frequented these games. In 1948 Camacho, then 20 years old, signed a contract with the St. Louis Browns and was assigned to the Belleville Stags of the Class-D Illinois State League, where one of his teammates was 17-year-old pitcher Bob Turley, who in later years contributed to several New York Yankees pennants. Camacho put together a decent year while playing second base and shortstop, hitting .259 with two home runs in 118 games. Promoted to Globe-Miami of the Class C Arizona-Texas League, he became a teammate of another pitcher who became a Yankee legend, 19-year-old Don Larsen. After playing in 38 games, Camacho suffered a broken ankle in a collision at home plate, and the Browns released him. After recovering he signed with Ogdensburg (New York) of the Class-C Border League and hit .304 with three home runs in

43 games. He returned to Ogdensburg in 1950 and enjoyed his best professional season, hitting .311 in 117 games with 22 doubles, 3 triples, and 10 home runs. After the season he married his high-school sweetheart, Patricia Margaret Carey.

Camacho's baseball career was interrupted when he was drafted into the US Army during the Korean War. Camacho was able to play baseball while stationed in Germany and earned the MVP award in a service tournament called the G.I. World Series.

Resuming his professional career in 1953, Camacho signed with the Cleveland Indians, who sent him to the Fargo-Moorhead Twins of the Class-C Northern League. At the age of 25, Camacho was one of the elder statesmen on a young, dominating (86-39) team that included 18-year-old Roger Maras. Camacho batted .296 with 35 doubles, 7 triples, and 11 home runs. During the season, he and Maras became close friends. This friendship continued as they were teammates while moving up the Indians farm system and rooming together at local YMCAs. Maras, who later changed the spelling of his last name to "Maris," gained fame in 1961 as the first player to hit 61 homers in a season.

Camacho reached Double-A Mobile (Southern Association) in 1957, batting .238 in 50 games. At the age of 29, it was obvious to him that he was never to get that shot at the big leagues. Typecast as a career minor leaguer at 29 years old, missing his family, which now included a young son, Michael (born in 1954)[1], he concluded that it was time to move on to another career, and retired as a player.

After getting out of the Army in 1953, Camacho had enrolled at Bridgewater (Massachusetts) State College under the GI Bill. Continuing his studies, he earned a bachelor's degree in 1959 and a master's degree in education in 1961. He became an elementary-school teacher and eventually the principal of his boyhood elementary school, the Sarah D. Ottiwell School in New Bedford. A second son, James, born in 1958, helped further transform his life from that of the vagabond, grinding through a long baseball season, into a contented and happy full-time husband, father, and teacher. However, baseball was still to find a place in his life.

In 1963 Camacho was hired as the baseball director at the Ted Williams Baseball Camp in nearby Lakeville, Massachusetts. The job at the baseball camp led him, if only for a short time, back into professional baseball. Camacho later recalled, "The camp would run in the summer only. School would end about the middle of June and the camp would start, lasting about 8 to 10 weeks. The kids were from 8 to 18 and came to the camp from all over the country. We were able to bring our families and children. Ted was naturally very involved and, and as always, full of enthusiasm. We became friends and up until his death we would talk quite a bit, at least once a week."[2] Joe considered Ted a friend and was unaware this friendship would bring him back into professional baseball and even into the major leagues, not as a player as he once dreamed but as a coach.

According to Gordon Edes, then a *Boston Globe* sportswriter, "When Ted Williams was named manager of the Washington Senators before the 1969 season, one of the first calls he made was to former teammate Johnny Pesky. 'I was doing radio and TV for the Red Sox,' Pesky said. 'A week earlier, I would have been with Ted. My wife Ruthie and her mother were in the kitchen when he called. He said, 'I need you. Can you come down?' I wanted to do it and break my contract but the general manager said it was too late. They had me reading the football scores in the winter to work on my voice, and they had done all this PR stuff for me.'"[3]

When Pesky turned Ted Williams down, Williams asked Camacho, still an elementary-school principal, to become his bench coach. The minor-league player who never made it to the majors resigned his position at the school and joined the Senators' coaching staff. Of this turn of events, Camacho commented, "All minor leaguers feel they should have been big leaguers, but I didn't make it into the big leagues. I made it as a coach under Ted. He must have felt that I knew what I was doing."[4]

The Camacho family plan for the summer of 1969 was for parents and sons to spend eight weeks in Lisbon as part of a Portuguese cultural exchange program. However, the chance to return to professional baseball in the major leagues, to work more closely with his friend Ted Williams, and the promise of becoming the farm director of the Washington Senators when Williams moved up to be team president after five years of coaching proved to be too much to turn down. Camacho became one of the first coaches to be called a bench coach. To claims that he was the first, some baseball historians cite Pete Reiser serving as Walt Alston's "bench-riding coach" in 1962 and Christy Mathewson serving John McGraw of the New York Giants in the 1919-21 seasons as his "assistant manager."[5] Without dispute, however, is that Camacho served Ted Williams in the same manner as all of the current bench coaches, while Reiser and Matheson held positions that only resembled the present concept of that coaching position. Before 1969 no team had such a position on its coaching staff. Now they all do.

Camacho brought a special desire and understanding to the coaching ranks that was unique to him. His minor-league experience, his association with the Ted Williams Baseball Camp, and his work as an educator combined to make him a valuable resource as well as a positive example for young players in the Senators farm system. One of them was Bill Madlock, a four-time batting champion in the National League. When he was honored in January of 1980 at a Hot Stove League dinner in Boston, Madlock made a point to bring Camacho along just to say thanks for how much Joe had meant to his career.

In 1969, Camacho's first year with the Senators, the team got off to a promising start, finishing fourth in the AL East with a record of 86-76. But it was the only winning season in the expansion Senators' history. The next season, 1970, was a step backward as the Senators fell to last place in the AL East with a 70-92 record. Camacho became convinced that the owner, Bob Short, wanted out of Washington. "For some reason Short wanted to get out of there and that Denny McLain trade was one of the worst things that happened to the club," Camacho said. "Certainly Ted didn't want that trade. We gave up Joe Coleman, Aurelio Rodriguez, Eddie Brinkman, and they ended up in Detroit winning the pennant (1972) with Billy Martin."[6] In 1971 the Senators won only 63 games and lost 96. They were spared the indignity of a last-place finish by the Cleveland Indians (60-102). Camacho, believing that some of the players on the club had "mailed it in" and undermined all that Ted Williams brought to the club, later said, "Probably the ringleader of what I called the 'underminers club' was Denny McLain. Consider the source. He was a hell of a pitcher at one time but he's been in trouble all his life. He's done everything. I haven't heard anybody speak poorly of Ted, as manager."[7]

Camacho's suspicions were not paranoia when you consider the deteriorating financial position of Bob Short, principal owner of the franchise, in 1970. Clearly the mood from the top down appeared to be "do anything that will get us out of this situation!" Affirming this, Eric Nadel, in his authorized history of the Texas Rangers, noted, "By the end of the 1970 season, Short was struggling financially and was under pressure to relocate from other team owners, who earned little money from their share of the meager gate receipts when their team played at RFK Stadium. Well aware of Short's predicament was the mayor of Arlington, Texas, Tom Vandergriff."[8]

So it came to pass, Joe Camacho followed his friend and manager, Ted Williams to Texas in 1972. But it was only to watch the team continue its slide in 1972. With a record of 54-100,[9] they occupied sixth and last place in the newly structured AL West, 38½ games out of first.[10] In four years the team had seen its win total shrink from 86 to 70 to 63 to 54. Camacho to the end was loyal to Williams. "It's easy for sports people to say great players don't make great managers – well, there are extenuating circumstances in everything, you know," Camacho said. "If you have good ballplayers – Casey Stengel, he was with the old Boston Braves and the New York Mets. When he was with the Yankees, they won everything."[11]

After the 1972 season, Ted Williams resigned. Camacho, weighed heavily by the three consecutive years of losing seasons, each worse than the last, was very happy to return to his family and the familiar surroundings of New Bedford. Ted returned to his beloved fishing. Joe Camacho, finding a job as principal of the Elwyn G. Campbell Elementary School available for the 1973 school year, returned to education in New Bedford. He held the position until he retired in 1986.

In an interview in 1997, Camacho summarized his experience with the Senators/Rangers. "The owners wanted to get out of there, and we had a good year the first year or so, but then (Short) made a few bad trades and moved to Texas, and that was the end of everything. I'm retired now. I've been a widower[12] since 13 years, I have a boy at home so I cook and take care of him. My mother-in-law, she's 85 years old and she is in a nursing home so we visit her daily."[13]

As of early 2016, Joe, experiencing some ill health in his later years, resided in a nursing home in Fairhaven, Massachusetts, just across the Acushnet River from New Bedford. His oldest son, Michael, a widower since 2001, has four grown stepchildren and resided in Myrtle Beach, South Carolina. James, his youngest son, worked as a supervisor for the Massachusetts Office of the State Auditor, residing near Joe in Fairhaven at the family residence, looking after the affairs and well-being of his father. Joe Camacho died at the age of 90 in Fairhaven, Massachusetts on December 27, 2018.

Sources

In addition to the sources cited in the Notes, the author consulted the following:

The Baseball Encyclopedia, ninth edition (New York: Macmillan, 1993).

Baseball-Reference.com.

Thomas, Buddy. "Looking Back: Joe Camacho's Big Finale," *New Bedford Standard-Times*, August 31, 2004.

Thomas, Buddy. "A Closer Look at the Legend of Joe Camacho," *New Bedford Standard-Times*, November 13, 2014.

The author is also grateful for a telephone interview with Joe's son, James Camacho, on January 4, 2016, and email correspondence from January 4-12, 2016.

Notes

1. Michael was a very good high school baseball player as well as a star in basketball and football. In 2008 he was inducted into the Fairhaven High School Hall of Fame. In 2003, Michael became a pro-golfer and now is working as a club repair expert for Golfsmith.
2. Interview with Joe Camacho by Bill Nowlin, May 21, 1997.
3. Gordon Edes, "Bench Coaches: More than Just a Job," *Baseball Digest*, July 1, 2008.
4. James Camacho interview.
5. Stuart Miller, "Next to the Manager, but a Bit Ahead," *New York Times*, August 18, 2012.
6. James Camacho interview.
7. James Camacho interview.
8. Eric Nadel, *Texas Rangers: The Authorized History* (Dallas: Taylor Publishing Company, 1997), 51.
9. A players strike at the start of the season canceled the first eight games of the 162-game schedule.
10. The American League was restructured to accommodate the geography of the club's move to Texas from Washington. The Milwaukee Brewers were moved to the AL East and the Rangers placed in the AL West.
11. Interview with Joe Camacho by Bill Nowlin, May 21, 1997.
12. Joe's wife, Patricia, died at age 54 from breast and lymphatic cancer.
13. Interview with Joe Camacho by Bill Nowlin, May 21, 1997.

NELLIE FOX

BY ROBERT W. BIGELOW AND DON ZMINDA

Nellie Fox was the heart of the 1959 Go-Go White Sox, the team that brought Chicago's South Side its first pennant since the tarnished Black Sox season 40 years earlier. The image of Little Nel in his batting stance has become iconic – a choked-up grip on his bottle bat with a wad of chewing tobacco bulging in his cheek. Fox was an unimpressive physical specimen at 5-feet-9 without much innate athletic ability, but determination and opportunity helped a gritty kid with a burning love for the game become a perennial all-star and ultimately a Hall of Famer. Nellie Fox won a Most Valuable Player Award, spent 12 years as an All-Star, won three Gold Glove Awards, and was a dominant force at his position for over a decade

Jacob Nelson Fox – he was always known by his middle name – was born on Christmas Day 1927 in St. Thomas, Pennsylvania, a small town in Franklin County about 30 miles west of Gettysburg. Nellie's father, Jacob L. Fox, known as Jake, was born on a farm but earned his living as a carpenter. Jake loved baseball and played second base on the St. Thomas town team. He was known as a hard-nosed player and a good bunter, traits he passed on to his son. The Fox family has a picture of young Nelson at the age of 2, holding a homemade bat designed by his father. Even then, Fox was swinging the bat left-handed.

Nelson was the youngest of three brothers. One of them, Frank, died tragically at the age of 3; the other, Wayne, who was seven years Nelson's senior, shared the Fox family's love for baseball. As a boy Nelson was often called by the nickname Pug; he wasn't referred to as Nellie until he began his professional baseball career. Nelson loved all sports, but baseball and soccer were his favorites. "I think I liked soccer better than baseball for a while," Fox told a writer. "I was only about 130 pounds, but I liked the contact. I liked to mix it up."[1]

Fox soon turned most of his attention to baseball, starting out as the mascot and batboy for the St. Thomas town team. He constantly pressured his father and the St. Thomas coach to put him into a game, and when he was given his first opportunity at the age of 10, he amazed everyone by getting a pinch-hit single off a pitcher who was considered the best in the area. Eventually he joined his dad in the St. Thomas lineup, playing first base while Jake manned second. He played ball almost anywhere he could find a team: on the St. Thomas High School team, in American Legion ball, and in the nearby Chambersburg Twilight League. As a teenager he also took on a lifelong habit that would become of his trademarks: chewing tobacco.

Fox was never much of a student: In class he was known to hide sports books or magazines in his notebook and read them when he was supposed to be studying. By the age of 16 he had decided that he wanted to make baseball his career. "I had to be a ballplayer," he said. "I wasn't very good at school and I didn't have any outside hobbies. I played ball. That's what I did."[2] His mother, Mae, was concerned about Nelson's future, and one day early in 1944, she wrote a letter to Connie Mack, owner/manager of the Philadelphia A's. "My boy is baseball crazy," she wrote. "He won't study in school. … He worries me to death. … All he talks about is you and the Athletics."[3] Mack wrote back that if her son actually had talent, it was possible to make a living playing ball. "I may one of these days be able to help him," Mack wrote.[4]

Due to wartime travel restrictions, the A's were holding 1944 spring training in Frederick, Maryland, about 50 miles from St. Thomas, and like most major-league teams, the club was holding open tryouts in an effort to fill its war-depleted farm system. With the encouragement they'd received from Mack's letter, Jake and Mae decided to take Nelson to the camp to try out for the team. Though they didn't tell Nelson, the Foxes hoped that the A's would tell their son that he would be better off staying in school.

So in a story that seems like something out of a 1940s B movie, Jake and Nelson drove to Frederick, found the A's hotel, introduced themselves to Connie Mack, and got a chance to try out for the team. (Fox later squelched the oft-repeated story that he showed up at the A's camp smoking a big cigar.) According to Philadelphia sportswriter Stan Baumgartner, "(Coach) Earle Mack had difficulty finding a small enough uniform to fit the boy."[5] Though he was almost ridiculously short for a first baseman at no more than 5-feet-6, Fox made a good impression on Mack. According to a story in the *Frederick Post*, "Connie Mack liked the way the youth conducted himself at the plate and his technique of handling low throws to the initial sack."[6] To Jake and Mae's surprise, the A's decided to offer the 16-year-old Fox a contract to join their minor-league system. "(Mack) probably thought the boy was good enough for Class D," said Jake, "and that he would get as much education by being around with a baseball team as he would in high school."[7]

After using him in a few exhibition games, the A's sent Fox to the Class-B Interstate League's Lancaster Red Roses, managed by Lena Blackburne. Fox immediately showed some talent, batting .325 while playing both first base and the outfield. It was no surprise that he was not a slugger, with no home runs in 24 games, though he did drive in 12 runs. Nellie was later sent down to the Jamestown Falcons of the Pony League (Class D) for 56 games and hit .304, again with no home runs.

Fox was back with Lancaster in 1945 and hit .314 in 140 games. Moved to second base, the position he would play for the rest of his career, he led the league in hits and runs and hit his first professional home run. However, Fox did not have an opportunity to immediately follow up on this strong showing, as he spent the 1946 season in the military, stationed in Korea. Perhaps the most notable occurrence in his life that year was his engagement to Joanne Statler on Christmas Day 1946. The two had met when both were in high school; "I was a freshman and he was my first date," said Joanne, recalling that they attended a Christmas dance.[8]

Fox was again with Lancaster in 1947, hitting .281 with one home run and 22 RBIs. He was called up to the Athletics very briefly that year and appeared in seven games, going hitless in three at-bats. He spent the 1948 season at Lincoln of the Class-A Western League, hitting .311. He led the league in hits and was named to the All-Star team. He and Joanne were married in Lincoln on June 30; the couple would have two daughters, Bonnie and Tracy. Later in the season, Fox was called up to the big club again and played three games at the end of the season, hitting .154 in 13 at-bats.

In 1949 Fox stayed with the Athletics all year, playing behind Pete Suder, who was in his seventh year with the club and had long had a lock on the second-base job. Fox played 88 games and hit .255 with no homers and only eight extra-base hits. He had desire but there were holes in his game, most significantly the inability to produce consistently at the plate. Connie Mack, often a masterful judge of talent, must have felt that Fox was never going to be more than a journeyman, because the A's put him on the trade market after the season. Connie Mack badly underestimated Nellie Fox.

Shortly after the 1949 season, the A's traded Fox to the White Sox for catcher Joe Tipton. This could not have been terrific news for Fox, who was leaving a Philadelphia team that had a solid, professional second baseman in Suder in front of him to a club that had Cass Michaels, the American League's starting second baseman in the 1949 All-Star Game, patrolling the middle.

After beginning the 1950 season as a backup to Michaels, Fox caught a break when the Sox traded Michaels to Washington on May 31 in a multiplayer deal which netted them slugging first baseman Eddie Robinson. Infielder Al Kozar, who came along with Robinson as part of the deal, was expected to be Michaels' replacement, but Kozar promptly hurt his back hitting a home run against the Yankees. Given an opportunity to play every day, Fox was a bust, hitting .247 with no home runs and 30 RBIs in 130 games. His most impressive traits continued to be his determination and competitive fire. "Nellie was the greatest competitor I ever played with," recalled Billy Pierce, Fox's longtime teammate as well as his roommate for 11 years. "Baseball, gin rummy, bowling … whatever he played, he just loved to compete."[9] Getting Fox to hustle and work was never an issue for any man who ever managed him. If anything, those who managed Fox wanted him to take an occasional break.

The White Sox were training in Pasadena, California, in 1951, and Fox was anything but a lock to make the Opening Day roster. "Nellie called me at home from spring training that year," recalled Joanne Fox, "and said, 'I don't think they're going to keep me. It looks they're going to send me back to the minors.'"[10] And in fact the White Sox had already made a tentative decision to sell Fox to the Portland club of the Pacific Coast League. But Fox had a supporter in White Sox coach Ray Berres. Berres told new manager Paul Richards, "He can play. He'll play for you if he has to play on crutches."[11]

Richards adopted Fox as a project. Former Yankee second base great Joe Gordon worked with Fox on his fielding. A particular focus was turning the double play. "It was brutal the way Fox was pivoting," Richards commented later. "I'm surprised he didn't get hurt making the pivot the way he was dragging his foot across the bag."[12] The drills with Gordon paid off, thanks in good part to Fox's determination. "He made himself into a good second baseman just by working so hard," said Billy Pierce.[13]

As a hitter, Fox did have one amazing ability – making contact with the ball. He struck out only once in every 48 plate appearances during his career, and never more than 18 times in a season. But the rest of his offensive game needed work, and White Sox coach Doc Cramer took Fox under his wing. The former Athletics/Red Sox/Tigers outfielder worked with Fox on his hitting, particularly stopping him from lunging at the ball. Cramer also suggested the use of a bottle bat. "Prior to that Nellie had been using a thin-handled bat," said Billy Pierce. "He was pulling the ball too much, but after Cramer gave him a thicker-handled bat, Nellie began spraying the ball all over the field."[14] Richards also worked with Fox on bunting, and before long, according to Pierce, Fox was the best bunter in baseball among left-handed hitters.

The 1951 season was the turning point in Fox's career. One-third of the way through this breakout year, he was hitting .364 and the Sox were in first place. That July he was the American League's starting second basemen in the All-Star Game. He hit only four home runs with 55 RBIs but finished this stellar season with a .313 batting average which was good enough for fifth in the AL. He also tied for second in the league in both hits and triples. His performance helped the club improve to an 81-73 record after seven sub-.500 seasons, finishing in fourth place. This season was the template for the next decade for the Sox and for Nellie Fox – gritty, solid, fundamentally sound baseball. Sox fans had a burgeoning star that they could identify with.

The breakthrough season in 1951 established Fox as a star, and he continued to embellish his reputation over the next decade. Making the American League All-Star team every year from 1951 through 1961, Fox led the league in hits four times during the 1950s and scored 100 or more runs in four straight seasons (1954-57). In the field, Fox led AL second basemen in total chances for nine straight seasons (1952-60), in double plays five times and in fielding percentage four times. In the eight-season span from 1952 through 1959, Fox finished in the top 10 of the American League's Most Valuable Player voting six times.

But while Fox's career continued to flourish, the 1950s were often a maddening time for the White Sox and their fans. The 1954 season was typical. Fox had one of the best years of his career, setting career highs with 201 hits, 111 runs scored, 16 stolen bases, and a .319 batting average. He also led the league in games played with 155 while striking only 12 times in 706 plate appearances. Fox's performance helped the White Sox win 94 games, the most for any Sox club since 1920. But the team still finished a distant third behind the Indians and Yankees.

Paul Richards left the White Sox to take over the Baltimore Orioles at the tail end of the 1954 season, and Marty Marion took over as manager. Neither Richards nor Marion could break the club's streak of third-place finishes, which reached five in a row in 1956, but on August 6, 1955, Marion did break Fox's streak of consecutive games played at 274. Giving Nellie a day off did not sit well with Fox. While Fox referred to it as "the most miserable day I ever spent in baseball," Marion said, "It was the most miserable day of my life too – having to listen to him gripe from the bench."[15] The next day Fox started a new streak that lasted 798 games – an all-time record for second basemen.

The third-place finish under Marion in 1956 marked the arrival of rookie shortstop Luis Aparicio, who took over after Fox's previous double-play partner, Chico Carrasquel, was traded to Cleveland. Though Carrasquel had been a four-time All-Star, it was immediately evident that the Sox had something special in Aparicio. Luis won the Rookie of the Year award in 1956 and stole 21 bases.

Another important man came to the White Sox in 1957, when Al Lopez took over as manager after one pennant and five second-place finishes with Cleveland. Fox celebrated Lopez's South Side debut by leading the league in hits, batting .317, and topping AL second basemen in putouts, assists, and double plays. He also became major-league baseball's first Gold Glove winner at second base and finished fourth in the league's MVP voting behind Mickey Mantle, Ted Williams, and Roy Sievers. Better still, the Sox finally broke out of their third-place rut by moving up a notch to second place.

After another second-place finish in 1958, the Sox added a final key element when a shrewd new owner, Bill Veeck, bought controlling interest in the team. Veeck brought flamboyance, enthusiasm, and a knack for making things happen to a team that was ready to reach the top, and it all came together for the Sox in 1959.

With Veeck and Lopez providing sound management as well as a belief that the mighty Yankees could finally be had, the White Sox broke out of the gate strongly in '59 and never looked back. On the field, the club was led by the determined veteran Fox, the speed of Aparicio and Jim Landis, and the solid catching and power hitting of veteran receiver Sherm Lollar. The pitching staff was excellent with Early Wynn, Billy Pierce, and Bob Shaw leading the starting rotation. The bullpen featured two relief aces in Jerry Staley and Turk Lown.

Fox batted .306 with two homers and 70 RBIs in 1959. He was first in the AL in at-bats and second in both hits and doubles. He batted .383 with runners in scoring position. In the field he led the league in putouts, assists, and fielding average while being voted the league's starting second baseman in the All-Star Game for the fifth straight year. The importance of Fox to this team could not be overstated. Owner Veeck put it well when he wrote that the Sox needed Nellie "no more than your baby needs milk."[16]

After beating out the Indians and Yankees for the American League pennant, the Sox faced a Dodgers team making their first World Series appearance since the move to Los Angeles the year before. This was not a dominant Dodgers team of the Brooklyn years but one that took the pennant – barely – with only 88 victories. Two of those wins had come in a best-of-three playoff series with the Milwaukee Braves, who had tied the Dodgers for first place. Sox fans had reason to be hopeful.

The Series began in Comiskey Park, and Game One could not have gone better for the White Sox, who crushed the Dodgers, 11-0, behind the pitching of Early Wynn and two homers from late-season addition Ted Kluszewski. Fox contributed by going 1-for-4 with a walk and two runs scored. But the Dodgers took Game Two by 4-3, then won Games Three and Four as the Series moved to the Los Angeles Memorial Coliseum, a football stadium whose left-field wall was less than ideal for Chicago's pitching-and-defense club. The Sox kept the Series alive by beating Sandy Koufax, 1-0, in Game Five, but back in Chicago, the Dodgers routed Wynn and wrapped up the Series with a 9-3 victory in Game Six. It was a disappointing finish, but the White Sox could hardly blame Fox, who led the team with a .375 World Series batting average. Fox wrapped up a memorable year by winning another Gold Glove, then being selected as the American League's Most Valuable Player.

But 1959 turned out to be a peak for both Fox and the White Sox, who would not reach another World Series for 46 years. Veeck made a flurry of deals prior to the 1960 season, trading away young talent to acquire power hitters Minnie Minoso, Roy Sievers, and Gene Freese, but the Sox dropped back to third place while Fox's average dropped 17 points to .289. In 1961 the Sox fell to fourth place and the 33-year-old Fox was showing signs of age, as his batting average fell to .251. The decline of the Sox continued in 1962, when the team fell to fifth place. Fox raised his batting average to .267, but failed to make the AL All-Star team for the first time since 1950.

In 1963, the White Sox rebounded to a second-place finish, with Fox batting .260 and again leading AL second basemen in fielding average. He was named an All-Star for the 12th and final time. But the White Sox were trying to break in younger players, and Fox's 14-year stint with the club finally came to an end in December of 1963, when he was traded to the Houston Colt .45s for pitcher Jim Golden and outfielder Danny Murphy. There were indications that had Fox remained with the Sox, he might no longer have had his starting position.

In Houston, Fox was reunited with Paul Richards, now general manager of the fledgling Colt .45s. Fox got into 133 games for the ninth-place .45s in 1964 and batted .265, but he was nearing the end of his playing days. In 1965 he lost the second-base job to future Hall of Famer Joe Morgan. Fox played in only 21 games, hitting .268 before being released by Houston (now known as the Astros) on July 31.

Remaining with Houston, Fox coached for the Astros in 1966 and 1967 under manager Grady Hatton. Joe Morgan credited Fox with helping him maximize his potential as a player, and the two remained friends until Fox's death. When Morgan was inducted into the Baseball Hall of Fame in 1990, he said about Fox, "I played with him, and I wouldn't be standing here today if it wasn't for what I learned from him. ... Above all, Fox impressed upon me the importance of going to the park every day bringing something to help the team. ... Nellie Fox was my idol."[17]

After leaving Houston, Fox was offered a chance to manage the Braves' Triple-A farm team at Richmond by Paul Richards, who had become Atlanta's general manager. Fox turned down the offer, instead joining the Washington Senators' staff as a coach under Jim Lemon, a former White Sox teammate. Fox remained a Senators coach when Ted Williams took over as manager in 1969, accompanying Williams to Texas when the club became the Texas Rangers in 1972. Fox was highly regarded by the club and given credit for helping several Senators/Rangers hitters, including Frank Howard and Ed Brinkman. Williams thought so highly of Fox that he recommended that Fox replace him as manager when he resigned after the 1972 season. Instead, the job went to Billy Martin. It wasn't the first time Fox had failed to get an opportunity to manage a major-league club. He had previously been a candidate to manage the White Sox when Don Gutteridge was let go late in the 1970 season, but lost out to Chuck Tanner.

Fox was offered a chance to remain with the Rangers as a minor-league manager, but decided to retire instead. Returning home to St. Thomas, Fox co-owned and operated a bowling center, Nellie Fox Bowl, which he had opened in 1956 in nearby Chambersburg (the bowling center was still in operation with the same name in 2008, long after the Fox family had sold its interest). He also played an occasional round of golf and hunted deer and small game with his beagles, Barney and Nellie. A hometown friend, Clark Gillan, recalled, "Nellie was a dead shot. Man, he could hit anything."[18] Fox also loved Penn State football and frequently attended Nittany Lions' home games.

"I believe that if (Fox) had not gotten sick, that he would have gotten back into baseball after a couple of years," said Joanne Fox.[19] But in the summer of 1975, Nellie was diagnosed with lymphatic cancer. Many former teammates visited him at the University of Maryland's Baltimore Cancer Research Center. After Bill Veeck came home from seeing him, his wife, Mary Frances, said, "That was one of the few times I saw Bill cry."[20] At the time Veeck was involved in negotiations to repurchase the White Sox, and, according to Joanne Fox, he told Fox that he wanted him to manage the team for him.

It wasn't to be; Fox died on December 1, 1975, 24 days before what would have been his 48th birthday. Jim Lemon commented that the cancer "had to be incurable because if it wasn't, Nellie would have beat it."[21] Fox was buried in his hometown at St. Thomas Cemetery.

Nellie Fox's posthumous road to the Hall of Fame was reminiscent of his struggles as a player fighting and scraping for his spot in baseball history. He barely missed election in 1985, his final year of eligibility in the annual BBWAA balloting, finishing with 74.7 percent of the vote and falling just two votes short of the requisite 75 percent, the smallest margin in the history of the Hall of Fame. Veteran Chicago writer Jerome Holtzman argued that, in line with baseball's tradition of rounding off percentages, Fox should have been credited with the necessary total of 75 percent, but Hall of Fame officials disagreed.

Fox's Hall of Fame candidacy then moved to the Veterans Committee, and another lengthy battle ensued. For several years Fox fell short in the committee voting, and there were reports that his former manager Al Lopez, a committee member, was working to block Fox's induction (or at least doing nothing to help it). In 1996, with Lopez now gone from the committee, Fox finally received the necessary 75 percent of the vote, but the committee was allowed to elect only one candidate per year; Jim Bunning had received one more vote than Fox, so Nellie missed again.

However, Fox's fans never gave up and many people lobbied for his election. In 1997, he finally landed his place in Cooperstown. Speaking at Fox's induction ceremony that August, Joanne Fox said: "He played with all his heart, all his passion, and with every ounce of his being – that was the best way he could show his appreciation to all those who helped him learn the game that became his life."[22] It was never the easy way for Nellie Fox but, as always, determination and grit would get him there.

Sources

http://www.baseball-almanac.com/deaths/nellie_fox_obituary.shtml

http://web.baseballhalloffame.org/hofers/vetcom.jsp

http://www.baseball-reference.com/bullpen/Interstate_League

http://www.baseball-reference.com/bullpen/Nellie_Fox

http://www.jockbio.com/Classic/Fox/Fox_bio.html

http://www.philadelphiaathletics.org/event/fox2001.html

http://www.philadelphiaathletics.org/trail/fox.html

http://www.retrosheet.org/

Alexander, Charles C. *Our Game* (New York: Henry Holt and Company, Inc., 1991).

The Baseball Encyclopedia (Toronto: Macmillan Publishing Company, 1993).

Enders, Eric. *100 Years of the World Series* (New York: Barnes & Noble Publishing, Inc., 2003).

Johnson, Lloyd and Brenda Ward. *Who's Who in Baseball History* (Westport, Connecticut: Brompton Books, 1994).

Johnson, Lloyd and Wolff, Miles. *The Encyclopedia of Minor League Baseball* (Durham NC: Baseball America, Inc., 1997).

Vanderberg, Bob. *From Lane and Fain to Zisk and Fisk* (Chicago: Chicago Review Press, 1982).

Ray Berres interview, March 8 and 19, 1996, SABR Oral History.

Notes

1. David Gough and Jim Bard, *Little Nel: The Nellie Fox Story* (Alexandria Virginia: D.L. Megbec Publishing, 2000), 16.
2. Gough and Bard, 20.
3. Ibid.
4. Gough and Bard, 24.
5. Gough and Bard, 23.
6. Gough and Bard, 25.
7. Gough and Bard, 26.
8. Don Zminda interview with Joanne Fox, July 18, 2008.
9. Don Zminda interview with Billy Pierce, July 18, 2008.
10. Joanne Fox interview.
11. Ibid..
12. Neil R. Gazel, "Nellie Does Right by White Sox," *Baseball Digest*, August 1951.
13. Billy Pierce interview.
14. Ibid.
15. Dave Condon, *The Go-Go Chicago White Sox* (New York: Coward-McCann, 1960), 132.
16. Bill Veeck with Ed Linn, *Veeck As In Wreck* (Chicago: The University of Chicago Press, 2001; originally published 1962), 342.
17. Gough and Bard, 288.
18. Gough and Bard, 271.
19. Joanne Fox interview.
20. Gough and Bard, 277.
21. Associated Press, "Nellie Fox Succumbs of Cancer," *High Point* (North Carolina) *Enterprise*, December 2, 1975.
22. Gough and Bard, 9.

SID HUDSON

BY JOHN BENNETT

When Tom Brokaw wrote about the "greatest generation," he might have easily selected the life of Sid Hudson as one of its shining examples. Although he was never a baseball great, Hudson's work in the sport spanned seven decades, stretching from the humble beginnings of Depression-era sandlot ball to the multibillion-dollar game of the present day. Hudson overcame many obstacles along the way, while serving his country in World War II and finishing as a teacher of the game to a new generation of ballplayers.

The story of Sidney Charles Hudson began in 1918 – or more precisely, 1915. For many years he listed his date of birth as January 3, 1918, and it was not until the early 1990s that it was corrected in baseball reference guides. Sid remained hazy on this subject, saying he cannot remember exactly when and how it got mixed up. His place of birth also brings some confusion. Early references cite his place of birth as Oliver Springs, Tennessee, while contemporary sources place his first appearance in nearby Coalfield. His father, Henry Hudson, a carpenter, died when Sid was 7 years old. Sid's mother, Addie, was left with a large family to raise. Sid helped as much as possible, eventually cutting short his schooling in his junior year of high school to work as a clerk in a grocery store. Before then, he had displayed a remarkable athletic talent for his basketball team and as a first baseman on the baseball team.

Hudson still managed to fit sports into his work schedule, playing when he could for several local amateur teams. Eventually he came to play for the East Lake team in the Chattanooga City League. Sid played mostly at first base, with his 6-foot-4 height helping him with tough throws. A decent batter, Hudson later took great pride in his batting during in his major-league career finishing with a .220 career average including several chances as a pinch-hitter. Hudson attracted the attention of Guy Lacy, a former Cleveland Indians player who was now managing Sanford in the Class-D Florida State League. Lacy signed Hudson for the 1938 season, and put him at first base, where he got off to a slow start. The team did poorly as well, and Lacy was replaced as manager by Bill Rodgers. A right-handed thrower, Sid had a fastball, hard curve, and, later, a changeup he developed with advice from future Hall of Famer Ted Lyons, who at the time was pitching for the rival Chicago White Sox.

Rodgers had brought another first-baseman with him and Hudson had a seat on the bench. A week later, the team was far behind in a game against Palatka. Rodgers asked Hudson if he could go in to pitch a few innings. Sid agreed and struck out the last six batters of the game. He was in the rotation for the rest of the season, winning 11 games for a last-place team and filling in at first base and third base. By the end of the year, Rodgers had turned Sid into his favorite project, working with him daily on pitching and fielding drills.

In 1939, the extra tutelage paid off as Hudson turned in a brilliant season. He won 24 games, with a 1.80 ERA, lost only 4, and completed all 27 of his starts. He continued to play part-time in the infield, batting .338. He started four more games in the league playoffs and completed and won them all. His extraordinary season caught the attention of the Washington Senators and Cleveland Indians, each of which tried to sign him for their minor-league teams. Sid chose the Senators, noting that with Mel Harder and Bob Feller on the Cleveland staff, his opportunities would be greater in Washington.

In 1940, Hudson went to spring training in Orlando, Florida, with the Senators, along with his Sanford teammate and fellow 20-game winner Harry Dean. The organization had coach Benny Bengough the catcher for the 1927 Yankees) work with each of them, and planned to send both to the club's Charlotte affiliate. Bengough worked closely with Hudson on throwing the curve and changeup, and Sid was surprised to find himself a member of the Senators starting rotation. In just two years, he had gone from the sandlots to the majors.

Hudson started the second game of the season against a very tough Boston Red Sox lineup, featuring four future Hall of Famers, Jimmie Foxx, Joe Cronin, Bobby Doerr, and Ted Williams. The Red Sox prevailed, 7-0, behind a home run by Foxx, but the Washington press lauded the rookie's poise and character in such a difficult debut assignment. Hudson won two of his next three starts, but then lost seven decisions in a row. Fully expecting to be sent to the minors, he was surprised when he received nothing but encouragement from owner Clark Griffith and coach Bengough. Hudson was told he was overthrowing, and to get back to basics – in Bengough's words, to "rare back and burn the ball in."[1]

Taking the mound against St Louis on June 21, 1940, Hudson walked the first three batters, but then went to his fastball and retired the Browns without a run scoring. He then shut them down completely, taking a no-hitter and 1-0 lead into the ninth inning. Although Rip Radcliff spoiled his bid with a double, Hudson won the game and turned his season around. He won his next five games, including a second one-hitter, against Philadelphia on August 6; the no-hit bid was spoiled by Sam Chapman's seventh-inning single.

On September 2, Hudson faced the Red Sox' Lefty Grove in what Sid later called one of the highlights of his major-league career. The two battled in a 0-0 duel through 12 innings, with Hudson pitching out of numerous jams, until the Senators broke through and gave him the win in the bottom of the 13th inning. The victory capped a remarkable rookie season. Fresh out of Class D ball, Hudson had won 17 games for a team that won only 64. He threw 19 complete games, three of them shutouts, and won nine one-run decisions. He finished second, by a scant three votes, to Lou Boudreau in the Rookie of the Year voting held by the Chicago baseball writers.

In the next two seasons, Hudson continued to be a pitching mainstay for the Senators. Despite losing records, he was selected to the All-Star team both years. In the 1941 game, he was briefly on the hook for the loss until Ted Williams won the game with a three-run homer in the ninth inning. Hudson was a workhorse for the Senators, completing 17 games in 1941 and 19 in 1942. Although his numbers were respectable (13-14, 3.46 ERA in 1941; 10-17, 4.36 in 1942), the Senators slumped in both seasons. Hudson enjoyed another favored career moment at the end of the 1941 season, when he shut out the Yankees in the last game of the season. Hudson had one of the 13 strikeouts that season of Joe DiMaggio, whom he considered the best all-around player he ever faced.

America was soon in World War II and Hudson spent the next three years in the Army Air Force, finishing his service time with Special Services on Saipan. In his 38-month tour of duty, Hudson pitched hundreds of innings in service games and also ran calisthenics for cadets five times daily. When he came back to the majors in 1946, his arm was fatigued and he developed a bone spur on his shoulder. Pitching with great pain, he turned in a decent 1946 season (8-11, 3.60 ERA), but as his arm worsened, his record declined along with it. His ERA rose to 5.60 in 1947, although he had one great moment, defeating

Spud Chandler and the Yankees, 1-0, on April 27, Babe Ruth Day, when more than 58,000 fans packed Yankee Stadium to honor Ruth, who was suffering from the cancer that would take his life a year later. Hudson had first met Ruth at a benefit game during the war, and remembered feeling sorry that April day to see one of his heroes in such poor health. Matching zeroes with Chandler into the seventh inning, Hudson won his own game by singling and scoring on a base hit by teammate Buddy Lewis. In 1948, he continued to slump, falling to a 4-16 record with a dismal 5.88 ERA with twice as many walks as strikeouts. A worried Hudson went to Johns Hopkins Hospital in Baltimore to have his arm examined by specialists. He was given a choice: opt for surgery without any guarantees that he would recover fully, or try pitching with a different delivery. Hudson chose the latter, changing to a side-arm style. The transformation paid off slowly – he led the league with 17 losses in a tough-luck 1949 season – but by 1950 he had returned to form, winning 14 of the team's 67 victories and earning attention as one of the season's best comeback stories.

In 1951, Sid slid backward with a 5-12 record and a 5.13 ERA, but in 1952, he got off to a strong start with the Senators, completing six of his seven starts with a 2.73 ERA. Seeking pitching help, the Red Sox acquired him in a trade on June 10, 1952, for pitchers Walt Masterson and Randy Gumpert. Although sad to leave Washington, Hudson welcomed a trade to a team with a better lineup, and also noted years later that he enjoyed escaping the humidity of the Washington summers. He went on to win seven and lose nine games for the Red Sox, pitching for manager Lou Boudreau, who had edged him out for the unofficial Rookie of the Year award in 1940. Hudson finished his career in a variety of roles for the Red Sox over the next two seasons. Still relying on his side-arm delivery, he went 6-9 in 1953 as a starter and reliever. His adjusted ERA of 119 (100 is average) was the best of his career.

Sid also enjoyed playing with, Ted Williams, a teammate he greatly admired. On September 17, 1953, Hudson was trailing Ned Garver and the Detroit Tigers 1-0 in the eighth inning at Fenway Park. As Sid recounted years later, Williams told him "he'd hit that little slider into the right-field seats and win the game."[2] And, just as he had done for him in the 1941 All-Star Game, Williams bailed out Hudson with a dramatic two-run, game-winning home run.

In 1954, now 39 years old and the third oldest player in the league, he worked mostly out of the bullpen, winning three games and saving five. The Red Sox slumped badly that season, with their lowest win total (69) since 1943. Among other changes, after the season Boudreau was replaced as manager by Mike Higgins, and Hudson had thrown his last major-league pitch. He went to spring training with the Red Sox in 1955, but was released before the start of the season. This ended a career in which Hudson had often pitched well for below-average teams. He had won 104 games, lost 152, and completed 123 of his 279 major-league starts.

The 1954 season may have been Hudson's last as an active major-league pitcher, but it was far from the end of his time in major-league baseball. Indeed, his release merely ushered in a new phase of his career. The Red Sox kept Hudson as a scout, a position he held for five years. In 1961, he returned to his baseball roots by accepting a job as a pitching coach for the expansion Washington Senators. Hudson remained in that organization for 25 years, following the team to Texas in 1972. He worked as a pitching coach at both the major- and minor-league levels and served under six different managers, including Gil Hodges, Billy Martin, and his old friend Ted Williams.

In 1964, while working with the Senators' Geneva farm team in the New York-Penn League, Hudson devised a contraption known as the "gadget." The device consisted of a leather strap that went around the pitcher's wrist. Attached to the strap was a strip of elastic with loops for the third finger and thumb. The loops pulled the finger and thumb to the ball and the strap allowed for the arm to stretch straight while throwing but then pulling in at the moment of release. According to Hudson, the gadget got the pitcher used to the feel of throwing a curveball in practice, which then made it more effective in a game.

Hudson had always demonstrated patience in his baseball career, and had valued all the coaching tips given him. Therefore, it was no surprise that he was able to make positive contributions as a coach. Former Senators pitcher Jim Hannan credited Hudson with helping him achieve the three best years of his career, recalling, "He really understood what goes through a pitcher's mind and how you have to handle pitchers."[3]

One of his last projects was working with a 39th-round draft choice in 1982. That pitcher, a young left-hander, caught Hudson's eye because of his loose, live arm. (According to Sid, "There was no substitute for those young, live arms.") However, when he asked him to throw from the stretch, the prospect replied "What's that?" Hudson patiently explained it to him.[4] Twelve years later, that pitcher – Kenny Rogers – threw a perfect game for the Rangers as part of a career in which he won more than 200 games and recorded more pick-offs than any other pitcher in history.

After leaving the Rangers organization in 1986, Hudson finished his baseball life by becoming the pitching coach at Baylor University. Sid spent six years there, advising his young pitchers on the nuances of the game, and becoming infamous for his painstakingly long walks to the mound. His pitchers included Scott Ruffcorn, who starred for Baylor and was a No. 1 draft choice for the White Sox in 1991. In 1992, at the age of 77, Hudson finally hung up his spikes for good. His personal connection to the game continued through his grandson Sam Hays, who was drafted by the Seattle Mariners and spent several years in their organization.

Sid spent the final part of his life living in Waco, Texas, fully relishing the memories of his baseball career. He and his wife had raised two daughters. He still received numerous letters from fans young and old, most of them autograph requests that he faithfully answered. Hudson enjoyed sharing stories with visitors, treating them to his "baseball room," which contained a large collection of memorabilia. In 2008, his beloved wife of 63 years, Marion, died. Sid followed his wife in death just a few months later, succumbing to strokes and melanoma on October 10, 2008, at the age of 93. He had dedicated his life to baseball – and enjoyed every minute of it.[5]

Sources

In addition to the sources in the Notes, the author consulted Retroheet.org, Baseball-Reference.com, and Sid Hudson's player file at the National Baseball Hall of Fame Library.

Edwards, Henry P., press release on Sid Hudson from the American League Service Bureau, January 5, 1941.

Richman, Milton. "Comeback of the Year: Sid Hudson," *Baseball Digest*, August 1950.

Shelton, Julie. "Former Major Leaguer Sid Hudson Dies at 93," (http://www.kwtx.com/blogs/all/30830304.html, October 10, 2008. Shelton is Sid's granddaughter-in-law.)

Norman Macht graciously shared his superb draft article and interview with Sid Hudson. Gabriel Schechter and Eric Enders kindly assisted in acquiring research materials from the Hall of Fame Library. SABR members Rod Nelson, Tom Hufford, and Matthew Bohn all provided help in sorting out the discrepancies between Sid's "dates" of birth.

Notes

1. Brent Kelley, "An SCD Interview with Sid Hudson," *Sports Collectors Digest*, January 17, 1992.
2. Norman Macht, "Sid Hudson" (unpublished interview article shared with this author)
3. Joe Holley, "Sid Hudson, 93; Pitched For Senators in 1940s," *Washington Post*, October 24, 2008.
4. Kevin Sherrington, "A Life Full of Curves," *Dallas Morning News*, October 26, 2008.
5. Author interview with Sid Hudson, via mail, 2003. Thanks to Jason for help with this.

GEORGE SUSCE

BY DAVID E. SKELTON

In 1955 *Cleveland News* sportswriter Ed McAuley noted that "[George] Susce is a man of many admirable qualities, but the ability to hit a baseball frequently was not among his assets."[1] At the time this was offered, Susce was 11 years removed from his last major-league appearance and well along into a coaching career that extended into the 1970s. Remembered with the rather incongruous moniker of "Good Kid" – a reputation seemingly earned only after he retired – Susce (pronounced SUE-see) reportedly engaged in over 37 fights – losing 36 of them – during the first six years of his career. Despite the terrible won-lost record, he continued throwing fists, often at his own teammates. (This was possibly due to another nickname ascribed to him by his mates: "Sweet Susie.") This combative behavior eventually hampered his career, something Susce readily acknowledged years later when he said, "I guess I was too aggressive in those days."[2]

George Cyril Methodius Susce was born in Pittsburgh on August 13, 1907, the youngest of two sons of Paul and Mary V. (Yager) Susce. His Slavic ancestry helps to explain his middle names – the ninth-century brothers Cyril and Methodius were the patron saints of the Slavs. Susce's parents were born in Austria-Hungary in the second half of the nineteenth century and emigrated from the crumbling empire to the United States in 1902. (They married that same year.) Paul went to work in Pittsburgh's thriving steel mills, where he labored for more than 40 years. The family lived three miles east of the confluence of the Allegheny, Monongahela, and Ohio Rivers, and one mile south of Forbes Field, home of the Pittsburgh Pirates. The ballpark opened two years after George was born and he passed it every day on his way to Schenley High School in Pittsburgh's North Oakland neighborhood. The industrious child owned a year-round morning and evening newspaper route and, during the baseball season, was a batboy for a semipro team while hawking peanuts and soft drinks at Forbes Field.

Susce was a gridiron star in prep school[3] and went on to play one season at St. Bonaventure University in Allegheny, New York. Playing on offense and defense as a fullback and defensive back, he received honorable mention as an All American.[4] But football paled in comparison to his true passion, baseball. Blessed with a strong arm, Susce spurned attempts by the Schenley Spartan coaches to move him from his preferred catching spot to the mound. His exploits on the high-school diamonds attracted major-league scouts – most notably St. Louis Cardinals executive Branch Rickey – but Susce chose college instead. (His ambition was to become a dentist.) But in early 1929, after just one year at St. Bonaventure, he had a change of heart. Discovered on the semipro sandlots in Pittsburgh, Susce was invited to a tryout with the Philadelphia Phillies, where he quickly caught the attention of manager Burt Shotton. Having sold the contract of reserve catcher Johnny Schulte in January, the Phillies were in need of a replacement. Susce was signed by Joe O'Rourke and immediately assigned to the parent club. It took little time for Susce to engage in his first altercation. During an at-bat against Philadelphia Athletics righty Eddie Rommel in a Florida exhibition, the youngster charged the mound when he thought the veteran hurler was intentionally throwing at him. Innings later the A's mild-tempered outfielder Bing Miller tried to choke Susce after a hard collision at the plate.

On April 23, 1929, Susce made his major-league debut, against the New York Giants in the Polo Grounds, as an extra-inning defensive replacement for starting catcher Walt Lerian. He got his first plate appearance the next day, striking out as a pinch-hitter against future Hall of Fame lefty Carl Hubbell. Susce played in just 15 more games the rest of the season. Except for a June 25 starting assignment against the Boston Braves in the nightcap of a doubleheader at Braves Field – a game in which Susce connected for his first major-league home run, a solo shot against Braves lefty Bunny Hearn – he was used solely as a defensive replacement or pinch-hitter. A .294 average in limited play may have warranted additional play, but his belligerent disposition, which Philadelphia fans took to be colorful, was less welcome among his teammates. During the offseason – presumably after the Phillies acquired catcher Harry McCurdy – Susce was assigned to the Buffalo Bisons in the International League.

It is unclear how much playing time, if any, Susce got in Buffalo. The 1930 Bisons used as many as five catchers with the lion's share of play devoted to future AL backstop Frank Grube. Midway into the season Susce was returned to the Phillies, who released him on July 30. Immediately signed by the Giants, Susce was assigned to the Kansas City Blues in the American Association.[5] The 22-year-old demonstrated an aptitude at the plate – .304 in 125 at-bats – but drew considerable criticism behind it, both in his handling of pitchers and with his strong but inaccurate arm. The next year Susce reported to the Blues spring training as, at best, the club's number-three catcher. In June he was demoted to the Springfield (Illinois) Senators in the Three-I League, where he handled the bulk of the catching responsibilities for the Class-B club. During the offseason he was obtained by the Beaumont Exporters, the Detroit Tigers affiliate in the Class-A Texas League.

That same offseason saw the departure of catchers Johnny Grabowski and Wally Schang from the Tigers roster around the time the club was also engaged in negotiations that would have sent a third backstop, Ray Hayworth, to the Washington Senators. Though Hayworth remained with the club, eventually wrestling the starting job from 36-year-old Muddy Ruel, the unsettled and ever-changing developments prompted the club to break its 1932 spring camp with Susce as insurance. He made two late-inning defensive appearances through May 13 before being assigned to the Montreal Royals in the International League. There he shared the catching responsibilities with Grabowski and veteran backstop Lee Head through the remainder of the season.

In 1933 Susce narrowly missed an opportunity to make the parent club before the Tigers opted for minor-league catching prospect Frank Reiber instead. Demoted to Beaumont, Susce suffered a broken shoulder, which sidelined him through most of the year. He torpedoed his chances the following spring after telling Tigers third baseman Marv Owen, "[y]ou'll soon be in the sticks where you belong."[6] When Mickey Cochrane got wind of the remark, the rookie manager immediately optioned Susce to the Milwaukee Brewers in the American Association. Though he hit very well – .370-1-30 in 154 at-bats – Susce's stay in Milwaukee proved short-lived after he nearly came to blows with outfield teammate Tony Kubek. He split the rest of the season between Beaumont and the Hollywood Stars in the Pacific Coast League.

By 1935 Susce had built a reputation as overly "spirited ... to the point of militancy"[7] to the extent that when the Tigers offered Brewers manager Allan Sothoron the option of taking the 27-year-old catcher back, the offer was declined. Susce was sold to the Toledo Mud Hens in the American Association, where, despite an all-star campaign, he again wore out his welcome after refusing a pinch-hit assignment. Toledo manager Fred Haney immediately suspended him for the rest of the season.

Susce earned all-star honors in each of the next three seasons while moving among five clubs (mostly in the Texas League). More importantly, over this time he developed into a fine defensive catcher. "Susce is one of the best receivers in the minors," said *The Sporting News* contributor Charles J. Doyle. "[F]or some reason the scouts pass him up ... [yet] yell about the shortage of catchers."[8] After the 1938 season Susce arranged his release from the Tulsa Oilers in order to negotiate directly with the major-league clubs.

Susce found a quick welcome from his hometown. After the Pirates traded veteran backstop Al Todd to the Boston Bees in December 1938, their roster consisted of two catchers who had averaged fewer than 60 games per season over the preceding three years. On February 15, 1939, Susce signed with the Bucs. Given an opportunity to compete for the starting job, he ended up serving behind the catching platoon of Ray Berres and Ray Mueller and did not get into a game until August, when the pair were sidelined by injury and illness. He had just one hit in his first 16 at-bats and barely climbed above .200 with a 3-for-3 day at the plate on the last day of the season.

Though Susce reported to Pirates spring training in 1940, his fate was likely sealed by the club's October 1939 acquisition of Spud Davis. Susce was released by the Bucs on March 20. He was picked up by the St. Louis Browns the next day. The move was a surprise to many observers; the Browns skipper was Fred Haney, the manager who had suspended Susce five years earlier. But coming off a 111-loss season in 1939, the club seemingly had few options. Moreover, Susce's improved work behind the plate included the ability to handle the knuckleball – a much-needed skill after the club acquired 36-year-old knuckler Johnny Niggeling. In 1940 Susce made a career-high 61 appearances for the Browns before being released at the end of the season.

Parallel events unfurling more than 500 miles to the northeast would have a major effect on Susce's future. After Cleveland Indians manager Ossie Vitt resigned following the 1940 season, the Indians were in the hunt for a new skipper and coaching staff. In January 1941 they hired Susce as their bullpen coach and, if necessary, spare receiver. Over the next four years Susce appeared behind the plate 35 times, briefly holding down the starting job in 1944 before he was sidelined by injury. But his full-time responsibilities were aiding in the development of his younger assigns and he took this job very seriously. Susce also provided the club with "a top-flight bench jockey,"[9] and even with his advanced age he was still quite capable of picking a fight. In 1943 he suffered a broken nose and damaged eye, the likely result of this very propensity, and years later reportedly threatened to take on an entire team singlehandedly. Susce also had an amusing reputation among the men in blue. In 1942 he capably filled in as an emergency spring-training umpire and did a fine job. "I don't know why he wouldn't," cracked umpire John Quinn. "He umpired from the catcher's position for 19 [actually up to that time just 13] years."[10]

In 1942 Susce was reunited with his first professional manager, Burt Shotton, in guiding 24-year-old player-manager Lou Boudreau through Boudreau's inaugural season as a skipper. With the exception of 1948, when Susce spent one season as manager of the Indians' Class-D affiliate in the Pennsylvania-Ohio-New York League, he remained in Cleveland through most of Boudreau's tenure as the Indians manager, later reuniting with the future Hall of Famer in Boston and Kansas City as well. "Susce was a force in the formation of the Boudreau dynasty," said *Cleveland Press* sports editor Franklin Lewis.[11] Arguably Susce might have relished the opportunity to remain in Cleveland throughout his entire coaching career had a dustup not developed regarding one of his many athletically inclined children.

Shortly before launching his professional career Susce had married Pennsylvania native Anna Theresa Pendro. A year his senior, Anna worked for the National Biscuit Company (now Nabisco) which sponsored a semipro club in Pittsburgh. They met while both attended one of its games. The union produced two daughters and four sons, with three of the boys eventually surfacing among baseball's professional ranks.[12] George Daniel, Susce's eldest son (a/k/a "Junior"), was a standout baseball player at his father's alma mater, Schenley High School. A superb pitcher and hitter, Junior was invited to work out at Cleveland Stadium on numerous occasions as the Indians aggressively pursued him. But in January 1950, after graduating from high school the previous June, Junior instead signed with the Boston Red Sox. Shortly after the signing, Susce was released by Cleveland. "[W]e should have received better treatment than that from a fellow who had been part of our Indian family as long as George had," complained Indians GM Hank Greenberg.[13]

Susce followed his son into the Red Sox fold and was appointed manager of the club's Marion (Ohio) affiliate in the Class-D Ohio-Indiana League. On June 30, 1950, one week after Steve O'Neill replaced Red Sox manager Joe McCarthy, Susce was advanced to the parent club as Boston's bullpen coach (he and O'Neill had developed a close friendship as fellow coaches in Cleveland). Susce was reunited with Boudreau when the latter replaced O'Neill in 1952 and followed the future Hall of Famer to Kansas City after a dismal 69-85 Red Sox finish in 1954. (Ironically Susce's dismissal came shortly after the Red Sox purchased his son's contract from their Triple-A affiliate.) Susce spent two years in Kansas City, only to be released under circumstances eerily similar to his Cleveland departure. In 1956 Susce's second oldest son, Paul, was an All-American pitcher at Auburn University. After his graduation that spring, the Athletics aggressively pursued the youngster. When Susce insisted that the club offer his son a three-year contract, management balked and Paul signed with the Pirates. Susce was released shortly thereafter.

Susce returned to the major leagues on April 6, 1958, replacing Milwaukee Braves bullpen coach Bob Keely (who had resigned a month earlier). He remained with the Braves through the 1959 season and stayed with the organization the following year as a coach with the Triple-A Louisville Colonels. In 1961 he was hired by the expansion Washington Senators. Except for 1968, when he signed for one season with the Jacksonville Suns in the Triple-A International League, Susce continued with the franchise through its 1972 move to Texas.

Susce's longevity as a major-league coach stemmed in part from the friendships he forged with Boudreau, O'Neill, and, later, Ted Williams. But Susce's credentials extended far beyond mere friendship. A tireless worker, he lived and breathed baseball. "He forced [me] to think baseball constantly," said Cleveland catching prospect Hank Ruszkowski. "'Make every second count,' Susce would say. 'If you were behind the plate right now, what pitch would you call?' It would go on like that all day."[14] Despite a mere .228 major-league batting average, Susce was well respected for the batting tips he offered. Moreover, he was credited for his work with pitchers, particularly Art Ditmar and Bennie Daniels, who praised him in learning to throw a slider.

But above all Susce was known as a stickler for conditioning. A disciple of calisthenics, he drew commendations from slugger Frank Howard and lefty hurler Jim Kaat for his ability to keep them in top shape. In 1964, when the Senators were on a West Coast swing, Sandy Koufax sought Susce out during a period when the future Hall of Fame southpaw was suffering from a sore arm. Not everyone was on-board with Susce's strict exercise regimen. Future Hall of Fame second baseman Joe Gordon and lefty hurler Mel Parnell were among his skeptics, and Boston manager Steve O'Neill once cracked, "Okay, George, you take the calisthenics while we watch."[15] But Susce would not be dissuaded. When he was close to 60 he could put his hands flat on the ground and touch his ankle with his nose without bending a knee. He could, it was reported, "out-exercise any fellow half his age."[16] He took his conditioning zeal outside of baseball by conducting calisthenics classes for the University of Pittsburgh track team in 1958, and the Pompano Beach Ladies Recreation Department exercise class nine years later.

After the 1972 season, Susce was released by the Texas Rangers after Ted Williams begged out of the final year of his managerial contract. The agile 65-year-old tried to secure another major-league coaching job, to no avail. In 1974 Susce helped in the conditioning of the Chicago White Sox during spring training. Observing his regimen, manager Chuck Tanner remarked, "[W]atching him go through exercises every day, I have to believe this man's never going to die."[17] In September of that year Susce worked as an instructor at the Ted Williams Baseball Camp in Lakeville, Massachusetts.

In 1950 Susce had moved his family from Pittsburgh to Sarasota, Florida. He spent many an offseason in construction and on at least two occasions barnstormed with the famed all-star squads of Dizzy Dean (1934) and Bob Feller (1946). He had always made time for youth baseball programs but, after his wife died of cancer in 1973, Susce immersed himself deeper into these programs. "I get a bang out of it," he said. "I've always enjoyed seeing somebody improve. All my life, I've been trying to help people. … [The] busier I am the better."[18] In 1977 Susce married a divorcee, Brooklyn, New York, native Jean Eva (Urbanowicz) Percy, but the union ended in divorce seven years later.

A strong family man, in the early morning of February 12, 1947, Susce had to rush his wife and children out of their Pittsburgh home when the house caught fire. Caused by an overheated furnace, the fire was quickly contained. Eight years later the importance he placed in family became even more clear when Susce listed them as his hobby for the Athletics' press programs. "I figure a hobby is what you like to do most in your spare time. There's nothing I'd rather do with it than to spend it with my family. So that must be my hobby," he explained.[19]

Susce established a wide network of friends both in and out of baseball. With a keen sense of humor, he was much prized on the rubber-chicken circuit in both western Pennsylvania (where he shared podiums with Hall of Famers Stan Musial and Honus Wagner) and Florida. Susce was also very generous with his time. In 1946 he accompanied his Indians teammates to Cleveland's Crile Veterans Administration Hospital to cheer the veterans. In the years following he participated in countless old timer's games – often accompanied by his sons – that benefited the Hospitalized Veterans Fund, the March of Dimes, and many youth baseball programs. In 1966 Bob Addie wrote in *The Sporting News* that Susce was the genuine article, the " 'Good Kid,' as generations of ball players from Abner Doubleday's time have called [him]."[20]

Susce contracted a lung ailment that led to his passing in Sarasota on February 25, 1986. Despite his advanced age (78) his death came as a shock to his immediate family because Susce never smoked or drank and remained in top physical shape. He was buried at Sarasota Memorial Park. Two decades later his son Paul, then a baseball coach and teacher at George Wythe High School in Richmond, Virginia, helped coordinate with local police and parks and recreation departments the establishment of a youth baseball program for at-risk children. Paul played a pivotal role in renaming the program, formerly known as Strike Out Substance Abuse, in honor of his father: The George Susce "Good Kid" Clinics and Camps.

In 1940 Susce had nearly half of his 268 major-league at-bats playing for the lowly St. Louis Browns. Considered at best a third-string catcher, as a young man Susce negated his chances of a longer career with his firebrand nature. He eventually mellowed to become one of the most endeared and longest-serving coaches in baseball.

Sources

In addition to the sources cited in the Notes, the author also consulted Ancestry.com and Baseball-Reference.com, and conducted two interviews:

George Susce interview with Dr. Eugene Murdock, January 4, 1980 (bit.ly/29Hs4mn).

Paul F. Susce interview, July 8, 2016.

The author wishes to thank SABR member Bill Mortell for his valuable research.

Notes

1. "Strategy - Sometimes It's Smart, Sometimes It's Senseless," *The Sporting News*, May 11, 1955: 14.
2. Ed Pollock, "Playing the Game - George Susce Is a Family Man Now," *The Sporting News*, March 30, 1955: 20.
3. Dan Rooney, the brother of future Pittsburgh Steelers owner Art Rooney, was among Susce's high-school teammates.
4. "George Susce ... There Was Only One Way to Play the Game," *Sarasota Herald-Tribune*, May 29, 1974: 35.
5. Baseball-Reference suggests Susce split the remainder of the 1930 season between Kansas City and Newark, New Jersey, a matter the author was unable to verify.
6. Edgar G. Brands, "Between Innings," *The Sporting News*, October 25, 1934: 4.
7. "Ginger Snap for the Tigers," *The Sporting News*, November 17, 1932: 1.
8. Charles J. Doyle, "Buc Fan Consensus Supports Traynor," *The Sporting News*, September 23, 1937: 3.
9. "Publications," *The Sporting News*, May 15, 1941: 6.
10. "Training Camp Notes," *The Sporting News*, April 2, 1942: 8.
11. Franklin Lewis, "Susce's Departure Marks Conclusion of Another Era," *The Sporting News*, January 18, 1950: 5.
12. The sports bloodline did not end there. In 1968 Susce's grandson appeared in the College World Series before launching a three-year professional pitching career. In the 1950s Susce's daughter Helene did promotional work for KDKA-Pittsburgh, the broadcast station for the Pirates; she was briefly engaged to a grandson of Connie Mack before marrying Boston College fullback and Detroit Lions draftee Emidio "Turk" Petrarca. The author discovered a Larry Susce pitching for the Palestine Pals in the East Texas League in 1938 but was unable to make a familial connection.
13. Ed McAuley, "Indians Release Coach Susce; Accepted Red Sox' Bid for Son," *The Sporting News*, January 18, 1950: 5.
14. Hal Lebovitz, "Embree Acts on Top by His Ex-Roomie," *The Sporting News*, January 14, 1948: 14.
15. Stan Baumgartner, "Knicknacks Nixed for Phils' Training," *The Sporting News*, February 4, 1953: 15.
16. Bob Addie, "Pilot Gil Lauds Work of Nat Tutors – Rehires All Five," *The Sporting News*, November 7, 1964: 24.
17. "George Susce ... There Was Only One Way."
18. Ibid.
19. Ed Pollock.
20. Bob Addie, "Capital Coaches Earn Repeat Engagement," *The Sporting News*, October 22, 1966: 22.

WAYNE TERWILLIGER

BY C. PAUL ROGERS III

A baseball lifer, Wayne Terwilliger found himself with more notoriety at age 80 than he had garnered in his previous 56 seasons in Organized Baseball combined when he agreed to return for the 2005 season as manager of the Fort Worth Cats in the independent Central League.[1] In doing so, he joined the legendary Connie Mack as the only 80-year-old managers in baseball history. And after he led the Cats to the Central League championship that year, he became the only manager in his 80s to manage a championship team. After that season, Terwilliger gave up the managerial reigns but returned to the Cats as the first-base coach, still pitching batting practice and jogging to the first-base coaching box before every inning.

Terwilliger's years with the Cats were the culmination of a journey that began when he was born on June 27, 1925, in the small central Michigan town of Clare, about 85 miles north of Lansing. He was the oldest of two children born to Ivan and Doris Terwilliger. When he was about a year old his family moved to Charlotte, Michigan, a slightly larger town about 20 miles south of Lansing. His father ran a bar in town while his mother played the piano and violin and wrote poetry. On Sundays when the bar was closed, Wayne's father listened to the Tigers games on the radio and Wayne began listening as well when he was about 5 or 6. Charlie Gehringer, the Tigers' great second baseman of the 1930s, soon became his hero. Ivan took Wayne to a couple of Tigers games in Navin Field and he also went annually to a game with his Cub Scout troop. Once, as father and son sat in the upper deck of the right-field bleachers, Lou Gehrig blasted a home run right at them, landing only a couple of rows in front.[2]

Early on, Terwilliger developed his hand-eye coordination by bouncing a rubber ball against the front steps of his house, hour after hour, day after day, imagining that he was playing in a big-league game. In high school, basketball became his best sport, although he wasn't very tall. He also played football and by his senior year had "ballooned" to 147 pounds and made all-conference playing quarterback in a single-wing offense on a team that finished 6-1-1.[3]

Baseball remained Wayne's favorite sport, although it was not his best sport. He made the high-school varsity as a utility infielder as a freshman, even though he had skipped a grade. Terwilliger's team won the conference championship his senior year and he played well enough to decide to focus on baseball during college.

He graduated from Charlotte High School in 1942 and headed for Western Michigan College of Education in Kalamazoo (now Western Michigan University) just after he turned 17. Terwilliger wasn't ready for the rigors of college academically. He flunked a course in Western Civilization in the fall, which made him ineligible to play baseball in the spring. With World War II well underway, Terwilliger, after he learned he would be ineligible, went straight to the Marine Recruiting Office in Kalamazoo and joined the Marines. He was not yet 18 so he went home and waited.[4]

In August 1943, two months after his 18th birthday, Terwilliger was ordered to report to boot camp in San Diego. After boot camp, he trained to be a radio operator and a machine gunner in an amphibious tank unit.[5] In March 1944 he was assigned to the 2nd Armored Amphibian Battalion of the 2nd Marine Division, where he learned to operate amphibious tanks. Their role was to lead the way for the infantry assault on the Pacific Islands the military needed for airstrips. Terwilliger saw heavy action on Saipan, Tinian, and later Iwo Jima.[6] On Saipan, his tank became bogged down in a mortar shell hole while under heavy fire, forcing its evacuation.[7] It took 26 days of intense fighting to secure the island. On Iwo Jima Terwilliger's tank unit led the way for the infantry who captured Mount Suribachi and eventually took control of the entire island.[8] In fact, Terwilliger was in one of the first tanks, if not the first, to go ashore there.[9]

After the Marines secured Saipan, Terwilliger was able to play some baseball on the island on makeshift fields and his battalion team went 28-0 to win the 2nd Division championship.[10] Even though he had not played above high school, he was chosen to go to Guam to play in an all-star game.

After Iwo Jima, Terwilliger's unit was sent to Maui to prepare for the expected invasion of Japan. He was playing baseball there when he heard that the Japanese had surrendered.[11] After returning to the mainland, he was discharged from the service in Chicago on December 5, 1945, and hitchhiked the 200 miles home to Charlotte, Michigan.[12] In February 1946 he married Mary Jane Locke, whom he had started dating after high school, and thanks to the GI Bill enrolled at Western Michigan for the spring term.[13] The couple were married for 25 years before divorcing and had two children, Marcie and Steve.

In Terwilliger's first year back at college, he played end on the freshman football team and played varsity basketball and baseball. He excelled on defense in basketball and had an outstanding game against Indiana State with steals, assists, and a few baskets. Afterward, the Indiana State coach complimented Twig on his great game. He turned out to be John Wooden, who would leave to coach UCLA in a couple of years.[14]

Playing baseball in the Marines had helped Terwilliger's confidence and he developed into an outstanding second baseman who hit about .350 in college. In 1947 the Terwilliger-led Western Michigan team twice beat Michigan State and its future Hall of Famer Robin Roberts. In 1948, Terwilliger's final year, the Broncos defeated both Michigan State and Michigan and finished 16-5, just missing out on the Mid-American Conference championship.[15]

In the summers during college Terwilliger played for the semipro House of David team in Benton Harbor, about 50 miles from Kalamazoo. In addition to playing in the semipro Michigan-Indiana League, the club also played a number of exhibition games against barnstorming Negro League teams. Terwilliger had planned to return to Benton Harbor for the 1948 summer, but by then he had attracted some professional scouts. After a tryout in Wrigley Field for the Cubs, the club offered him $450 a month to play for the Des Moines Bruins in the Class-A Western League.

Terwilliger signed but then played sparingly in Des Moines because he was blocked by Red Treadway, a former major-league second baseman who was hitting well over .300.[16] His first professional RBI occurred when he was beaned with the bases loaded.[17] Remarkably, however, in 1949 Terwilliger jumped from not playing in Class A the previous year to becoming the starting second baseman for the Los Angeles Angels in the Triple-A Pacific Coast League. He started the season like a house afire and three weeks into the season was hitting a robust .412. Although his average tapered off, he was selected to play in the PCL All-Star game in Seattle, in which he doubled, scored a run, and played well defensively.[18]

Terwilliger was hitting .275 in 115 games and 432 at-bats for a last-place team when on July 31 the Chicago Cubs purchased his contract after an injury to their second baseman, Emil Verban. It was a little over a year since Twig had signed a professional contract and then not been able to crack the lineup in Class-A Des Moines. He first appeared in a major-league game on August 6 as a late-inning pinch-hitter for Gene Mauch in a game the Cubs were winning 10-0 against the Boston Braves in Wrigley Field. He struck out against Braves bonus baby Johnny Antonelli on three swinging strikes.

The next day Terwilliger relieved Mauch at second base with the Cubs losing 7-0 and, after flying out to left field in the sixth inning, connected for his first big-league hit, a blooper to right field against Bill Voiselle. He got his first big-league starts on August 10 and 11 against the Pittsburgh Pirates, going a combined 2-for-6. Then, beginning with his last two at-bats in a game against the Pirates in Pittsburgh, Twig ran off eight straight base hits to become only the fourth rookie to have eight or more consecutive base hits.[19] The string upped his batting average to .364 after just 11 games in the major leagues.

Terwilliger tailed off from that hot start and hit .223 in 36 games and 112 at-bats in his abbreviated rookie campaign. Included in that hit total were his first two big-league home runs: a three-run shot against Dave Koslo in the Polo Grounds on August 23 and another three-run blast against the Pirates' Bob Chesnes in Wrigley Field on September 4.

The Cubs had finished in last place in 1949 and were committed to a youth movement in 1950 under manager Frankie Frisch. Terwilliger had a strong spring and won the starting second baseman job. A month into the season he was hitting about .290 but for the season leveled off to .240 in 480 at-bats in 133 games. Although listed at 5-foot-11, 165 pounds, he showed surprising power, slugging 10 home runs and connecting off the likes of Curt Simmons, Don Newcombe, Larry Jansen, and Dave Koslo. He also showed good baserunning ability, stealing 13 bases. Late in the season his hometown and surrounding communities gave him a Wayne Terwilliger Day before a Sunday afternoon game in Wrigley Field.[20]

Terwilliger began the 1951 season as the Cubs' regular second baseman, but struggled at the plate, batting only .214 in 50 early-season games. Then on June 15, the trading deadline, the Cubs made a major trade and dealt him and Andy Pafko, Johnny Schmitz, and Rube Walker to the Brooklyn Dodgers for Joe Hatten, Bruce Edwards, Gene Hermanski, and Eddie Miksis. Once with the Dodgers, Terwilliger played sparingly since somebody named Jackie Robinson was manning second base there.[21] On July 21 he did win a game for the Dodgers with a bases-loaded pinch-hit single off Harry Brecheen of the Cardinals. In 37 games, Twig hit .280 in just 50 at-bats. He was on the Dodgers bench when Bobby Thomson hit the famous Shot Heard 'Round the World to snatch the pennant away from the Dodgers on October 3.

Terwilliger faced stiff competition to make the Dodgers in 1952 with Rocky Bridges and Bobby Morgan also on the roster and so was sent to the St. Paul Saints of the American Association just before the season began. Once there he played behind Jack Cassini, who was having an outstanding year at second base.[22] During the season, Terwilliger saw firsthand the fierce rivalry between the Saints and the Minneapolis Millers, suffering a beaning that he believed was intentional.[23] Terwilliger finished the season with a hot bat and by going 3-for-3 the last day of the season, boosted his average to .312 in 125 at-bats.

His performance with the Saints caught the attention of the Washington Senators, then officially called the Nationals, who purchased his contract from the Dodgers and ordered him to report to their 1953 spring training in Orlando.[24] In that spring training he beat out Mel Hoderlein and a rookie named Leroy Dietzel for the starting position at second base.

Terwilliger started the season with a hot bat and was hitting .360 a week into the season before cooling off. On May 28, he smashed a first-inning home run on a hanging slider from Whitey Ford of the Yankees in a game the Senators lost 7-2. In later years, Twig recalled that home run as his greatest individual thrill in baseball.[25] He played well in the field in 1953 and continued to get timely hits, including a 10th-inning game-winning bloop single against Satchel Paige of the Browns on June 3. Two days later Twig hit the only grand slam of his career, off Saul Rogovin in Chicago against the White Sox. That blast even caught the attention of President Dwight Eisenhower, who, when told of it, said, "And isn't that Terwilliger playing grand ball?"[26]

Terwilliger slumped in July and Senators owner Clark Griffith arranged for Ted Williams, who had just returned from active duty in Korea, to work with him before a game in Boston. It was the beginning of a very positive relationship between the two. Terwilliger finished 1953 with the best season of his career, hitting .252 in 134 games and 541 plate appearances, both career highs. He smacked four home runs and drove in 46 runs, also tops in his career, as the Senators finished in fifth place with a 76-76 record. A Washington team would not have another .500-plus season until 1969 when Ted Williams was the manager and Terwilliger was his third-base coach.[27]

During the offseason Terwilliger and his wife returned to Kalamazoo where Twig worked in the paper mill and officiated high-school basketball games to keep in shape. For his efforts in 1953 he finally received a $500 raise to $8,500 for the '54 season.[28] He began the season as the Nationals' regular second baseman but struggled at the plate. In late May he hit home runs in three consecutive games against the Philadelphia Athletics in Connie Mack Stadium, but hit only .208 for the season in 106 games. He even suffered the indignity of batting ninth in the lineup late in the year, behind pitcher Mickey McDermott.[29]

After the season, the Senators sold Terwilliger to the New York Giants, who promptly optioned him to the Minneapolis Millers of the American Association. Terwilliger played well on a team loaded with former and future major leaguers and was batting .297 in late June when the parent Giants came to Minneapolis for an exhibition game. Giants second baseman Davey Williams was having back problems and so after the game, Giants manager Leo Durocher told Twig, "Get on the bus, you're coming with us."[30]

In his first game with the Giants, Terwilliger made a brilliant backhand play on a hard grounder by Red Schoendienst with two outs in the ninth and the tying and winning runs on to preserve a 1-0 victory. He went on to field .985 in 78 games to tie Schoendienst for the highest fielding percentage in the league by second basemen.[31] He struggled at bat after his callup, hitting in the low .200s until he was seriously beaned by Johnny Klippstein of the Cincinnati Reds. The pitch broke the batting helmet but kept Terwilliger out of the lineup for just three days.[32] When he returned, Frankie Frisch, who was then a radio announcer for the Giants, suggested that he back off from the plate a little more than usual until he got back into the swing of things. It turned out to be good advice because Twig hit .300 for the last two months of the season and finished at a solid .257 in 80 games.[33]

Terwilliger played sparingly early in the 1956 season as new Giants manager Bill Rigney started the season with Daryl Spencer at second base. Twig had only 18 at-bats by mid-June and requested reassignment to Minneapolis so he could play.[34] Once back with the Millers, he batted .245 in 344 plate appearances. That winter he ventured to Venezuela and played for the Maracaibo Centauros in the Venezuelan Winter League.[35]

Terwilliger returned to the Millers in 1957 as the regular second baseman and batted .270 in 144 games and 614 plate appearances while leading the American Association in fielding at second base. That winter he accepted an offer from longtime baseball man Salty Parker to play with Los Leones del Escogido in Santo Domingo, the capital of the Dominican Republic, where his teammates included a 19-year-old Juan Marichal as well as several of his teammates on the Millers such as future major leaguers Felipe Alou, Ozzie Virgil, Bill White, and Willie Kirkland. The loaded team swept to the league championship.

After the 1957 season the Giants traded Terwilliger to the Detroit Tigers for fellow infielder Jack Dittmer. Although Terwilliger had grown up rooting for the Tigers, he was not destined to play for them. Instead he was assigned to the Charleston, West Virginia, Senators, the Tigers' Triple-A team in the American Association. There he had a banner year for a team that won the American Association regular-season championship. He led the league in virtually every defensive category as well as in runs scored with 103 and stolen bases with 24. Although his batting average was just .269, he was named the league's Most Valuable Player for 1958.[36]

That performance convinced the Kansas City Athletics to take Terwilliger in the Rule 5 draft heading into the 1959 season. Although plagued by a midseason finger injury, Twig hit .267 in part-time duty in 74 games, the highest average of his major-league career. Highlights included a solo home run in Detroit's Briggs Stadium against future Hall of Famer Jim Bunning on May 9.

Terwilliger began the 1960 season with the A's but early in the season wrenched his back trying to field a bad-hop groundball. He stayed in the game and popped up in his only at-bat before telling the trainer about his back injury. That at-bat would be the final one of his big-league career.[37] He was sold a few weeks later to the New York Yankees who promptly optioned him to their Richmond Triple-A farm club. He played regularly for the Virginians for about a month before reinjuring his back, which limited his playing time. For the year he batted .206 in 277 at-bats.

Late in the season the Yankees asked Terwilliger if he would be interested in managing their Class-B team in Greensboro, North Carolina. Terwilliger was 35 years old and plagued with a bad back, so he accepted the offer.[38] He immediately loved managing and drew upon what he had learned from his major-league managers. Those included Frankie Frisch, Bucky Harris, Leo Durocher, Eddie Stanky, Harry Craft, and Charlie Dressen. His first team finished third in the Carolina League with a 70-68 record but, perhaps because the team had won the pennant by 10½ games the year before, the Yankees fired him at the end of the season.[39]

The Washington Senators' farm director, Hal Keller, however, soon offered Twig a job managing their Pensacola club in the Class-D Alabama-Florida League.[40] Pensacola had a banner year under Terwilliger's tutelage and won the pennant by a whopping 22 games, finishing with a 79-38 record.[41] That earned Twig a promotion for the 1963 season to Wisconsin Rapids in the Class-A Midwest League. He then spent two seasons, 1964 and 1965, managing the Geneva Senators in the Class-A New York-Pennsylvania League. In 1966 he was back in the Carolina League managing the Burlington, North Carolina, Senators.

Burlington finished in second place with a 76-62 record and earned Terwilliger a promotion all the way to the Triple-A Hawaii Islanders of the Pacific Coast League for 1967. The Senators moved their Triple-A affiliate to Buffalo for 1968 and Terwilliger moved with them. Although the team finished in seventh place, Twig was set to return to the Bisons in 1969 when Ted Williams intervened.

Williams had been named manager of the parent Senators when Bob Short purchased the club after the 1968 season. Terwilliger went to spring training with the parent team to help out before his Buffalo team reported. Twig impressed Williams with how much energy and hustle he displayed so one day Williams sidled up to him and told him he was going to be his third-base coach with the Senators.[42] That year the team won 21 more games than the year before and finished 10 games over .500 with an 86-76 record as Williams was named American League Manager of the Year.[43]

Terwilliger continued to coach with Williams for three more years, including 1972 when the Senators moved to Arlington, Texas, and became the Texas Rangers. That was also the year when Terwilliger and Mary Jane, his wife of 25 years, separated and divorced.[44] Although out of his big-league job when Williams resigned as manager, the Houston Astros hired Twig to manage their Columbus, Georgia, club in the Double-A Southern League for the 1973 season. The club finished in third place, just below .500 with a 69-70 record.

Terwilliger stayed out of baseball in 1974, returning to his hometown, Charlotte, Michigan, and taking over and running his father's tavern full-time. He also rewed, marrying a woman named Lin whom he had met in Arlington. When Hal Keller called and offered Terwilliger the opportunity to return to baseball in 1975 and manage the Rangers' Lynchburg, Virginia, farm club in the Class-A Carolina League, he eagerly accepted.[45] He moved with the Rangers' Class-A affiliate to Asheville, North Carolina, in 1976 and managed the Tourists in the short-season

Western Carolinas League for four years through 1979, finishing with a winning record each year.

That stretch earned him a promotion to the Tulsa Drillers of the Double-A Texas League for 1980, where he managed future big leaguers Wayne Tolleson and Nick Capra. The following year Twig was back in the big leagues and back with the Texas Rangers as the third-base coach for manager Don Zimmer.[46] He remained with the Rangers for five seasons, working under four managers.[47] When Texas manager Bobby Valentine decided not to bring Twig back for 1986, Minnesota Twins manager Ray Miller quickly hired him to work with the club's young infielders and to coach first base.

Tom Kelly replaced Miller as manager late in the season and kept Terwilliger on his coaching staff for 1987. It turned out to be a monumental year for the Twins as they won the American League West Division by two games, defeated the Detroit Tigers for the American League pennant, and then beat the St. Louis Cardinals in an exciting seven-game World Series. Terwilliger remained on the Twins coaching staff for a total of nine years, including 1991, when Minnesota again won the World Series, defeating the Atlanta Braves in another thrilling seven-game Series.

Late during his time with the Twins, he began experiencing excruciating pain from two of his toes while pitching batting practice. He very much wanted to be able to continue to throw batting practice, and eventually had parts of the two toes amputated to relieve the pain.[48]

Terwilliger's run with the Twins ended after the strike-shortened 1994 season. The Twins let it be known that Twig would be "retiring" and on August 10, the day before the strike began, the Twins players and coaches surprised him with a fishing boat and accessories in a pregame ceremony. He was 69 years old.[49]

Terwilliger was not long retired because in November St. Paul Saints owner Mike Veeck hired him to coach first base under manager Marty Scott.[50] The Saints had been re-established in 1993 and played in the independent Northern League. Terwilliger spent the next eight years coaching for the Saints, who were a perennial pennant-winner or contender in their league. During his years there, the Saints had many former major leaguers, including Jack Morris, Darryl Strawberry, Glenn Davis, Dan Peltier, and Matt Nokes. J.D. Drew, the first pick in the draft in 1997, played for the Saints that season when he could not come to terms with the Phillies, who had drafted him.[51]

Late in the 2002 season Terwilliger announced that he would not return to the Saints. He was moving back to Texas with his wife, Lin, because her father was ailing. On Labor Day of that last season, the Saints held a day for Twig and officially retired the number 5 that he had worn for the organization.[52]

Terwilliger was 77 years old when he left the Saints and settled in Weatherford, to the west of Fort Worth. Marty Scott, the manager Twig worked under in St. Paul, was also back in Texas as the president of the Fort Worth Cats of the independent Central League. Although Terwilliger had not managed in 22 years, he approached Scott and Cats owner Carl Bell about managing the Cats and, after a lunch meeting, they agreed. Thus, in 2003 Terwilliger became the oldest minor-league manager in baseball history and the second oldest ever, after Connie Mack, who retired from managing the Philadelphia Athletics at 87. His first season he hired former major leaguers Toby Harrah and Dan Smith as his coaches and the club won the second half of its division before losing in the playoffs.

In 2004 Terwilliger returned to manage the Cats and the team finished 51-43 but just missed the playoffs.[53] He was diagnosed with bladder cancer that year, but after surgery recovered and was back managing the Cats in 2005.[54] That year the team won its division in both halves of the season and then defeated Pensacola and San Angelo in the playoffs to win the league championship for their 80-year-old manager. Not surprisingly, the league named Terwilliger manager of the year and he drew coverage in the *New York Times* for his accomplishment.[55]

Twig stepped down as manager after the season, finishing with a combined 162-120 won-lost record for his three seasons as Cats manager. However, new Cats manager Stan Hough, who had been Terwilliger's third-base coach with the Cats, persuaded him to return as his first-base coach. The Cats had joined the now independent American Association, named for the Triple-A league that Terwilliger had played in in the 1950s. He stayed on as a coach for the Cats for five years before retiring from baseball for good after the 2010 season.[56]

In 2006 Terwilliger published his autobiography, *Terwilliger Bunts One*. It was written with the help of two longtime St. Paul Saints fans, Nancy Peterson and Peter Boehm. The title arose from Annie Dillard's memoirs called *An American Childhood*. In it, Dillard wrote that her mother once heard "Terwilliger Bunts One" on a radio broadcast of a game and asked, "Is that English?" Thereafter, her mother repeated the phrase regularly.[57]

Altogether, Terwilliger spent 62 years in professional baseball before retiring to his home in Weatherford, Texas, to play golf. Four years later he made news when, tired of sitting at home, he re-entered the workplace in 2014 at age 88, going to work sacking groceries at a local grocery store.[58]

Notes

1. Ira Berkow, "At 80, a Manager Keeps Going and Going and …," *New York Times*, December 7, 2005: D-1.
2. Wayne Terwilliger with Nancy Peterson and Peter Boehm, *Terwilliger Bunts One* (Guilford, Connecticut: Insiders' Guide, 2006), 8-12.
3. Terwilliger, 14.
4. Terwilliger, 17-18.
5. Terwilliger, 17-18.
6. Terwilliger, 19-38.
7. Terwilliger later described what happened: "We had to abandon the tank. Everybody scattered into the nearest foxholes. But at just about that time a Jap tank rolled up and began blasting away. I knew I had to get out of there, so I ran for the beach, zigzagging in and out with the tank chasing me. I'm sure I'd be lying out there somewhere now, if it hadn't been for one of our own tanks, which luckily showed up while I was doing all that broken-field running. They knocked out the Jap tank." baseballinwartime.com/player_biographies/terwilliger_wayne.htm.
8. Terwilliger, 34-37.
9. Steve Wilstein, "Time Rolls On and So Does Twig Terwilliger," Boston.com, February 3, 2005.
10. Terwilliger, 32-33.
11. Terwilliger, 37.
12. Terwilliger, 38.
13. Terwilliger, 39.
14. Terwilliger, 40.
15. Terwilliger, 40-41.
16. Treadway ended up hitting .352 for the year at Des Moines.
17. Ray Buck, "At 88, Wayne Terwilliger Forgets to Act His Age," *Fort Worth Star Telegram*, February 19, 2014.
18. Terwilliger, 49-56.
19. Babe Herman had nine straight hits as a rookie in 1926 while Ted Williams (1939) and Glenn Wright (1924) also had eight consecutive hits as rookies. Terwilliger later recalled that one of his hits went right through Ted Kluszewski, who was one of the best fielding first basemen in the league. "They probably gave me a break on that call," he remembered. Brent Kelley, "Wayne Terwilliger Interviewed: It Took 40 years to Get to the Top," Sports Collectors Digest, May 1, 1992: 120
20. Terwilliger, 70-71.
21. Terwilliger considers Dodgers manager Charlie Dressen to be the worst manager he ever played for. According to Twig, Dressen just ignored him for the 3½ months he was with the Dodgers in 1951. Buck.
22. Cassini hit .308 for the year for the Saints and was one of a number of Dodgers infield prospects blocked by the team's outstanding major-league infield of the 1950s. He played 14 years in the minor leagues, but had a very abbreviated major-league career, appearing in eight games for the 1949 Pittsburgh Pirates, all as a pinch-runner.
23. Terwilliger, 95.
24. Bucky Harris was the Nationals manager and asked the club to buy Terwilliger's contract. He had seen Terwilliger play in the Pacific Coast League in 1949 when he managed the San Diego Padres. Terwilliger, 96.

25 Drew Davison, "After 62 Years in Baseball, Twig Ready to Step Away," *Fort Worth Star-Telegram*, August 6, 2010.
26 Eisenhower was attending the annual Congressional baseball game in Washington and was sitting with Senators owner Clark Griffith when word came about the Senators win and Terwilliger's grand slam. Terwilliger, 99-100.
27 The Washington Senators that Terwilliger played for moved to Minneapolis after the 1960 season to become the Minnesota Twins. The Washington Senators team that Terwilliger later coached for was actually a different team, formed in 1961 as an American League expansion franchise.
28 Clark Griffith initially offered Terwilliger no raise, but increased the offer just prior to spring training. Terwilliger, 107-08.
29 Terwilliger 109.
30 Terwilliger, 111-12.
31 Terwilliger did not, of course, play in enough games to officially tie for the lead. He also turned 70 double plays in his 78 games at second.
32 It was the third and, thankfully, last time Terwilliger suffered a beaning in his baseball career, although the first time he had been hit with a batting helmet on. Unfortunately, the third beaning was the most serious. Terwilliger, 117.
33 Terwilliger, 117.
34 Terwilliger, 122.
35 Terwilliger, 128-29.
36 Terwilliger, 137.
37 Terwilliger's final major-league batting average was .240 in 666 games and 2,091 at-bats. He had 501 hits, 93 doubles, 10 triples, and 22 home runs spread over his 10-year big-league career.
38 Terwilliger, 144, 146-47.
39 Terwilliger, 149-50.
40 Don Keller was the third baseman on Terwilliger's Greensboro team and told his father, Charlie Keller, the former Yankees slugger, that he liked Terwilliger as a manager. Charlie Keller passed that information on to his brother Hal Keller, who was the farm director for the Senators and Hal hired Terwilliger. Terwilliger,150.
41 Pensacola did, however, lose to the Selma Cloverleafs in the league playoff finals.
42 Terwilliger, 169; Berkow.
43 One day Williams was talking hitting with Terwilliger and asked him what he looked for when he was at the plate. Terwilliger answered, "Fastball." Williams said, "Why only fastball?" Terwilliger said, "Because I couldn't hit that other thing [curve]." Williams replied, "Hmm. That's a good answer." Berkow.
44 Terwilliger, 193-94.
45 Terwilliger, 200.
46 Terwilliger considers Zimmer to be the best manager he ever worked under. Terwilliger, 205-06.
47 They were, in addition to Don Zimmer, Darrell Johnson, Doug Rader, and Bobby Valentine.
48 Terwilliger, 283.
49 Terwilliger, 233-34.
50 Morley Safer of CBS's 60 Minutes did a feature on the Saints in 1995 in which Terwilliger was prominently featured.
51 Drew hit 18 home runs in 44 games for the Saints in 1997.
52 Terwilliger, 256.
53 Kevin Sherrington, "Twig Knows His Way Around," *Dallas Morning News*, June 27, 2004.
54 Ray Richardson, "Book It: Twig's Story Is Unique," *St. Paul Pioneer Press*, May 26, 2006; Terwilliger, 282-83.
55 Berkow.
56 Davison: 1.
57 Berkow.
58 Buck.

BOB SHORT

BY BOB WHELAN AND STEVE WEST

Bob Short was a buyer and a seller. Involved in law, business, and politics, he bought and moved two sports franchises. He earned the ire of the two cities that he left, but earned millions when he sold the teams.

Robert Earl Short was born on July 20, 1917, in Minneapolis. His father, Robert Lester Short, was a fireman, and his mother, Frances (Niccum), was a telephone operator. Two of his grandparents were born in Canada, one on each side, and there was Irish ancestry. Robert had an older sister, Kathryn, and a younger brother, Richard. As a young man Short saw Ted Williams play for the Minneapolis Millers in 1938. "He said he had worn holes in his pants sitting on the bleachers watching me hit," Williams said.[1]

Short graduated from the College of St. Thomas in St. Paul, then attended law school at the University of Minnesota and Fordham University. He enlisted in the US Navy in 1942, and saw World War II action in the Pacific on the aircraft carrier Intrepid, rising from ensign to commander. While posted as a legislative officer at the US Naval Gun Factory (now Washington Navy Yard) after the war, he met and married Marion McCann of New York in 1947.[2] He also graduated from the Georgetown University Law School that year.

Discharged from the Navy, Short moved into law, working as an assistant United States attorney in the District of Columbia, before moving back to Minneapolis and taking the same position there. He began investing in business, borrowing $15,000 to buy an interest in the Mueller Transportation Company, a trucking firm.[3] Over the years he purchased several other trucking companies and merged them into Admiral Transit. Through numerous mergers the company, now known as Admiral Merchants Motor Freight, eventually covered the Eastern half of the United States.[4]

Through the years Short continued investing, and owned real estate in downtown Minneapolis, as well as several hotels. His family grew, too, as he and his wife had seven children throughout the 1950s. His first big investment thrust him into the public eye, where he remained until his death.

The Minneapolis Lakers won five titles in six seasons between 1949 and 1954, but after the retirement of star center George Mikan, they struggled. After a few seasons of poor performance on and off the court, owners Ben Berger and Maurice Chalfen decided to get out. A group from Kansas City, led by former St. Louis Cardinals shortstop Marty Marion, agreed to buy the NBA franchise and move it.[5] Berger, loyal to his city, said he would give any local buyers a week to match the offer.

"Short had wanted a major-league sports team in the worst way," former Lakers general manager Sid Hartman said. "He looked at football and baseball, but nothing was available there. Then he and Ryan read that Ben Berger was hoping to sell the Lakers to out-of-town of-town interests."[6] Short and college friend Frank Ryan gathered a group of 30 investors in a few days and raised $150,000 to buy the Lakers. Short was named president of the team.

Quickly the new owners discovered how much trouble they were in. They immediately had to inject another $50,000 just to keep the team afloat. The team began trading and selling players to cut expenses, a practice Short would follow for the rest of his career as a sports owner. Not long after, the team needed even more money, and when none of the other owners stepped up, Short purchased the remaining unissued stock of the company for $40,000.[7]

With the loss of top players, the team fell to the bottom of the league. Fans stopped coming to games at the rundown arena, and the Lakers regularly had crowds of under a thousand. But the luck of the draft saved the Lakers. With the first pick of the 1958 draft, they selected Elgin Baylor. Despite concerns over his signability, Short persuaded Baylor to leave the University of Seattle after his junior season, paying him $22,000 to come play for the Lakers. It was a last throw of the dice. "If Elgin had turned me down, I'd have gone out of business," Short said.[8]

Baylor paid immediate dividends, earning the Rookie of the Year Award while taking the Lakers to the NBA finals, where they lost to the Boston Celtics. With Baylor spending half of the next season on Army Reserve duty, the team slumped again. This time the Lakers ended up with the second pick in the draft, which they used to select Jerry West. The duo of West and Baylor led the Lakers for the next decade, with each ending up in the NBA Hall of Fame. The team became incredibly successful on the court, going to the NBA finals six times in the 1960s, although they lost every time to the even more successful Celtics.

Off the field, momentous events were happening. The first rumors of moving the team were heard in 1957. Chalfen had watched as the Brooklyn Dodgers moved to California, and wanted to follow suit, but Berger insisted on staying in Minnesota. Now, Short picked up Chalfen's idea. In January 1960, the Lakers headed to California to play games in San Francisco and Los Angeles. Sellout crowds made up his mind, although he appeased Minneapolis by saying that he would stay if he could sell 3,000 season tickets.[9]

However, in April Short and Ryan asked an NBA owners meeting for permission to move the team to Los Angeles. Not wanting the additional expense of trips to the West Coast, they voted 7 to 1 against the move. By great coincidence, at lunch that day Short saw a newspaper headline. Abe Saperstein, owner of the Harlem Globetrotters, had tired of waiting for the NBA to give him a promised franchise, and announced he was forming the American Basketball League, with a team in Los Angeles. NBA owners immediately realized they did not want to lose that territory, and voted again that afternoon. This time Short won 8-to-0 approval to move the Lakers to Los Angeles.[10]

Short himself decided to remain in Minneapolis. He hired Lou Mohs to be general manager, and to set up the team operation out west. As with his other operations, Short ran the team in Los Angeles on a shoestring. "Bob Short gave me three specific instructions," Mohs said. "'Go out there and don't let me hear from you; if you have any money left send it back to me; if you need any money forget where you came from.'"[11] The team was so poor that Mohs had to borrow chairs just to have something to sit on; his wife, Alice, washed the players' jerseys; and his children counted tickets.[12] He created a mailing list of potential season-ticket holders. "Luckily, we got season-ticket orders totaling $150,000," Mohs said. "If that money hadn't come in we would have been through."[13]

Things started slowly in Los Angeles – just 4,008 showed up to the inaugural Los Angeles Lakers game – but soon picked up. As the team kept winning, the crowds came to see them play, and by the end of the season the Lakers were selling out every night. Making the playoffs every year, they lost the NBA finals to the Celtics in 1962, 1963, and 1965. By that time the team was profitable, making $500,000 in 1965, and Short decided it was a good time to sell.[14]

Canadian millionaire Jack Kent Cooke approached Short to buy the team. Short initially demurred, then decided to take a long shot. Since the Celtics had been sold for $3 million, Short asked Cooke for $5 million. Surprised when Cooke said yes, Short said he also wanted half of the season-ticket money they'd already sold. "I told him he was holding me up, but I wanted the Lakers, so I agreed to it," Cooke said. That made the final sales price $5.175 million.[15]

There was still a wrinkle in the deal. "Walter O'Malley … warned me that Cooke was a tough, smart businessman, to be careful," said Ryan. "Walter said we should make him pay cash." They did, and bank guards rolled a cart with the money from one bank to another in New York. After the money was counted, Ryan and Short got a certified check and walked away from the Lakers.[16]

Short had long been interested in politics. "My Dad always wanted to be a politician," his son Kevin said. "He grew up a poor Irish kid in Minneapolis. And (former Farmer-Labor Governor) Floyd B. Olson was his hero. My dad idolized him."[17] In 1946 he ran for Congress in Minneapolis, finishing a distant second in a three-way Democratic-Farmer-Labor (DFL) primary. He worked on several Hubert H. Humphrey campaigns during the 1950s and 1960s.

Short's next attempt at politics came in 1966, when he ran for lieutenant governor. He lost again in a close race, 51 percent to 49 percent, as voters repudiated the efforts of then Vice President Humphrey. Short was not put off politics, though, and became the treasurer of the Democratic National Committee in 1968 for the Humphrey presidential campaign.

In 1978 Senator Humphrey died in office, and a special election was held to replace him. Short barely received the nomination from the DFL Party, squeaking through the primary with 48 percent of the vote to Congressman Donald Fraser's 47.4 percent. Many in the party had voted against his conservative views on abortion and local issues. "There's no doubt (the primary) damaged my dad," Kevin Short said. "It was bloody and divisive. The party had been thrown into such turmoil that it was hard to put back together."[18]

With the party split and many DFL voters switching sides just to vote against him, Short was trounced by Independent-Republican David Durenberger, gaining just 34.5 percent of the vote. It was part of a huge defeat for the DFL, as Minnesota Republicans gained Senate seats for the first time in almost two decades.

The Washington Senators of 1968 were not the Senators of old. Curiously enough, those Senators moved to Minnesota and became the Twins, just months after Short had moved the Lakers to California. In both cases the owners had cited an inability to make money in their original location. In its wisdom, baseball had decided to put an expansion team in Washington to replace the team that had moved. Now the Senators were struggling again, and Short saw an opportunity very similar to the one he had seen in basketball: a team struggling in one market that would be worth much more elsewhere.

Washington attorney Stanley Bregman was a member of the legal firm that represented the Senators and knew that owner James Lemon was looking to sell the team. Bregman (grandfather of future major leaguer Alex Bregman) had also been a director in the Humphrey presidential campaign, and knew Short from his time as DNC treasurer. Knowing Short had made a lot of money selling the Lakers, Bregman said, "Why don't you use some of that money and buy the Senators?"[19] Short agreed on a purchase price of $9.4 million with Lemon. At a luncheon welcoming Short to Washington, his political friend Humphrey joked about it. "I'm sure it's only a coincidence but when Bob Short was our party treasurer, we went into the hole for $9 million. That's just the amount of money it cost him to buy the Washington Senators."[20]

Later investigations by *The Sporting News* and others found that Short was very creative in raising the money. First, he got Lemon to agree to keep 10 percent of the team in preferred stock, at a value of $1.1 million. Next, he arranged a bank loan for $2 million, providing securities as collateral. He then added loans secured by the team itself, and, finally, he arranged unsecured loans for the rest of the money, at heavy interest rates.

The *Washington Post* claimed that Short's total cash outlay for the Senators was just $1,000, and that was used to pay the legal costs of setting up the new company. The Post said that Short's trucking company then loaned the Senators $1 million to cover their operating costs, at a 9.75 percent interest rate. And economists Roger Noll and Benjamin Okner showed that Short's other companies were eligible for tax writeoffs of $4 million over the next five years, due to player depreciation.[21]

Short denied it was all that cheap for him. He claimed that the collateral he put up was equity. "If the loan goes bad, I can be out $2 million. If that isn't equity, what is?" he said.[22] He added that the trucking-company loan was at his risk. And he claimed that the team had $3 million in cash losses from 1969 through '71. The Washington Post analysis showed that much of that loss was in fact depreciation, while other parts of his claimed cash losses were dubious, since he hadn't actually paid the bills. "He was always cash-poor," Bregman said. "Lots of rich men are. But he started having real cash problems here. Slid by for a year or so."[23]

When Short took over the team after the 1968 season, he appointed himself general manager, and hired Ted Williams to manage the team. Williams at first declined the offer, but Short talked him into it, giving him a five-year no-cut contract, $1.5 million over five years, with an option to purchase 10 percent of the team, and the ability to manage on his own terms. Williams liked Short from the start, calling him "the smartest man I ever met," and saying, "He was not only dynamic, but he was imaginative about baseball, though he had never been involved in it before, and he was damned persuasive."[24] Williams took the job "against my better judgment" but was bowled over by the force of Short's personality. "[H]e just happened to be a guy I couldn't refuse. I kept saying 'no' until I heard myself say 'yes.'"[25]

In its first season, the Senators improved by 21 games, although they still finished in fourth place, 23 games behind the 109-win Baltimore Orioles. They drew 918,106 fans, the second highest attendance of either iteration of the Washington Senators.

The success was short-lived, though, as over the next two seasons the team and attendance both fell back. In 1971 Short began a serious campaign of bad-mouthing the city, in an attempt to win approval to move. He complained that fans wouldn't come to the ballpark because it was in a crime-ridden neighborhood (ignoring the fact that he was charging among the highest prices in the league to see one of the worst teams). He complained that the ballpark contract with the D.C. Armory Board meant that he was losing money. And he complained that the radio and television contracts were among the worst in the league.[26]

Commissioner Bowie Kuhn later described a late-night phone call he received from Short in April of 1971:

"No one can keep me in Washington, not Nixon, not Cronin, not Kuhn," he said. "I will cannibalize the club if necessary. I own it and I will take it to St. Paul if I want. I have lawyers too. I will move wherever I want. ... Ted says Washington is a horseshit town and I've gotta get out. I'll go elsewhere before I'm forced into bankruptcy like Seattle. I know I had my eyes wide open when I went to Washington, but I told the American League that I wouldn't keep it there forever."[27]

Short was at least partly right about the team's problems, although he deliberately avoided doing the one thing to eliminate them: improve the team. Instead, he seemed to be running it down just so he could move the team to more profitable vistas. Short made several curious baseball decisions, such as trading for Denny McLain,[28] a one-sided deal that was later said to be made in order to secure the Tigers' vote for the approaching Senators move.[29]

By 1971 Short had settled on a destination and was working to be allowed to move there. Arlington, Texas, was a small town midway between Dallas and Fort Worth, and Mayor Tom Vandergriff had decided to attract a major-league baseball team to improve the town's economy. He had been working since the late 1950s to get an expansion team, or persuade someone to move, without luck. He had built a minor-league ballpark designed to be easily expanded to meet major-league requirements. He talked to several teams about moving, and finally got in touch with Short.

Short was easily convinced of the riches waiting him in Arlington. He was promised fans, a ballpark, civic support, broadcasting deals, everything he was missing in Washington. The biggest swing factor was the radio and television contracts. The city of Arlington said it would buy 10 years of broadcasting rights up front, at $750,000 per year. That $7.5 million would pay off all of Short's debts and loans in Washington, ensuring that he would come out with a healthy profit when he sold the team.

In July an American League owners' meeting heard how Short was losing money in Washington, had no possibility of improving there, and wished to move the Senators to the Dallas-Fort Worth area. AL President Joe Cronin decided to research solutions and report back to a joint meeting with the National League in August. They suggested trying to find local buyers, but the price Short demanded included covering all his claimed losses over the last few years. He strung along one buyer to the last minute, but despite some debate, the owners approved the move. Quickly turning into a pariah in Washington, Short got out of town and looked toward the new location. He also persuaded Ted Williams to stay on for another season as manager.

The 1972 season began with a stumble, as the players went on strike to start the season. Short saw his first Opening Day for the newly christened Texas Rangers disappear, but wasn't too worried. He backed the players in the strike, and promised that a million fans would come see the Rangers that season. He was wrong, as the team was terrible, but it drew a few thousand more than the previous season in Washington, which Short claimed as a success.

Williams quit after the season, and Short appointed Whitey Herzog as manager. They described a multiyear rebuilding plan, but that plan received multiple blows, because Short kept trading players for cash. Worse, Herzog had been manager for barely half a season when Short fired him. He hired the newly available Billy Martin, figuring that he would be a good gate attraction. In another shortsighted move, the team acquired high-school sensation David Clyde in the June amateur draft, and rather than send him to the minors to learn, Short brought him to the Rangers for a quick boost to the gate. When Clyde was successful in his first start, Short kept him on, which helped with attendance but arguably destroyed Clyde's long-term viability as a pitcher.

In early 1974, it was announced that Short was selling the team to local businessman Brad Corbett. Despite his previous denials, the sale occurred just a few months after the fifth anniversary of Short's buying the team, lending credence to the accusations that he was just interested in the tax writeoffs that were available for that period.

The purchase price was listed as $9 million, and Short retained 10 percent of the team. He claimed that the price meant he would barely break even, but the 10 years of broadcasting rights had already paid off his debts, so in reality Short made a significant profit.

Short wasn't out of baseball for long. In early 1976, the Stoneham family announced the sale of the San Francisco Giants to the Labatt's Brewery company, which planned to move the team to Toronto. After weeks of legal and financial maneuvering, Short and Robert Lurie, a minor shareholder in the Giants, partnered to keep the team in San Francisco. "Mr. Lurie and Mr. Short are going to make baseball go in San Francisco," Mayor George Moscone said.[30]

The plan was for each man to put up $4 million to buy the team. While they worked to complete their agreement, things came unstuck. Short said he had assumed that Lurie "would lean heavily on my experience in the operation of two baseball teams."[31] The National League owners, wary of Short's history, said they wanted to have one majority owner – and they didn't want it to be Short. Short withdrew, believing that would put pressure on Lurie and the league to bring him back and save the Giants. Instead, Lurie got lucky. Bud Herseth, a Phoenix meat-company owner said he would not only put up $4 million, but he'd be happy to have 49 percent of the team and make Lurie the majority owner. The National League quickly voted to approve the deal.

And that was it for Short. Despite rumors over the years that he would return, including that he would buy back the Rangers in the late 1970s, the attempt to buy the Giants was his last real involvement in baseball. He turned to his other businesses, and had his ill-fated Senate run in 1978. He had joined the Notre Dame Law School Advisory Council in 1974, where he remained until his death. Several of his children attended Notre Dame, earning a total of 10 degrees between them, and a number of his grandchildren also went there. He and his wife also endowed the Robert and Marion Short Chair in Law at the university.

Short contracted cancer and died on November 20, 1982. Marion took over his positions in his companies and on the Notre Dame Council upon his death.

Notes

1. Ted Williams with John Underwood, *My Turn at Bat* (New York: Fireside, 1988), 241.
2. Wedding announcement, *Washington Evening Star*, October 8, 1947: B3.
3. washingtonpost.com/archive/local/1982/11/22/robert-short-ex-owner-of-senators-team-dies/6d6b5733-1445-4e76-8d0e-10b6cab3d-f29/?utm_term=.3d60d2e72411.
4. Admiral Merchants Motor Freight website, ammf.com, retrieved March 14, 2018.
5. "Looks Like Marion Will Get Lakers," *Sarasota* (Florida) *Herald-Tribune*, February 27, 1957: 17.
6. Roland Lazenby, *The Show: The Inside Story of the Spectacular Los Angeles Lakers in the Words of Those Who Lived It* (New York: McGraw-Hill, 2006), Kindle edition.
7. Ibid.
8. Ibid.
9. Ibid.
10. Ibid.
11. William Leggett, "Growing to Greatness," *Sports Illustrated*, October 29, 1962.
12. Jim Murray, "Remember Those Early Laker Days?" *Los Angeles Times*, June 28, 1985.
13. Leggett.
14. Lazenby.
15. Ibid.
16. Ibid.
17. Frank Rajkowski, "Flashback Friday: US Senate Race in 1978 Pitted Johnnie vs. Tommie," kstp.com/news/flashback-friday-david-durenberger-bob-short-us-senate-race-1978-tommie-johnnie/4610390/.
18. Ibid.
19. Ken Denlinger, "Washington's Storied Pastime Includes Unhappy Endings," *Washington Post*, March 3, 1991.
20. Bob Addie, "Addie's Atoms," *The Sporting News*, May 15, 1976: 14.
21. "Only $1,000 Cash Needed to Own Senators," *Indianapolis Star*, December 26, 1971: 74.
22. C.C. Johnson Spink, "Short Gives His Side of Deal for Senators," *The Sporting News*, February 5, 1972: 33.
23. Denlinger.
24. Williams, 240-41.
25. Williams, 240.
26. Bowie Kuhn, *Hardball: The Education of a Baseball Commissioner* (New York: Times Books, 1987), 95.
27. Kuhn, 94.
28. The Detroit Tigers traded third baseman Don Wert, outfielder Elliott Maddox, and pitchers Denny McLain and Norm McRae to the Senators for shortstop Ed Brinkman, third baseman Aurelio Rodriguez, and pitchers Joe Coleman and Jim Hannan.
29. Ted Leavengood, *Ted Williams and the 1969 Washington Senators* (Jefferson, North Carolina: McFarland, 2009), 187.
30. Art Spander, "'Green Plasma' Saves Giants in Last-Hour Heroics," *The Sporting News*, March 13, 1976: 33.
31. Art Spander, "Meat Packer Brings Home the Bacon for Giants," *The Sporting News*, March 20, 1976: 32.

ARLINGTON STADIUM

BY WILL OSGOOD

Arlington Stadium has a history that deserves to be told. It is a bit unknown, but certainly worthy of telling.

The story started in 1959 when residents of the Dallas-Fort Worth area voted to approve a bond for a small minor-league ballpark to be built in the centrally located suburb of Arlington, Texas. It was eventually decided that the site would be a 137-acre open area sitting adjacent to Six Flags Over Texas, one of the original high-scale theme parks in the country.[1] It would be 13 years from the time of the vote until the ballpark could gain anywhere near the traffic or revenue of its neighbor. But in 1972, after a long pursuit process led primarily by Arlington Mayor Tom Vandergriff, the Washington Senators made the move from D.C. to the up-and-coming Metroplex, changing their name in the process to the Texas Rangers.

The ballpark, though, built a few years after the vote passed, began as a 10,500-seat minor-league park called Turnpike Stadium. It hosted the Dallas-Fort Worth Spurs of the Double-A Texas League from 1965 to 1971.

Building the ballpark in its initial form cost $1.9 million. Through the years it would see many add-ons, which all told cost exactly 10 times that, $19 million.[2] To fulfill the requirements of hosting a major-league team, the City of Arlington organized efforts to alter the ballpark significantly. The changes began in 1970 two years before the Texas Rangers became a reality. In 1970 the ballpark capacity was doubled, to 20,000 seats. In 1972, the first season of its major-league life, the stadium capacity expanded to 35,739.

The first game at Turnpike Stadium was played on April 23, 1965. Seven years later, on April 21, 1972, the rebuilt and renamed ballpark hosted its first major-league baseball game, the Texas Rangers playing the visiting California Angels. The ballpark had been set to debut as a major-league park earlier, but the start of the season was delayed slightly because of a players strike. The Rangers' season began on April 15, when the team played the Angels in Anaheim. In the home opener on the 21st the Rangers enjoyed a fast start, when Frank Howard's first-inning home run became the ballpark's first major-league run and home run. The Rangers won the game, 7-6.[3]

The inaugural home game was one of the few bright spots in the team's opening season in Arlington. The Rangers limped along to a 54-100 record, including 31-46 at home. (Four of the 31 victories came in that opening series, as the Rangers swept the Angels, and ended the set tied for first in the AL West division.)

The tie lasted only one game, and was not achieved again during the 1972 season. But for a long weekend in mid-April, the Texas Rangers looked as if they might be a contender.

The attendance at the first contest at Arlington Stadium was 20,105, making it a poorly attended inaugural major-league contest. A night later 5,517 paid to watch the Rangers' second home game. Sunday's attendance was 11,586. Over the course of the season, the Rangers never neared a sellout. Only twice did they top 20,000.

The Rangers finished 10th out of 12 American League franchises in attendance, attracting 662,974 to the renovated minor-league park for big-league action. The play on the field may have been one major reason. The sparse crowds saw few wins, and especially few of the most exciting kind. The Rangers had only three walk-off wins in 1972. Those were the most exciting moments in the ballpark during the 1972 season. It is almost impossible to have so few walk-off wins. It is almost as if the team planned to torture their new home fans.

Other factors prevented the average fan from coming out to the ballpark. Among them was the heat. The Dallas Metroplex is among the hottest regions in the United States. Because of that, the Rangers schedule all but a few home games for nighttime.

The ballpark's construction did not help. The playing field was below ground level, with the stands ascending to the level of the parking lot. Warm air started at the playing level and rose to the top, creating an unfriendly atmosphere for players and fans alike. One writer called the outfield stands "the world's largest open-air roaster."[4]

When the upper deck was built in 1978, some fans would not walk down to their seats but would travel upward. But the rising heat remained and the ballpark never became a comfortable place to play in or watch a baseball game.

The evolution of the ballpark was extensive from its opening in 1965 to when it was replaced in 1994. The 1978 upper-deck expansion brought the seating capacity to 41,097. Further expansions after 1978 brought the capacity to 43,508 in 1985 and finally to 43,521 in the stadium's final season hosting Rangers baseball. The 43,000-plus capacity made for quite a contrast to the original Turnpike Stadium. The left-field façade above the field featured a scoreboard shaped like the state of Texas. It was replaced in 1983 with a more standardized Diamond Vision scoreboard.[5]

Some factors remained the same throughout. One was the outfield wall dimensions. The down-the-line right-field and left-field distances remained 330 feet throughout the Rangers' tenure in the park, and straightaway center field remained 400 feet. The only changes came in right-center and left-center, which began at 370 feet, became 383 for one season (1981), and then dropped three feet to 380 for the remainder of the ballpark's lifetime, making it still a tough power alley to traverse, especially in a day when home runs were not aplenty.[6] Turnpike Stadium, aka Arlington Stadium, was similar to other ballparks in another sense. As was common when it was built, the bullpens were crafted into the field of play, along the foul lines. The Rangers bullpen was down the right-field line, as their dugout sat on the first-base side.

Of all the games played in Arlington Stadium the one on Sunday, September 30, 1984, is by far the best-known. Mike Witt, lanky California Angels right-hander and four-year veteran, sliced through the Rangers' lineup with a combination of wicked curves (55), fastballs (37), and changeups (just two), to retire all 27 Rangers in a row. The perfect game was the ninth in what is commonly referred to as the modern era of baseball, and 11th overall (including Don Larsen's perfect game in the 1956 World Series). Witt's 94 total pitches were the fifth fewest thrown among the 21 modern-era perfect games (in Cy Young's perfect game the pitch total is not known, as is the case with the pre-modern-era games). Witt's brilliance – and that of his opposing pitcher, Charlie Hough, who gave up one unearned run on seven hits – was evident by the rapid nature of the 1-0 final, which ended in one hour and 49 minutes. Unfortunately few people witnessed this season finale, as only 8,375 fans paid to watch the historic performance.

Some of the game's most colorful personalities held a seat, and cast watchful eyes, in the first-base dugout over the years. Among the Rangers managers while the team played at Arlington Stadium were Ted Williams, one of the greatest hitters of all time (1972); Whitey Herzog, better known for leading the Kansas City Royals and St. Louis Cardinals to great success (1973); Billy Martin, who was hired and fired multiple times by the New York Yankees' mercurial owner George Steinbrenner (1973-75); Don Zimmer, one of the all-time characters and best-respected men in baseball (1981-82); and the always colorful Bobby Valentine (1985-92). The Rangers' manager in their final season in Arlington Stadium was Kevin Kennedy, who lasted two seasons (1993-94) and later became a broadcaster.

Some great broadcasters occupied the home broadcast booth at Arlington Stadium.[7] In the Rangers' inaugural season, Bill Mercer and Los Angeles Dodgers Hall of Famer Don Drysdale provided play-by-play and color commentary respectively for both radio and television. In 1978 Jon Miller began a short stint as play-by-play commentator for both television and radio. His tenure lasted just two years, but produced fruit beyond Miller's ascension to national prominence. It also provided an opportunity for Eric Nadel to gain experience behind the mike. He began in Miller's second season, as a television voice exclusively. The next year, 1980, he established himself as the pre-eminent radio voice of the Rangers. Thirty-five years after he began calling Rangers games from a creaky old broadcast booth in an unenthusiastic stadium, Nadel won the Ford C. Frick Award in 2014. The Frick honor is given annually to a baseball announcer who exudes excellence in his craft, courtesy of the National Baseball Hall of Fame.[8]

Tom Vandergriff, the mayor who was responsible for bringing the Rangers to Arlington, spent three seasons in the television booth next to Dick Risenhoover (1975-77). Vandergriff spent 26 years in the mayor's seat in Arlington. The last three coincided with the time he was calling Rangers games. But it is not as quirky as one might expect. When he was just 16, Vandergriff took a job as a radio broadcaster with KFJZ Radio in Fort Worth. Because of his work as a broadcaster, but more importantly for bringing the Rangers to Arlington, getting a ballpark built and then another one in 1994, Vandergriff was inducted into the Texas Rangers Baseball Hall of Fame in 2004.[9]

Vandergriff was clearly a man of vision and results. Yet it is difficult to assess whether he could have foreseen some of the oddball innovations coming out of Arlington Stadium. For instance, Arlington Stadium was the birthplace of ballpark nachos. The heated, juicy cheese dip and tortilla chips are now the most common and inexpensive food item available at most sports and entertainment venues.

Another mainstay in American sporting events is the dot race. It has evolved to a point where it is generally a series of culturally relevant artifacts taking semi-lifelike form and racing around the city in video form. Whatever form it takes nowadays, its genesis ought to be understood as being an Arlington Stadium creation.

Yet none of those innovations are as uniquely Texas as this: Arlington Stadium became the birthplace of unique culturally relevant songs being played, sung, and danced to between the top and bottom halves of the seventh inning. While "Take Me Out to the Ball Game" is the iconic fans' song, at some point the Rangers determined that replacing it with "Cotton Eye Joe" was a good idea. It turned out to be, as it was an almost instant hit, and of course uniquely Texas.

The ballpark was featured in the movie Bull Durham.[10] In the film it is the ballpark where Tim Robbins' character is interviewed after making it to the major leagues. But Arlington Stadium was not a hotbed for movie production or other kinds of attractions during its hosting the Rangers or after. Even the Six Flags next door could not bring people out to the yard. The 1991 season was the team's best in attendance at 2,297,720 paying customers. It still did not compare to Yankee Stadium or Dodger Stadium, which seated more spectators than the Rangers' eventual 43,000.

Then again, it is not incorrect to note how Arlington Stadium was not exactly the most aesthetically pleasing yard, even with its standard but beautiful Tifway 419 Bermuda sod[11] spread across the 110,000 square feet of playing surface.[12]

The ballpark did hold two other distinctions while it was in use. The outfield bleachers took up more space and spanned more of the ballpark than at any other major-league ballpark. Also, the outfield fences and other façade areas surrounding the playing field held more advertisements than any other ballpark. In today's world of marketing and commercialization it would not garner much attention, but in the 1980s the space given in the ballpark to advertising was quite noteworthy.

None of the advertising, seating capacity, or improved product on the field could keep Arlington Stadium from giving in to father time. It, like the "Ryan Express," had an expiration date. The expiration of the two coincided as one. Future Hall of Fame pitcher Nolan Ryan finished his career with the Rangers, making just 13 starts in 1993. And just as Ryan's career had an unsatisfactory ending, so too did the Rangers' time at Arlington Stadium.

On October 3, 1993, the Rangers played their final home game in the rundown stadium and lost. Future All-Star Kevin Appier held the Rangers to one run on four hits in eight innings while striking out 10 batters. Greg Gagne provided all the offense needed when he hit a two-run homer. It was a rather fitting end to the ballpark's existence. A game that began with much hope for victory had it swallowed away by the opponent. The Rangers needed a new ballpark if for no other reason than to turn the tide of their franchise. The remedy proved worthwhile, as the Rangers began an era of winning baseball almost immediately upon transitioning into their brand-new ballpark across the street.

While the new ballpark proved a welcome change for the franchise, it was not exactly good news for the old ballpark. Some ballparks survive years past their existence of hosting a professional team. Not Arlington Stadium. For a short time the Rangers' old home and new home existed alongside each other, with merely a street between them. But for the opportunity to create a more modern environment around the new stadium, the ballpark was allowed to decay. Weeds and erosion made it look more like a jungle than a former baseball field.

Some of the seats were torn out after the final out of the 1993 season, making room for the grass to overgrow and overflow into the abandoned stands. Mounds of dirt hills came into being, so that the yard could hold a motocross race. Arlington Stadium became ghastly in appearance. It was finally demolished in 1994, and the site as of 2016 was the parking lot for the new ballpark, with nothing remaining to indicate there was a ballpark there, not even a home-plate marker. All that is left behind is the memory of a tortured stadium that was too hot for comfort. Beyond anything, the memory of Arlington Stadium was the heat. Rangers fans today are happy to have a more weather-friendly stadium to go to for watching their hometown team play baseball.

Sources

Besides the sources cited in the Notes, the author consulted Baseball-Reference.com and "Tifway Bermuda Sod," supersod.com/sod/bermuda-sod/tifway-bermuda.html.

Notes

1. "Arlington Stadium," ballparksofbaseball.com/past/ArlingtonStadium.htm.
2. Ibid.
3. "Texas Rangers," sportsencyclopedia.com/al/texas/texrangers.html.
4. "Arlington Stadium," baseball-reference.com/bullpen/Arlington_Stadium.
5. "Arlington Stadium," ballparks.com/baseball/american/arling.htm.
6. "Arlington Stadium," seamheads.com/ballparks/ballpark.php?parkID=ARL01.
7. "All-Time Broadcasters," texas.rangers.mlb.com/tex/history/broadcasters.jsp.
8. Barry M. Bloom, "Rangers Broadcaster Nadel Wins Frick Award," m.mlb.com/news/article/64578256/.
9. "Hall of Mayors: Tom Vandergriff," arlington-tx.gov/history/hall-mayors/tom-j-vandergriff/.
10. "On Location … Bull Durham Filming Locations," fast-rewind.com/locations_bulldurham.htm.
11. "Arlington Stadium," ballparks.com/baseball/american/arling.htm.
12. "Arlington Stadium," seamheads.com/ballparks/ballpark.php?parkID=ARL01.

PLAYERS WHO HOMERED AT ARLINGTON STADIUM AS BOTH MINOR AND MAJOR LEAGUE PLAYERS

BY ALAN COHEN

In 1965, in an effort to attract a big-league team, Arlington, Texas, built a ballpark known as Turnpike Stadium. The original facility did not have the seating capacity of a big-league park, but it was built to facilitate enlargement once the big leagues came to town. For seven years the Dallas-Fort Worth Spurs played at Turnpike Stadium in the Double-A Texas League. In 1972, when the Washington Senators chose to move to Texas, the Dallas area was ready, expanding the ballpark and renaming it Arlington Stadium.

Not many players accomplished the feat of hitting home runs in Arlington Stadium as both minor leaguers and major leaguers. First, the Texas Rangers, as the Senators were renamed, were in the American League, and as late as 1968, the only Texas League team affiliated with an American League team was the El Paso Sun Kings, Double-A affiliate of the California Angels. Second, the percentage of Double-A players who make it to the majors is not particularly high. Lastly, relatively few homers were hit by anyone at Arlington Stadium during the minor-league years.

However, the Dallas-Fort Worth team switched its affiliation from the Chicago Cubs to the Baltimore Orioles in 1969, and the parent team had a fairly good season. What was in the pipeline?

During the first three years of major-league play in Arlington, only two Rangers with Texas League connections had homered, while 11 former Texas League players had homered as visitors.

Although the enclosure of the ballpark and the addition of an upper deck would increase home-run productivity when the Senators moved in and became the Rangers, home runs were not flying out of the park during the minor-league days. During the first few games, it appeared that the ballpark was hitter-friendly with seven homers in the first six games. Then things turned around and for the whole 1965 season, only 29 homers were hit at Turnpike Stadium by an assortment of players, none of whom would replicate the feat as major leaguers.

Home runs at Turnpike Stadium were far harder to come by for anyone in 1966, as 21 homers, all told, were hit at Turnpike Stadium. One El Paso player, a first-round draft pick of the Angels, spent three seasons at El Paso, improving each year. So it was no great surprise that Jim Spencer had homered on June 8, 1966, in a 1-0 El Paso win over Dallas. In 1967 he hit two more home runs in Arlington, and the Angels called him up to the major leagues in 1968. By 1972 Spencer was a regular major leaguer, but he had a down year, hitting just one home run all season. That homer came on April 24 at Arlington off Don Stanhouse in a 6-4 loss to the Rangers. Traded to the Rangers in 1973, he achieved the distinction of homering as both a visiting and home player at Arlington when he homered off Pat Dobson of the Yankees on August 19. Over the course of his major-league career he had 13 homers at Arlington.

Home-run numbers didn't change much over the next two years. In 1967, the count was up to 31, which was to be the highest ever for a season at Turnpike Stadium, while in 1968 it was down to just 19, the lowest season total.

One of Spencer's teammates on the 1967 team had a particularly good year playing third base. His name was Leo Rodriguez and he tagged 11 homers for the Sun Kings. Were any home runs hit during the 14 games at Arlington? Nope. Of course, Leo Rodriguez went on to become Aurelio Rodriguez and accomplished the feat of homering at the same ballpark in the minors and majors at Seattle's Sick's Stadium.

But most of the big hitters in 1967 were with National League farm teams, and sluggers like Amarillo's Nate Colbert, who had a league-leading

28 homers (two at Arlington) would not return to Arlington as major leaguers.

One future National League star homered at Turnpike Stadium on July 20 and July 22, 1967, as a member of the Amarillo Sonics, the farm club of the Houston Astros. Bob Watson played with Houston until 1979, clubbing 139 homers. He was traded to the Boston Red Sox that June, and visited Arlington Stadium shortly thereafter. On July 27, 1979, Watson homered off Steve Comer in a lopsided Rangers win over the Red Sox. After the 1979 season, he became a free agent and signed with the Yankees. His second and last major-league homer at Arlington Stadium came on April 11, 1980, off Ferguson Jenkins. He concluded his playing career with Atlanta in 1984 with the distinction of having homered in two ballparks (San Diego and Arlington) in the minors and majors.

Albuquerque was linked with the Dodgers organization for many years. The Albuquerque Dodgers of 1965-71 included some great names, but most of those players spent their careers in the National League. The Albuquerque team leader in homers in 1968 had been signed by the Dodgers in 1964 and worked his way up through the organization, landing in Albuquerque in 1967. On June 25, 1968, Bill Sudakis slammed his ninth homer of the season, at Arlington Stadium, in a 4-3 win over the Spurs. Sudakis made it to the big club at the end of the 1968 season and stayed in Dodger Blue through 1971, when knee injuries resulted in his being waived out of the organization. In 1972 he was with the Mets, who traded him to Texas prior to the 1973 season. In his one season with the Rangers, mostly as a DH, he had 15 homers (his best as a major leaguer). The first of six 1973 Arlington Stadium homers came on May 14 off Jim Kaat of the Twins in a 7-6 Rangers win.

Occasionally, one comes across a player who seems to be a sure thing. One such player was in the Baltimore Orioles farm system in 1969. At first, however, my research into Don Baylor's homers at Arlington came up empty. Homer after homer was hit on the road. But persevere I did. I went through issue after issue of the San Antonio Light, as they had the box scores for all Texas League games. Much was going on in July 1969, but on the evening of July 11, 1969, in a 7-6 win over Amarillo, Don Baylor stroked his sixth homer of the year, and first at Arlington Stadium. It was to be his only homer at Arlington that season. His other 10 homers were hit on the road. Indeed, as I was to discover, the combined homer count at Turnpike Stadium in 1969 was only 21.

Baylor had 338 career major-league homers, including 18 at Arlington Stadium. His total was the third highest (behind Reggie Jackson and George Brett) for a visiting player at Arlington. His first Arlington blast came on June 10, 1972, off Casey Cox, as the Orioles defeated the Rangers 5-2.

I stumbled onto the story of a player who had 280 minor-league homers, including a league-leading 43 at Tacoma in 1971. The prior year, 1970, he had hit a league-leading 29 with San Antonio in the Texas League. And the year before that, 1969, you guessed it, he led the league with 24 with Shreveport. In 1969, his 22nd homer came at Arlington on July 30 in a 9-3 win over the Spurs. In 1970 he was fighting for the home-run title as San Antonio played a four-game series at Arlington in late August. In the space of four games, he had four homers, his 28th of the season coming on August 26 in an 8-2 win over the Spurs in the final game of the series. He accounted for four of the 29 homers hit at Arlington Stadium in the 1970 season. Adrian Garrett played minor-league ball for 16 consecutive seasons for 14 different teams. In six seasons, he had 20 or more homers. After his major-league career was over, he went to Japan and hit 102 homers over the course of three seasons. He also played winter ball in the Dominican Republic, leading the Dominican League with 9 homers one season. All told, he had more than 400 professional home runs.

Garrett's major-league career was relatively unsung, though, as he played in just 163 games over eight seasons, for four different teams, with just 11 home runs. His 1975 season with the Angels was the "best" of his major-league career; he batted .262 with six homers. On consecutive days, August 2-3, 1975, he homered at Arlington Stadium. He victimized Bill Hands and Steve Hargan, respectively.

The Albuquerque team leader in homers in 1970 had been drafted by the Dodgers in the eighth round in 1968, and Albuquerque was the third stop on his ladder to the big leagues. On May 14, 1970, Joe Ferguson homered for the Albuquerque Dodgers at Arlington Stadium in a 7-4 Dodgers win. He was the only Albuquerque player to homer in the Spurs' home park all season. Most of his years were in the National League with the Dodgers, but when he was released in 1981, he signed with the California Angels. In parts of three seasons with the Angels, he had four homers, and on September 23, 1982, he hit his last major-league homer. It came at Arlington Stadium off Mike Mason. It was his only major-league homer at Arlington.

On Saturday August 8, 1970, the Amarillo Giants, the farm club of the San Francisco Giants, had defeated the Spurs at Arlington on the strength of two homers. The homer that put them in front was slugged by a man who was to go on to a 16-year major-league career during which he slugged 442 homers and was named to three All-Star teams. Dave Kingman's first stop in Organized Baseball was Amarillo, where he slugged 15 homers in 60 games. Kingman spent most of his career in the National League with the Giants, Mets, and Cubs, but in 1977, he was a man of many uniforms. He started the season with the Mets and was traded to the Padres in June. The Padres placed him on waivers on September 6, and he was claimed by the California Angels. Not long after he had unpacked and got used to his new surroundings, the Angels traveled to Arlington Stadium and, on September 13, 1977, he homered off Gaylord Perry and Bobby Cuellar as the Angels came from behind to score eight runs in the seventh inning (two on a homer by Kingman) and win 12-7. Two days later, Kingman was traded back to New York, this time to the Yankees, where he proceeded to homer in his first three games with the Bombers. Kingman wrapped up his career with a three-year stint at Oakland. In each of those last three years with Oakland, concluding in 1986, he had at least 30 homers. During his years with Oakland, he homered at Arlington another four times, bringing his career total at the Rangers' ballpark to six.

For the entire 1971 season, the hometown Spurs had 8 homers at home. It was so rare an occurrence for a Spur to homer there that when Steve Turigliatto got his first homer of the season on August 15, he was so disoriented that he stumbled while running the bases, broke his elbow, and was out for the season. Turigliatto never played another game in Organized Baseball.

Visiting teams did not do particularly well, either, slugging out just 18 homers. San Antonio, the Cubs affiliate, visited Arlington Stadium for 19 games that season. Their center fielder was best known for his speed, stealing 47 bases in 1971, but he banged out 10 homers that season, including one at Arlington Stadium on June 22 in a losing cause. At the end of the 1972 season, Billy North was traded to Oakland, where he stole 229 bases over the next five seasons. On June 26, 1973, North led off the third inning with a homer off Jim Merritt for his only Arlington Stadium major-league homer. The homer broke a 1-1 tie, and the A's went on to defeat the Rangers, 6-2.

Of course, when you are researching a topic, you invariably stumble across something else, and in 1971 the Dallas-Fort Worth Spurs were, indeed, part of history. They were playing the Albuquerque Dodgers in Albuquerque on August 4. On that night, Tom Walker, their starting pitcher, went 15 innings and pitched what at the time was the longest no-hitter in baseball history. The final score was 1-0.

And on September 21, 1971, it was announced that the Senators were coming to Texas. Arlington Stadium had hosted its last minor-league ballgame. Over the course of seven seasons, spectators at Turnpike Stadium had witnessed just 176 homers. During the 1972 major-league season, 74 homers were hit at the expanded Arlington Stadium, and over the years, eight players who homered there as minor leaguers homered there as major leaguers.

Sources

In preparing this article, the author used Baseball-Reference.com, the *Dallas Morning News*, and the *San Antonio Light*.

DALLAS-FORT WORTH BASEBALL MEDIA IN 1972

BY STEVE WEST

The media market in North Texas was changing in 1972, just as the rest of the country was. With the advent of television, newspapers had felt the pinch as advertising dollars shifted to the new medium. Now, a couple of decades after the arrival of television, newspapers were beginning to fold or merge with others. Instead of multiple outlets, cities were left with just one or two papers to give fans the latest news on their team.

THE MARKETS

In 1972 Dallas and Fort Worth were still very distinct cities, far more so than they are today. The ongoing feud between the two towns was summarized by Amon Carter, owner of the *Fort Worth Star-Telegram*, who once said, "Fort Worth is where the West begins, and Dallas is where the East peters out."[1] Relations between the two cities were thawing, though. After decades of bickering, the federal government had finally forced Dallas and Fort Worth into partnership on a new airport. Naturally they had argued about location, so the future Dallas Fort Worth International Airport was under construction midway between the two cities, just north of Arlington.

In media, the two markets – Dallas and Fort Worth – were defined separately by the Federal Communications Commission, although things were changing. The Arbitron ratings company issued separate radio ratings for the two cities until 1973, when they were combined. Radio had figured out that a single market, with central antennas, was much better for ratings and thus how much they could charge advertisers. Television was slowly moving the same way. In the 1950s the town of Cedar Hill had become established as an antenna center for the Dallas-Fort Worth market. South of Arlington and situated on one of the highest points in the Metroplex,[2] it was ideally located for broadcasting into both cities. KRLD-TV and WFAA-TV combined to build a 1,500-foot antenna, so their signals could be received over a wide area. A signal broadcast from the downtown area of each city could be received over a much smaller footprint. Over time, numerous other television and radio stations built antennas in the same area, which inevitably led to the markets combining.

THE NEWPAPERS

Newspapers, however, were much more parochial, focused on their home areas, which they still do. In 1972 the newspaper market leaders were the *Dallas Morning News* and the *Fort Worth Star-Telegram*, with several other papers taking up smaller but still important roles. Those papers were owned by conglomerates that also owned television and radio stations.

Alfred Belo, owner of the *Galveston Daily News*, had sent his employee, George Dealey, to Dallas to start the *Dallas Morning News* in 1885. Dealey ran the business, eventually becoming owner in 1926 of the parent Belo Corporation. The company expanded into radio with WFAA in 1922, and in 1950 started WFAA-TV as the Dallas ABC affiliate. In the 1960s the company bought several suburban newspapers, and thus owned a significant portion of the Dallas media market.

Their major newspaper competitor in Dallas was the *Dallas Times Herald*, founded in 1888. It had also expanded into other media, buying radio station KRLD in 1926 and television station KRLD-TV in 1949. In 1970 the Times-Mirror corporation, owner of the *Los Angeles Times*, bought the company, and attempted to compete more aggressively with the *Morning News*. At that time KRLD-TV was renamed KDFW.

In Fort Worth the *Star-Telegram* ruled, having been founded in 1909 by a merger between two struggling papers. Owner Amon Carter also moved the company into radio, founding WBAP in 1922, and in 1948 creating WBAP-TV as the first television station in the South. Their biggest newspaper competition was the *Fort Worth Press*, founded in 1921 as a Scripps-Howard newspaper, but it always struggled against its larger neighbor.

THE TEXAS RANGERS

The Rangers arrived in 1972 largely because of an unusual broadcasting deal. To get the Senators to move to Arlington, Mayor Tom Vandergriff agreed that the city would pay owner Bob Short enough money to pay off his debts in Washington. The city did this by buying the Rangers' broadcasting rights for the first 10 years, at $750,000 per season. The $7.5 million paid up-front to Short ensured that the team would come to Texas, but also that the city would lose a lot of money.

Arlington set up a company to handle broadcasting, and in the first season ended up with a 30-station radio-broadcast network. KRLD in Dallas became the flagship station. It hired Bill Mercer, well-known to locals as the radio announcer for the Dallas Cowboys and the minor-league Dallas-Fort Worth Spurs, and former pitcher Don Drysdale, who had spent the previous two seasons broadcasting in Montreal, as the two announcers.

KDFW got the limited television rights, showing just 24 games during the first season. Only five of them were home games, as Short believed that showing home games on television would reduce the attendance at the ballpark. Dick Risenhoover, a longtime broadcaster, was the lead announcer, with Drysdale and Mercer alternating innings in the television booth with him.

The second game played that season was intended as the first telecast of a Rangers game. Due to the players strike at the start of the season, the television people canceled the game coverage and planned other shows. By the time the strike was settled, two days earlier, it was too late to change their plans and show the game. Rangers fans thus missed the opportunity to see the first-ever win for the team, 5-1 over the California Angels.

The Rangers' first season, 1972, was a terrible one on the field, and there were plenty of struggles off it, too. Arlington had committed to $750,000 a year in radio sales, but fell short, leaving taxpayers on the hook for the balance. In his book *Play-by-Play*, Mercer blamed a combination of inexperience and poor salesmanship. The inexperience was based on a group of people coming together at the last minute to try to build a major-league broadcast network. Although they all had radio experience, none of them had worked together before. In addition, Mercer claimed that the lead salesman was more interested in having fun on the radio expense account than in actually selling advertising.

These failures led to big changes in 1973. The radio network fell apart, with stations unhappy at the losses. From 30 stations in 1972, the network was down to 16 in 1973. Drysdale moved on, deciding at the end of the 1972 season to take a broadcast job with the Angels. This angered Short, who had expected Drysdale to stay, but Drysdale pointed out that he had a one-year contract and it had ended. Risenhoover moved into the radio booth alongside Mercer, and others came in over the years. Mayor Vandergriff even got involved, spending three years in the booth, paying his own way and not taking a salary, just so the network could try to break even. Broadcasting in North Texas seemed to be as much a cowboy operation as the Rangers were.

On the newspaper scene, each of the papers had its own writers covering the team. For the *Dallas Morning News*, the lead writer was Merle Heryford, who had covered the minor-league teams in Dallas for decades. He was backed by a young feature writer, Randy Galloway, who occasionally spelled Heryford as the beat writer. Galloway went on to write about the Rangers for years, eventually becoming the premier sportswriter in North Texas, and expanding into radio and television as well. David Fink and Harry Gage were the primary writers for the *Dallas Times Herald* in 1972.

Harold McKinney and Bob Lindley were the writers for the *Fort Worth Star-Telegram*, while Mike Shropshire and Tommy Love wrote for the *Fort Worth Press* (Shropshire moved to the *Star-Telegram* in 1973). Press writers later described how they, as an afternoon paper, had more time to write in-depth articles than the morning *Star-Telegram* did.

THE FUTURE

Ironically, given the animosity between the two cities, they combined in 1974 to buy the Rangers. A group led by Brad Corbett purchased the team from Short. The group contained equal numbers of investors from each side of the Metroplex, and included the son of the founder of the *Star-Telegram*, Amon Carter Jr., who had just sold his late father's newspaper (he remained as publisher) and was looking for something to do with the money.

Ultimately, as in much of the country, the battles for media control in the Metroplex would end up in just a few hands. After years of struggling, the *Dallas Times Herald* ended up losing a circulation war against the *Morning News*. In 1991 Belo Corporation, owner of the *Morning News*, bought and closed the *Times Herald*, leaving the *Morning News* as the sole major newspaper in Dallas.

The Star-Telegram was bought by Capital Cities Communications, Inc., in 1974. The paper quickly won its citywide battle against the Press, which folded in 1975 after decades of unprofitability. The two major cities were eventually down to one major newspaper each, and both struggled through the long, slow decline of the newspaper industry.

In the meantime, the rise of cable and of sports broadcasting as a staple of programming led to a corresponding rise in television rights fees. In 2015 the Rangers signed a 20-year deal with Fox Sports Southwest for $1.6 billion, or $80 million a year. Essentially, they were receiving about a half-million dollars for every game they played. This was just for local cable rights, and didn't include national rights fees, or anything from radio.

The Rangers were also being run by savvy financial people by that time. In 2016 the team was talking to the financial markets, looking to sell a billion-dollar bond against that huge rights deal. The aim was to hedge their bets, making sure the team would receive the $80 million a season regardless of what changes might happen over time with the television contract. Who knows what changes might happen in baseball broadcasting in 20 years?

Bob Short thought he'd done a great deal to get $7.5 million in rights fees from Arlington, and to sell the team at a profit. What would he think of the numbers being thrown around today?

Sources

Mercer, Bill. *Play-by-Play: Tales from a Sports Broadcasting Insider* (Latham, Maryland: Taylor Trade Publishing, 2007).

Shea, Stuart. *Calling the Game: Baseball Broadcasting from 1920 to the Present* (Phoenix: Society for American Baseball Research, 2015).

Shropshire, Mike. *Seasons in Hell: With Billy Martin, Whitey Herzog, and "The Worst Baseball Team in History" – the 1973-1975 Texas Rangers* (New York: Diversion Books, 2014).

Notes

1 June Naylor, *Insiders' Guide to Dallas & Fort Worth* (Guilford, Connecticut: Morris Book Publishing, 2010), 3.

2 The word "Metroplex," a term that has both admirers and detractors, was coined by a local adman in the early 1970s. Denoting a metropolitan area that has more than one significant anchor city, it is a squashing-together of the words "metropolitan" and "complex." Tim Rogers, *Texas Monthly*, February 2013.

BILL MERCER

BY BO CARTER

Ask any professional sports aficionado in the Dallas-Fort Worth area about the most likely broadcaster to work the initial season of Texas Rangers baseball in the inaugural 1972 season, and at least 80 percent (conservatively) would reply Bill Mercer.

William A. "Bill" Mercer was born in February 1926 in Muskogee, Oklahoma, on February 13, 1926, to Frank Mercer, a physician's assistant, and Maynie Mercer, a homemaker. He spent most of his early life in Muskogee before serving in the US Navy from 1943 to 1946, participating in five Pacific invasions during World War II. Discharged, he studied under the GI Bill of Rights at Northeastern State in Oklahoma and received a broadcasting degree from the University of Denver in 1949.[1]

By 1972 Mercer was one of the true veterans of minor-league baseball broadcasts. Other such notables include Larry Munson of the Double-A Nashville Volunteers (and later Vanderbilt and Georgia football and basketball and Atlanta Braves baseball), Ernie Harwell of the Double-A Atlanta Crackers and decades with the Detroit Tigers, and Joe Buck of the Triple-A Louisville Colonels, the St. Louis Cardinals, and later Fox Sports.[2]

The Muskogee native began his baseball broadcasting career after covering general sports beats in the Muskogee area, then moving to the Dallas-Fort Worth area in 1958. He called the games of the Dallas Rangers of the American Association (1959-64) and the Dallas-Fort Worth Spurs of the Texas League (1965-71) before joining the Rangers broadcast crew in 1972.

Mercer's first Rangers broadcast partner was former Los Angeles Dodgers All-Star and World Series hero Don Drysdale. Drysdale had begun his career behind the mike with the Montreal Expos expansion team in 1970 and '71 and more than welcomed the move back to warmer climates in the Metroplex in 1972. After two seasons with the Rangers, Mercer moved to the Chicago White Sox with Ford Frick Award winner Harry Caray in 1974 and '75.

Because of contracts in effect when the Washington Senators made the move to Texas, a third member of the '72 broadcast team was Arlington Mayor Tom Vandergriff, the 26-year (1951-77) leader of the team's home city, dubbed the "Boy Mayor" when he was first elected in 1951 at the age of 25.[3] Vandergriff had been an avid fan of the Dallas Steers/Rebels in the 1920s and 1930s as a youngster growing up in nearby Carrollton and utilized his smooth delivery and University of Southern California communications training to become an instant hit in the broadcast booth.[4]

"It was just a thrill to be on those early broadcasts," the mayor and future congressman said in 1998. "Working with people like Bill Mercer and Don Drysdale made me appreciate the time and effort it took to produce a quality broadcast, and we tried to weave some local stories and Texas baseball history into almost every broadcast. (Manager) Ted Williams was always extremely colorful, you might say, especially when he had a 'minor' disagreement with the umpires."[5]

Vandergriff, Mercer, Drysdale, and executives from KRLD radio (which carried the games in 1972 before giving way to WBAP radio in 1973) were joined by a former basketball and baseball coach, Dick Risenhoover.[6] Along with Bill Merrill, they handled all games on radio and many local telecasts before the days of cable (Home Sports Entertainment, Prime Sports, and Fox Sports Southwest from 1982-present). Risenhoover brought a work ethic and love of baseball from working as a sportscaster in Amarillo for 13 years.[7] KDFW-TV brought Risenhoover from Childress High School in Amarillo to the Metroplex as a sports director in 1971, and he moved into the number-two analyst's post besides Mercer in 1973. The Rangers added area broadcaster Terry Stembridge as a third man in the radio booth that same season.

The beloved Risenhoover laid the groundwork for Mercer to take the Rangers position and continued in his post through the 1977 season when he began encountering some health problems (notably fainting spells) and later was diagnosed with multiple cancers in January 1971.[8] Just hours before the Rangers' home opener on April 8, 1978, he died in an Arlington hospital. Before his death he was so dedicated that he had his wife bring a recorder to the hospital so he could give Rangers preseason updates. Mercer and hundreds of others mourned his passing.[9]

When Mercer moved to Chicago for 1974 and '75, former major leaguer and Chicago White Sox broadcaster Jim Piersall joined the Rangers longtime public-relations director and traveling secretary Burt Hawkins and handled color commentary for Texas telecasts.

"Bill Mercer brought so much to the broadcast every day and night," remembered the late Fred Graham, sports information director at the University of North Texas, who worked with Mercer while Mercer was the lead play-by-play broadcaster from 1969 to 1988. "And Bill brought so many great broadcasters into the profession while he was an instructor at UNT and when he allowed the students to work with him on broadcasts for many years."[10]

"Bill was the consummate professional," Graham said, "and you really could not tell if he had been broadcasting the game from the North Texas radio booth or the opponent's vantage point. Yes, he did get excited when the Mean Green scored or made in big play in football and basketball, but he gave credit to the other teams throughout the games."[11]

Mercer was noted for the tales he spun for print and broadcast sports journalists at their frequent lunches at the historic Old Mill Inn, some 200 yards from Cotton Bowl Stadium on the Texas State Fairgrounds in Dallas.[12]

"Things were pretty rudimentary when they started the Rangers broadcasts in the 1970s and especially in the first season in '72," Graham recalled. "They were using a remodeled version of Turnpike Stadium (later to become the now-demolished Arlington Stadium) with the minor-league team's press box and just the basic radio gear for the longest time. Still, Bill, Don Drysdale, and Dick Risenhoover gave the fans a professional broadcast."[13]

Mercer, though, probably was best known for broadcasting hundreds of wrestling matches from the old Sportatorium in downtown Dallas after being called upon in an emergency situation as a wrestling sportscaster in Muskogee in the early 1950s.[14]

He was a folk hero on radio in the Dallas-Fort Worth radio market for years even before he took on the additional duties of sports director at KVIL radio on the morning drive-time program with the late fellow Texas Radio Hall of Fame broadcaster Ron Chapman.[15]

It was there, in the University of North Texas classrooms, high-school football stadiums, and basketball gyms, and Fouts Field and visiting football arenas that Mercer brought along the likes of sports radio greats such as George Dunham, Craig Miller, Craig Way, Dave Barnett, Brian Briscoe, Mark Followill, and dozens of others while giving them on-air experience and honest critiques after their live radio efforts.[16]

"Bill was a mentor to so many of us," Dunham noted, "and he gave us the tools for a lifetime of sports broadcasting. We are forever grateful."[17]

His live coverage of the Kennedy assassination and its aftermath in November 1963 received rave reviews. That led to publication of a book, *When The News Went Live* in 2004, before he authored *Play-by-Play: Tales from a Sportscasting Insider* in 2007, with numerous tales from the 1972 Rangers days and hundreds of other events from the Cotton Bowl Classic to wrestling matches by the fabled Von Erich family.

Mercer also continued to be a well-known banquet and educational speaker for decades after his 1972-73 stint with the Rangers. Those fledgling broadcasts laid the groundwork for the likes of the late Mark Holtz, Frick Award recipient Eric Nadel, Merle Harmon, Merrill, Risenhoover, Mel Proctor, Vince Cotroneo, Brad Sham, Bill Schoening, Barnett, and Scott Franzke to work on Rangers radio broadcasts.[18]

Mercer amazingly had a brief guest stint in the Rangers radio booth with Eric Nadel and Matt Hicks in April 2016 at the age of 90. His smooth delivery in that cameo included stories of re-creating minor-league baseball games from 1959 to 1971 for various Dallas radio stations and then working play-by-play duties with Drysdale and Vandergriff during that first Rangers season in Arlington in 1972. He is credited with teaching Drysdale the ins and outs of baseball play-by-play.[19]

He also told stories of the early days of professional wrestling and pointed to an anticipated crowd of 100,000-plus for WrestleMania at AT&T Stadium down the street in coming weeks.

One of Mercer's pride-and-joy stories was about his granddaughter Emma Tiedemann, who graduated from the University of Missouri in broadcast journalism and took her grandfather's lessons into the radio booth as play-by-play announcer for the Medford (Oregon) Rogues of the Great West Baseball League.[20]

"Bill could handle everything from pro baseball to pro wrestling to pro football (he was Dallas Cowboys radio commentator for a number of seasons in the 1960s) to tiddlywinks," Graham said with a laugh in that 1991 conversation. "He is the ultimate professional broadcaster, and he has literally touched the lives of millions during his career."[21]

Bill Mercer lives on in Texas Rangers lore – not just as the inaugural 1972 broadcaster but also for his contribution to radio sports nationally as a member of the Texas Radio Hall of Fame.[22]

Notes

1. Bill Huffaker, Bill Mercer, George Phenix, Wes Wise, and Dan Rather (foreword), *When the News Went Live: Dallas 1963* (Dallas: Taylor Trade Publishing, 2004), 1-28.
2. Author interview with Bill Mercer, January 21, 1994.
3. Southern Arkansas University Magale Library Archives presentation, November 20, 2014. web.saumag.edu/library/bill-mercer/.
4. Interviews with Wes Wise, May 23, 2002, and Mike Jones, March 10, 1988. See also Huffaker et. al.
5. Conversation with Tom Vandergriff, July 12, 1998.
6. Ibid.
7. Ibid.
8. Author interview with Bill Mercer, January 21, 1994.
9. Conversation with Tom Vandergriff.
10. Author interview with Fred Graham, June 24, 1995.
11. Ibid.
12. Ibid. See also author interviews with Sam Blair, June 24, 1995, and October 8, 1996, and Bill Mercer, *Play-by-Play: Tales from a Sportscasting Insider* (Dallas: Taylor Trade Publishing, 2007), 37.
13. Fred Graham interview. See also Sam Blair interview, and author interviews with Dr. Roy Busby and Jo Ann Ballantine, August 12, 2007.
14. Mercer, *Play-by-Play*," 22-26.
15. Author interviews with George Dunham and Craig Miller, February 5, 1997. See also Mercer, *Play-by-Play*, 1-4.
16. George Dunham and Craig Miller interviews.

17 Ibid.
18 Huffaker, *When the News Went Live*, 4; Mercer, *Play-by-Play*, 45.
19 Ibid.
20 Allbookstores.com/Bill-Mercer/author.
21 Fred Graham interview.
22 *The North Texan Alumni Newsletter*, Denton, Texas, September 4, 2012.

DON DRYSDALE

BY JOSEPH WANCHO

*"Hitters would dig a hole and really get anchored with their back foot.
Willie Mays dug in sometimes with both feet and he looked up and realized it was Drysdale.
I don't think he was even thinking at the time. He called time out and filled up the hole as if to say,
'I made a mistake. I didn't realize he was pitching.' VROOOOM, down he went."*
Jeff Torborg Los Angeles Dodgers catcher[1]

*"He hit me more than anyone else. He kept me going like a rocking chair.
That night, I always felt like I had been wrestling a bear. I was so tired when I left the ballpark.
But I respected him for the way he went about his job."*
Frank Robinson, Cincinnati Reds[2]

*"I know Don Drysdale is trying to hit me. He'll even come to the batting cage and say,
'Where do you want it today, big boy?'"*
Mickey Mantle, New York Yankees[3]

The first World Series game at Dodger Stadium was played on October 5, 1963. The ballpark had opened its gates the previous season. Over the following six decades Dodger Stadium served as the backdrop for some of the greatest moments in major-league history. On October 5, the Dodgers' opponent was the New York Yankees. The Yankees were a particular thorn in the side of the Dodgers, going back to their days in Brooklyn when the Bronx Bombers won six of seven World Series from the neighboring borough.

But as Don Drysdale took the hill for Game Three, his teammates had to be feeling quite confident. Los Angeles had won the first two games of the Series at Yankee Stadium, in rather convincing manner. Sandy Koufax struck out 15 batters in the 5-2 Dodgers win in Game One. Johnny Podres was not as overpowering in Game Two, but still won, 4-1. In starting the two left-handers at Yankee Stadium, Dodgers manager Walt Alston pushed Drysdale, the winner of 19 games and the reigning NL Cy Young Award winner, back to Game Three.

The Dodgers reached the Yankees' Jim Bouton for a run in the bottom of the first inning. Jim Gilliam walked, went to second base on a wild pitch, and scored on a single by Tommy Davis. But that was all the offense the Dodgers could muster. Drysdale would have to be on top of his game to bring home the win. In the top of the third, Tony Kubek reached base on an error by Maury Wills. Not to worry; Drysdale picked Kubek off.

The final out caused the most angst for Drysdale and the Dodger fans. With two outs Joe Pepitone lifted a fly ball to left field. Left fielder Ron Fairly drifted back to the track, just short of the fence in front of the Yankees bullpen, to haul it in. "Pepitone hit it real good and I saw Fairly going back until he was almost touching the fence," Drysdale said. "Then he stopped and put his glove up and I knew I had won the game."[4] Drysdale struck out nine and scattered three hits while going the distance to stake the Dodgers to a 3-0 advantage in the series. "The extra rest helped me," Drysdale said. "I felt strong. I know I was pitching high, but the Yankees were apparently looking for low stuff, so I just stayed high."⁵ Alston praised his right-handed hurler, saying, "He had the left-handers to contend with and he didn't make a mistake all through the game. His control was never better."⁶

Donald Scott Drysdale was born to Scott and Verna Drysdale on July 23, 1936, in Van Nuys, California. Scott Drysdale was a repair supervisor for the Pacific Telephone Company, which provided a comfortable middle-class upbringing. Scott had a brief career as a minor-league pitcher in 1935, the year before Don was born.

Drysdale credited his father with his early love of baseball. "We played catch in the afternoon," he said. "Often we'd go to the playground and Dad would hit me grounders and flies and I would take batting practice. He really taught me the game."⁷

It was not until his senior year at Van Nuys High School that Drysdale tried his hand at pitching. He posted a 10-1 record. Brooklyn signed the former second baseman to a $4,000 bonus contract. He was assigned to Bakersfield of the Class C California League. An astute observer, Branch Rickey, then with the Pittsburgh Pirates, scouted the 17-year-old pitcher and on June 15, 1954, wrote:

"A lot of artistry about this boy. Way above average fast ball. It is really good. Direction of the spin and the speed of rotation the same on all fast ball pitches. Angle of delivery is the same, stride is wide and his body is in all pitches. The pitching hand, and placement on fast and curve ball needs no coaching. He is good."⁸

Drysdale pitched well enough at Bakersfield (8-5, 3.46) to earn a promotion to Montreal of the International League in 1955. He started the season 10-2, but injured his right hand, and continued to pitch with the pain. It proved to be a broken bone and Drysdale lost nine games in the second half of the season to go 11-11. The next year he was promoted to Brooklyn, although Drysdale conceded that it took some good fortune to land him there. "I never would have made the majors the next season if luck wasn't with me," he wrote. "The Dodgers lost Johnny Podres to the Navy, and Billy Loes, Don Bessent, and Karl Spooner got hurt. Stuck for pitchers, the club took me, in desperation."⁹

It may have been luck that got Drysdale to Brooklyn, but it was skill that kept him there. He pitched in 25 games, mostly as a spot starter and reliever. But he showed enough (5-5, 2.64) to stay with the team all season. Trailing Milwaukee by one game, the Dodgers won the pennant by sweeping the Pirates as the Braves lost two of three at St. Louis. In the World Series, they took a 2-0 lead against the Yankees. But their old nemesis took four of the next five games to win the world championship.

Drysdale was promoted to starter in 1957 and led the club with a 17-9 record. His 2.69 ERA was tied for second in the league with Warren Spahn, right behind his teammate Podres' 2.66. Drysdale's best effort was a two-hitter against Philadelphia. He struck out six and gave up an unearned run in the 5-1 Brooklyn victory.

The young side-armer was getting a reputation as a headhunter in only his second season. With his 6-foot-6, 190-pound frame, Drysdale was an intimidating sight to most batters. On June 13, 1957, against the Milwaukee Braves, "Big D," as he was often called, was not having one of his better days. Bill Bruton homered to begin the game. In the second inning Bobby Thomson doubled and came home on a double by Carl Sawatski. Bruton followed with his second round-tripper. The Braves were up 4-0. "Johnny Logan was up next," recalled Drysdale. "He was strutting around up there and digging in and showing me his teeth and acting like he owned the place. A charge went right through me. I look at this guy and tell myself, 'Okay Buster, you asked for it.' And I aim one inside to let him know who's boss."[10] The baseball nearly took Logan's head off his shoulders as he spun out of the way and got hit at the base of his neck. Logan jogged to first base, all the time jawing at Drysdale and Don giving it right back. As Logan took his lead off first, Drysdale threw over in a pickoff attempt. First baseman Gil Hodges stuck out his glove, but missed the ball. Johnny was beaned yet again. Logan charged the mound and set off one of the biggest donnybrooks in years. There was a near-riot as both benches emptied. Drysdale was attacked from all sides, and when the dust cleared, he and Logan were ejected. The Braves had their own nickname for him, the Shooting Gallery Kid.

That 1957 season was a watershed year for major-league baseball. Although expansion had been a movement in recent years, no team moved west of St. Louis or the Mississippi River. Brooklyn Dodgers owner Walter O'Malley and New York Giants owner Horace Stoneham both saw the infinite possibilities for growth on the West Coast. Even though the Dodgers had drawn more than a million to Ebbets Field in 1955, O'Malley was not fond of the park, which was surrounded by a congested and deteriorating neighborhood. The Dodgers moved a handful of home games to Roosevelt Stadium in Jersey City in 1956 and 1957. With cities like Hoboken and Union City to draw from, it also had 10,000 parking spaces, compared with several hundred at Ebbets.

Although the move of games to Jersey was a ploy to strong-arm Brooklyn for a new ballpark, in September 1957 the Dodgers signed a deal to move to Los Angeles for the following season. They would build a new ballpark on 300 acres of land within Chavez Ravine. Similarly, Stoneham moved the Giants to San Francisco.

From 1958 through 1961 the Dodgers played their home games at the Los Angeles Memorial Coliseum. The Coliseum was one of the great football stadiums of all time, serving as the home field for the Los Angeles Rams and the University of Southern California Trojans. The seating capacity was 90,000 and it easily set baseball attendance records. Because it was built for football, and was in the shape of an oval, it lent itself to some strange dimensions. It was 250 feet to left field, 320 feet to left-center, 425 feet to center field, and 440 feet to right-center field. Hence, 260-foot home runs and 430-foot fly outs were a common sight for the fans.

The 1958 Dodgers finished under .500 for the first time since 1938 (not including the 1944 war year record of 69-85) with a record of 71-83. It was not all bad for Drysdale, though. He married Ginger Dubberly, a model and former Rose Bowl Parade Queen, in September 1958. They had one child, a daughter, Kelly.

In 1959 Drysdale led the team in wins with 17 and the league in strikeouts with 242. He also led the league in hit batsmen with 18. He made the first of nine All-Star Game appearances on July 7 at Pittsburgh's Forbes Field, as he got the starting assignment for the National League and pitched three hitless innings. (There were two All-Star Games that season. Drysdale also started the second one, on August 3, and took the loss, giving up three runs in three innings.)

The Dodgers finished strong in 1959, coming from third place on September 14 to overtake the Braves and the Giants for the pennant. They won 9 of 11 down the stretch. Their opponent in the World Series was the Chicago White Sox, a team built on pitching, defense, and speed. The White Sox drubbed LA in the opener, 11-0 behind Early Wynn. But the Dodgers came back to win the next four of five, with Drysdale picking up the 3-1 victory in Game Three.

Over the next three seasons the Dodgers fell short in their bid to return to the World Series. Drysdale led the league again in strikeouts in 1960 with 246 and hit batsmen with 10. The following year he hit 20 batters to pace the senior circuit.

Drysdale put it all together in 1962. He posted a 25-9 record with a 2.83 ERA. He led the league in wins, starts (41), innings pitched (314⅓), and strikeouts (232). His 41 starts were the most by a Dodgers hurler since Oscar Jones started 41 games in 1904. It was the first of four straight years in which Drysdale led the NL in starts. "Batting against him is the same as making a date with the dentist," said Pittsburgh's Dick Groat.[11] "Drysdale has simply got more stuff than ever before," said Alston.[12] Drysdale won the Cy Young Award and was named *The Sporting News* Player and Pitcher of the Year.

Sandy Koufax, who like Drysdale began his career back in Brooklyn, was mostly a .500 pitcher until the 1961 season, when he hurled his way to an 18-13 record. Beginning in 1962, he led the National League in ERA for five straight seasons. He gave the opposition a much-dreaded combination of power pitchers, one right-handed and Koufax left-handed. He didn't intimidate batters the way Drysdale did by plunking them. Koufax had 18 hit batsmen in his career. He intimidated them with his speed, as he was considered one of the fastest pitchers to ever toe the rubber in the major leagues.

Drysdale may have felt his 1962 awards bittersweet. The Dodgers had put together a seven-game winning streak to take a four-game lead over San Francisco on September 15. But they could muster only three more wins the rest of the season, which placed them in a tie with the Giants at the end of 154 games. The Giants won a best-of-three playoff in three games and advanced to the World Series.

After celebrating the world championship in 1963, the Dodgers slumped in 1964, finishing two games under .500. But they resurfaced to win the pennant in 1965. Drysdale (23 victories) and Koufax (26) accounted for more than half of the team's 97 victories. "When you've been pitching on the same staff for as long as we have, you know when the other one is doing something right or wrong," said Koufax. "We're quick to tell the other one about it, too."[13] Drysdale threw a one-hitter against Bob Gibson and St. Louis on May 25. He was no slouch at the plate that season, tying his career high with seven home runs, driving in a career-best 19 runs, and batting .300.

Going into September, the Dodgers sat atop the standings with a 1½-game lead over San Francisco and two games over Milwaukee and Cincinnati. But a 22-8 record, which included a 13-game winning streak (from September 16 to 30) helped LA distance itself from the others.

The World Series started off bleakly for the Dodgers. They dropped the first two games to Minnesota at Metropolitan Stadium, Drysdale and Koufax taking the losses. Both pitchers won their next game; Drysdale fanned 11 Twins in a 7-2 win in Game Four. Koufax won the seventh game, 2-0, to secure another world championship for Los Angeles. "I threw one bad pitch and Harmon Killebrew hit for a home run and I got a curve up high on Tony Oliva and he smacked it out," said Drysdale after his victory in Game Four. "When I saw my breaking stuff wasn't working too well early in the game, I went to my fastball. But the main thing was that I kept moving the ball around, inside and out, and I thought I was setting up the batters pretty well."[14]

After battling San Francisco again in 1966, the Dodgers won the pennant again in 1966, but were swept by the Baltimore Orioles in the World Series. Drysdale (13-16) had his first losing season since 1958. He lost two World Series games. He pitched well in Game Four, but was outdueled, 1-0, by Dave McNally, on a home run by Frank Robinson.

An arthritic elbow forced Koufax to retire after the 1966 season, prematurely ending his great career at the age of 30. Even though the Dodgers were not an offensive power, the great pitching of Koufax, Drysdale, and Claude Osteen had always given the team a chance to win.

From May 14 to June 8, 1968, Drysdale set a record for consecutive scoreless innings pitched. His new mark was 58⅔ innings, breaking the record of 55⅔ innings set by Walter Johnson in 1913. In three of the games during the streak, the margin of error was slim. Drysdale beat the Cubs and the Astros by a 1-0 score. He topped the Cardinals in another, 2-0. The string ended when Philadelphia scored a run in the fifth inning of a 5-3 LA win at Dodger Stadium. "I have two things to say about Drysdale," said Phillies manager Gene Mauch. "He's a hell of a man and the most knowledgeable pitcher in the game. We didn't think much about the record but I know he was thinking about it, and has for a long time. He's been through a hell of an emotional strain."[15]

The Phillies' Roberto Pena grounded out to third baseman Ken Boyer to begin the third inning, which gave Drysdale the record. "I wanted the record so bad," said Drysdale, "but I'm relieved that it's over. I could feel myself go 'blah' when the run scored. I just let down completely. I'm sure it was the mental strain."[16]

Twenty years later, Drysdale was working in his first year as a broadcaster for the Dodgers. On September 28, 1988, Orel Hershiser was zeroing in on Drysdale's scoreless-innings record. When Hershiser tied the mark pitching against San Diego, he asked to be removed from the game, out of respect for Drysdale. But manager Tommy Lasorda and pitching coach Ron Perranoski persuaded him to go for the record, and he set a new record: 59 scoreless innings. (Hershiser pitched 10 scoreless innings in that game.) When Drysdale was told that Hershiser wanted to be taken out of the game, he said "I would have gone out there and kicked him in the rear."[17]

Recurring shoulder injuries slowed Drysdale down. He was an ironman as pitchers go, as he started 35 or more games for nine straight seasons. His injury, which was diagnosed as a torn rotator cuff, never got better. After making just 12 starts in 1969, Drysdale retired as a player. In 14 seasons, all with the Dodgers, he compiled a record of 209-166 with an ERA of 2.95. He struck out 2,486 batters, posted 49 shutouts and hit 154 batters. He struck out 200 or more batters six times. Drysdale hit 29 home runs, sixth all-time for pitchers. He was 3-3 in the World Series, with an ERA of 2.95. He pitched in eight All-Star Games.

Drysdale never left the game. He went right to the broadcast booth. Drysdale was a radio and TV color man for the Montreal Expos (1970-1971), Texas Rangers (1972), California Angels (1973-1979, 1981), Chicago White Sox (1982-1987), and the Dodgers (1988-1993). He broadcast regional and national telecasts for both NBC and ABC. For ABC he contributed to *Wide World of Sports and Superstars*. His good looks made him a natural for television shows. He made cameo appearances on *The Brady Bunch*, *Beverly Hillbillies*, *Leave It to Beaver* and the *Donna Reed Show*, among others.

Don and Ginger divorced in 1982. In 1986 Drysdale married Ann Meyers, a college basketball player who was an All-American at UCLA and is a member of the National Basketball Hall of Fame. She was the only woman to be signed to a professional contract in the NBA, with the Indiana Pacers in 1979. They had three children – two boys, Don Jr. and Darren, and a daughter, Drew. "I won't play against her, she's too tough one-on-one," said Drysdale.[18]

On August 12, 1984, Drysdale was elected to the National Baseball Hall of Fame with Harmon Killebrew, Pee Wee Reese, Rick Ferrell, and Luis Aparicio. Drysdale was in his 10th year of eligibility and received 78 percent of the vote.

In 1990 Drysdale published his autobiography, *Once a Bum, Always a Dodger*, written with Bob Verdi. Drysdale gave readers a candid look into his baseball career and his personal life.

Drysdale died on July 3, 1993 of a heart attack in Montreal, where he was with the Dodgers to broadcast a Dodgers-Expos series. A week earlier, the Dodger family had lost Roy Campanella, also to a heart attack. "I think God need a battery, because he got one of the best that heaven could have ever accepted," said Dodgers manager Tom Lasorda.[19]

On July 9, 1961, the Cincinnati Reds were playing the Dodgers at the LA Coliseum. The Reds were atop the National League standings, and the Dodgers were four games behind them in second place. Drysdale came into the game in the fifth inning as a reliever. When the Dodgers came to bat, they were down 7-2. Reds second baseman Don Blasingame was knocked down on a pitch that whizzed by his head, courtesy of Drysdale, to lead off the sixth inning. Big D received a warning from home-plate umpire Dusty Boggess.

Blasingame popped out and the next batter was Vada Pinson, who doubled. Frank Robinson stepped to the plate.

Drysdale's offering was an inside pitch that sent Robinson sprawling. Boggess again came out to warn Drysdale. "Shit, Dusty," said Drysdale. "What do you want me to do? Lay the ball right down the middle so he can beat my brains in?"[20] Drysdale came inside with the next pitch, and hit Robinson on the right forearm. Boggess immediately ejected Drysdale.

The next day, Drysdale was given a five-game suspension and fined $100 by National League President Warren Giles. Drysdale decided to pay his debt in person. The next time the Dodgers were in Cincinnati, where Giles had his office, Drysdale stopped at a bank and got $100 worth of pennies. He emptied all of the pennies into a sack, walked to Giles' office, and placed them on the desk of Giles' secretary. He walked back to his hotel room, feeling proud of himself, when the phone rang and he was summoned back to Giles' office. The conversation was amiable and it ended with Giles saying, "And by the way, I want you to take those pennies of yours and roll them back up for me."[21] Drysdale spent the next few hours cursing and rolling pennies.

Don Drysdale may have been rolling pennies, but to Dodger fans, he was a million-dollar pitcher.

Notes

1. *When It Was a Game III*, HBO Sports, 2000.
2. Ibid.
3. "Suddenly, Don's Gone Too," *New York Daily News*, July 5, 1993: 48.
4. "Drive by Pepitone Produced One of Big Thrills of Game," *The Sporting News*, October 19, 1963: 27.
5. "Drysdale Sparkles, Blanks Bombers With 3-Hit Gem", *The Sporting News*, October 19, 1963: 27.
6. Bill Becker, "Drysdale Had Visions of Pepitone's Last-Out Drive Going Into the Seats", *New York Times*, October 6, 1963: S-3.
7. Melvin Durslag, "L.A.'s Fiery Strike-Out Artist," *Saturday Evening Post*, July 1, 1961: 56.
8. Branch Rickey Papers at the Library of Congress; Don Drysdale player file at the National Baseball Hall of Fame.
9. Drysdale player file.
10. Al Stump, "Headhunter With a Horsehide," *True Magazine*, May, 1980: 102.
11. Bob Hunter, "Drysdale Crowned Slab King of Year," *The Sporting News*, November 17, 1962: 1.
12. Huston Horn, "Ex-Bad Boy's Big Year," *Sports Illustrated*, August 20, 1962.
13. Bob Hunter, "Sandy and Big D Super Stoppers," *The Sporting News*, July 17, 1965: 4.
14. "Speed-Boy Dodgers Force Twins Into Key Blunders," *The Sporting News*, October 23, 1965: 27.
15. Al Goldfarb, "Don Drysdale: What Does He Do for an Encore?" *Complete Sports*, May 1969.
16. Ibid.
17. Steve Wulf, "Deep Roots," *Sports Illustrated*, December 19, 1988: 69.
18. Ross Forman, "Don Drysdale Reflects on HOF Career," *Sports Collectors Digest*, June 28, 1991: 111.
19. Associated Press, July 13, 1993, in Drysdale player file.
20. Don Drysdale with Bob Verdi, *Once a Bum, Always a Dodger* (New York: St. Martin's Press, 1990), 181.
21. Drysdale and Verdi, 182.

RANDY GALLOWAY

BY NORM KING

Suppose they started a baseball season and nobody came?

That was indeed the situation at the beginning of the 1972 season when a players' strike, the first in baseball history, delayed the start of the campaign. Fans and media everywhere were disappointed, of course. Nowhere was this truer than in Dallas-Fort Worth, where major-league baseball was about to become a reality with the Washington Senators relocating to the area and being renamed the Texas Rangers.

Among the scribes itching to cut his teeth on the baseball beat was Randy Galloway of the *Dallas Morning News*. Galloway was a rookie at covering professional baseball in 1972, and even though his introduction to the majors had to wait a little longer than normal – the Rangers missed their first regularly scheduled games – covering the team turned into one of the great learning experiences of a long career as a Dallas sports reporter and broadcaster.

George Randolph Galloway was born on January 19, 1943, in Mayfield, Kentucky, one of three children of Parker and Margaret (Bingham) Galloway. Parker was a construction and oil-field worker, while Margaret was the one who passed on the journalistic genes to her son. She had a 50-year career as an ink-stained wretch, with stints as women's editor at the *Arlington* (Texas) *Citizen Journal*, and as a writer/editor with the *Dallas Morning News* and the *Grand Prairie* (Texas) *Daily News*.

Parker moved the family moved around the South to wherever the jobs were available. The Galloways settled in Odessa, Texas, for one year where Randy played football. He also lived down the street from four guys who formed a band called *The Wink Westerners*. "We played football with three of the band members and one guy would never play," recalled Galloway. "He would just kind of sit on the porch and he'd watch us play football across the street in the park. He had real thick glasses."[1] His name was Roy Orbison.

The family moved to Grand Prairie, a suburb of Dallas, in 1956. Randy attended Grand Prairie High School, where he met his future wife, Janeen, at the local Dairy Queen; he was a senior and she was a junior. They married in 1964 and celebrated their 50th anniversary in 2014.

Randy studied journalism at Sam Houston State University and began getting immersed in the world of sportswriting, working part time at the weekly *Grand Prairie Banner* and the *Grand Prairie Daily News*. After he got married, he did some construction work while continuing his apprenticeship. He did part-time work with the *Dallas Morning News*, followed by his first full-time job with the daily *Port Arthur* (Texas) *News*, in Cajun country near the Louisiana border, in 1965. The Port Arthur job lasted 14 months, but Galloway remembered the town and the people there fondly. "I loved it down there," he said, referring to Port Arthur. "I learned the Cajun culture and they're still my favorite people."[2]

He returned to the Morning News in 1966, this time as a full-time sportswriter – he stayed there until 1998, when he joined the *Fort Worth Star-Telegram* – and when the Rangers came to town, he became their beat reporter, even though his only experience in writing about professional sports had come from covering the Dallas Chaparrals of the old American Basketball Association.[3] Still, that time reporting on the "Chaps" helped him prepare for covering baseball. "I did the Chaps for four years, and that was a great foundation for what was to come with the Rangers," he said.[4]

Covering the 1972 Rangers was a daunting task for any reporter, partly because they were a terrible team – they had a 54-100 record in the strike-shortened season – but also because their manager was Ted Williams, who was notorious for his relations with the media. Nevertheless, Galloway got along well with the Splendid Splinter.

"For whatever reason, Ted took a liking to me early in the season," Galloway recalled. "I don't think he knew or cared who I was during six weeks of spring training. But Ted treated me wonderfully. So, obviously, based on his media reputation, I was shocked."[5]

Obviously it's more fun to write about a pennant contender, but writing about a lousy team taught Galloway that if a journalist writes something negative about a player, he'd better be willing to stand behind it. "I learned quickly that when you write negative on someone, be sure to be there early in the clubhouse the next afternoon. Show your face," he said. "What you write, you own. Players do notice if you are hiding out after a negative story."[6]

As a sideline to reporting on the Rangers that year, he also became one of the team's official scorers, despite never having covered baseball. This was back in the days before free agency, and players who had no problem with anything negative you wrote about them were unforgiving if you gave them an error on a play because that could affect their contract negotiations for the next season. The grief he contended with wasn't worth the $50 per game he received, so he quit doing the job early in the 1974 season. By that time Billy Martin was managing the Rangers, and on hearing that he had quit, a disappointed Martin told Galloway that he was the best scorer the team had – three days after tearing a strip off him by phone from the dugout and calling him the worst scorer in all of baseball.

Any glitz and glamour that came from being a beat writer for a major-league ballclub was tempered by the fact that Galloway was away from home a lot, leaving Janeen to take care of their two young daughters, Gina and Jennifer.

"I really did have to do a lot of it on my own, because he was on the road a week or two at a time, and when they were in spring training, he would leave for six weeks," Janeen remembered. "But I think with him being gone so much, [the children] appreciate all the time they have with him now."[7]

As he accumulated more experience covering the Rangers, Cowboys, and other Dallas teams as a print journalist in the 1970s, Galloway also began doing occasional guest spots on sports-talk radio shows. His on-air colleagues felt that he was a natural for the airwaves. "Randy had a lot of things going for him," said fellow radio host Norm Hitzges. "He was smart; he had a folksy style; and he had a very recognizable voice."[8]

Those attributes eventually led to a regular program on WBAP-AM in 1985; the show was called, to give you an idea of the man, *Wimp-Free Sports Talk*. Galloway was successful on the show because he, as Howard Cosell would have said, "told it like it is."

"Well, he has strong opinions, and that's what makes a successful talk-show host, no matter if it's sports or news issues," said Tyler Cox, a WBAP operations manager when Galloway worked there. "Randy is a host that a lot of people love to hate."[9]

He switched over to ESPN radio in 2003, calling his show *Galloway and Company* until he retired from radio in 2008. His retirement prompted some of his colleagues to say some very nice things.

"When Randy was the lead columnist for the *Dallas Morning News*, he was the best colleague a beat writer like myself could have, as he was in the know on a lot of things and passed them along without expecting any credit for whatever story came from the tip he provided," said Ed Werder of ESPN.[10]

"My mom died unexpectedly of lupus in 1997. Ironically, Galloway's brother died the same week," recalled Jean-Jacques Taylor of ESPNDallas.com. "Still, Galloway made it a point to come by my house and offer his condolences to me and my family. That the most important columnist in Dallas-Fort Worth would make time to get my address and show up unannounced in my time of grief meant a lot."[11]

As of 2015, Dallas residents might no longer hear Galloway's voice on radio, and he might not generate the emotions that can build up through the intimacy of radio, but don't confuse retirement with inactivity; he remained a vital part of the Dallas sports scene with his column for the *Star-Telegram*.

His fondness for sports, and his aversion to wimps, for that matter, went beyond baseball, football, and basketball. He became part-owner of Wimp Free Racing Stables in 1995 —maybe it's the Kentucky blood. A feature on Galloway in *The Texas Thoroughbred* captured how he feels about the Sport of Kings.

"I've been there when the (Dallas) Cowboys have won five Super Bowls and all, but I've never come close to being as pumped up as when our horse is about to run in a $10,000 claiming race at Trinity Meadows," Galloway said. "There's no finer feeling on Earth."[12]

Sources

In addition to the sources cited in the Notes, the author used the following:

Legacy.com.

Vipfaq.com.

Notes

1 Robert Philpot, "Retirement Will Be a Relative Term for Randy Galloway," *Fort Worth Star-Telegram*, December 21, 2013.
2 Philpot.
3 The Chaparrals were one of the ABA's flagship franchises in 1967. They became the San Antonio Spurs in 1973, and joined the NBA when the two leagues merged for the 1976-77 season.
4 Email from Randy Galloway to the author, September 28, 2015.
5 Galloway email.
6 Galloway email.
7 Philpot.
8 Philpot.
9 Mike Shropshire, "Randy Galloway: King of Sports Radio," *D Magazine*, December 1997.
10 Richard Durrett, "More Than a (Galloway &) Co. Man," ESPNDallas.com, October 7, 2013.
11 Durrett.
12 Anne Lang, "Texas Profile: Randy Galloway," *The Texas Thoroughbred*, May 1996.

TOM VANDERGRIFF

BY GREG CHANDLER

Tom Vandergriff was the central figure in bringing major-league baseball to North Texas, but that was just one of many significant achievements during his 26 years serving as mayor of Arlington. Under his leadership, the city of Arlington grew from a small rural town of about 7,500 people to a large city of 125,000 with a vibrant entertainment district. There are many towns between Dallas and Fort Worth, but Mayor Vandergriff said Arlington would be the hyphen in D-FW.[1]

The Vandergriff family moved from Carrollton, Texas, to Arlington in 1937 when Tommy, as he was known as a child, was 11 years old. Tommy's grandfather, father, and uncles had been in the auto business since 1912, repairing horseless carriages in the early days, and then opening a Chevrolet dealership in Carrollton in 1920. Tommy's father, W.T. "Hooker" Vandergriff, opened a new dealership in Arlington and a few years later took over all of the family's auto business and opened a furniture store.[2]

The family business was doing well as Tommy grew up, but selling cars was not his interest. Tommy loved sports and radio. At the age of 16, having a deep, mature voice for his age, he became an announcer for a Fort Worth radio station. After graduating from Arlington High School in 1943, he pursued a degree in speech, first at Northwestern University in Evanston, Illinois, then at Southern Methodist University in Dallas, and then finally at University of Southern California, where he received a degree in broadcast journalism in 1947. He had continued to work in radio during his college years, but after graduating returned home and returned to the family business for a couple of years. Though he grew up around the car business, that was not where Tom's passion or talents lay. He would soon make the decision that would change his life and the future of Arlington.

Vandergriff was president of the Arlington Chamber of Commerce when he learned that General Motors wanted to open an assembly plant in Middle America. Realizing that his current position was insufficient to broker a deal of this magnitude, he decided to run for mayor. At the age of 25, he won his first bid for public office and promptly negotiated a deal to open a General Motors assembly plant in Arlington. He had secured a 250-acre tract with a promise from the state to build a road to the new facility. The plant opened in 1953, just two years after he was elected.

The plant immediately changed economic conditions in Arlington, creating a lot of new jobs. It also brought new demands on infrastructure and the need for water. Mayor Vandergriff's next major success was the creation by means of a dam of Lake Arlington, which would serve as the city's primary water supply for the next couple of decades. Voters approved the bond package to build the dam which was completed in just over a year. It was expected that it would take two years for the lake to fill, but heavy rains filled it in just 26 days.

Mayor Vandergriff led the way on a number of other civic projects during his 26-year tenure as mayor, including raising funds for Arlington Memorial Hospital and lobbying for Arlington State College, a two-year college, to be added to the University of Texas system and expanded into a four-year university. With the Dallas-Fort Worth Turnpike opening in 1957 making travel across the metroplex through Arlington much easier, Vandergriff started working on projects to establish Arlington as a tourist destination.

Mayor Vandergriff visited Disneyland not long after it opened and thoroughly enjoyed it. He encouraged Angus G. Wynne Jr., a developer who was planning to build a large industrial park in Arlington and neighboring Grand Prairie, to visit. Wynne was also impressed, and tried to persuade Walt Disney to build a second park on his land in Arlington. Unable to convince Disney, Wynne, with Vandergriff's support, decided to open his own park. Six Flags Over Texas opened in 1961.

The second major entertainment option Mayor Vandergriff sought was a major-league baseball team. Minor-league baseball had been successful in both Dallas and Fort Worth. With both the National and American Leagues expanding westward, Vandergriff led a coalition of North Texas mayors and leaders in developing a plan for major-league baseball. Arlington offered land beside the new turnpike about halfway between the two cities. The group won approval to sell $9.5 million in bonds to build the first-ever air-conditioned stadium. In the fall of 1960, they made their first pitch to expansion committees of both leagues, but both would choose other cities. Over the summer of 1962, Vandergriff and Charley Finley, the owner of the Kansas City A's, discussed moving that franchise to Arlington, but the league did not approve.

Unable to land a major-league team, Vandergriff initiated construction of a county-owned ballpark on the proposed site. Turnpike Stadium became the home of a Texas League team, the Dallas-Fort Worth Spurs. Its initial capacity was just over 10,000, but it was built with plans to easily expand it to 50,000 seats if a big-league franchise was granted. The ballpark opened in 1965. It was expanded to 20,500 seats in 1970, to 35,700 in 1971, and to about 40,000 seats with the addition of an upper deck in 1978. The stadium was renamed Arlington Stadium. The last game was played there on October 3, 1993, with the opening of The Ballpark in Arlington in the spring of 1994.

The new ballpark was just part of the mayor's continuing efforts to attract major-league baseball. He made another pitch to both leagues in 1968, but was denied again. It seemed doubtful that additional teams would be added in the next several years, so Vandergriff focused on luring a struggling franchise. In 1971 Bob Short, the owner of the Washington Senators, was threatening to move the team from Washington if the rent on RFK Stadium was not reduced. When no deal could be reached, Short and Vandergriff met with the American League owners and received approval to move the team. After 13 years, Tom Vandergriff's dream of major-league baseball in Arlington was fulfilled when the Texas Rangers moved into their new home, Arlington Stadium, in 1972.

As mayor, Vandergriff continued to pursue his passions for broadcasting and sports. He volunteered as the public-address announcer for Arlington High School and University of Texas at Arlington football. From 1975 to 1977, he was the color commentator for the Rangers. He took no pay and even paid his own expenses when traveling with the team.

Vandergriff accomplished much during his 26 years as mayor, but not everything was successful. One of the biggest failures was Seven Seas, an amusement park with a marine theme. It had dolphins, killer whales, and other sea life. The park was not popular and it closed after only three years.

Vandergriff was still extremely popular when he surprised the city council by announcing his resignation at a council meeting in January 1977. He did have detractors over the tax burden from the stadium, Seven Seas, and the Texas Rangers Broadcast Network. People were also critical of Arlington for being one of the largest cities in the country without public transportation, something Vandergriff would admit that he regretted.[3]

"I don't consider what happened as a 'personal achievement,'" he once said. "... It was an era when, for example, if we needed a hospital we could build it, or if we had to have a lake for our water supply we constructed it. If we wanted our junior college to become a university we had the ability to see that it was done. In other words, a spirit developed that if we as a community wanted something strongly enough, we could reach that goal. ... During those years a feeling emerged that anything was within our reach if we wanted to attain it."[4]

A few years after stepping down as mayor, Vandergriff returned to politics. In 1982 he was elected to the US House of Representatives and served one term. He was well enough regarded, but as a Democrat was overwhelmed by the Republican landslide in the 1984 election. In 1990 he ran for Tarrant County judge and won. During this time, in addition to his responsibilities as county judge, he actively campaigned for taxpayer funding of a new stadium for the Rangers. To a lesser degree, he was also involved in the Dallas Cowboys building a new stadium in Arlington. He finally retired at the end of 2006 at the age of 80. "When asked why he was retiring, Vandergriff said, "Well, I'm 80 years old and I haven't spent much time with my wife these last several years." Vandergriff's wife, Anna Waynette Vandergriff, died in 2009 two weeks after being diagnosed with leukemia."[5] They were high-school sweethearts and married in 1949, two years after he graduated from USC. They had four children – daughters Vanessa, Valerie, and Vivica, and son Victor.

Vandergriff continued to support the Texas Rangers in the final years of his life. Despite battling a variety of illnesses, he made his last public appearance at a 2010 ALCS game when the Rangers beat the Yankees to advance to their first World Series. After getting home that night, he fell and fractured his hip. Vandergriff died two months later, on December 30, 2010.

Fort Worth Mayor Mike Moncrief said Vandergriff's death "closes an important and prosperous chapter" in Tarrant County's history. "Although Tom will undoubtedly be remembered for putting Arlington on the map with the GM plant, Six Flags, and the Texas Rangers, it will be those personal experiences working alongside Tom that Rosie and I will never forget," he said. "Tom was a champion for Tarrant County, and he was a respected statesman who lived a full, complete, and meaningful life. It was a life dedicated to making our quality of life the best it could be. He certainly succeeded in that."[6]

Sources

In addition to the sources cited in the Notes, the author also consulted:

Schrock, Susan, and Gordon Dickson. "Visionary Leader Tom Vandergriff Put Arlington on Map," *Fort Worth Star-Telegram*, December 30, 2010. (star-telegram.com/living/family/moms/article3827034.html).

"38 Things to Know About Arlington," mediaroom.arlington.org/trivia.

"City of Arlington Hall of Mayors," arlington-tx.gov/history/hall-mayors/tom-j-vandergriff/.

Notes

1 Ray Hutchison, "The Texas Rangers' First Hero," *Dallas Morning News*, November 26, 2010.
2 Joe Simnacher and Elizabeth Zavala, "Former Arlington Mayor Tom Vandergriff Dies at 84," *Dallas Morning News*, December 30, 2010.
3 Simnacher and Zavala.
4 Susan Schrock, "Arlington Remembers Tom Vandergriff, the Man Who Built It," *Fort Worth Star-Telegram*, January 7, 2011.
5 Elvira Sakmari, "Arlington Legend Tom Vandergriff Dead at 84," *Fort Worth Star-Telegram*, December 30, 2010.
6 Simnacher and Zavala.

JOE BURKE

BY STEVE WEST

Joe Burke broke into baseball with help from his wife, and spent the rest of his life in the game. He was involved in the business side of the game in both the minor and major leagues, and is best remembered as general manager and president of the Kansas City Royals teams that won six division titles, two American League championships, and the 1985 World Series.

Joseph Roy Burke was born in Louisville, Kentucky, on December 8, 1923. Descended from Irish immigrants, he was the second of five children of Joseph E. Burke, a shipping clerk, and Lillie Morris. Among Burke's memories of his youth, one of his favorites was seeing Pee Wee Reese playing softball before he signed for his hometown team, the Double-A Louisville Colonels.[1]

In 1943 Burke enlisted in the US Army, and his enlistment form stated that he had four years of high school, and was an unskilled worker in beverage production. He performed well in the Army, eventually being promoted to staff sergeant while assigned to the Intelligence Division of the Troop Carrier Command. With this assignment he traveled extensively in Europe, North Africa, and South America.

Coming out of the Army after the war, Burke had few prospects. His father had died of heart problems during the war, and his mother could not afford to send him to college, so he took a job at the post office while taking night classes to become an accountant.[2] Burke played softball, and one of his teammates introduced him to Mary Hayden, who soon became his wife. Mary worked as treasurer for the now Triple-A Colonels, and in December 1948 Joe asked her to arrange a meeting with the new club president, Ed Doherty.

"I went in and asked him for a job. I told him I had no qualifications whatsoever. He said he had only one job – working in the ticket office. It meant a cut in pay from my post-office job, but I took it."[3] It was the beginning of a long association between Burke and Doherty.

Beginning with Louisville in the 1949 season as a ticket seller, Burke quickly rose through the ranks. A year later he was promoted to head of ballpark operations; in 1952 he became business manager; in 1953 he was traveling secretary; and in 1956 he became acting general manager, a position he gained full-time in 1958.

Many years later Burke told the story that in 1951 he had left Louisville to take a job with an unidentified minor-league club as general manager, with Doherty's approval. However, when he and his wife arrived and got a look at the club's books, they found "the club he wanted me to run was $30,000 in debt. He owed bills from spring training the year before. ... After 11 hours on the job I quit. ... I went back to Louisville. ... Doherty said to get back to work and forget it."[4]

The 1950s were a tough time for Louisville. With poor teams on the field, they were unable to draw crowds, so the team was beset with financial problems. When they were sued by the University of Louisville in 1956 for unpaid rent, Burke said the team had $50,000 in debt. By juggling debts here and there, he staved off the creditors that time, but the problems continued.

Burke became general manager on January 14, 1958, and immediately got to work on the money problems. He began a program he called "Operation Survival," designed to raise enough money to pay the team's bills for the season. The team planned to raise $50,000 from local businesses, but managed to collect only $17,000. Still, this was enough for the American Association to step in and provide an emergency fund of $24,000 to keep the team going through the season.[5] In addition, Kentucky Governor (and former Baseball Commissioner) Happy Chandler stated that he would arrange for the team to use Fairgrounds Stadium rent-free for the season, which saved the club $10,000.[6]

At the end of the season Burke was given the task of saving the Colonels by the board of directors. With on- and off-field failures, the team was in dire trouble, even borrowing money from the Baltimore Orioles just to keep the business office open through the end of the year.[7] Burke managed to find a solution. In November Milwaukee Braves officials announced that they had reached an agreement for the Colonels to become their top farm club, saving the team that was virtually defunct. (Legally, the Louisville club was dissolved and Milwaukee moved its Wichita franchise to Louisville, taking the old club's name.) Burke was retained as assistant to new general manager Lynn Stone. "I know Louisville has been a great baseball town and will be again," said Braves vice president Birdie Tebbetts.[8]

The team flourished in 1959, but at the beginning of 1960 Stone resigned, and Burke got the job once more. His efforts then, and over the previous years, brought him reward after the season, when the Louisville Baseball Writers Association honored him at its annual dinner as Man of the Year. It was a bittersweet moment for both Burke and the writers; shortly before being honored, Burke had left the team, moving another step up the baseball ladder.

Doherty had left the Colonels in 1953 to become president of the American Association. Burke had made a great impression on him: "After I worked with him for three or four years, he told me if he ever went to the major leagues in any capacity he would take me with him."[9] Sure enough, when Doherty became general manager of the expansion Washington Senators, Burke got a call, and became Doherty's assistant in charge of stadium operations.

By now, moving was a big deal for Burke, as his family had grown over the years. Along with his wife, he took his seven children (one other child had died shortly after birth) and moved to a large home in McLean, Virginia, just outside Washington.

After two seasons in charge of the Senators, Doherty was fired as general manager. Team President Pete Quesada hired former Yankees outfielder George Selkirk to replace Doherty and moved Burke to business manager. Burke, who had been considered the leading candidate for the GM job, received a two-year contract extension with a salary increase, but set his sights higher: "I hope to be a general manager some day, either with Washington or some place else, and will work hard toward that position."[10]

"There aren't many more knowledgeable baseball people than Burke," one writer wrote at the time. In that 1962 story, Burke listed cities he felt were ready for major-league ball: Atlanta, Dallas, Toronto, Seattle, Buffalo, and Denver. He wasn't too far off in his expansion plan either – Burke thought there would be four six-club leagues in the future.[11] He was less successful in his prognostications a couple of years later. While he correctly predicted the coming of pay-TV and a free-agent draft, his misses included envisioning that Congress would pass antitrust laws for baseball, and that there would be a single minor league, with all players instead going through greatly expanded college ranks, similar to the way football works.[12]

At the beginning of 1963 the team was bought by investment bankers James Johnston and James Lemon, who informed Selkirk, Burke, and manager Mickey Vernon that they would not only keep their jobs but would have expanded authority with the club.[13] In mid-1964 Johnston gave a strong vote of confidence in Selkirk and Burke, extending their contracts, which he did again in 1967.

Johnston died at the end of 1968, leaving his partner, Lemon, in charge of the team. In a boardroom reorganization, Burke was promoted to vice president and treasurer. Everything changed at the end of the year when Lemon sold the team to Bob Short. Short came in and quickly disrupted things, firing Selkirk and announcing that he would act as general manager himself. He decided that Burke could stay, but adjusted his position to be vice president for administration.

Burke quickly became an adviser to Short on baseball matters. By 1972 both were referring to "us" and "we" when talking about trades, as in "They have not offered us anything we feel would make a square deal," which Burke said when talking about a possible Denny McLain trade.[14] During 1972, after the Washington club became the Texas Rangers, Burke was officially named general manager, although his influence with Short was limited as long as the dominant Ted Williams was manager. Once Williams resigned at the end of the 1972 season, Burke grew in power.

Burke and Short interviewed at least 25 candidates to succeed Williams, and eventually chose Whitey Herzog, who had been backed by Burke.[15] "The Rangers are a triumvirate, including Mr. Short, Whitey, and me. Decisions are made only after we've studied all the angles," Burke said just a month later.[16]

It was notable that during the Williams era Burke developed a strong farm system, ran the spring-training complex in Florida, and did what he could to be involved in places that Williams was not. With Herzog, Burke found a manager who shared many of his ideas, such as giving young players a chance and avoiding platooning where possible. Burke's ideas began to take root.[17]

But it didn't last long. Burke surprised everyone, not least Short, by resigning on September 2, 1973, to take a position with another club. Short had tried to talk Burke out of the move for three months, before accepting his resignation.[18] Just five days later Short fired Herzog, Burke's man, and brought in Billy Martin as manager.

Burke's new role turned out to be as vice president of business operations for the Kansas City Royals. Owner Ewing Kauffman had decided to split the general manager's role, leaving Cedric Tallis in charge of the baseball side of things, and giving everything else to Burke.

"It was a difficult decision to leave the Rangers," Burke said. "All of my life I wanted to be a general manager. I am thankful to Bob Short for giving me that opportunity. But this is a new challenge that I couldn't turn down."[19] Burke later said that the ongoing instability in Texas was a big reason for his leaving. "I spent too much time with clubs that didn't offer security."[20]

Burke's time out of the general manager position lasted less than a year. On June 11, 1974, Kauffman demoted Tallis and promoted Burke to executive vice president and general manager of the Royals, saying, "Mr. Burke will be responsible only to me for the entire operation. Mr. Burke was selected over Mr. Tallis because of the ever-increasing complexities of the operation of a baseball club. Mr. Burke has the business and baseball experience that makes him well qualified for the new position."[21]

Kauffman pointed out that the Royals had lost $900,000 in 1973 (and would lose an estimated $1 million in 1974), and wanted Burke to bring them back even, a goal that probably gave Burke flashbacks to his time in Louisville. Even so, he said he planned few changes, because he had been surprised by the decision the day before. Still, he said, "I'm not egotistical, but I'm not afraid of my new job. I know what's involved, and I know the key is delegating authority to the right people."[22]

Burke quickly signed manager Jack McKeon to a two-year contract extension. By the winter he was deep in trade discussions, trying to obtain pitching. In a surprising move, given his history of player development, he cut three farm teams (leaving the Royals with four), and joined the Major League Scouting Bureau, cutting his own scouting staff from 23 to 6.[23] These moves were intended to reduce operating costs, and along with an increase in ticket prices, designed to stop the team's losses.[24]

During the 1975 season the team struggled to perform as well as expected, and at the end of July Burke made the decision to fire McKeon even though the team was in second place (11 games out). He brought in Whitey Herzog, his old friend from Texas, to be the manager. Burke made it clear that in both the firing and hiring decisions, Kauffman had no involvement other than to approve Burke's recommendations.[25] For his part, McKeon held no grudges. "Ewing Kauffman and Joe Burke are good people. I can't say anything except good things about them. Both of them have been fair and honest to me."[26]

Things improved over the rest of the season, but they ended the season seven games behind Oakland, and Burke knew he had seen enough to make changes. "We know where we stand and what we have to do to improve. I feel certain we'll make some changes."[27] They did, promoting Lou Gorman to assistant general manager and John Schuerholz to farm director. Burke then released veteran Harmon Killebrew, let pitcher Lindy McDaniel retire, and made it clear that several other veterans would be cleared out to make way for young players from the farm system.

With the Messersmith-McNally decision coming down during the winter, big changes were on the way to baseball. Pitchers Andy Messersmith and Dave McNally claimed that the standard reserve clause in their contracts meant they were free agents, after playing out a season without a contract. In December 1975 an arbitrator agreed, making those two players free agents, and potentially allowing any other unsigned player to follow suit. Burke moved quickly to sign many of his players, to avoid looming problems. One advantage he had was in being fair to players: "I've never believed in playing games with people. When we sit down to talk, my first offer is one I believe to be fair and reasonable. I think that when management takes this approach, the player tends to be realistic."[28]

But owners began a lockout in spring training, which lasted a couple of weeks and ultimately ended up with owners and players agreeing on the beginnings of free agency. Burke was considered a moderate in the dispute because he accepted that there would be modification of the current system. He declined to comment during the lockout, though. "I feel we have an excellent attitude on this club and that there is harmony between the players and the front office," he said. "We've worked too hard to build up a positive attitude and I'm not going to start destroying it now."[29]

Burke then changed the Royals' attitude to contracts. Although the Royals had never previously given out more than a two-year deal, Burke surprised everyone by handing outfielder John Mayberry a five-year contract for more than a million dollars.[30] He realized that what would work in the age of free agency was signing young and upcoming players to long-term deals, and did so with a number of his players over the next year.[31]

On the field in 1976 the Royals started slowly, but once they got going everything clicked. They moved into first place in mid-May and pushed their lead as high as 12 games by early August. They faded the rest of the way, but hung on to win their first-ever division title by 2½ games over Oakland. Then followed a thrilling ALCS, which the Yankees won three games to two on a home run by Chris Chambliss in the bottom of the ninth of Game Five.

Looking to boost the team for the future, the Royals looked at several free agents, but weren't able to sign any. This pattern played out consistently over the next few years, with the core of the team coming from the farm system that Tallis had set up. A conservative policy from Kauffman said that they wouldn't pay free agents more than they paid their own stars, but that meant they were never likely to be in on top free agents.[32] Talking on how players would use others' big contracts to boost their own value, Burke said, "We should not be held accountable for what New York and California do."[33]

More honors came to Burke at the end of 1976, when he was named The Sporting News Executive of the Year. The publication cited his "strong, stable leadership" in improving the team on and off the field. They described how the club was split between the baseball and business sides before he arrived, and there was conflict among several personalities in the organization. Burke had united the club and removed conflicts, turned the financial side around, made a solid team and a productive farm system.[34]

As he often did, Burke played down his own role in receiving the award. He said, "I've never been one to seek publicity or notoriety. In this business you cannot do it alone. … The credit should go to the organization, not to one person. … I think the award I have received is a tribute to everyone in our organization and to the type of ownership provided by Mr. and Mrs. Kauffman."[35]

The 1977 season proved to be better than 1976. The Royals took over first in mid-August, and a 16-game win streak in September helped push them to 102 wins for the season, easily winning the division. Once more they faced the Yankees in the ALCS, and once more they lost three games to two, despite winning two of the first three games and leading, 3-1, in the final game, which they lost 5-3.

Despite their success, they knew they couldn't stand still. Both Burke and Kauffman said that the prior season had been about taking care of the club's current players, but that for 1978 they would bring in a couple of free agents. "You have to improve your club every year. I just don't believe in disrupting the club during the season, making a flock of changes, bringing players in and out," Burke said.[36] But they still didn't make any big signings or trades, and Burke was dismayed at the criticism they received. "We haven't made any spectacular trades, so right away people say we're a stand-pat club. We're going to have five or six new faces on our team this year, just like we did last year."[37] On the other hand, third baseman George Brett gave the front office credit at the end of the regular season for believing in the players they had: "Joe Burke … showed a lot by not going out and getting a lot of big-money players in the free-agent market."[38]

The Royals finished the 1978 season 10 games worse than the previous season, but with 92 wins they won their division by five games, and were matched with the Yankees for a third consecutive ALCS. This time they lost the series three games to one, with their only highlight being Brett hitting three home runs in Game Three. After elimination, the tune changed, with several players and manager Herzog openly questioning why the team hadn't signed some free agents to put them over the top. "We need to have some quality players," DH Hal McRae said, adding that Burke and Kauffman "are going to have to decide if they want a good team or a great team." Said Herzog: "In spite of what the top echelon says, we've got to get off our rears."[39]

The conservative approach stayed in place, and the team didn't make any serious moves for 1979 either, which came back to haunt them as the predictions of falling behind came true. They contended all the way, but finished three games behind the Angels for the division title. Burke knew where he wanted to place blame, firing Herzog right after the season ended. "It is a decision that is mine and one for which I accept full responsibility. … I am not giving any specific reason other than that I believe we need the change." Herzog himself blamed player grumbling for the move, with a number of veterans feeling they would have won the pennant if he had played them.[40] He also slammed the front office, saying that he had wanted them to get involved in the free-agent market. "I figured when they fired me they'd go out and sign a couple of pitchers, but I guess they don't want to. They're not going after free agents like they really want to sign them."[41]

A few weeks after firing Herzog, Burke hired Orioles first-base coach Jim Frey as manager. "He has extensive background in baseball and has dedicated his life to the game. We feel Jim is the man to continue our development of the Royals," Burke said.[42] The move worked, as with a 97-65 record they cruised to winning their division, then finally won an ALCS, sweeping the Yankees in three games before losing the World Series to the Philadelphia Phillies in six games. Burke said that the Royals had come of age three years earlier, but the stakes were now higher. "We're not losers. We're not going to let anybody put that tag on us again."[43]

Burke still wouldn't get involved in the free-agent market, though. Not wanting to spend big money, he stayed away from the top free agents, and wasn't even interested in lesser ones. "You can't take a chance on a middle-range player anymore. One or two players are not going to turn around a club."[44] This attitude began to rebound as some of his star players approached free agency, as Burke looked to hold the line against them too. Hal McRae, second baseman Frank White, and pitcher Dennis Leonard all talked of frustration that the Royals weren't moving quickly, and that they weren't offering the money the players could get elsewhere.[45]

In the late 1970s Burke became a member of the owners' Player Relations Committee. Players and owners were beginning work on a new Basic Agreement, with the two sides seemingly preparing for war. That war arrived in 1981 with a strike by players, which wiped out a significant part of the season. By now Burke and the Royals were hardliners in terms of player relations, although he denied this. "I've never been a hawk on anything. I wouldn't call Ewing Kauffman a hawk, either. He has strong feelings, but he always is concerned with the best interests of the game."[46]

A few weeks after the strike ended, Burke fired manager Jim Frey. The team was 10-10 in the second half, and Burke felt something was missing. "It has been apparent during most of the year that the winning combination has not been present," he said.[47] He quickly hired former Yankees manager Dick Howser to run the Royals. The Royals then raced away to win the second half of the split season, but were swept in the Division Series by Oakland.

In August 1981 Burke was diagnosed with lymphoma, and began to undergo chemotherapy to treat the disease. In October he was promoted to team president, a less demanding position to help in his recovery. The Royals promoted his assistant, John Schuerholz, to general manager.

At the end of 1980, Kauffman had allowed Burke to become the first stockholder in the team other than Kauffman and his wife. This was his way of showing his appreciation for the way Burke had operated the team.[48]

Over the years Burke had become more involved in the league side of baseball. Apart from his involvement in the Player Relations Committee, in 1981 he testified at a National Labor Relations Board hearing, stating that management did not completely control salaries, because some players went to arbitration, where a third party chose the salary. He also said that fans pressured teams to re-sign players, which was an indirect influence on salaries.[49]

Later, in 1987, Burke was a member of the American League expansion committee. One of the complaints he dismissed was that there weren't enough players good enough to play if the major leagues expanded. "Even when we had eight teams in each league, everyone was crying about not having enough left-handed pitching. No matter how many teams there are, there will be the same talent complaints."[50]

Burke dealt with other off-field problems, too. As general manager in 1980 he was approached by catcher Darrell Porter, who admitted to having drug and alcohol problems. Burke helped him get admitted to rehab, and supported his return to the team.[51] In 1983, while president, he helped deal with the fallout from the arrests of four Royals players for cocaine possession. And in 1986 Royals manager Howser was diagnosed with cancer, and left the team for surgery and recovery. He came back the following spring, but was too weak to continue as manager, so he officially resigned, and died later that summer. During his ordeal, Burke stood right by him, to help him get through it. Having experienced it himself, Burke knew just how much work it would take to recover. Burke was also the one to tell Howser that it was time to resign, when he saw what a physical toll managing was taking.[52]

In the early 1980s the team stumbled a little, but the drug scandal helped them reboot, and 1985 finally produced the breakthrough they had been waiting for. After a 91-win season, they went to the ALCS against the Blue Jays. Down three games to one, they won three in a row – the last two in Toronto – to go to their second World Series, this time against the in-state rivals St. Louis Cardinals. Again they found themselves down three games to one, and again they rallied to win all three and get their first championship.

Burke celebrated with his team, and even got in a dig at Kansas City's reputation. To the 300,000 fans at the victory parade he said, "Across the country, when everyone awoke this morning and read the newspapers, they realized that everything is up to date in Kansas City."[53]

Burke had suffered through several health issues in his later years, apart from the cancer. He had had surgery in 1979 to repair ruptured discs in his neck, and in 1985 had his gall bladder removed. The cancer returned in 1992, and while undergoing treatment, Joe Burke died at the University of Kansas Medical Center on May 12, 1992.

Burke was eulogized across baseball as a good and honorable man. "Joe Burke was not only a great man in baseball, but was a great one individually and toward all other human beings. I shall miss him very much personally and professionally," said Kauffman.[54]

Commissioner Fay Vincent said, "Joe was one of the most beloved figures in baseball. Joe gave the game a measure of dignity and grace that long will be remembered."[55]

"Joe Burke has been a pillar of strength in our organization for many years. He has touched all of us in a very special way while providing direction and leadership," Royals GM Herk Robinson said,[56] while one of his former players, George Brett, said, "He was like a father to me when I first came up. Joe gave me fatherly advice all the time. … When you walked out of his office you felt good."[57]

"The thing I remember most was his patience with any situation," said Hal McRae. "People were always putting pressure on him to make trades. Joe would always say sometimes the best trade is the one you never made."[58] Burke's former assistant general manager, Lou Gorman, said that Burke "was a kind, thoughtful and gentle man with an extremely pleasant personality."[59]

Notes

1. Joe McGuff, "Royals' Joe Burke Gains Executive of the Year Honor," *The Sporting News*, December 11, 1976: 36, 40.
2. Ibid.
3. Bill Fuchs, "Marriage Got Burke Into Baseball," *Washington Evening Star*, March 25, 1962: G7.
4. Ibid.
5. Frank Haraway, "One Worry Eased, Another Increased," *The Sporting News*, May 21, 1958: 29.
6. Johnny Carrico, "Chandler Takes Step to Lower Colonels' Rent," *The Sporting News*, May 21, 1958; 29.
7. "Burke Told to Try to Save Colonels," *Lexington* (Kentucky) *Herald*, October 31, 1958: 8.
8. "Braves Promise Finest Talent for Colonels," *Lexington* (Kentucky) *Leader*, November 15, 1958: 8.
9. Fuchs.
10. Merrell Whittlesey, "Selkirk Open to Deals for Any Senator," *Washington Evening Star*, November 22, 1962: G1.
11. Francis Stann, "Win, Lose or Draw," *Washington Sunday Star*, January 14, 1962: C2.
12. Dave Brady, "Nats Looking Ahead; Ink TV Pact Hinging on New Package Plan," *The Sporting News*, February 22, 1964: 22.
13. Shirley Povich, "Quesada cashes In – All's Quiet Again Along the Potomac," *The Sporting News*, February 9, 1963: 14.
14. Randy Galloway, "Deal for Denny Is Still a Possibility," *The Sporting News*, January 29, 1972: 36.
15. Randy Galloway, "Rangers' Bats Weak, Skipper Herzog Admits," *The Sporting News*, November 18, 1972: 39.
16. Merle Heryford, "Ranger Burke Covers More Ground," *The Sporting News*, December 30, 1972: 44.
17. Ibid.
18. "O'Brien Succeeds Burke in Rangers' G.M. Chair," *The Sporting News*, September 15, 1973: 4.
19. "Joe Burke Joins Royals," *The Sporting News*, September 22, 1973: 15.
20. Sid Bordman, "Royals Promote Burke to G.M. Post," *The Sporting News*, June 29, 1974: 12.
21. Ibid.
22. Ibid.
23. "Royals Cut Scout Staff, Farm System," *The Sporting News*, November 23, 1974: 61.

24 Joe McGuff, "Royals See Chance to End Red-Ink Flow in 1975," *The Sporting News*, March 1, 1975: 46.
25 Joe McGuff, "Tiffs with Players, Press End Mckeon Reign at K.C.," *The Sporting News*, August 9, 1975: 9.
26 Ibid.
27 Joe McGuff, "Lindy's Exit Could Start Royal Housecleaning," *The Sporting News*, October 11, 1975: 21.
28 Joe McGuff, "Quick Signings Viewed as Flag Sign in K.C.," *The Sporting News*, February 28, 1976: 37.
29 Joe McGuff, "Slow-Starting Mingori Major Victim of Lockout," *The Sporting News*, March 13, 1976: 44.
30 Joe McGuff, "Royals' New Pact Makes Mayberry a Millionaire," *The Sporting News*, April 3, 1976: 42.
31 Peter Gammons, "Money Can't Buy Me Love," *Sports Illustrated*, April 23, 1990: 34.
32 Joe McGuff, "Free Agents Slow Royals' Trade Talk to a Crawl," *The Sporting News*, December 4, 1976: 60.
33 Joe McGuff, "Royals Hoping for Compromise on Salaries," *The Sporting News*, January 22, 1977: 41.
34 Joe McGuff, "Royals' Joe Burke Gains Executive of the Year Honor," *The Sporting News*, December 11, 1976: 36, 40.
35 Ibid.
36 Sid Bordman, "Security and Pride Cited as Keys to Royal Success," *The Sporting News*, October 15, 1977: 12.
37 Del Black, "Foes Stronger, Royals Are Too, Says Herzog," *The Sporting News*, April 22, 1978: 24.
38 Sid Bordman, "Champion Royals Calmly Sip Champagne," *The Sporting News*, October 14, 1978: 31.
39 Sid Bordman, "Cracks in Royals' Castle? Herzog, Players Complain," *The Sporting News*, October 28, 1978: 11.
40 Del Black, "'Why?' Folks Ask at Whitey's Exit," *The Sporting News*, October 20, 1979: 29.
41 Del Black, "Whitey Rips Royals' Milquetoast Style," *The Sporting News*, December 15, 1979: 51.
42 Sid Bordman, "Frey Expects to Win in 1980 with Royals," *The Sporting News*, November 10, 1979: 46.
43 Mike DeArmond, "After a Taste of Series, Royals Want It All," *The Sporting News*, November 8, 1980: 38.
44 Mike DeArmond, "Porter Only Free-Agent Fish in the Sea for the Royals," *The Sporting News*, November 29, 1980: 46.
45 Mike DeArmond, "Leonard, K.C. – Big Silence," *The Sporting News*, January 31, 1981: 52; DeArmond, "'McRae-White Plan' Upsets Royals," *The Sporting News*, January 24, 1981: 51.
46 Mike McKenzie, "Royals: Gura Growing," *The Sporting News*, August 22, 1981: 44.
47 "Royals Fire Frey; Howser to Manage," *The Sporting News*, September 12, 1981: 75.
48 Mike DeArmond, "Hurdle in Dark Over His Role with Royals," *The Sporting News*, January 10, 1981: 39.
49 William R. Barnard, "Envelopes May Have Key to Settling Strike," *Lexington* (Kentucky) *Leader*, July 10, 1981: C1.
50 Paul Attner, "Big Bang," *The Sporting News*, March 18, 1991: 19.
51 Mike DeArmond, "An 'Aware' Porter Tells His Story," *The Sporting News*, July 12, 1980: 19.
52 Bob Nightengale, "Howser: Battle Over, War Begins," *The Sporting News*, March 9, 1987: 27.
53 "300,000 Hail Royals During 2-Hour Parade," *Augusta* (Georgia) *Chronicle*, October 29, 1985: 13A.
54 "Royals President Joe Burke Dead at 68," *Ellensburg* (Washington) *Daily Record*, May 14, 1992: 12.
55 Dick Kaegel, "Kansas City Royals," *The Sporting News*, May 25, 1992: 26.
56 "Royals President Joe Burke Dead at 68."
57 Ibid.
58 Ibid.
59 Lou Gorman, *High and Inside: My Life in the Front Offices of Baseball* (Jefferson, North Carolina: McFarland, 2007). 130.

HAL KELLER

BY NELSON "CHIP" GREENE

Hal Keller was 12 years old in 1939 when his brother Charlie became a hitting sensation for the New York Yankees. "I was in sixth grade when he played in his first World Series," Hal remembered 71 years later. "I was proud as a peacock. They were all day games, and the teacher brought a radio in the classroom and we'd listen."[1] As the Yankees swept Cincinnati in four games, Charlie Keller, in his rookie season, batted .438 and hit three home runs, and that performance served notice that the man the press had dubbed King Kong was well on his way to a brilliant major-league career.

Little could Hal have imagined at the time the path his own life would take. If he never reached the level of stardom that his celebrated brother experienced nor even became a household name among fans, still, in a baseball career that stretched over 50 years as a player, manager, farm director, and front-office executive, Keller enjoyed success at every level of the professional game. Indeed, as Keller, then 82 years old, told a reporter in January 2010, "Baseball was good to me, no two ways about it."

Perhaps it was inevitable that he would be a ballplayer. Born July 7, 1927, on a farm in Middletown, Maryland, a rural community in the western part of the state, Harold Kefauver Keller was the youngest of four children and the third son born to Charles Ernest and Naomi Kefauver Keller. Hal was 11 years younger than Charlie, and by the time Hal began to hone his skills his brother had already left home and was gaining renown in college and the minor leagues. So Hal developed as a player without much input from the future Yankees slugger.

In addition to Charlie and Hal (a sister, Ruth, was the oldest child), another brother, Hugh, two years Charlie's junior and nine years older than Hal, was also a gifted ballplayer. Hugh was a shortstop, and a cousin, Jack Remsberg, who grew up with the Kellers in Middletown, remembered him as "a great hitter."[2] As Charlie had before him, Hugh starred at the University of Maryland. During World War II Hugh entered the service, and by the time he got out he was too old to pursue a baseball career. (When Hugh was a star in the local Frederick County League, Hal served as a batboy on Hugh's team. Later, Hugh became a high-school coach and also played semipro baseball.) With older brothers like those, it was only natural that Hal, too, would take an interest in the game.

Growing up on a farm, the brothers of course had plenty of chores to do. Through their daily labors both of Keller's brothers had developed powerful physiques that formed the foundation of their hitting power, and Hal was no exception; fully grown, the left-handed slugger reached 6-foot-1 and weighed 200 pounds. Unfortunately for the Kellers, during the Depression they lost their farm to foreclosure, so Hal worked instead on the Remsbergs' neighboring tract, milking cows each evening after school. He also accompanied Jack Remsberg to fairs, where the finest of the cattle were displayed.

Still, there was always time for play. Given the age disparity between Hal and his brothers, their influence on him was minimal, so he was largely on his own when it came to developing fundamentals.

"I learned to play ball in a church parking lot in Middletown," Keller recalled during a phone conversation with the author in 2010. "However many kids showed up, that's how many played – even two on a side, if need be, although there were usually three or four. If you hit the ball to the opposite field, you were out. I think that was better than the pressure of Little League." Later, as his brothers had, Keller attended Middletown High School, where he played second base on the baseball team.

During those years Charlie's celebrity understandably provided some advantages for his little brother. Charlie often visited home when the Yankees traveled to Washington to play the Senators; Middletown is about 50 miles from Washington. Hal said Charlie never brought any of his teammates to Middletown, but during a series in 1939, his rookie season, 12-year-old Hal attended a game and met Lou Gehrig. Despite having already been diagnosed with his fatal disease Gehrig was still traveling with the team, and Hal was mesmerized by the introduction. The meeting remained as vivid to Hal more than seven decades later as it did the day it took place.

While Charlie Keller became a schoolboy legend at Middletown High School, ten years later circumstances were different for Hal. With the effects of World War II being felt across the nation, gas rationing dictated that teams had to reduce their travel. As a result, Hal remembered, he played in only three or four games throughout his high school career. Nonetheless, his name carried significance. Both Charlie (1934-36) and Hugh (1939-40) had starred at the University of Maryland playing for coach Burton Shipley, and once Hal graduated from high school in 1944, coach Shipley, in Hal's words, "wanted to see what the next Keller could do." So the coach secured a $500 scholarship for Hal from Sears Roebuck, got him a job in the dining hall, and the last of the Keller brothers enrolled at the University of Maryland. He played there during the 1945 season, shuttling between catcher and center field.[3]

That year Keller's fortunes took a dramatic turn. Early in 1945 coach Shipley, who was a friend of Senators owner Clark Griffith, took Hal to Griffith Stadium for a tryout overseen by Washington's general manager, Ossie Bluege. Bluege expressed interest in signing him, but Keller told him a baseball career would have to wait, because he was soon to enter the military.

"Soon" turned out to be the following year. Keller received an appointment to the Merchant Marine Cadet School, in San Mateo, California (Charlie had served in the Merchant Marine the previous two years). Hal headed off to become what was the equivalent of a plebe at the Naval Academy. After a year, however, with no opportunity to play baseball, Keller left the school and enlisted in the Army. That year he also married his first wife, Marietta, with whom he eventually produced five children. (Their marriage ended in divorce.)

Throughout 1947 Keller played baseball in the Army. Early in the year he joined the Sixth Infantry Division team as a catcher in South Korea, and that experience, he recalled, "was my real introduction to baseball." The Sixth won a service title in 1947 and went to Hawaii to play in the FEC tournament, a service championship series among Army teams. "Those teams had older guys," Keller recalled, some as old as 35, and the Sixth eventually lost. Nonetheless, the 20-year-old had gained invaluable experience, and he returned home eager to begin his professional career.

Keller was discharged from the Army on February 28, 1948. He had agreed to join the Senators in Orlando, Florida, for spring training the following week, but first he returned home to visit his family. He and his wife arranged for veterans housing in Frederick, 10 miles from Middletown. On March 6 Keller reported to training and signed a contract for the 1948 season.

For the next five years Keller remained in the Washington organization and tried to establish himself as a major leaguer. When he broke in, he hadn't really played a lot of organized baseball; nonetheless the Senators considered Keller, in the words of owner Clark Griffith, perhaps their hottest prospect,[4] and they were optimistic about his future. What they were not completely sure of, however, was what position the hot prospect would play. So divided had the Senators had been over Keller's defensive abilities that it took them two seasons to decide. While he had spent some time at the University of Maryland playing in the outfield, he had been used most often at catcher. Many of the scouts who watched him at College Park considered it his strongest position. But General Manager Bluege, as well as several others in the Senators organization felt strongly that Keller possessed the speed and skills to play the outfield. So as the 1948 season got under way, that's where he began his professional career.

His first season in pro ball proved only moderately successful. He split time between two teams in Class-B leagues, Charlotte in the TriState League and Hagerstown in the Interstate League, 30 miles from his Frederick home. Playing in both left field and center field, Keller usually batted third or fourth yet often struggled, hitting a combined .258 with a slugging mark of just .354. In spring training in 1949 it came out that during his time in the service Keller's coaches had altered the stance and swing he had learned at Maryland, and so he had spent 1948 trying to "rearrange himself." When he finally got his timing and mechanics restored, the Senators got the production they had hoped for, and 1949 turned out to be Keller's finest season as a ballplayer. Back with the Hagerstown Owls, he batted .322, sixth highest in the league, with a .434 slugging average and 95 RBIs for a last-place team; typically batting fourth, he led the team in almost every offensive category. On defense Keller was shifted to right field, where he played the position, wrote one sportswriter, "like a veteran … pulling down line drives and sky balls that used to drop in for base hits."[5]

"Equipped with one of the strongest throwing arms in the league,"[6] a newspaper said, Keller "[threw] to third and home from his post in right field as if he was pitching strikes."[7] By the end of the season he was considered "one of the best outfielders in the league."[8] Not surprisingly, when the rosters expanded on September 1, Keller received a callup to the major leagues.

The 22-year-old made his major-league debut on September 13, 1949. Entering as a pinch-hitter for pitcher Joe Haynes in the eighth inning at Griffith Stadium, Keller singled off Randy Gumpert of the Chicago White Sox ("I was leading the league in hitting for about 12 hours," he laughingly remembered) and moments later he scored the second run of a 3-2 Senators loss. His only other appearances that month were two more pinch-hitting appearances, both unsuccessful.

Keller's career year at Hagerstown before his call-up wasn't completely serene. In August he stayed behind when the Owls departed on a road trip. He had a back problem and, a sportswriter reported, "is in Washington undergoing special treatments under the supervision of the Senators' trainer."[9] As Keller was at the time "highly regarded by Washington's front office,"[10] the article said, the team was "taking no chances with the future of the big boy."[11] As it turned out, the Senators had been less than impressed with Keller's speed, and decided to make him a catcher. (In anticipation of the move, Keller had played 27 games at the position at Hagerstown.) In a 2010 interview Keller said he had reconciled himself to the move. Still, he felt the Senators had made a big mistake allowing him to "waste" two years in the outfield if they intended to make him a catcher. Still, he went home that winter prepared to compete for a roster spot the following spring. He didn't make it. Keller never again was more than just a prospect at the major-league level. In retrospect, he said, "I was probably a pretty good Triple-A hitter, nothing more," even though "I considered that my best asset - hitting."

But there was to be one more highlight before he was through. Failing to make the Senators out of training camp in 1950, Keller was assigned to Augusta in the Class-A South Atlantic League, where he remained for the entire season, posting solid batting and slugging averages of .296/.427. When the

Senators expanded their roster in September, they again recalled Keller and this time he got on the field, appearing in eight games behind the plate. Of his six hits, one was memorable. On September 29, in the top of the eighth inning at Fenway Park, the Senators trailed the Boston Red Sox 6-4 with a runner on base and one out. On the mound for Boston was a 29-year-old rookie right-hander named James Atkins, who was making his major-league debut.[12] With three Senators having already homered, manager Bucky Harris sent Keller to the plate as a pinch-hitter, and the 23-year-old promptly homered against Atkins to tie the game, 6-6. (Boston eventually won, 7-6, in the bottom of the ninth.) It was Keller's only major-league home run.

In 2010 Keller couldn't remember the name of the pitcher who gave up the home run. However, he recalled with pride one thing quite clearly. After hitting the home run, Keller went behind the plate in the top of the ninth. That inning, when Ted Williams came to bat, Williams turned to Keller and said, "Didn't that feel good?"

Keller spent all of the 1951 season with Chattanooga in the Double-A South Atlantic League (he never played for Washington that year), and began the 1952 season there as well. In July, when an injury sidelined Washington's backup catcher, Clyde Kluttz, Keller was recalled to the Senators for what turned out to be the final time, and he saw action in his final 11 major-league games, the last of them on July 28. On August 7 Keller, now out of options, was sold to Toronto in the International League. His five-year Washington career was ended. He played three more seasons in the minors. In the first of them, 1953, Keller finally felt the effects of the back injury he had suffered in 1949, his second year in baseball. "I just couldn't run anymore," he recalled. In October 1953, after playing first in Toronto and later in Kansas City, Keller underwent surgery to repair a herniated disk.

In 1954, on loan from Toronto, Keller spent his last full minor-league season playing with the Memphis Chicks and, ironically, it was one of his best (.321 with 15 home runs). Toward the end of the season Toronto needed a catcher and recalled Keller. He got into one game and walked in his only appearance.

The next season, his last as an active player, Keller was playing for Oshawa, Ontario, in an outlaw league, when Toronto summoned him again. "They signed me to help out," he remembered, "but I was essentially a bullpen catcher." And with that, his playing career was ended.

It took Keller only a year, however, to set the remainder of his life in motion. In 1948, after his stint in the Army, he had returned to the University of Maryland to renew his education; he enrolled that year in the fall semester and for the next five years earned the equivalent of six semesters' credits ("I'm very proud of that," he said) and qualified for a degree in agricultural economics (the same degree as Charlie's) in January 1953. Also, while still playing Keller had spent his winters substitute-teaching in Frederick County. With his playing career over, Keller became a full-time teacher and the baseball coach at Frederick High School.[13] Charlie, too, had settled in Frederick after his career ended, purchased 300 acres of land and begun Yankeeland Farms, where for the remaining 35 years of his life he bred champion trotters and pacers. Both of Charlie's sons, Charlie Keller III and Donald, attended Frederick High School and were coached by their uncle Hal.

One afternoon Hal's friend and former teammate, Joe Haynes, who scouted for the Senators, came to Frederick High School to watch Charlie's sons play, and Hal suggested to Haynes that he wouldn't mind returning to the game in some capacity. "I wasn't making much money," Hal remembered, "and I told Joe if he had a Rookie League job, I wouldn't mind managing." Hal hadn't necessarily had any aspirations to manage; he simply wanted to make more money.

In 1958, Keller became the manager of the Senators Rookie League team in Superior, Nebraska, a town with a population of about 3,000, where, he recalled, "you could shoot a cannon down Main Street and never hit a soul." The team dressed in a high-school gym, drew a total attendance of 8,953, and finished last in the Nebraska State League with a record of 22-41. Other than as a player, it was the only on-field job Keller ever held in professional baseball.

The following year he took on an even bigger challenge. After the season Keller boldly asked Senators farm director Sherry Robertson for a job, and Robertson offered him the position of assistant farm director. ("I talked myself into two jobs," Keller told me, referring also to his managerial stint.) Keller held the position for the next two years.

During our interview there was one point about which Keller was adamant. "I want you to highlight this when you write," he said. "The Griffiths had a reputation for being cheap. They were never cheap. They did everything first class – what they could afford." In fact, he said, the team took the entire front office, including secretaries, to both Mexico City and Hawaii for the winter meetings.

As Keller began his front-office career, for several years he continued to live in Frederick and commute to Washington. Throughout, he and Charlie remained close. "He was kind of a quiet guy," Hal said. "He didn't like people talking too much; he would say someone was 'popping his bill when he should have been listening.'" They remained close even after Hal later moved 50 miles away, to the Washington suburb of Greenbelt, Maryland.

In his two years as an assistant, Keller learned the ropes of player development. Then, when the "original" Senators moved to Minneapolis after the 1960 season, Keller was named farm director of the expansion Senators team that replaced them. He remained in that position until October 1962.

As farm director Keller assumed broad responsibilities, effectively serving as both director of scouting and player development. Back then, he recalled, "you had all those responsibilities under one hat. Now they have five guys."

During his first year in the position the Senators spent $300,000 in bonuses and Keller doubled the size of his scouting staff. When the bonus money was cut in half the following year, Keller no longer felt he had the tools to operate successfully. So in October 1962, he left and took a position with the Minnesota Twins as their Eastern scouting supervisor. There, Keller soon fell victim to the hit-or-miss horrors of scouting. In 1964, he traveled to New York to watch a young second baseman play for a team sponsored by a department store. Later, he discussed the prospect with one of his scouts.

"I said I thought [the prospect] would make a pretty good second baseman," Keller remembered almost 50 years later. "But I questioned whether he could hit." Eventually, Keller said, "he became a much better hitter than he was a second baseman." The player was Rod Carew. "So that goes to show how smart you are." Still, he eventually recommended signing the future Hall of Famer.

After two years with the Twins, in October 1964, at the urging of Washington general manager George Selkirk, Keller returned to the Senators as farm director. At the time Washington had about 130 players in the organization, including 40 at the major-league level, many of whom Keller had brought to the organization during his first go-round, including Eddie Brinkman and John Kennedy, an infielder whose development later allowed the Senators to trade for Frank Howard.

As farm director, Keller recalled, he maintained a simple philosophy. "I always tried to do two things. I tried to place a player high enough that it was challenging, but not too high he couldn't succeed; and I tried never to send a player down. If he was hitting .200 at Double-A, I'd rather he stayed there and finish at .240, rather than hit .300 at A.

"I never liked to promote them, either. If [a player] was having a good year, I'd rather he finish with a good year and then have him jump a class at the beginning of the next season."

And there was one final credo Keller adhered to, the one he was most proud of: "I never told a lie to a ballplayer. I always felt that at that stage you're screwing around with a man's life." It was a sentiment that served him well for a very long time.

Within the farm system, decisions about a player were democratic among all minor-league personnel, Keller said, but he always reserved veto power over managers who wanted to place a player too high.

And he continually sought innovative ways to teach. In fact, he may have been a trend-setter. "I think I was the first man to use a radar gun," he said. Sometime in the early '70s, Michigan State baseball coach Danny Litwhiler, who used the gun, wrote to each major league team suggesting that they also might benefit from its use. Keller was intrigued, and bought one. Although he and Joe Klein, a former Senators minor leaguer then working in the front office, initially used the gun as a scouting tool, they soon found it had coaching possibilities, and so the radar gun as a teaching tool for Rangers' prospects was born. Each scout in the organization was given a radar gun.

By January 1979 Keller had been with the organization almost 15 years. When Senators owner Bob Short moved the club in 1972, Keller moved with the team to Arlington, Texas, where the Senators became the Rangers, and retained his position. He had no nostalgia about relocating the franchise, he remembered, saying, "I was being paid, so I didn't care." Besides, "I thought Washington was a dead end."

While in Texas Keller oversaw the drafting of such future major leaguers as Mike Cubbage, Dave Righetti, Roy Smalley, Bill Madlock, and Len Barker, as well as the blossoming of Jeff Burroughs, whom Keller had earlier developed in Washington. Keller was unhappy when new owner Brad Corbett began trading them away ("they wanted to trade Jim Sundberg too," Keller recalled, "but I wouldn't let them"), and "I got discouraged." So when the new Seattle Mariners came along with a job offer, "I took it."

On January 22, 1979, Keller was named director of player development for the Mariners. He and Mariners President Dan O'Brien had worked together for five years in Texas, and when O'Brien left Texas to head the Mariners, Keller was the first person he considered to run Seattle's farm system. Keller "has proven his ability to put together a farm system in an expansion franchise setting, one which is currently producing top quality major league players," O'Brien said. By then more than 50 players whose development Keller had at one time supervised had played in the major leagues.[14]

Keller retained his post for the next four years. During that time he oversaw the drafting and development of such future Seattle stars as Spike Owen, Harold Reynolds, Phil Bradley, Mark Langston, Bud Black, Darnell Coles, and the 1984 American League Rookie of the Year, Alvin Davis.

A final front-office challenge awaited Keller. In 1983, after the Mariners finished with a dismal record of 60-102, Dan O'Brien, the team president and general manager, was fired, and the 56-year-old Keller was named vice president of baseball operations and general manager. The Mariners won 74 games in each of the next two seasons. But the everyday demands of his new position soon became too great. "I didn't like being the GM," Keller recalled in January 2010. "It's a pressure-packed job. I would have liked it ten years before." Negotiating contracts "was much tougher with the players than it was in the old days, and I felt the pressure. My blood pressure felt it," he said. As well, "the game had kind of passed me by." In July 1985, "I thought it was best for me to retire."

Keller remained away from the game for three years. By 1989, though, he felt an urge to return and joined the Detroit Tigers as a national cross-checker, evaluating players who had already drawn the attention of other scouts, a job in which "You try to rate the cream of the crop for the draft." Later, he performed the same scouting function for the California Angels.

In 1998 Keller underwent a heart bypass, and the following year he finally retired for good. During his years in the Mariners' front office he had resided in the town of Issiquah, outside Seattle. In 1999 he and his second wife, Carol, whom he had married in 1967, moved to Sequim, Washington, near the Olympic Mountains. In addition to five children by his first wife and two stepchildren from Carol's first marriage, Carol and Hal also had one child together. There were 11 grandchildren and five great-grandchildren.

A few years after he retired Keller's right leg was amputated below the knee. In 2010, he said, "I'm not at all active but I have people that call. . . . I try to keep up with what my acquaintances are doing. You need to. They move around a lot more now than they used to."

On January 16, 2010, in a ceremony in Los Angeles, Keller received the George Genovese Lifetime Achievement Award from the Professional Baseball

Scouts Foundation for "long and meritorious service in the world of professional baseball scouting." Keller, said foundation chairman Dennis Gilbert, was a natural choice to receive the award. "He is a very well thought-of person in the baseball community," Gilbert said.[15] It was a just reward for a life well spent. About receiving the award, Keller said, "When you recognize talent, you like to see them develop. That's the fun part of the business."

In his last years, Keller's health markedly declined. In addition to battling the diabetes that had caused the amputation of his foot, he also developed a growth on his vocal cords, which was eventually diagnosed as esophogeal cancer. After enduring chemo and radiation therapies, in May 2012 he was hospitalized due to dehydration brought on by an inability to intake enough liquid. On Thursday, May 31, Keller finally asked to go home to Sequim, Washington, where during the early hours of June 5, 2012, he died peacefully in his sleep.

That afternoon, Keller's wife, Carol, related to the press, "He told three doctors he had a wonderful life and had done everything he wanted to do. He said he wanted to go home. He said he didn't want to spend 10 years in a nursing home."[16]

It had indeed, been a fantastic life.

On June 30, 2012, a memorial service was held for Keller at the American Legion in Frederick, Maryland. Very few baseball people attended. Among those who did were Keller's good friend, Joe Klein, and Darnell Coles, one of the featured speakers.

Hal Keller was cremated and his ashes were scattered over his birthplace, his beloved Middletown Valley.

Sources

My sincerest thanks to Hal Keller for personal phone interviews on May 21 and 22, June 4, and August 30, 2010.

My sincerest thanks to Jack Remsberg, Hal Keller's cousin, for a personal interview at Remsberg's home, July 2, 2009

E-mail exchanges on May 24 and August 18, 2010, with Randy Adamack, vice president of communications, Seattle Mariners.

Telephone conversation with Carol Keller on July 21, 2012.

Many thanks to Jason Speck, an archivist at the University of Maryland Archives, for information on Keller's career at the university.

The author also consulted Baseball-Reference.com, Retrosheet.org, the Hal Keller player file from the National Baseball Hall of Fame, and the following newspapers:

News-Post (Frederick, Maryland), *Pacific Stars and Stripes*, *The Sporting News*, *Oakland Tribune*, and www.sportsillustrated.cnn.com, , and http://www.powerset.com/explore/semhtml/Nebraska_State_League

Notes

1. Unless otherwise noted, all quotations from Hal Keller were from interviews the author conducted between May 21 and August 30, 2010.
2. Authors interview with Jack Remsberg, conducted July 2, 2009.
3. According to University of Maryland archives, during the later war years (1943-45) Maryland did not field a varsity team. The team was considered 'informal', and no varsity letters were awarded during those years. Additionally, the team mostly played local service units and not colleges and universities. No records exist of the 1944 team; however, in 1945 the team went 2-9. Hal was a starter at both catcher and centerfield and routinely hit in the middle of the lineup. On June 2, 1945, Hal faced off against Hugh, who was playing for a team at Ft. Myers, Virginia, and Maryland won, 10-9. Also, as had Charlie, Hal, too, played basketball at Maryland (during the winter of 1944). "I wasn't a good shooter," he remembered, "but I was a good rebounder."
4. "Senators Consider Hal Keller Hot Prospect," *Wisconsin State Journal*, March 8, 1948.
5. Dick Kelly, "The Spotlight on Sports," Hagerstown (Maryland) *Daily Mail*, May 27, 1949: 14.
6. Ibid
7. Frank Colley, "The Colley-See-Um of Sports," Hagerstown (Maryland) *Morning Herald*, April 21, 1949: 22.
8. Dick Kelly, "The Spotlight on Sports," Hagerstown (Maryland) *Daily Mail*, September 30, 1949: 14.
9. Dick Kelly, "The Spotlight on Sports," Hagerstown (Maryland) *Daily Mail*, August 5, 1949: 12.
10. Ibid
11. Ibid
12. This would be Atkins' only appearance in 1950. Two years later he appeared in three more games for Boston, including one start, before finishing his career with a 0-1 record and 3.60 ERA in 15 total innings pitched.
13. One of Keller's players was an outfielder named Don Loun. Impressed by the young man's strong left arm, Keller switched Loun from the outfield to pitcher. Later, when Keller became Farm Director of the Senators, he drafted Loun for Washington. On September 23, 1964, Loun tossed a complete game shutout against Boston in his major league debut, and he ended his career with two appearances for the Senators, posting a 1-1 record and 2.08 ERA.
14. Among those players were: Bill Madlock, Mike Hargrove, Bump Wills, Toby Harrah, Tom Grieve, Dick Bosman, and Len Barker.
15. "Sequim resident, former Mariners general manager, to receive lifetime achievement award this weekend," Peninsula Daily News, http://www.peninsuladailynews.com/sports/sports-sequim-resident-former-mariners-general-manager-to-receive-lifetime-achievement-award-this-weekend, accessed February 10, 2018.
16. "Keller remembered as top-notch scout," Fox Sports, https://www.foxsports.com/mlb/story/hal-keller-obit-baseball-scout-radar-gun-060512, accessed February 10, 2018.

BILL ZEIGLER

BY CHARLIE GRASSL

On June 24, 1945, seven weeks after the German Wehrmacht surrendered to the Allied armies and on the same day more than 40,000 Russian troops paraded through Moscow's Red Square to celebrate their victory over the Nazi invaders, a son was born to Mary and Ralph Zeigler in Greencastle, Pennsylvania, on June 24, 1945. William Harry Zeigler (pronounced Zeeg-ler) was to be their only child due to Mary's medical issues associated with childbirth. Greencastle was a small town south of Harrisburg, just across the Mason-Dixon Line from Maryland that for a brief time in 1863 had been occupied by Robert E. Lee's Confederate troops during the Gettysburg Campaign, was the environment of Bill Zeigler's childhood. His father worked in a milk-processing plant whose product was shipped to nearby Hershey to become a key part of the Hershey's Milk Chocolate Bar. Bill grew to become a very good basketball and baseball player at Greencastle High School. Those skills would take him to Florida, initially at Manatee College (1963-65) and the at Florida State University (1965-68).

It was at Florida State that Ziegler learned his baseball skill level would most likely not take him past the college game. Married, with a young son he named Ted Williams Zeigler, he traveled with a friend to the White Sox spring-training facility in Sarasota. The facility was home to four of the White Sox' minor-league clubs after the big-league club had gone north for the start of the 1968 season. Through his friend's personal connection, Bill discovered the need for an additional trainer to help with these four clubs. Needing a job, he was quick to accept a job offer after being told previous experience was not an issue. After a brief time, he discovered he really enjoyed the work and pursued a student trainer's position with Don Fauls, head trainer at Florida State. Fauls provided Zeigler the opportunity to learn and practice the skills needed to be an athletic trainer.

One day, while visiting in Fauls' office, he picked up a copy of *The Sporting News* and read about the Washington Senators trainer, Tom McKenna, leaving the club for a similar position with the New York Mets. Encouraged to pursue this opportunity by Fauls, Zeigler contacted Nellie Fox, then a Senators coach and someone he knew locally in Pennsylvania. Fox had him submit a résumé and helped get the résumé into the right hands. Anticipating and excited about an interview with his boyhood hero Ted Williams, who now was manager of the Senators, Zeigler instead received a phone call from Joe Burke, the general manager. Zeigler was in Dayton, Ohio, with Florida State's basketball team when Burke called. To his surprise Burke offered him the job solely on the basis of his résumé and Fox's endorsement. There would be no interview with Ted Williams. Instead he would work for his boyhood idol and the man he named his first son after. The 1970 season was to be the first of 22 seasons as trainer for the major-league club that in 1972 became the Texas Rangers.

In those 22 years, Zeigler found stability as he enjoyed the interesting events associated with a major-league team: its owners, its players, and its managers. Ted Williams, Whitey Herzog, and Billy Martin. Lenny Randle, Jim Kern, and Mickey Rivers. Bob Short, Brad Corbett, and Eddie Chiles. All were colorful and provided an interesting background to many exciting major-league games that enfolded, almost each summer day, before and around him. Zeigler enjoyed the work associated with interesting people and days that were unpredictable, challenging, and anything but routine. He was a constant presence in a place of constant change for those 22 years, as people moved in and out of the roles associated with a major-league baseball team.

Zeigler was able to share the good fortune this life provided for him with his three sons, Ted, Kim, and David. All three were batboys for the Rangers and each benefited from video evaluations of their hitting styles by none other than Ted Williams. Zeigler's influence, though, went far beyond his family, into the many lives of those he encountered along the way.

Zeigler described a lunch in Milwaukee in 1985, with Rangers outfielder, minor-league manager, and coach Bobby Jones.[1] In his words, "Bobby was one of the nicest men I've ever known. Calm, affable, steady, helpful to all around him. Always respected by all his teammates. Well, Bobby, the night before our lunch, had met up with some of his Army buddies he had served with in Viet Nam. They had enjoyed a few brews and reminisced about their wartime experiences. I was sitting at a table in the hotel restaurant and saw him approaching the table. Usually smiling and energetic, I could see Bobby was severely troubled and upset. Sitting down, he began to visibly and uncontrollably shake and begin to tell me he was having visions of dead bodies and other scenes from his time in Viet Nam. I knew that Mike Stone, then the president of the Rangers, had some knowledge of psychology so I quickly brought Bobby to Mike as this situation was more serious than anything I could handle. Mike was able to walk Bobby through this flashback of the horrors of war he had experienced. It was scary but as far as I know Bobby never experienced this again."[2]

In a November 9, 2011, interview with St. Louis Cardinals senior medical adviser Barry Weinberg, Andrew Gershman of the *Jerusalem Post* described how Zeigler had influenced Weinberg's career as a trainer in the major leagues. "Growing up in Silver Spring (Maryland), Barry Weinberg was a fan of the Washington Senators. One of Weinberg's inspirations was Bill Zeigler. He remembers writing Zeigler a letter about leaving school and joining Zeigler's training staff on the Senators. Zeigler responded with words of encouragement and a recommendation to stay in school. Weinberg did just that and five years later they were on opposing benches, Weinberg with the Yankees and Zeigler with the Rangers. The two have remained friends to this day, and Weinberg still credits his friend for the inspiration to pursue his dream."[3]

A 1987 *New York Times* article credits Zeigler with championing facial protection for batters.[4] He worked with Rangers catcher Don Slaught, who was severely injured when struck by an Oil Can Boyd pitch that broke a couple of bones in his face. From this experience, Zeigler became an outspoken advocate of better protection for this most vulnerable part of a player's body.

There were many thrills for Zeigler in baseball, such as working for Ted Williams, standing next to Joe DiMaggio at the 1977 All-Star Game, and becoming friends with Nolan Ryan. However, in the fall of 1991 he and Rangers manager Bobby Valentine had a parting of the ways. He decided it was time to step away from baseball. Zeigler politely referred to the incident: "We just didn't see eye-to eye."[5] On December 19, 1991, the MLB Transaction page noted, tersely and without explanation, "Texas Rangers – Fired trainer Bill Zeigler." For the first time in 22 years Zeigler was out of baseball. But since 1981 he had been working in the baseball offseason as a trainer at Professional

Rodeo Cowboys Association events. After continuing to work part-time in the 1992 PRCA season, which includes some 130 yearly rodeo events, he took on a full-time job for the Justin Boot Company,[6] which sponsored a truck/trailer combination that contained medical and training equipment and traveled the PRCA circuit. This became Zeigler's new "office" and work space. Traveling by car in place of airplanes, he still was ministering to athletes, helping them resume their careers after an injury. "In baseball if a guy can't play, you have the disabled list and guaranteed contracts. Here, if they can't perform they can't make money. You make suggestions but you can't tell them not to play," Zeigler said in a 1993 interview.[7]

Zeigler's yearly travels ranged from Fort Madison, Iowa, in the north to Jackson, Mississippi, in the east, to Corpus Christi, Texas in the south, and Santa Fe, New Mexico, in the west. Never looking back, Zeigler said he did not regret leaving baseball. In fact, he said, "I got out of baseball just in time. I got out two years before José Canseco came on board."[8] (Canseco joined the Rangers in 1992.) Later retired from the rigorous travel of the rodeo circuit, he said, "I once thought I was just a lucky man but now I know I am really just a blessed man!"[9] After hearing a preacher from the Aledo (Texas) Cowboy Church at a wedding, he and his wife became active members of the church.

A resident of Azle, Texas, Zeigler continued to follow the Rangers, the Boston Celtics, and the rodeo circuit. His second wife, Jill, was Nolan Ryan's personal secretary when Zeigler met her. His three sons and two stepsons reside in the Dallas-Fort Worth area, affording the couple to spend time with their grandchildren.

From the athletic fields to the training tables of baseball players and bull riders, Zeigler has been a quiet servant of those in need of healing, a "first responder" on the field or the arena, bringing comfort to those whose livelihood depends upon the perfect physical functioning of all of their body parts. His affable and confident manner brought peace, assurance, and hope in times of uncertainty to those in need.

Sources

The author would like to express his thanks to Bill Zeigler for a telephone interview on January 24, 2016.

Notes

1. Bruce Markusen, "Cooperstown Confidential: Baseball and Viet Nam," September 17, 2010, hardballtimes.com/cooperstown-confidential-baseball-and-vietnam, accessed January 29, 2016.
2. Author interview with Bill Zeigler, January 24, 2016.
3. Andrew Gershman, "Cards Trainer Sheds Light on Magic Run," *Jerusalem Post*, November 9, 2011.
4. William Schmidt, "Protecting Faces From Errant Pitches," *New York Times*, July 19, 1987.
5. Larry Yanos, "Taking Care of Rangers and Cowboys," *Hagerstown* (Maryland) *Herald-Mail*, November 26, 2007.
6. Bryan Painter, "Rodeo Is a New Game for Zeigler," October 3, 1993, newsok.com/article/2443875, accessed January 25, 2016.
7. Painter.
8. Yanos.
9. Author interview with Bill Zeigler, January 24, 2016.

RANGERS THROW AWAY THEIR FIRST-EVER GAME: APRIL 15, 1972: CALIFORNIA ANGELS 1, TEXAS RANGERS 0 AT ANAHEIM STADIUM

BY STEVE WEST

The opening of the 1972 season was unforgettable in many ways, but especially for North Texas. The Washington Senators were moving to Arlington, Texas, to become the Texas Rangers, and the fans were looking forward to Opening Day.

The Rangers spent their spring in Pompano Beach, Florida, trying to sort out who was going to play where. Manager Ted Williams had numerous gaps to fill in the field, and while he had the players, he didn't know which position was best for each of them. To make matters worse, his ace pitcher, Denny McLain, had spent the whole winter complaining and was eventually traded in the middle of spring training; and his top slugger, Frank Howard, was holding out in a contract dispute, which wasn't resolved until March 29.

The California Angels were at their spring-training camp in Palm Springs, California, where the biggest story was the appointment of Del Rice as the new manager. The Angels had struggled the previous year, far below expectations. The team had been made over, with several comings and goings both on- and off-field as they tried to improve. Because of this, there were several positions open for competition during the spring, especially at catcher and in the outfield.

But on April 1 everything came to a stop. On that day the Major League Baseball Players Association called a strike, the first player strike in major-league history. Players were demanding an increase in pension payments, something the owners refused. As the days dragged on, the players were locked out of ballparks and training facilities, and ended up gathering in self-organized sessions. The leagues started canceling games as the scheduled Opening Day of April 5 came and went. Rice was disappointed that his managerial debut would be delayed. "All I ever wanted was to become a big league manager. I finally get the job and the players quit."[1]

The Rangers were hurt more than most. Having just moved the franchise, owner Bob Short was looking forward to a grand extravaganza at home on April 6, to introduce the team to the North Texas public. As it was, manager Ted Williams was at the ballpark that day with a group of media, to talk about the prospects for the season, but the players and fans waited things out. Williams wasn't sure about his team's prospects: "We'll be running more, squeezing more, and I'll be praying more," he said.[2]

Finally the strike ended on April 13, with games scheduled to start on Saturday, April 15. Both sides lost money in the short term, the players from lost pay and the owners from lost revenue, and the league lost a number of games from the schedule, something that would come back to haunt some teams by the end of the season. For the Rangers, their new first game was now scheduled to be played in Los Angeles instead of at home. On Friday morning the Rangers worked out at Arlington Stadium for the first time, then flew to California in the afternoon to be ready for Saturday night's game. Williams watched that practice and admitted that the team looked as if it needed a couple more weeks' work.[3]

The first game was attended by a crowd of 13,916, a surprisingly low figure for Opening Day, but obviously hampered by the strike and the reaction of fans to it. During player introductions there were scattered boos, but mostly cheers for the home team. Fred Haney, former major-league player and manager, and the first general manager of the Angels, threw out the first pitch.

The Rangers went with Dick Bosman, starting his third consecutive Opening Day for the franchise, while the Angels countered with Andy Messersmith, a 20-game winner the year before. The two pitchers lived up to their billing, putting zeroes on the scoreboard all day, proving Williams's suggestion that because of the strike the pitchers would be ahead of the hitters at the start of the season. Bosman pitched well for the visitors, as in the first eight innings he let just one runner reach third and one other get to second. Through eight innings he allowed five hits and had six strikeouts, two each in the first, second, and fifth innings.

Messersmith was better. He kept the Rangers hitless through six innings; Hal King led off the seventh with a single to break up the no-hitter, and Toby Harrah's single in the eighth was the only other hit the Rangers got. Messersmith finished with nine strikeouts – all by the sixth inning – and five walks. The walks were the closest the Rangers came to his undoing, when in the fifth Messersmith got two strikeouts but then walked Joe Lovitto (making his major-league debut) and Harrah. With two on, Bosman struck out to end the threat.

In the bottom of the ninth, with the game still scoreless, Bosman tired, walking leadoff batter Sandy Alomar. Mickey Rivers bunted, catcher Hal King fumbled the ball, and both runners were safe. Another walk, to Leo Cardenas, and Bosman was done. Williams went to the bullpen, bringing in lefty Paul Lindblad to face left-handed batter Jim Spencer. Spencer fouled off the first pitch, then Lindblad bounced the next pitch in front of the plate. It skipped past King to the backstop, allowing Alomar to run home and score on a walk-off wild pitch.

"Boy, for an opener that was all right. … I wasn't sure how sharp I'd be. Everything just fell into place," Messersmith said.[4] "I was thinking about a no-hitter from the fourth inning on. I had such good stuff and I felt so good I thought I might make it."[5] Catcher Jeff Torborg said, "He was actually throwing harder in the ninth inning than he was earlier. He had everything."[6]

For the Rangers it was an embarrassing way to lose their first-ever game. The game would be symbolic of their entire season: They couldn't hit, and although they had decent pitching they would be undone by mistakes. Opening Day was just the start of a long and difficult road.

Notes

1. Dick Miller, "Ex-Steel Union Boss McDonald an Angels Fan," *The Sporting News*, April 29, 1972: 21.
2. Don Merry, "Only 13,916 See Andy Tame Texas on 2-Hitter," *Long Beach Independent Press-Telegram*, April 16, 1972.
3. Merle Heryford, "Out of Cocoon Into the Limelight," *Dallas Morning News*, April 15, 1972.
4. Merry.
5. Joe Hendrickson, "Messersmith Flips 1-0 Gem," *Pasadena Star News*, April 16, 1972.
6. Merry.

BROBERG'S EIGHT STRONG INNINGS GIVE RANGERS FIRST WIN IN CLUB HISTORY: APRIL 16, 1972: TEXAS RANGERS 5, CALIFORNIA ANGELS 1, AT ANAHEIM STADIUM

BY GREGORY H. WOLF

On April 16, 1972, Apollo 16, NASA's eighth of nine manned lunar missions, took off from Cape Canaveral, Florida. On that same day, some 3,000 miles away in Anaheim, California, there was another blast-off of sorts. The Texas Rangers, behind eight strong innings by hard-throwing right-hander Pete Broberg, won their first-ever game.

After 11 mainly disappointing seasons in the nation's capital, the Washington Senators relocated to Arlington, Texas, a city between Dallas and Fort Worth, and were rechristened the Rangers for the start of the 1972 baseball season. Led by Ted Williams since 1969, the Senators had finished with a dismal 63-96 record (fifth place in the AL West) in 1971; however, Texas seemed to have the talent to notch a winning season, something they had done just once as the Senators. "We were excited to start the season," Broberg told the author. "We had some young players like me on the club, Toby Harrah, Lenny Randle, Jeff Burroughs, and some older guys and veterans, Frank Howard, Dick Billings, and Dick Bosman. We had a good mix."[1]

Notwithstanding the players' excitement, the 1972 season was delayed by 13 days when the players union, the Major League Baseball Players Association, called the first strike in baseball history, resulting in 86 canceled games. "We expected to do well," recalled Broberg about the start of the season despite the layoff. "We had some success against the Angels the year before (8 wins, 4 losses), and we knew we could hit them. [Dick] Bosman pitched a great game in the season opener and lost."[2] In that game, Angels right-hander Andy Messersmith, who would play a central role in another showdown between the players' union and baseball owners three years later, outdueled Bosman, blanking the Rangers, 1-0, on two hits. "Both Andy and Broberg are overpowering pitchers," said Angels pitching coach Tom Morgan in anticipation of a tough afternoon against the Rangers. "[T]hat type will have less trouble coming back from the long layoff."[3]

"I felt right at home on the club," Broberg recalled. "I was more mature, was with the club for about four months in '71, and had just had my first spring training with them."[4] Originally chosen second overall by the Oakland A's in the 1968 draft, Broberg rejected a reported $150,000 bonus and instead enrolled at Dartmouth College, where he earned All-American honors. On June 8, 1971, Washington chose him with the second pick of the secondary draft. The 21-year-old Broberg made his big-league debut 12 days later, tossing three-hit ball and yielding two runs in a 6⅓-inning no-decision against Boston. "He can be as good as anybody pitching today," said Williams of Broberg, who concluded his rookie campaign with a 5-9 record and a 3.47 ERA in 124⅔ innings. "He has tremendous ability and intelligence."[5]

Toeing the rubber for first-year skipper Del Rice's Angels was 31-year-old southpaw Clyde Wright. An All-Star in 1970 when he finished with a 22-12 record, Wright had fashioned a 58-55 record in parts of seven big-league seasons.

A sparse crowd of 6,556 turned up at the Big A, as Anaheim Stadium was known, for a Sunday afternoon of baseball. Attendance had been down all over baseball on the belated opening weekend as thousands of fans mounted their own informal strike.

Only 13,916 attended the Angels' season opener the night before.

"No more two-hitters against us," said skipper Williams before the game. "We're gonna get some blankety-blank hits."[6] The Rangers might have taken the Splendid Splinter's words to heart as the first five batters reached base. Randle led off with a walk, moved to third on Dave Nelson's single, and scored the first run in Rangers history when, 6-foot-7, 275-pound "Hondo" Howard lined a single to right field. Texas was counting on a productive season from Howard, who Williams claimed hit "left-handers as well as – probably better than – anyone in the league."[7] After smashing a big-league-most 136 home runs from 1968 through 1970 and leading the AL in round-trippers in '68 and '70, Howard belted 26 in 1971. Billings followed with a single to drive in Nelson. After Tom Grieve bunted to third base to load the bases, rookie Joe Lovitto hit a grounder to shortstop Leo Cardenas, who opted for a 6-4-3 double play instead of risking a throw home to nab Howard, who was running on contact and scored. [Lovitto was not credited with an RBI]. Wright fanned Elliott Maddox to end the frame.

The Angels came out swinging against Broberg. Leadoff hitter Sandy Alomar lined a single to center and moved to second on a wild pitch. While the rugged, 6-foot-3, 205-pound right-hander retired the next three hitters, Alomar scored what proved to be the Angels' only run on Cardenas's one-out grounder to Harrah.

Wright regained his composure to retire all six batters he faced in the second and third innings. The Angels managed to get a runner to second base with two outs in both innings, yet came up empty-handed both times.

With two outs in the fourth, Maddox got the game's only extra-base hit, a double to right field. He moved to third on Wright's wild pitch with Harrah at the plate, and scored the Rangers' fourth run on a passed ball charged to catcher Jeff Torborg.

After yielding a leadoff hit to Ken McMullen in the fourth, Broberg went on a roll. Described as "dazzling" and "baffling" by sportswriter Leo Noonan of the *Los Angeles Herald-Examiner*, Broberg did not yield another hit in the fourth through eighth innings.[8] He did issue three walks, but also started a double play in the fifth when he made a fine fielding play on Mickey Rivers' bouncer to the mound, and threw to Harrah to erase the speedy Alomar at second. Harrah then rifled to Howard for the inning-ending twin killing.

The Rangers maintained a 4-1 lead until the ninth inning. Two innings earlier they had had runners on second and third with two outs against Tom Murphy in his second inning of relief. But the former starter, who had lost his spot in the rotation with the acquisition of fireballer Nolan Ryan from the New York Mets in a blockbuster trade in the offseason, induced Howard to ground out. Larry Biittner led off the ninth with a shot to shortstop Cardenas, who misplayed it for his second error of the game. After Broberg's one-out sacrifice bunt moved Biittner into scoring position, Randle followed with an infield single off reliever Lloyd Allen, in his second inning of work, to drive in Biittner and increase the Rangers' lead to 5-1.

Broberg's afternoon ended when McMullen led off the ninth with a single. Rubber-armed southpaw Paul Lindblad, who would lead the AL with 66 appearances in '72, retired left-handed hitter Vada Pinson, still a dangerous batter in his 15th big-league season. Right-hander Horacio Pina, whom beat writer Merle Heryford of the *Dallas Morning News* affectionately called "the Latin pretzel" because of his tall and lanky appearance, retired the last two batters to preserve Broberg's victory and earn his first of what would be a team-high 15 saves.[9]

"I thought Broberg pitched a good game, a strong game, especially since he hadn't worked in two weeks and hadn't gone more than five innings this spring," said Williams.[10] Broberg yielded five hits, walked four, and struck out three in eight impressive innings. Said Ross Newhan of the *Los Angeles Times* after the game, "the pitchers are clearly ahead of the batters."[11] Angels beat reporter Leo Noonan equated Broberg's stuff with his staff's 20-game winner from the previous season, opining, "[Broberg] pitched the same kind of game Messersmith did on opening night."[12]

In the days before pitchers were monitored so closely, Broberg told the author, he never thought much about pitch counts and could not remember how many pitches he threw that day. *The Los Angeles Times* reported that Broberg was wound up and visually excited on the mound. "I had a lot of nervous energy I couldn't burn off," Broberg told the paper.[13]

After losing their next two games, in Chicago facing the White Sox at Comiskey Park, the Rangers finally had their home opener on Friday April 21, against the Angels. Bosman pitched just well enough (nine hits, four runs, three earned, in 5⅓ innings) to pick up the win, 7-6. The following afternoon, in front of just 5,517 spectators in Arlington Stadium, Broberg tossed the first shutout in Rangers history, blanking the Angels on four hits.

Notes

1. Author's interview with Pete Broberg on June 29, 2015.
2. Ibid.
3. Leo Noonan, "Gates Creaking at Anaheim Stadium," *Los Angeles Herald Examiner*, April 17, 1972: D2.
4. Author's interview with Pete Broberg on June 29, 2015.
5. Ross Newhan, "Broberg Too Slick for Angels, 5-1," *Los Angeles Times*, April 17, 1972: Part 3, 1.
6. Merle Heryford, "Rangers, Broberg Jail Angels, 5-1. Texas Wins No. 1 With Quick Start," *Dallas Morning News*, April 17, 1972: B1.
7. Ibid.
8. Noonan.
9. Heryford.
10. Ibid.
11. Newhan.
12. Noonan.
13. Newhan.

FANS CELEBRATE THE ARRIVAL OF MAJOR-LEAGUE BASEBALL IN NORTH TEXAS: APRIL 21, 1972: TEXAS RANGERS 7, CALIFORNIA ANGELS 6 AT ARLINGTON STADIUM

BY DUANE VICTOR KEILSTRUP

There on the ball diamond in Arlington, Texas, was Teddy Ballgame himself – Ted Williams, dramatically symbolic of dreams having come true for thousands of North Texans. It was a Friday evening, April 21, 1972, when Frank Howard, "the Washington Monument," as he was known in Washington before the franchise migration, and his Texas Rangers teammates took the field for the first time in Arlington.

"The game climaxed 20 years of effort for [Arlington Mayor Tom] Vandergriff and other local leaders who tried to bring major league baseball to the area."[1] One writer recalled that "It was Sept. 21 when Vandergriff stood before AL President Joe Cronin and the club owners and confidently told them a 35,000 seat park would be ready for this team in April. Sincere as the Arlington mayor was, he must have felt like Elmer Blurt, the character on the old Fibber McGee and Molly radio show, who would say something and add, 'I hope-I hope-I hope-I hope.'"[2]

The Houston Astros owner, Judge Roy Hofheinz, had earlier cast a costly negative vote so Vandergriff told the crowd on opening night, "Let's make our cheers heard all the way to Houston tonight."[3] The first ball that Vandergriff pitched to home plate to start the historic game is now in the National Baseball Hall of Fame at Cooperstown.

Rangers players' names like Lovitto, Biittner, Randle, Grieve, Harrah, Maddox, Nelson, and Billings were new and virtually meaningless to most of the fans in "neat, tidy modern Arlington Stadium" (formerly Turnpike Stadium).[4] But what mattered was the game itself and the reality of major-league baseball in the Fort Worth-Dallas Metroplex. No longer did baseball fans have to rely on radio play-by-play broadcasts of games for their only touch to major-league action – on-the-scene reports by great announcers like Harry Caray, Vin Scully, Red Barber, Ernie Harwell, Mel Allen, and Jack Brickhouse. Suddenly it seemed as though colorful action photos from *Sports Illustrated* were magically bursting forth from its pages as second basemen leaped high to turn double plays and batters were swinging for the fences for real.

Newspaper wire reports would no longer be the only reading accounts of yesterday's games at the breakfast table. The Texas Rangers and their fans were now part of the daily drama called major-league baseball. And soon teams with even more impact would be on their way to Arlington Stadium – historic teams like the Yankees, the Red Sox, the Tigers, the Orioles, and the Indians would be taking the field. And visions of exhibition old-timer games with Hall of Famers like DiMaggio, Mays, Feller, Musial, and Mantle, along with World Series and All-Star games, were already flashing magically on screens in the corners of many fans' minds. Truly, on this day any hits, runs, and errors by the Texas Rangers and the visiting California Angels were far less meaningful than the historic significance of the grand game of baseball itself.

American League President Joe Cronin was in attendance and observed, "This is the best-lit park in the major leagues. ... It is remarkable that they put together such a complete product in so short a time. I was here several weeks ago and it didn't look anything like this," to which California manager Del Rice added, "It's a lot like Fenway Park in Boston."[5] Shortstop Toby Harrah said, "This park is beautiful.

… I was expecting a Double-A park but this is one of the best in the league. … It's nice to play behind a crowd like this."[6]

The team had played its first four games on the road and returned to Arlington with a record of 1-3, while the Angels came in at 2-2.

As it turned out, the most exciting moment for the Rangers came in the first at-bat by the Rangers' Frank Howard, who sent a high slider from left-hander Clyde Wright beyond the farthest point in the park, landing an estimated 480 feet from home plate. Most of the 20,105 fans in attendance gave Howard a standing ovation, and the Rangers went on to take the game, 7-6. Third-base coach Wayne "Twig" Terwilliger said the Howard home run is what he remembered most vividly about that first game.[7]

The Angels tied it up in the top of the second, on a Rangers error and a couple of singles off the Texas starter, right-hander Dick Bosman. The Rangers added two more in the bottom of the third, two in the fourth, and single runs in the fifth and sixth.

Bosman weakened in the top of the sixth, charged with three runs. Casey Cox relieved. The Angels got two more off Cox in the eighth. Paul Lindblad pitched to the final batter in the ninth, striking him out and earning a save.

Another Ranger contributing to the win was Lenny Randle, who went 3-for-4 and drove in four runs. In addition to Howard's homer, Dave Nelson hit one out of the park in the fifth inning. Toby Harrah batted in three runs with three hits, and committed one error in five chances. Winning his first game of the year was Dick Bosman, whose pregnant wife left the game early to give birth to a baby girl. Leading the Angels were first baseman Jim Spencer, catcher Art Kusnyer, and left fielder Vada Pinson with three hits apiece; the duo of Mickey Rivers and Sandy Alomar added two more. Wright was the losing pitcher, his second loss of the season.

The 1972 baseball players strike, which caused a loss of eight games and postponement of the opening game, did not dampen the enthusiasm of Rangers fans. Owner Bob Short commented, "It was a great beginning,"[8] and added, "I think we've found a home."[9] Frank Howard said he was happy with his home run, but "Let's hope that the win is the memory the fans take home and not just what I or anyone did."[10]

From the perspective of Ted Williams' close friend, "Twig" Terwilliger, a veteran major-league player, coach, and manager over a period of some 60 years, probably the best thing about Ted Williams, the manager, in Texas and during his career, was "his passion for the game, his competitiveness, his incredibly detailed way of analyzing the hitting game, his larger-than-life personality, his way of taking over a room just by walking into it, and his sense of humor – more than once I saw him laugh so hard tears just streamed down his face." Terwilliger also related what a special honor it was for him to coach for Williams, who unexpectedly gave him the responsibility not only to coach at third base but also for deciding whether batters should bunt. When Williams first called him about coaching, Twig said he experienced pretty much the same thrill as avid baseball fans felt at that first game in seeing Ted Williams in person.[11]

At the conclusion of that home opener, following Frank Howard's lead, Williams preferred to focus comments on the victory and Lenny Randle's performance. He never did wear the cowboy hat or the cowboy boots with gold baseball cleats presented to him in pregame ceremonies. Rangers fans in attendance at that first home game, however, couldn't have cared less, for they were still filled with the stirring historic baseball magic of that night, and no doubt most of those fans still living will forever keep that in their personal "hall of fame" memory. This writer was one of those first-nighter fans. As Twig wrote in his book and no doubt would say now, "Nuf said."

Notes

1. "Cowboy Hats, Rangers, Empty Seats Mark Debut," *Stars and Stripes*, April 23, 1972: 23.
2. Sam Blair, "A Smile a Minute," *Dallas Morning News*, April 21, 1972: B1.
3. "Cowboy Hats, Rangers."
4. "Opening Act Went Well for Rangers," *Kittanning* (Pennsylvania) *Leader Times*, April 22, 1972: 10.
5. "Rangers Win Texas Debut," *Benton Harbor* (Michigan) *News Palladium*, April 22, 1972: 14.
6. "Ball Park, Fans Draw Praise From Rangers After Opening Night Win," *Arlington* (Texas) *Daily News*, April 23, 1972: 9.
7. Author interview with Wayne Terwilliger, December 11, 2015.
8. "Opening Act Went Well for Rangers."
9. "Rangers Win Texas Debut."
10. "Ball Park, Fans Draw Praise."
11. Wayne Terwilliger with Nancy Peterson and Peter Boehn, *Terwilliger Bunts One* (Guilford, Connecticut: Globe Pequot, 2006), 163-164.

BROBERG, RANGERS SUFFER HARD-LUCK LOSS TO ORIOLES: MAY 10, 1972: BALTIMORE ORIOLES 1, TEXAS RANGERS 0 AT MEMORIAL STADIUM

BY FREDERICK C. BUSH

In baseball, as in every team sport, the team with the better players has an obvious advantage over its opponent; however, sometimes the line between winning and losing is a thin one, and it may also hinge to some degree on pure, dumb luck. Such was the case on May 10, 1972, when the Texas Rangers took on the defending American League champion Baltimore Orioles before a sparse crowd of 6,617 fans at Memorial Stadium.

The Rangers had no reason to be optimistic about their chances against the powerhouse Orioles, who had won over 100 games each season from 1969 to 1971 and had claimed the AL championship each year as well, as well as a World Series victory in 1970. The Rangers, on the other hand, had lost over 90 games in each of the past two seasons, when they were still the second incarnation of the Washington Senators, and would end up losing 100 games in 1972.

In addition to the obvious disparities between the two franchises, the Rangers were up against noted Senators-slayer Dave McNally, a 20-game winner in each of the previous four seasons. McNally had a career 23-4 record against the Senators/Rangers; since 1968, he was 17-1 against the franchise and had beaten them 13 times in a row.[1]

Rangers manager Ted Williams sent righthander Pete Broberg to the mound in the hope that he could play the role of David against McNally's Goliath. Broberg, an Ivy Leaguer from Dartmouth College, had been the Senators' first-round draft pick in June 1971 and had posted a 5-9 record with a respectable 3.47 ERA over 18 starts in his rookie season.

Broberg was projected for future stardom and appeared on the cusp of fulfilling his potential as he entered the game with a 1.86 ERA. After he suffered a tough loss to the Cleveland Indians on May 3, the result of two unearned runs, Rangers pitching coach Sid Hudson said, "There's a great deal of difference in Pete this season compared to last year. More confidence, more maturity. ... The only thing he's lacking now is being able to put that ball where he wants it every time. ..."[2] Hudson had no idea that his words would be prophetic; Broberg would suffer a worse fate against the Orioles on this evening due both to a sudden inability to find the strike zone and a freak error in the bottom of the ninth inning.

The Rangers' best chance to score came in the top of the first as Dave Nelson and Frank Howard hit back-to-back one-out singles, but they were stranded when McNally got Ted Ford to fly out and retired Tom Grieve on a grounder to third. After that, the Rangers demonstrated an innate ineptitude on the basepaths the few remaining times they actually had a baserunner.

In the top of the fourth, Lenny Randle reached base on a two-out single but was picked off by McNally. Two innings later, Ford demonstrated the Rangers' lack of learning that so frustrated their manager, Williams, when he suffered the same fate as Randle, hitting a two-out single and being picked off by McNally.

After Grieve led off the seventh inning with a single, he at least was gunned down at second base by Orioles catcher Andy Etchebarren rather than being picked off at first. In any case, Grieve's lack of base-stealing success quickly quenched any hope of a Rangers rally.

Perhaps lost amid the Rangers' misadventures on the bases was the fact that Broberg was matching McNally zero-for-zero through the game. Entering the ninth inning, the Orioles had managed only a single by Etchebarren in the third and a walk to Don Buford in the sixth. In fact, since the Rangers' half of the first inning, neither team had managed to get a man as far as second base.

Unfortunately, the wheels quickly fell off the Broberg Express in the bottom of the ninth. After Buford hit a one-out single, Broberg lost his composure and walked Merv Rettenmund and Boog Powell to load the bases. (Powell was walked on four pitches.) Brooks Robinson stepped to the plate, and it seemed a certainty that he would knock in the winning run one way or another. With the count at 3-and-1, Robinson appeared discontent with the idea of drawing a walk for the victory and took a hack at a Broberg fastball. The result was a tailor-made double-play ball to Nelson at third base.

Nelson threw to home for the easy force out on Buford, but then bad luck stepped in to thwart the Rangers' chance to end the inning and extend the game. Catcher Ken Suarez, who was making his first start of the season, threw to first, where he would have had an easy force out except for the fact that he stepped on Robinson's bat just as he threw the ball. Suarez's throw hit Robinson on his left side and caromed into right field.

Randle chased after the ball from his second-base position as Rettenmund raced home with the winning run. Though Randle made a throw home, the play was not even close and the Orioles escaped with a 1-0 victory. It was one of 13 walk-off losses this inaugural Rangers squad would suffer in 1972 compared to only three such victories.

In addition to the on-field shenanigans that had cost the Rangers a chance at a win, there was additional drama in the stands that added insult to injury. This series was the first for the team in the Baltimore-Washington area since the Rangers had departed for Texas after the 1971 season, and a number of angry Senators fans had made the 30-mile trip from Washington just to express their opinion of Rangers owner Bob Short, who was at the game.

In the sixth inning, a disgruntled female Senators fan poured a cup of beer over Short's head as he viewed the game in a box seat behind the Rangers' dugout. Jerrold C. Hoffberger, the Orioles' chairman, had been sitting with Short, and he pursued the woman. Eventually, Hoffberger and security officers "grabbed the woman at the top of the stairs and she was hauled away."[3]

After the ignominies on the field and in the stands were over, Broberg demonstrated the maturity Hudson had credited to him as he handled the tough defeat by simply stating, "When you're snakebit, you're snakebit."[4] He tried to deflect some of the blame from Suarez, urging the reporters, "And say something good about Suarez. Man, he caught a hell of a game for me. I've never handled Baltimore like that before. Suarez brought out the best in me."[5]

In spite of his "best," it was Broberg's second consecutive loss on unearned runs, and his inability to throw strikes at the right time had contributed greatly to the late-game fiasco. Los Angeles Dodgers pitching great Don Drysdale, a Rangers radio announcer in 1972, said a few days later, "And that's very important. Being able to put a pitch exactly where you want it is what separates the average and the great pitchers."[6]

As destiny would have it, Broberg was unable to control his pitches and never achieved major-league greatness. He finished the 1972 season with a 5-12 record and a 4.29 ERA. After posting an 0-4 record with an 8.07 ERA in an injury-riddled 1974 season, he was traded to Milwaukee; there he went 14-16 in 1975, a season in which he walked more batters (106) than he struck out (100). Following stints with the Chicago Cubs and Oakland A's, the 28-year-old Broberg's career was over after the 1978 season.

Sources

In addition to the sources cited in the Notes, the author also consulted Baseball-Reference.com.

Notes

1. Deane McGowen, "Roundup: Broberg Loses Two-Hitter on Error, 1-0," *New York Times*, May 11, 1972.
2. Randy Galloway, "For Rangers' Broberg Stardom in the Future?" *Dallas Morning News*, May 6, 1972.
3. "Fans Give Short Beer Baptismal," *Dallas Morning News*, May 11, 1972.
4. Randy Galloway, "Orioles Back Into 1 to 0 Win," *Dallas Morning News*, May 11, 1972.
5. Ibid.
6. Randy Galloway, "Broberg Makes Own Orbit," *Dallas Morning News*, May 16, 1972.

RANGERS WIN 18-INNING MARATHON: MAY 17, 1972: TEXAS RANGERS 4, KANSAS CITY ROYALS 3 AT MUNICIPAL STADIUM

BY FREDERICK C. BUSH

The Rangers' May 17 game against the Royals in Kansas City was their 11th consecutive road game and the eighth in eight days. The team was already fatigued from their travels, as was evidenced by their four-game losing streak, and had not planned on playing the equivalent of a doubleheader on this evening, but they prevailed 4-3. As center fielder Joe Lovitto said, "Nobody wants to play five hours and lose. ... that one should give us a lift."[1] Lovitto was correct; the 18-inning win over the Royals propelled the Rangers to five straight victories, their longest winning streak of the season.

The cliché "the first one is the hardest one" certainly held true for the first victory in the Rangers' win streak as manager Ted Williams used 20 players – one fewer than his counterpart Bob Lemon employed – during the 4-hour 56-minute marathon. The Rangers continually squelched Royals rally attempts, so that those Kansas City fans from the crowd of 7,114 who remained to the end went home disappointed.

The Royals' Jim Rooker had pitched a 5-0 shutout against the Rangers on May 16, but this time the Texas offense started with a bang against Kansas City's starter, Dick Drago. Dave Nelson smashed a one-out triple and was followed by Don Mincher, who was mired in a zero-for-28 slump. Mincher seemed to be cursed, and not only at the plate. On the previous day, three of his front teeth, "all permanent caps, just fell out for no apparent reason, leaving the first baseman with a gaping smile – if he had any reason to smile."[2]

Fortunately, Mincher gave himself a reason to flash his now gap-toothed grin as he lined a double to the left-center-field wall that drove in Nelson for the game's first run. Hal King followed with a double of his own and later scored on Lovitto's two-out single to give the Rangers a quick 3-0 lead.

The fact that Lovitto also began the game with a hit was an encouraging sign for the 21-year-old center fielder and his team after he had missed time with a back injury and then had been held out of the lineup in favor of Elliott Maddox until the preceding game against the Royals. Williams, whose own storied hitting career was known to all, said of Lovitto, "We think he has a great future in this game. ... But the question is whether he's ready to hit now or not."[3] On this night, Lovitto, who started in right field, acquitted himself admirably.

Kansas City began to chip away at the lead in the bottom of the second when Cookie Rojas led off with a single against Rangers starter Dick Bosman. Ed Kirkpatrick followed with an RBI double that plated Rojas and reduced the Royals' deficit to 3-1. They recouped another run in the bottom of the fourth when Lou Piniella led off with a double and Rojas, the next batter, knocked him in with his second base hit of the game.

Drago, after his rough first inning, had settled down and kept the Rangers from adding to their lead during the remainder of his seven-inning stint on the mound, which included retiring the side in order in the fourth through sixth innings. When Bosman walked John Mayberry to start the bottom of the seventh, the Royals capitalized on the opportunity as Gail Hopkins, pinch-hitting for Drago, doubled to drive in the tying run against reliever Mike Paul, who had just entered the game. With the game now tied, neither team would score for the next 10 innings.

The Royals' lack of runs from this point on was not due to a lack of scoring opportunities. In the bottom of the ninth, Mayberry and Paul Schaal greeted Paul Lindblad, the fourth Texas pitcher of the game (who had recorded the last out of the eighth), with back-to-back singles. Pinch-hitter Ron Hansen was intentionally walked to load the bases, a gamble that worked out for the Rangers in this instance. Freddie Patek flied out as did Amos Otis. Mayberry tried to score on Otis's out. Maddox made an offline throw from center field, but catcher Rich Billings grabbed the ball on one bounce and applied the tag to Mayberry to send the game into extra innings.

In the bottom of the 10th, Lindblad again found himself in a jam after surrendering a one-out single to Piniella and a double to Rojas. Dennis Paepke was intentionally walked to load the bases once more for Kansas City. Williams's managerial strategy paid off as planned when Mayberry hit a grounder to Lenny Randle at second base. Randle fired the ball home to get the force out on Piniella, and Billings doubled up a lollygagging Mayberry, who "didn't run out the play," at first base.[4]

The bottom of the 11th was not quite "déjà vu all over again" (as Yogi Berra may or may not have said), but there were enough similarities to the prior two innings that Williams may have felt trapped in a time warp. With Lindblad still pitching for Texas, Nelson hit a one-out single and advanced to second on a sacrifice bunt by Patek. Otis then became the third Royals batter to receive an intentional walk in the past three innings as Williams returned to what was becoming a tried-and-true tactic. Richie Scheinblum, a former Rangers farmhand, looked to thwart the Rangers skipper's strategy when he singled to center field, but Maddox fielded the ball and rifled a perfect throw to Billings to cut Nelson down at home plate for the third out.

If good things come in threes, that was not the case for the Royals in this game. That was three intentional walks in three consecutive innings that resulted in three runners being out at home. The three runs on which the Royals remained stuck would turn out to be insufficient for victory.

In the meantime, the Rangers' offense had gone into an even greater slumber than it had in the previous night's shutout. After their three-run barrage in the first, the Rangers went 16 innings without a run, a time during which they managed only five hits (they had accumulated four, including three extra-base hits, in the top of the first!). It was fitting, therefore, that the Rangers would win the game in the 18th inning without managing a hit of any kind.

Ted Abernathy, the fourth Royals reliever, who had entered the game in the top of the 17th inning, got Larry Biittner to fly out for the first out of the 18th. Lovitto reached first on catcher's interference by Paepke. Rangers reliever Jim Panther, who had pitched the 17th, batted for himself and reached safely when Abernathy threw his bunted ball away as he tried to get the force at first; the error allowed Lovitto to advance to third and put Panther on second. Lemon tried Williams's approach for ending potential rallies when he had Abernathy issue an intentional walk to Jim Driscoll, who had entered the game at second base in the 16th. With the bases now loaded, Lemon brought in Tom Murphy to pitch to Toby Harrah.

Harrah lined a shot that deflected off Murphy's glove and was fielded by shortstop Patek, who flipped to the second baseman Rojas for the force out. Driscoll's slide took out Rojas so that he was unable to make a throw to first to complete the double play, and Lovitto crossed home plate with an unearned run that gave the Rangers a 4-3 lead. Maddox flied out to end the Rangers' "rally," and Panther set the Royals down in order in the bottom of the inning to preserve a hard-fought victory. Mayberry, who had a night to forget, made the Royals' final out on a grounder to second.

If there was a hero of the game, it may have been Lovitto, who had two hits, two walks, and an RBI, and scored the game-winning run. Observers believed at the time that "Lovitto epitomizes the Ranger youth movement – an outstanding young talent with a can't-miss tag, but still there's the matter of proving himself."[5]

One game does not make a career, however, and Lovitto never did prove himself. He managed a lowly .216 batting average in only 763 at-bats over parts of four seasons with Texas, and his playing career ended after the 1975 campaign. On May 17, 1972, he at least had a moment in the spotlight of the Rangers' longest game of the season.

Sources

In addition to the sources listed below, the author also consulted Baseball-Reference.com.

Notes

1. Randy Galloway, "Needed: Good Joe," *Dallas Morning News*, May 19, 1972.
2. Randy Galloway, "Skin of Don's Teeth," *Dallas Morning News*, May 18, 1972.
3. Galloway, "Needed: Good Joe."
4. Randy Galloway, "Rangers Go Late to Win, *Dallas Morning News*, May 18, 1972.
5. Galloway, "Needed: Good Joe."

NELSON, RANDLE HELP RANGERS SUBDUE TRIBE IN 12 INNINGS:
JULY 16, 1972:
TEXAS RANGERS 3, CLEVELAND INDIANS 2 AT ARLINGTON STADIUM

BY FREDERICK C. BUSH

After going 28 consecutive innings without scoring a run, the anemic Rangers offense gave starter Pete Broberg a two-run lead in the first inning of their July 16 game against the Cleveland Indians at Arlington Stadium. Broberg eventually allowed Cleveland to tie the score and did not receive a decision for his 8⅓ innings of work. Instead, the Rangers became involved in their second extended contest against the Tribe in three nights, and the goats of their 14-inning loss to the Indians on July 14 – Dave Nelson and Lenny Randle – found redemption as heroes of this evening's 12-inning victory.

Broberg scattered eight hits and surrendered five walks to make things more interesting at times than his manager, Ted Williams, likely wanted them to be. The top of the first inning was one such occasion as Broberg managed to work around two walks and a single to escape the inning unscathed, thanks largely to catcher Rich Billings' throwing out Jack Brohamer on an attempted steal of second base.

In the bottom of the first, the Rangers' futility with their bats finally came to an end against Cleveland's starter Mike Kilkenny. Ted Kubiak hit a one-out single, and Ted Ford drew a walk to put runners at first and second. Ford was picked off at first by catcher Ray Fosse as Billings was batting, but Billings drew the Rangers' second walk of the inning, which Frank Howard and Joe Lovitto followed with back-to-back RBI singles that gave the Rangers a 2-0 lead before Elliott Maddox struck out to end the inning.

Both pitchers avoided trouble over the next two innings, but Broberg's propensity for surrendering walks contributed to the Indians tying the game in the fourth. Fosse was the recipient of a one-out free pass, and he advanced to second on a two-out single by Frank Duffy. Cleveland manager Ken Aspromonte sent Lou Camilli, a switch-hitter, to pinch-hit for Kilkenny since he could bat left-handed against the right-hander Broberg.

Left fielder Maddox played the third-base line to try to prevent "the wrong-field extra-base hit," but he also played "extremely shallow, no more than 100 feet behind third base."[1] Thus, Maddox was helpless when Camilli lofted a double, which should have been "a routine fly ball,"[2] to straightaway left field that rolled to the wall and knocked in both Fosse and Duffy to knot the score at 2-2. Broberg retired Del Unser on a fly ball to end the inning, but the damage had been done courtesy of the walk to Fosse and Maddox's poor positioning in the outfield.

Reliever Ray Lamb took the mound for Cleveland in the bottom of the fourth and pitched seven outstanding innings against Texas. Lamb retired the Rangers in order four times, allowed harmless two-out singles in both the 7th and 10th innings, and worked around two Texas singles in the ninth.

Broberg kept the Indians from taking the lead, and received some fine fielding support in the top of the eighth that kept the game deadlocked. Tommy McCraw had hit a one-out double and was still on second – now with two outs – when Buddy Bell hit a grounder to the hole at shortstop. Kubiak, filling in at shortstop for All-Star selectee Toby Harrah, who had injured a shoulder two nights earlier, made a diving stop of the ball that held Bell to a single and forced McCraw to hold up at third base.[3] Billings then threw out Duffy, who was attempting to bunt his way on, to end Cleveland's scoring threat.

Broberg was replaced by Paul Lindblad in the ninth inning after surrendering a one-out single to Unser. Lindblad allowed the Indians' second hit of the frame to Brohamer before striking out both Chris Chambliss and Graig Nettles to quash any thoughts Cleveland might have had of a late-game rally. In the Rangers' half of the inning, Billings led off with a single and advanced to second on Maddox's two-out base hit, but that was the farthest any runner advanced against Lamb, and Randle struck out to send the game to extra innings.

The relief pitchers' duel continued with Lindblad and Lamb pitching the 10th inning for their respective teams. Horacio Pina took over the mound duties for Texas in the top of the 11th, and Ed Farmer did the same for the Indians in the bottom of the frame; both hurlers did well in their first inning of work, but then created excitement in the 12th inning.

Pina walked Brohamer to open the 12th, but Brohamer was forced at second base on a Chambliss grounder. Nettles then singled, and Pina issued his second walk of the inning, to McCraw, to load the bases. With the Indians on the cusp of taking the lead, Rangers infielders demonstrated some deft glove work. First, Fosse hit a grounder to Kubiak and the shortstop fired home to get the force on Chambliss. Next, Bell shot a grounder up the middle that looked as though it would be a base hit, but "Randle backhanded the ball, then flipped to Kubiak at second to just nip Fosse for the third out."[4]

As is often the case when a player has made an outstanding play in the field, the momentum carries over to the plate. Such was the situation for Randle in the bottom of the 12th as he hit a one-out single and advanced to second when Pina, looking to help his own cause, laid down a perfect sacrifice bunt. Nelson stepped to the plate and watched as Farmer uncorked a wild pitch that enabled Randle to advance to third. With the winning run only 90 feet away and a 3-and-0 count at the plate, Nelson swung away and lashed a single to center field that knocked in the final run of what was now a 3-2 Rangers victory.

To anyone who was surprised that Nelson, who had been hitless in five previous at-bats in the game, swung on 3-and-0, he explained, "No way I'm going on my own in that situation. … I'm definitely checking with the dugout."[5] After Williams gave the sign to swing away, Nelson got the pitch he was looking for and ended the game on a positive note for himself and his team.

For both Nelson and Randle, their roles in the 12-inning victory were a sweet reversal from two nights earlier when they had made errors on back-to-back batted balls that had resulted in two unearned runs to give the Indians the win in a 14-inning contest. The two players exemplified the 1972 Texas Rangers, whose roster was filled with athletes who had the potential to be future stars; unfortunately for the Rangers and their fans, most of the players' potential would remain unfulfilled.

In the case of Nelson, no less an observer than Williams, the "Splendid Splinter" himself, had appraised him as a potential .280 or .290 hitter and had raved, "If he hits that and makes 75 attempted steals, he can get 50 stolen bases. … That guy can be a helluva asset and player in this league."[6] Nelson's best season would be 1973 when he batted .286 and stole 43 bases, coming close to Williams's projections, but he was traded to the Kansas City Royals for pitcher Nelson Briles after the 1975 season and was out of the major leagues after the 1977 campaign.

Randle, who had scored the winning run, had also started to earn accolades. Though Williams had commented, "He's got that little flip throw to second trying to start a double play that I wish he'd forget,"[7] Randle's fielding acumen had been in evidence on this night. As for Randle's batting, he had begun switch-hitting in 1972 and Williams observed, "I think this has helped him at the plate. I'll tell you, I'm sold on this kid now."[8]

As fate would have it, of all the 1972 Rangers who failed to have successful careers, Randle was the only one to go down in infamy. After losing his starting job at second base to Bump Wills during spring training in 1977, he punched manager Frank Lucchesi in the face three times, sending Lucchesi to the hospital.

Randle was fined $23,407, suspended for 30 days, and then traded to the New York Mets on April 26, 1977, but he "never could shake the label of a hothead who had once broken his manager's cheekbone."9

Sources
In addition to the sources listed below, the author also consulted Baseball-Reference.com.

Notes
1. Randy Galloway, "Rangers Win in 12th, 3-2," *Dallas Morning News*, July 17, 1972.
2. Ibid.
3. Ibid.
4. Ibid.
5. Ibid.
6. Bob St. John, "Price You Pay," *Dallas Morning News*, May 23, 1972.
7. Merle Heryford, "Switch in Time, Randle Closer on Left Side," *Dallas Morning News*, March 14, 1972.
8. Randy Galloway, "He's So Out, He's In," *Dallas Morning News*, April 25, 1972.
9. Patrick Mondout, "Lenny Randle Slugs Manager After Losing Job (3/28/1977)," baseballchronology.com/Baseball/Years/1977/March/28-Frank-Lucchesi-Lenny-Randle.asp, accessed October 21, 2015.

RYAN OVERCOMES 107-DEGREE HEAT AND FATIGUE TO SHUT OUT RANGERS AND FAN 14:
JULY 27, 1972:
CALIFORNIA ANGELS 5, TEXAS RANGERS 0 AT ANAHEIM STADIUM

BY GREGORY H. WOLF

"It was nothing," wrote Randy Galloway of the *Dallas Morning News*, about the record 107-degree temperature at Anaheim Stadium for the matchup between the Texas Rangers and California Angels, "compared to the heat generated by Nolan Ryan."[1] A Texas native who was accustomed to the blaring sun, Ryan held the Rangers hitless for 7⅔ innings, and finished with a sparkling two-hit shutout while striking out 14 despite "feeling awful" before the game.[2]

"I felt tired and sluggish when I got to the ballpark," admitted Ryan. "I hadn't done anything for a few days."[3] The hard-throwing 25-year-old, acquired from the New York Mets in the offseason in what proved to be one of the most lopsided trades in major-league history,[4] seemed fatigued in his first season as a full-time starter after serving as a swingman and reliever for most of the previous four seasons. In his three last starts, all losses on the road, Ryan had been clobbered for 19 hits and 18 runs in just 18⅓ innings, dropping his record to 11-8 and raising his ERA to 3.14. But pitching at home in Southern California was a different story. In his 11 starts at Anaheim Stadium, the Ryan Express had spun five shutouts, thrown a one-hitter, a three-hitter, and two four-hitters, and had fanned 16 twice. Facing "one of the least distinguished batting orders in baseball," opined Ron Rapoport of the Los Angeles Times, was just what the doctor ordered to get Ryan back on track.[5]

A crowd of just 8,715 spectators braved the sweltering heat for an intradivision contest between two sub-.500 teams on Tuesday, July 27, at the ballpark affectionately called the "Big A" because of its gigantic, 230-foot A-frame scoreboard adorned with a halo. Playing their first game since concluding a 12-game road swing on July 23, rookie skipper Del Rice's Angels were reeling, having lost 10 of their last 14 games to fall to 40-52, fifth place in the AL West. The Rangers, led by the immortal Ted Williams in his fourth and final campaign as skipper, matched California's record in its last 14 games. The cellar-dwellers were 37-53, 18½ games behind the eventual world champion Oakland A's.

Ryan started the game by fanning Dave Nelson before running into trouble. He walked the next two batters, Joe Lovitto, who promptly stole second, and Larry Biittner, both of whom moved up on a wild pitch. With "perhaps the liveliest fastball in the majors," according to Randy Galloway, Ryan fanned Dick Billings and Ted Ford to escape what proved to be his biggest jam of the game.[6]

California loaded the bases with one out in the first against starter Mike Paul when Leo Cardenas and Andy Kosco singled and Bob Oliver walked. Paul, a 27-year-old southpaw acquired in the offseason from Cleveland, was arguably the Rangers' best hurler thus far in '72 with a 3-2 record and 1.94 ERA as a spot starter and reliever. He punched out Ken McMullen before Billy Parker, playing in his first game since being recalled from Triple-A Salt Lake City, singled to right to drive in Cardenas and Kosco.

Ryan, who had walked almost as many batters as hits he surrendered thus far in his career, issued a free pass to Bill Fahey, who was making his first plate appearance of the season since his call-up from Texas's

Triple-A affiliate, the Denver Bears. Undeterred, Ryan fanned the next three hitters.

The Angels added a run in the bottom of the third when left fielder Billings misplayed Cardenas's fly ball, enabling the five-time All-Star from Cuba to reach second. After Bob Oliver was intentionally walked with one out, California native Ken McMullen derailed Paul's plan to play for an inning-ending twin killing by driving in Cardenas on a single to left. It was déjà vu all over again as Billings fumbled the fly for his second error of the frame, permitting Oliver to advance to third, where he was stranded.

While Ryan mowed down the Rangers with 11 strikeouts without surrendering a hard-hit ball through five innings, the Angels nicked reliever Bill Gogolewski for another run in the fifth, though it could have been worse. Oliver led off with a walk, moved to third on McMullen's single, and subsequently scored on Ken Berry's one-out force-play grounder. With Berry on second via a stolen base and John Stephenson reaching on a hit by pitch, Ryan grounded out.

The Angels held their collective breath in the top of the seventh when Ryan grabbed his elbow after retiring Fahey on a fly to left with Ford on first via a walk. Racing to the mound, manager Rice and trainer Freddie Federico inspected Ryan, who shook his arm and seemed to shrug off the pain. "I can't say I lost anything due to it," said Ryan after the game. "It popped like that before, maybe three or four times a year. It bothered me on three or four pitches after that."[7] Ryan fanned the next batter, Jim Mason, and dispatched Vic Harris on a grounder to first.

In the bottom of the seventh inning, Berry's two-out double down the left-field foul line led to the Angels' fifth and final run. Gogolewski intentionally walked Stephenson to face Ryan, among the worst-hitting pitchers in baseball history.[8] The mild-mannered Texan slapped a fastball down the right-field line, driving in Berry, for his second of 10 career doubles.

Following Ryan's two-out walk to Lovitto in the eighth, Biittner broke up Ryan's no-hitter on a clean double just out of the reach of right fielder Andy Kosco, who fired a bullet to home plate to keep Lovitto from advancing and thus preserving the shutout. Ryan ended the inning by fielding Billings' tapper back to the mound and firing to first baseman Oliver.

Ryan's league-leading sixth shutout of the season was not without another tense moment in the ninth. After punching out leadoff batter Ford and retiring Fahey on a grounder, Ryan yielded a single to Mason. To the plate stepped pinch-hitter Frank Howard, a two-time home run champion and once one of the most feared sluggers in the AL. According to Randy Galloway, Howard sent Ryan's offering into the gap in deep right-center field. Center fielder Ken Berry made a spectacular "diving catch" to end the game in 2 hours and 37 minutes.[9]

The Angels scored five runs or more in a game for only the sixth time in their last 35 games by victimizing Rangers pitchers for 11 hits and eking out five walks, but also leaving 12 runners on base in their 5-0 victory. The story of the game, however, was the club's star pitcher. Overcoming the elbow scare in the seventh inning, Ryan finished with a two-hitter and fanned 14, the seventh time in 23 starts thus far in '72 that he whiffed at least 10 in a game; he also walked six batters. "I was able to stay away from them with my fastball all night," Ryan told the *Los Angeles Times*.[10] Dick Miller of the *Los Angeles Herald Examiner* wrote excitedly that Ryan made the Rangers, whose .217 team batting average in 1972 was the second lowest in the live-ball era, look like "Execution Row."[11]

"I feel comfortable here," said Ryan about pitching in Anaheim Stadium, where the victory improved his record there to 9-2 with a sub-1.00 ERA and six shutouts. "This was a big game after the way I pitched in my last three innings."[12] An All-Star for the first of eight times in 1972 (he did not pitch in the game), Ryan surpassed his career-high innings set the previous year with the Mets, with more than two months of the season remaining. "I never have been a good second-half pitcher," he told the Times. "And I didn't want to have another lapse."[13] And he didn't. Over his last 17 starts of the campaign, Ryan posted a 1.41 ERA in 140⅔ innings and held opponents to a .156 batting average, yet split his 16 decisions. He concluded the season with a 19-16 record and a 2.28 ERA, and led the AL in strikeouts (329), shutouts (9), hits per nine innings (5.3), and strikeouts per nine innings (10.4), but also paced the circuit in walks (157) and wild pitches (18).

"That's the first time I ever had a shot at a no-hitter," said Ryan of his victory over the Rangers. "I've never gotten that close before."[14] His skipper, Del Rice, a former big-league catcher who played on World Series winners in St. Louis (1946) and Milwaukee (1957), knew it was just a matter of time before the speedballer would achieve the feat. "He'll get more than one no-hitter when he's consistent with his control and has his curveball," Rice said.[15] The following spring, on May 15, Ryan held the Kansas City Royals hitless at Royals Stadium to notch his first of a big-league record seven no-hitters.

Sources

In addition to the sources cited in the Notes, the author also accessed Retrosheet.org, Baseball-Reference.com, SABR.org, and *The Sporting News* archive via Paper of Record.

Notes

1. Randy Galloway, "Ryan Blanks Texas," *Dallas Morning News*, July 28, 1972: 4B.
2. Dick Miller, "Aches 'n Pains. Ryan Rockets Back to Top," *Los Angeles Herald Examiner*, July 28, 1972: C1.
3. Ibid.
4. On December 10, 1971, the Mets shipped Ryan, catcher Frank Estrada, pitcher Don Rose, and right fielder Leroy Stanton to the Angels for aging, six-time All-Star shortstop Jim Fregosi. While Fregosi played in only 146 games in two years, Ryan developed into a Hall of Famer and Stanton served as a dependable outfielder, often in a platoon role, for the next five seasons.
5. Ron Rapoport, "Ryan Loses No-Hitter in 8th, Then Wins, 5-0," *Los Angeles Times*, July 28, 1972: III, 1.
6. Galloway.
7. Rapoport.
8. Leading up to this game, Ryan had batted .137 (27-for-197) and finished with a .110 average on 94 hits in his big-league career.
9. Galloway
10. Rapoport.
11. Miller.
12. Miller. In his last outing, Ryan lasted just 3⅓ innings in the second game of a doubleheader against New York at Yankee Stadium, yielding six hits and seven runs.
13. Rapoport.
14. Ibid.
15. Ibid.

RANGERS MANAGER TED WILLIAMS TEES OFF IN BATTING PRACTICE AT FENWAY: AUGUST 25, 1972: BOSTON RED SOX 4, TEXAS RANGERS 0 AT FENWAY PARK

BY BILL NOWLIN

As Red Sox owner Tom Yawkey was sometimes wont to do, the Boston Red Sox announced that all proceeds from the Friday night, August 25 game against the visiting Texas Rangers would go to the Jimmy Fund, to aid in the fight against cancer in children. The Jimmy Fund was a favored cause of Ted Williams, dating back to 1947, and the official charity of the Red Sox since they inherited the mantle after the Boston Braves left town in 1953. There was a hitting contest scheduled before the game with older players such as Dom DiMaggio, Walt Dropo, Ted Lepcio, Frank Malzone, and Johnny Pesky.

Ted Williams was in town as manager of the Texas Rangers. It was far from the first time he'd visited Fenway with another team; he'd managed the Washington Senators in 1969, 1970, and 1971. The Rangers had been to Fenway in mid-June, but this time there was the Jimmy Fund component. And a hitting contest.

Ben Bradlee Jr. writes that Tom Yawkey had paid a visit to Ted before the contest.[1] It wasn't a total surprise that Ted took up a bat; he'd told Clif Keane of the *Boston Globe* the day before that he'd be taking at least half a dozen swings.[2]

Williams had been out of the game for a dozen years and was just five days shy of turning 54 years old. The old slugger said, "I may have a heart attack. I haven't swung all year, so it may be tough." Keane suspected he might have done a little hitting the day before, when the Rangers were in Milwaukee.

The 6:30 P.M. contest before the regularly scheduled game was to feature some 10 radio personalities and former Red Sox players.

The others all took their cuts, but around 7:15 the crowd started chanting, "We want Ted!"

It made it appear that he hadn't been scheduled to be in the competition but was drafted by popular acclaim. Williams was described by the *Globe*'s Keane as "obese" and by the *Boston Herald*'s Fred Ciampa as "portly." Keane said Ted "dragged his bat, as ever, shaking his head and pointing out to [pitcher] Lee Stange of the Red Sox to 'bring it.'"[3]

Williams didn't just grab any old bat, apparently. Bill Zeigler handed him one of Tom Grieve's bats, a W183 Louisville Slugger, the same model Williams had used as a player. He was wearing number 9, but his jersey bore the name "Williams" on the back; it was a Rangers jersey. The Red Sox, even more than 40 years later, do not wear their names on their uniforms at home.

Texas Rangers catcher-left fielder Dick Billings said, "It was the most electrifying thing I've even seen in my life. He hit line drive after line drive. He hit them everywhere. He hit them off the wall. He hit a home run that was just foul [to right field]. Everything was a shot. Guys in the dugout were just looking at each other. Staring. How old was he? You would have thought he was 22. I never have seen a batting practice exhibition like that from anyone of any age."[4]

Though Williams struck the ball well, Billings may have been guilty of a bit of hyperbole. The one he said was off the wall was actually off the front wall of the Rangers bullpen, hitting it on one bounce. The *Boston Herald* did write that he hit one "clearing the right-field fence."[5] The *Los Angeles Times* wrote that Number 9's timing was understandably off: "He fouled off several pitches, but also hit some solid shots, including one to the base of the 380-foot sign in right field. Ted also pulled one down the right-field line which appeared foul by inches."[6]

So maybe he didn't actually hit a home run. Everyone felt good. And regarding the ball that went near the Pesky Pole, it was ruled a home run. "[T]he 'official scorer' ruled that the drive hit the foul pole, so the Jimmy Fund, Ted's pet charity, was enriched by another $250 donation from Yawkey for the 'homer.'"[7] Ted Lepcio did hit a homer, into the netting atop the left-field wall. Walt Dropo hit one out, too. (It was noted that Lepcio had been working out at Fenway for two weeks.)

Keane concluded, "Layoffs don't mean a thing if you still have that swing." Tom Grieve of the Rangers had a memory paralleling that of Billings. "The players were just stunned."[8]

In the game that followed, Luis Tiant threw a four-hitter and the Red Sox won, 4-0. It was his fourth start in a row that resulted in a complete-game win. He'd allowed a total of 16 hits in the four games. His next two starts were shutouts as well.

Ted's hitting well after a layoff was reminiscent of the show he put on back in 1953 for a nearly empty ballpark and not the 33,551 present in 1972. He'd just come back from serving in the Korean War, including 39 combat missions, forced to crash-land his jet once and barely limping back with a badly damaged plane another time. He hadn't held a bat, or been on a ballfield, for more than a year. *Cambridge Chronicle* reporter George Sullivan recalled that Williams took a few swings at Paul Schreiber's pitches … and then hit nine balls in a row out of the park. "It was one of the greatest things I ever saw. I always said it was one of the greatest things I ever saw, how many balls he hit out of the ballpark. My nose was up almost to that batting cage. I noticed during the end of it that there was blood streaming down Ted's hands. Just superficial, from his hands not being calloused from hitting a baseball."[9]

Notes

1 Ben Bradlee Jr., *The Kid; The Immortal Life of Ted Williams* (Boston: Little, Brown, 2013), 562. Bradlee reported the account of Rangers trainer Bill Zeigler.
2 Clif Keane, "Williams Leads Jimmy Hitters," *Boston Globe*, August 25, 1972: 53.
3 Clif Keane, "Ted Swings, and Fans Love It," *Boston Globe*, August 26, 1972: 21.
4 Leigh Montville, *Ted Williams: The Biography of an American Hero* (New York: Doubleday, 2004), 301-302.
5 Fred Ciampa, "Williams Homers for Jimmy Fund," *Boston Herald*, August 26, 1972: 2.
6 "There Was No Mistaking Him When Williams Came to Bat," *Los Angeles Times*, August 27, 1972: C2.
7 Ibid.
8 Montville, 302.
9 Author interview with George Sullivan, October 3, 2014.

GOGO TOSSES ONE-HITTER AND OUTDUELS THE RYAN EXPRESS: SEPTEMBER 12, 1972: TEXAS RANGERS 3, CALIFORNIA ANGELS 0 AT ANAHEIM STADIUM

BY GREGORY H. WOLF

"Any time Nolan Ryan pitches," reported the Los Angeles Times, "there's a chance for a no-hitter. But this time it was a different pitcher."[1] That "different" pitcher was the Texas Rangers' 24-year-old right-hander Bill Gogolewski who mowed down the first 20 batters he faced, and later yielded a two-out double in the eighth inning to settle for a one-hitter in the game of his life. It was an incredible game," Gogolewski told the author. "I made one bad pitch, one bad decision, and it cost me a hit."[2]

The Rangers were in a freefall, having lost 10 of their last 12 games when they arrived in Anaheim to kick off an 11-game road swing. Fourth-year skipper Ted Williams's squad was in last place in the AL West (51-84), and would finish last among the 12 AL teams in most offensive categories in '72, including home runs (56), batting average (.217), and slugging percentage (.581). The club's pitching staff matched their offensive counterparts by finishing last in team ERA (3.53), complete games (11), shutouts (6), and of course, losses (100) in the strike-shortened season. The Rangers' dismal record kept their division opponents, the California Angels, out of the cellar. Led by first-year pilot Del Rice, the Halos (63-72) were in fifth place.

Toeing the rubber for the Angels was Nolan Ryan, whom Merle Heryford of the *Dallas Morning News* described as "probably the fastest man in the league."[3] The Angels had acquired the 25-year-old speedballer, along with three other players from the New York Mets in exchange for Jim Fregosi in an offseason trade that has been considered among the most lopsided in baseball history. While Ryan posted a pedestrian 29-38 record in limited action in parts of five seasons with the Mets, he transformed into one of the AL's best pitchers in '72, entering the game with a 16-13 record and 2.53 ERA. In 33 starts, he had struck out at least 10 batters on 12 occasions, and had thrown a one-hitter, two two-hitters, and three three-hitters.

While Ryan made national headlines with his 100-mph heater, Oshkosh, Wisconsin, native Bill Gogolewski hurled in relative obscurity. Chosen in the 18th round of the 1965 amateur draft, "Gogo," as his teammates called him, debuted as a September call-up for the Washington Senators in 1970. The following season he was arguably the Senators' most effective pitcher, winning six of 11 decisions and posting a robust 2.75 ERA in 124⅓ innings as a part-time starter and reliever. But in the Rangers' first season in Texas, the 6-foot-4, 200-pound hurler had struggled thus far in '72 (3-9, 4.39 ERA in 121 innings) and had not notched a victory since he tossed a five-hitter against Minnesota on May 19.

Gogolewski recalled that he was looking forward to starting against Ryan. "We pulled into Anaheim Stadium and on the marquee it said 'Nolan Ryan vs. the Texas Rangers.' And I thought, 'the rest of the team isn't going to show up, or what?' That was an incentive." In fact, Gogolewski had been pitching his best ball of the season, surrendering just 15 hits and six earned runs in his last 22 innings, though he came up winless in those three starts.

The Tuesday evening match-up between two sub-.500 teams drew a sparse crowd of 4,292 to Anaheim Stadium, known as the "Big A" for the 230-foot-tall letter A that served as the park's main scoreboard. The Rangers came out swinging against Ryan. Leadoff hitter Dave Nelson lined a single to right field and reached second when Leroy Stanton juggled the ball for an error. Nelson moved to third on Toby Harrah's fly ball and scored on Ryan's wild pitch.

After Gogolewski set the Angels down 1-2-3 in the first, the Rangers took their cuts at Ryan's fastball. Joe Lovitto sliced a one-out single to center field and moved to second on another wild pitch by Ryan, who led the majors with 18 wild ones in '72. Bill Fahey, batting a meager .150, hit a bouncer past first base to drive in Lovitto for a 2-0 lead. It looked as though Ryan was on the ropes. Fahey moved to third on a single by rookie Vic Harris (batting .106), who stole second with Gogolewski at the plate. After "Gogo" fanned, Ryan walked Nelson to load the bases, but punched out Harrah to end the threat. "It was amazing how quick [Ryan's] fastballs got to you," recalled Gogolewski, who whiffed in each of his three plate appearances against Ryan. "By the time you react, it's at you. But I wasn't worried about those strikeouts."

No batter for either team reached base again until Ryan issued a one-out walk to Nelson in the fifth. Nelson took advantage of Ryan's high leg kick to swipe the 40th of his career-high 51 steals that season. Then, in a dazzling display of speed, Nelson took off on a hit-and-run with Harrah at the plate. Harrah hit a grounder to third base that Ken McMullen fielded cleanly and threw to Bob Oliver at first. Not slowing down, Nelson rounded third and slid home just beating Oliver's throw.

Gogolewski "yawned through the first six innings," opined Rangers beat reporter Merle Heryford.[4] The Angels pounded Gogolewski's devastating slider into the dirt, making 12 infield groundouts and hitting only five outfield fly outs in the entire game.

Texas threatened in the seventh when Fahey was hit by a pitch on his right elbow and stole second. Still smarting from the blow, Fahey departed for pinch-runner Dalton Jones, and went to the hospital for x-rays. Nelson beat out a two-out infield single, moving Jones to third, and swiped another base to put two men in scoring position. Ryan reared back and fanned Harrah to end the frame.

The Angels' Sandy Alomar attempted to break up Gogo's no-hitter by bunting to lead off the seventh. Gogolewski fielded the tapper back to the mound and fired a strike to first baseman Larry Biittner. When umpire George Maloney called Alomar out, Angels skipper Del Rice burst onto the field to protest, but to no avail. Vada Pinson drew a two-out walk to end Gogolewski's perfect game, but the tall right-hander set down the next batter.

After issuing a walk to McMullen to lead off the eighth, Gogolewski fielded Stanton's chopper back to the mound to initiate a 1-6-3 double play. Billy Parker, who entered the game batting a paltry .171, stepped to the plate. "Fahey got hurt and Dick Billings came in [from left field to catch in the bottom of the seventh]," explained Gogolewski. "He said to me, 'I'm not calling your pitches.' He knew I had a no-hitter going. He had put down a slider for Parker. But I thought, 'No, they'll be looking for it because they knew that that was my out pitch.'" Parker blasted a clean double over center fielder Lovitto's head. "It was supposed to be a fastball inside and it was a fastball belt-high outside," said Gogolewski. "And Parker drove it to right center." Parker's hit, which both the Dallas and Los Angeles papers described as the Angels' only hard-hit ball of the game, ended Gogolewski's quest to throw the first no-hitter in franchise history. A good-natured Midwesterner, Gogolewski took a deep breath, and then retired pinch-hitter John Stephenson on a popup to second base.

After Ryan pitched a scoreless ninth, Gogolewski tossed a 1-2-3 frame to complete the game in 2 hours and 11 minutes. In what was described as a "brilliant performance" by Merle Heryford, Gogolewski finished with a one-hitter, issued two walks, and struck out three in what proved to be his second and final shutout in his six-year major league career (1970-1975), during which he went 15-24.[5] Gogolewski's career day, opined sportswriter Don Merry of the *Long Beach* (California) *Independent*, "was more surprising than it was overpowering."[6] A tough-luck loser, Ryan yielded six hits and only two earned runs, and struck out 15. Ryan concluded the campaign in a blaze, making five more starts, striking out 54 in 44 innings, while yielding only 21 hits and five earned runs (1.02 ERA) to finish the season with a 19-16 record and a 2.28 ERA. He led the league in shutouts (9), strikeouts (329), and fewest hits per nine innings (5.3).

Gogolewski's gem was one of the Rangers' last highlights of the '72 season. The club lost its next 15 games, and finished with a major-league worst 54-100 record, 38½ games behind the division champion Oakland A's.

Notes
1. "Gogolewski One-Hitter Too Much for Ryan, 3-0," *Los Angeles Times*, September 13, 1972: III, 1.
2. Author's interview with Bill Gogolewski on August 17, 2015. All quotations from Gogolewski are from this interview.
3. Merle Heryford, "Gogo 1-Hitter Defeats Angels," *Dallas Morning News*, September 13, 1972: 4B.
4. Ibid.
5. Ibid.
6. Don Merry, "Ryan Fans 15, but Rangers Win, 3-0," *Independent* (Long Beach, California), September 13, 1972: 43.

DICK BOSMAN BEATS THE WHITE SOX, ENDING RANGERS' 15-GAME LOSING STREAK: OCTOBER 1, 1972: TEXAS RANGERS 1, CHICAGO WHITE SOX 0 AT ARLINGTON STADIUM

BY MICHAEL HUBER

The Texas Rangers hosted the Chicago White Sox on October 1, 1972, three days before the end of the strike-shortened season.[1] Last-place Texas had lost 15 consecutive games, dating back to September 13, and only three times in that span did the Rangers score more than three runs. They came into this game with a record of 52-99. Chicago was in second place in the American League West, 20 games above .500 with a record of 85-65, but they had been eliminated from the pennant race two days earlier.

On this Sunday afternoon, before an Arlington Stadium crowd of only 5,121, Chicago's Wilbur Wood was looking for his 25th win of the season. Facing him was Dick Bosman, who had an ERA of 3.83 but a record of only 7-10. Bosman had not won a game for the Rangers since August. In his last start, on September 25, he had pitched well, allowing only two runs on five hits in eight innings, but Nolan Ryan and the California Angels bested Bosman and the Rangers 2-1.

The game against the White Sox started off well for Bosman. Three up and three down in the top of the first, including a strikeout of leadoff batter Lee Richard. In the Rangers' first inning, leadoff batter Dave Nelson walked and stole second base. Toby Harrah lifted a fly ball to center for an out, and Nelson motored to third base after the catch. Ted Ford then singled to right field, and the Rangers had a quick 1-0 lead. Dick Billings lined to third baseman Hank Allen, who threw to first to double up Ford for the third out.

Bosman struck out the side (Tony Muser, Jay Johnstone, and Allen) in the second. Wood was equally effective. His defense made two errors in the second, but Wood retired the side with no hits or runs. In the top of the third, Rudy Hernandez singled to center with one out but was stranded there. An inning later, after Bosman struck out Jorge Orta, he allowed back-to-back singles by Pat Kelly and Muser. Then Johnstone flied out and Allen forced Muser at second to end the threat. Those two hits in the fourth were the last given up by Bosman in the game.

The Rangers got a hit by Vic Harris in the fifth inning, but he was forced at second when Bosman grounded to short. Bosman and Wood traded zeroes inning after inning. In the bottom of the sixth, Wood faced the top of the order. Nelson singled to right and again stole second base. Harrah walked. Rangers manager Ted Williams put on the sacrifice, and Ford bunted. Wood fielded the ball and threw to first, where Orta was covering. With one out, Texas had runners at second and third. Billings was intentionally walked to load the bases. Wood prevailed, though, striking out Larry Biittner and getting Tom Ragland to ground into a force out, short to second.

The only other play of note occurred in the top of the seventh inning. Johnstone was called out on strikes and argued the call. Home-plate umpire Bill Kunkel ejected the Chicago left fielder. He was replaced by Walt Williams.

The rest of the game consisted of the pitchers facing three batters each inning and giving up no walks or hits. In the top of the ninth, Orta reached on an error by Texas second baseman Harris, but he was caught stealing on the next play. Kelly struck out and Muser fouled out to third baseman Ragland to end the game, which was completed in 1 hour 58 minutes.

Both pitchers pitched well enough to earn the victory. Each had pitched a complete game and allowed only three hits, all singles. Wood had walked three and Bosman had issued one free pass. Wood got 12 groundball outs in the game, and Bosman struck out at least one White Sox batter in every inning except the sixth, for a total of 13.

The victory for Bosman was his only complete game and shutout of the season. The three hits he gave up were the fewest since he allowed one hit in six innings on June 6. Wood, with a record of 24-17, finished second in the 1972 American League's Cy Young Award vote. (The winner was Cleveland's Gaylord Perry.) In this loss, he failed for the seventh straight time in his quest for victory number 25.[2] After the game, Chicago manager Chuck Tanner gave Wood the rest of the season off, meaning that he did not play in the White Sox' final three games.

Nelson and Ford provided the offense for Texas, with a walk, stolen base, and single in the first inning. Two of the key Rangers players (Bosman and Ford) were linked after this season as well. On May 10, 1973, they were traded by the Rangers to the Cleveland Indians for pitcher Steve Dunning. The 1973 season was Ford's last in the major leagues.

In defeating the White Sox, Texas had ended its 15-game losing streak (which would remain the franchise record through 2015). They beat the Kansas City Royals in their next game, on October 3, but they lost their final game of the season to the Royals, 4-0, to give them 100 losses for the season.

In 1972 the Washington Senators had left the nation's capital to become the Texas Rangers. They brought their manager, Ted Williams, with them. Williams managed the Senators for three years (1969 to 1971), and after this one awful 1972 season in Texas, the Hall of Famer hung up his uniform.

Sources

In addition to the sources mentioned in the notes, the author consulted baseball-reference.com, mlb.com, and retrosheet.org.

Notes

1   baseball-reference.com/bullpen/1972_strike. The players union struck from April 1 to April 13, 1972. The 86 games lost were not made up, so most teams played 154, 155, or 156 games. Both the Rangers and White Sox finished the season with 154 games played.
2   "Sox Lose 1-0, Wood Ends Season," *Chicago Tribune*, October 2, 1972.

MINOR-LEAGUE BASEBALL IN THE DALLAS-FORT WORTH AREA

BY BRUCE BUMBALOUGH

Minor-league baseball in the Dallas-Fort Worth Metroplex is virtually synonymous with Texas League professional baseball in the region. The small parts not connected to the Texas League are the rise and fall of black baseball in the area and the brief sojourns of the Fort Worth and Dallas teams in other leagues. (The Metroplex is the local sobriquet for what the US government calls the Dallas-Fort Worth-Arlington Metropolitan Statistical Area.)

Black baseball came and went in a span of about 30 years. In 1916 Fort Worth's Hiram McGar worked to form the Colored Texas League. He also managed the Fort Worth Black Panthers. Dallas had a team in the league. The Black Panthers played at McGar Park, just south of the old Panther Park in Fort Worth. The old Panther Park was located in the Northside of Fort Worth between the West Fork of the Trinity River and North Throckmorton Street near NW Seventh Street. It is not known how long the league lasted or how the Black Panthers fared in their efforts. In 1920 McGar was again involved in organizing a black league. The Dallas Black Giants and the Fort Worth Black Panthers were a part of the Texas Negro League. The league lasted to 1927. In 1929 another league was born. Again Dallas and Fort Worth belonged. At one game in Dallas, possibly at Riverside Park, some 8,000 fans turned out to watch the Black Giants and Black Panthers play. In the later incarnations of the black leagues, the Black Panthers played at Panther Park and LaGrave Field. That league died in 1932 during the Great Depression, and fans of black baseball saw only barnstorming traveling teams in the years. Two such barnstorming teams were the Fort Worth Black Cats and the Dallas Brown Bombers. The barnstormers played all over Texas and featured players who later played in the Negro National League and the Negro American League. With the arrival of Jackie Robinson and the integration of the major leagues in 1947, the death knell for black baseball sounded in Texas. Play continued into the 1950s as the major and minor leagues slowly integrated, but eventually black professional baseball died out.[1]

Cleburne, Dallas, Fort Worth, and Frisco have all hosted Texas League teams at some point in the league's history and each has won at least one championship. Dallas was also very briefly a member of the Southern League in 1899. Both Dallas and Fort Worth played in the American Association in 1959. A team representing both cities played in the American Association in 1960-62 and the Pacific Coast League in 1963. In 1964 Dallas had an entry in the PCL and Fort Worth in the Texas League. From 1965 to 1971 Dallas-Fort Worth played in the Texas League.[2]

Under the minor-league playoff system, the league champion could be, and often was, a team that finished lower than first place in the regular season. The Texas League would sometimes split the season to create greater interest in the pennant races. At times the decision to split the season came during the season itself if one team was running away with the race. If the owners did split the season and one team won both halves, that team was declared the champion. If two teams each won a half, a playoff determined the champion. Texas League officials adopted the Shaughnessy playoff system in 1933. Under that system the first- and fourth-place teams were paired in one bracket and the second- and third-place teams in another. The winners of those brackets played for the league championship. That system has been replaced by divisions and half-seasons for playoff teams. The remainder of this chapter will concentrate on the years in which a Metroplex team emerged as the league champion. The years when Dallas, Fort Worth, Cleburne, or Frisco were not champions are included when other significant events require mention. Brief summaries of the nonwinning years in the American Association and Pacific Coast League are included to note the teams' presence in those leagues.

The Dallas and Fort Worth franchises in the Texas League were among the original teams. Others were Galveston, Houston, Austin, San Antonio, and New Orleans. The league had as few as four members and as many as eight throughout its existence. The history of the Dallas and Fort Worth teams is so intertwined that separating them into separate narratives harms the overall picture. Dallas and Fort Worth were archrivals long before baseball in the Texas League came to be. The baseball rivalry came to symbolize the rivalry between the two cities in other aspects of life and played no small part in making minor-league baseball successful in the area.

The Dallas Hams (55-29) won the first Texas League championship, in 1888. They played in Oak Cliff Park, across the Trinity River from downtown. The championship came outright as there was no playoff. Several of the original teams, including Fort Worth, folded during the season. Fort Worth had a record of 20-28 when it stopped play on June 25. The Panthers' home was an unnamed park located near the Texas and Pacific Railroad reservation south of downtown and near the notorious Hell's Half Acre.[3]

The Texas League did not operate in 1891, 1893, or 1894. The Fort Worth Panthers won their first league title in 1895. Although the Dallas Steers finished the overall regular season in first place and won the first half, Fort Worth won the second half and then a 13-game playoff series, seven games to six. Dallas (13-7) was in first place in 1898 when league magnates called off the season due to the Spanish-American War. Dallas's brief venture in the Southern League resulted from the reduction of the Texas League to four teams in 1899. When Dallas's bid to return to play was rejected by the league out of fear of increased travel costs, the Steers joined the Southern League only to see it fold shortly afterward.

When the Texas League re-formed in 1902, Dallas and Fort Worth returned the Dallas Griffins and the Fort Worth Panthers. Joe Gardner bought the Griffins in 1902. W.H. Ward owned the Panthers.

The Dallas Giants took the 1903 pennant by defeating Waco in a 10-game playoff series. The title fell into dispute, however, because Corsicana had claimed Charlie Barrett, who played for Dallas in the series. Corsicana and Dallas were thus named co-champions.[4]

Fort Worth (71-31) had the best overall record in 1904. The Panthers were an amazing 40-10 in the second half, finishing 12 games ahead of the Dallas Giants. Taking on the Corsicana Oilers in a 19-game playoff series, the Panthers were able to win only eight of the games, and Corsicana was the league champion.[5]

Fort Worth repeated as champion in 1905 in a wild finish. The Panthers trailed the Temple Boll Weevils by four games with seven to play on August 29. Fort Worth won seven straight games, including four from Temple, to close out the year at 72-60, a half-game ahead of the Boll Weevils. There were no playoffs.[6]

Cleburne won its title in 1906, the only year the Railroaders were a Texas League team. In that year, the playoffs put the first-half winner against the second-half winner. Fort Worth's Panthers (78-46) took the first half with a record of 42-20 and finished second in the second half with a mark of 36-26. Cleburne's Railroaders (77-49) finished third in the first half at 38-24, but won the second half at 39-25. Fort Worth refused to play the Railroaders in the playoffs, handing the championship to the Cleburne nine. Future Hall of Famer Tris Speaker played for the Railroaders and hit .268. He also pitched, appearing in 11 games with a 2-7 record.[7]

Neither Dallas nor Fort Worth took a league championship until the Giants of Dallas (83-57) broke through with a narrow win in 1910, finishing one game ahead of the second-place Houston Buffaloes. The season came down to a doubleheader between Dallas and Fort Worth and a rare tripleheader (five innings each game) between Houston and Galveston. Dallas won both its games while Houston lost the first game, won the second, and was given the third game by forfeit when Galveston left the field fearing a riot. There were no playoffs.[8]

Dallas and Fort Worth's greatest era in Texas League baseball began with the 1917 season. Joe Gardner, Dallas owner since 1902, sold the team in 1916 to a group of veteran players headed by Hamilton Patterson. W.K. Stripling and Paul LaGrave bought the Panthers with Stripling becoming president and LaGrave team secretary. (Team secretaries then were the equivalent of general managers of today.) The two teams won eight of nine league titles and six of seven Dixie Series titles in the years between 1917 and 1926. The Dallas Giants took the first of two consecutive titles with a 96-64 record in 1917. There were no playoffs in 1917. James "Snipe" Conley, a spitballing right-handed pitcher, was the key to the pennant as he won 25 games, including 19 straight victories and a no-hitter.[9]

In 1918, with the United States involved heavily in the World War, owners elected to stop play on July 7. Dallas, in first place with a 53-37 record, was named the champion team.[10]

Shreveport broke the DFW string with a championship in 1919. The Gassers ran away with the first half, recording a 44-21 mark. Fort Worth, showing the beginnings of the greatness that was to follow in the next six seasons, took the second half at 56-30. The Gassers dropped from first to fifth at 38-39 in the second half, but came alive to take the playoffs four games to two.[11]

In 1920 the Panthers (108-40) began their six-year domination of the Texas League. Managed by Jake Atz and having a combination of great pitching and hitting, they won no fewer than 96 games in each of the six seasons and twice won 109 in a season. Atz was a former major-league infielder who had signed as manager with Fort Worth in 1914, left in 1916, returned in 1917, and stayed until 1929. He was considered the greatest manager in the history of the Texas League. The Panthers took the 1920 first half by 8½ games and the second by 12 games. Joe Pate, who would pitch briefly in the majors in 1926 and 1927, and Paul Wachtel, who had pitched for Brooklyn in 1917, won 26 games each and had ERAs of 1.75 and 2.45 respectively. After the season, and in hopes of moving up from Class B to Class A, the Texas League challenged the Class A Southern Association to a playoff between the two league champions. That was the beginning of the Dixie Series. The Panthers defeated Little Rock, four games to two. The next year the National Association raised the Texas League to Class A.[12]

The rampage of the Panthers (107-51) through the Texas League continued in 1921 as they once again ran away with both halves of the season. The Memphis Chicks fell to the Panthers four games to two in the Dixie Series. Pate led the league with a 30-9 mark and a 2.68 ERA. Wachtel and Bill Whitaker each won 23 games. Augie Johns added 20 wins. Clarence Kraft led the league in hitting with a .352 average and hit 31 home runs.[13]

The 1922 season brought more of the same to the Panther fans. The beloved home team racked up another runaway first-place finish. After rolling through the first half with a remarkable 50-22 record, the Panthers (109-46) outdid themselves in the second half with a 59-24 mark, setting a league record for victories. Mobile's Bears cast a bit of darkness over the campaign when they took the Dixie Series four games to two. Pate dropped from 30 wins to 24 and Wachtel had 26 and Johns 21. Kraft won the home-run title with 32 and had 131 runs batted in. He hit .339 but missed the Triple Crown.

In 1923 the Panthers (96-56) suffered a slower start. League executives decided the race was tight enough to not split the season as they had at times in the past. Nonetheless Fort Worth ran away from the other teams, benefiting from an August surge, and downed second-place San Antonio by 13½ games. The Panthers redeemed themselves for the 1922 loss in the Dixie Series by beating the New Orleans Pelicans four games to one. Kraft repeated as home-run champion with 32. Lil Stoner led the Panther staff with 27 wins while Pate continued his string of 20-win seasons with 23.[14]

Clarence "Big Boy" Kraft had a career season in 1924. The first sacker led the Panthers (109-41) to another Texas League title. He hit 55 home runs, drove in 196 runs and batted .349. His efforts again fell shy of a Triple Crown. He led the league in home runs and RBIs, but failed to catch Butch Weiss of Wichita Falls, who hit .377. Kraft retired from baseball after the season. His league record of 196 RBIs still stands. Fort Worth got out to a much better start than it had in 1923. The Panthers were nine games ahead of second-place Houston at the break with a 51-23 mark. They bested that in the second half with a 58-18 record. Pate once again won 30 games and Wachtel 22. In Dallas, Steer Park burned on July 19. The Steers played a game at Riverside Park, home of the black team, before finishing the season at the State Fair Ground racing facility. There an attendance record (16,484) was set when the Steers and Panthers played on August 3. The Panthers took the Dixie Series from Memphis in seven games.[15]

The final year of the Fort Worth Panthers' streak began with the usual expectation that Fort Worth would again easily surpass the other teams. League officials anticipated a split based on that assumption. The situation nearly backfired, however, because they did not anticipate the improvement of the Dallas Steers in the second half. The Panthers charged to the first-half winner's circle, leading second-place Houston by 7½ games. The Steers finished fifth in the first part of the season. Dallas came on hard after the break and Fort Worth fell to earth. When the half was over, the two teams were deadlocked at 49-26. A best-of-three playoff for the second-half title went to Fort Worth in a sweep. The Panthers then won the Dixie Series for the fifth time in six years, downing Atlanta in six games. Paul Wachtel again led the league in victories with 23 while Johns had the lowest ERA at 2.74. Johns and Pate also racked up 20 wins each. Ed Konetchy, a former major leaguer who replaced Kraft at first base for the Panthers, led the league in home runs with 41 and RBIs with 162.[16]

In 1926 Conley, now a player-manager, led the Steers (89-66) to the Texas League crown, ending the six-year title streak of the Panthers. Dallas finished first by 3½ games over San Antonio. Fort Worth finished third, 6½ games back of the Steers. The Steers downed the New Orleans Pelicans, four games to two, to claim the Dixie Series. Individual performances for the Steers included Charlie Miller leading the league with 30 home runs and 118 RBIs, and Slim Love winning the strikeout race for the third straight year with 216.[17]

In the winter of 1928-29 Paul LaGrave, the longtime team secretary of the Panthers, died in El Paso. W.K. Stripling honored him by renaming the Panthers home field LaGrave Field. The new field, which had opened in 1926, was a few blocks east of the old one at Seventh and Commerce Streets, had more seats and was closer to the levees on the Trinity River. It remained as the home of the Panthers/Cats until their demise after the 1964 season. It was destroyed a few years afterward. In 2002 a new LaGrave Field was built on the site of the original and was home to the independent Fort Worth Cats through the 2014 season.[18]

Dallas won its next championship in 1929 when the Steers (91-68) won the first half and defeated the Wichita Falls Spudders for the title. The Steers had a record of 47-33 in the first half, but fell to 44-36 in the second. The Spudders led the league with an overall record of 94-65, three games ahead of Dallas. Dallas took the playoffs three games to one. Birmingham's Barons beat the Steers four games to two for the Dixie Series title.

W.K. Stripling sold controlling interest in the Panthers to a group headed by S.S. Lard and Ted Robinson in the early days of the 1929 season. Later in the year, with the Panthers languishing in the second division, longtime manager Jake Atz was fired and replaced by Frank Snyder. The death of LaGrave, the sale of the club by Stripling, and the firing of Atz brought to an end the triumvirate that had created the greatest single stretch of athletic success in Fort Worth history.[19]

Fort Worth returned to the championship ranks in 1930. Wichita Falls pulled away from the rest of the league by 8½ games to take the first half. Fort Worth, faced with a lengthy road stretch at the end of the year, won 13 of 18 road games to overtake Wichita Falls for the second-half title. The Panthers then took the playoffs in three games. Fort Worth beat Memphis four games to one in the Dixie Series. Dick McCabe and Dick Wentworth each won 20 games to lead the league in victories for Fort Worth. In an effort to lure more fans to games, Waco's Navigators installed lights in Katy Park. The first night game resulted in a 13-0 drubbing of the Panthers. Other teams soon followed and night baseball was on its way to being the dominant way the game was played in the Texas League. Only Beaumont held out, largely at the behest of the Detroit Tigers, and did not install lights in Briggs Stadium until 1948.[20]

The 1937 season saw the Cats (85-74) return to the championship ranks. They finished the regular season in third place. The Cats eliminated Tulsa three games to two in the first round and knocked out Oklahoma City four games to two in the finals. The Cats defeated Little Rock in the Dixie Series, four games to one.[21]

The 1939 season saw a return of both Dallas (now the Rebels) and the Cats to the playoffs, and was the first time the four largest cities in Texas appeared in the playoffs. Houston won the regular season with a 97-63 record. Dallas and San Antonio tied for second at 89-72. Dallas won the coin flip for second place. Fort Worth finished in fourth place, two games behind Dallas and San Antonio. Fort Worth drove the Houston Buffaloes from further play with a three games to two win in the first round. Dallas did the same with San Antonio. That set up a Cats-Rebels final. Fort Worth won, four games to one. The Dixie Series trophy came to Fort Worth, which defeated Nashville in seven games.[22]

The Rebels (80-74) returned to the playoffs in 1941. They finished the season in fourth place. Houston's Buffaloes were the runaway winner at 103-50. Dallas swept the favored Buffaloes in the first round of the playoffs, and then sent Tulsa home in the title round. Nashville swept the Rebels in the Dixie Series.[23]

The Cats and Rebels returned to the playoffs in 1946, the first year of play after a three-season suspension of play because of World War II. Dallas finished the regular season in second place with a 91-63 mark, 10 games behind the Cats (101-53). In a style reminiscent of their 1920s dominance, the Cats took an early lead and were never headed. Fort Worth disposed of Tulsa three games to one and Dallas eliminated San Antonio three games to two in the first rounds. Dallas erased the Cats four games to one in the finals. The Rebels then moved to the Dixie Series, where they kept their series winning streak alive with a four-game sweep of Atlanta. Prince Oana, a future Detroit Tigers pitcher, led the league with 24 victories for Dallas. Fort Worth's Johnny Van Cuyk recorded 207 strikeouts and posted an ERA of 1.42. The Rebels' Bob Moyer had 24 home runs and 102 RBIs.[24]

In 1948 Kilgore oilman Richard Burnett bought the Dallas Rebels for $555,000 and later bought Rebel Field for $265,000. He renamed the team the Eagles, and Rebel Field after himself as Burnett Park. It was located at Colorado and Jefferson Streets in Dallas. Burnett enlarged the seating capacity to almost 11,000 and made it one of the better minor-league parks in the nation. As was the case with Fort Worth's LaGrave Field, it lasted until Turnpike Stadium was built for the Dallas-Fort Worth Spurs. Burnett Park, like its Fort Worth counterpart, was demolished about 1965. The site is now an empty field. On the west side of the Metroplex, the Brooklyn Dodgers offered backup catcher Bobby Bragan the opportunity to manage the Cats. He quickly accepted. He led the team to what would be its final Texas League title in his first year as a player-manager. The Cats finished the season in first place with a 92-61 mark, a game and a half ahead of Tulsa. Houston was third and Shreveport (76-77, .49673) and San Antonio (75-76, .49688) finished in a virtual tie for fourth, with Shreveport winning the final playoff spot by a whisker. Fort Worth, despite being injury-riddled, knocked out Shreveport in six games and then downed the hard-hitting Tulsa Oilers in the finals in six games. The Cats dropped the Dixie Series to Birmingham in five games. The 1948 win was the final championship recorded by the Cats.[25]

The most significant event of 1949 in Fort Worth was the flood that began on May 17. It was perhaps the worst of many that the city endured since it was established in 1873. Nine people died, more than 13,000 were left homeless, and damage exceeded $25 million. Among the flooded spots was LaGrave Field. The flood was the second disaster suffered by the Cats in a week. Two nights earlier, a fire broke out in the grandstand and more than 10,000 seats were destroyed. Damage from the fire was estimated at $3 million. The Cats were hosting San Antonio when the fire broke out. Notwithstanding the fire, the teams continued the series the next day. The right-field pavilion and bleachers down the third-base line had not been damaged. Portable seats, including some metal folding chairs, were set up down the first-base line. Some series in the rest of the season were moved to the other team's site with the Cats acting as the home team. Others were played at the damaged LaGrave. The Cats also hosted the Texas League All-Star Game at LaGrave Field just two months after the fire and flood. The Cats (100-54) continued their defensive-minded mastery of the league. Tulsa again gained the second spot. Both clubs easily dispatched their opponents in the first round and Tulsa turned the tables on the Cats to win the league championship. Once again the finals went the full seven games with Tulsa winning the deciding game 4-1 in 11 innings.[26]

In the offseason after the 1949 campaign, the Dodgers rebuilt LaGrave Field. The new ballpark was much improved over the old one. It had a seating capacity of 13,005, better seats, more restrooms, fewer posts to obstruct the view of fans, better concessions and a press box that contained TV broadcasting space. The Cats (88-64), still under the leadership of Bragan, continued their playoff streak. They finished second to Beaumont, but were eliminated by Tulsa in the first round.[27]

Dallas owner Burnett signed Dave Hoskins, a veteran of the Negro National League, to pitch for the Eagles in 1952. Hoskins was the first black player to work for a Texas League team. He led the league in victories with 22 and pitched for the Cleveland Indians the next two seasons. Dallas (92-69) and Fort Worth (86-75) finished the 1952 campaign in first and second place respectively but fared poorly in the playoffs. The Cats lost to ultimate winner Shreveport while the Eagles were eliminated by Oklahoma City. Shreveport's Sports then defeated the Indians to win the league title. The Sports dropped the Dixie Series to the Memphis Chicks, four games to two.[28]

In 1953 the prospects for a major-league franchise in Texas became a bit more likely when the Boston Braves left for Milwaukee. The next year, the St. Louis Browns moved to Baltimore to become the Orioles. Although neither of the moves struck new ground for baseball, they were indicative of the need for change in the location of the game. It was the first change in the major-league team structure in 50 years. Four years later, the New York Giants and Brooklyn Dodgers left the East Coast for the West Coast, landing in San Francisco and Los Angeles respectively. (The move of the Dodgers affected the Cats directly. Seeking a farm club closer to their new West Coast base, the Dodgers traded their Fort Worth franchise to the Chicago Cubs for the Cubs' farm team in Los Angeles.[29])

The Dallas Eagles (88-66) won their final Texas League title in 1953. Tulsa was second at 83-71. Fort Worth was third at 82-72 with Oklahoma City fourth. Tulsa ended the Cats' chances while Dallas gained revenge for the previous-season loss to Oklahoma City with a four games to three win. Dallas trailed the Indians, three games to none, before taking the final four. Dallas eased past Tulsa in five games and then won the Dixie Series over Nashville in six games.[30]

The Brooklyn Dodgers sent Maury Wills and Eddie Moore to the Cats in 1955 and the pair had the distinction of integrating Fort Worth professional baseball.[31]

Neither the Eagles nor the Cats won another Texas League title. The Cats finished fourth in 1954 but were taken out of the playoffs by the ultimate winner, Shreveport. Dallas was a first-place club in 1955, but lost to Houston in the first round. Dallas and Fort Worth were second and third respectively in 1956. Dallas won 102 games in 1957, the most ever by a Dallas team, but was beaten by Houston in the finals. Fort Worth's final first-place finish came in 1958, but the Cats were erased from the playoffs by Corpus Christi.

Leaving the Texas League after the 1958 season, the Cats and Eagles moved up to the Triple-A

American Association. They played separately in 1959 and combined as the Dallas-Fort Worth Rangers in 1960-1962. The American Association folded after the 1962 season, forcing the Rangers to find a new home. In 1963 they played in the Pacific Coast League. Fort Worth returned to the Texas League in 1964 while Dallas played separately as the Dallas Rangers in the Pacific Coast League. From 1965 to 1971, the two teams again combined – this time as the Dallas-Fort Worth Spurs – and played in the Texas League. They were very popular with fans in the Metroplex, drawing well over 200,000 each season and occasionally reaching 300,000. Their attendance was routinely at or near three times the next highest total. The Spurs played in Turnpike Stadium, located along Interstate 30 in Arlington and near the present Globe Life Park that is home to the Texas Rangers. Turnpike Stadium was intended as a demonstration of the support the area would give to a major-league franchise. The Spurs were never more than an also-ran in their seven years of existence, but drew more fans than the winning teams. In 1972 the Washington Senators came to Texas and began play as the Texas Rangers, ending the tenure of minor-league baseball in the Metroplex for three decades.[32]

Frisco's Roughriders came to that Dallas suburb from Shreveport in 2003 and won the only Texas League championship in their history the next year. The Roughriders came on strong to win the second half of the East Division race after Tulsa had taken the first. Round Rock won both halves in the West and so advanced to the championship. The Roughriders downed the Drillers in three games to move on against the Express. The Express fell to the Roughriders in five games.[33]

Minor-league baseball provided fans in the Metroplex with wonderful entertainment in the more than 110 years that it has been played in the area. The Fort Worth teams of 1920-1925 rank among the very best minor-league teams ever to step on a baseball field. The intense rivalry between Dallas and Fort Worth ensured outstanding attendance any time the teams met. Minor-league baseball also paved the way for Major League Baseball to put a team in the Dallas-Fort Worth area. Without the outstanding attendance at the Turnpike Stadium for the Dallas-Fort Worth Spurs, the Texas Rangers might never have come to the Metroplex.

Notes

1. Mark Presswood, "Black Professional Baseball in Texas," *Texas Almanac* (texasalmanac.com/topics/history/black-professional-baseball-texas), accessed October 7, 2015.
2. Larry G. Bowman, "Dallas-Fort Worth Minor-League Baseball," *Handbook of Texas Online* (tshaonline.org/handbook/online/articles/xod03), accessed October 9, 2015.
3. Wright, 7-13; John C. Holady and Mark Presswood, *Baseball in Dallas* (Charleston, South Carolina: Arcadia Books, 2004), 115.
4. Larry G. Bowman, "Dallas-Fort Worth Minor-League Baseball"; Ruggles, 26, 84-86; O'Neal, *Texas*, 233.
5. Ruggles, 90-91.
6. Ruggles, 97-98.
7. William B. Ruggles, *The History of the Texas League of Professional Baseball Clubs 1888-1951* (Texas League of Professional Baseball Clubs, 1951), 101-102, 202; Bill O'Neal, *The Texas League 1888-1987: A Century of Baseball* (Austin, Texas: Eakin Press, 1988), 221-224; Marshall D. Wright, *The Texas League in Baseball, 1888-1958* (Jefferson, North Carolina: McFarland, 2004), 92-97.
8. Ruggles, 114.
9. Ruggles, 125-128; Wright, 176-190; Snipe Conley Player Page, baseball-reference.com, accessed October 12, 2015; O'Neal, *Texas*, 53.
10. Wright, 184.
11. Ruggles, 129-130.
12. Wright, 198-199.
13. Ruggles, 130-131; Wright, 206-207.
14. Ruggles, 135; Wright, 223-224.

15 Ruggles, 136; Wright, 232-233.
16 Ruggles, 137-138; Wright, 240-241.
17 Wright, 249-256; Snipe Conley Player Page.
18 Bruce Bumbalough, "LaGrave Field," SABR Bio-Project, Society for American Baseball Research (sabr.org/node/37719), accessed ctober 15, 2015.
19 O'Neal, *Texas*, 233; Ruggles, 143-145; O'Neal, *The Southern League: Baseball in Dixie, 1885-1994* (Austin, Texas: Eakin Press, 1994), 307-308.
20 Ruggles, 145-147; Wright, 285.
21 Ruggles, 160-162.
22 Ruggles, 165-167.
23 Ruggles, 170-172.
24 Ruggles, 179-181; Wright, 395.
25 Ruggles, 184-186; Larry G. Bowman, "Burnett, Richard Wesley," *Handbook of Texas Online* (tshaonline.org/handbook/online/articles/fbuws), accessed October 20, 2015; Wright, 417-418; Holaday and Presswood, 115.
26 Bumbalough, "LaGrave Field"; Ruggles, 188-189.
27 Presswood and Holaday, 95; Ruggles, 190-191.
28 Wright, 457; Dave Hoskins Player Page, baseball-reference.com, accessed October 21, 2015.
29 Fran Zimniuch, B*aseball's New Frontier* (Lincoln: University of Nebraska, 2013), 3; Wright, 466; Presswood and Holaday, 76.
30 Wright, 466-467.
31 Presswood.
32 Lloyd Johnson and Miles Wolff, eds., *Encyclopedia of Minor League Baseball Third Edition* (Durham, North Carolina: Baseball America, 2007), 489, 493, 497, 501, 506, 511, 515.
33 Tom Kayser email to author, October 26, 2015.

EMBRACING THE FUTURE: THE TRANSACTIONS OF THE 1972 TEXAS RANGERS

BY WILLIAM SCHNEIDER

There are a number of reasons teams complete transactions in major-league baseball. While the goal is clearly to improve the team, the exact nature of that improvement varies considerably, based on the circumstances in which the team finds itself. A contending team will look for upgrades in the field or on the mound in the near term, while a rebuilding team will seek to cash in current assets for future value. A financially strapped team might attempt to unload high-salaried players, and a poorly attended team might try to make a splash to boost fan interest and (presumably) attendance. Interestingly, the 1972 Texas Rangers appeared to pursue several of these goals at the same time.

Ostensibly the Rangers were in the midst of a well-publicized youth movement with an eye toward future competitiveness. Owner Bob Short was also struggling financially, and could be expected to try to cut costs. On the other hand, the team wanted to create fan interest in the first season in Dallas, and manager Ted Williams's competitive drive was an established fact.

YOUTH MOVEMENT

When the Washington Senators were surprisingly competitive in the 1969 season, they were led by a number of veterans. The average age of the team's position players was 27.8, above the American League average of 27.3. Similarly, the Senators' pitchers averaged 27.0 years old against an American League average of 27.1. By 1971, the Rangers ranked as the youngest team in the league in both categories. The transactions pursued by the team before and during the 1972 season, in aggregate, would make the team younger still.

Despite the youth movement, however, Ted Williams was not throwing in the towel on fielding a competing club as of the start of the 1972 season. Williams outlined his thinking in *The Sporting News*'s season preview: "We could be a little better than anyone thinks. I think we've plugged some defensive gaps, and our pitching should be stronger."[1] By the season's midpoint, however, the skipper was ready to embrace the future more vigorously.

COST CUTTING

The move to Dallas from Washington was motivated by money, notably the inability of Bob Short to remain financially viable in the nation's capital. While a full treatment of Short's struggles is beyond the scope of this article, his money problems were anything but low key. Sports Illustrated described Short in 1971 as an "impoverished millionaire,"[2] and he was in danger of failing to meet the team's financial obligations. Short's budget problems showed up in the transaction register. At the start of the 1972 season, the Rangers' highest-paid player was Frank Howard at $120,000 for the year. Consistent with Sports Illustrated's observation that Short had in previous years "economized by peddling off players in the middle income range,"[3] the next highest-paid player was Don Mincher at $47,000. Both Howard and Mincher would be gone by season's end, as well as the player with the fourth-highest salary (Ted Kubiak, $31,000).

NEAR-TERM IMPROVEMENTS

The Rangers moved a number of depth pieces for small upgrades. The veterans acquired in these trades did not necessarily support the next great Rangers team, but did offer the potential for improved results in 1972. Their limited upside made any significant impact in the standings unlikely, however.

MAKE A SPLASH

In his tenure as owner of the Senators, Bob Short had made a good-faith effort to attract fans to RFK Stadium. In fact, *Sports Illustrated* noted in 1971 that "Short stages as many promotional extravaganzas as any other owner in baseball, including that formidable showman Charles O. Finley."[4] This desire to attract attention spilled over into transactions as well, as Short had pursued a number of personnel moves aimed at garnering attention for his struggling team while in Washington. Two of the more prominent were the hiring of Ted Williams as manager of the team before the 1969 season and a trade for former 30-game winner Denny McLain before the 1971 season. The Rangers' 1972 acquisitions did not include any of these noteworthy moves, but the trade of McLain (see below) did undo the least successful of Short's splashy transactions.

NOVEMBER 3, 1971

Traded Joe Grzenda to the St. Louis Cardinals. Received Ted Kubiak.

TYPE: NEAR TERM IMPROVEMENT

Thirty-four-year-old Joe Grzenda was a very good relief pitcher in 1971, appearing in 46 games with a record of 5-2 and an ERA of 1.92. This season stood as an outlier, however, as his ERA was 3.88 in 1969 and 5.00 in 1970. The 29-year-old Ted Kubiak was a good-fielding, mediocre-hitting infielder who appeared in 121 games in 1971, mostly as a starting second baseman, for the Brewers and the Cardinals. Kubiak had been responsible for 1.4 WAR, batting .232 with four homers. Williams was reportedly enamored of Kubiak's potential as a starting second baseman, and oversaw a spring-training battle between him and youngster Len Randle.[5]

Result: In 2017, this trade would be considered a savvy move by the Rangers. The trade of a fluky good reliever for a starting position player is looked on as a sure win for the acquiring team. Grzenda, as could be expected, reverted to form. He had an ERA of 5.66 for the Cardinals in 30 games in 1972 and was finished as a major leaguer. Kubiak did not hit well enough to remain a starter at second base, though. He started about one-third of the Rangers' first 66 games, hitting only .224, before being traded to Oakland. Overall, this trade was inconsequential for the Rangers.

DECEMBER 2, 1971

Traded Paul Casanova to the Atlanta Braves. Received Hal King.

TYPE: NEAR TERM IMPROVEMENT

Paul Casanova was a 29-year-old career backup catcher who had spent his career to that point with the Senators. He was sub-replacement in 1971, hitting a mere .203 with five homers.

Hal King, a 27-year-old backup catcher with Atlanta, had similarly hit .207 in 1971 with five homers, albeit in fewer at-bats than Casanova. King did bat left-handed, however, and therefore would serve as a better platoon partner for incumbent catcher Dick Billings and newly acquired Ken Suarez than the righty-swinging Casanova.

Result: Manager Williams tried King as a starter against right-handed pitching in the early part of the season, but Hal had "hit" his way to a .125 batting average by May 20. Thereafter, his playing time was spotty until he was optioned to Triple-A Denver in July. He did not appear in another game for the Rangers, being packaged in a trade with the Reds after the season. His contributions to the Rangers amounted to 150 plate appearances, a .180 batting average, 4 home runs, and a .333 on-base percentage due to a strong ability to take a walk. Casanova appeared in 49 games for the Braves with a .206 average, and did not contribute above replacement level for the remaining years of his career. This trade proved inconsequential to the Rangers' fortunes.

DECEMBER 2, 1971

Traded Bernie Allen to the New York Yankees. Received Gary Jones and Terry Ley.

Traded Gary Jones, Terry Ley, Denny Riddleberger, and Del Unser to the Cleveland Indians. Received Roy Foster, Rich Hand, Mike Paul, and Ken Suarez.

TYPE: YOUTH MOVEMENT

After the aforementioned minor transactions, the Rangers pulled off a big deal with the Cleveland Indians. Per Ted Williams, the Rangers hoped to acquire "more versatility, more depth, and more pitching potential"[6] and moved a number of veterans to the Indians in the quest to meet those needs.

Gary Jones and Terry Ley were young nonprospect pitchers for the Yankees who were destined to spend less than a day under Rangers control. Jones and Ley were acquired for the services of third baseman Bernie Allen and immediately flipped to the Indians as part of the larger trade. Therefore, from the Rangers' perspective the trade consisted of Allen, Riddleberger, and Unser for Foster, Paul, Hand, and Suarez.

Del Unser was the key to the deal from the Indians' perspective. The 27-year-old had been a four-year starter at center field for the Senators, finishing second in Rookie of the Year voting in 1968, and batting .255/.325/.355 for 2.5 WAR in 1971. Denny Riddleberger, a 26-year-old left-handed reliever, had shown flashes of potential in 1971. Denny had appeared in 57 games for the Senators, striking out 7.2 batters per nine innings and registering a 3.23 ERA. Allen, a 32-year-old utility infielder, had had a pretty good season at the bat in 1971 while appearing in games at both second and third base. Bernie's hitting was good for a 115 OPS+ as he had a .359 on-base percentage while playing passable defense.

22-year-old right-hander Rich Hand was the key figure in the trade from the Rangers' perspective. The original trade had been held up for three days until the Indians agreed to include the former first-round pick in the 1969 June secondary draft. In 1971, Hand had gone 8-2 with a 1.88 ERA in Triple A before going 2-6 with a 5.79 ERA with the big club. In his 1970 rookie season he had shown strong potential though; Rich had allowed only 132 hits in 159⅔ innings with an ERA of 3.83.

Paul was a 26-year-old left-hander who had been a regular pitcher for the Tribe since 1968. In 1971, he had struggled to a 2-7 record with a 5.95 ERA and had similarly struggled to a 4.37 ERA in Triple A.

Foster, the other principal piece headed west in the trade, was the American League Rookie of the Year in 1970. He had followed up his stellar first season with an 18-homer effort in 1971, although his average had dropped to .245 and his defense was considered suspect. At the time of the trade, manager Williams was hoping for big things from his new outfielder. Williams stated that he always liked Foster's potential and opined that "he may hit even better and more home runs in Texas."[7]

Ken Suarez was a right-handed-hitting backup catcher. 28 years old, he had batted a mere .203/.310/.285 in 146 plate appearances in 1971.

Result: The trade initially worked out well for the Rangers from the pitching perspective, as both Hand and Paul had some success as starters for the 1972 Rangers. Hand proved to be the Rangers' best starter in 1972, going 10-14 with a 3.32 ERA in 28 starts. Paul surprised, given his track record, by chipping in with 20 starts good for 8-9 and a 2.17 ERA. Neither, however, would prove to be a long-term solution. Paul reverted back to the journeyman hurler he had always been in 1973 (5-4, 4.95 ERA for the Rangers), and Hand was unable to build on his 1972 season. He went 6-6 with a 4.39 ERA in 1973 to finish up his major-league career.

Foster, in a bizarre twist, never appeared in a regular-season game for the Rangers. He was traded back to the Indians in April (see below). Suarez played for a couple of seasons for the Rangers without distinction.

Unser proved to be the most impactful player included in the trade. He played for 11 more seasons, including five as a major-league regular. He accounted for 11.5 WAR over the remainder of his career. Riddleberger went 1-3 with a 2.50 ERA for the Tribe in 1972 and then exited the major leagues for good. Bernie Allen hit .227 in part-time duty for the Yankees in 1972, then finished his major-league career in 1973 as a sub-replacement player in limited action.

In the final analysis, the Rangers gave up a peak-year center fielder, a valuable commodity, in their quest for depth, versatility, and pitching potential.

They received in return a brief glimpse of that potential but nothing else of significance.

BEFORE 1972 SEASON

Lew Beasley received from the Baltimore Orioles in an unknown transaction.

TYPE: YOUTH MOVEMENT

Beasley was a 22-year-old outfielder in the Orioles system. A second-round pick in 1967, he had a strong season in Class A in 1971, hitting .303/.347/.392 with 24 steals. It is not recorded what the Rangers gave up to acquire him.

Result: Today, the fact that Beasley was 22 years old in Class A would cast doubt on the predictive power of his strong season at the bat. Those doubts proved to be well founded.

MARCH 4, 1972

Traded Denny McLain to the Oakland Athletics. Received Jim Panther and Don Stanhouse.

TYPE: YOUTH MOVEMENT

As previously mentioned, owner Bob Short had acquired the enigmatic McLain prior to the 1971 season in an attempt to attract attention for his struggling club. His payoff had been a 10-22 season with a 4.28 ERA, a season-long dispute between McLain and Williams over the structure of the Senators' pitching rotation, and a pitcher who was thought to be a disruptive influence on the Rangers' younger players.

On the advice of Rangers Triple-A manager Del Wilber, the Rangers pursued Don Stanhouse and Jim Panther. Wilber was particularly high on Stanhouse's potential, stating, "If you can get Stanhouse even up for McLain, make the deal."[8] Stanhouse was a first-round draft pick in the 1969 draft and had gone 7-4 with a 3.74 ERA at AAA in 1971. He was considered the outstanding pitching prospect in an Oakland A's system that had recently produced Catfish Hunter and Vida Blue.

Jim Panther, 26, had gone 10-10 with a 3.63 ERA for Triple-A Iowa in 1971. He was too old to be considered a strong prospect, but offered the versatility to pitch as both a starter and reliever.

Result: Enticing the normally astute Charlie Finley to give up his number-one pitching prospect for the washed-up McLain was a coup for the Rangers. Stanhouse came out of the gate strong in 1972, fanning 12 batters in his first 12⅔ innings with the Rangers after striking out the side against the Chicago White Sox in his major-league debut. However, he hurt his elbow and was forced on to the disabled list. His overall 1972 season consisted of 16 starts with a 2-9 record and a 3.78 ERA. Panther made a limited contribution to the Rangers, going 5-9 with a 4.13 ERA in 58 games before being moved to Atlanta in a postseason trade. The McLain-Stanhouse trade, much like the trades described above, did not prove to be a needle-mover for the Rangers franchise.

MARCH 7, 1972

Released Tim Cullen.

TYPE: COST CUTTING

Tim Cullen was a 30-year-old middle infielder who had appeared in 125 games for the Senators in 1971, batting a mere .191 and fielding just well enough to account for .6 WAR. He was obviously not a part of the Rangers' future and in the absence of a likely trade market, he was released. He was signed by Oakland and appeared in 72 games in 1972 to finish out his career.

APRIL 3, 1972

Traded Roy Foster and Tommy McCraw to the Cleveland Indians. Received Ted Ford.

TYPE: YOUTH MOVEMENT

After his acquisition in the blockbuster deal with the Indians, Roy Foster had hit .302 in spring training. Despite this, Ted Williams was not a fan. "I just couldn't stand his moping around all the time," said Williams. "That's not my kind of player."[9]

30-year old Tommy McCraw was a nine-year veteran who had been acquired by the Senators before the 1971 season. He had played 122 games for them, batting .213/.291/.382 in 234 plate appearances. It was clear to him during 1972 spring training that he was not in Ted Williams's plans. McCraw commented, "Heck, he only gave me four at-bats all spring training. How could I prove anything to him?"[10]

The Rangers were excited by the potential of the 24-year-old Ted Ford. "I personally made this trade, I think it's a damn good one," said Ted Williams.[11] said Ted Williams. "I think we got the best end of it in age on the one hand and enthusiasm on the other." Ford had been a first-round pick in 1966, and had torn up Triple-A pitching to the tune of a .326 average with good power in 1970 and a .330 average, .404 on-base percentage, and .500 slugging percentage in 1971. He had struggled upon his callup to the Indians in 1971, though; he hit .194 with no power in 206 plate appearances.

Result: Ford had the best year of his career for the Rangers in 1972. After hitting a three-run homer in his first game on April 28, he went on to hit 14 homers, knock in 50 runs, and bat .235. His career faded quickly after that, as he hit only .225 in 40 at-bats in 1973 and exited the majors for good after that season. McCraw came out of the gate strongly for the Indians. The Tribe surprisingly surged into first place in May, prompting Cleveland manager Ken Aspromonte to say, "I don't know where we'd be today if it weren't for Tom McCraw. He has been a tremendous addition."[12] The discerning fan would be skeptical that a 31-year-old with a previous high of 2.6 WAR in any of his previous seasons, and that all the way back in 1967 as a 26-year-old, would suddenly flash MVP potential, and would be proved correct. McCraw finished 1972 with a .258 average and accounted for 2.0 WAR, not bad but certainly not the linchpin of a playoff team. He went on to play three more seasons as a decent hitting (on-base percentage ranged from .336 to .343), poor fielding part-time player before leaving the majors after the 1975 season. Foster was used primarily as a pinch-hitter for the Indians, and his poor performance confirmed Williams's estimate of his potential. The 1972 season was his last in the majors.

This trade proved to be another that had limited short-term and no long-term impact for the Rangers.

MAY 8, 1972

Signed Tom Robson as a free agent.
TYPE: YOUTH MOVEMENT

Tom Robson was a 25-year-old outfielder who had hit 16 homers and delivered a .274/.347/.445 slash line in Double A in 1971 in the Reds system. The Rangers signed him after he was released by the Reds in April. His major-league career totaled 54 undistinguished plate appearances in the 1974 and 1975 seasons.

MAY 30, 1972

Traded Norm McRae to the Detroit Tigers. Received Dalton Jones.
TYPE: NEAR TERM IMPROVEMENT

Norm McRae, a 23-year-old who had been a throw-in in the 1971 acquisition of Denny McLain, went 6-13 with a 4.89 ERA for Triple-A Denver in 1971. He was not viewed as a prospect of note.

Dalton Jones was a 27-year-old utility infielder for the Tigers. He had appeared in 83 games for them in 1971, batting .254.

Result: McRae failed to return to the major leagues (he had played briefly with Detroit in 1969 and 1970), while Jones served his utility role in undistinguished fashion for the Rangers in 1972 and never again appeared in a major-league game.

JULY 20, 1972

Traded Ted Kubiak and Don Mincher to the Oakland Athletics. Received a player to be named later, Vic Harris and Marty Martinez. The Oakland Athletics sent Steve Lawson (July 26, 1972) to the Texas Rangers to complete the trade.
TYPE: YOUTH MOVEMENT

It had been about eight months since the Rangers' last big trade. With the team mired in last place in the American League West at the All-Star break, owner Bob Short finally was able to persuade Ted Williams to embrace the youth movement full force. Per Short, "We think we are now putting a young, aggressive, and attractive team out there, one that with experience can be a contender in future years."[13] Veterans Ted Kubiak and Don Mincher were not the last to exit the Rangers' stable over the following few weeks.

Kubiak had been acquired from St. Louis as a potential starting second baseman in November of 1971. He had received regular playing time for the Rangers, but with a .550 OPS was clearly not someone to continue playing with a full-fledged youth movement underway.

Don Mincher, who was 34 years old, had been the Senators' leading hitter in 1971 after coming over in a trade with Oakland. In 100 games for the Senators, he had hit 10 home runs, knocked in 45 runs, and hit .291. He was still effective in 1972, although this was due more to a high on-base percentage driven by walks than by his customary home-run power. He had hit only six homers in 243 plate appearances at the time of the trade, and was batting at a .236 clip.

Steve Lawson was a 21-year-old left-hander working at Oakland's Triple-A farm club at the time of the trade. A third-round pick in the 1969 draft, he had excelled at Class A in 1971, going 7-2 with a 3.07 ERA while striking out nearly a batter an inning. He jumped from Class A to Triple A for the 1972 season, and was struggling against the tougher competition (7-9, 4.57 ERA in 20 starts). However, Denver manager Del Wilber was very high on Lawson's potential. Per Bob Short: Wilber "advised us to take Lawson head up for both Kubiak and Mincher. That's how much he thinks of this kid."[14]

Vic Harris, the A's first-round draft pick in 1970, had stolen 39 bases while batting .291/.392/.419 at Class A in 1971. The A's had moved him through Double A and Triple A in 1972 and he was still performing well, batting a combined .293/.355/.419 with 18 steals and 7 triples. He seemed to offer a nice package of speed and batting eye as a middle infielder.

Marty Martinez was a 30-year-old utility player who was hitting .125 for the A's at the time of the trade. His last regular playing time had been 150 at-bats with the Astros in 1970. He was the epitome of a throw-in.

Result: Steve Lawson appeared in 13 games in relief for the Rangers in 1972. While his ERA was a solid 2.81, he walked 10 batters in only 16 innings.

Despite Del Wilber's assertion that he "has all the equipment," he would struggle with control in Triple A in 1973 and was destined not to appear in another major-league game.

Vic Harris debuted for the Rangers in 1972 as well. He batted only .140 in 61 games. In 1973, he became the Rangers' starting center fielder and appeared in 152 games. He batted .249 with eight home runs, but struggled in the field and on the basepaths (he stole 13 bases against 12 times caught stealing). The Rangers traded him after the 1973 season, and although he played through 1978 he had the unusual distinction of never finishing a season with a positive WAR.

Martinez played in 26 games for the Rangers in 1972 without distinction to finish off his playing career.

Mincher served as a pinch-hitter for the A's for the balance of the 1972 season. He appeared in the A's World Series victory over the Reds, getting a hit in his only at-bat, before hanging up his spikes for good. Kubiak continued to play his utility-infielder role for the A's and Padres through 1976, but had negligible impact on his teams' fortunes.

This was yet another Rangers youth bet that did not pay off. Given the negligible cost, however, nothing was really lost or gained.

AUGUST 31, 1972

Sold Frank Howard to the Detroit Tigers.
TYPE: COST CUTTING

Frank Howard was a star for the Senators in 1971, slugging 26 home runs to lead the team and delivering a 145 OPS+ and 2.7 WAR. He fell from those lofty heights in 1972, being reduced to a .244 average with nine homers on August 30. He had still managed a 116 OPS+ in the reduced offensive environment of the time, but with his high salary was a luxury the rebuilding Rangers no longer thought necessary. He played for the Tigers through the 1973 season, but his days as a major contributor were over.

AUGUST 31, 1972

Traded Casey Cox to the New York Yankees. Received Jim Roland.

TYPE: NEAR TERM IMPROVEMENT?

Casey Cox, 30, had been with the Senators since his major-league debut in 1966. He had enjoyed several solid years with the team, but since the end of the 1969 season had toiled as a below-replacement-level spot starter and reliever. Through August 30, he was 3-5 with a 4.41 ERA in 1972.

Jim Roland had been pitching in the majors since debuting as a 19-year-old in 1962. He was still an effective reliever through the 1971 season, but his performance had fallen off noticeably in 1972. With the A's and Yankees, he had sported an ERA around 5.00 in limited innings.

Result: Neither Cox nor Roland pitched effectively for his new team in 1972. Cox threw one inning for the Yankees in 1973 and then exited the major leagues for good, while Roland never appeared in another game in the majors after 1972. This trade was completely irrelevant for both clubs.

SEPTEMBER 7, 1972

Purchased Rich Hinton from the New York Yankees.

TYPE: YOUTH MOVEMENT

Rich Hinton had the unusual distinction of being drafted five different times before finally signing with the White Sox in 1969. At the time of his purchase from the Yankees, he was 25 years old and had yet to distinguish himself in either the minors or in his brief major-league callups.

Result: Hinton got into five games for the Rangers in September 1972, but those would be the only games he played for them. The Rangers traded him to the Indians before the 1973 season. He pitched in the majors through 1979, but exceeded replacement level only in 1978. Hinton was another young pitcher lottery ticket that failed to pay out.

OVERALL SUMMARY

The Rangers made a number of transactions before and during the 1972 season, most in pursuit of young cost-controlled talent. The team placed a particular emphasis on the accumulation of pitchers with strong potential, while also adding outfielder Ted Ford and infielder Vic Harris to their youthful roster.

Unfortunately, the net effect of all that player movement was negligible. Most of the acquisitions made the strongest contributions they would make to the Rangers in the 54-win 1972 season. Rich Hand (10-14, 3.32 ERA in 1972), Mike Paul (8-9, 2.17 ERA), Don Stanhouse (2-9, 3.78 ERA), and Steve Lawson (0-0, 2.81) all either washed out or moved on without contributing any more significantly. Similarly, outfielder Ted Ford generated 2.3 WAR with 14 homers in 1972 before turning into a pumpkin while infielder Vic Harris never delivered on his potential.

On the other hand, of the players the Rangers gave up in trade, only Del Unser achieved any significant post-Texas success. Unser's 11.5 post-trade WAR was the most accumulated by a significant margin by any player included in the transactions described above.

Although the Rangers' bets on youth did not pay off, in my opinion the attempt was still worthwhile. Retaining Del Unser would not have made the team competitive in the near-term anyway. Perhaps they shouldn't have listened to Del Wilber's advice on pitching prospects, though, as none of his recommendations (Stanhouse, Lawson, Panther) panned out.

POSTSCRIPT

The Rangers 1972 talent drive was not a complete wash. In the 1972 June entry draft, the Rangers selected third baseman Roy Howell (10.9 career WAR), catcher Jim Sundberg (40.5 career WAR), and first baseman Mike Hargrove (30.3 career WAR). It would take a while, but better days were indeed on the way in Arlington.

Notes

1. Merle Heryford, "Rangers' Youth Fails to Shatter Ted's Optimism," *The Sporting News*, April 8, 1972: 11.
2. Ron Fimrite, "Bad Case of the Short Shorts," *Sports Illustrated*, August 9, 1971.
3. Ibid.

4   Ibid.
5   Merle Heryford, "Rangers' Youth."
6   Merle Heryford, "Rangers Size Up Foster as Home-Run Threat," *The Sporting News*, December 18, 1971: 47.
7   Ibid.
8   Randy Galloway, "Youth Drive? 'Bunk!' Says McClain," *The Sporting News*, March 18, 1972: 52.
9   Randy Galloway, "Rangers Prefer Their Ford over a Rolls Royce," *The Sporting News*, June 24, 1972: 20.
10 Russell Schneider, "Injuns Shudder: Where Would They Be if Not for McCraw," *The Sporting News*, June 3, 1972: 9.
11 Randy Galloway, "Rangers Prefer."
12 Russell Schneider, "Injuns Shudder."
13 Randy Galloway, "Ranger Roster a Cross-Word Puzzle," *The Sporting News*, August 12, 1972: 24.
14 Ibid.

TEXAS RANGERS 1972 SEASON SUMMARY

BY STEVE WEST

Unless otherwise noted, all headlines are from the next day's edition of the *Dallas Morning News*.

April 15. ANGELS BEDEVIL RANGERS' DEBUT, 1-0.

Delayed by two weeks because of the players strike, the Rangers finally played their first game, in California against the Angels. The game was a pitchers' duel between Dick Bosman and Andy Messersmith, remaining scoreless into the bottom of the ninth. A tiring Bosman loaded the bases on two walks and an error, and was replaced by Paul Lindblad. Lindblad's second pitch bounced in front of the plate and past the catcher, allowing Sandy Alomar to score on a walk-off wild pitch.

April 16. RANGERS, BROBERG JAIL ANGELS, 5-1.

The first five Rangers hitters reached base in the top of the first, giving Pete Broberg a three-run lead, which was more than enough. He pitched eight strong innings, giving up a run in the first but allowing only two Angels to get as far as second base the rest of the way.

April 18. RANGERS THRASHED BY WHITE SOX, 14-0.

Wilbur Wood's three-hit shutout was overshadowed by his hitters in the White Sox home opener. Bill Gogolewski and Jim Panther gave up all the runs in the first five innings, with Carlos May having four hits and six RBIs by that point.

April 19. RANGERS FALL LATE.

Once again the Rangers failed to hit, wasting a good start by Don Stanhouse, who struck out nine in 6⅔ innings in his major-league debut. In the bottom of the ninth, catcher Hal King fielded a throw to the plate and threw to second to try to get the runner there, which allowed Carlos May to score the winning run from third when Lenny Randle couldn't hold the ball, the White Sox winning 2-1.

April 21. RANGERS SOUND LAST HARRAH, 7-6.

In the first-ever major-league game played in North Texas, the Rangers broke out to a 6-1 lead and hung on to win. Frank Howard homered and Toby Harrah scored three runs, each time driven in by Lenny Randle, who had four RBIs.

April 22. FOUR-HITTER BY BROBERG BLANKS ANGELS.

Pete Broberg threw the team's first shutout and the Rangers batters bunched six extra-base hits to win comfortably, 5-0.

April 23. TEXAS CLIPS ANGEL WINGS, 5-2.

When starter Gogolewski left with a blister after just four batters, Panther lucked into his first major-league win when Don Mincher hit a three-run home run off Nolan Ryan in the bottom of the first. Horacio Pina came in and pitched six innings to finish the game, allowing just four hits to get the save.

April 24. CALIFORNIA DREAMIN'.

In a back-and-forth game, Larry Biittner's bases-loaded two-run single in the seventh put the Rangers on top for the first time, and they held on for a 6-4 win. That completed the four-game sweep of the Angels and put the Rangers in a tie for first place, the only day they would be in that position all season.

April 25. LOLICH THROWS A MICKEY.

Tigers starter Mickey Lolich gave up a run and left the bases loaded in the first, but allowed just three singles after that, throwing a complete game and beating the Rangers, 4-1.

April 26. DETROIT SHOWERS TEXAS, 8-1.

Joe Coleman gave up three hits, none after the second inning, and a five-run fifth gave the Tigers an insurmountable lead.

April 28. NEW FORD MAKES DEBUT IN TEXAS.

Ted Ford made himself a hero in his Rangers debut, hitting a three-run home run off Bob Bolin in the seventh to give the Rangers a 9-6 win over the Boston Red Sox.

April 29. RANGERS STEAL SOX OFF BOSTON.

After several lead changes, the game was tied in the middle of the ninth. Dave Nelson led off the bottom with a single, then stole second and third. The Red Sox walked the bases loaded, but Ken Suarez singled over the drawn-in outfield to complete a 7-6 win.

April 30. RANGERS SHELLED IN TENTH BY BOSOX.

Jim Shellenback and Lew Krausse matched zeroes all day, Shellenback working in and out of trouble while Krausse allowed just two hits. But it took until the top of the 10th to break the tie, when Panther gave up three doubles and the Red Sox won, 3-0.

Standings at the end of April:

	W	L	GB
Minnesota Twins	8	3	-
Oakland Athletics	7	4	1
Chicago White Sox	8	5	1
Texas Rangers	7	6	2
Kansas City Royals	6	8	3½
California Angels	5	8	4

May 2. TRIBE TRADE WINDS BLOW DOWN RANGERS.

Gaylord Perry struck out 12 batters in 7⅔ innings, and although the Rangers scored twice in the eighth it wasn't enough as Cleveland held on for a 4-2 win.

May 3. TRIBE BURIES RANGERS, 2-1, ON BOOT HILL.

Milt Wilcox threw a complete game and Pete Broberg went seven innings, while the two teams combined for five errors and none of the runs in the game were earned.

May 5. RANGERS HOLD ON, 2-1.

Gogolewski threw his best game of the season so far, keeping the Tigers hitters down into the eighth inning, and the Rangers held on for the win.

May 6. DETROIT STRIKES IT RICH IN FIRST.

The Tigers scored three in the first on a single past a shifted second baseman, and comfortably kept the lead the rest of the way to win 4-1, with the Rangers bats quiet once more.

May 7. TIGERS SLOG RANGERS, 7-4.

The Rangers managed 11 hits, all singles, against Mickey Lolich, but he spread them out to keep the score down. The Tigers took advantage in the fifth inning with five runs from three singles, three walks (two intentional), a hit by pitch, and an error.

May 9. Texas at Baltimore rained out.

May 10. ORIOLES BACK INTO 1 TO 0 WIN.

Pete Broberg gave up just a single and a walk in the first eight innings, but got into trouble in the ninth. He loaded the bases with one out, and got a grounder to third for a double play. Third baseman Dave Nelson threw home for the first out, but catcher Ken Suarez stepped on the bat as he threw to first, causing him to sail the throw, which hit the runner and bounced away, allowing Baltimore to score the winning run.

May 11. RANGERS KEEP BIRDS ON GOGO, 3-1.

Jim Palmer walked in a run and another scored on an error in the first, all that Gogolewski needed as he allowed just one run in 7⅓ innings. The Rangers bullpen then held on as the Orioles left five runners on base in the last two innings.

May 12. RANGERS PUT OUT FIRE IN WIGWAM, 3-1.

Pitching and defense were again the rule as the Rangers scratched two runs off Cleveland starter Milt Wilcox in the first two innings, and rode Dick Bosman's six innings to the win.

May 13. TRIBE SHELLS HAND.

A three-run homer by Alex Johnson was the highlight of a six-run third inning for the Indians, but even though the Rangers got three runs in the eighth, they were too far behind, losing 7-3.

May 14. RANGERS FALL IN 10TH.

Frank Howard was always a tradeoff of defense for power, and it cost the Rangers in the seventh inning when he couldn't reach a ball that allowed the tying run to score. In the 10th Chris Chambliss hit Cleveland's third solo home run of the day for the walk-off 4-3 win.

May 15. ROYALS EDGE RANGERS, 5-4.

Pete Broberg gave up four runs in four innings, but the Rangers fought back to tie, until a Cookie Rojas double in the eighth gave Kansas City the winning run.

May 16. FIVE-LEAK BOOTS MIRE RANGERS, 5-0.

Jim Rooker, making his first start of the season, threw a four-hit shutout against the hapless Rangers batters, while Rich Hand battled both the Royals and his own defense to take the loss.

May 17. RANGERS GO LATE TO WIN.

The Rangers scored in the first and last innings to win 4-3. That is, they got three runs in the first, and the winning run in the 18th inning, still the longest extra-inning game in Rangers history (through 2017). Both teams had opportunities throughout extra innings and wasted them. The Rangers eventually won without a hit, with Joe Lovitto reaching on catcher's interference, moving to third on an error, then scoring when Toby Harrah hit a ball that tipped the pitcher's glove and bounced to short, where the shortstop got a force at second but the Royals couldn't complete the double play.

May 19. MINNESOTA SPECIAL DERAILED IN TEXAS.

A pitching battle between Gogolewski and Jim Kaat ended in the Rangers' favor, with Gogo throwing a complete game to win, 2-1.

May 20. PETE EASES PAST TWINS FOR 5-1 WIN.

Pete Broberg retired 17 in a row at one point, but tired in the ninth and gave up a run before being relieved.

May 21. RANGERS MAKE TWINS SEE DOUBLE.

In the first-ever doubleheader in Arlington, the Rangers beat the Twins twice, 5-2 and 3-1, to complete their four-game sweep of the league leaders. The bullpen threw six shutout innings to win the first game, and starter Jim Shellenback gave up one run in seven innings to win the second.

May 22. RANGERS FALL, 7-6, TO CHISOX IN 10TH.

Ted Williams made a double-switch in the ninth. Did he reverse the player positions or not? Williams said he did, the umpire said he didn't, and that caused the rallying Rangers to lose an out in the bottom of the 10th on a batting out of turn. That may or may not have been decisive, but what was decisive was

May 23. RANGERS LOSE 2 TO 1 AS DARING FAILS.

All the runs scored in the first inning, but the game ended when Lenny Randle was thrown out at the plate trying to score from second base on a single to second, where the second baseman had fallen down just trying to stop the ball.

May 24. CHISOX RAKE GOGO, GRAB A SWEEPER.

The White Sox got just one hit after the first inning, a single in the eighth, but they had done all the damage already as they batted around in the first. Umpire Jim Evans was hit in the eye by a throw home from Joe Lovitto, which bounced off catcher Rich Billings' glove, and had to leave the game, which ended in a 5-1 loss for the Rangers.

May 25. TWINS SQUEEZE BY.

In a back-and-forth game, the Rangers lost 6-5 when Minnesota squeezed home the winning run in the bottom of the seventh.

May 26. TWINS BLANK RANGERS.

The Twins strolled to a 7-0 victory as Bert Blyleven threw a five-hit shutout against the Rangers.

May 27. RANGERS' EXPLOSION RIPS MINNESOTA, 16-2.

The Rangers had a season-high 16 runs on 15 hits and 7 walks, doing all the damage early. They sent 14 batters to the plate in the second and scored nine runs, and another 11 batters in the third scored six runs. The 16 runs would remain as a franchise record until they scored 19 in one game in 1986.

May 28. RANGERS REEL, 7-2.

Harmon Killebrew's grand slam in the third was the highlight, putting him just one behind Ted Williams in the all-time home-run record books.

May 29. A'S TWICE TOO POWERFUL.

The streaking A's came to Arlington and won both games of a doubleheader. They hit two home runs in each game to win, 4-1 and 7-1.

May 30. RANGERS WIN.

In the seventh Ken Suarez singled, then Dave Nelson pinch-ran, went to second on a sacrifice, stole third, and scored on a sacrifice fly to defeat the Athletics, 3-2, behind Rich Hand's 8⅔ innings for his first win of the season.

May 31. TEXAS CAN'T HOOK CATFISH.

The Rangers put 15 men on base during the game, but the A's Catfish Hunter worked around all that trouble to win the complete game, 5-1.

Standings at the end of May:

	W	L	GB
Oakland Athletics	25	12	-
Minnesota Twins	23	12	1
Chicago White Sox	22	16	3½
California Angels	18	23	9
Texas Rangers	17	24	10
Kansas City Royals	13	24	12

June 2. BREWERS TOPPLE RANGERS.

Multiple rain delays, totaling 2:47, slowed the game to a crawl. A 2:24 delay in the first removed Gogolewski, who had already given up four runs. Milwaukee led 7-0 after five, and while the Rangers rallied to score five in the top of the sixth and make it 7-5, that was all the scoring.

June 3. RANGERS FALL AGAIN TO MILWAUKEE, 3-1.

Rangers bats were silent again as Bill Parsons scattered five hits for his complete-game victory.

June 4. RANGERS WAKE UP, RIP BREWERS 10-0.

A six-run first inning was more than the Rangers needed, as three pitchers combined for a six-hit shutout.

June 6. RANGERS RIP YANKS.

Another day with everything working, as the hitters got 14 hits and the pitchers gave up just four on the way to a 6-3 victory, Frank Howard's first home run since April 29 being the highlight.

June 7. YANKEES DOWN RANGERS, 7-5.

Defense let the Rangers down with four errors overall, but six straight singles contributed to a six-run third inning for the Yankees. The Rangers came back, but Sparky Lyle had 3⅔ innings of one-hit ball to get the save.

June 8. TEXAS NABS SERIES.

Rich Billings homered in the first, and Pete Broberg and Paul Lindblad combined to allow just five hits as the Rangers beat the Yankees, 6-2.

June 9. ORIOLES FIND THEY LIKE IT HERE.

The Orioles got ahead early and stayed there, winning 7-2, with the highlight for the Rangers being another Frank Howard home run.

June 10. ORIOLES SLAM RANGERS.

Dave McNally held the Rangers down while Brooks Robinson homered to lead the Orioles to a 5-2 victory. Joe Lovitto's first major-league home run wasn't enough to get the Rangers back into the game.

June 11. O'S RALLY TO NIP RANGERS.

If the 53-minute rain delay in the sixth had lasted longer, the Rangers would have won 1-0, but when the rain stopped, the Orioles started scoring, ending up 3-1 winners behind a complete game by Jim Palmer.

June 12. RANGERS FIND POWER ALLEYS.

Another night of rain delays, this time the Rangers were not interrupted as they beat Milwaukee 7-1, with Don Mincher and Dalton Jones both homering.

June 13. BROBERG FIRES BLANKS, 4-0.

Pete Broberg received his college degree from Dartmouth three days earlier, and celebrated by throwing a three-hit shutout and hitting a two-run double against the Brewers.

June 14. RANGERS GET HELPING HAND.

The Rangers had a six-run fourth inning, and Rich Hand threw seven innings in the 7-1 win over Milwaukee.

June 15. NEW ASTROS. Exhibition.

The Rangers headed to Houston for the first "Texas Major League championship game," an exhibition they lost 2-1.

June 16. Rangers at Yankees rained out.

June 17. RANGERS LOSE TWO.

Steve Klein threw a five-hitter to win the first game, 2-0, and Mel Stottlemyre pitched into the eighth inning in the second, winning 3-1. Sparky Lyle struck out the side with the bases loaded to preserve the second win.

June 18. Rangers at Yankees rained out.

June 19. RED SOX SHELL BROBERG.

The Red Sox hit four home runs and Sonny Siebert threw a three-hit shutout as the Sox beat the Rangers, 12-0.

June 20. JONES' BLAST KEYS WIN.

Dalton Jones homered against his former team, leading the Rangers to a 5-2 win over the Red Sox.

June 21. BOSOX GET BIG ASSIST IN 10-9 WIN.

Three errors helped the Rangers throw away a six-run lead, then another two-run lead, before losing in the 11th inning.

June 23. RANGERS HALT WOOD, CHISOX.

Ted Ford and Frank Howard homered, and four pitchers combined to hold the White Sox in a 4-3 win.

June 24. IT'S BILLINGS AGAIN! RANGERS RIP CHISOX.

Pete Broberg struck out 11 in 7⅓ innings, but wasn't around for the win as the Rangers scored five in the eighth to win, 6-1.

June 25. CHISOX HOT ITEM FOR RANGERS.

With a 104-degree game-time temperature, the White Sox struck early, scoring seven runs in the fourth, including a Carlos May grand slam, to lead 9-0. The Rangers came back, but it was too little too late as they lost, 10-5.

June 26. 10C BEER, NICKEL BATS.

10-cent beer night probably helped drown some sorrows, as the Rangers went quietly in a 3-0 loss to Oakland.

June 27. A'S HOMER PAST TEXAS IN 9-3 WIN.

Rollie Fingers threw four innings in relief and hit his second career home run as the A's eased past Texas.

June 28. FARM YIELDS SLOW CROP.

Exhibition. The Rangers went to Denver for their annual exhibition game against their Triple-A team, the Bears, and were pounded 11-4.

June 29. ANGELS FIND GOLD.

A six-run third inning was the highlight for the California Angels as they rolled to a 12-4 win.

June 30. NO PLACE LIKE HOMERS.

The five through nine hitters combined for 10 hits for the Rangers, with Larry Biittner's first career home run the highlight of a 7-3 win over the Angels.

Standings at the end of June:

	W	L	GB
Oakland Athletics	42	23	-
Chicago White Sox	39	27	4
Minnesota Twins	35	29	7
Kansas City Royals	31	33	11
California Angels	31	37	13
Texas Rangers	27	38	15½

July 1. RANGER STICKS SILENT AGAIN; KC WINS IN 11TH.

The Rangers got 10 hits, but did little when it counted, and although they tied the game in the ninth, the Royals won 3-2 in the bottom of the 11th.

July 2. RANGERS SPLIT WITH ROYALS.

The Rangers had 15 hits in the first game of the doubleheader, winning 7-5, but Kansas City got to Pete Broberg early in the second game, winning 8-3 for the split.

July 3. RIGHT COMBINATION WORKS.

The Rangers were outhit 11-7 by the Royals, but the pitchers worked their way out of trouble all night, hanging on for the 2-1 win.

July 4. ONE PITCH TOO LATE.

A game dominated by pitching was lost by one mistake, when John Lowenstein homered off Rich Hand to win the game for Cleveland, 2-0.

July 5. Rangers at Indians rained out.

July 6. TEXAS FALLS.

Cleveland won both games of the doubleheader caused by the rainout, 4-2 and 6-5.

July 7. RANGERS TAP ORIOLES, 5-4.

The Rangers blew an early 4-0 lead before Jim Panther threw five shutout innings in relief to carry the team to victory.

July 8. RANGERS GIVE BIRDS BATH TWICE.

The Rangers swept the Orioles in a doubleheader, 2-1 and 3-1. In the first game Rich Hand beat Pat Dobson in a battle of complete games. In the nightcap Lenny Randle's three-run homer in the eighth was all the Rangers needed.

July 9. RANGERS 'KIDS' SWEEP ORIOLES.

The Rangers completed a four-game sweep of the Orioles, winning 3-2 largely thanks to Joe Lovitto's RBI triple in the eighth and RBI double in the 11th.

July 10. TIGERS RIP TEXAS, 8-3.

Joe Lovitto starred again with four hits, but Don Stanhouse had given up seven runs in five innings to put the game out of reach.

July 11. TIGERS WIN A SLUGFEST.

The Rangers blew a 4-1 lead, and both sides combined for 24 hits, but the Rangers couldn't get them when they counted and lost, 6-5.

July 12. TIGERS CLIP RANGERS, 3-1.

Rookie Bill Slayback gave up eight hits, but again the Rangers couldn't bunch enough of them to make a difference in the game.

July 13. RICH GETS A HAND.

Four runs in the first were all Rich Hand needed, as he threw a shutout in the 5-0 win.

July 14. ERRORS HELP INDIANS WIN.

Scoreless for 13 innings – Indians starter Gaylord Perry throwing all of them – it took back-to-back errors by the Rangers to give the 2-0 win to Cleveland.

July 15. RANGERS FALL, 7-0.

Another rookie did the job for Cleveland, this time Dick Tidrow throwing a shutout while the offense scored six in the second to make it easy.

July 16. RANGERS WIN IN 12TH, 3-2.

Fielding helped the Rangers get to extra innings against the Indians, and they won playing small ball. Randle singled, was bunted to second, went to third on a wild pitch, and scored the winning run on Dave Nelson's single.

July 17. FLUBS FELL TEXAS.

Just as the fielders won the game before, they lost this game. The Orioles beat the Rangers, 3-1, their three runs each scoring thanks to a mistake – a fly ball lost in the sun, a throwing error, and a passed ball.

July 18. ROBBY FELLS TEXAS IN 15.

Dave McNally gave up one run in nine innings for the Orioles, and Rich Hand gave up one run in 10 innings for the Rangers, but neither got the decision as it took until the 15th for Brooks Robinson to single home the winning run in the 2-1 Rangers loss.

July 19. RANGERS WIN.

Two Orioles mistakes in the eighth – an error at second and a missed double play – gave the Rangers the tying and winning runs in their 3-2 win.

July 20. TIGERS CUFF TEXAS, 5-1.

For the second time in eight days Bill Slayback dominated the Rangers, striking out 13 as he threw a complete game.

July 21. TIGERS CROWD TEXAS.

Mickey Lolich won his 17th game and had his 17th complete game of the season, comfortably handling the Rangers, 3-1.

July 22. TIGERS TRIP RANGERS, 6-2.

A third straight complete game for Tigers pitchers against the Rangers; this time former Senator Joe Coleman shut them down with little difficulty.

July 23. BUM'S RUSH FOR TIMMY.

Tom Timmermann couldn't follow his Tiger rotation mates, giving up three runs in just two-thirds of an inning, and while three other Tigers pitchers didn't allow a run, Rich Hand and Horacio Pina combined to give up just one run for the 3-1 Rangers win.

July 25. ALL-STAR GAME.

No Rangers players were at the All-Star Game in Atlanta, after the team's only selection, shortstop Toby Harrah, had been injured a few weeks earlier. The team's sole representative was therefore bullpen coach George Susce.

July 27. RYAN BLANKS TEXAS.

The Rangers started slowly out of the All-Star break, with Nolan Ryan throwing a no-hitter for 7⅔ innings, before settling for a two-hitter with 14 strikeouts, and winning 5-0.

July 28. ANGELS LEAD RANGERS.

The Rangers came back from 2-0 to tie the score in the top of the ninth, but a double play with the bases loaded cost them dearly when Leo Cardenas doubled home the winning run in the bottom of the ninth, the Angels winning, 3-2.

July 29. ANGELS AGAIN TOO MUCH FOR RANGERS, 8-1.

The Rangers took a 1-0 lead in the third, but it was all Angels after that, helped by poor pitching and fielding from the Rangers.

July 30. RANGERS WIN!

Dave Nelson got four hits, and four steals, and drove in two game-winning runs as the Rangers swept a doubleheader in Oakland, 2-1 and 4-2.

July 31. BLUE GETS UPPER HAND IN 2-0 TILT.

Vida Blue gave up two hits, Rich Hand and two relievers gave up two hits, but it was fielding mistakes that cost the Rangers both runs in the loss to Oakland.

Standing at the end of July:

	W	L	GB
Oakland Athletics	59	38	-
Chicago White Sox	53	43	5½
Minnesota Twins	47	45	9½
Kansas City Royals	46	49	12
California Angels	44	53	15
Texas Rangers	39	57	19½

August 1. TEXAS CORNERS ZERO MARKET.

Dick Woodson threw a three-hit shutout as the Twins beat the Rangers, 3-0. Pete Broberg pitched decently but failed to get the win for the 10th consecutive start.

August 2. RANGERS CLIP TWINS, 4-1.

A throwing error by Twins starter Ray Corbin led to three unearned runs, all the difference in the game.

August 3. PERRY STOPS RANGERS, 9-1.

Jim Perry didn't give up a hit until the sixth inning, or a run until the ninth, and by then the Twins were far out of sight.

August 4. RANGERS LOSE IN 9TH, 3-2.

Dick Allen lined a double off the wall in the bottom of the ninth, driving in the winning run for the Chicago White Sox.

August 5. RANGERS GO WILD.

The Rangers scored their second highest run total of the season so far, beating the White Sox, 11-5, paced by Ted Ford's five RBIs.

August 6. RANGERS LOSE TWIN BILL.

The Rangers slumped to a doubleheader loss against the White Sox, 10-1 and 7-1.

August 7. TWINS PREVAIL ON 5-0 COUNT.

Confusion over an infield fly cost the Rangers a double play, but that was just one of the lowlights as they failed once again.

August 8. TEXAS FALLS AGAIN.

Ted Ford homered off Bert Blyleven to tie the game with two out in the top of the ninth, but the Twins loaded the bases and scored on a two-out single by Danny Monzon in the bottom of the 10th to win 6-5.

August 9. RANGERS END SKID.

Don Stanhouse gave up just five hits in his complete game, while the Twins committed five errors, making all the Rangers runs unearned in the 3-2 win.

August 11. EX-RANGER, YOUNG ROGER WIN FOR KC, 2-0.

Pitching dominated, with the Rangers getting just three hits off Royals pitcher Roger Nelson, and the Royals four hits off Rich Hand and Horacio Pina, but two of the Royals hits were solo home runs for the win.

August 12. HOWARD BLASTS RANGERS TO 3-0 WIN.

Rain ended the game with two out in the bottom of the seventh, but Mike Paul had allowed the Royals just two hits to get the win, while Frank Howard hit his first home run since July 18.

August 13. RANGERS ERUPT, 13-4.

Despite hitting into a triple play, the Rangers knocked 17 hits on their way to a comfortable win over the Royals.

August 14. Rangers at Texas League All-Stars, Alexandria, Louisiana (Exhibition).

The Rangers beat the Texas League All-Stars, 4-3, but the big news was shortstop Toby Harrah's appendectomy, which put him out of action for several weeks.

August 15. REGGIE, BOSOX TOO MUCH.

Reggie Smith hit two home runs and John Curtis threw a three-hit shutout as the Red Sox beat the Rangers, 3-0.

August 16. RANGERS GIVE BOSOX GRIEVE.

In a back-and-forth game that included a Reggie Smith grand slam, Tom Grieve homered in the bottom of the 10th for the 9-8 Rangers win.

August 17. SMITH, BOSOX NIP RANGERS.

Reggie Smith's three-run homer in the eighth – his fourth in three games in Arlington – was the difference as the Red Sox came from 3-1 down to win, 4-3.

August 18. RANGERS SPANK YANKS, 11-2.

A seven-run fourth inning was the big blow for the Rangers as they comfortably beat the Yankees.

August 19. YANKS STOP TEXAS.

The big inning went to the Yankees this time, scoring four early on their way to a 6-2 win.

August 20. THROW-AWAY FOR TEXAS.

Frank Howard's bad throw home allowed the Yankees to score the first run in the top of the 10th, and they added another to win, 2-0.

August 22. RICH BACKHANDS BREWERS.

Rich Hand took a one-hitter into the ninth but had to turn it over to the bullpen, with Casey Cox coming on to save the 2-1 win.

August 23. Rangers at Brewers rained out.

August 24. RANGERS DIVIDE TWIN BILL.

The Rangers and Brewers split a doubleheader, with the Rangers winning the first game, 4-1, and the Brewers the second, 4-3.

August 25. TIANT BLANKS RANGERS.

Luis Tiant threw a four-hit shutout as the Red Sox won, 4-0.

August 26. BOSTON RALLY STOPS TEXAS.

The Rangers wasted a good start by Bill Gogolewski, who allowed two runs in seven innings. Their 6-2 lead going into the bottom of the ninth turned in a 7-6 loss as the bullpen fell apart.

August 27. BOSOX BLITZ RANGERS, 10-3.

The Red Sox scored three in the first and never looked back after that, Rico Petrocelli and Carlton Fisk homering on the way to a comfortable win.

August 29. RANGERS WIN NIGHTCAP TO EARN SPLIT.

In the first game the Rangers blew a couple of leads before finally losing 7-6 in the 11th inning, the Yankees' Bobby Murcer hitting for the cycle. Ted Ford homered in each game, with his homer in the second game giving the Rangers the lead for good as they won, 7-4.

August 30. RANGERS LOSE, 3-1.

Johnny Callison saved the day for the Yankees, reaching into the crowd to pull back a Tom Grieve shot that would have tied the game in the eighth inning.

August 31. YANKEE POWER TOO MUCH, 7-0.

Home runs off Rich Hand in the first and second innings pushed the Yankees ahead to stay. Casey Cox, traded to the Yankees before the game but not joining them until after, pitched for the Rangers and gave up two runs in three innings.

Standings at the end of August:

	W	L	GB
Oakland Athletics	73	51	-
Chicago White Sox	71	52	1½
Minnesota Twins	61	60	10½
Kansas City Royals	60	63	12½
California Angels	57	67	16
Texas Rangers	49	79	24½

September 1. ANOTHER ZERO FOR RANGERS.

The Rangers were shut out for the second day in a row, Brewers pitcher Jim Colburn throwing a three-hitter to win 3-0.

September 2. RANGERS LOSE, 6-2.

Pete Broberg took his eighth straight loss, giving up five runs in five innings.

September 3. TEXAS' HOT TIME.

Mike Paul's complete game led the Rangers over Milwaukee, 4-1.

September 4. RANGERS' RALLY FALLS SHORT.

The Rangers tried to come back, scoring three runs in the last three innings, but it wasn't enough as the Royals held on to win, 4-3.

September 5. ROYALS TAP RANGERS AGAIN, 7-2.

Only 3,011 fans, the smallest crowd of the season so far, showed up to see the Rangers scuffle their way to another loss.

September 6. GOOSE EGGED AGAIN.

The Twins' Dick Woodson threw a two-hit shutout to comfortably handle the Rangers, 2-0.

September 7. MORE HITS, NO RUNS.

The Rangers doubled their hit total from the day before, to four, but still couldn't get anything as the Twins won, 4-0.

September 8. EPSTEIN'S 3-RUN HOMER TAGS RANGERS, 6-3.

The Rangers managed to score runs, but pitching didn't help as the Athletics were easy winners.

September 9. RANGERS CLIP OAKLAND, 3-2.

Lightning knocked out half the lights, and rain caused delays, but the Rangers scored three runs in the first two innings and held on for the win.

September 10. TED LETS A'S GET OUT OF HAND.

Rich Hand gave up one run in seven innings, but the bullpen allowed six unearned runs in the eighth as the A's won 7-2.

September 12. GOGO'S 1-HITTER DEFEATS ANGELS.

In a game in which Nolan Ryan struck out 15, the headlines were stolen by Bill Gogolewski, who was perfect into the seventh inning and gave up the only hit in the eighth, as the Rangers won, 3-0.

September 13. RANGERS FALTER IN STRETCH, 6-5.

The Angels squeezed home two runs, making the difference in a tightly contested game that could have gone either way.

September 14. WRIGHT 2-HITS TEXAS.

Clyde Wright had two hits and two RBIs at the plate, and threw a two-hit shutout as the Angels comfortably beat the Rangers, 4-0.

September 15. ALOU LEADS A'S TO 12-3 VICTORY

(*Springfield* [Illinois] *State Journal-Register*). A late game on the West Coast. Ken Holtzman had a three-hit shutout going until the ninth, when he allowed four hits and three runs, but that did little to the final score.

September 16. BLUE BLANKS RANGERS ON TWO HITS AGAIN.

Vida Blue threw his second two-hit shutout of the season against the Rangers, the A's winning, 4-0, this time.

September 17. TEXAS HOOKED.

Catfish Hunter won his 20th game of the season, allowing a single to the first batter, then retiring 20 straight batters, finishing with a two-hitter in the 4-1 Oakland win.

September 19. RANGERS FALL.

With two out in the ninth, Cesar Tovar homered to complete his cycle and the Twins' 5-3 win.

September 20. MINNESOTA OVERCOMES TEXAS, 3-1.

The Rangers only had three hits, but improbably led 1-0 until the bottom of the eighth when things fell apart and the Twins scored all their runs.

September 22. RANGERS MAKE IT EIGHT.

Carlos May got things started with a bases-loaded triple, and Stan Bahnsen battled to his 20th win, the White Sox beating the Rangers 8-4.

September 23. RANGERS DROP NO. 9.

Each team managed 10 hits, but the White Sox won 4-3 as the Rangers losing streak continued.

September 24. ALLEN's HOMER RAPS TEXAS, 7-4.

Once again the Rangers were tied in the bottom of the eighth, and once again their bullpen gave up three runs to lose to the White Sox, as reports swirled that Ted Williams would not return as manager in 1973.

September 25. TEXAS FALLS AGAIN.

Nolan Ryan struck out 12, becoming the eighth pitcher in history to have 300 strikeouts in a single season. Dick Bosman battled him all the way, but each side had an unearned run as the Angels beat the Rangers 2-1.

September 26. RANGERS MAKE IT AN EVEN DOZEN.

Another pitching duel, broken up by an hourlong rain delay, ended with the Rangers losing once more. Andy Messersmith's three-hitter beat the nine hits Mike Paul scattered in eight innings, as the Angels again won 2-1.

September 27. TEXAS STREAKS TO 13TH.

Yet again it was pitching that dominated, the Rangers losing their 13th straight as Clyde Wright's six-hitter beat Don Stanhouse's five, the Angels winning, 3-1.

September 29. RANGERS OUTGUNNED.

The White Sox rested a bunch of regulars and still beat the Rangers, 5-1.

September 30. …LOSING CONTINUES.

Headline writers gave up as the Rangers lost their 15th straight game. Gogolewski gave up two hits through six innings, but then fell apart in the seventh as the White Sox scored all their runs in a 5-3 win.

October 1. SURPRISE! SURPRISE! RANGERS WIN, 1-0.

The official announcement that Ted Williams would not return as manager in 1973 was no surprise. The surprise was Dick Bosman throwing a three-hitter to beat Wilbur Wood's own three-hitter, Bosman's 13 strikeouts defeating the White Sox and ending the losing streak.

October 3. RANGERS BLANK KANSAS CITY, 3-0.

Mike Paul and Bill Gogolewski combined to blank the Royals, the first time all season that the Rangers had back-to-back shutouts.

October 4. RANGERS FALL TO LOSE 100.

The Rangers lost 4-0 to the Royals to lose their 100th game of the season, in the final game played at Kansas City's Municipal Stadium. Dave Nelson stole three bases to briefly give himself the AL lead, but he lost the race when Bert Campaneris stole two later in the day to win the title, 52-51.

Final Standings:

	W	L	GB
Oakland Athletics	93	62	-
Chicago White Sox	87	67	5½
Minnesota Twins	77	77	15½
Kansas City Royals	76	78	16½
California Angels	75	80	18
Texas Rangers	54	100	38½

BY THE NUMBERS

BY DAN FIELDS

TEXAS RANGERS IN 1972

0
Active players from the Rangers on the AL squad at the 1972 All-Star Game. Shortstop Toby Harrah was selected as a reserve but was replaced because of injury.

0.2
Home runs per nine innings pitched by Mike Paul, best in the majors.

1
Hit allowed in a shutout by Bill Gogolewski on September 12 against the California Angels.

1.361
Walks and hits per nine innings pitched by the 1972 Rangers, highest in the AL.

2.17
ERA of Mike Paul, sixth-lowest in the AL.

3
Doubles by Larry Biittner on August 13.

3
Stolen bases by Toby Harrah on June 20 and Dave Nelson on October 4.

3.53
ERA of the 1972 Rangers, highest in the AL.

4
Runs scored by Elliott Maddox on May 22 (10-inning game) and Dave Nelson on August 5.

5
RBIs by Toby Harrah on May 27, Ted Ford on August 5, and Dick Billings on August 13.

6.8
Strikeouts per nine innings pitched by Pete Broberg, eighth in the AL.

10
Assists as a right fielder by Ted Ford, most in the AL.

11
Complete games by Texas pitchers, the fewest in the majors.

13
Batters hit by Pete Broberg, most in the majors. He hit three batters on June 24. Broberg also had 14 wild pitches, second in the AL.

13
Double plays as catcher by Dick Billings, most in the majors.

15
Consecutive losses by the Rangers from September 13 to September 30. For the month, the team went 3-23 (.115) and was outscored 116-53.

15
Saves by Horacio Pina, sixth in the AL.

27
Times that the 1972 Rangers were shut out. They shut out their opponents eight times.

51
Stolen bases by Dave Nelson, second in the AL. He was caught stealing 17 times, most in the league.

54-100

Record of the 1972 Rangers. Their .351 winning percentage was the lowest in the majors.

56

Home runs by the 1972 Rangers, fewest in the majors. The only player in double digits was Ted Ford, with 14.

66

Games played by reliever Paul Lindblad, most in the majors. Horacio Pina (60 games) and Jim Panther (58 games) were in the top 10 in the AL.

103

Walks allowed by Rich Hand, third in the AL. Pete Broberg (85 walks) was tied for sixth.

126

Stolen bases by the 1972 Rangers, most in the AL. The team led the majors with 73 runners caught stealing.

.217

Batting average of the 1972 Rangers, lowest in the majors. Larry Biittner and Toby Harrah led the team with a .259 average.

.290 / .290 / .581

On-base percentage, slugging average, and OPS of the 1972 Rangers. The on-base percentage was the lowest in the AL, and the slugging average and OPS were lowest in the major leagues.

461

Runs scored by the 1972 Rangers, the second fewest in the majors.

.972

Fielding percentage of the 1972 Rangers, lowest in the majors.

662,974

Attendance at Arlington Stadium in 1972, an average of 8,160 per game. The Rangers were 20th out of 24 major-league teams.

AROUND THE MAJORS IN 1972

0.871

WHIP of Roger Nelson of the Kansas City Royals, lowest in the majors. Don Sutton of the Los Angeles Dodgers had the lowest in the NL (0.913).

1ST

Pitch faced in the majors, on which Don Rose of the California Angels hit a home run off Diego Segui of the Oakland Athletics on May 24. Rose, the starting pitcher, also got the only win of his major-league career.

1ST

Career save by Rich Gossage of the Chicago White Sox, on June 7 against the Boston Red Sox. He retired in 1994 with 310 saves.

1ST

All-Star Game to be played in Atlanta, on July 25. The Braves had previously hosted the midsummer classic while playing in Boston (1936) and in Milwaukee (1955). In the 1972 game, Hank Aaron thrilled the hometown crowd with a two-run homer off Gaylord Perry in the sixth inning. The NL won 4-3 in 10 innings. Joe Morgan, who singled to drive in the winning run, was selected as the game's MVP.

1ST

Career home run by Mike Schmidt of the Philadelphia Phillies, on September 16 off Balor Moore of the Montreal Expos. Schmidt hit his 548th and final home run on May 2, 1989, off Jim Deshaies of the Houston Astros.

1ST

Player on a last-place team to win the pitching Triple Crown or the Cy Young Award: Steve Carlton of the Phillies. He led the majors in wins (27, accounting for 45.8 percent of the team's 59 wins) and had the lowest ERA (1.97) and most strikeouts (310) in the NL. Carlton also led the majors in complete games (30) and led the NL in games started (41), innings pitched (346⅓), and ratio of strikeouts to walks (3.56). He won 15 consecutive games from June 7 through August 17.

1ST

Player to win the AL Rookie of the Year Award by a unanimous vote: Carlton Fisk of the Red Sox. He was tied with Joe Rudi of the Athletics for most triples in the league (with 9), was second in slugging average (.538) and OPS (.909), was fourth in extra-base hits (59), and finished in the top 10 in doubles (28), home runs (22), batting average (.293), on-base percentage (.370), and total bases (246). He also won a Gold Glove Award as catcher.

1.91

ERA of Luis Tiant of the Red Sox, lowest in the majors.

2.32

ERA of NL Rookie of the Year Jon Matlack of the New York Mets, fourth lowest in the league. He had a 15-10 record, 169 strikeouts, and four shutouts.

2ND

NL MVP Award won by Johnny Bench of the Cincinnati Reds, who was only 24 years old during the 1972 season. He led the majors in home runs (40), RBIs (125), and intentional bases on balls (23) and won his fifth consecutive NL Gold Glove Award as catcher. Bench homered in five consecutive games (including two multi-homer games) from May 30 through June 3.

3

Consecutive games won by the Detroit Tigers on 11th-inning home runs, on August 26 and 27 (both games of a doubleheader) on the road against the Minnesota Twins.

3

No-hitters thrown in 1972, by Burt Hooton of the Chicago Cubs (in his fourth career game) on April 16 against the Phillies, Milt Pappas of the Cubs on September 2 against the San Diego Padres, and Bill Stoneman of the Expos on October 2 (first game of doubleheader) against the Mets. Pappas retired the first 26 batters before walking pinch-hitter Larry Stahl. Hooton and Stoneman each gave up seven walks.

4

Players who hit for the cycle in 1972: Dave Kingman of the San Francisco Giants on April 16, Cesar Cedeno of the Astros on August 2, Bobby Murcer of the New York Yankees on August 29 (first game of doubleheader; 11-inning game), and Cesar Tovar of the Twins on September 19.

4

Home runs in the 1972 World Series by catcher Gene Tenace of the Athletics. He homered in his first two at-bats in Game One, both off Gary Nolan of the Reds. After the A's topped the Reds in seven games, Tenace was named the Series MVP. During the regular season, he hit five home runs in 82 games.

5 AND 13

Home runs and RBIs, respectively, by Nate Colbert of Padres in a doubleheader on August 1 against the Braves. In six consecutive games from July 30 (second game of doubleheader) through August 3, he had 8 home runs and 19 RBIs.

5.26

Hits allowed per nine innings by Nolan Ryan of the Angels, the lowest in a single season in major-league history (through 2015).

6

RBIs by Rico Petrocelli of the Red Sox on June 21 (11-inning game) and again on August 5.

6

Home runs by the Phillies on October 3 against the Cubs. Bill Robinson homered in the second inning, Don Money and Greg Luzinski hit back-to-back homers in the third and fifth innings, and Terry Harmon homered in the eighth inning. The Phillies won 11-1.

6TH

Consecutive season with at least 20 wins by Fergie Jenkins, all with the Cubs.

8

Runs scored by the Yankees in the 13th inning against the White Sox on June 3. Bobby Murcer scored twice during the inning and had five runs for the game. The Yankees won, 18-10.

8

Consecutive batters struck out by Nolan Ryan in the first, second (nine pitches), and third innings on July 9 against the Red Sox. He struck out a total of 16 batters during the game.

9

Shutouts by Nolan Ryan and Don Sutton, tied for most in the majors.

11

Walks allowed by Jimmy Freeman of the Braves in a complete-game win on September 1 (second game of doubleheader) against the Phillies. He gave up eight hits and five runs, but the Braves scored 11.

12

Consecutive home losses by the Padres from May 22 through June 10.

12

Runs allowed (only four earned) by Bill Singer of the Dodgers in 3⅔ innings on July 30 (first game of doubleheader) against the Braves.

12TH

Consecutive Gold Glove Award as outfielder by Roberto Clemente of the Pittsburgh Pirates, to match the mark set by Willie Mays.

13

Innings pitched by Clay Kirby of the Padres on June 7 (second game of doubleheader), Gaylord Perry of the Cleveland Indians on July 14, and Don Wilson of the Astros on September 7.

13

Runs scored by the Braves in the second inning on September 20 against the Astros. During the frame, Dusty Baker doubled, hit a three-run home run, and grounded out against three different pitchers. The Braves won 13-6.

13

Triples by Larry Bowa of the Phillies, most in the majors.

14

Wins in relief by Mike Marshall of the Expos, against eight losses.

14TH

Career grand slam by Willie McCovey of the Giants, on July 2 off Don Sutton, to tie Hank Aaron and Gil Hodges for the NL record.

15

Years since Willie Mays had played for a New York team. On May 11 the 41-year-old Mays was traded from the Giants to the Mets. In his debut with the team on May 14, he hit a solo home run off Don Carrithers of the Giants. Mays was with the New York Giants from 1951 through 1957.

17

Seasons together with the Pirates by Roberto Clemente and Bill Mazeroski, from 1956 through 1972.

20TH

Season with the Tigers by Al Kaline, who hit .313 in 106 games.

21

Losses by Steve Arlin of the Padres, most in the majors. On July 18 he was one strike away from a no-hitter against the Phillies when Denny Doyle singled. Pat Dobson of the Baltimore Orioles and Mel Stottlemyre of the Yankees tied for most in the AL with 18.

22 AND 55

Home runs and stolen bases, respectively, by Cesar Cedeno. He became the second player (after Lou Brock in 1967) with at least 20 home runs and 50 stolen bases in a season.

22.75

Percentage of San Diego's runs that Nate Colbert drove in (111 of 488).

24

Wins by Gaylord Perry of the Indians and Wilbur Wood of the White Sox, tied for most in the AL. Perry (1.92 ERA, 234 strikeouts) edged Wood (2.51 ERA, 193 strikeouts) for the AL Cy Young Award.

25

Double plays grounded into by Lou Piniella of the Royals, most in the majors. Marty Perez of the Braves led the NL with 21.

26

Hits by the Yankees in a 16-inning game on August 27 (second game of doubleheader) against the Royals. Bobby Murcer and Celerino Sanchez had four hits each. The Yankees won 9-8.

29

Complete games by Gaylord Perry, most in the AL.

34

Baserunners allowed in eight innings by the Mets in an 18-5 loss to the Cubs on September 16. Five pitchers yielded 17 hits and 15 walks and threw two wild pitches. Starter Tom Seaver faced 18 batters, 12 of whom got on base.

37

Innings in two consecutive games between the Milwaukee Brewers and the Twins. In a game begun on May 12, suspended by curfew after 21 innings, and resumed on the 13th, the Brewers won 4-3 in 22 innings; the Twins didn't score after the fifth inning. In the regularly scheduled game on May 13, the Twins won 5-4 in 15 innings. Rod Carew of the Twins had eight hits and four walks during the two games.

37

Saves by Clay Carroll of the Reds, a major-league single-season record at the time. Sparky Lyle of the Yankees led the AL with 35 saves, a new league record.

37 AND 113

Home runs and RBIs, respectively, by AL MVP Dick Allen of the White Sox – both tops in the league. He made a run at the Triple Crown, finishing third in batting average (.308). Allen led the majors in on-base percentage (.420), led the AL in slugging average (.603), and led the majors in OPS (1.023). He was tied with Bobby Murcer for most extra-base hits in the AL (70) and tied with Roy White of the Yankees for most walks (99). Allen hit two inside-the-park home runs on July 31, becoming the first player since 1950 to accomplish this feat in one game.

39

Doubles by Cesar Cedeno of the Astros and Willie Montanez of the Phillies, tied for most in the majors. Lou Piniella led the AL with 33 doubles.

40⅓

Consecutive innings without allowing a run by Luis Tiant, from August 19 to September 8.

41

Consecutive batters retired by Jim Barr of the Giants on August 23 (last 21 Pittsburgh batters) and August 29 (first 20 St. Louis batters), a record for two consecutive starts.

49

Games started by Wilbur Wood, most in the majors since 1908.

63

Bases stolen by Lou Brock of the Cardinals, most in the majors. Bert Campaneris of the Athletics led the AL with 52.

65

Games played by Clay Carroll and Mike Marshall, tied for the most by an NL pitcher.

77

Extra-base hits by Billy Williams of the Cubs, most in the majors.

86

Total games canceled at the beginning of the 1972 season (April 1 to 13) owing to the first general strike by the Major League Baseball Players Association.

115

Walks drawn by Joe Morgan of the Reds, most in the majors.

122

Runs scored by Joe Morgan, most in the majors. Bobby Murcer led the AL with 102.

145

Strikeouts by Bobby Darwin of the Twins and Lee May of the Astros, tied for the most by a major-league batter.

157

Walks allowed by Nolan Ryan, most in the majors. Steve Arlin led NL hurlers with 122 walks.

198

Hits by Pete Rose of the Reds, most in the majors. Joe Rudi led the AL with 181 hits.

228TH

And final career save by Hoyt Wilhelm of the Dodgers, on April 17 against the Braves. He held the career record for saves until 1980. When Wilhelm played his final game, on July 10, he was about two weeks shy of his 50th birthday.

329

Strikeouts by Nolan Ryan, most in the majors. It was the first of six seasons during his career that Ryan had at least 300 strikeouts.

.333

Batting average of Billy Williams, highest in the majors. Rod Carew led the AL with a .318 average; he was the first batting champion in the junior circuit to hit no home runs.

348

Total bases by Billy Williams, most in the majors. Bobby Murcer led the AL with 314.

376⅔

Innings pitched by Wilbur Wood, most in the majors in 1972 and most in the AL since 1912.

.417

On-base percentage of Joe Morgan, highest in the NL.

.606

Slugging average of Billy Williams, highest in the majors.

645

At-bats by Pete Rose, most in the majors. Bert Campaneris led the AL with 625.

731

Plate appearances by Pete Rose, most in the majors. Bert Campaneris led the AL with 681.

.750

Winning percentage of Catfish Hunter of the Athletics (21-7) and Gary Nolan (15-5), tied for highest in the majors.

1.005

OPS of Billy Williams, highest in the NL.

3,000TH

And final hit by Roberto Clemente, on September 30 off Jon Matlack of the Mets. On December 31 he died in the crash of a plane taking supplies to earthquake victims in Nicaragua.

Sources

Nemec, David, ed. *The Baseball Chronicle: Year-by-Year History of Major League Baseball* (Lincolnwood, Illinois: Publications International, 2003).

Society for American Baseball Research. *The SABR Baseball List and Record Book* (New York: Scribner, 2007).

Solomon, Burt. *The Baseball Timeline* (New York: DK Publishing, 2001).

Sugar, Burt Randolph, ed. *The Baseball Maniac's Almanac* (third edition) (New York: Skyhorse Publishing, 2012).

baseball-almanac.com.

baseball-reference.com.

retrosheet.org.

thisgreatgame.com/1972-baseball-history.html.

THE FIRST TWO DOZEN YEARS: BAD MANAGEMENT, WORSE BASEBALL

BY JOE STROOP

The dominant characteristics of the Texas Rangers' early history were inept management, pitiful baseball, and terrible attendance. The team proved incapable of coming up with a workable plan and sticking with it. This premise was stated well by a presumably neutral observer, veteran Chicago sports columnist Bernie Lincicome: "Texas has been a franchise governed by impulse, impatience and poor judgment."[1]

Frankly, though, it didn't take a lot of baseball acumen to figure that out – you just had to watch what was going on.

The team's first year in Texas was **1972**, after owner Bob Short and Arlington, Texas, Mayor Tom Vandergriff persuaded the other American League owners to let the franchise relocate from Washington, where the team had been terrible for years. As early as 1909, writer Charles Dryden had coined a legendary phrase: "Washington – first in war, first in peace, and last in the American League."[2]

The franchise's final season in Washington, 1971, featured yet more poor performance from the Senators, punctuated by rioting in the final game by fans angry that Short was moving the team.[3]

That first season after the move from D.C., the Texas Rangers lost 100 games, finishing – where else? – last in the American League West Division, 38½ games out of first place. The best player was a journeyman pitcher, Mike Paul. Hall of Famer Ted Williams completed his fourth year as manager of the team, and wearily decided that it would be his last.

A few names on that first Texas team might be familiar to Rangers baseball fans: slugger Frank Howard, slugger-to-be Jeff Burroughs, infielder Toby Harrah, and rookie Tom Grieve. Burroughs would soon earn the American League MVP Award and Grieve would become the team's general manager after his playing days were over. Grieve and Harrah are members of the Rangers Hall of Fame.[4]

The rest of that team was players who were hoping to make it, or trying to hang on. It was a sad, futile season that drew fewer than 700,000 Texas baseball fans, which put owner Short in a near-desperate financial situation. He had bought the team hoping to duplicate the windfall he had reaped when he bought the NBA Minneapolis Lakers for $500,000, moved them to Los Angeles and sold them five years later for $5 million.[5]

But without good attendance, then the primary source of revenue, Short had two problems: funding operating losses from his own pocket, and attracting eager buyers. Naturally, he spent considerable time calculating how to pull fans to Arlington Stadium. And since he had anointed himself general manager, Short's chores also included hiring a new manager and acquiring better players.

For a manager, Short chose the New York Mets farm director, Dorrel Norman Elvert "Whitey" Herzog, who had no previous managing experience. Herzog asked Short for time to build the Rangers for long-term, not immediate, success, and Short agreed. To his lasting regret, Herzog believed him.

The Rangers, by virtue of their terrible regular-season record, would have the first pick in the coming player draft, but Short had no intention of waiting until then to beef up the roster. Between the July trading deadline and the end of the year, he traded away nine players and sold two others (one of them Frank Howard), getting a like number in return.

But the only big name the Rangers acquired in all that commotion was former batting champion Rico Carty from the Braves. For Texas, he hit a miserable .232 and was gone after just 86 games – a harbinger of things to come. This high-volume roster churn in search of big-name stars who would draw fans would dominate the Rangers' approach for most of the decade.[6]

To boost attendance while the team wasn't winning, Short resorted to giveaways and other promotions. During the 1973 season, he bought thousands of cheap giveaways and used them to stage numerous promotions. There were Cap Nights, T-shirt Nights, Calendar Nights, Rangers Keychain Nights, a Panty Hose Night, even a Hot Pants Night, for which the entrants outnumbered the paying fans.[7]

The most successful promotion, in terms of fan acceptance, had to be scrapped almost immediately: Bat Night. Any youngster who attended a game would be given a Little-League-sized bat, which, of course, the kids enjoyed bashing against the old stadium's metal seats and barriers all game long. The racket was a huge distraction. Quickly, the Rangers wised up and gave the kids coupons they could redeem for bats after the game.[8]

But the biggest promotion of the new season was centered on a player the Rangers acquired in the draft. Two separate agendas were in play. General manager Joe Burke and manager Whitey Herzog were looking for a player to build a franchise around. Short was looking for someone to fill the seats.

With high-school left-hander David Clyde, they could have had both if they'd handled it right. Clyde was the best pitching prospect most scouts had seen that year. He had two plus pitches – a buzzing fastball and a hammer curve. The Rangers chose him ahead of Dave Winfield and Robin Yount. He agreed to terms before he graduated and made his first major-league appearance six days after his senior prom, wearing jersey number 32 in honor of Sandy Koufax.[9]

Herzog had wanted to send Clyde to the minors for seasoning, of course, but Short wanted him on the mound in Arlington Stadium, promising it was only for a few games.

June 27, 1973, was Clyde's debut and Short's biggest, best promotion yet. It was almost a circus. The pregame celebration featured Clyde's family, three hula-dancers, a papier-mâché giraffe on wheels, a character in a half-bird, half-fish costume and two live lion cubs. It was a standing-room-only sellout. Clyde walked the first two batters, then struck out the side – and the Rangers won. After the game, Short said, "According to my calculations, on gate receipts alone, in two starts I will have earned back Clyde's entire … signing bonus."[10]

The next night, fewer than 4,000 fans came to the park, so Short told Herzog the youngster would be with the Rangers for the rest of the year. It was shortsighted and, predictably, detrimental to Clyde's development. He lasted less than five years in the majors.

Looking back on it, Grieve said, "It was the dumbest thing you could ever do to a high-school pitcher. In my opinion, it ruined his career. Bob Short did it because he needed the money. So David served a purpose for Bob Short, at the expense of what I firmly believe would have been a nice 12- to 15-year big-league career."[11]

The Clyde extravaganza wasn't the final splash of the season. In September Short made more headlines when he fired Herzog to replace him with the mercurial Billy Martin, who himself had just been fired by the Detroit Tigers. Here again, Short was looking toward the box office.[12]

At the news conference announcing the hiring of Martin, Short said, "If my mother were managing the Rangers and I had the opportunity to hire Billy Martin, I'd fire my mother."[13]

It was Short's last major decision with the team. Just before the new season began, he sold out to a local group led by Fort Worth millionaire Brad Corbett, who had parlayed a small-business loan into a multimillion-dollar plastic-pipe business.

As the 1974 season began, it didn't take long for the brash Corbett and the equally brash manager Martin to collide. Martin, like Whitey Herzog before him, demanded that young Clyde be allowed some time in the minor leagues, and Corbett, like Short, refused – so Martin simply refused to play the youngster. This further stunted Clyde's development, physically as well as emotionally.

But even without Clyde, positive things were happening on the field. Jeff Burroughs had a career year in his second big-league season, batting .301 with 25 home runs and a league-leading 118 RBIs, to win the 1974 American League Most Valuable Player Award.

Another breakthrough player was Mike Hargrove, the Rangers' first native Texan. He made the jump from Class A ball to hit .353 and earn the AL Rookie of the Year Award. He was joined by rookie catcher Jim Sundberg, who went to the All-Star Game. Veteran right-hander Ferguson Jenkins, acquired from the Cubs, won 25 games, was named Comeback Player of the Year and finished second in the Cy Young Award voting. And young right-hander Jim Bibby tossed the team's first no-hitter.

The Rangers finished the season 84-76, second in the AL West, and drew 1,193,902 fans, fourth in the league. Thanks to a quality manager in Martin and some on-field talent, the team had become relevant for Dallas-Fort Worth sports fans.

Corbett, like Short, preferred the instant gratification of showy transactions over the hard work of player development. For example, his deal for Jenkins had cost the team future four-time batting champion Bill Madlock. In 1974, through trade, sale, or release, the Rangers got rid of 25 players and acquired 17 others.

Corbett put it to the floorboard in **1975**, with offseason deals that landed aging outfielder Willie Davis and left-hander Clyde Wright, a 20-game loser the prior year, at the cost of top pitching prospects Pete Broberg and Don Stanhouse, plus slick-fielding shortstop Pete Mackanin. Then, shortly after the season began, Corbett sent pitchers Jim Bibby, Jackie Brown, and Rick Waits, plus $100,000 to Cleveland for 36-year-old spitballer Gaylord Perry.

It wasn't enough. In July, with the Rangers at 44-51 and Martin constantly sniping at Corbett's personnel decisions, Corbett fired the manager. To succeed Martin, he named third-base coach Frank Lucchesi, whose only prior managerial experience had been leading the 1970-72 Phillies to a dismal 166-233 record. The Rangers finished that season 79-83, third in the division.

And **1976** was even worse. Pitchers Jenkins, Wright, and Bill Hands were sent packing. Perry was a year older and no one else picked up the slack. At the deadline, Corbett sent youngsters Mike Cubbage, Jim Gideon, Bill Singer, and Roy Smalley along with $250,000 to the Minnesota Twins for pitchers Bert Blyleven, who finished the year at 9-11, and Danny Thompson.

The team never found first gear and finished 76-86, tied with the Angels for fourth place in the AL West. The team had some players – rising fan favorites Harrah, Grieve, and Sundberg, who won his first Gold Glove. But Burroughs' production fell as the league's pitchers caught up with him.

As the **1977** season approached, Corbett signed two big-name free agents, former A's shortstop Bert Campaneris and former Braves right-hander Doyle Alexander. He also shuffled Burroughs off to Atlanta for five players, only one of whom, pitcher Adrian Devine, made a positive contribution.

But the season's highlight came in spring training when fiery infielder Lenny Randle violently assaulted his manager. Rookie Bump Wills – son of Maury – had supplanted Randle at second base. Randle, unhappy over the demotion, asked Lucchesi for a few words, then suddenly knocked the skipper to the ground and punched him until teammates intervened. Lucchesi was hospitalized for a week. Randle was fined, suspended, charged with assault, and quickly shipped off to the Mets for, in effect, nothing in return.

If that weren't enough, the Rangers also went through four managers in six days. As the team languished, Corbett fired Lucchesi, chose coach Connie Ryan as interim manager until he hired Eddie Stanky – who quit after one game! Finally, Billy Hunter joined the team from Earl Weaver's Baltimore staff.

Some good things did happen that year. Harrah and Wills had back-to-back inside-the-park home runs on consecutive pitches in Yankee Stadium; the team turned its first triple play and got a no-hitter from Blyleven. Under Hunter, the Rangers rallied to win 21 of their last 31 games for a 94-68 record, the team's highest win total ever, but not good enough to catch the red-hot Kansas City Royals.

For the **1978** season, Corbett signed free agent Richie Zisk, who had belted 30 homers and knocked in 101 runs for the White Sox. Corbett also traded away Clyde, Perry, and slugger Willie Horton for no substantial return.

Then, at the winter meetings, Corbett went into orbit, orchestrating a four-team deal that sent five players packing, including Blyleven and Grieve – the last original Ranger – for outfielder Al Oliver from the Pirates and lefty Jon Matlack from the Mets, plus some spare parts. Then in May, he traded for Bobby Bonds.

Despite the constant roster churn, the Rangers did enjoy a rare, brief sort of stability during the 1978 season – there were no changes in ownership, the front office, the manager, or the coaching staff – and finished tied for second in the division. Sundberg earned another Gold Glove and another All-Star Game berth. Matlack had his best year as a Ranger: 15-13, 2.27 ERA in 270 innings.

But, as always, you couldn't have a 1970s Rangers season without some significant controversy, this time courtesy of the newly acquired and ever-erratic pitcher Dock Ellis. After a fight broke out on a team charter, manager Hunter imposed a no-alcohol rule. Ellis, a controversial sort, said he would bring his own booze. He characterized Hunter as a tyrant, telling reporters, "He may be a Hitler but he ain't makin' no lampshade out of me."[14]

After the season, Hunter and the front office wanted Ellis gone, but Corbett believed Ellis was amusing and good for publicity – so he fired Hunter instead.

Another new season, **1979**, saw another new manager – this time, it was tough-as-nails Pat Corrales, who had been a catcher for nine years in the National League. This was his first managing job and he took the team to a third-place finish, at 83-79. Buddy Bell, acquired from Cleveland, became one of the team's steadiest, best players for the next six years. Bell earned a Gold Glove and finished among the top 10 vote-getters for the MVP. Corbett, continuing his habit of shopping for big names, also added closer Jim Kern and three big-name former New York Yankees: Oscar Gamble, Mickey Rivers, and Sparky Lyle.

One move turned out to be more significant than it seemed at the time – original Ranger Tom Grieve retired as a player, joined the Rangers front office, and began getting ready for the next season's duties as the color commentator for the team's TV broadcasts.

INTERIM

One thing should be noted at this point: The 1970-1979 decade was the very last time that major-league baseball was openly tolerant of what were euphemistically called "characters" – perpetrators of the goofy, nutty behavior that had been so typical of players, managers, and owners alike. The reason is simple: money. In 1970 the average player salary was about $29,000, and total TV revenue was about $176 million. By 1982, the average player salary had grown to $245,000, and TV revenue exceeded $250 million.[15] Baseball started to slowly squeeze out those who treated the game as a game. It was a serious, money-making business.

During the 1980 season, the Rangers continued a pattern that had been established before the franchise even moved to Texas: One good year under a new manager, then a quick slide back to mediocrity, or even worse. After finishing four games over .500 for Corrales the previous season, the Rangers fell to 76-85, finishing fourth. That was finally enough for Corbett, as he and his partners sold the team to Fort Worth oil millionaire Eddie Chiles.

Fun, flamboyant American League umpire Ron Luciano provided the perfect commentary on Corbett's turbulent ownership tenure: "Brad thinks his ballplayers are like his plastic pipes – they need to be flushed all the time."[16]

Among the season's on-field highlights, homegrown right-hander Danny Darwin – nicknamed the Bonham Bullet for his fastball and his North Texas hometown – posted a 13-4 won-lost record with a 2.63 ERA in his first full season. Meanwhile, veteran Jenkins became the fourth pitcher to win 100 games in each league.

The **1981** season saw the beginning of the conflicted relationship between the flint-hard new owner Chiles and his chosen new manager, Don Zimmer, a baseball lifer. Zim spent more than 60 years in pro baseball, from 1949 until his death in 2014. He claimed he never took a paycheck outside of pro ball except for some Social Security payments.

Chiles, born in Itasca, Texas, clawed his way to the top of the oil business. He started his business, the Western Company, in 1939 with two trucks and three employees. He grew it to become one of the wealthiest men in Texas. At one point, he ran a series of radio commercials with the tagline, "If you don't have an oil well, GIT ONE! You'll love doing business with Western."

Chiles was determined to run the Rangers the way he ran his business – which meant concrete, "attainable" goals with frequent individual reviews. Zimmer thought that was ridiculous and threw Chiles' written instructions in the trash.

The 1981 season was interrupted by a players' strike. At the time, Zim's Rangers were just 1½ games out of first place. But the strike lasted 50 days and when the season resumed, the team never regained its momentum. It finished 57-48, five games back of eventual division champion Oakland.

General manager Eddie Robinson decided that what the Rangers needed for 1982 was an athletic outfielder who could hit, prompting him to make one of the worst trades in the team's history. He sent two promising young pitchers, Ron Darling and Walt Terrell, to the Mets for Lee Mazzilli. Darling had been the team's number-1 draft pick, and Terrell was their number-1 pitching prospect at the time. Mazzilli? He hated Texas from the minute he arrived. When Zimmer tried to put him in left field, Mazzilli said, "Left field is an idiot's position."[17]

Mazzilli pouted all year and was hitting .241 when the team finally shipped him to the Yankees for aging shortstop Bucky Dent. Meanwhile, over the next six seasons, Darling and Terrell combined to win 146 games for their new teams.

When the Rangers came home from a four-city July road trip that featured 10 losses, Chiles told Zimmer he was fired, but asked him not to tell anyone and would he please stay on until Wednesday? Even worse, Chiles chose Doug Rader to manage the team, which turned out to be one of the worst personnel decisions in the history of the franchise. Rader proved to be a complete failure as a manager, and the man who was runner-up in the interviews was Jim Leyland, who later won pennants in both leagues and a World Series.

The 1982 team finished 64-98, second worst in the division. There were two on-the-field bright spots: Outfielder Larry Parrish hit three grand slams, with 19 RBIs, in one week, and rookie outfielder Dave Hostetler – nicknamed "The Hoss" – bashed 10 home runs in June, 22 in his first 76 games that season. Unfortunately for Hostetler, that's when big-league pitchers found the holes in his swing, and he was off the team by 1984.

Rader's first full year as manager, 1983, saw the team leap to 11 games over .500 in the early going, then – as Rader began to assert his "personality" – struggle to finish in third place, at 77-85. Rader became a disaster with players, fans, and the media. Several years later, Rader admitted he had done a "terrible" job. He actually instigated feuds with his most experienced players, with the beat writers, even the fans. Rader later admitted he was a terror, that no one wanted to play for him, and he didn't blame them.[18]

In 1984 the team finished 69-92, last in the division and 14½ games out of first. Even worse, Rader ran off longtime fan favorite Sundberg, citing a lack of toughness. Sundberg went to Milwaukee for Brewers catcher Ned Yost. At the time, Rader said, "We made the deal because Ned Yost is a better catcher than Jim Sundberg. Period."[19]

HERE ARE THE FACTS:

Sundberg won six consecutive Gold Glove Awards. He consistently led AL catchers in fielding percentage, putouts and assists. He was Rookie of the Year and made three All-Star teams. He averaged 126 games a year in 12 seasons. His caught-stealing rate was 41 percent. His bWAR with the Rangers was 34.7.[20]

Ned Yost lasted one season with Texas. He caught 78 games. His caught-stealing rate was 17 percent. His bWAR with the Rangers was -2.4.[21]

On the positive side of the ledger, third baseman Bell earned another All-Star Game appearance, his sixth consecutive Gold Glove and a Silver Slugger Award. Tom Grieve was named farm director.

In **1985** Grieve took over as general manager and chose his pal Bobby Valentine to replace Rader. The team finished 62-99, last again, but Valentine had more polish than Rader, was better with the fans and media, and was committed to working with Grieve to build some success.

On the field, rookie outfielder Oddibe McDowell became the first Ranger to hit for the cycle. Smooth, powerful right-hander Jose Guzman made his major-league debut. He would post four double-digit winning seasons for Texas before shoulder problems ended his career.

The next season under Valentine, **1986**, saw the Rangers challenge for the division title, finishing second at 85-75. Valentine finished second in the Manager of the Year Award voting. Two rookies, outfielders Pete Incaviglia and Ruben Sierra, added their muscle to that of veterans Parrish and first baseman Pete O'Brien to form the Rangers' power parade. Incaviglia had made a big impression during spring training when he hit a line drive through – not over, but through – the left-field fence. Looking at the hole in the fence, Valentine said, "That's one-inch plywood. Awesome."[22]

Ageless wonder Charlie Hough – holder of the team career records in wins and strikeouts – was a 17-game winner for those Rangers, while 22-year-old rookie Bobby Witt went 11-9. And on the business front, the Rangers turned an operating profit for the first time.[23]

The next season, **1987**, was not quite as much fun, even from the beginning. The Rangers opened the season 1-10, including nine straight losses. McDowell, at the team's "Welcome Home" banquet and fan fest in late April, cut his hand trying to butter a dinner roll. Closer Greg Harris, who had demanded a 100 percent raise based on his 20 saves the year earlier, missed three weeks in August and September with a strained elbow, sustained when he flicked sunflower seeds at a friend in the stands one afternoon.[24]

The big-four bats continued to thump – Parrish had 32 home runs, Sierra 30, Incavigilia 27, and O'Brien 23. The Rangers outscored every other American League West team, but still fell back into the cellar, at 75-87. Pitching coach Tom House recommended subliminal tape recordings to free up a pitcher's subconscious so he could find the strike zone, and having pitchers warm up by throwing footballs to each other. Asked if the football drill was helping his pitching motion, the veteran Hough replied, "No, but we lead the league in third-down conversions."[25]

On the business side, owner Chiles bought Arlington Stadium from the City of Arlington.

The team continued to struggle in **1988**. Slugger Parrish needed knee surgery before the season started, his bat never recovered, and he was gone before the All-Star break.

Closer Harris was gone after the sunflower-seed stunt. Budding starter Edwin Correa tried to come back from a sore shoulder but could not pitch through the pain – he would eventually have career-ending surgery.

The team had eight straight wins in May, but then lost 19 of 31 games. The Rangers' only bright spot the second half of the year was fireballer Bobby Witt, who had been demoted in May for his inability to throw strikes. He came back up in July, having added a forkball to his repertoire, and rattled off nine straight complete games.

Nonetheless, the team finished two games out of the cellar, at 70-91. It was the worst record of Valentine's tenure to date, but Chiles gave him a two-year extension.

Looking ahead to **1989**, GM Grieve decided standing pat was not working, so he went on a buying spree. The team traded six players, including closer Mitch Williams, to the Chicago Cubs for three players – primarily young first baseman Rafael Palmeiro, who had hit .307 the previous year. Also, the Rangers sent three players, including starters McDowell and O'Brien, to Cleveland for second baseman Julio Franco, a career .295 hitter at the time. Then, Grieve made a trade he later regretted – three players, including future superstar Sammy Sosa, went to the White Sox for DH Harold Baines, who never found his stride with Texas.

In December the team made local headlines with the signing of free-agent pitcher Nolan Ryan, who was immediately installed as the staff ace, and fans' expectations rose tremendously. Joining Ryan were newcomers Kenny Rogers and Kevin Brown. The Rangers' busy offseason was noticed around the league, with Oakland GM Sandy Alderson saying, "The most important byproduct of all that change is the change in their image. And self-image."[26]

Ryan won 16 games and led the American League with 301 strikeouts, including career strikeout number 5,000. New closer Jeff Russell led the league in saves and posted a 1.98 ERA. Sierra led the league in triples, RBIs, slugging percentage, and total bases, was named to his first All-Star team and captured the Silver Slugger Award.

This season also marked the major-league debut of 19-year-old outfielder Juan Gonzalez. He would play 13 years with Texas, win the AL Most Valuable Player Award twice, play in three All-Star Games and win the Silver Slugger Award six times. As of 2016 he held the team record for home runs and RBIs.

The team improved to 83-79, but three other West Division teams won 90 games or more and Texas finished fourth, 16 games off the pace.

Shortly after the 1990 season began, owner Chiles – whose oilfield company was being pummeled by the energy crisis – sold the Rangers to an investment group fronted by future President George W. Bush. It was the fourth new ownership team in 17 years but proved to be the most stable up to then.

The group announced plans to build a new stadium – The Ballpark In Arlington. Arlington voters loved the idea and, the following year, approved a sales-tax increase to help fund it.

During the season Ryan again led the league in strikeouts, became the oldest pitcher to throw a no-hitter and earned his 300th career win. Bobby Witt won 17 games and Incaviglia bopped 24 home runs, but the team finished third, at 83-79.

Catcher Ivan "Pudge" Rodriguez made his debut in the 1991 season at age 19. Rodriguez grew to become one of the finest catchers in the game. He was named to 10 All-Star teams in his 12 years with the Rangers, and won 10 Gold Gloves, six Silver Sluggers and one AL Most Valuable Player Award.

In May Ryan threw his seventh career no-hitter, three more than any other pitcher. Gonzalez hit 27 home runs and drove in 102 runs, while Palmeiro batted .322 and chipped in 26 homers.

Construction began on the new stadium in 1992, as the Rangers finished the season eight games under .500, at 77-85. The poor play earned Valentine the boot as manager in July, with coach Harrah taking over in the interim.

At the trading deadline, Grieve completed another blockbuster trade, sending Sierra, Witt, and Russell to Oakland for controversial outfielder Jose Canseco, who brought the national spotlight to Texas, and not in a good way. In a game against Cleveland, Canseco lost sight of a fly ball, which bounced off his head and over the fence for a home run. But the primary attention Canseco brought to Texas came later, from his 2005 book, *Juiced* – his personal account of his own steroid use and those of teammates, including accusations against many Rangers.

On a more positive note, Grieve persuaded ownership to give scouting director Sandy Johnson a contract extension, cementing the team's commitment to do a better job of developing its own players.

Kevin Kennedy took over the dugout in 1993 as the Rangers' new manager – the team's 15th since 1972. Kennedy got to preside over one of the most memorable events in franchise history, one still talked about today. On August 4 against the White Sox, Ryan plunked third baseman Robin Ventura on the arm with a fastball. Ventura took a moment to think about it, then charged the mound. Ryan caught him in a headlock and punched him six times before the benches emptied and knocked both men to the ground.

Sadly, Ryan's season and career ended abruptly in September, when he ruptured an elbow ligament in a game against Seattle. He elected to retire at age 46 rather than go through surgery. The team finished second in the division at 86-76.

The Rangers' new ballpark, modeled after the retro-look Camden Yards in Baltimore, opened in 1994 to great fanfare. It was a big success with fans, who turned out in record numbers – 2.5 million for the strike-shortened season.

In July lefty Kenny Rogers tossed the team's first perfect game. The Rangers signed first baseman-DH Will Clark to replace Palmeiro and he led the team in batting at .329, while Canseco added 31 home runs. But the team finished 10 games under .500, at 52-62 – technically "first place" in the division because the season was cut short by the players' strike that resulted in the first World Series cancellation since 1904.

The poor record led to Grieve's dismissal as GM. He was replaced by Doug Melvin, who chose Johnny Oates to replace Kennedy as manager. Oates would lead the Rangers to their first postseason action just two seasons later.

The team's first year under Oates, **1995,** saw continued success at the plate and mediocre pitching at best. Four hitters reached double-digit home runs, paced by Gonzalez with 27, and Clark added 92 RBIs.

On the mound, lefty Kenny Rogers had a fine 17-7 record, but no other pitcher finished above .500.

The Ballpark in Arlington hosted the 66th All-Star Game in the middle of the year, providing a new kind of excitement for fans, who saw the National League beat the American League, 3-2. For the regular season, also shortened by the players' strike to 144 games, Texas finished in third place at 74-70, 4½ games behind Seattle.

After two decades featuring varying degrees of futility, frustration, and failure, the **1996** Texas Rangers clinched their first postseason appearance in franchise history, winning the Western Division by 4½ games with a record of 90-72. It was their first 90-win season since 1977. Attendance was a record 2.88 million.

Oates was named co-Manager of the Year, tied with Joe Torre of the Yankees. Gonzalez was the American League MVP with 47 home runs and 144 RBIs. Seven other players had double-digit homers, including newcomers Mickey Tettleton and Dean Palmer.

The Rangers faced the Yankees in the American League Division Series, and won Game One in New York, 6-2, with home runs by Gonzalez and Palmer, and a complete game from John Burkett. However, the Yankees took the next three games to win the series.

This seems an appropriate stopping place, now that we have followed the Rangers from their inception as (in the salty words of Whitey Herzog during a private spring-training conversation) "the worst ****ing team in baseball," to champion of the American League West. The team would win two more division titles in the next three years. From 1996 through 2015 the Rangers earned seven playoff appearances and two American League pennants. Fun, in the early years, came mostly from off-the-field activities. Mercifully for Rangers fans, their fun can now be found between the lines.

Notes
1. Bernie Lincicome, "Rangers Fire Rader for Losing Ugly," *Chicago Tribune*, May 17, 1985.
2. baseballhall.org/discover/awards/j-g-taylor-spink/charles-dryden.
3. washingtonpost.com/wp-srv/sports/redskins/history/rfk/articles/baseball.htm.
4. texas.rangers.mlb.com/tex/history/rangers_hall_of_famers.jsp.
5. en.wikipedia.org/wiki/Bob_Short.
6. baseball-reference.com/players/c/cartyrio1.shtml.
7. Mike Shropshire, *Seasons in Hell* (New York: Donald I. Fine Books, 1996), 67.
8. Rusty Burson, *100 Things Rangers Fans Should Know & Do Before They Die* (Chicago: Triumph Books, 2012), 237.
9. Josh Lewin, *Ballgame* (Chicago: Triumph Books, 2012), 16.
10. Shropshire, 69.

11 dallasnews.com/sports/texas-rangers/headlines/20130622-townsend-40-years-after-memorable-debut-ex-ranger-david-clyde-recalls-a-career-cut-short.ece.
12 baseball-reference.com/managers/martibi02.shtml.
13 Phil Rogers, *The Impossible Takes a Little Longer* (Dallas: Taylor Publishing, 1990), 12-13.
14 en.wikipedia.org/wiki/Dock_Ellis.
15 eh.net/encyclopedia/the-economic-history-of-major-league-baseball/.
16 dmagazine.com/publications/d-magazine/1979/march/march-up-front.
17 Rogers, 27.
18 articles.latimes.com/1989-02-26/sports/sp-1045_1_texas-doug-rader.
19 articles.latimes.com/1989-02-26/sports/sp-1045_1_texas-doug-rader/3.
20 baseball-reference.com/players/s/sundbji01.shtml.
21 hbaseball-reference.com/players/y/yostne01.shtml.
22 Burson, 75.
23 Burson, 173.
24 star-telegram.com/sports/mlb/texas-rangers/article3846157.html.
25 Lewin, 19.
26 Rogers, 124.

CONTRIBUTORS

Marc Z Aaron is a Certified Public Accountant and Certified Valuation Analyst practicing in Randolph, Vermont and living in Hull, Massachusetts. He is an avid baseball fan from his childhood growing up in The Bronx, and remains to this day a born and bred Yankee fan. Marc has four sons and coached Little League for six years. He is a contributor to the SABR bio-project and his first book was *Who's on First: Replacement Players in World War II* with co-author Bill Nowlin. Marc loves tennis as much as baseball and is a tournament tennis player on the local, regional and national levels. He has been a ranked player in New England for his age grouping. A fantasy baseball player in a countless number of leagues, Marc is also an adjunct professor of economics at Vermont Technical College. Most recently Marc has joined a senior softball league and found that running from third to home makes one more injury prone than tennis.

Mark Armour writes baseball from his home in Oregon's Willamette Valley.

John Bennett has contributed biographies to *Green Mountain Boys of Summer*, *Deadball Stars of the American League*; *Deadball Stars of the National League*; *Lefty, Double-X and the Kid*; and to *The National Pastime*. He is also the co-author of *Johnny Podres: Brooklyn's Only Yankee Killer* and admits to dabbling in pro football research as well. A SABR member since 1993, he has taught social studies at the high school level in Vermont for 25 years.

Robert W. Bigelow is an attorney and educator practicing law in New York and New Jersey. He has served on the faculty of the School of Business at Capella University since 2004. He contributed to *Go-Go to Glory: The 1959 Chicago White Sox* (ACTA Publications, 2009), *Deadball Stars of the American League* (Potomac Books, 2006), and SABR's 2004 convention journal *Baseball in the Buckeye State*. Robert lives in New Jersey with his wife Madeline. They have two grown children, Will and Emma.

Maurice Bouchard, a SABR member since 1999, has worked as an author, editor, and fact-checker on many "team" books for the BioProject, starting in 2005 with *'75: The Red Sox Team that Saved Baseball*. He has also contributed to full-length biographies of Willie Keeler, Hugh Casey, and Dixie Walker. Bouchard and his wife Kim live with their two dogs in the woods of Westford, New York, just a 10-minute drive from 25 Main Street, Cooperstown.

Bruce Bumbalough is a life-long Detroit Tiger fan. He attended his first Tiger game in 1952 with his mother and younger brother. His life's work has been in public libraries where he is beginning his 42nd year as a librarian. He holds a master of Library Science degree from the University of Mississippi and a Bachelor of Science degree from the then Memphis State University. He has done additional graduate study in history at the University of North Texas.

Frederick C. (Rick) Bush, his wife Michelle, and their three sons Michael, Andrew, and Daniel live in the greater Houston area, where he teaches English at Wharton County Junior College. He was an ardent fan of the 1977 Texas Rangers while living in Fort Hood, Texas, and relived many a childhood memory while writing about Toby Harrah for this book. He and Bill Nowlin co-edited *Bittersweet Goodbye: The Black Barons, the Grays, and the 1948 Negro League World Series* and are currently co-editing a book about the 1946 Newark Eagles, a team that featured four Hall of Fame players in addition to the only woman enshrined in the HOF, co-owner Effa Manley.

Bo Carter is a 26-year SABR member and former media relations director of the Southwest and Big 12 Conferences. He has been a member of the SABR College Baseball Committee and has been a co-author or contributor for seven books, including 2016's *Dizzy: Dean of Baseball and My Podnah* with the late Gene Kirby and Mark McDonald. He lives in Carrollton, Texas.

Greg Chandler is a database developer and project development consultant for Solomon Associates in Dallas, Texas. He was born into a family that loved baseball, especially the Texas Rangers, and has continued that tradition with his wife and two children. Many of their summer vacations are planned around visiting ballparks around the country. Greg is active in his church and has been on several short-term mission trips. He also enjoys hiking and snorkeling. This writing is his first contribution to a SABR publication.

Alan Cohen has been a SABR member since 2011, serves as Vice President-Treasurer of the Connecticut Smoky Joe Wood Chapter, and is the datacaster (stringer) for the Hartford Yard Goats, the Double-A affiliate of the Colorado Rockies. He has written more than 40 biographies for SABR's bio-project, more than 30 games for SABR's games project, and has contributed stories to *The National Pastime* and the *Baseball Research Journal*. He has expanded his BRJ article on the Hearst Sandlot Classic (1946-1965), an annual youth All-Star game which launched the careers of 88 major-league players. He has four children and six grandchildren and resides in West Hartford, Connecticut with his wife Frances, a cat (Morty) and a dog (Sam).

Rory Costello has been to quite a few major-league parks but has not yet had the good fortune to see a Rangers game. He lives in Brooklyn, New York, with his wife Noriko and son Kai.

Dan Fields is a senior manuscript editor at the *New England Journal of Medicine*. He loves baseball trivia, and he enjoys attending Boston Red Sox and Pawtucket Red Sox games with his teenage son. Dan lives in Framingham, Massachusetts, and can be reached at dfields820@gmail.com.

Paul Geisler is an ordained minister of the Evangelical Lutheran Church in America. He serves as pastor of Christ Lutheran Church in Lake Jackson, Texas, where he lives with his wife and their three children. For his entire life, Paul has enjoyed all aspects of baseball - playing, watching, coaching, researching, and writing. He became a Houston Astros fan from the team's first year in 1962, and then a Texas Rangers fan 1971, when the Senators moved to Texas. He attended seminary in Chicago, where he added another favorite, the Cubs of Wrigley Field.

Joseph Gerard has been a lifelong Pittsburgh Pirates fan. He grew up hating the Yankees despite being born in Newark, New Jersey – his biggest regret in life is that he was only 2 years old in 1960. Because of Roberto Clemente, he developed an interest in Latin-American baseball history and has contributed biographies of several Latin players to SABR's BioProject. He lives in New York City with his wife Ann Marie and their two children, Henry and Sophie.

Charlie Grassl is a retired electrical engineer and former high school shortstop whose love of the game of baseball has been a strong current in the flow of his life. After 33+ years with Westinghouse, Texas Instruments and Raytheon he discovered SABR and deepened his enjoyment of the game. The articles in this book are his first for SABR. He grew up in San Antonio following the Texas League "Missions" but now resides in Arlington, Texas with his wife Carole following the Texas Rangers. He moved to Arlington in 2004, from Dallas, to be nearer his daughters and grandchildren but all three daughters believe it had more to do with the location of the Rangers ballpark.

Chip Greene joined SABR in 2006. A long-contributor to the Biography Project, he lives with his wife, Elaine, in Waynesboro, Pennsylvania.

Paul Hofmann, a SABR member since 2002, is the Associate Vice President for International Programs at Sacramento State University. He is a native of Detroit, Michigan and lifelong Detroit Tigers fan. Paul currently resides in Folsom, California.

Chris Holaday is a writer and photographer based in Durham, North Carolina. A native of Dallas and a life-long Rangers fan, he discovered a love for minor league baseball while a student at the University of North Carolina-Chapel Hill. His first book, *Professional Baseball in North Carolina*, won the 1999 Sporting News-SABR Baseball Research Award. In the years since he has written several other books and was co-author, with Mark Presswood, of *Baseball in Dallas* and *Baseball in Fort Worth*. His most recent books are *The Tobacco State League* and a cookbook titled *Southern Breads*, which is surprisingly unrelated to baseball.

SABR member **Mike Huber** is Professor of Mathematics at Muhlenberg College in Allentown, Pennsylvania. He has published his sabermetrics research in several books and journals, including *The Baseball Research Journal, Chance,* and *Base Ball,* and he genuinely enjoys contributing to SABR's Baseball Games Project. In his only visit to Arlington, Texas, he was fortunate enough to see Nolan Ryan.

Gordon Janis is a first-time contributor to the BioProject. He remembers his childhood heartbreak when the Mets traded his idol Tom Seaver for a Farrah Fawcett poster, a pack of pop rocks, a buffalo nickel, and dryer lint. That stinging disappointment combined with his frequent attendance at Yankee Stadium with his season ticket-holding uncle turned his loyalties to the Bronx Bombers. He was on hand to witness Reggie Jackson's magical night of three first-pitch home runs in Game Six of the 1977 World Series. An avid lifelong baseball card collector, he is glad he acquired his childhood neighbor's entire collection of 1973-74 baseball cards in exchange for his own collection of Wacky Packages. He currently lives in Alexandria, Virginia and enjoys attending Nats games with his daughter who was born the same year baseball returned to the nation's capital.

Chris Jones is an attorney at Phelps Dunbar where he practices in the area of commercial litigation, with a focus on property rights, eminent domain, real estate disputes and contract disputes. He is a lifelong baseball fan and a member of SABR since 2015. The highlight of his playing days was being drafted by the Toronto Blue Jays in the 2001 amateur draft. He resides in the Dallas/Fort Worth area with his wife and four children. For firm information please visit www.phelpsdunbar.com, or contact Chris directly at chris.jones@phelps.com.

Maxwell Kates is an accountant who lives and works in midtown Toronto. A SABR member since 2001, he writes a monthly baseball column for the Houston-based *Pecan Park Eagle*. He has spoken at SABR conventions and regional meetings in Seattle, Montreal, and Houston. He and Bill Nowlin are co-editing *Baseball's Expansion Teams*, which is expected to be published before the end of 2018. Favourite baseball teams: Montreal Expos, Detroit Tigers, Houston Astros.

Duane Victor Keilstrup, a lifelong baseball fan, has closely followed the Texas Rangers since their home opener on April 21, 1972. He is Professor Emeritus at The University of Texas at Arlington and holds a Ph.D. from The University of Nebraska at Lincoln. He is editor emeritus of an international professional journal and has written several scholarly works, along with autobiographical essays in his book *The Christian Professor in the Secular University: Singing & Soaring on Paths of Joy*. Keilstrup also produces a weekly vintage big band radio show online on The Olde Tyme Radio Network. He resides in Arlington, Texas with Glenda, his wife of 56 years.

In one of the smartest moves of his life, **Norm King** joined SABR in 2010. Norm, who grew up in Montreal but lives in Ottawa, Ontario, has focused his SABR research on his beloved Montreal

Expos. He has written a number of biographies of Expos players, and that has given him the chance to meet some of his heroes, including Steve Rogers, Warren Cromartie, Hall of Fame broadcaster Dave Van Horne, and Gary Carter's widow, Sandy. In 2016, SABR published *Au Jeu/Play Ball: The 50 Greatest Games in the History of the Montreal Expos*, for which Norm was senior editor and lead writer. It was SABR's top-selling book of the year.

Bob LeMoine grew up in Maine and has lived and died with the Red Sox for most of his life. He joined SABR in 2013 and has contributed to several SABR book projects. He is currently a co-editor with Bill Nowlin on a future SABR book on the Boston Beaneaters of the 1890s. Having a love for both history and baseball, he rarely says no to contributing a biography or article for any SABR book. Bob lives in Rochester, New Hampshire and works as a high school librarian and adjunct professor.

Len Levin remembers seeing the Rangers play when they were the Washington Senators and playing Sunday doubleheaders at Fenway Park. A retired newspaper editor, he currently does his editing for the Rhode Island Supreme Court, as well as SABR.

Francisco Rodriguez Lozano never had the pleasure of seeing Horacio Piña in action, because he was not born until five years after the pitcher's pro career ended. Paco is a journalist based in Torreón, Mexico.

Chad Moody is a nearly lifelong resident of suburban Detroit, where he has been a fan of the Detroit Tigers from birth. An alumnus of both the University of Michigan and Michigan State University, he has spent 25 years working in the automotive industry. Chad's first foray into baseball research occurred as a teenager, when he had a letter published in *Baseball Digest*. From that humble beginning, he has since frequently contributed to SABR's BioProject and Games Project. Chad and his wife, Lisa, live in Northville, Michigan, with their children, Jacob and Jessica, and dog, Daisy.

Bill Nowlin has always felt a certain sort of tie to the Texas Rangers because of the Ted Williams connection. The author of eight books on Ted Williams, his most recent one is *Ted Williams: First Latino in the Baseball Hall of Fame*. Co-founder of Rounder Records way back in 1970, he has in the past few years devoted most of his time to helping edit books for SABR.

Will Osgood is 31 years old, and recently moved to Dallas, Texas. He has been a part of SABR for over two years, and his favorite team is the Chicago Cubs. Will is especially interested in the Negro Leagues, and biographical information for other players who hail from Southeast Louisiana. He is also fascinated by the intersection of baseball and religion and race. Will is halfway through a Master's degree in Theology and plans to start churches and one day obtain a PhD in Sociology.

Carl Riechers retired from United Parcel Service in 2012 after 35 years of service. With more free time, he became a SABR member that same year. Born and raised in the suburbs of St. Louis, he became a big fan of the Cardinals. He and his wife Janet have three children and is the proud grandpa of two.

Francisco Rodríguez is a journalist based in Torreón, in northern Mexico. He currently works as a correspondent for *Vanguardia* newspaper and for *El Universal* newspaper. He has been a fellow of the Sociedad Interamericana de Prensa and a fellow of the Global Investigative Journalism Conference. He was honored with the National Journalism Award of Science in 2014 and 2015, and the National Prize of Journalism "Rostros de la Discriminación" (2017). He is also a journalism teacher at Universidad Iberoamericana.

Paul Rogers is co-author of several baseball books including *The Whiz Kids and the 1950 Pennant* with boyhood hero Robin Roberts and *Lucky Me: My 65 Years in Baseball* with Eddie Robinson. Most recently he co-edited *The Whiz Kids Take* *the Pennant – The 1950 Philadelphia Phillies* and *The Team That Time Won't Forget – the 1951 New York Giants*, SABR team projects with Bill Nowlin. He is president of the Ernie Banks – Bobby Bragan DFW Chapter of SABR and a frequent contributor to the SABR BioProject, but his real job is as a law professor at Southern Methodist University where he served as dean for nine years. He has also served as SMU's faculty athletic representative for over 30 years.

Ray Rossi is a retired accountant who lives with his wife Connie in Mesquite, Texas. A SABR member since 2015 and attends the quarterly meetings at the ballpark in Arlington. He was also a Pony Baseball Inc. coach for 10 years. His son attended the Arlington school of baseball back in 1988 and was taught by Mike Bascik Sr. Rossi grew up in Pittsburgh and is a longtime Roberto Clemente fan. This is his first work for SABR.

A native Texan, **Kris Rutherford** has a natural connection to the Rangers, who were coming of age about the time he realized what a baseball was. He is a Texas League historian with three books on Pre-WWII TL baseball to his credit as well as dozens of articles, many published in the Texas League Newsletter. He is also a youth sports novelist, editor, and ghostwriter. Today he lives near Little Rock, Arkansas.

Rick Schabowski is a retired machinist from Harley-Davidson and is currently an instructor at Wisconsin Regional Training Partnership in the Manufacturing Program, and is a certified Manufacturing Skills Standards Council Instructor. He is President of the Ken Keltner Badger State Chapter of SABR, Treasurer of the Milwaukee Braves Historical Association, and a member of the Hoop Historians.

William Schneider has been a baseball fan since receiving his first pack of baseball cards in 1974. An engineer by profession, Bill recently began writing about baseball in addition to avidly reading about and watching the game. He has a particular interest in the strategic aspects of team building and roster construction.

From an early age **David E. Skelton** developed a lifelong love of baseball when the lights from Philadelphia's Connie Mack Stadium shone through his bedroom window. Long removed from Philly, he resides with his family in central Texas where he is employed in the oil & gas industry. An avid collector, he joined SABR in 2012.

Mark S. Sternman roots for the Yankees, but, as a greater Boston resident, attends at least 10 Red Sox games each year. He has few ties to Texas. His brother-in-law and Fenway seatmate both hail from Dallas. In college basketball and football seasons, Sternman roots for the Oklahoma Sooners. Sorry.

Joe Stroop, retired, spent 55 years as a professional communicator, beginning at age 15 when he took an after-school job as a DJ at the local radio station (best job ever). He earned a degree in journalism and worked at Dallas-Fort Worth radio/TV stations covering local news and sports, including the Texas Rangers' first opening day. He joined the Associated Press, covering every Rangers home game for several seasons, including the tumultuous Doug Rader era, and was awarded that Holiest of Grails, a BBWAA membership card. Somehow, he was enticed to join the public relations department of a Fort Worth-based airline, later managed his own PR firm, and retired as a regional PR manager for a San Francisco-based national bank. He has continued to write about baseball, contributing "throwback" articles for a Rangers web site and SABR projects. Today, he, his gorgeous wife and two brilliant, successful children are all DFW residents.

Wayne Strumpfer is Of Counsel with the law firm Young, Minney & Corr in Sacramento, California. His life-long love of baseball started at the age of 7 when Gaylord Perry, then of the San Francisco

Giants, tossed him a baseball at Candlestick Park. He has contributed as an author on several stories for the SABR Games Project including writing about the 1970 All-Star Game and the seventh game of the 1971 World Series.

Clayton Trutor is the chairman of Vermont's Gardner-Waterman SABR chapter. He teaches at Northeastern University and is completing a PhD in U.S. History at Boston College. He is the author of 15 player biographies and the co-editor of *Overcoming Adversity: Baseball's Tony Conigliaro Award*, which SABR published in 2017. He also covers Cincinnati Bearcats athletics for SB Nation at *Down the Drive*. Follow him on Twitter: @ClaytonTrutor

Dale Voiss is a longtime Milwaukee Brewer fan who has been a SABR member since 2009. He has written several biographies for the SABR BioProject and currently resides in Madison, Wisconsin.

Joseph Wancho lives in Westlake, Ohio, and is a lifelong Cleveland Indians fan. He has been a SABR member since 2005 and serves as the chair of SABR's Minor Leagues Research Committee. He was the editor of the book *Pitching to the Pennant: The 1954 Cleveland Indians* (University of Nebraska Press, 2014) and authored *So You Think You're a Cleveland Indians Fan?* (Sports Publishing, 2018). In 2019, SABR will publish his book on the 1995 Cleveland Indians, *The Sleeping Giant Awakes*.

Steve West vividly remembers the first time he stepped into the seating bowl at The Ballpark in Arlington, and saw the vast expanse of green grass spread out in front of him. Along with his wife and son, he has been a season ticket holder for many years. He is halfway to his goal of collecting a baseball card of each of the more than 1,000 players who have been Texas Rangers.

Bob Whelan is a retired professor of public administration and city planning. Most recently, he taught at the University of Texas-Dallas. He is co-author of *Urban Policy and Politics In A Bureaucratic Age*, and author and co-author of numerous academic articles, book chapters, and papers. Bob is a lifelong fan of the San Francisco Giants. Willie Mays is his hero. He has authored or co-authored several articles and book chapters related to baseball topics.

A lifelong Pirates fan, **Gregory H. Wolf** was born in Pittsburgh, but now resides in the Chicagoland area with his wife, Margaret, and daughter, Gabriela. A professor of German studies and holder of the Dennis and Jean Bauman Endowed Chair in the Humanities at North Central College in Naperville, Illinois, he has edited eight books for SABR. He is currently working on projects about Wrigley Field and Comiskey Park in Chicago, and the 1982 Milwaukee Brewers. As of January 2017, he serves as co-director of SABR's BioProject, which you can follow on Facebook and Twitter.

A SABR member since 1979, **Don Zminda** retired in 2016 after two-plus decades with STATS LLC, where he served first as Director of Publications and then Director of Research for STATS-supported sports broadcasts that included the World Series, the Super Bowl and the NCAA Final Four. Don has also written or edited over a dozen sports books, including the SABR BioProject publication *Go-Go to Glory: The 1959 Chicago White Sox*. He is currently working on a book about Harry Caray's broadcasting career. A Chicago native, he lives in Los Angeles with his wife Sharon.

www.ingramcontent.com/pod-product-compliance
Lightning Source LLC
Chambersburg PA
CBHW081717100526
44591CB00016B/2409